ASIAN THOUGHT:
TRADITIONS OF INDIA, CHINA, JAPAN & TIBET

Volume II

CONFUCIANISM
TAOISM
BUDDHISM IN CHINA
SHINTO
BUDDHISM IN JAPAN

Robert B. Zeuschner, *Ph.D.*
Professor of Philosophy
Pasadena City College

ECHO POINT BOOKS & MEDIA, LLC
Brattleboro, Vermont

Published by Echo Point Books & Media
Brattleboro, Vermont
www.EchoPointBooks.com

Asian Thought (volume II)
ISBN: 978-1-63561-703-0 (paperback)

Cover design by Alicia Brown
Cover image: Golden wood statue of Guan Yin with 1000 hands by pixtawan,
courtesy of iStock

BUDDHIST SITES IN INDIA

INDUS VALLEY SITES IN INDIA

CHINA AND JAPAN

TURKESTAN

MONGOLIA

TIBET

PAKISTAN

CHINA

Yellow River

Yangtse River

CHINA

INDIA

MYANMAR

KOREA

JAPAN

TAIWAN

LAOS

THAILAND

VIETNAM

CAMBODIA

MALAYA

PHILIPPINES

BORNEO

SUMATRA

Table of Contents

INTRODUCTION TO VOLUME II

CONFUCIANISM
TAOISM
BUDDHISM IN CHINA
SHINTO
BUDDHISM IN JAPAN

Asian Thought: Vol. I and *Asian Thought, Vol. 2*, are intended to serve as an introduction to some of the most important and enduring religious, spiritual and intellectual traditions of India, China, Tibet, and Japan. Because this material is introductory, these discussions cannot be exhaustive or comprehensive. Consequently, the chapters do not go into extensive detail into any specific subject although the author has tried to provide enough detail so that key concepts are not distorted.

This book is not concerned with trying to persuade the reader to change his or her religious orientation. The author has no interest in encouraging you to be more spiritual, to take religion more seriously, to make you more religious, or less religious, and has no interest in converting you from one religion to some other religion. What the author does want is for you, the student, to find the topic of Asian[1] thought to be interesting, stimulating and challenging. These systems provide new perspectives to enrich and broaden one's world-view, new possibilities of thought which seem obvious to other civilizations, but often unrecognized or under-appreciated by the wide variety of Western traditions. There is much to appreciate in non-Western traditions. Studying religion requires us to be objective, to commit ourselves to rigorous academic standards, with the goal to be an appreciation of the complexities found in the non-Western traditions.

The focus in **Volume 1** is South Asia, stressing India and Tibet. The importance of the traditions of this area is evident when one considers that the South Asian subcontinent (including India, Pakistan, and Bangladesh) contains twenty-percent of the world's population. In this book, **Volume 2**, we focus on East Asia, specifically China and Japan. We will begin with China, where we find Confucianism, Taoism, Legalism and other early thought systems, plus later developments in Chinese Buddhism and Neo-Confucianism. In Japan we will focus on the several varieties of Buddhism, including the Pure Land and Zen, and the ancient religion of Shinto. Each and every one of these various traditions is quite complex, and so the author cannot avoid using generalizations. Whenever we make historical, cultural, and philosophical generalizations, there are always exceptions.

Although most books freely and uncritically use the English term "religion" to describe many of these systems, this book does so only hesitantly, firstly because in defining religion we tend to make the Eurocentric assumption that there must be some universal essence to all the things we call religions, and despite numerous attempts to find and define that essence, no such essence has ever been found. In addition, in assuming that all religions share important commonalities, we feel safe and comfortable using Western

---

[1] Some books refer to this area as "Oriental," however "Oriental" has been used to describe areas as widespread as northern Africa, the Middle East, eastern Europe, and Persia, as well as India, China, Korea and Japan. That is quite diverse. As noted above, the focus of these two books will be India, China, Japan, and Tibet.

assumptions to predetermine the forms that questions will take before those questions are even posed, such as questions about a "god" or a "savior."

The problem is that we discuss systems of thought that are much broader than the limited meaning for the term "religion" as it is used uncritically in Western Christian cultures. The author has found that many of his Western students tend to assume that anything called a religion will be sectarian and centered around beliefs in some divinity. Isn't a religion simply a belief system with a list of things one must accept on faith, the major difference being that other religions use a different name for the divine being they worship? The answer is "no." Many of the systems of thought traditionally described as Asian religions stress actions over belief or faith, and encourage critical responses. As used in the field of world religions, the term "religion" is incredibly more broad than concepts like "belief" and "faith" would suggest.[2]

WHAT ARE RELIGIONS?

In recent decades, it has become recognized that even asking the question "What is religion?" assumes that there exists something universal that all civilizations call "religions." This is based on assumptions that are not as straightforward as we used to think. In fact, these assumptions are quite controversial. The religious categories we use to answer the question "What is religion?" are historically specific and culturally relative, not universal.[3] Some scholars have argued that the word "religion" is too Western in its associated meanings to be useful.[4] Leading scholars have pointed out that both "religion" and "religious experience" are not universal categories of human experience, but instead are a relatively late and distinctively Western invention, which certainly will cause problems for any author trying to create a textbook introducing world religions.[5]

These issues of the general nature of religion as discussed by scholars in the field of religious studies go well beyond the purposes of this textbook.[6] There are dozens of definitions for "religion" yet there is no single agreed-upon definition for this central term. This textbook will gently sidestep these scholarly controversies, and instead use the term "religion" as a general albeit vague term, flexible enough to have some relevance to both Western civilizations and non-Western civilizations.

---

[2] "Belief appears as a universal category because of the universalist claims of the tradition in which it has become most central, Christianity." Donald S. Lopez, Jr., "Belief," in Mark Taylor, ed., *Critical Terms for Religious Studies* (Chicago: University of Chicago Press, 1998), p. 33. In assuming that all religions are alike, that they are universal in some important way, then we can safely assume that because "belief" is important in Western religion, then "belief" must also be an important element in non-Western religions, and we will put special energy in looking for something which would play the same, or a similar role in non-Western religion. We look for "belief." In doing so, we distort the non-Western tradition with our presuppositions.

[3] The introduction to Brent Nongbri's *Before Religion: A History of a Modern Concept* (Yale University, 2013) states "For much of the past two centuries, religion has been understood as a universal phenomenon, a part of the 'natural' human experience that is essentially the same across cultures and throughout history. Individual religions may vary through time and geographically, but there is an element, religion, that is to be found in all cultures during all time periods. Taking apart this assumption, Brent Nongbri shows that the idea of religion as a sphere of life distinct from politics, economics, or science is a recent development in European history—a development that has been projected outward in space and backward in time with the result that religion now appears to be a natural and necessary part of our world. . . . in antiquity, there was no conceptual arena that could be designated as 'religious' as opposed to 'secular'."

[4] Daniel Dubuisson, *The Western Construction of Religion: Myths, Knowledge, and Ideology* (Johns Hopkins University Press, 2007).

[5] The issues are complex, but several excellent discussions are available. See "Experience" by Robert H. Sharf, and "Religion, Religions, Religious" by Jonathan Z. Smith, both in Mark C. Taylor, ed., *Critical Terms for Religious Studies* (Chicago: University of Chicago Press, 1998). Should we understand religion through the lens of modernism, post-modernism, structuralism, post-structuralism, or some other methodology? Professor Taylor's introduction to the volume summarizes the most important issues in this debate.

[6] For example, see Tomoko Masuzawa, *The Invention of World Religions: Or, How European Universalism Was Preserved in the Language of Pluralism* (University of Chicago Press, 2005), or Brent Nongbri, *Before Religion: A History of a Modern Concept* (Yale University, 2013).

In the West[7], there is a tendency to assume that world religions share some common essence with Western religions, perhaps involving unquestioning reverence for an institutionalized ancestral dogma.[8] In the West there is a tendency to believe that the categories based on a divinity who requires submission, adoration, belief, and faith, are universal categories. However, recent scholars have argued that this cluster of ideas is related specifically to Western culture, and does not apply universally to many non-Western religious traditions. For many in the area of religious studies, religions are concerned with how we respond to fellow humans and to the world in which we live. It may be impossible to separate out religion from philosophy, history, politics, economics, art, literature, sociology, psychology and anthropology, although we in the West have attempted to do so. Can religion be separated from cultural institutions? As pointed out previously, early human civilizations seem not to have made any distinction between religion, culture, economics and political structures.[9]

Are religions just a list of beliefs one must accept on faith? Certainly, some of the systems we call religions fit this description. However, there is much more to religion than accepting beliefs generated from ancestral dogmas, or even accepting supernatural beings. In Western religions, religious questions often involve theories of human nature (do we possess a soul and how can we tell? is soul different from mind or consciousness?), morality (is something good because God commands it, or does God command it because it is good?), mortality (is there life after death? reincarnation, heaven, hell, or something else?), society (how can we apply the Golden Rule to our neighbors and to other cultures?), history (who are the real authors of our scriptures? is the universe really six-thousand years old?), and anthropology (did humans evolve over the millennia or are humans some kind of special creation?). In fact, religions serve many purposes and fulfill many functions.[10]

All civilizations attempt to explain what humans could not explain. Questions about the causes and meaning of an eclipse, an earthquake, a flood or tsunami, an illness, about the possibility of some life after death, or the general meaning of existence, are in need of explanation. Out of these kinds of questions come systems of symbols which encapsulate a world-view which will guide the choices and lives of those who participate in the system.

THE MANY FUNCTIONS OF ASIAN THOUGHT

Western people tend to draw a distinction between religions and philosophies, but these lines are due to conditions unique to Western thought, and are artificial and inappropriate when used on non-Western traditions discussed in these volumes. Rather than try to impose the Western distinction between religion and philosophy on Asian thought systems to which the distinction is foreign, in these books more often we will use an Asian category. In Chinese and Japanese there is a two-character compound **ssu-hsiang**, or **shi-so** 思 想 which we render in English as "thought." It can include what we call spirituality, or philosophy, and what we call religion as well.[11] Thus, the title of this book is *Asian Thought*.

---

[7] The term "West" is quite problematic, for there is no single unitary religion or philosophy typical of all the countries included by the term "West." It is not even clear precisely which groups or nations are included in the umbrella term "West." We cannot restrict "West" to just North America, or just North America and Europe. It would have to include South America and many other regions. In this book, the term "West" is intended to refer to a vague yet still useful generalization whose purpose is to contrast typical Greek, Roman, Christian, Northern European Anglo-Saxon-descended cultures, and North American assumptions with the religions and systems of thought of India, China, Japan, and Tibet. The term "West" is also used in the study of societies. For example one might study "WEIRD" societies, that is, "Western, educated, industrialized and democratic."

[8] This is how Christian missionaries explained the meaning of the Western term "religion" to the Japanese and Chinese.

[9] For more on this, see Brent Nongbri's *Before Religion: A History of a Modern Concept*.

[10] The student might find it instructive to read the first chapters of several different textbooks on world religions, and notice the great variety of definitions for the term "religion." There is no single agreed-upon standard definition for this important term. There is even disagreement about the meaning of the Latin root for the term.

[11] In Japanese the term *shukyo* renders "religion," however the Japanese two-character compound *shukyo* (*zongjiao* in Chinese) is not ancient; it was created by Jesuit Christian missionaries in Japan. Because the Japanese did not have words for anything quite like Christian beliefs, the missionaries made up the two-character compound in an attempt to capture the Western concept of religion as an institution with authority

Over many centuries, Western people traveled to Asia and noticed that many Asian practices and rituals resembled what Christians do in the West, and that these practices and rituals seemed to fulfill functions similar to Western religion. They found a wide variety of very different creation myths and sacred stories. Sometimes there were explanations of the universe or the origin of good and evil. There were sacred texts and goals that guided individual behavior and choices. In the West, these sorts of activities tended to fall under the category of religion. Consequently, Western people called these Asian systems "religion," assuming that in essence, these were similar to Western religions. However, despite similarities, westerners did not realize that these non-Western systems simply did not have similar presuppositions, did not share the same concerns or ask the same questions that those Judeo-Christian religious traditions asked.

For example, many of the non-Western systems did not wonder if a single god existed, and explicitly rejected the idea that a single god created all of reality. They did not conceive of a divinity who required submission and adoration. They did not interpret the world as a battleground between an omnipotent good god and an evil being or devil. They did not believe that humans needed a divine savior. For some of these thought systems, the question of the existence of a god was simply not interesting. Some wondered "where did god come from?" and searched for the impersonal ultimate source of all divinity and considered worship of a god to be spiritually immature.

Athens versus Jerusalem

Non-Western systems tend not to have the same tensions between faith and reason which are part of the history of Western religion. The history of Western thought could be described as an ongoing tug-of-war between ideas originating in Athens and ideas originating in Jerusalem. In this book we will explore thought traditions whose world-view does not originate in either the Jerusalem of Judaism, Christianity, and Islam, but also neither do these traditions have their origins in the Athens of Socrates, Plato, and Aristotle. In religions originating in Jerusalem, obedience and faith tends to be valued over reason, over empirical observation, over science. In Athens, it is reason, critical thinking, empirical observation, and science which tend to be valued over faith.

In India, China, Japan, and Tibet, there never was anything like the sharp tension between these two approaches of Jerusalem and Athens, the tension between reason and faith, between science and religion, which dominates the history of Western thinking. Thus the demarcation in the West between religion and philosophy applies perfectly well to the history of Western Christian civilization, but dividing non-Western thought into these two rigid categories is simply an inappropriate structure to impose upon these non-Western traditions of thought. It gives us a distorted understanding of the ideas and their assumptions.

The tension between science and religion in the West is found only recently in Asian systems and it arose in modern times as a result of conscious political manipulation, not devotional conflicts. We cannot assume that Asian thought systems are opposed to critical philosophical analysis, or opposed to science and contemporary scientific discoveries.[12]

Westerners who have never taken a course in world religions tend to assume that anything that is called a religion will be like Christianity. It will have a god or gods as its central core, and would believe that this divinity lays down moral and social rules, believe that humans have an eternal soul, and that there is life after death when one will be judged. Similar concepts are true for a few Asian thought systems, but not all.[13]

Some Asian thought systems do have similarities with Western Christianity, but also have significant differences. Asian and Western systems are both filled with creative insights and have inspired countless followers to guide their lives by some features of each system. In Asia what we might call religion, philosophy, and even proto-science have interfused and interacted in many fecund ways. This is what we will explore in this book, and try not to get distracted by the issue of how to use specifically Western labels to describe non-Western systems.

---

derived from a historical lineage (such as that of the Catholic pope). Interestingly, the literal meaning of *shukyo* is something like "essential principle-lineage teachings," "tenets-teachings," "sectarian-tenets" or "lineage-teaching," a respected teaching handed down in a line of teachers. According to Professor Dan Lusthaus, the compound implies reverence for an institutionalized ancestral dogma. The Chinese borrowed the two-character compound from the Japanese.

[12] A book which deals with how Chinese Buddhists understood the relationship between Western science and their doctrines is Erik J. Hammerstrom, *The Science of Chinese Buddhism: Early Twentieth-Century Engagements* (New York Columbia University Press, 2015).

[13] For example, see Stephen Prothero, *God is Not One: The Eight Ritual Religions That Run the World – And Why Their Differences Matter* (New York: HarperOne, 2010).

We must be careful also not manipulate one religion to appear better than another. One easy way to do that is when we compare the **ideals** of one religion with the actual **practices** of another. Some people say "My religion says that we should not kill, but followers of your religion do kill." To be accurate, we should compare the ideals of one religion with the ideals of another. Then we may discover that both teach "do not kill." We can also compare the actual practices of one religion with the practices of another. Then we may discover that both have had followers who killed in the name of their religion.

RELIGION: THE GRAND TRADITION AND THE LITTLE TRADITION

In recent times some Western scholars have pointed out that there is a way to think about religions that is not related to content or beliefs, but a more sociological understanding related to the attitudes and training and social position of those who hold the religious beliefs.[14] Some sociologists have pointed out that religious understanding in a culture may vary depending upon wealth and education. There is a continuum of beliefs and practices between the literate and powerful minority at one extreme, and the illiterate yet hard-working majority at the other extreme. This distinction is *not* between ancient tribal traditional followers and modern industrialized religious followers. In contemporary America we find both traditions existing side-by-side.

The religious understanding of those elite members of the well-educated segments of society are those people who are not only literate, but also familiar with a wide variety of world views, acquainted with critical thinking and philosophy, knowledgeable about current science, and this segment of society attempts to understand religion in a way that is consistent with the best science and philosophical and critical traditions. The religious beliefs of this group are perfectly compatible with science, with evolution, with the age of the universe, with the fact that the earth is not the center of the universe, with quantum physics, with anthropology, with the findings of geology, with the wide variety of human sexuality, and evolutionary biology. For many of these thinkers, if god did create the universe and everything in it, then science will be discovering the details of the mechanisms which god used to make our world and our selves. Thus science and religion must be compatible. This compatibility is not generated by rejecting science, but rather by offering skillful interpretations of sacred scripture.

It is often the case that the religious leaders of the major Christian churches and denominations are educated at high-quality secular universities taking classes in science, philosophy, critical thinking, anthropology and history alongside the scientists and philosophers, and the views and understanding of this group has been referred to as the **Grand Tradition** of religion. Thus, the term Grand Tradition refers to the elaborate ideas, teachings, values, and practices of the well-educated elite members of the institutional churches.

The Grand Tradition will be interested in trying to date accurately when their sacred scriptures were composed, and perhaps debate the actual authors of these sacred texts, and in doing so they utilize a complex array of scientific tests, combined with linguistic and historical data. Because of their education, social position, and wealth, often these same people may wield political power as well as religious power. If one considers this as a continuum, at one extreme are those scholarly in ancient languages and ancient history, as well as other well-educated members of the religion, and at the other end of the continuum, at the other extreme, are those who never had the benefit of a quality education and may never have encountered many people whose ideas were different from those of their own insulated community. Of course the majority of people belong in the in-between area. This distinction between Grand Tradition and Little Tradition lies along a continuum, with the majority of the people in the vast in-between grey area.

Until very recently in human history, the majority of people in a civilization were not literate and had very little formal education, no training in scientific methods or the mathematical underpinning basic to science, little understanding of empirical testing and how science works, and had little interest in historical methods, or critical thinking. The religious beliefs and attitudes of this segment of society tends to be interestingly different from the explicit beliefs of the Grand Tradition church leaders. These are groups of basic religions whose followers preserve their religious beliefs in stories, in oral form. They could not, or have not preserved their ideas in written form. In fact, in general this aspect of religion is not focused on the historical analysis of texts, or focused on beliefs and ideas at all; rather it tends to be about behavior. Popular religion is less concerned with the conceptual justification of what people think and believe, but rather tends to be about what people do.

---

[14] This distinction began with Max Weber in his *The Sociology of Religion* (Boston: Beacon Press, 1963) but has been discussed extensively by Robert Redfield, *Peasant Society and Culture* (Chicago: University of Chicago Press, 1973). Examples of the application of this dichotomy are found in Robert Ellwood, *Cycles of Faith* (New York: AltaMira Press, 2003).

This popular oral manifestation of religion is at the other extreme of the continuum, and is often referred to as "Folk Religion" or the **Little Tradition**. The term "little" is not meant to be demeaning to popular folk religion. Some scholars prefer to refer to the Little Tradition religion as Popular Religions, Oral Religions,[15] or Basic Religions.[16]

The Little Tradition covers a quite wide range of trends and practices, but tends to be more focused on personal needs, subjective spiritual feeling, visions, dreams, spirit beings, personal experience, anecdotes and pious tales, and has little interest in abstract theology or theory. Religious tales and scriptures are taken at face value and the conclusions of informed historical analyses are rejected. History and mythology are not clearly distinguished. The Little Tradition has greater reliance upon ongoing miracles, stressing apparitions and relationships with a spirit realm filled with divinities or angels who can provide concrete blessings in response to rituals, personal sacrifice or devotional vows. Little Tradition religion can see images of saints and divinities in an oil slick, in a pattern of wood on a door, in a cheese sandwich. This is "popular religion" or "folk religion."

The Little Tradition can be conveyed with song, with dance, with celebrations, and community festivals. The Little Tradition is transmitted orally through family and community, transmitted through charismatic figures who are often local church officials, or perhaps "holy men" and "holy women," who might include miracle workers who enter trance-like states. It might include such activities as "speaking in tongues" or ecstatic states where the participants may believe that they can predict the future.

Shamanism

The Little Tradition also includes shamans. **Shamanism** is the name for the world-view of those who believe that there are two realms which make up reality: the physical world that humans inhabit and a parallel realm inhabited by a wide variety of spirits who can intrude into our world to communicate with us, to help us, or to hurt us. Things with spirit could be animals, trees, stones, rivers, mountains, seas, human beings who have died, and heavenly and underworld beings. People who claim to "channel" spirits or communicate with the dead belong to this tradition.

Shamanism holds that these spirit beings can bless or curse humans. Thus spirits provide an explanation for why bad things happen to us. These spirits can enter and possibly take over the body of a human and cause illness. Often, the shamans explain that dreams are a connection between us and the spirit realm. **The shaman is the person who has the ability to interact with these spirits, to enter the spirit realm and communicate with and perhaps manipulate these dangerous forces.** Contemporary people who claim to offer us the opportunity to communicate with departed family members are modern inheritors of the shamanistic tradition.[17]

Shamans must be concerned with practical matters as well. Success in hunting and in planting and harvesting are central, but so too is dealing with evil spirits, curing pain and disease by bringing about spiritual healing and expelling demons. Evil spirits can sometimes be frightened off by fearful gestures or by loud noises, like the sounds of firecrackers. Sometimes the shaman may have to leave his or her body and travel to the realm of spirits. Sometimes the spirit will take up residence in the body of the shaman and the shaman will speak with the voice of the spirit.

Shamans provide talismans[18] which can ward off sinister or evil forces and shamans can interpret dreams for supernatural significance. The shamanistic aspect of religion places its stress on a world filled with unseen realms and invisible spirits who can cause our lives to change for the better or worse. Illness and bad luck must be the result of negative forces and spirits. Using rituals and various devices to induce a trance-like state,[19] the shaman is able to perceive and communicate with these spirits, hopefully to improve the lives of the individual or community. These are the kinds of activities which are the domain of the shaman.

---

[15] Michael Molloy, *Experiencing the World's Religions: Tradition, Challenge and Change* Second Edition (Mountain View, CA: Mayfield Publishing Company, 2002).

[16] For example, see chapter one of Lewis M. Hopfe and Mark R. Woodward *Religions of the World*, 10th edition (New Jersey: Pearson-Prentice Hall, 2007).

[17] Shamanism is found in movies, in books, in popular entertainment. Any movie with ghosts or demons is drawing on shamanism. One cannot but note that Grand Tradition religious leaders show little interest in this aspect.

[18] A talisman is some physical object which is believed to have magical powers, or perhaps will confer powers or protection on the bearer. Something that will ward off evil influences because of its protective powers is a talisman. A good luck charm is a talisman.

[19] These devices could include ingesting psychoactive substances, chanting, drumming, dancing, isolation, fasting, sleep deprivation and meditation.

Although "Grand Tradition" and "Little Tradition" are merely the extremes of a grand continuum with almost all religious people falling somewhere in the middle, we can discuss some qualities associated with each extreme. The questions which dominate the Grand Tradition tend to be the abstract ones. What is the meaning of existence, what is the nature of the sacred, why are we here, what is our purpose, how should human beings relate to supernatural beings, or relate to one another? They might ask why we human beings suffer? What is it that we are ignorant of that causes human beings such misery? Why is there something instead of nothing? The Grand Tradition might attempt to define the nature of the supreme being, or explain how a trinity of gods is monotheism, or attempt to explain how a universe created by a perfectly good deity could have so much undeserved evil in it.[20] The Grand Tradition might ask why a divine being would create a universe with so many flaws—what was the plan or purpose? Literacy and reason are important tools of the Grand Tradition.

Generally, followers of the Grand Tradition understand how reason works, and understand what makes some reasons good and other reasons worthless, understand the difference between a good explanation and a poor explanation, know why some arguments are logically very strong, and other emotionally appealing arguments can be weak or invalid. In a weak or invalid argument, the evidence offered does not support the conclusion.

The Little Tradition questions tend to be more literal, more immediate, personal and practical. For the Little Tradition believers, if one's sacred text says that giants mated with human women at the beginning of the world, then this must have happened. If one's sacred text says that a deity took three steps across the universe, creating morning, noon, and night, then this must have happened. If the sacred text says that a god came to earth and incarnated as a chariot driver on a battlefield, then this must have happened. Generally, practical questions dominate the Little Tradition of religion. For example, how can we influence deities to bring rain, or cure grandmother's illness? How can we ensure that our next child will be male, or how can I improve my luck when I gamble? If I sacrifice something of value as an offering, will the spiritual beings respond with blessings, with protection, with what I desire?

There is a tendency for the followers of the folk traditions to regard the Grand Tradition as too liberal and too abstract. If science is incompatible with their interpretation of doctrines and beliefs, then it must be science that is mistaken and empirical evidence and empirical testing are irrelevant. The followers of the Little Tradition are the ones who perform magical conjurations to summon the rain or bring about a miracle that could cure an illness or save the crops from insects. Often this is the realm of the shaman.

All the world religions exhibit both Grand and Little Tradition aspects, including Western Christianity. Hinduism and Buddhism have the intellectual component, but among the majority of people it is a wide range of folk religion which dominates. China and Japan also have these two traditions. The various Grand Traditions of these civilizations can be compared with one another very fruitfully, but the many Little Traditions are more varied and less conceptual, and thus more difficult to explore. As noted before, this distinction between Grand Tradition and Little Tradition is a continuum, not an either/or relationship.

Emic and Etic

"Emic" and "etic" are useful technical terms in the field of religious studies. Scholars of religion use the term **"emic"** to denote the understanding of a religion as explained by a committed believer, or possibly a priest, a minister, a pope or bishop. These people provide an insider's sympathetic view of a religious tradition, an appreciative view, a committed view. However, the view of one insider within a religion might be wildly different from the view of another insider. Insiders within the same church will often disagree vigorously with one another. Sometimes insiders will not acknowledge the legitimacy of other ways of practicing the very same religious tradition. For a clear understanding of a particular religious tradition, we cannot restrict ourselves only to the emic perspective.

---

[20] The Grand Tradition might try to answer the question of undeserved evil (i.e., senseless murder of small children) with free will. The Little Tradition response might be to say that the undeserved evil is punishment by an angry god for the sins of those among us, that god wants us to change our ways. These two approaches are interestingly different.

The term "**etic**" is used for the knowledgeable outsider's view of a religion, the view of a scholar who wants to be respectful yet objective,[21] dispassionate and honest about the claims and practices of a particular religion, and also someone who wishes to make useful and reasonably accurate cross-cultural comparisons between religious traditions. To understand religions of different cultures, we need both **emic** appreciation and **etic** studies of religions. We need objectivity, but we also need empathy.

As the purpose of this book is to provide an appreciative scholarly study of Asian thought, the obvious stress will be on the etic, a scholarly study of the dominant literary Grand Traditions in India, China, Japan, and Tibet. However, there will also be discussions of the Basic Religions, the Oral Religions, or the Little Traditions in each culture as well.

Because this book on Asian thought is incorporating both religion and philosophy, and because this is directed primarily at students who are likely to have some background in Western ways of thinking about spirituality, let us begin with some distinctions that Western scholars might make between religion and philosophy.

DISTINGUISHING PHILOSOPHY AND RELIGION IN THE WEST

In using the phrase "Western Thought," the term "thought" is intended to encompass both religion and philosophy. Although neither the Chinese nor Japanese find a problem with the term "Asian Thought," in the West we have distinguished philosophy and religion. Let us pursue this distinction as it appears in contemporary European and American thought.

The origins of Western philosophy are found in Athens, roughly four-hundred years before the common era. The term "philosophy" has its roots in the Greek language, and literally it can be translated as "love of wisdom." For the Greek thinkers, philosophers seek wisdom. Socrates and Plato offer a new understanding of wisdom. Wisdom is not merely repeating fixed truths inherited from previous generations. Wisdom is the ability or skill to make careful choices which lead to a good life, a meaningful, worthwhile, and fulfilled life. Wisdom leads to happiness. For philosophy, this wisdom is acquired by a combination of critical thinking and knowledge gained by sense experience. Education was not mere memorization of culture; it was based on critical discussion.

The etymological roots of the term "religion" are in Latin, and the verb *religio* probably meant "bind" or "tie fast." A common explanation is that *religio* refers to that aspect of society which binds people together in a community-unifying attitude of respect for and cultivating a special relationship with various forces, powers, or divinities. The Roman world had numerous divinities, and was aware of the religious practices of other cultures, and never insisted that the Roman religious beliefs were the only true beliefs. The Latin term *religio* did not refer to an exclusive belief system or symbol system which rejected other religions. In this more ancient sense, religions, like cultures, bind us together into a common attitude of respect for powers that control human destiny. Quite often these forces were associated with forces of nature and not divine beings who had human-like personalities.[22] Some interpret *religio* to mean "binding" people to what is good, and avoiding evil.

However, for most people in the West religion is identified with the problems and viewpoint of Jerusalem, the original source of three major world religions. In general these are referred to as "followers of the book," the Jewish, Christian and Islamic followers. Among these groups, the term "religion" denotes an exclusive group to which

---

[21] The author is **not** suggesting that the emic perspective, that of religious believers, must be biased or that all outsiders are objective. The question of what objectivity is and whether it is even possible for anyone, is outside the purview of this book.

[22] An extended discussion of the numerous interpretations of the Latin *religio* can be found in many books. A good discussion is found in Steven Brutus, *Religion, Culture, History: A Philosophical Study of Religion* (CreateSpace Independent Publishing Platform, 2012). One might also consult the introductory chapter of David Hicks, *Ritual & Belief: Readings in the Anthropology of Religion* (New York: McGraw-Hill, 1999).

one belongs. In addition, throughout much of human history, religious education was memorization of sacred texts, not critical discussion of these texts.

Theology

Christianity is primarily a monotheistic devotional religion (many non-Western religions place little or no emphasis on gods or devotion to gods) and the intellectual aspects of Christian religion are explored in **theology**, the aspect of religion closest to philosophy. "Theology" is a Christian term derived from the Greek, and basically it means the study of the nature of the divine as explored by those committed to forms of Western religion including Christianity. Theology is the rational conceptual justification of what members of the religious group think and believe to be true. Theology uses reason to justify and explicate doctrines and dogma.

Many people assume that non-Western religious traditions are pretty much like Western religions. For example, almost all Western religions are exclusive, which means that in joining one religious group, one must reject all others as wrong, possibly as evil.[23] This is not common in non-Western traditions, which tend to be non-exclusive, and tend not to understand their own tradition as possessing the sole truth. Students are often astonished that in other cultures, one can easily move between two or three religious traditions without any problem.[24] This fact lends support to the position that non-Western systems are really not religions in the way the West uses the term.

Western Philosophy and Theology Share a Number of Basic Problems

There are several problems common to both religion and philosophy in the West such as concern with the fundamental nature of human beings, the existence of a single omnipotent creator god (if any), the source and structure of ultimate reality, the nature of the good life for human beings, and both have a shared concern with morality and the basis for morality (i.e., ethics), and questions of what we should value and why.

In terms of content, religion and philosophy also have problems that are unique to each and not shared. For example, the nature of valid inference or a cogent argument (in logic) and the explication of the notion of "cause" are purely philosophical; the function of baptism or the proper age for baptism is purely theological or doctrinal.

Although philosophy and religion share many common problems, neither are defined just by the content of what they study. It is more in the *approach* to these various problems that philosophy and theology differ so profoundly.

The Approach of Theology and Philosophy

To distinguish theology and philosophy is to distinguish the world-view of early Athens from the world-view of Jerusalem. These differences provide the historical foundations for the distinction we in the West make between philosophy and religion. What differentiates these two is the approach they take and the assumptions they make.

What Is Assumed to be True?

A major distinction between philosophy and theology lies in **what they assume to be true**. Christian theology begins by assuming the existence of a supernatural dimension of reality, traditionally interpreted as a single

---

[23] As with any generalization, there are exceptions. Scholars have noticed many of the students in Buddhist groups are Jewish and Buddhist simultaneously. Some Roman Catholic priests and nuns have been recognized as Zen Buddhist teachers (see the bibliography) at the same time. Often, Quakers and Unitarians feel that they belong to multiple traditions. Native Americans in the southwestern states will often follow both their own traditional religions and either Roman Catholicism or some form of evangelical Protestantism.

[24] It is common to note that in traditional China, everyone is Confucian in their moral, familial and political lives, Buddhist in the realm of matters of life and death, Taoist in matters of alchemy, medicine, and cosmology, and also participants in "Little Tradition" forms of popular religion including ghosts, spirits, and gods in heavenly realms. Nevertheless, in China politics was important for Confucianism, Buddhism, and Taoism, and because of power politics, each group separated itself from its rivals in the competition for political influence.

spiritual being who created and continues to sustain all that exists, and the transcendent realm inhabited by that being or beings. In English-speaking Christian cultures that spiritual being is called God (from the pagan pre-Christian German word "gott" or fluid) and this being is described as omnipotent, omniscient, omnibenevolent[25] and the creator of all that exists.

If a being with these characteristics does not exist, if in fact there is no supernatural dimension of reality, then theology is the study of things like the Marvel universe of the X-Men, like studying Middle Earth[26] or the civilizations of Barsoom[27] or the content of fantasy fiction novels such as the Harry Potter series. If there is no supernatural realm, then an expert in theology is like an expert in the history of and architecture of Hogwort's Academy. One can be an expert in unicorns or dragons as well. Such a person is a genuine expert in the area, but what she studies need not exist. Thus, theology assumes that God exists.

It is popular to say that philosophy demands justification for every claim; that nothing is simply assumed to be true. Since the days of Socrates and Plato four hundred years before the Christian era, philosophers have been very wary of accepting anything as true unless there is substantial evidence to justify the claim. Philosophy strives for clarity about what we think is true and why we think it is true, which means to be critical with respect to all assumptions and not accept a claim too easily. A thorough philosopher will require that all conclusions exhibit their truth or probability in the light of reason or sense experience before being accepted. It is very difficult to imagine any absolute assumptions without which philosophy would cease to be.

If you assert that a statement is true, the contemporary philosopher will think it is perfectly appropriate to ask how do you know? How do we know that the sun is 93 million miles from earth? How do we know that the square of the hypotenuse of a right triangle is equal to the sum of the squares of the other two sides? What evidence supports the claim that the universe is nearly fourteen billion years old, or that it is merely 6,000 years old? What evidence is there for the existence of free will, and what do we mean by the term "free will"? How do we know what year Henry VIII was born?

For a philosopher, before any statement can be accepted as true, there must be good reasons which justify and support the claim. For philosophy, the fact that authorities in the past asserted the claim, or that a sacred text makes such a claim, does not constitute good evidence or reasons (how does the authority know? sacred texts do not agree and highly regarded interpreters of sacred texts do not always agree).

Thus, the philosopher does not start out assuming that a god exists or that a god does not exist; rather the philosopher will ask the person or group which makes the assertion if there is any evidence at all which can justify the claim that such a being exists. And for those who hold that no god exists, the philosopher will ask if there are good reasons to conclude that, as defined, such a being is self-contradictory or impossible. Based on argument and evidence, some philosophers reject the existence of a divine creator, and others accept the claim as reasonable or probable. This philosophical approach is also found in some religious scholars (theologians) and it generated numerous attempts to find an argument which could prove that the God of Christianity exists, or at least provide some evidence or justification to make probable the claim that some sort of a god exists.

The Goals of Philosophy and Theology

The goals of philosophy and theology are interestingly different. The **goal of theology** is to understand the nature of the divine and the proper relationship between that divinity and human beings. The primary activity to accomplish that is the explication and interpretation of religious truth or religious doctrine as contained in sacred

---

[25] This standard list is glossed as infinitely powerful (omnipotent), knows all that is true (omniscient) and is infinitely and perfectly moral or perfectly good (omnibenevolent).

[26] A reference to J. R. R. Tolkien's classic book trilogy, *The Lord of the Rings*, which was made into a very successful movie trilogy by Peter Jackson. *The Hobbit* trilogy of films is also set in Middle Earth.

[27] A reference to Edgar Rice Burroughs' fantasy realm based on Mars, found in his classic novels *A Princess of Mars*, *The Gods of Mars*, and *The Warlord of Mars*. The realm of Barsoom was the setting for the 2012 Disney film *John Carter*.

scriptures from the past (for Christians this is the Bible), or found in the writings of the leaders of the tradition. In this sense, theology is not independent of religion; rather, theology serves religion. The basic orientation of both theology and religion is usually otherworldly and focuses in the ultimate direction of the eternal as opposed to the merely temporal.

In general, the **goal of philosophy** is wisdom (remember "philosophy" means "love of wisdom"). This wisdom is often interpreted as a clarity which provides the ability, knowledge or skill to live a good life. It is also the wisdom to realize how little we really know for sure, and philosophy makes us less confident in the simple answers accepted by those of the past.

Philosophers know that we cannot simply discard everything we think we know and start fresh. We must have confidence in our current understanding and use it to live in our world, and yet we cannot allow ourselves to be so confident that we are unable to modify our current understanding, or even to reject it when new compelling evidence is presented. Even our most cherished beliefs could be wrong (maybe the earth is *not* the center of the universe after all, maybe large amounts of vitamin C will not lessen the duration or intensity of a cold), and recognizing that is the strength of science. We must be willing to value evidence, and study it even if it leads to contradiction of some of our most deeply held beliefs.

We all realize that one group's or person's common sense can be another person's absurdity.[28] Philosophers understand that human thought is fallible; we may be wrong about what we believe to be true. Not only were ancient societies wrong about many of their beliefs, but when we analyze his arguments, we may conclude that Socrates may have been wrong. Plato and Aristotle may have been wrong. Kant may have been wrong. You and I may be wrong. Ideally, philosophers are willing to change their minds when an alternative view has very strong evidence to support it. Philosophers tend to think that wisdom is acquired by way of some kind of comprehensive intelligent and critical understanding of the nature of human beings, the nature of the world which human beings inhabit, and the relation between the two.

Attitude Towards Legitimate Sources of Knowledge.

Philosophy and theology have quite different attitudes towards sources of knowledge. Both philosophy and theology accept (1) **reason** and (2) **sense experience** as sources of relatively reliable knowledge. Reason tells us that the square root of 2 is ±1.41428 . . . , and sense experience tells us that the sun is shining outside our window.

But philosophy rejects two additional sources which theology accepts as a source of genuine knowledge. Theology accepts (3) **authority** and (4) **scripture** as sources of reliable knowledge. An important source of knowledge for the Christian tradition is pronouncements made by church dignitaries and officials.[29] For many Christians, when church authorities pronounce some practice praiseworthy, and a different practice to be sinful, most followers accept these authorities and accept the statements as true and certain, and use them to guide their choices and their lives. For many followers, scripture and church authorities are accorded a sacred status which exempts them from critical challenge.

Philosophers do not do this. Concerning authority, philosophers ask, "How does the authority know?" or "Where did the authority gain her knowledge?" or "When two different authorities disagree on a doctrine, how can we tell which of them is correct?" Thus philosophers do not treat authority alone as a reliable source of knowledge. Similarly, no scientist accepts a claim merely because some famous scientist has asserted it. A Nobel-prize-winning

---

[28] For much of the world, reincarnation or rebirth is common sense. For others, it seems to be absurd.

[29] It is common to observe that some Little Tradition church leaders imagine that science is simply *whatever scientists believe* thus turning science into a faith system like Christianity. Of course, no scientist accepts something as true simply because Newton or Einstein stated it. When one believes a statement to be true because there is sufficient evidence, we call that knowledge, not belief. The question scientists ask is: What is the evidence? Where does the evidence lead? Are there any possible observations which could show the claim false? What predictions are made by the hypothesis? Science does not produce certainty; rather it seeks for the best explanation consistent with reason and observation.

scientist may make a claim, and fellow scientists ask, "What is the evidence that supports the claim?" "What possible tests can confirm or disconfirm the findings?"

The second source of knowledge accepted by theology is the belief that the sacred scriptures of its tradition are without error. Sacred scriptures of Western religions are often called revelation, truths revealed by God. Revelation is treated as more certain than knowledge gained by reason or by sense experience. The philosophical approach rejects the *assumption* of the absolute truth of sacred texts. Philosophy does not blindly reject everything in scriptures, but neither does philosophy treat scriptural statements as sources of certain knowledge when properly interpreted.[30] From the point of view of orthodox Christian theology, properly interpreted revealed scripture cannot err, and thus any statement that contradicts revealed scripture (when properly interpreted) is necessarily false. Of course, the problem as to what a given scriptural statement really means is usually not an easy problem for the theologian. Scripture does not interpret itself. Thus, although scripture may be absolute, interpretations of scripture are diverse.[31]

So, in general theologians accept four reliable sources for knowledge, and philosophy (and science) accept only the first two of those, reason and sense experience. It must be obvious that when two groups disagree on the sources of reliable knowledge, meaningful discussion is very difficult. One group offers support for their claims by quoting scriptures or church authorities, and considers that certain and the issue settled. The other group rejects the claims of authority and scripture without additional empirical evidence to support the claims.

Attitudes Towards Truth

The attitude toward truth differs between philosophy and theology as well. For the theologian, the ultimate truth has been set forth once and for all and is to be discovered in special sacred writings or teachings of the past. For most Christians, the highest truth was laid out in the writings of the Old Testament (mostly the books treated as sacred in the Jewish religion) and the New Testament (the twenty-seven books originally written in Greek which relate to the message of Jesus, the anointed one).

For the philosopher, there is no one source of complete truth. Philosophy does not look to the past for the ultimate and final truth. Even the greatest thinkers have made questionable assumptions and logical mistakes; we are all fallible and we can and do make mistakes even today (and when these errors are recognized, the mistakes are corrected and not repeated). There are many valuable insights and truths discovered by studying thinkers of the past, but these insights are not ultimate; they can be improved. By studying the philosophers of the past, we find the mistakes committed and expect that we will not repeat those mistakes.

Suppose you are a Platonist, a person who looks to Plato as a great philosopher. Plato's philosophy has problems. Plato was clearly mistaken about many of his claims, and many of his arguments are not very strong or not logically valid. The modern Platonist selectively rejects and reconstructs Plato's positions. The Platonist philosopher does not accept something just because Plato wrote it any more than a scientist would accept something just because a respected fellow scientist like Newton or Einstein wrote it.[32]

The attitude of the creative philosopher will be a feeling of confidence with respect to her or his own views, not as absolute, but subject to revision when errors are revealed. A philosopher tries to start out having learned from the mistakes of the past, tries to establish her claims on as sound a footing as possible, and clearly moving in the right direction. The creative philosopher learns from the past, but also hopes that she or he can learn from and avoid the

---

[30] Do not make the mistake of thinking that philosophers assume that scriptures are false; they do not. Rather, they take a "wait and see" attitude, and test the empirical claims made by these sacred texts, not merely to confirm, but also to see if any observation could disconfirm the claims. This is the critical attitude of science in general, not just philosophy.

[31] For example, take "Thou Shalt Not Kill." This does require interpretation. Can we kill animals and eat them? Can we kill in times of war? Can we kill criminals in the name of the state and justice? Can we kill in self-defense? The early Christians were pacifists and did not fight when thrown to the lions. Note that different Christians disagree on each of these things. Interpretations vary.

[32] Remember that authority is NOT a source of reliable knowledge for science.

errors made by those in the past, and as a result can re-conceptualize and produce something more complete than what has ever been set forth before.[33]

ASIAN VIEWS OF SPIRITUALITY AND WISDOM

There is an amazing variety and diversity in what are called "world religions" which are not encompassed by the concerns of Western theology. In Indian thought, philosophy and religion are encompassed by (1) notions of social, ritual, moral and religious duty (called **dharma**), and (2) insight into the ultimate nature of reality (called **darshana**).[34] As we have already noted, in China and Japan, the terms for spirituality are **ssu-hsiang**, or **shi-so** 思想 and the closest English translation to this is just "thought."

The standard Western way to be religious focuses on faith in, obedience to, and devotion to the one Supreme Being, who is thought of as a supreme king or ruler who hands down laws that must be obeyed upon the threat of severe punishment. Indian models of spirituality include devotion, but are considerably broader than traditional Western models.

Four Ways of Being Religious

In the Indian model, there are at least four ways of being a religious human being living a spiritual life.[35] One can be spiritual by engaging in the pathway of right **action**, that is, certain special sorts of activities which certainly include performing rituals or ceremonies but it might also include one's social and moral duties, perhaps building homes for the homeless, donating money to social or religious groups, or feeding the hungry.

Another way of being spiritual is to engage in quiet, solitary **meditation**, in a deep and profound focusing of awareness until a transformation of ordinary consciousness is brought about. A third way of being religious is the pathway of **reasoned inquiry**. This is to use one's intelligence or reason to question, doubt, explore, challenge and ultimately to achieve liberating wisdom, or achieve profound insight into the nature of the way things truly are (here the student can see where the lines between religion and philosophy are blurring).

Finally, another way of being spiritual is the pathway of **devotion**. On this path one will worship the divine, one will love completely, rely upon, and pray to supernatural powers or beings, the majority of which in Asia are neither rulers nor creators.

Although all four of these can be found within the framework of Christianity, Western religion tends to place the greatest stress upon devotion, dogma, doctrine, and ritual out of these four pathways of spirituality. Many of the world's great spiritual traditions focus on the other ways of being religious. It is important to realize that what is typical of Western religion is not typical of all world spiritual pathways.

---

[33] The author is indebted to Prof. Harold McCarthy for many of the distinctions and points stressed here.

[34] *Darshana* is a term rich with meaning, including "focused religious viewing," which can mean having eye-contact with a sacred statue or an image of the divine, or viewing an image of one's spiritual teacher, or having a face-to-face meeting with one's spiritual guide, and ultimately seeing past the individual into the absolute reality. In modern times a follower can have live *darshana* by watching an icon of a divinity on the internet.

[35] In recent times Western scholars have suggested that there may be many different ways of being a religious human being living a spiritual life. For example, see Dale Cannon, *Six Ways of Being Religious: A Framework for Comparative Studies of Religion* (New York: Wadsworth Publishing, 1996), or Gary E. Kessler, *Eastern Ways of Being Religious* (Mayfield Publishing, 2000).

TERMINOLOGY

In this book, the reader will be led through the many ways of Asian intellectual thought, the many ways of Asian spirituality typical of India, China, Japan and Tibet. Some of these traditions will argue that there exists some sacred reality which interacts with humans, which rewards, which punishes, and which intervenes in human history with miracles. This is **theism**. Some assert that this sacred ultimate is plural or many. We can describe that as **polytheism**. Some will argue that the sacred is one divine being who cares about humans, interacts with humans, rewards, and judges, and we call that **monotheism**. Some assert that there is one divine being but that one divine being takes many different forms or incarnations throughout history; shall we call this one monotheism as well?

We will discuss some Asian spiritual systems which assert that all the world is sacred, everything in the world is sacred, including humans. Western scholars refer to these as **pantheism**. There is one view which seems comfortable with a divinity who gives form and shape to the chaotic universe, but that divine creator does not have any special affection for humans and does not answer prayers or respond to rituals; this is called **deism**. Some will argue that the genuinely real is oneness and when we perceive differences, we are misperceiving the highest ultimate truth. We might refer to these positions as **monism**. Some will argue that sacred reality cannot be numbered as one, as two, or as many, because all concepts are inadequate, including the concept of "oneness." Sacred reality cannot be described adequately as one or two or many. Some of these can be called **non-dualism**.

Some will argue that there is no convincing evidence that there exist sacred realities which transcend this world or are apart from this world, although if such evidence were produced they could change their minds. They often find the definitions and descriptions of a deity to be self-contradictory and therefore such a deity would be impossible. Because there is no good reason to accept a supernatural being, such people do not accept divinities. This would be **atheism**. Some find focusing on divinities counterproductive, irrelevant or useless for the achievement of a spiritual life. Often these are called **non-theistic**.

A person who is **agnostic** is someone who says although a divinity is possible, there is not sufficient evidence for either accepting or rejecting divinities, and so an agnostic is not sure whether there is any supernatural deity, and thus reserves judgment. It is also true that an agnostic could argue that it is impossible for any limited *finite* human to actually know that an *infinite* being exists.

ASIAN LANGUAGES

The technical ideas and concepts in this book are described in languages like Sanskrit (India), Tibetan, Chinese, and Japanese. In the discussions which follow, we shall find technical terms in many different languages, and we will use words that most students will not have heard of before. Those terms in Asian languages which seem to have fairly close equivalents in English will be rendered by English terms. We will encounter many important technical terms whose meanings cannot be accurately translated into English (i.e., *satori, koan, Nirvana* or *Tao*). Those we will simply describe and define and then proceed to use the foreign term in the text.

None of these Asian civilizations use the Latin alphabet, the "a" and "b" and "z" with which we are so familiar. So, these Asian technical terms and names need to be rendered using our alphabet, that is, *transliterated* into English so that we can pronounce them. This is also called *romanization*. Even simple things like capitalization is a product of Latin languages; there is no such thing as a capital letter in Sanskrit, Chinese, or Japanese. In their classical forms, these languages did not have commas, periods, or quotation marks.

Even when romanized, pronunciation will be a challenge. It is made even more difficult because there are different forms of transliteration into English, even for the same language. To complicate matters, some languages have sounds that do not exist in English, and scholars use numerous different technical marks (diacritical marks) which indicate subtle sounds that the great majority of students will not be able to hear easily. You may have seen *Ch'ang* and *Chang*, or *k'ung-fu* and *kung-fu*. How are we to pronounce these correctly?

For the Chinese language there are numerous transliteration systems, but there are two which are important currently in the English-speaking world. One is the Wade-Giles system which has been used in English-speaking countries for well over a hundred years, and the other is the Pinyin system, decreed by Chairman Mao in the 1950s and becoming more popular in this country since the 1980s.

This text book will use the Wade-Giles system as the primary system of transliteration of Chinese because it is what the Library of Congress uses, and every English book prior to the 1970s used only the Wade-Giles system. Important texts published this year still use the Wade-Giles system. However, the Pinyin romanizations are becoming increasingly popular and will be included as well for those familiar with that system. When appropriate, the author will also include an approximate guide to proper pronunciation because in many cases, neither the Pinyin nor the Wade-Giles romanizations will be pronounced correctly by the average English-speaking student.[36]

There is more than one way to transliterate Japanese terms, for example we can write kōan, or kooan, or koan (a *koan* is a puzzling question asked by a Zen teacher of the student). Many Japanese terms appear in English dictionaries, in which case we will use the English spellings. For all the others, the standard way to romanize Japanese terms, called the Hepburn system, is the one that will be used in this book.

"Before the Common Era"

Like the great majority of scholarly books in recent decades, this book does not use the calendar abbreviations "B.C." or "A.D." These two abbreviations for calendar dates seem to imply some special international status and privilege for the Christian religion. Why would a Chinese Marxist date Mao or Confucius by the birth of Jesus? To say that Siddhartha, the Buddha, was born in 563 B.C. (Before Christ) is not relevant to a Buddhist—why would a Buddhist want to date the Buddha by the Christian misunderstanding of the birth year of its founder?[37] In fact, in many Buddhist countries such as Sri Lanka, the current calendar date system is based on their understanding of the date of the death of the Buddha.

Similarly "A.D." means *anno domini*, "in the year of our Lord" — again a uniquely Christian calendar. Without intending to be disrespectful to Christian cultures, or disrespectful to non-Christian traditions, in this book we use the standard neutral abbreviations used in most recent scholarly history books: "Common Era" or **C.E.** and **B.C.E.** or "Before the Common Era."

WHY STUDY ASIAN THOUGHT?

At no time in this text will we argue that any particular religion is best. If you are already firmly convinced that your own personal religious outlook is perfect and cannot be improved, then the study of Asian thought has something valuable to offer to you. Stated simply, when you learn about spiritual systems which have different presuppositions from your own, which offer new possibilities of thought, this gives you the ability to better understand and appreciate your own religion from different perspectives. In articulating the beliefs of others, you can better articulate your own beliefs. As a result you can reflect about your own life and the world; you can try to clarify the basis of your own world-view.

Actually, that works just as well if you consider yourself non-religious. By studying the spiritual patterns of others, you can come to appreciate the variety of ways that human beings are spiritual, and again come to understand where your own views position you in regards to these deep and enduring issues.

---

[36] For example, it is not clear to the average reader how to pronounce the Chinese term "Qi" or "Xin" based on the Pinyin romanization, or "jen" or "k'ung-fu" and "kung-fu" in the Wade-Giles system. The term *foxing* in Pinyin is written *fo-hsing* in Wade-Giles. The issue is further complicated by the fact that there are very many dialects of Chinese, and the same term can be pronounced differently depending on where the speaker was born and lives in China.

[37] Christian historians are in fair agreement that Jesus was born between 6 and 4 B.C.E. because the most likely date for the death of King Herod (the ruler when Jesus was born according to the New Testament) is 4 B.C.E.

The primary purpose of this book is to help you understand ways of being wise or spiritual which arose in Asia (and are not the same as Judeo-Christian systems), but which at the same time have a long history of recognition of worth and importance to fellow human beings. I have learned much from each of these; I hope you will too.

ACKNOWLEDGMENTS

No book that aims to cover so much in so few pages can possibly satisfy all readers and any approach to such a vast task comes with advantages and drawbacks. The advantages have to do with the range of topics, and the drawbacks have to do with details. It should be obvious that the range of perspectives and traditions that this book covers is beyond the expertise of any single scholar, or many scholars. Some of the material in this book comes from personal travel and personal experience, but even more from approximately five decades of reading, studying, organizing, distilling, teaching and discussing Asian thought. It also comes as a result of studying with a great many excellent teachers, including Chang Chung-yuan, Chung-ying Cheng, David Kalupahana from Sri Lanka, K. N. Upadhyaya from India, Eliot Deutsch, and Harold McCarthy, at the University of Hawaii. I have benefitted greatly from ongoing conversations with colleagues at the University of California at Santa Barbara and the University of California, Riverside. I have had valuable discussions with David Chappell, Robert Doud, and others informally and at conferences. Dr. Philip Ricards graciously read early drafts of some chapters and made numerous suggestions and improvements from which I have benefitted. I have also learned from all the students who have taken my classes over the decades. Their questions have prompted me to do further research in many topics, and have allowed me to work on clarification of many obscure issues. I would like to express my appreciation to all of them.

I have tried to provide acknowledgments for each and every book and author whose ideas and words have influenced this text, but fifty years of reading and lecturing means that there is much which I may have remembered but lost track of the original source long ago. In the case of any omissions, please let me know and I will be very happy to make suitable acknowledgment of the sources in future editions.

Although I have learned so much from so many, it should be noted that no work of any size is free from errors. Certainly this volume will have more than its fair share. The author is responsible for all such errors.

TECHNICAL TERMS USED IN THIS CHAPTER

agnostic
: The term "agnostic" literally means "not know." An agnostic is someone who thinks a divinity might be possible, but does not claim to **know** that a divine being exists, and is not sure whether any such beings exist.

atheism
: Literally "not-theism;" the view that there is insufficient or no evidence to support the claim that there exists a divine being who performs miracles, interacts with humans, rewards, punishes, or judges. An atheist does not claim to possess certain knowledge of the fact that a divinity does not exist. Rather, the atheist concludes that there is not enough evidence to allow one to conclude that such existence is even probable. "Non-theistic" is used in this chapter to mean religious attitudes which acknowledge that gods may exist, but consider the existence of a god irrelevant to spiritual goals.

Bhagavad Gita
: The "Song of the Lord," "Song Supreme" or "Song Celestial," a sacred text for many Hindus which tells of Lord Krishna.

darshana
: This is to see directly the nature of the sacred, and is pronounced darshan.

emic	The insider's view of a religious tradition, the perspective of a devotee, a believer. These can vary from person to person.
etic	The outsider's view of a religion, the perspective of a scholar, a person trying to maintain an objective standpoint. Scholars of religion hold that both an emic and an etic perspective are required if one is to gain a useful understanding of any particular religious tradition.
monism	The view that all of reality is truly one, not many. All distinctions and differences which we perceive are, in some sense, not real.
omnibenevolent	All-good, perfectly good, infinitely good, perfectly moral.
omnipotent	All-powerful, infinitely powerful, unlimited in power.
omniscient	Knows all that is true, past, present, future.
pantheism	The view that all ("pan-") is sacred, or divine.
philosophy	The love of ("philo") wisdom ("sophia"). Philosophy is the branch of human endeavor which seeks clarity and justification for those things we are curious about, and which we believe to be true or false. The modern philosopher attempts to ask and answer "What do you mean?" and "How do you know?" "Does your conclusion follow logically from your evidence?"
polytheism	The view that there are two or more sacred beings who care about humans, may answer prayers, interact with history and perform miracles, reward and judge.
shaman	This is the specialist (often either a male or female village priest) who is believed to be able to communicate with and interact with spirit realms.
theism	The view that there exists one or more divine beings who interact with humans, who care about humans, who reward, punish, and judge, who perform miracles and answer prayers, and who preside over a heavenly realm.
theology	The intellectual study of the nature of the divine. In Christianity, the theologian is the believer who attempts to make intellectual sense of and find conceptual justification for the doctrines of his or her church.
Vedas	The ancient sacred scriptures of Hinduism, which includes (1) four volumes of sacred hymns, (2) the Brahmanas which discuss ritual, (3) the Books of the Forest Monks, and (4) the Upanishads (all of which are discussed in detail in succeeding chapters).

QUESTIONS FOR FURTHER DISCUSSION

1) It might be an instructive exercise to look up several different definitions of the term "religion" in reference works, and then see if those definitions will describe the beliefs and practices of non-Western religions.

2) Is it possible for a religion to exist only within the mind of a single person, or do religions require a culture and a group of followers? Of course we can say that "Sam makes a religion out of golf," but it is not clear that we use the term "religion" in the same way we might speak of the "Protestant religions." What do you think?

3) How important are shared systems of symbols to religion? Could a religion exist without any special religious symbols?

4) Many students find it nearly impossible to use the term "religion" to describe a group which has no concern with supernatural deities. Yet there are several non-Western groups that certainly appear to have all the

trappings of religions, but no concern with gods. Where do you stand on this issue? Is belief in a deity required for something to be called "a religion"?

5)   One can adopt an insider's view of a religious tradition (an emic view), or an outsider's view of a particular religious tradition (an etic view). Scholars of religion feel that both emic and etic views are essential to understanding a religion. Is the insider's view always biased, or prejudiced? If so, everyone who belongs to a religion is biased and prejudiced. Can this be true? Is the outsider's view automatically objective and unbiased? Should we trust whatever a scholarly non-believer says about your religion?

6)   We discussed the collection of religious attitudes called Shamanism, whose roots go back into ancient prehistory. Do you find any traces of Shamanism in Western religions or in Western culture? You might consider Hollywood films about ghosts and about people who communicate with the dead (i.e., the 1990 movie *Ghost* with Whoopi Goldberg playing a shaman, or the 1999 film *The Sixth Sense* with Bruce Willis).

7)   Do you think that belief in an afterlife is essential for something to be a religion? Western religions assert that there is some sort of life after the death for each individual, however this is not true for all non-Western religions. Some accept reincarnation or rebirth. Others assert that the individual is swallowed up in a great ocean of pure consciousness. Still others put their energy into this life because there is no life after death.

BIBLIOGRAPHY

RECENT DISCUSSIONS OF 'WHAT IS RELIGION?'

Brutus, Steven, *Religion, Culture, History: A Philosophical Study of Religion* (CreateSpace Independent Publishing Platform, 2012). ISBN-10: 1479109681.
Dubuisson, Daniel, *The Western Construction of Religion: Myths, Knowledge, and Ideology* (Johns Hopkins University Press, 2007)
Hicks, David, *Ritual & Belief: Readings in the Anthropology of Religion* (New York: McGraw-Hill, 1999)
Masuzawa, Tomoko, *The Invention of World Religions: Or, How European Universalism Was Preserved in the Language of Pluralism* (University of Chicago Press, 2005)
Nongbri, Brent, *Before Religion: A History of a Modern Concept* (Yale University, 2013)
Taylor, Mark, ed., *Critical Terms for Religious Studies* (Chicago: University of Chicago Press, 1998)

GENERAL INTRODUCTIONS TO ASIAN THOUGHT

Bonevac, Daniel, Phillips, Stephen, *Understanding Non-Western Philosophy* (Mountain View, Ca: Mayfield, 1993)
Cannon, Dale, *Six Ways of Being Religious: A Framework for Comparative Studies of Religion* (New York: Wadsworth Publishing, 1996)
Carmody, Denise and T. L. Brink, *Ways to the Center: An Introduction to World Religions*, 5th edition (Belmont, Ca: Wadsworth, 2002)
Coogan, Michael D., ed., *Eastern Religions: Origins, Beliefs, Practices, Holy Texts, Sacred Places* (New York: Oxford University Press, 2005)
Ellwood, Robert, *Cycles of Faith: The Development of the World's Religions* (New York: Alta Mira Press, 2003)
Fenton, John Y., Norvin Hein, Frank E. Reynolds, Alan Miller, Niels Nielsen, Jr., Grace Burford, *Religions of Asia*, 3rd edition (New York: St. Martin's Press, 1993)
Fieser, James, and John Powers, *Scriptures of the East*, 2nd edition (McGraw-Hill, 2002)
Hawkins, Bradley K., *An Introduction to Asian Religions* (New York: Pearson Longman, 2004)
Herman, A. L., *An Introduction to Indian Thought* (Prentiss-Hall, 1976)

Hicks, David, *Ritual & Belief: Readings in the Anthropology of Religion* (McGraw-Hill, 1999)

Hopfe, Lewis M., and Mark R. Woodward *Religions of the World*, 10th edition (New Jersey: Pearson-Prentice Hall, 2007)

Kessler, Gary E., *Eastern Ways of Being Religious* (Mountain View, Ca: Mayfield, 2000)

Koller, John, and Patricia Koller, *A Sourcebook in Asian Philosophy* (Macmillan, 1991)

Koller, John M., *Asian Philosophies*, 5th edition (New Jersey: Pearson-Prentice-Hall, 2007)

Koller, John M., *The Indian Way: Asian Perspectives* (New York: Macmillan, 1982)

Oxtoby, Willard G., *World Religions: Eastern Traditions*, 3rd edition (London: Oxford, 2009)

Potter, Karl H., *Presuppositions of India's Philosophies* (Englewood Cliffs, N.J.: Prentice-Hall, 1963, paperback Westport, CT: Greenwood Press, 1963)

Radhakrishnan, Sarvapali, *Indian Philosophy*, two volumes (London: Allen & Unwin, 1927; reprinted several times)

Schouten, Jan Peter, *Jesus as Guru: The Image of Christ among Hindus and Christians in India*, (Amsterdam/New York: Rodopi Press, 2008)

Van Voorst, Robert, *An Anthology of Asian Scriptures* (Belmont, CA: Wadsworth, 2001)

ASIAN THOUGHT:
TRADITIONS OF INDIA, CHINA, JAPAN & TIBET

PART III: CHINA

CHAPTER 13: THE ORIGINS OF CHINESE THOUGHT

13.1 OVERVIEW OF THE CHAPTER

For the past two-thousand years, official Western religions have been preoccupied with the relationship of human beings to the single sacred reality, to the divine sacred ultimate. People in China did not share these same religious assumptions as those in the West, nor did they share the religious outlook of India or Tibet. The impulses in the early Chinese civilization tends to be shamanism. That is, early Chinese concerns with the supernatural led to a focus upon contacting spirits, performing sacrifices to spirits, and utilizing *divination* or fortune-telling to know the future. The beings who transcend the natural world include gods (whose rules and whose homes resembled the earthly emperor's court), troublesome ghosts, departed ancestors, and legendary recluses who roamed the mountains and who were believed to be immortals. In addition there was the realm of Heaven itself which reacted to and responded to the sacrifices and rituals of the rulers. Heaven was not the home of an infinitely powerful ruler-god who created everything and then laid down rules for how humans ought to behave.

The Chinese wanted to enhance communication between Heaven and Earth using sacrifices and interpretation of natural signs or auguries. Some of this is found in Indian religions. However, the fundamental presuppositions of the Chinese world-view is profoundly different from the assumptions of India. The Chinese were primarily interested in practical concerns, with politics and ethics, and there was little interest in the human fate after death or metaphysical speculation about ultimate reality. The harmonious interrelatedness of all things, and the positive value of the world has been a presupposition which has continued throughout the history of Chinese religions. The Chinese viewed nature as a very positive force, and this is a bit surprising considering how difficult life has been in China throughout history.

The world around is filled with things that move but are not alive; there is wind, rain, thunderstorms, earthquakes, the movement of sun and moon across the sky. The Chinese were certain that they were surrounded by unseen forces, forces which are not a part of the material world we observe. These forces might reside in the sky overhead, but some seemed more local. Generally these forces correlate with natural forces, to be associated with wind, sun, sea, stars but they might possess some characteristics similar to those of human beings. It was the role of the emperor to interact with the most powerful forces for the benefit of the nation.

Since the earliest times, life in China has been uncertain, with danger coming from wars, rebellions, invasions, and not even the wealthy and powerful were free from uncontrollable and capricious violence. In wartimes, the military would draft any healthy male between twelve and fifty. But these men were the ones who plowed and cleared the land. With males gone, grandmothers, wives, and daughters had little chance of surviving the next winter, and little chance of growing enough food for the next springtime.

In China, punishments for lawbreakers were not simply prison. In addition to capital punishment, punishments included scarring and amputation of limbs, ears, noses, and other body parts. In addition to the suffering imposed by the imperial government and local government, the Chinese had to deal with the unpredictable forces of flood and famine. Every system of Chinese thought can be understood to be an attempt to deal with these uncertainties.

CHINESE DYNASTIES (early dates are approximate)

HSIA/XIA (c. 2205-1766 BCE).
SHANG (c. 1765-1122 B.C.E.).
CHOU/ZHOU (c. 1122-249 B.C.E.).
      King Wen, King Wu, Duke Chou.
        Interstate warfare after 771 B.C.E.
      Spring and Autumn Period 722-481 B.C.E.
        Lifetime of Confucius and Lao-tzu
      Warring States period 403-221 B.C.E.
        Lifetime of Mencius and Chuang-tzu/Zhuangzi
CH'IN/QIN (221-207 B.C.E.)
      Ch'in-shih Huang-ti/Qinshi Huangdi.
      China unified 221 B.C.E.
      Legalism adopted as official state policy.
      Burning of the books in 213 B.C.E.
      Central control and bureaucratic administration over China.
HAN (202 B.C.E.-220 C.E.)
      Confucianism comes to dominate Chinese government
      Buddhism enters China around 50 C.E.
CHIN (265-420 C.E.)
      China in a state of civil war.
SOUTHERN & NORTHERN DYNASTIES (420-589)
      Rebellions continue.
SUI (590-618 C.E.)
      Central control reestablished.
      Buddhism becomes very strong; major Buddhist schools established.
T'ANG/TANG (618-906 C.E.)
      An era of poetry, art and philosophy.
FIVE DYNASTIES (907-960)
SUNG/SONG (960-1279)
      Neo-Confucianism responds to the power of Buddhism.
YUAN (1280-1368)
      China controlled by the Mongols.
MING (1368-1644)
CH'ING/CHING (1644-1912)
REPUBLIC (1912-
    Republic of China in Mainland China (1912-1949)
    People's Republic of China (established by Mao Tse-tung) (1949-)

13.2 SOURCES OF CHINESE THOUGHT

The origins of Chinese religions go back to the time long before written languages. Chinese archaeologists have found hominid fossils that have been dated to over 500,000 years ago, and evidence of Homo Sapiens (our species) shows humans in China as long as 40,000 years ago. The shift from a hunting-gathering society to the domestication of rice seems to have begun about 10,000 B.C.E. This was especially in the Yellow River valley areas, where villages and communities began to develop.[1] We can only speculate about any possible religious ideas in that ancient past.

Chinese archaeological discoveries do reveal recognizable elements that we might term "religious" that go back at least 5,000 years. There have been discoveries that suggest that a mother goddess may have been significant in some groups. Near inner Mongolia a female statue of a pregnant goddess figure was discovered, dating to perhaps some time before 3000 B.C.E. A life-sized head of a female figure was also unearthed in a different location dating to about 3000 B.C.E.[2] These suggest that in the archaic past, there was at least one female goddess who played a role in some communities in the northern areas of ancient China.

It seemed obvious to the Chinese that things like illness, earthquakes, floods, famines, and celestial events happened which we could not explain, but those same events made sense if we assume that we shared our world with unseen yet very powerful spirits who interacted with human lives. These supernatural forces and beings affected our lives; rituals, sacrifices, ceremonies and rites could be used to appease these spirits. Some of these supernatural beings were departed ancestors, but not all of them. Some were minor gods specific to our local area, or regional gods, and even heavenly messengers. Over the centuries the heavenly spirits were thought of inhabiting a bureaucracy and the major gods became thought of as like the scholar-officials in the royal courtrooms. These shamanistic beliefs had a great influence upon the enduring traditions of popular Chinese religions.

In addition, certain symbols were especially important to our world because the secular world was not independent of the sacred realms; these two were in constant interaction and there was no clear distinction between them. The ruler claimed to have a special relationship with the forces of nature and gods, and rituals carried on by the emperor were believed to be essential to ensuring a good harvest and peace in the kingdom. The Chinese accepted the belief that the political ruler of the empire was an absolutely essential link connecting us to supernatural forces which could help us to achieve material and religious goals. No Chinese thinker seems to have even imagined the possibility of any other form of government than a monarchy.

What about the beginning of creation? How did everything arise? Unlike Western religions, the Chinese did not attribute creation to an all-powerful deity, but instead saw the universe as existing in chaotic form when heaven (*yang*) and earth (*yin*) were not yet separated. The universe was self-generating, self-sustaining, and self-regulating. Each part of our universe was related organically to the other parts. The realm of humans and the realm of spirits are interrelated and interdependent.

There was no single official creation myth in Chinese thought, but there are several which are popular. One of these is the story of an old mother Nuwa.[3] Another is the myth of P'an-ku/Pangu, the giant who arises out of the

---

[1] Archaeologists use pottery shards and burial remains to study these ancient cultures. Anthropologists find women playing important roles in these cultures, perhaps as shamans.

[2] Julia Ching, "East Asian Religions," in Willard G. Oxtoby, ed., *World Religions: Eastern Traditions*, Second Edition (London: Oxford University Press, 2002), pp. 322ff.

[3] There are different myths about the creation of human beings, most involving mother goddesses including Nuwa and another with Wusheng Laomu, literally "the Uncreated Old Mother." There is a legend of Nuwa making human beings out of the earth, taking care with the first figures she shapes, but later just dragging others through the mud on a string. The aristocrats were the ones made with care, and the common people were the ones made with less care.

undifferentiated primordial chaos:

> Heaven and Earth were in the chaos condition like a chicken's egg, within which was born P'an-ku. After 18,000 years, when Heaven and Earth were separated, the pure *yang* formed the Heaven and the murky *yin* formed the Earth. P'an-ku stood between them. His body transformed nine times daily while his head supported the Heaven and his feet stabilized the Earth. Each day Heaven increased ten feet in height and Earth daily increased ten feet in size. After another 18,000 years this is how Heaven and Earth came to be separated by their present distance of 90,000 *li*.[4]

Chinese Thought Did Not Have Two Sources

According to scholars of Indian religions, there were at least two different sources: the more ancient Harappan civilization and the later Aryan perspectives. The traditional Western view of the world comes from two sources as well: the contrast between the Greek world view grounded in rationality and logical inference, and the Biblical-Christian world view grounded on faith which supercedes reason.[5] Chinese religion did not arise from a tension between two completely different world-views, and does not reflect a tension between faith and reason.

The earliest Chinese religious views were a composite of many strictly regional cultures, but those cultures shared much in common by the time the central authority of the various Chinese dynasties were established. As pointed out above, there never was a clear distinction between the secular realm and the sacred realm in traditional China. At least a dozen different philosophical systems of Chinese thought arise out of that common and ancient world-view, including Confucianism, several forms of Taoism/Daoism, Legalism, the Yin-Yang school, the Mohists who followed Mo-tzu (Mozi), the School of Names, and others.[6] Historically, in terms of enduring importance and subsequent influence, the major indigenous philosophical systems are Confucianism and two rather different systems, both of which are called "Taoism" in English.

Approximately two thousand years ago Indian Buddhism entered China and in the following centuries influenced Taoism and Confucianism (and helped to produce what Western scholars call Neo-Confucianism). Ultimately, throughout the long history of China, the **Three Traditions** of Confucianism, Taoism, and Buddhism had immense influence on the life of the Chinese, both the Grand Tradition and the Folk Traditions.

13.3 SOME GENERAL CHARACTERISTICS OF CHINESE THOUGHT

China is large and geographically quite varied, and has always been the home of different ethnic groups and numerous different spoken languages and dialects. Until recently, the various regions in China were relatively isolated from one another because of deserts, large mountain ranges and major rivers. The fact that we call them all "China," is potentially misleading. There may be one word which names the large country, but this never was a homogeneous nation. In 2008 there were 55 officially recognized minority groups in China. China has always been multi-cultural with distinctively different dialects, different foods, clothing, customs, and different gods in each major region.

---

[4] N. J. Girardot, *Myth and Meaning in Early Taoism* (Berkeley: University of California Press, 1983), p. 193.

[5] Scholars have pointed out that the world-view of Europe and north America (the West) comes from two sets of different assumptions. We get our religious views from Jerusalem, and our philosophical views from Athens. This is the conflict between faith and reason. Thus, we distinguish religion and philosophy and sometimes have a conflict between science and Christian beliefs. Chinese thought has no such tension, and thus the distinction between religion and philosophy that seems so obvious to Westerners does not apply well to China.

[6] These are described and analyzed in detail in volume I of Fung Yu-lan, *A History of Chinese Philosophy* (Princeton New Jersey, Princeton University Press, 1952).

CHAPTER 13: ORIGINS OF CHINESE THOUGHT

Chinese civilization may have had multiple points of origin in the ancient past,[7] but the official history of China begins in the north. The high quality soil in the Yellow River basin provided a good agricultural life for the early inhabitants. The group who lived in the north along the Yellow (Huang) river were the Han Chinese, and the Han Chinese came to dominate Chinese politics. With wide variation in weather conditions and a dense farming population, very early China needed to control water with large-scale community projects, irrigation and flood-control projects. These sorts of activities need central authority to impress citizens into labor gangs and guide large numbers of workers. With central authority comes complex governmental institutions, which helps to explain why the problem of governing was central to the aristocracy and the intellectual elite of China.

When a powerful central authority began to emerge along the Yellow River in ancient China, the ruling clans were forced to deal with the political disunity generated by numerous different regional cultures. China has been heavily populated from early times. For any group to rule successfully, there needs to be a commonly accepted ideological framework. The result is that much of Chinese religion and thought focuses upon establishing harmony between rulers and the ruled, harmony within the community, harmony within the family, and harmony with nature.

Despite the incredible diversity within China, there seems to have been a world-view that many indigenous Chinese traditions drew upon for inspiration. In this chapter we will discuss this world-view focusing upon human beings and the human relationship with nature. We'll also consider the Chinese attitude towards cause and effect, and the role of abstract reasoning in Chinese thought. The first characteristic of Chinese thought concerns the attitudes towards human beings and nature.

Chinese Thinkers Focus Upon Human Beings in a Human World

In general, the shamanistic aspect of popular Chinese religion is its concern with gods and departed ancestors, but these gods are not totally "other" than humans. In traditional China, the gods are like us. The gods are made of the same stuff as humans and animals, called *ch'i/qi* ("vital energy'). In general, Chinese thinkers were primarily concerned with human beings, not supernatural beings. The Chinese believed that spirits share our world, and the heavenly realms are inhabited by these spirits and our deceased ancestors, but the supernatural beings who dwell there are humans or human-like with concerns like yours and mine. When the Chinese explored the nature of reality, they tended not to see human beings and the human realm as fundamentally different from nature and the sacred.

The focus was on the Chinese family, not the individual. We must be careful not to imagine a father, mother, and two children when we hear the word "family." Like the rest of Asia, Chinese cultural thinking is grounded in the extended family, and the local grouping of extended families to make up villages. The extended family meant that three or four generations of the same family occupied the same residential compound. Grandparents, parents, uncles and aunts, and cousins, all shared the same compound, which included servants as well.

In a family-based system, it is considered appropriate that the individual should place the benefits of the group over his or her own personal desires. This is obvious when we consider the ancient Chinese virtue of "filial piety" or "filiality" (respect of younger members of the family for older ones) which was a highly regarded virtue throughout all levels of Chinese society. It was not the individual who was important, it is the group. The most important members of the group are the eldest males.

Due to the presuppositions of the Judeo-Christian religious traditions, Western people tend to see a profound and ultimate difference between humans and nature. Western people tend not to see this world as our home, but only a temporary way-station. In the West we talk about "bending nature to our will." This is not typical of the traditional Chinese worldview. In traditional Chinese thought, there is an assumed sense of harmony, a sense of continuity between human beings and nature. This world is our home. We humans are not separate from nature. Human beings are ripples in the complex system of ever-changing interactions that make up nature. All of reality is rolling change

---

[7] Julia Ching, "East Asian Religions," in Willard G. Oxtoby, ed., *World Religions: Eastern Traditions*, Second Edition, pp. 319ff.

and we humans are a part of waves and patterns.

The Chinese would say that human beings share a relationship with heaven and earth. Humans are important, and may be central in some sense, but everything in the universe is somehow very much like us. We and nature are a seamless process. When we build a dam or a bridge, we participate in the works of nature. It is nature which supplies the materials and the valleys which support the dam or bridge. We human beings grow out of nature as a flower or plant grows out of nature; we humans flower as a rose flowers. There is no external deity imposing structure and order on nature; nature develops slowly and gradually. Nature is organic, like a growing plant, and possesses its own organizational principle and its own creative energy. Matter is not inert and not totally different from humans; we are like the rest of the universe.[8] Nature is our home. We belong here. The order of nature is built into nature itself, and all of reality is created by natural patterns. This is quite different from Indian assumptions, and Western assumptions concerning humans and nature.

Common Assumptions in Indian Thought

In India, ultimate reality transcends our world. As was discussed in Volume I, a common assumption in India is that this world cannot be the source of human happiness. Some in India advocate realizing our original unity with the sacred ultimate Brahman which transcends our world, a world which might even be the product of illusion (*maya*). Some advocate freeing our true immaterial eternal soul (*purusha*) from this world of matter (*prakriti*). Some advocate practicing devotion to a supernatural heavenly being (*deva*) in the hope that the worshiper will be able to live in the heavenly realm with the divinity. The goal of liberation means liberation **from** this world. The Buddhists seek nirvana, but the evidence is that most in India understood that as liberation **from** our realm of birth-and-death (*samsara*).

Common Assumptions in the Judeo-Christian Traditions

In the traditional Judeo-Christian world-view, God is the supreme ultimate, the creator of everything and everything that exists was created out of nothing. Directly below the creator are numerous layers of angels, and then human beings (who possess souls created in the image of God). For many in the Judeo-Christian tradition, nature is subhuman and decidedly inferior to human beings because God created all of physical reality for the benefit of humans, and no creature in nature possesses a soul except for humans. The ultimate home for humans is not in this world; rather it is in a heavenly realm after we die. For many in the Western Christian view, nature is not intrinsically valuable. Things in the world have value only in so far as they are of use to human beings (i.e., we are advised not to drive species to extinction because the species may be of use to humans later on).

The Chinese did not share these assumptions

It should be clear that the early Chinese world view did not share these Western perspectives:

> The harmonious cooperation of all beings arose, not from the orders of a superior authority external to themselves, but from the fact that they were all parts in a hierarchy of wholes forming a cosmic pattern, and what they obeyed were the internal dictates of their own natures.[9]

Of course, Chinese farmed and built water-management projects, but tended not to think of themselves as conquering nature in the process. They worked *with* the processes of nature. Note that the traditional view of nature

---

[8] If we assume that the human realm is very much **like** the rest of the world, then we will tend to use analogical thinking, seeing similarities and the relatedness of things. A is **like** B; A has property X; therefore B is likely to have property X as well. Chinese philosophers tend to rely on analogies. Analogies can be based on observations, on abstraction, on words, on phrases, on proverbs, and on metaphors.

[9] Joseph Needham, "Human Laws & Laws of Nature," *Journal of the History of Ideas*, 1951, vol. 12-1/2, p. 230.

in ancient China described above is not the same as in the present. Contemporary China tends to share the Western view that nature is to be exploited, and contemporary China seems to be as hard on the land as Western cultures have been.[10]

The Chinese Attitude Towards Human Beings and Rationality

The Chinese in the past understood human nature to be in harmony with the rest of nature, and human reason was of value, but not the ultimate value. In the attitude toward abstract reason there is a clear contrast with Western attitudes. We in the West are the inheritors of the Greek traditions of Plato and Aristotle, where the stress is on abstract reason and logic as that aspect of the human mind which is most important, most reliable as a source of knowledge, and that part which should control one's feelings, desires, and inclinations. Although Socrates and Plato would not have thought that pure reason could answer all questions, following the time of Descartes (1596-1650) there was a tendency in the West to stress abstract principles, abstract reasoning, pure mathematics, pure logic, and pure philosophy as the proper tools to solve all of life's problems. Reason (exemplified most clearly in philosophy and science) should be the ultimate guide to life.[11] The conclusions which we should accept are the ones that result from a process of critical thinking based on valid inferences. There is a tendency to undervalue other kinds of thinking in the process of trying to make sense out of life. In the West we also have a tendency to think of mind as the same as consciousness, and a tendency to think of consciousness as something profoundly different from our physical bodies.[12] For many in the West, the mind is independent of and separate from the body.

In China, mind is not sharply separated from the physical, and the value of reason is in its ability to aid in the harmonization of human relationships. Pure abstract reason is not the ultimate source of wisdom, but it does aid in the ultimate fulfillment of a human being. A spontaneous and creative intelligence is more important than abstract logic. Humans use many kinds of thinking besides purely logical reasoning, such as thinking by analogy, correlation, and imaginative simulation. Chinese thinkers used all of these. Instead of giving pure deductive and inductive reason the highest authority, in Chinese thought the focus tends to be on the totality of human nature, not upon reason to the exclusion of our other mental faculties. Another way to put it is that the value of reason is found in being reasonable, not pure intellect divorced from the rest of our conscious life.

In China, reason encompasses feeling as much as anything else. For example, the Chinese character *hsin* (*xin* in the Pinyin system of romanization) is usually translated as "mind," but in its original form, it is a picture of the human heart, the seat of emotions, feelings and desires. In the West, if I ask you where your mind is located, you tend to point to your head. If I ask you where your feelings are located, you tend to point to your chest where your heart is located. From the Chinese perspective, Western people have mistakenly separated *mind* into two (reason in the head, emotions in the chest). From the Chinese perspective, reason and emotions are both contained in mind and reasonableness. And these are thought of in physical terms. The mind and the functioning of the body are not separable. Translators often translate *hsin* as "heart-mind" in an attempt to capture the broad range of meanings.

---

[10] See Judith Shapiro, *Mao's War Against Nature: Politics and the Environment in Revolutionary China* (Cambridge University Press, 2001).

[11] If you have ever studied Western philosophy, you may have encountered Immanuel Kant (1724-1804). Kant sat in his study each day, thinking about the ultimate nature of reality, what can be known, and how the mind works. This was not done with exploration of the physical world or using sense-experience. Kant sat at his desk in his study, analyzing the nature of reality without investigating nature. In the middle ages, medieval scholiasts discouraged sense experience; if you wished to know something about the world, you were advised to read the writings of Aristotle.

[12] In Western thought we have the area called "philosophy of mind," which wrestles with problems created by this sharp dualism. We also have psychology which has attempted to study mind and consciousness using empirical methods capable of observation and falsification.

CHAPTER 13: ORIGINS OF CHINESE THOUGHT

Causality is Organic, not Mechanical

Metaphysics is the area of philosophy which studies the nature of reality, and the cause-effect relationship is a cornerstone of metaphysics. Until recently, Western science has done very well conceptualizing the relationship between cause and effect on the model of a machine, especially something like a clockwork mechanism. That is, causality has been understood as purely mechanical. One billiard ball strikes a second ball, and mechanically and externally forces the second ball to roll. All things influence one another by acts of mechanical causation, by pushing, forcing, or bumping, and we can experimentally ascertain the laws which describe these causal sequences, and those laws allow us to predict many new mechanical sequences. We often think of "laws of nature" as making or forcing things to happen in the world, or perhaps these laws of nature were imposed by an all-powerful being who dictated these laws.[13]

Until Einstein, the model in the West for the past four-hundred years has been nature as a kind of exceedingly intricate clock like mechanism which we can figure out, and then manipulate. If you know how to manipulate the machine, then you can change the nature of reality. This attitude has been a very powerful archetype which has allowed the West to excel at science and technology.

The Chinese did not share this view. They looked for mutually reinforcing patterns in our environment. For the Chinese, cause and effect arise together as co-participants in a rather organic environment. I say "good morning," and you respond "good morning." I wave to you, and you wave back. If we are introduced for the first time, we might bow, or in the West, I hold out my hand to shake yours, and you respond. In holding out my hand, I have caused you to extend yours as a consequence. But, **no mechanical external cause has forced or made something happen**. There is a cause-effect relationship, but this was not like a mechanical clockwork. I did not grab your arm and put your hand in mine. Rather, the two of us are participating in a social ceremony where my action evokes a response from you; the polite response is to shake hands. The plant responds to the sunlight, but not by mechanical pushing or pulling. The model of mechanical causation does not work well with these cases. The Chinese adopted a model of causality of stimulus and response, a model closer to social politeness, and closer to organic growth processes observable in nature.

The Chinese tendency was to look for resonances, patterns and order where one thing influences another and the two participate in a sort of reciprocal social ceremony. This kind of causal thinking places things side-by-side in patterns, and things influence one another by mutual influences. If I am grouchy and cranky, after a while my wife and children will begin to be grouchy as well, snapping back at me. This is mutual resonance; we resonate and affect one another in that way.

In the Chinese world-view, all things in the universe form part of one colossal resonating responsive pattern. A thing's identity is determined by its place in the total pattern, and nothing is independent of the total pattern. All things were therefore parts or processes, in existential dependence upon the whole world-as-organic-process. All things react to one another, not so much by mechanical causation, but rather by a kind of mysterious resonance. Joseph Needham[14] has pointed out that since the Han dynasty, the Chinese thought of the universe as self-generating, not caused externally. They thought of the universe as self-sustaining, and so no deity was needed to keep things in existence. The universe is self-regulating, the way a plant or tree is self-regulating. There are rhythms to the seasons and rhythms in growing things, like birth, growth, sustaining, and finally death. Each of these ever-flowing rhythms interact with all the other cycles that make up reality. We humans are an important part of these rhythms and cycles.

In the Chinese world-view events are **not uncaused**. But things are not just mechanically and externally

---

[13] In modern science, the "law of gravity" does *not* make things fall. Rather, it *describes* how things behave.

[14] Joseph Needham, *Science and Civilization in China*, Vol. II (London: Cambridge University Press, 1956), pp. 279–289.

caused either. The causal pattern of the whole is more organic and less like a machine. Each individual thing depends upon the totality of the system and yet at the same time each creates the ripples that make the pattern. The order and pattern we see all around us is organic, and things arise because they are part of the pattern and respond to the pattern. Things arise the way grass grows in the spring, spontaneously and organically responding to the weather, the sun, and the soil.

Harmony Is the Nature of Reality

If we want to know what is ultimate reality, we must look around us at the world. When in the past the Chinese looked around, they saw that the basic theme in all of nature was harmony. All things exist as contributors to a gigantic continually undulating pattern which in its very nature is in constant resonant motion and simultaneously everything is intrinsically harmonious. The Chinese saw a swinging and alternating movement which provides a pathway of continual change. The universe is one vast interdependent system whose basic nature was a moving harmony.

All parts of the universe are essential to the process of nature; human beings and what the Chinese called the "ten-thousand things" are continuous, without radical distinctions. Differences between humans, gods, spirits and nature are differences of degree rather than differences in kind. The world is better described as a continuum rather than a disjunction. In that continuum there is a correct and completely natural pattern of behavior for everything in the universe.

The Ultimate Reality is Tao

The name that the Chinese give to this entire cosmic order, for that total grand pattern, is **Tao/Dao**.[15] Tao/Dao is the pathway or pattern that the stars make as they wheel overhead year after year, and also the way humans behave when they behave appropriately and correctly, and are in harmony. The term Tao/Dao can also denote the resultant harmony of all the apparently separate patterns. The basic meaning of the Chinese character Tao/Dao is road, path, or pathway. The most common translation is the "Way." However, the word is much richer than any English translation can suggest. Here is one attempt to clarify the meaning of Tao:

> Vast indeed is the Ultimate Tao,
> Spontaneously itself, apparently without acting,
> End of all ages and beginning of all ages,
> Existing before Earth and existing before Heaven,
> Silently embracing the whole of time,
> Continuing uninterrupted through all eons,
> In the East it taught Father Confucius,
> In the West it converted the "Golden Man" [the Buddha]
> Taken as pattern by a hundred kings,
> Transmitted by generations of sages,
> It is the ancestor of all doctrines,
> The mystery beyond all mysteries.[16]

Do not think of Tao as a divine being or a god. Tao/Dao is free from action, thought, feeling and desire; it

---

[15] In the Wade-Giles system of romanization, the Chinese character is written "Tao" in English, but it is an unaspirated "T" so it sounds like Dao. The Pinyin system writes it *Dao*.

[16] A sixteenth century Ming dynasty rock inscription, translated in Philip Rawson and Laszlo Legeza, *Tao: The Eastern Philosophy of Time and Change* (London, Thames and Hudson Ltd., 1973), p. 8.

does not have goals or purposes. There is no special relationship between Tao and humanity, as there is between humans and the divinity in the West. In fact, according to the Taoist/Daoist philosopher Chuang-tzu/Zhuangzi, a lump of manure is as close to Tao as human beings are. Tao does not respond to devotion or rituals, does not answer prayers, or have favorites. The Tao does not issue commands, does not engender miracles to influence human history, and does not relate to individual people. Tao does not create things out of nothing. In fact, the Chinese never had a creator divinity and firmly rejected the hypothesis that things could ever come from nothing.

In the Chinese world-view, the world itself is not created; rather it arises out of a primordial chaos which gradually becomes unified and undergoes continual cyclical and organic change. As we shall discover, although the different various Chinese traditions and their schools share this impersonal aspect of Tao, nevertheless they have differing ideas about how the Tao is to be conceived, known and followed.

The Goal of Chinese Thought is to Acquire Wisdom

For the Grand Traditions of Chinese thought, which stress human beings, we can understand that the goal of the intellectual traditions in China is to be effective as an instrument for the cultivation of human beings. In Confucianism, a system is successful if it leads to human harmony, family harmony, social harmony, and political harmony. The Confucian ideal human is the sage, who is a role model for harmony and wisdom. In Taoism, a system is successful if it leads to spiritual and creative freedom. The Taoist sage is in harmony with nature whereas the Confucian sage seeks harmony with society.

Spirituality, whether we think of it as religious or philosophical, leads to the liberation of human beings within this world. The goal is *to be* a certain sort of wise human being, and not just to *know* something, or to *believe* something. The worthy thinker in China is not someone who knows esoteric concepts. Rather, the worthy thinker achieves the exalted status of sage, the wise human who lives life fully and completely in this world. Such a person is worthy of imitation, worthy of emulation.

The Ideal of Chinese Thought is Harmony

What is the ultimate value to cultivate if we want a good life? The goal of Chinese thought is **harmony**.[17] The ideal is when all things are in accord with the flowing pattern of Tao, that is, operate in a cosmic harmony; and that is when peace and order are found in human affairs and in nature. However, human behavior (especially the un-virtuous behavior of the emperor) can disturb the cosmic harmony and we must then work to re-establish this equilibrium. When harmony is lessened, when nature is unbalanced, the world is dangerous and death and destruction can occur without warning and without sense. For thinkers like the Confucians and the Taoists/Daoists, we must lessen the chaos and work towards harmony. Although this harmony depends most strongly upon the emperor, it also depends upon your behavior and mine. Heaven, earth, and human beings form a balanced flowing tension, and with the full attainment of equilibrium all the things in the world can flourish and be nourished. The harmonious interrelatedness of all things, and the positive value of the world, have continued throughout all the Chinese religions.

13.4 THE EARLY MYTHOLOGICAL HISTORY OF CHINA

In the legendary history of China before 2500 B.C.E., there were myths about the Three Sovereigns (Fu-hsi, Shen-nung, Yen Ti), followed by the Five Emperors (the Yellow Emperor or Huang-ti, Chuan Hsiun, Khun, and Yao,

---

[17] The goal of a good life for the Chinese was harmony; the ultimate goal of a good life was happiness for Aristotle and the Greeks.

who passed the throne on to the virtuous sage Shun). The Yellow Emperor, Huang-ti (Huangdi),[18] who tradition dates to about 2,500 B.C.E. is one of the most important. If that date is even remotely accurate, this mythological figure would have lived during the Stone Age, perhaps five hundred years before the Bronze Age in China (approximately 2000–771 B.C.E.). Legends attribute many important cultural innovations to the Yellow Emperor, including establishing an early form of government, revealing to humans how medicine works and he is reputed to be the author of an early text of folk medicine. In the myths, Huang-ti was as much a shaman as a ruler. Legends say that a goddess appeared to the Yellow Emperor and provided him with a magical book which allowed him to summon tigers, bears, and other wild animals to come and fight for him.[19] Not just a folk hero, the Yellow Emperor was treated as an important divinity by the rulers in the third century Ch'in/Qin and seventh-century Tang dynasties.

Traditionally, the Chinese understood all human history as a succession of royal dynastic eras, with each dynasty ruled by an imperial family with unquestioned authority. Every now and then an army general would win his way to the royal throne, overthrow the existing power structure and establish himself as the new emperor. All of his sons and descendants who rule comprise his dynasty. When another new general successfully battles his way to the throne, the dynasty changes.

The earliest dynasty in Chinese history is the **Hsia/Xia** (pronounced like Sha), and it is prior to 1600 B.C.E. (maybe 2200 B.C.E.), which is during the transition of the Stone Age, the Neolithic era, to the Bronze Age. This is pre-history. There are no writings from this period; our knowledge comes primarily from archaeology. It is thought that northern China was a loose confederation of independent agricultural settlements, including separate ethnic groups, and even when one group gained dominance, it is not likely to have resembled the sorts of rulership associated with later dynasties. The "palaces" were made of earth platforms and wood posts whose walls were woven fibers plastered in mud. It seems likely that the religious attitudes of the era were ritualistic and shamanistic. Remember that the Hsia period and all the legendary names prior to the Hsia are just before the Bronze Age, before the invention of bronze, mining of copper and tin, and other metals. Metals will make important technological and social changes to Chinese civilization during the succeeding Shang dynasty.

It was during the following **Shang** dynasty, and the succeeding **Chou/Zhou** dynasty when many of the basic insights of the Chinese intellectual tradition solidified.[20] It is following the collapse of the Chou dynasty that the traditions of Confucianism, philosophical Taoism, Mohism and the others took shape. Let's first look at the roots of these traditions in the Shang and Chou dynasties.

13.5 THE SHANG DYNASTY (c. 1766–1122 B.C.E.)[21]

The Shang clan did not rule all of the area we call modern China, or even all of northern China. The Shang dynasty kingdom was located in north-central China, centered around the Yellow River (the Huang river, pronounced Hwang). The Shang civilization was primarily agricultural with the major crop being wheat and millet. The Shang people also created many large fortified towns. The Shang developed a written language which is the prototype of modern Chinese ideographs. The Shang era is the Bronze Age, and the Shang were the first people of Asia to emerge

---

[18]   There are various dates for the Yellow Emperor: 2698 B.C.E. and 2711 B.C.E. Do not confuse the Yellow Emperor (Huangdi) with the much later first emperor of China named Qinshi Huangdi (Ch'in-shih Huang-ti) who lived ca. 220 B.C.E., two-thousand years later.

[19]   Martin Palmer, *The Elements of Taoism* (Rockport, MD: Element Books, 1991), p. 17.

[20]   An excellent treatment of early Chinese history up to the Shang is by Li Liu, *The Archaeology of China: From the Late Paleolithic to the Early Bronze Age* (New York: Cambridge University Press, 2012).

[21]   1766 B.C.E. is the legendary date, but archaeologists find a date of about 1500 B.C.E. to be more reasonable.

from the Stone Age — they were highly skilled in creating bronze implements, including weapons, cooking vessels and wine containers, and sacrificial ritual containers for major ceremonial functions. Offerings of food were placed on bronze utensils and presented to the royal ancestors by members of the ruling family.

The aristocracy of the Shang dynasty believed that the personal life of the emperor (whether he was virtuous or immoral), and ritual sacrifices which the emperor performed, affected the harmony between nature and human life. Like the shaman, the emperor mediated between the heavenly forces above and the earth below. The emperor's performance of sacrifices affected the crops, affected the maintenance of law and order in society, affected the weather, flood and drought, and could even be the occasion for natural disasters like earthquakes. This became an unquestioned truism in China for thousands of years.

The emperor was thought to have a special resonance with the force of Heaven. The ruler was the only one who connected impersonal Heaven to the human realm; he was the only conduit through which the blessings of Heaven flowed. The emperor was necessary if there was to be harmony between Heaven and earth, and this harmony was maintained when the emperor did the proper rituals, performed the proper sacrifices, and made proper offerings to the supernatural forces. The ruler could communicate with ancestors and spirits, and was the only human who could perform these rituals. The reason the ruler had such an important role was because Heaven had given the ruling family the authority and mandate to rule.

In the Chinese world-view, heavenly life, human life, and animal life are interconnected. The gods depend on the sacrifices to sustain themselves as gods,[22] and devotees depended on the gods to grant their requests. All earthly living things participate in the same cosmic cycles. There is the time for seeding, a time of growth, and then flourishing and harvest, and these times describe human and animal lives as well as crops. Following that, all living things return to the earth to make way for the next generation. Thus it was especially important that the emperor perform the correct rituals during the winter solstice so that the movement of nature could swing away from the cold dormant winter and nature could give way to the warmer spring. Similarly, the rituals and sacrifices of the emperor could guarantee that the shortest day of the year could reverse its course and that longer days would follow.

Agriculture and Reverence for Ancestors during the Shang

During the earliest centuries the Shang ruling family had special reverence for their legendary first ancestor, a being they called "Lord-on-High" or *Shang-ti/Shangdi*. He was the human founder of the Shang clan. As the centuries went by, the status of that primordial ancestor was elevated to the status of one divinity among many, and then the highest god of all, and special rituals were carried on in honor of Shang-ti.[23] Shang-ti was like an emperor in heaven, and he presided over a large collection of subordinate nature gods like rain, mountains, rivers, directions of the compass, and other awesome natural energies. Shang-ti could grant fruitful harvests, and assist troops to victory in battle. Shang-ti ruled over epidemics, drought, the person of the emperor, and thunder. The wind was the messenger of the Shang-ti, and Shang-ti ruled over the spirit powers. These served Shang-ti in the same way ministers serve the emperor who presides over his court.[24] If there was an eclipse of the sun, or the moon, it was believed that Shang-

---

[22] In 823, poet Po Chu-i (772–846) wrote that "You depend on us for your divinity. Beings are not divine on their own account, it is their worshipers that make them so." If people stopped performing sacrifices, the shrines would be bare, the god's name forgotten, and a new god would step in and take his place.

[23] Shang-ti can also be described as a deified totem figure as well as the supreme ancestor of the royal clan.

[24] The parallels between those spirits in heaven who serve Shang-ti and those celestial angels of Christianity who serve God and act as messengers of God, should be obvious.

ti/Shangdi was displeased. The human Shang royal court had access to the spirit realms, so they would ask questions of departed ancestors using methods of divination, such as "Is this a good time to begin a military campaign?" or "Will the rice harvest be good this year?" Questions were asked more than once, and records were kept about the accuracy of the answers.

The Shang dynasty rulers wanted to produce bountiful harvests, and they believed that an important element of this involved ritual respect for their own first ancestor. Through proper performance of sacrifices and rituals in honor of the first ancestor of the Shang clan, a virtuous emperor could assure healthy crops season after season. *Shang-ti* did not create the world or human beings, and was not a personal divinity who answered prayers. *Shang-ti* was remote and impersonal, but did respond when the Shang rulers performed proper rituals and sacrifices.

Shang-ti sent the rain down to the earth, but Shang-ti could also send down drought and famine instead. Shang-ti brought victory to the army, brought good fortune upon the world and its people, but Shang-ti was also the source of major misfortune as well. If Shang-ti was the ancestor of the ruler, then the ruling family could have special influence over these sorts of events. Also, even if you did not belong to the Shang dynasty ruling family, if one's ancestors sat in the heavenly court near Shang-ti, perhaps they could influence this divinity to benefit one's own clan.

The Shang rulers believed that it was possible to contact spirit forces or their departed Shang-ti ancestor, and more recently departed ancestors, and get information about the future, and obtain advice on how best to proceed in governmental affairs. This process of fortune-telling to know the future is called *divination*.[25] Divination is a common thread in popular Chinese religion. Even into modern times, people believed that one could ask questions of spirits and departed ancestors, who could respond with brief and vague explanations for events such as eclipses of the sun and moon, floods, fires, and drought. One well-known application in ancient China was to take an empty tortoise shell, scratch the Chinese characters for "yes" and "no" in various places on the shell, ask a question and then touch the shell with a hot poker. The resulting cracks on tortoise shells were answers which would then be interpreted by professional diviners.

Another option for the ruler was to try to predict the future by consulting with the clan ancestors. A more common divination text still in use today is the Chinese classic entitled the *I Ching* or "Book of Changes" which uses the random generation of hexagrams (six horizontal lines, both solid *yang*-lines and broken *yin*-lines) on the assumption that synchronicity between nature and apparently random events will give us a glimpse into the patterns of nature, and thus, into the future.

In the earliest periods, it was just the ancestors of the Shang emperor who were offered sacrifices. In succeeding centuries, other aristocratic clans began to maintain family temples containing wooden tablets with the names and accomplishments of their own clan ancestors inscribed on them. These family temples became focal points for rituals which offered food and drink in exchange for guidance and blessings.

Although respect and reverence for ancestors originated among the ruling families, later the practice came to permeate all of China and became an important part of the everyday life of almost every Chinese. The result is that family and the clan gradually became more and more important in Chinese society. As the centuries passed, for all levels of Chinese society, family ancestors were consulted on important decisions, and were kept informed about worldly affairs of their descendants (spring and autumn were especially good periods for doing this).

Life After Death

In early Chinese religion, the Chinese were not much concerned with details about human life after death. There were no official or orthodox statements about what precisely happened after death. It was a common popular belief that there was some sort of survival, but this survival was understood to be just a pale and shadowy afterlife. Some believed the afterlife was in heavenly realms, but others placed it in somewhere nearer, known as the Yellow

---

[25] Things like astrology, reading tea leaves, determining auspicious days for weddings or other events, or interpreting ambiguous ancient texts to get clues to the future are modern forms of divination. One form of Chinese divination is *feng-shui*, originally used to determine burial sites using concentric circles, and compass points. In English, these sorts of practices are called geomancy.

Springs. This afterlife was like human life on earth, but not as vigorous. Life after death was not a heavenly paradise; ancestors needed the assistance of descendants to make it tolerable. Life after death for ancestors was an unsatisfactory reflection of earthly existence.

The Chinese were quite sure that at least one small part of the ancestors did survive and did interact with descendants. Over the centuries popular belief was that ancestors lived in heavenly realms and could shower benefits upon their descendants, such as long life, good luck, many sons, wealth, and health. This became a two-way relationship. Ancestors helped out, and in return, humans offered ceremonies and food which were genuinely necessary for the ancestor to have a happy life in heavenly realms. If these family ceremonies were not performed regularly and properly, ancestors could be harmed, and become angry and punish their descendants. Ancestors depended upon descendants for the proper sacrifices and rituals which supported their lives in heaven; the descendants depended upon the ancestors for advice, for knowledge of the future, for things such as health and other benefits, and protection.[26]

One of the consequences of respect for ancestors is that it provided most Chinese with a sense of connectedness with the ancestral clan and ancestral lineages. As a result of family rituals participated in since early childhood, you would know the names and deeds of ancestors for seven or eight generations back, and perhaps longer; and you knew that your descendants would also recall your deeds for many generations. Such traditions became very powerful controls over behavior. A proper son would never want to bring shame upon himself, or upon his family, clan, or upon his ancestors. It was not the individual who was important; it was the family and the clan.

Sacrifices were offered to the forces of nature, and these included sharing food with the gods and ancestors. Animals were sacrificed including cattle, young bulls, goats, and pigs. These ritual sacrifices were intended to please spirits, but in the interaction with spirits there was little concern with questions of morality. Historians believe that in the ancient past human sacrifices were offered as well. When rulers passed away and were buried, the servants would accompany their masters into the next world. Sometimes the wife or concubine would be included in the tomb. The tomb of the founder of the Ch'in dynasty is believed to contain the bodies of the ruler's many wives and children, in addition to the world famous terra cotta army of approximately 8,000 soldiers. In later centuries, instead of living animals, shamans made use of effigies of animals made of straw, such as a straw dog. These were used in sacrifices in place of live animals.

---

[26] Thus, a family without a male heir would have no one to continue the sacrifices supporting departed ancestors; the husband must have a male child. The solution was to provide a male heir by either taking a second or third wife, or adopting a son of a concubine, or adopting a son from outside the family.

The terra cotta army of the emperor of the Ch'in dynasy

13.6 THE CHOU/ZHOU DYNASTY 1122–771 B.C.E.

As the Shang families who ruled became very comfortable, slowly they ignored their leadership duties and responsibilities. A farming group living about 300 miles south-west of the Shang kingdom overthrew the Shang dynasty somewhere around 1045 B.C.E. and established their own Chou/Zhou (pronounced something like "Joe") dynasty. The Chou instituted a feudal system in which each lower member owed allegiance to the higher people on the pyramid. The Chou rulers preserved Shang social and religious practices, and continued to perform sacrifices to Shang ancestors and especially Shang-ti/Shangdi, the divine first ancestor. The Chou preserved the Shang written language, and used it for poetry, ritual, law, history, philosophical and political wisdom writings.

The Chou people shared the key Shang values of order and harmony. It was believed that if the ceremonies (especially spring and autumn rituals) were carried out properly by the emperor, the spirits would confer on the Chou people abundant crops, few calamities, and other blessings. Proper ritual sacrifices and offerings to ancestors was absolutely essential.

Several hundred years later, during the Age of the Hundred Philosophers (approximately 500 B.C.E., the time of the flourishing of Confucianism and Taoism), sacrifices also demonstrated to one's ancestors that their descendants were prospering. Although filial rituals might seem directed exclusively to the departed ancestors, many Confucian scholars offered a slightly different interpretation of ceremonial rituals: sacrifices are about the person making the sacrifice, are about the community of the living, and are not really about dead ancestors.[27]

Throughout later Chinese history, the Chou/Zhou dynasty prior to 800 B.C.E. was seen as the ideal political

---

[27] Later Chinese thinkers like Confucius and Hsun-tzu say that sacrifices arise from within and demonstrate the state of mind of the sacrificer, demonstrate his loyalty, love and respect. Only common people regard sacrifices as a service rendered to spirits of the dead. Arthur Waley, *The Way and Its Power* (London: George Allen & Unwin, 1968), pp. 24-25.

kingdom.[28] The main rulers were seen as ruling with great virtue: King Wen, King Wu, and the Duke of Chou became legendary moral exemplars. The Chou era was looked upon as a Golden Age where everyone lived together in harmony and the kingdom was peaceful, where families lived orderly harmonious lives, and the world was perfectly virtuous.

In addition to the divine "Lord on High," Shang-ti, the Chou/Zhou royal family had their own divinity, called Heaven,[29] or ***T'ien*** (*Tian* in Pinyin, pronounced tea-en), who becomes of great importance during the later Chou/Zhou period. The spherical vault of the sky overhead was Heaven, and it was not only a place where heavenly spirits lived, but also seen as an impersonal force in its own right, and that force was the origin of natural order and moral order. In Indian thought Heaven was not thought of as having power, or agency. In China, however, Heaven responds.

Heaven, *T'ien/Tian* is above this world, even divine, but *T'ien* is not like the divine first ancestor, Shang-ti. *T'ien* was never an ancestor. *T'ien* is an impersonal sacred power which is natural, and which regulates all. It is transcendent yet it is also an organic system which is aware of the human realm and interacts with people through the dynastic emperor. In later times *T'ien* extends to encompass "all under Heaven," or what we would call nature and the world.

During the Chou/Zhou, in popular religion, *T'ien* is thought of as an agency, an impersonal force that can make things happen. *T'ien* is also all the forces (and ancestors) who live in Heaven, ruled over by *Shang-ti*. We can tap into those forces using shamans, using magic spells, with lucky omens, by doing sacrifices, and conforming to the Way of Heaven. Conforming to the Way of Heaven gives power to those who have the ritual knowledge, allowing them to manipulate some of the spirits.[30]

The Mandate of Heaven

T'ien, or Heaven, serves another function as well. Suppose we ask the emperor, "Why should you be emperor and not me? Why should I obey you? I'm smarter than you are, and I'm stronger than you are." The Chou dynasty emperors had an answer: the Chou had the authority to rule because *T'ien* recognized that the Chou royal family were people of extraordinary virtue, and in recognition of the virtue of the family, *T'ien* presented the right to rule, a "Mandate of Heaven" (*t'ien-ming; tianming*) to the rulers. This Mandate of Heaven (or Decree of Heaven) gave the Chou family the moral authority and heavenly power-connections to rule. The Will of Heaven is simultaneously the Way of Heaven and it legitimizes the great power and responsibility conferred on the rulers of the Chou/Zhou.

The Heaven of the Chou dynasty was not a personal being who created this world, and not a personal being who cared about humans. Instead, Heaven is a cosmic moral force, an impersonal natural force which is responsive to the socio-political world of the rulers and the court. Heaven makes sure that these institutions and leaders resonate with the larger rhythms of a universe functioning in natural harmony with moral principles.[31] Heaven can express displeasure and intervene in human history if the rulers do not maintain conditions of peace, prosperity and justice.

The emperor mediated between the cosmic force of Heaven and the everyday world. For Confucians, moral values are intrinsic to the structure of the universe. Later Confucian thinkers believed that whenever a ruler became

---

[28] Like most major civilizations, the Chou considered the land that they ruled over as the center of the empire, and ultimately, the center of the universe. The Chinese believed that the entire universe revolved around the emperor of China, and it was in the Chou land that the emperor dwelt. In Chinese, the name of China is *Chung-kuo* (pronounced Jung-guo, the Central Kingdom), which reflects this idea of the center of the universe. Of course, just about every civilization thought of itself as located in the center of the universe and many contemporary civilizations still do hold that view. The author suspects that politicians in Washington D.C. in London, in Paris, in Moscow, all share the view that their realm is the center of everything that is important.

[29] When used to name the impersonal sacred force which responds to the emperor, the term will be capitalized: Heaven. When used to name the sky overhead, or the realm where spirits and divinities reside, we will use a lower-case: heaven.

[30] For more remarks on shamanism in ancient China see Laurence G. Thompson, *The Chinese Way in Religion*, ch. 5.

[31] See Herlee Creel, *The Origins of Statecraft in China*, volume 1, chapter 5, "The Mandate of Heaven" (Chicago: University of Chicago Press, 1970), pp. 81–100.

tyrannical or otherwise morally unfit to exercise rule, heaven would display its disfavor by manifesting ominous portents such as an eclipse or an earthquake, and eventually floods, droughts, and other natural disasters.[32] If the situation became critical enough, heaven would withdraw its mandate, disorder would increase, and the political order would fall into chaos. As long as the emperor's behavior was ceremonially appropriate and in accord with the social norms of cultural morality and ritual correctness, Heaven, *T'ien*, supported the emperor and gave him and his descendants the Mandate of Heaven, the authority to rule.

This Mandate of Heaven doctrine explained political change. Suppose a general leads a rebellious army against the ruling family. The leader of the group that wins the final battle must have the Mandate of Heaven, whether it be a rebellious general or the reigning dynasty. Without the Mandate, a general could not defeat the ruler of the previous dynasty. Ultimately the later Chou emperors identified the Shang divinity, Shang-ti, with the Chou divinity, *T'ien*.

Shamanism

For the early Chinese, and continuing on into the later folk religion in China, popular religion was shamanistic. In shamanism, the universe is alive with countless spirits, some in heaven and some on earth, some beneficent, some malevolent, some indifferent. In addition there are a host of minor nature deities worshiped in various parts of the country. Among the variety of deities are wind, cloud, sun and moon and the cardinal directions of north, south, east, and west, and deities of mountains and rivers. In the early world of farms and farming the importance of agriculture and deities of fertility were also critical to a healthy harvest.

The Jade Emperor

The most important of the heavenly deities resembled the hierarchy of governmental ministers in the Chinese imperial court. For Chinese religion, the divine world was very much like the earthly bureaucracy but on a heavenly scale. The Chinese gods were governing celestial officials, influencing the lives of their worshipers exactly like China's own imperial and local bureaucrats governed the worldly lives of the citizens. Various deities tend to be portrayed as dressed in the clothing worn by imperial officials in the distant past.[33] The most important ruling god is the Jade Emperor, Yu-huang, or Yu-ti/Yudi, the leader and controller of the heavenly organization. In the same way the earthly emperor ruled under the protection of Heaven, so too Heaven had a supreme ruler, the Jade Emperor. The Jade Emperor was usually depicted as sitting on his throne, wearing robes embroidered with dragons, the ceremonial robes of an ancient emperor. The Jade Emperor is responsible for determining events both in the heavens and on earth, but uses underlings to carry out his commands. The Jade Emperor lives in a palace with a door-keeper and court functionaries, and he has ministers who preside over the various departments concerned with human activities.

Not all divinities were heavenly. There are household spirits, spirits of the hearth, spirits of the well, the stove god, a kitchen divinity of the cupboard and the household fire, divinities which can help provide for the prosperity and security of the family. Many things that happen to us, and that happen in our world, are explained as the actions of spirits. Dreams can be interactions with spirits. Strange sensations in one's body are the result of spirits. Buzzing in the ears, twitching of eyelids, itching, and unexplained movements of things in the world are communication from Heaven. In addition, by observing the behavior of birds, insects, animals, and attending to thunder, lightning, and the stars, one can receive messages.[34] Human beings seek harmony, not only with one another, but also hope to establish

---

[32] Even in the twenty-first century there are some Americans who interpret such catastrophes as punishment from the Christian God.

[33] When Western artists depicted the single God of the Bible, they never dress such a being in a suit and tie. Instead, the being wears the robes of ancient patriarchs and rulers and may sit on a golden throne. Similarly, Chinese images of the divine wear ancient robes of ancient rulers and sit on a royal golden throne.

[34] Arthur Waley, *The Way and Its Power*, p. 22.

the coveted relationship of harmony with the forces of nature. In addition to being bureaucrats, these local divinities were also personally interested in us, perhaps as patrons or parents or guardians, and these local spirits could provide protection in exchange for reverence and sacrifice.

In classical China there were people who communicated with spirits, but there was no professional and powerful priestly guild, or caste (nothing like the Brahmin caste in India). There were people who claimed special knowledge of supernatural powers, and some who claimed that their spells and incantations could influence the spirits. They included both males and females. These people were shamans, not priests in the sense that Western religions understood the term. These people prayed for the blessings of the divinities, for male offspring or for good crops or rain. It is thought that the very ancient kings of regions in China were shamans or perhaps claimed descent from shamans.

Tao/Dao, Yin and Yang Develop During the Chou Dynasty

In the period around 800 B.C.E., the great majority of people were farmers. You and I would most likely have been born on a farm, would have grown up on a farm, married a fellow farmer, raised crops and a family, and finally, died on a farm and then we would be buried on the farm land. Later on, our descendants would perform proper rituals for our welfare for at least eight generations.

Living on a farm means living intimately with cycles of nature. Nature is manifest as patterns, monthly patterns of full moons, patterns of the seasons, cold and hot, wet and dry, planting and harvesting, with a regulating pattern of growth-harvest-dormancy. Spring and summer are bright, warm, and the period of active growth of plants. Fall and winter are dark and cold, and it is the time for plants to become dormant. In nature, we go from summer to winter and then back to summer: reversal is inevitable. It cannot be avoided by anything a human being might do.

Imagine graphing a sine wave, curving up and down. In the Chinese world, all of the patterns around us can be plotted on such a graph of successive risings and fallings. At the top of the mountain it is bright, and at the bottom of the valley it is cool and dark. At the high point of the sine curve, we have the hot summer. At the bottom low point, we have winter. Spring and fall can be found in the midway points, as the year moves from hot to cold, and then back from snow to summer sun. Animals are born weak (the low part of the curve) and slowly gain strength until, at some point, they achieve maximum strength. Then, as they age, they get weaker and weaker, until they die. High noon is the sun overhead, and midnight is the cold and dark. During the day there is a time when you are most awake (the high part of the sine wave), and another time of the day when you have trouble keeping your eyes open (the low point of the sine wave). As we have seen, Tao/Dao is the continuous field in which all the rising and falling multiplicities are harmonized.

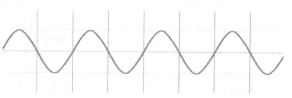

The Chinese gave names to the particular high points and low points. The high bright place they call **yang** (yah-ng), and the low, dark point they called **yin**. The alternation and interaction of *yin* and *yang* is how the principles of change were explained in classical Chinese thought. The interaction of *yin* and *yang* provides a causal explanation for why things change in the regular patterns which are so immediately observable to anyone living in touch with natural rhythms.

The universe cycled back and forth between poles of *yin* (covered by clouds; dark, hidden, secret, receptive, cool) and *yang* (bright and shinny; light, open, assertive, warm). The high point of the curve, *yang*, is not heavy so it went upwards to form the heavens. *Yang* is light, fire, life, movement. The *yin* is heavy and descended to form the earth we inhabit. *Yin* is water, death, stillness. These are two opposite but complementary forces or tendencies inherent in all things. We can study and understand how things are and how they have changed in the past, and how they will change in the future. *Yin* might dominate for a while, but then it will go into decline and be replaced by *yang*. But, note that nothing in our universe is completely *yin* or completely *yang*, and neither state is permanent. Neither state is complete by itself, but each needs its complement to become complete.

The same pair can be applied to male and female. The *yang* is the male, and it is active, bright, assertive, logical and rational. The feminine is *yin*, which is hidden, creative, passive, non-aggressive, obscure, intuitive and yielding. These two are not at war with one another. *Yin* and *yang* are modalities of the flowing reality we call "Tao," they are equal and opposite forces, one active and one quiescent, continually alternating.[35] Every real thing is a dynamic fusion of these opposites, a fusion of *yin* and *yang*.

Tao/Dao is another name for the continually changing yet harmonious movement from *yin* to *yang* and back again. Chinese numerology also utilizes this: odd numbers are *yang* and even numbers are *yin*. The color red is a *yang* color; black is the *yin* color.[36] The penetrating, the celestial, the mountains, are *yang*; the receptive and the earthly, the valleys, are *yin*. These concepts are essential to understanding Chinese culture and are prominent in Chinese art, especially black ink landscape art.[37]

For the philosophical Taoists and Confucians, the abstractions which *yin* and *yang* symbolize are not related as a good-evil pair. Neither of the two is goodness, and neither is bad, or evil. *Yin* and *yang* are each essential, each necessary; they are mutually dependent. When *yin* and *yang* are in dynamic harmony and actively balance one another in a series of alternating processes, this is good. When *yin* and *yang* are out of balance, with an excess of one and a deficiency of the other, this is trouble, this is a lack of balance, a lack of harmony, this creates problems. For traditional Chinese medicine, an imbalance of *yin* and *yang* is the explanation for ill-health, and ill-health is evil. Good is the proper flowing harmonious mixture of both *yin* and *yang*; evil is an unbalanced excess of either.

The continual motion of *yin* and *yang* are the threads which weave Tao/Dao. Tao, the Way, or the Path, was understood to be the ultimate ordering principle of the world, the way the world works, the path of nature, the pattern of the stars in the sky, the path of celestial change, the path of all natural patterns. The Chinese scholars kept calendars which recorded these patterns, and emphasized the idea of order, in which every thing and every activity had its proper time according to the season.[38]

The Tao which Taoism knows, and with which its art is concerned, is a seamless web of unbroken movement and change, filled with undulations, waves, patterns of ripples and temporary 'standing waves' like a river. Every observer is himself an integral function of this web. It never stops, never turns back on itself, and none of its patterns of which we can take conceptual snapshots are real in the sense of being permanent, even for the briefest moment of time we can imagine.[39]

---

[35] See Robin R. Wang, *Yinyang: The Way of Heaven and Earth in Chinese Thought and Culture* (London: Cambridge, 2012)

[36] Black is the color of the sky before dawn, it is the new moon, it is the color of the heavenly beings, all *yin* forces. Some Taoists associate blue-green with *yin*.

[37] See George Rowley, *Principles of Chinese Painting: Revised Edition* (Princeton, NJ: Princeton University Press, 1974).

[38] Joseph Needham, *Science and Civilization in China*, Vol. II (London: Cambridge University Press, 1956), pp. 279–289. The second volume of this amazing series deals with ancient Chinese civilization and its religious ideas. Needham's books points out that the incredible scientific achievements of China are not well-known in the West. For example, the Chinese had the world's first printed book using movable type, seven hundred years before Gutenberg's bible printed in the 1450s. In addition to gunpowder and the compass, Chinese made advances in mining technology, silk production, ceramics, astronomy, mathematics, and medicine. Joseph Needham's monumental series of books is highly recommended. See also Deng, Yinke, *Ancient Chinese Inventions* (New York: Cambridge University, 2011). An abridged version of Needham's classic is Carl Ronan, *The Shorter Science and Civilization in China* (London: Cambridge University Press, 1980)

[39] Philip Rawson, Laszlo Legeza, *Tao: The Eastern Philosophy of Time and Change*, p. 10.

CHAPTER 13: ORIGINS OF CHINESE THOUGHT

The Tao/Dao provides the sacred ultimate in classical Chinese thought, but Tao is not just transcendent and above this world: ultimacy is found in ordinary things and ordinary events in the world.[40] Human lives are not in conflict with the sacred. The sacred ultimate does not just transcend our world. It is not separate and apart from earth. The sacred ultimate is immanent, found in everyday life, and even found within the individual. However, some people and some places were thought to be more sacred than others — especially forces of nature and revered ancestors. In addition, kings, emperors, and living persons of high status were especially sacred.

The relationship between the sacred ultimate and the human realm was not limited primarily to a vertical relationship between a deity above and humans human below, but rather was found in the horizontal net of interrelationships that included all living things.

13.7 THE PERIOD OF THE WARRING STATES (771–221 B.C.E.)

In 770 B.C.E., northern barbarians sacked the capital, killed the Chou emperor and central government disappeared in northern central China. The existing remnants of the Chou government was forced to move its capital east, and they lost control over much of their empire. A period of civil and cultural crisis resulted. Remnants of the royal family could not re-establish control in the north and China divided into independent kingdoms. In the past, the rulers of those independent realms were called "dukes" (someone ruling on behalf of the ruler) but now they called themselves "king." These kingdoms were soon warring with one another for control of China. There were many dozens of small vassal states, each with its own independent king. With central authority gone, each local king was potentially the new emperor of all of China, and the founder of a new imperial dynasty.

The kings of these feudal kingdoms were untrustworthy and corrupt, and the result was social and economic deterioration everywhere. Life for everyone was appallingly dangerous. The more powerful state would attack another, weaker kingdom, and boundaries and borders were constantly shifting. When armies move, they take the food they need from their own farmers who lose everything, and starve. Taxes were unbearable. Healthy males were drafted to fight and their farms fell into disrepair. Those with power oppressed those without power. China was a land of tumultuous change and continuing violence which escalated with each passing century.

War became much more practical, more realistic, than it had been in the past. It was no longer just the clan aristocrats battling with one another. During the early years of the previous dynasty (1045–771 B.C.E.), warfare between groups and kingdoms was at least partly a demonstration of aristocratic values. There were rules of chivalry, of honor. Military battles were somewhat ritualized and provided a chance for someone to distinguish himself as a mighty warrior or a hero.[41] This was no longer the case during this period of civil wars.

Throughout human history periods of civil and cultural crisis tend to provoke a re-thinking of the meaning of human existence. Such times are fertile for the development of military strategy, but also for the development of new religions, new traditions, and new perspectives on the world. Responding to the chaotic times, Chinese scholars and teachers offered some revised traditional theories and some radical new theories which attempted to capture a deepened understanding of nature, human beings, and their interrelationship.

The result was many schools of thought appeared: Confucianism, several forms of Taoism, Mohism, the Yin-Yang school, the School of Names ("Dialecticians"), Logicians (Neo-Mohists), and Legalism. Among the most important of the many religious schools to arise during this time of conflict was Confucianism, and several varieties of Taoism.

---

[40] This is especially true for the Chinese Taoist philosopher Chuang-tzu (Zhuangzi).

[41] Andrew Seth Meyer, *The Dao of the Military: Liu An's Art of War* (New York: Columbia University Press, 2012). See also Andrew Seth Meyer, John Major, Sarah Queen, and Harold Roth, *The Essential Huainanzi* (New York: Columbia University Press, 2010).

Confucianism and Taoism both began during the Period of the Hundred Philosophers (which roughly corresponds to 570–221 B.C.E.). According to tradition, Confucius, and the founder of philosophical Taoism/Daoism, Lao-tzu, were both alive approximately 500 B.C.E. However, no single system became dominant during this time period. Historically, politically and socially things got worse and worse and the fighting was relentless. Marauding armies destroyed everything they encountered. Entire provinces were massacred. Famines caused by war and by flood were widespread.

13.8 THE CH'IN/QIN DYNASTY 221–206 B.C.E.

The political decay and destruction which followed the collapse of the Chou/Zhou dynasty in 771 B.C.E. continued on until 221 B.C.E. when the ruthless ruler of the Ch'in/Qin kingdom finally defeated all six of the remaining rival kingdoms, and established himself as the first emperor of an expanded and unified China, the first in five hundred years. The new Ch'in dynasty adopted the Chinese philosophy of Legalism as the official philosophy of the government, and this resulted in a merciless "Law and Order" society of unprecedented strength. The law codes were unified, weights and measures were standardized, axle width was standardized, coinage was standardized, and the written language was standardized. The empire was unified by brute force.

One consequence of adopting Legalism was the Ch'in emperor's ruling in 214–213 B.C.E. that all the classical literature of China (all of which was written on bamboo strips held together with heavy string) which was in conflict with Legalism, or which suggested ideas other than Legalist ideas be burned, resulting in the near total destruction of almost all the great Chinese classics. These were reconstructed later from memory, but with varying success.[42] The Ch'in emperor accused scholars of venerating the past instead of venerating his new dynasty, accused them of entertaining ideas other than Legalism, and so he buried alive four-hundred and sixty scholars and historians to ensure that the intellectuals would not contradict his politics. These same intellectuals would have memorized the ancient forbidden texts, and by burying them alive, the memories would be lost as well.

Ch'in-shih Huang-ti/Qinshi huangdi (259–210 B.C.E.), the first sovereign emperor, started numerous great projects, including linking the highways and the waterways with a series of canals, creating the greatest inland water communication system in the world. His most famous project was inaugurating the construction of the Great Wall of China to protect northern China from raiding Mongolian nomads. It was in 214 B.C.E. that the immense project of building the Great Wall of China began.

---

[42] There has been great debate about these ancient texts before the Ch'in burning. Luckily for scholars, a number of very ancient texts from about 300 B.C.E., written on bamboo strips, have been discovered and are in the process of being studied and occasionally translated into English. For example, there is Sarah Allan, *Buried Ideas: Legends of Abdication and Ideal Government in Early Chinese Bamboo-Slip Manuscripts* (New York: State University of New York Press, 2015), Dirk Meyer, *Philosophy on Bamboo: Text and the Production of Meaning in Early China* (Leiden: Brill, 2011); Matthias L. Richter, *The Embodied Text: Establishing Textual Identity in Early Chinese Manuscripts* (Leiden: Brill, 2013); Edward L. Shaughnessy, *Unearthing the Changes: Recently Discovered Manuscripts of the Yi Jing (I Ching) and Related Texts* (New York: Columbia University Press, 2014); Wang Zhongjiang, *Daoism Excavated: Cosmos and Humanity in Early Manuscripts* (Three Pines Press, 2015; now on Kindle).

In the northern frontier there already existed scattered fortifications; the emperor proposed a wall connecting the fortified towers. Historians believe that 300,000 forced laborers were used to build the Great Wall. A great many of them died, and the legend is that their bodies were buried inside the walls so their spirits would act as a protective barrier against demons.[43] The emperor heavily taxed all parts of China to pay for these projects. Starvation was rampant. Unorganized dissent spread throughout the empire (Legalism and the Great Wall became symbols of imperial oppression for two thousand years). The emperor then ordered the construction of a gigantic tomb or mausoleum and one report suggests that 700,000 workers were brought to the project. Part of this tomb includes the 8,000 terra cotta warriors which were buried underground and only discovered in 1974. The tomb (the size of a small mountain) has never been opened, but is the focus of sustained research. It is believed to contain sizable amounts of mercury, the fumes of which would be damaging or deadly to any who opened the tomb.

The emperor Ch'in-shih Huang-ti believed that it was possible for a human being to live for many centuries, and in an effort to achieve immortality, he brought religious Taoist/Daoist alchemists into the capital to brew an elixir of immortality. The magical potions the alchemists brewed are believed to have included mercury and phosphorus. The emperor became successively more irrational, and it is likely that Ch'in-shih Huang-ti died from ingesting these concoctions brewed for him by his royal alchemists. Immediately after his death, the emperor's advisors killed his eldest son who was in the north, and then put the more pliable second son on the throne. Peasant uprisings followed, and the second son died on the battlefield. The Ch'in dynasty came to an end, to be replaced by the Han.

13.9 THE HAN DYNASTY 202 B.C.E.–220 C.E.

The Han dynasty[44] began following the spectacular collapse of the Ch'in/Qin dynasty, and adopted a combination of Confucianism, practical Legalism, and Taoism for its political life, and certain alchemical and cosmological aspects of religious Taoism continued to be important. Confucianism was primarily a moral and political system for people who were in a position to be politicians, and it served the religious needs of China's elite ruling class, and became state orthodoxy until about 200 C.E. The harshness of Legalism was tempered, but it was recognized as a practical tool for governing. At that point, Taoism gained in importance, both to the non-elite peasants and common

---

[43] Scholars think this is a myth. Human bodies buried in the wall would have weakened it over time, and the Chinese rulers did not want their wall to be weak at any location.

[44] A very detailed analysis of the Han dynasty is Michael Loewe, *Divination, Mythology and Monarchy in Han China* (New York: Cambridge University Press, 1994). This explores the symbols of the Han, the authority of the emperors, astronomy, the role of dragons in the Han, bones and stalks used for divination, and even imperial tombs. An excellent thorough analysis of the Ch'in/Qin and Han based on recent discoveries is Michael Nylan and Michael Lowe, eds., *China's Early Empires: A Re-Appraisal* (Cambridge University Press, 2010).

people, and continued on as the backbone for Chinese popular religion.

Chinese astronomers developed a very sophisticated way of mapping the stars during the Han dynasty, because they believed that the positions of the stars foretold auspicious times for birth, marriages, and battles. They were sure that there were correspondences between heaven and earth. An eclipse was a message of warning sent from the heavens, and the first Chinese astronomers were the ones who interpreted these signs. The Chinese were the first civilization in history to record ancient supernovae explosions and the birth of nebula.

Paper was invented during the Han dynasty, produced by crushing bamboo, soaking the bamboo mush in bleach, and then grinding it into pulp. The ancient Chinese discovered the world's first cast iron which allowed for mass production of farm equipment. But cast iron is fairly brittle, and further experimentation produced the much harder steel. By 150 C.E., the early Chinese had worked out a sensitive mechanism for detecting earthquakes as they were occurring, because earthquakes were a message from heaven about how the ruler was ruling.

The Chinese believed that their emperor was the center of the entire human world, not just the empire of China. Chinese astronomers believed that the universe circled about the north star, and by extension the entire world must go around the emperor who occupied the center of creation. Thus, the court officials must always be south of the emperor who is always to be seated to the north. The throne room had to be built so that the royal throne faces south, and cities were built on a precise north-south axis. Determining north was the task of the court alchemist-magicians who experimented with ways to determine true north. Later in the T'ang/Tang dynasty (618-906 C.E.) the Chinese worked out the magnetic properties of lodestone, and used it to create the magnetic compass which was used to lay out Chinese cities.

When the Han dynasty collapsed in 220 C.E., Confucianism was no longer seen as the single best way to rule the country, and the emperors of the succeeding dynasties became patrons of both Taoism and Buddhism. For the next six-hundred years, Confucianism, Chinese Buddhism and Taoism uneasily shared access to the rulers, and shared influence. This period includes the incredible artistic flowering during the Sui (590–618 C.E.) and T'ang (618–906) dynasties, and the following early Sung dynasty (to about 1200 C.E.).

As the centuries progressed, the political influence of Taoism and Buddhism began to wane, and a re-invigorated Buddhist-influenced newer form of Confucianism became more important. Western scholars call this "Neo-Confucianism" and it dominated the religious, political, and cultural life of China from about 1200 to the start of the twentieth century — when Western influences (Marxism among others) began to have a profound influence on Chinese thinkers. When the Marxist Chairman Mao took control of China in 1949, he considered all forms of religion to be detrimental to the state, and the government did its best to stamp out all forms of religious practices except those deifying the Communist state and its Communist leaders. Contemporary China has a present population of 1.3 billion people, making it the most populous country in the world (India's population is estimated to be 1.1 billion).

13.10 SUMMARY OF THE CHAPTER

We have discussed the early sources for the traditional Chinese world-view in the period from the stone age up to the Ch'in/Qin and Han dynasty (202 B.C.E.–220 C.E.) which followed the Ch'in. The Shang dynasty is the earliest mention of reverence for ancestors and an acknowledgment of a world filled with spirits including Shang-ti, the first ancestor of the ruling family. The belief that the moral virtue of the emperor was essential for the harmonious operation of the world was also taking shape during the Shang.

In the succeeding dynasty, the Chou, belief in the heavenly force called *T'ien/Tian* became important, and the belief that the royal family received its right to rule from heaven (*T'ian-ming*) because of the virtue of the family. The Chou also saw a strengthening belief in the regularity of the patterns found in nature was added to the world-view. The chief value was putting oneself into harmony with the Tao/Dao, the regular pattern of nature found in every aspect of the world, found in human and animal life, and even found in politics. The active, bright, aggressive, logical aspect of Tao/Dao was called *yang*, and the passive, cool, receptive, intuitive aspect of Tao was called *yin*. Chinese thinkers used the movement from *yin* to *yang* and back again to *yin* as a model for all aspects of life, including traditional

Chinese medicine.

During the politically chaotic Period of the Hundred Philosophers, approximately 570–220 B.C.E., numerous schools of Chinese thought became established, the two most important of which were the teachings of Confucianism and Taoism. Later on after the collapse of the Han dynasty, approximately 400–500 C.E., forms of Chinese Buddhism became more influential in Chinese political life and in the private lives of the people. Many forms of devotional, meditative, and philosophical Chinese Buddhism and religious Taoism were particularly important for the next five hundred years during the Sui and T'ang dynasties. Finally, beginning around the year 1000 C.E. Confucianism became reinvigorated, adapted some Buddhist ideas, and slowly regained dominance over Chinese political life. This dominance continued until the twentieth century. Since the T'ang/Tang dynasty (618-906 C.E.), popular Chinese religion was a combination of shamanistic folk religion, Confucianism, varieties of religious Taoism, and devotional Buddhism, however these were discouraged by the Maoist government in China after 1950 C.E.

13.11 TECHNICAL TERMS

divination   Any process of fortune-telling designed to reveal the future is called *divination* (astrology and crystal balls are a modern form of divination).

Shang-ti   The first ancestor of the Shang rulers; later elevated to godlike status. It can be romanized as Shangdi, and is pronounced Shang-dee.

Tao   The Way, the Pathway of all things in nature; the way things ought to be. It is pronounced "dow."

T'ien   Heaven, the deity of the Chou dynasty, later identified with Shang-ti. Properly pronounced tee-en.

Yang   The energetic up movement of Tao; the active, the male, the bright.
Yin   The passive down movement of Tao; the cool, dark, intuitive, creative.

13.12 QUESTIONS FOR FURTHER DISCUSSION

(1)   We have seen that harmony with nature, and harmony within society, were important values in Chinese civilization. Did European and American civilizations ever value harmony with nature and within society? What was the attitude in the West during the Middle Ages? During the Renaissance? In contemporary times?

(2)   The Chinese talk about the Three Traditions as the backbone of Chinese life. What are these three? Did they conflict, or could they work together?

(3)   Modern anthropology seems to discover genetic and biological similarities between human beings and the other living things on the planet. According to European and American thinkers, are humans profoundly and fundamentally different from other living things, or are we very much like the other living things (as the Chinese believed)?

(4)   This chapter pointed out that there has been a tendency in Western thought to assume that pure reason, rationality, especially as exemplified by contemporary science, should be able to solve every problem. Science

has been very successful in many areas (medicine, technology, cosmology and astronomy, and so forth) but seems not to make much headway in other areas (one's personal relationships, settling moral issues like capital punishment and abortion, legalization of drugs, etc.). Where do you stand on this issue? Is human flourishing to be found in rationality (as Western people often think), or is human flourishing to be found in reasonableness (as the Chinese used to believe)? Maybe it is to be found somewhere else, such as humility or righteousness? Discuss.

(5) Respect of youth for old age, and reverence for departed ancestors, have been very important to Asian civilizations. Do Western cultures have any similar traditional and enduring values?

(6) Consider the properties of *yin* and *yang* in the Chinese world view. The Chinese believe that males are *yang* and females are *yin*. Question: are males completely *yang* with no *yin* at all? Are females completely *yin* with no *yang*? Or is it a case of shifting proportions of *yin* and *yang*?

(7) If I see you in the morning and say "hi," you will respond "hi." This relationship is clearly one of cause and effect. How does Western thought account for this causal interconnection? Is it mechanical? If not, then what is the connection between cause and effect? Discuss.

(8) Is a wise human being someone who knows a lot of information? Is a wise human someone who has faith and believes what tradition and authority assert? Is a wise human someone who behaves in certain ways that society approves of? Is it something else? How do classical Chinese and contemporary Western people understand wisdom?

SELECTED BIBLIOGRAPHY

Overview of Early Chinese Thought

Balazs, Etienne, *Chinese Civilization and Bureaucracy* (1964).

Bokenkamp, Stephen R., *Ancestors and Anxiety: Daoism and the Birth of Rebirth in China* (Berkeley: University of California, 2009) Development of the Indic idea of rebirth into Chinese Taoism and popular religion.

Creel, Herlee, *The Origins of Statecraft in China* (Chicago: University of Chicago Press, 1970)

Deng, Yinke, *Ancient Chinese Inventions* (New York: Cambridge University, 2011)

Fung Yu-lan, *History of Chinese Philosophy*, 2 volumes (Princeton, NJ: Princeton University Press, 1952)

Girardot, N. J., *Myth and Meaning in Early Taoism* (Berkeley: University of California Press, 1983).

Hansen, Chad, *A Daoist Theory of Chinese Thought* (New York: Oxford University Press, 1992)

Hymes, Robert, *Way and Byway: Taoism, Local Religion, and Models of Divinity in Sung and Modern China* (Berkeley: University of California, 2002)

Kohn, Livia, *Daoism and Chinese Culture* (Magdalena, New Mexico: Three Pines Press: 2001)

Lagerway, John and Marc Kalinowski, eds., *Early Chinese Religion: Part One: Shang Through Han* (1250 BC–220 AD) (Leiden & Boston: Brill, 2011)

Lagerway, John and Lu Pengzhi, eds., *Early Chinese Religion: Part Two: The Period of Division* (220 AD–529 AD) (Leiden & Boston: Brill, 2010)

Li Feng, *Early China: A Social and Cultural History* (New York: Cambridge University Press, 2013)

Loewe, Michael, *Divination, Mythology and Monarchy in Han China* (New York: Cambridge University Press, 1994)

Loewe, Michael, *Everyday Life in Early Imperial China* (1968).

Meyer, Andrew Seth, *The Dao of the Military: Liu An's Art of War* (New York: Columbia University Press, 2012)

Munro, Donald, *The Concept of Man in Early China* (Stanford, CA: Stanford Univ. Press, 1969)

Needham, Joseph, *Science and Civilization in China*, Vol. II (London: Cambridge University Press, 1956)

Needham, Joseph, *Science in Traditional China* (Harvard University Press, 1981)

Oxtoby, Willard G., ed., *World Religions: Eastern Traditions*, Second Edition (London: Oxford University Press, 2002)

Rawson, Philip, and Laszlo Legeza, *Tao: The Eastern Philosophy of Time and Change* (London: Thames & Hudson, Ltd., 1973)

Ronan, Carl, *The Shorter Science and Civilization in China* (London: Cambridge University Press, 1980)

Temple, Robert, *The Genius of China: 3000 Years of Science, Discovery and Invention* (Inner Traditions, 2007)

Van Norden, Bryan W., *Introduction to Classical Chinese Philosophy* (Cambridge: Hackett Publishing, 2011)

Waley, Arthur, *Three Ways of Thought in Ancient China* (New York: Doubleday, 1956)

Wang, Robin R., *Yinyang: The Way of Heaven and Earth in Chinese Thought and Culture* (London: Cambridge, 2012)

Yü Ying-shih, "Life and Immortality in the Mind of Han China," *Harvard Journal of Oriental Studies* 25 (1964–1965), pp. 80–122.

CHAPTER 14: THE AGE OF THE HUNDRED PHILOSOPHERS

14.1 OVERVIEW OF THE CHAPTER

The time period the Chinese called the Age of the Hundred Philosophers began in the middle of the sixth century B.C.E. and ended when the first emperor, Ch'in-shih huang-ti/Qinshi huangdi, conquered the remaining kingdoms of China in 221 B.C.E. using the harsh theories of Legalism. During his reign he ordered the death of hundreds of scholars who disagreed with him, and he ordered the destruction of the classical literature of China. So many of the important Chinese thinkers lived during this turbulent period prior to the Ch'in/Qin dynasty that it is called the Period of the Hundred Philosophers, or The Age of the Hundred Philosophers.

The Age of the Hundred Philosophers is one of the most fertile for the development of Chinese thought, both religion and philosophy in China. The major developments in Chinese thought originate during this time, and many of the popular religious ideas also take hold among the general population in this era. This label, Period of the Hundred Philosophers, is not a reference to dynasties or to a specific political period. It includes the last part of the historical era called the Spring and Autumn Period (770–476 B.C.E.), a period of feudalism where kings and lords battled to expand their kingdoms, using both military forces and political intrigues and assassinations.

The Age of the Hundred Philosophers begins in the sixth century B.C.E. which was a time of civil war and chaos. Life was difficult, and the energy of thinkers of the time was focused upon questions of why the world was so unfair and painful, and how we can bring about a well-ordered harmonious society. Most of the great Chinese philosophers during this period in Chinese history wrestled with this problem.

The central authority of the Chou dynasty had disintegrated nearly two hundred years before the Age of the Hundred Philosophers, and China was undergoing continuing economic changes, military imbalances, and wars between competing kingdoms to establish a new emperor. The Spring and Autumn period was the era of Confucius and early Taoism. Things did not improve after the Spring and Autumn period.

The Chinese refer to the next period as the Warring States Period (475–221 B.C.E.), where the remaining kingdoms were constantly at war. Politically and militarily, it was a world of assassinations and attempted assassinations, ambushes, battles, sneak attacks, swift raids, and reprisals. It was a world of treaties, pacts, truces, and alliances which lasted very briefly, and then were broken whenever it was an advantage to one side or the other. Political alliances could not be relied upon to bring peace. The world was in disorder and the ancient harmony so much stressed in the Chou dynasty was no longer visible in Chinese civilization. The ongoing warfare reduced feudal kingdoms down to seven super-kingdoms, each attempting to defeat the others. Each ruler of the kingdoms wanted to unify China, but to unify China with himself as sole ruler.

This violent era is the period of Confucius and Mencius, the thinkers who provided the backbone of Confucianism. But it is also the period of Mo-tzu/Mozi, who advocated universal love and egoless sacrifice. The law-and-order philosophy of Han-fei-tzu/Hanfeizi was particularly important, and was adopted by the ruler of the Ch'in/Qin kingdom. One Chinese thinker advocated pleasure and what was of benefit to the self. This was the hedonist philosopher Kung-sun Lun/Gongsunlun. The famous military strategy of Sun-tzu/Sunzi was developed during this time of war. Finally, the greatest Taoist thinkers lived during this period, Lao-tzu/Laozi and Chuang-tzu/Zhuangzi.

In addition, this was the time when the most basic beliefs about gods, ghosts, and departed ancestors solidified within the popular folk religion of China.

CHAPTER 14: THE HUNDRED PHILOSOPHERS

14.2 THE HUNDRED PHILOSOPHERS (roughly 551 B.C.E.–221 B.C.E.).

The era called the Age of the Hundred Philosophers generally begins with the birth of Confucius in 551 B.C.E., and then extends into the political period of the Warring States, which began in 403 and ended in 221 B.C.E. It was one of the truly great creative periods in Asian thought, in religion, philosophy, morality and political thought, where the decline of the Chou/Zhou leadership re-opened the question "What is the Way that we should follow if we want to reestablish harmony?" "Which Path will unify all of China?" Whatever that path or "Way" was, the Chinese thinkers did not believe it was centered only on humans. That Way would be the foundation of both earth and heaven. It would be the potential source of all reality. It would be the root of existence. It would be the sacred ultimate.

At the beginning of this time period Chinese society could be divided into two main groups: the aristocratic ruling class, and the common class. During the Age of the Hundred Philosophers, a third group emerged, the elite scholars, who were people of superior birth which gave them access to a good education, but who did not have wealth or power or political connections of the aristocrats. Scholars tried to earn their living using the skills that come with education. They offered theories of governing, theories on the nature of reality, the nature of society, and theories about how to extend one's life and how to achieve harmony with Nature. Scholars and teachers offered some revised traditional theories and some radical new theories reflecting a deepened understanding of nature, human beings, and their interrelationship. There were many new ideas being discussed and argued, and only a few actually became separate schools with a lineage tradition. In the interests of clarity, we will discuss these as "schools of thought." The two most important were (1) Confucianism, and (2) Taoism (in Wade-Giles romanization) or Daoism (in the Pinyin system of romanization).[45]

14.3 THE MAJOR SYSTEMS OF THE HUNDRED PHILOSOPHERS

THE YIN-YANG SCHOOL

The earliest coherent system of ideas (or schools) to develop was most probably the Yin-Yang cluster of concepts which interpreted everything in terms of pairs of complementary opposites and as forces which resonated sympathetically with one another. The vision of this school endured throughout Chinese history and influenced all subsequent Chinese world-views. This school perceived nature to be composed of two pervasive yet opposite forces, two forces which work together and complement one another, each equally essential. The universe cycled between poles of *yin* (covered by clouds; soft, moist, dark, earthly, hidden, shadowy, secret, receptive, passive, cool) and *yang* (hard, bright and shiny; heavenly, light, dry, open, assertive, active, warm). The interaction of *yin* and *yang* provides a causal explanation for why things change in the regular patterns which are so immediately observable to anyone living in touch with natural rhythms.

Metaphysics: The Nature of Ultimate Reality

The Yin-Yang school was sure that to understand reality, we should study the two complementary forces or tendencies inherent in all things, The Yin-Yang school was certain that we can study and understand how things are and how they have changed in the past, and how they will change in the future. *Yin* and *yang* are modalities of Tao, equal and opposite forces, one active and one quiescent. The two act together in complete harmony — not strife. We can study and understand how things are and how they have changed in the past, and how they will change in the future.

The Yin-Yang teachers were concerned with the origin, evolution and structure of all things, as well as more practical questions which could be considered proto-scientific, such as questions about the chemical and physical

---

[45] An excellent summary of these schools is found in A. C. Graham, *Disputers of the Tao* (LaSalle, Illinois: Open Court, 1989).

nature of all things in the world. If we ask "Where did the universe come from, and how did it originate?" the answer is that all things grow, or arise organically out of Tao itself and all things are a combination of a *yang* element and a *yin* element.

The interaction of *yin* and *yang* produces **Five Agencies**, Five Phases, or Five Processes (sometimes called the Five Elements): wood, fire, earth, metal, and water.[46] Those things in the world which shared these fundamental tendencies would then resonate with one another, and an event occurring in one place actually was connected organically with similar events elsewhere else, and the Chinese thinkers speculated on the details of how the world was interconnected.

This made sense to all the following Chinese thinkers, not just the Yin-Yang school. They were sure that the things of our ordinary world are produced by the interaction of these five and thus *yin* and *yang* provide a causal explanation of what things are made of, and why they change in the regular patterns that we observe around us. These five are the natural forces which consecutively alternate, resonate, and recombine to produce the orderly changes within nature that happen each year.

When WOOD is dominant, we have the season of spring; when FIRE is dominant, we have summer; when METAL is dominant, we have fall; when WATER is dominant, we have winter rain. In late summer, EARTH is dominant. Each of these five is a phase of Tao, each overcomes and replaces the next in line.

These five resonate with similars and interact in cycles, and understanding their complex interactions would help explain what is likely to happen next in the empire. Earth blocks water, water overcomes fire, and so forth. These are the backbone for much of Chinese divination (fortune-telling) and medicine. Chinese emperors also adopted these five to explain dynastic succession: since water extinguishes fire, the Chou (fire) dynasty was replaced by the Ch'in (water); in turn the earth Han dynasty (earth dams up water) replaced the Ch'in. Since wooden tools dig up earth, the next dynasty will be wood. Since fire burns wood, the next dynasty will be fire.

Another aspect of the Yin-Yang school was the search for a process which would turn base metals into gold (a process called **alchemy**) and turn the base decaying physical body of a human being into an immortal (gold-like, untarnished) being — this search became identified with religious Taoism. Thus the Yin-Yang school provided the basic conceptual framework by which all later Chinese thought dealt with human nature, including human biology and which turned into traditional Chinese medicine.

CONFUCIANISM: A Brief Introduction

The period of the Hundred Philosophers was a period of social and moral chaos and this occupied the talents of many of the major thinkers of the period. For example, Confucius (551–479 B.C.E.) focused on political rulers and on social and familial ethics. He thought that the primary cause of disorder was rulers who exerted their power without any moral principles to guide them, and used their power just for their own benefit.[47] Confucius was certain that this went against the pattern of Heaven (*t'ien/tian*). People lacked the proper moral role models, and were even ignorant about the great virtuous leaders of the past.

Confucius saw a solution for the chaos: social reform so that the government would be run by virtuous rulers

---

[46] The Greeks had four basic elements: earth, air, fire, water. The Chinese did not have air in their list of five, but the Chinese did have *ch'i*, or *qi*, the air-like spiritual substance pervading all material things which was the life-essence.

[47] For almost all of Chinese history, Chinese thinkers assumed that the only possible form that a government could take was an all-powerful dynastic ruler, perhaps because this emperor was the only one who could channel the blessings of Heaven onto earth. They presuppose the rule of an absolute monarch who seeks to enact his will through an elaborate bureaucratic apparatus. Ideally the ruler would have the blessings from and authority from Heaven (*t'ien*) to rule. It seemed clear to Chinese thinkers that everything in the world should be unified under one single monarch. Whoever could unify China and maintain harmony was legitimate in the eyes of both the elites and the people. A valuable book which discusses this is Yuri Pines, *The Everlasting Empire: The Political Culture of Ancient China and Its Imperial Legacy* (Princeton, NJ: Princeton University Press, 2012). A previous volume by Professor Pines on the same topic is *Envisioning Eternal Empire: Chinese Political Thought of the Warring States Era* (2009)

who would bring peace and harmony to the empire. The rulers needed to rule from a position of moral authority, not military might. All persons in a position of authority must cultivate the seeds of their own morality, develop their humanity and benevolence, master the rules of ritual and ceremonial interaction, and then serve as a role model for those subordinates beneath them and for succeeding generations. People need to work on themselves first, develop themselves morally and socially, and then one can help guide those living in our local environment. Only then could one try to reform the government. The Confucians asserted a version of the Golden Rule: "Never do to others what you would not like them to do to you."[48]

For the Confucians (like the Greek philosophers), the foundation for human morality and goodness is found within nature and within human beings, and is not located in commands from some supernatural power. If we want our world to change into a realm of harmony, we cannot simply impose peace and harmony by laws and regulations. To improve society morally requires internal moral self-transformation from each of us. We must cultivate goodness within ourselves. As a result of those changes, we are in harmony with our fellow human beings and we are in harmony with the Tao/Dao.

TAOISM/DAOISM: A Brief Introduction

Scholars generally feel that the origins of Taoism lie in the ancient past, originating from shamanistic roots. These amorphous currents gradually separated into two strands, religious and philosophical. Like Confucianism, **philosophical Taoism/Daoism** begins in the rather chaotic Age of the Hundred Philosophers, about 500 B.C.E. Unlike the Confucians, the philosophical Taoists /Daoists were more concerned with the nature of an ultimate reality which is fully natural yet transcends humanity.[49] The philosophical Taoists believed that all the things under heaven moved spontaneously according to their own nature, and resonated with the general patterns of nature, and just this was the deepest reality. However, human beings had lost touch with their own spontaneous natural humanity because humans put so much faith in, and stress upon the use of tools like words, concepts, artificial rules and logic. When we rely too much on these, they insulate us from the real world that these tools are used to denote or symbolize.

The *Tao Te ching/Daodejing* is a Taoist classic, a poetic collection of insights indicating that we should look to the natural world for our role models, and the result would be re-establishing our original harmony with nature, which then would result in peace in the kingdom and personal contentment. Give up the profit motive, discard trying to be too clever, stop trying to outdo others, to fool others, to swindle others, to "get ahead." Instead of making things more complex, we should simplify. We human beings are not separate from nature; we are as natural as everything else in the world, and we need to return to harmony with the flow of Tao/Dao, alternating between the complementary poles of *yin* and *yang*. We are at home in this world. The philosophical Taoist has no interest in extending one's life or achieving immortality. There needs to be a single ruler, but that ruler should simplify and take action as infrequently as possible.

Genuine human freedom lies in spontaneity. We need to become free of society's rigid and artificial rules and develop our spiritual and creative freedom. We need to break free of our fear of death and our irrational desire to extend life at all costs; instead we can and must fearlessly face and embrace death as the universal process of nature.

The **non-philosophical religious forms of Taoism/Daoism** included those priests who regarded Lao-tzu as a god, and rejected the philosophical Taoist attitude of going along with the flow. The religious Taoists sought installation of a Taoist saint who should be the single ruler of China. They tended to utilize alchemy, stressing extending one's life, perhaps achieving immortality, and cultivating sexual and physical exercises for health. The roots

---

[48] The Analects of Confucius: 12:2 and 15:23.

[49] In the West, this area of philosophical concern is called ontology or metaphysics.

of religious Taoism are very clearly shamanistic. There are Taoist priests who interact with and control spirits using magic, and there are Taoist church-like temples. The alchemical Taoists sought eternal life by mixing various compounds and then cooking them over fire. They mixed compounds like mercury, sulphur, saltpeter, and various plants.[50]

The physical exercise aspect of religious Taoism was closer to a modern aerobics class, or a gym or health club where one engages in stretching exercises and repetitive exercises so one can get into shape or regain flexibility to maintain health. Later developments in religious Taoism brought about social, political and military movements designed to establish a Taoist/Daoist theocracy ruled by a Taoist priest who was the earthly incarnation of the heavenly divinity, Lao-tzu/Laozi.

MOHISM

The philosopher Mo-tzu/Mozi (ca. 470–376 B.C.E., pronounced Mow-zu) is the founder of Mohism (Mo-ism). Mo-tzu disagreed with Confucius, and drew inspiration from folk and popular religion. He understood Heaven (t'ien/tian) to be a personal deity who cared about us, who watched over the affairs of human beings and meted out rewards and punishments. This deity was not the creator of all things but was a part of the natural order. The will of Heaven is the ultimate guide to human existence, and heavenly gods and spirits were the instrument of Heaven. Mo-tzu rejected lavish funeral rituals as being of no particular value to human beings.

Mohism appealed to those with little social prestige, little worldly power, and no wealth. Mo-tzu built his philosophy on the concept of utility, or usefulness, stressing the general welfare of the common people. On the scale of usefulness, he found Confucianism to be lacking. It was just too theoretical.

Mo-tzu/Mozi held the view that Heaven loves all equally, and so he established his thought upon a foundation of **universal love**, and criticized the graduated-love political and social solution of Confucius and Confucianism. For the Confucians, one loves one's family and puts them first; then comes extended family, neighbors, and finally villagers and outsiders. Mo-tzu's doctrine of universal love or universal altruism asserted that we must love one another equally.

Mo-tzu/Mozi tried to be very practical. Mo-tzu focused on actual physical changes in the social and political realms. The motto of the Mohist was "promote general welfare and remove evil." The criterion for measuring human happiness was usefulness, interpreted as "useful to the people," or "bringing benefit to people." Usefulness, and benefits refers to measurable things like wealth, population, and contentment.

Mo-tzu could be described as a militant pacifist. He wanted the smaller states to gain military knowledge so they could defend themselves. His idea was to use defensive warfare to produce a state of non-war. A state strong in defensive techniques should lessen the aggressive wars that were so prominent during this period.

His positions seem to have been too extreme for the general population. By the beginning of the Han dynasty (202 B.C.E.), Mohism had ceased to exist.

SCHOOL OF NAMES

The literal meaning of the Chinese characters denoting this group of Chinese thinkers is "School of Names," however, some scholars have tried for more descriptive philosophical terms. The Chinese scholar Fung Yu-lan prefers "Dialecticians" and "Sophists"; the scholar W. T. Chan calls them "Logicians" and each of these labels captures an aspect of the function of this tradition of Chinese thought. The interest in this school was mostly theoretical and abstract: what is the relationship between the real world and the abstract names and concepts we use to understand the real world?

---

[50] When the alchemists finally added charcoal to their mixtures, they accidentally discovered gunpowder (perfected about 1000 C.E.). Around 1270 C.E. Marco Polo reported to skeptical Europeans about the powers of Chinese gunpowder.

CHAPTER 14: THE HUNDRED PHILOSOPHERS

The School of Names was influenced by Confucianism, but was much more interested in the actual abstract relationship between (a) the names we give to things and (b) reality. They also wondered if the <u>hardness</u> of a white stone can be separated from the <u>whiteness</u> of the white stone. Each conceptual division seems to lead to a self-contradiction. This abstract school was very intellectual and as such, it did not have the utilitarian stress of the Mohists.

LEGALISM: THE SCHOOL OF LAW AND PUNISHMENT

Around 250 B.C.E., toward the end of the chaotic and destructive Warring States period, new philosophical ideas became the guiding influence upon the ruler of the Ch'in/Qin kingdom. This was the school of *fa* (law), referred to as Legalism. The philosophers Han-fei tzu (d. 233 B.C.E.) and Hsun-tzu/Xunzi (ca. 300–238 B.C.E., pronounced Shun-zu) developed a vision of human nature that was not very romantic but decidedly practical.

Hsun-tzu/Xunzi argued that human beings are innately selfish ("evil") and as a result, they must be controlled by strict laws and punishments. Since people are fundamentally selfish, they will always ask "what's in it for me?" and once we realize this, we can utilize and manipulate this innate selfishness to control people. It is simple: reward people when they do what we want; punish people when they do not do what we want.

If we apply this to governing the nation, we get Legalism, a "law-and-order" approach, which assumes that because each person is self-centered, we cannot trust them to do what is best for the society as a whole, but we can control them using a "carrot and stick" approach to governing. Every human being goes where he is sent, does what he is told, and is judged by how well he does it There are no mitigating circumstances, no excuses. The punishments for failure were very harsh, but everyone knew in advance what the punishments would be if one broke the law. Ideally, it made no difference whether one were a wealthy minister, or a poor farmer. The law was black and white, and very harsh.

The fundamental theory of Legalism is that common people exist to serve the ruler. The ruler has absolute power, and has no responsibilities to his people. The people have duties towards the ruler. The ruler must use extreme and ruthless techniques to control everyone: reward them when they do their job, punish them when they do not live up to their job description. Everyone must follow the letter of the law in every detail; no creative responses were desired. If you did less than expected of your job description, you were punished very severely. No excuses were possible. If you did more than expected of your job description, you were punished also. No one was allowed to take any initiative; the rule was follow orders, do what you were told, no more and no less. The kingdom belonged to the king, and all the people were to serve and obey the ruler.

The Ch'in/Qin Ruler becomes the First Emperor of all of China

The king of the Ch'in/Qin adopted the Legalist strategy of rewarding people who do what you require of them, and severely punishing those who do not fulfill their job requirements. Using this strategy he managed to impose effective central control, to unify his own army and kingdom and defeat the remaining kingdom of Chu about 225 B.C.E. He then set himself up as the new Emperor of a unified China and in 221 B.C.E. called himself Ch'in-shih Huang-ti/Qinshi huangdi (pronounced something like Chin-shur Hwang-dee), the First Emperor of the Ch'in/Qin, the lord of the world. The Ch'in/Qin dynasty started in 221 B.C.E. and then collapsed about 207 B.C.E., after only fourteen years.

The Ch'in dynasty produced profound changes in Chinese society. The bureaucracy was centralized in a way never seen before in Chinese dynasties. The government standardized wheel-axle size for carts, thereby standardizing the roads and allowing carts and wagons to pass one another in villages and highways everywhere in the kingdom. The Ch'in imposed standardization on coinage throughout the empire. The Ch'in also standardized the Chinese written language for the first time. The people were mobilized under the direction of the government and a vast network of canals and roads built. The Great Wall of China began construction under the leadership of the Ch'in-shih Huang-ti to protect northern China against the invasions of the nomadic Mongol tribes that were always a danger to northern communities.

CHAPTER 14: THE HUNDRED PHILOSOPHERS

When the Ch'in/Qin dynasty collapsed, Legalism was blamed for the evil excesses of the regime and few scholars openly encouraged the adoption of Legalism afterwards. But Legalism continued to be studied and continued to exert influence upon Chinese political thinking. Legalism did encourage Confucians to strengthen their idea of ritualized ceremonial interaction (*li*) by writing social and moral rules into rigid laws, thereby adding a dimension of legality to Confucian morality.

The schools we have talked about in this chapter are the Grand Tradition religions, but there is another dimension to Chinese religion, the Little Tradition. Ancient religion in China is decidedly shamanistic in character.

14.4 GODS, GHOSTS, and DEPARTED ANCESTORS

Even before the Age of the Hundred Philosophers, the early Chinese religion was a composite of many regional cultures, but they had some shared nature myths, they practiced divination or fortune telling, men and women cultivated trance states, and kings and queens had ritual roles to interact with a hierarchy of divinities, supernatural energies or powers, mostly in semi-human forms. These beings could be either male or female, but they resembled human beings and share our world.

One important group were the divinities who reside in heavenly realms. In addition there is the realm of departed ancestors. The human world we inhabit has beings who are negative, like ghosts, demons, and devils. There was also the fourth realm of those humans who used magical foods or exercises to extend their lives to hundreds of years, and might even become immortal.

THE GODS IN HEAVEN

The heavens are continuous with the human world, not completely separate or different. The realm of the deities is very much like the human realm, and in the same way that on earth, high above ordinary working people there are aristocratic ruling families and an emperor, similarly high above the human emperor are the heavens which have **shen**, or divinities who are like government officials who rule the spiritual worlds. *Shen* are kindly or neutral with regards to human goals and aims. They are like humans but occupy the divine realms, and none have powers like omnipotence or omniscience. The English term "gods" is misleading if one associates it with deities who transcend the physical universe and who created the cosmos out of nothing.

The gods are made of *ch'i/qi*

Many of the *shen* are beings of great power, but the gods are made of the same basic stuff as humans. This stuff is called *ch'i/qi* (pronounced "chee"). *Ch'i* is a difficult concept because of the wide variety of meanings: originally it meant vapor, or steam, and then comes to mean the vital force, the life-breath or the energy of life and the stuff of matter. All things that are alive possess *ch'i* as life-energy. The Neo-Confucian philosopher Chu Hsi/Juxi writes: "All men's capacity to speak, move, think, and act, is entirely derived from *ch'i* . . ."[51] It was believed that *ch'i* circulated throughout the body, like blood, but *ch'i* could not be observed. Blood was thought to be part of the body's *yin-yang* balance. The Chinese also believed that the universe had the same *yin-yang ch'i*, which constitutes the Tao. Like water when heated, *ch'i* could expand into vapor or mist, which is mind and the spiritual. But like water when frozen, *ch'i*

---

[51] Chang Chung-yuan, *Creativity and Taoism: A Study of Chinese Philosophy, Art, and Poetry* (New York: Julian Press, 1963, reprinted Harper Colophon Books, 1970 and again by Jessica Kingsley, Publishers, Philadelphia PA: 2011), p. 65. I have substituted "*ch'i*" where the translator used "ether."

could condense into physical stuff. Thus *ch'i* is the fundamental essence of life, but it is also the fundamental building block of all that exists.

The *shen* in the heavenly realms most resemble powerful governmental bureaucrats; they are like human officials who have the power to grant or withhold favors, within the limits of their own jurisdiction. For example, these beings determine the length of life allotted to each person. Like human politicians and bureaucrats, the *shen* respond to flattery, gifts, and bribes. So these heavenly *shen* were celestial officials who governed the fate and fortunes of those on earth in the same way that China's own aristocratic bureaucracy governed their worldly lives.

The divine hierarchy of Heaven was never the central focal point of religious life for the majority of Chinese people. Many important Chinese deities are known only by the titles of their official position in the heavenly hierarchy. These beings exist, they may influence the country or our personal lives, but the great majority of them are too remote to be relevant to us.[52] There are two analogies that can be drawn to illuminate their status. We might compare *shen* to federal politicians in democracies, or we might compare *shen* to the angels of popular Christianity.

Consider the role that important politicians in the capital city play for most of us. We know the names of the two or three most important federal political leaders and possibly the names of a few of our local representatives, but the majority of us pay little attention to the names and titles of the majority of the politicians who make our laws and influence our lives. We know that there are numerous federal and state judges, but unless the court affects us personally, we do not know the names of these judges. We may have heard of the Ninth Circuit Court of Appeals, but have no idea of the names of the judges who sit on that court. The *shen* in their heavenly courts might be like those judges and politicians for our world.

Another way to think of *shen* is to use the idea of angels. *Shen* play a role similar to the role angels play in popular Christianity. A good Christian might know the names of a few of the most important angels (i.e., Michael, Gabriel),[53] but most angels are unnamed. You may believe that you have a guardian angel, but not have any idea of the name of that angel or have any idea of what that angel does when not looking after you. Many *shen* are very much like this. Like guardian angels, the majority of the *shen* have limited realms of influence because most *shen* are local. Often *shen* are limited to one geographic area, a village or urban neighborhood. A few *shen* had a larger range of influence.

The heavenly realms shared the same basic structures as the human world, because the aspects of the world which are supernatural take their origins from the same source as our natural world. We need not be concerned with the heavenly beings unless there was an occasion where a heavenly official might be of some help in our worldly concerns. Most Chinese rituals were family rituals, and did not require the services of professional priests.

Local *shen* are close to the people in villages. The earth god is the lowest ranking official in the heavenly hierarchy, and protects the villages and also controls wealth and good fortune. The earth god is most often on the altars of common folk. He is portrayed as having a staff and usually a cup with gold in it.

Many *shen* are associated with natural forces such as wind, clouds, sun, and moon. There are *shen* ruling over the cardinal points of north, south, east, west. There are *shen* associated with mountains and rivers. Some *shen* are deities of thunder and fire.

The Jade Emperor is the Ruler of Heaven

In the same way the earthly emperor ruled, under the protection of Heaven, so too Heaven had a supreme ruler, the Jade Emperor. The Jade Emperor sits on his royal throne, dressed in the ceremonial robes of an ancient

---

[52] However, there were also *shen* who were more personal, who functioned as patrons or guardians. These *shen*, who offered protection in exchange for ritual sacrifice and reverence expressed towards them, will be discussed in the next section.

[53] In the Christian and Jewish holy texts, angels perform miraculous feats and have supernatural powers. In this respect they are similar to the Chinese *shen*.

emperor. He is responsible for determining events both in the heavens and on earth, but uses court underlings to carry out his commands, including ministers who preside over the various departments concerned with human activities.

The Jade Emperor was concerned only with the problems of the worldly emperor; he is never concerned with ordinary mortals.[54] It was his ministers who dealt with the problems of lesser mortals. Once a year the Jade Emperor calls all the subordinate gods to his palace, which is in the highest of the heavens. The *shen* would then be allocated new positions, according to how they had performed their duties during the previous year. The heavenly ministers oversee everything, including rain, water, time, war, and wealth.

The Jade Emperor has a wife, the Queen Mother of the West. She presides over the west, and is sometimes portrayed riding on a crane. She wears a crown and is served by the Jade maidens. She lives in a nine-story palace of jade far off into the west, with a golden wall more than a thousand miles long. She knows the secrets of immortality, and in fact she grows the peaches of immortality in her garden, but the tree bears fruit only once every 3,000 years. It was during the Han dynasty that widespread worship of the Queen Mother of the West began.

Lao-tzu/Laozi, the philosophical author of the *Tao Te Ching*, was officially deified in 165 C.E. and he joined the pantheon of *shen* or deities in the heavenly realm. He was now known as the Supreme Ultimate Lord Lao. During the T'ang dynasty (618–906 C.E.), the royal family claimed a genealogical descent from Lao-tzu.

14.5 THE EARLY CHINESE VIEW OF LIFE AFTER DEATH

The Early Chinese understanding of "soul"

In Chinese thought, there was nothing corresponding to the Western concept of an eternal unitary soul created in the image of the divine god, and nothing corresponding to the Hindu idea of an unchanging eternal *atman*. For the Chinese, humans have numerous aspects that function something like multiple souls and Chinese thinkers were very vague about what happens to these various parts of a human after death. Of course, all things that exist arise out of both the *yin* and the *yang*, and are the product of the continuous interaction of *yin* and *yang*, and that includes human beings. Human beings are not the special creations of a god, and the essence of a human being is not identical with the Sacred Ultimate (i.e., the way Brahman is identical with *atman* for the Vedanta school in India). All things, including souls and the heavens, are combinations of the Five Processes (wood, fire, earth, metal, and water).

There were several conflicting views about life after death in early China. The Chinese never conceived of a heavenly realm as a reward for having faith or for believing the right things. Heaven was never given as a reward by some deity. The Chinese had no concept of hell[55] where a deity might condemn those who did not worship him. Gods were not particularly relevant to life after death in classical China. What was relevant were rituals and birth-status. Some Chinese thought that there was the possibility of one aspect of the human soul to live on in the tomb. Some members of the powerful families believed that after death the common people might travel to the Yellow Springs, huddled in darkness, but kings and aristocracy might live on in the heavenly realms near Shang-ti, the Lord on High. Some might live in dark prisons below the earth, where they would slowly fade away. Later on the Chinese did adopt the concept of hells once Buddhism came to permeate Chinese civilization, but the Chinese-Buddhist hells were never permanent.[56]

---

[54] If we are having a problem with international laws or governmental bureaucracy, we might ask for and expect help from our local elected representative, but we would not expect the President of the United States to intervene in a local problem.

[55] In the Han dynasty (206 B.C.E. – 220 C.E.) the Chinese talked about an underworld which was governed by underground bureaucrats, but it was not a realm of torture and punishment for those who had lived immoral lives, or for those who believed the wrong things.

[56] In Buddhism, one remained in the hellish realm until one's bad karma was paid off, and then would be reborn in higher realms.

CHAPTER 14: THE HUNDRED PHILOSOPHERS

Even after the introduction and development of Indian Buddhist ideas of heaven, hells, and karma in China, the Chinese tended to be quite unconcerned about the details of life after death. There was a vague unfocused cluster of beliefs but nothing official and nothing corresponding to doctrine or dogma. It simply did not seem to be important to work out the details.[57] For some, the afterlife was to live on as an immortal inhabiting a mountain paradise or abiding in special magical islands off the coast of China. For some, the afterlife was the paradise in the west ruled by the Queen Mother of Heaven. We already mentioned the possibility of the Yellow Springs under the earth. For some, the afterlife was returning to the great Tao, the great pattern or way of nature.

For most Chinese, the immediate and important goal was a long and healthy existence in this life, with less concern about an afterlife. If descendants performed the proper rituals, the afterlife would be reasonably comfortable. In fact, the Chinese have Five Blessings: a long life, riches, health, love of virtue, and a natural death. As mentioned above, after Buddhism began to affect popular religious beliefs, the idea of hellish realms were also included in the list of possible afterlives. As the centuries progressed, in later popular Chinese religion the most common goal was to join one's ancestors in the heavenly realms.

An early locus for the Chinese view of what makes a person a human is the *Tso Chuan* (Tso's Commentary on the *Spring and Autumn Annals*, Duke Hsi, 5th year), which states:

> In man's life the first transformations are called the earthly aspect of the soul (*p'o*). After *p'o* has been produced, that which is strong and positive is called the heavenly aspect of the soul (*hun*). If he had an abundance in the use of material things and subtle essentials, his *hun* and *p'o* will become strong. From this are developed essence and understanding until there are spirit and intelligence. When an ordinary man or woman dies a violent death, the *hun* and *p'o* are still able to keep hanging about men and do evil and malicious things.[58]

The ideas behind the two parts to the soul arise from the concept of the pattern of nature, Tao/Dao, functioning through the interaction of *yin* and *yang*, which then produces both the human physical body and the finer more subtle spiritual manifestations. Humans, as a combination of these two, do not have a unitary substance or soul; rather they have a spiritual essence with a *yin* part and a *yang* part, each with several sub-parts, in a constant dynamic yet stable unity.[59]

Hun is the positive heavenly *yang* aspect, and *p'o* is the negative earthly *yin* aspect to the self. *Hun* is the brighter *yang*-spirit of a human's vital force, expressed in intelligence and breathing. Some texts describe the *hun* as having three smaller component parts.[60] *P'o* is the coarser *yin*-spirit of our physical nature, expressed in bodily movements.[61] The finer *hun* was venerated in family shrines and occupied heavenly realms and was the "luminous soul" aspect of an ancestor which influenced the family and succeeding generations. The *p'o* was earthly and more physical, but there were at least seven varieties of *p'o*.[62] Among royalty, the buried body would be accompanied by things that would be useful for the more physical aspect of the self, things like clothing, food, sacred texts, sculptures of musicians,

---

[57] When Buddhism became established in China, Buddhist priests tended to be seen as specialists in matters dealing with funerals, with answers to questions about the ultimate nature of reality and questions about life after death.

[58] Translation by Wing-tsit Chan, *A Source Book in Chinese Philosophy* (Princeton, NJ: Princeton, 1963), p. 12.

[59] Lawrence G. Thompson, *Chinese Religion*, 4th ed. (Belmont, CA: Wadsworth Publishing Company, 1989), pp. 10–11.

[60] Michael Saso, *Taoism and the Rite of Cosmic Renewal* (Washington State University Press, 1972), p. 12.

[61] Wing-tsit Chan indicates that religious Taoist/Daoist texts interpret the *hun* as semen, and the *p'o* as the (dark) inside of the female sex organ. W.T. Chan, *The Way of Lao Tzu*, p. 117, note 2.

[62] Michael Saso, *ibid.*, pp. 12-13.

maps of sacred realms, works of art, and sometimes servants and guardian warriors were killed and their bodies were put in royal tombs.

14.6 ANCESTORS ARE MOST IMPORTANT

Not all *shen* (heavenly beings) are bureaucrats. At least some *shen* can also be departed ancestors. The mechanism behind this transformation is the idea that the self has a *yin* part and a *yang* part, which are separable. It is possible for the *yang* aspect, the *hun*, to travel to the heavens. When alive we have a *hun* but after death it becomes *shen*.[63] When humans died, they moved to another realm that was not too far and not too different from the earthly one inhabited by descendants.

One part of the personality, the brighter and positive *yang* part of the person, the parts that make up the *hun*, rose up to join previous ancestors in Heaven. The coarser and negative *p'o* aspect (there may be as many as seven *p'o*) lingered by the grave until it weakened, sank down into the earth and gradually expired. The third part of a human, the animating part of the personality, was the *ch'i*, the "life-breath" which simply dispersed at death.[64]

The Duty of Filial Piety

Descendants had a religious duty to perform rituals venerating departed ancestors. Reverence and respect for parents and ancestors is called *hsiao/xiao*, or the virtue of filial piety. If the descendants nourished the *hun* of the departed ancestor on the domestic altar with offerings of food, then it could intervene on their behalf in heaven (for things like blessings, crops, long life, medical cures, and male offspring). If descendants neglected ceremonial offerings to the *p'o*, it might become malevolent and dangerous. It was essential that the sons of each family do the proper rituals for ancestors. The ancestors may have died, but they remain family members. They have moved to a new realm and interact with their earthly family members at appropriate times. For those ancestors of many generations ago, they tended to fade into the pantheon of heavenly gods or spirits.

As we have seen, in the traditional Chinese world-view there are several parts to a human being and none of these is equivalent to a Hindu *atman* or a soul as in Christianity. The Chinese did not think that these parts could be reassembled, any more than we could recapture the helium atoms that were in a balloon after the balloon had been popped with a pin.

Every child within a family participates in numerous rituals for departed ancestors, and most Chinese are conscious of belonging to a continuing line of ancestors and descendants. Rarely has this been questioned by classical Chinese thinkers. There is an interaction between those who had passed beyond and those who remain behind. There is a mutual cooperation. At the very least, departed ancestors provide a spiritual and psychological "glue" that connects later generations together, treating each generation with the proper respect.

In popular Chinese religion, the belief was that departed ancestors offer blessings if the appropriate sacrifices are performed properly. Sacrifices to ancestors ensured that the ancestors would have a continuing existence in a spiritual condition in the other dimension, not far removed from the mortal world. Reverence for ancestors was the best chance for the ancestors to achieve immortality, and for you, their descendant, to achieve immortality.

. . . the rites of burial and sacrifice were sanctioned both by fear of the dead becoming a vengeful
    demon [*kuei*] and by hope that the dead would become a benevolent god. Such a fear and such a hope

---

[63] Michael Saso, *ibid.*, p. 13.

[64] The branch of religious Taoism concerned with immortality provided most of the details on the *yin* and *yang* parts of a human being, which supported the cult of ancestors.

underlie all of Chinese religion.[65]

As long as a person was remembered and the proper rites of respect were performed regularly by descendants, the bright part of their soul (the *hun*, the *yang* element) would continue to exist after death. Respect or reverence for ancestors involved home ritual offerings of food, incense and "spirit money" which ancestors could use to pay for food and pay for rent in the heavenly realms. This is illustrated in one of the most ancient poetry collections, Ode 279 from the *Book of Odes*:

> Abundant is the year, with much millet and much rice.
> And we have tall granaries,
> With hundreds of thousands and millions of units.
> We make wine and sweet spirits
> And offer them to our ancestors, male and female,
> Thus to fulfill all the rites.
> And bring down blessings to all.[66]

In the early time periods, ancestor rituals were the exclusive province of rulers and members of the aristocracy. Over the centuries the religious rituals in honor of ancestors became an essential part of every Chinese family. There were memorial rituals as part of state religion, and rituals as a family practice. If the family had an ancestral temple, the first rituals were performed there. Rituals were performed at grave sites, and at the family altar. Wine and food were offered to ancestors, and deep bows were performed before the tablets which had the name of the departed. These rituals were performed frequently for the first years, and then annually after the first three years. When a young man achieves manhood, there is a ritual where he is presented to his ancestors. Announcements of weddings and births are shared with ancestors as well. These family religious rituals are associated with Confucianism in China, but are not really what Confucius taught to his followers.

14.7 GHOSTS AND DEMONS

In addition to the *shen* comprised of celestial gods and ancestors, there are also negative beings who share our earthly world. If the proper funeral and family rituals are performed, the *hun* will go to the realm of ancestors to send down blessings to the surviving family members and the negative *p'o* (the *yin* part) will rest peacefully in the grave. Without a suitable burial ritual and continuing family rituals, the *p'o* could turn into a vengeful ghostly being who is not well-disposed towards human beings. This negative force was called a *kuei* in Wade-Giles, or *guei* in the Pinyin romanization (pronounced something like gu-way).

The negative *kuei/guei* is a pale shadow of the living person, usually invisible, but capable of horrifying people by appearing before them as a grotesque caricature of the mortal form.[67] These are normally invisible to humans, yet they disrupt the harmony and flow of the human realm. These *kuei/guei* are spirits, ghosts, demons, or devils which arise from the negative *p'o*.

A *kuei/guei* may take revenge on those who mistreated them while they were alive. An untimely death can produce a *kuei/guei*; a suicide, death in childbirth, drowning, or murder. It was thought that anyone who had a sudden

---

[65] Lawrence Thompson, *Chinese Religion*, 4th., p. 12.

[66] Bradley K. Hawkins, *Introduction to Asian Religions* (New York: Pearson Longman, 2004), p. 182.

[67] Thompson, *Chinese Religion*, 4th., p. 11.

and violent death had not completed the life-cycle assigned to them by heavenly bureaucrats, so they had to live out the balance of their lives as ghosts. A child who died young could be a dangerous ghost. A ghost is an unhappy, lonely hungry being which can be recognized because a *kuei/guei* casts no shadow.

These *kuei/guei* provide a convenient and popular explanation for personal and communal tragedies. Every family had members who had passed away while still young. Every family could explain bad fortune as the result of the curse of a *kuei/guei*. Illness can be due to a *kuei/guei*. Even minor problems like unexplained anxiety or insomnia are the workings of *kuei/guei*. *Kuei/guei* are a disruptive influence over the individuals and over the community. Sometimes the evil spirits would masquerade as a beautiful woman, seduce a man, and do evil at his expense.[68] At prescribed times during the year, the village will perform rituals to propitiate the *kuei/guei*, including offerings of food and drink, and gifts.

Later in Chinese history, Indian Buddhist theories of karma and hells came to influence popular Chinese folk religion. The *p'o/hun* duality dominated for ancestor reverence, but Buddhist beliefs came to provide the framework to understand funerals, mostly performed by Buddhist priests. Heaven is the home of Buddhas, bodhisattvas, *arhats* (followers of the Buddha who achieved nirvana), worthy celestial beings, immortals, emperors, empresses, kings, gods and goddesses.

After the Chinese added hells to their divine realms, like heaven, hell was ruled by an elaborate bureaucracy where punishments were made to exactly match the original crimes.

14.8 THE IMMORTALS

There is one additional class of supernatural being: those humans who by mastery of esoteric rituals or ingesting secret foods and elixirs, have achieved very long lives, or even gained eternal life in a physical body. These are *hsien/xian*. The *hsien* are the immortals of religious Taoism/Daoism, and many of these will become very important in the Ch'in/Qin (221-207 B.C.E.) and later Han (202 B.C.E.–220 C.E.) dynasty. Although born as human beings, these beings won magic powers and immortality through the practice of spiritual exercises, or physical hygiene. By purifying their *ch'i* (breath, activating essence), they acquired immunity to fire and water, could ride the wind, could live many hundreds of years and even became immortal. If the follower could only get their attention and their favor, the *hsien* might teach the ruler, the supplicant, or even the student how to attain the same skills and powers.

The immortals were generally believed to lead solitary lives in remote mountains, and mountains and rivers were often regarded as sacred places by the Chinese. Cloudy mountains were often believed to control the regularity of the seasons. These mountains are sacred places, and the hermits who lived in these areas were believed to have extra long lives, and perhaps supernatural powers.

14.9 SUMMARY OF THE CHAPTER

Following the Shang and Chou/Zhou dynasties, the earliest periods in recorded Chinese history, central authority disappeared and China dissolved into warring states. The time of the Hundred Philosophers is a reaction to this situation of chaos and violence. The various schools of Chinese thought were concerned with many different issues, but paramount among them was the problem of how to establish harmony within the empire, and harmony among the people who comprise the family, the village and the kingdom. The Chinese political thinkers all agreed that a single ruler who unified and controlled the world was the only possible political system. But how to work out the details was the question.

The schools of Confucianism, Taoism/Daoism, the Yin-Yang, the Mohists, and even the Legalist School of

---

[68] Anthony Christie, *Chinese Mythology* (N.Y.: Paul Hamlyn, 1968), p. 105

CHAPTER 14: THE HUNDRED PHILOSOPHERS

Law all dealt with this problem to varying extents. Their solutions varied considerably, as we have seen the Law and Order philosophy of rewards and punishments used by the Ch'in/Qin ruler ultimately enabled Ch'in-shih Huang-ti/Qinshi Huangdi (259–210 B.C.E.) to conquer the few remaining states and establish himself as the first emperor of the newly unified China. The harsh governmental punishments were at least partially responsible for the ultimate collapse of the Ch'in/Qin empire. After the fall of the Ch'in dynasty, the Legalist philosophy was rejected, and Confucian ministers and Taoist/Daoist minsters shared an ever shifting dynamic interdependent relationship of who had the ear of the ruler, and who exerted the most influence upon those in power.

The Chinese view of gods, ancestors, and demons became firmly established into the Little Tradition, or folk religion (but supernatural beings were minimized in the Grand Traditions of the philosophers). Although the Chinese "Little Tradition" imagined a universe filled with supernatural beings, they are not ultimately very much different from us. Gods, or *shen*, share much in common with humans, and departed ancestors are much like their still-living earthly descendants. Even the realm of unhappy and vengeful ghosts was made up of the negative parts of human beings, and were motivated by much the same sorts of things that motivate those who inhabit the human realm.

There are numerous tales of immortals who roamed the mountains far from civilization, but these were humans who had purified themselves so wondrously that they could do many miraculous feats, including having a very long life.

14.10 TECHNICAL TERMS

hun	the *yang* part of the living essence of a human
hsiao/xiao	the virtue of filial piety, reverence for elderly and especially departed ancestors
kuei/guei	vengeful ghosts, demons, and spirits who are not well-disposed towards human beings
Mo-tzu/Mozi Mohism	
p'o/po	the *yin* or physical part of the essence of a human being
shen	a deity, a departed ancestor, a heavenly being
Tao/Dao	the fundamental pattern of all reality
t'ien/tian	Heaven, an impersonal force which responds to human affairs
Yang	the bright, masculine, logical, aggressive aspect of reality
Yin	the cool, dark, shadowy, feminine, intuitive, receptive aspect of reality

14.11 QUESTIONS FOR FURTHER DISCUSSION

(1)   It is easy to see why early Chinese civilization understood the universe as a continuous alternation of the *yin* force and the *yang* force. Early Western civilization tended to interpret apparently opposing forces as being at war with one another. The Chinese saw these as merely co-dependent movement between two poles. Which view is closest to your own? How do modern people explain the apparent alternation between night and day,

bright and dark, male and female, high and low, etc.?

(2) Early Chinese civilization attempted to understand nature as a progressive interaction and alternation of Five Processes (sometimes called the Five Elements): wood, fire, earth, metal, and water. The Greeks had four elements: earth, air, fire, and water. Could there be additional processes or elements that should be added to the list, in order to explain the world?

(3) The Greek philosopher Plato distrusted the democracy of Athens, and instead wanted a king to rule, but a king who was wise. Those Greeks who loved wisdom were the philosophers, and thus Plato wanted a Philosopher-King to rule wisely. Confucius thought that there must be a single powerful ruler, but the problem was that the kings and rulers of his era lacked virtue, and ruled for the benefit of their own group or their own personal pleasures. He felt that they lacked a proper attitude of respect for moral values. Is a wise ruler to be preferred over a system which allows us to vote for representatives who may not be wise, but who can make a good impression on a digital device or a television or while giving a speech? Which is most important in a ruler or politician, wisdom, or virtue? Or would you prefer some other quality in your ideal politician? Discuss.

(4) The philosophical Taoists/Daoists advise us to accept death as we accept life, and to fear neither. Religious Taoists/Daoists worked very hard to find methods which could extend one's life, or even bring about immortality. What do you think? Would an immortal life be a goal worth pursuing? Why, or why not?

(5) In the Middle Ages and after, many European explorers sought the Holy Grail or the Fountain of Youth, believing that there was something somewhere that a person could drink, or eat, which would give them immortality. In contemporary times, we read about new medical discoveries which might extend our lives to 100 years, or maybe beyond. Are modern people still seeking immortality? What do you think?

SELECTED BIBLIOGRAPHY

Overview of Early Chinese Thought

Balazs, Etienne, *Chinese Civilization and Bureaucracy* (1964).

Bokenkamp, Stephen R., *Ancestors and Anxiety: Daoism and the Birth of Rebirth in China* (Berkeley: University of California, 2009) Author traces development of the Indic idea of rebirth into Chinese Taoism and popular religion.

Chang Chung-yuan, *Creativity and Taoism: A Study of Chinese Philosophy, Art, and Poetry* (New York: Julian Press, 1963, reprinted Harper Colophon Books, 1970 and again by Jessica Kingsley, Publishers, Philadelphia PA: 2011)

Christie, Anthony, *Chinese Mythology* (New York: Paul Hamlyn, 1968)

Fung Yu-lan, *History of Chinese Philosophy*, 2 volumes.

Girardot, N. J., *Myth and Meaning in Early Taoism* (Berkeley: University of California Press, 1983).

Graham, Angus C., *Disputers of the Tao* (LaSalle, Illinois: Open Court, 1989)

Hansen, Chad, *A Daoist Theory of Chinese Thought* (Philosophy), (New York: Oxford University Press, 1992)

Hawkins, Bradley K., *Introduction to Asian Religions* (New York: Pearson Longman, 2004)

Hymes, Robert, *Way and Byway: Taoism, Local Religion, and Models of Divinity in Sung and Modern China* (Berkeley: University of California, 2002)

Kohn, Livia, *Daoism and Chinese Culture* (Magdalena, New Mexico: Three Pines Press: 2001)

Lagerway, John and Marc Kalinowski, eds., *Early Chinese Religion: Part One: Shang Through Han* (1250 BC -220 AD)

(Leiden & Boston: Brill, 2011)

Lagerway, John and Lu Pengzhi, eds., *Early Chinese Religion: Part Two: The Period of Division* (220 AD -529 AD) (Leiden & Boston: Brill, 2010)

Li Feng, *Early China: A Social and Cultural History* (New York: Cambridge University Press, 2013)

Loewe, Michael, *Everyday Life in Early Imperial China* (1968).

Moorey, Teresa, *Understand Chinese mythology* (London: Hodder Education: 2012)

Munro, Donald, *The Concept of Man in Early China* (Stanford, CA.: Stanford Univ. Press, 1969)

Needham, Joseph, *Science and Civilization in China*, Vol. II (London: Cambridge University Press, 1956)

Pines, Yuri, *Envisioning Eternal Empire: Chinese Political Thought of the Warring States Era* (2009)

Pines, Yuri, *The Everlasting Empire: The Political Culture of Ancient China and Its Imperial Legacy* (Princeton, NJ: Princeton University Press, 2012)

Saso, Michael, *Taoism and the Rite of Cosmic Renewal* (Washington State University Press, 1972)

Thompson, Lawrence G., *Chinese Religion*, 4th ed. (Belmont, CA: Wadsworth Publishing Company, 1989)

Van Norden, Bryan W., *Introduction to Classical Chinese Philosophy* (Cambridge: Hackett Publishing, 2011)

Waley, Arthur, *Three Ways of Thought in Ancient China* (New York: Doubleday, 1956)

Wang, Robin R., *Yinyang: The Way of Heaven and Earth in Chinese Thought and Culture* (London: Cambridge, 2012)

Yü Ying-shih, "Life and Immortality in the Mind of Han China," *Harvard Journal of Oriental Studies* 25 (1964–1965), pp. 80-122.

CHAPTER 15: CONFUCIANISM

15.1 OVERVIEW OF THE CHAPTER

The person people in the West call Confucius lived during the sixth century B.C.E. during the Age of the Hundred Philosophers (roughly 551–220 B.C.E.), and had more influence upon Chinese thought and the Chinese world-view than any other human being. Confucianism, the system inspired by Confucius, became inseparable from Chinese society, and provided the matrix out of which the identity of the nation is grounded. For two-thousand years, to be Chinese was to be Confucian, but not exclusively Confucian.[1]

Scholars have described Confucianism as arguably the longest and most influential ethical and spiritual tradition in human history, stressing self-cultivation and learning of the heart and the mind. The Way of the Confucians will lay the theoretical groundwork for family and social morality for all of China (and most of S. E. Asia). The Confucian will stress study and learning as a process for self-cultivation, and stresses the responsibility of a cultivated man to engage in social involvement, to be a service to society and take a leadership role in political activities. For the Confucian, there must be a harmonious balance between individual cultivation and political involvement. This follows naturally from becoming a cultivated superior person.

The sixth century B.C.E. was a period of acute cultural chaos; the central authority of the Chou dynasty had disintegrated two hundred years before, and economic changes brought on by the widespread use of iron in military weapons and in farming made for a civilization undergoing major changes, including military imbalances and ongoing civil wars. The Chinese world was sinking into barbarism, violence, and Chinese thinkers could see the eventual collapse of civilization. China disintegrated into civil war and chaos for the next five hundred years. This included the historical era called the Spring and Autumn Period (770–476 B.C.E.), a period of feudalism where kings and lords battled to expand their kingdoms, using both military forces and political intrigues and assassinations. Things did not improve after the Spring and Autumn period. Everyone knew that the Chou dynasty had been a succession of wise rulers, but after a few hundred years, everything had turned into chaos. What had gone wrong? How could we return to the golden age of the Chou ruling systems? What can be done to repair the situation?

Confucius believed he had re-discovered the secret of the Chou rulers. Confucius was sure that he knew how to repair the situation and his solution was grounded in how human beings ought to interact with one another. We humans share in a network of relationships involving family responsibilities and social duties. Confucius thought that one of China's great cultural heroes of five hundred years before, the Duke of Chou/Zhou, had behaved towards others in such a sagely fashion that his behavior unified and ultimately brought civilization to the Chinese world. However, the insights and discoveries of the Duke of Chou had faded and were forgotten and the need was to re-establish and restore world-order on the past. Confucianism will stress order, control, and hierarchy in the family and in the state, all grounded in the ancient past.[2]

Confucius wandered throughout China seeking a political position, trying to convince various kings and rulers to change the ways they behaved, to recognize that they are involved in reciprocal relationships with responsibilities

---

[1] Like other Asian systems Confucianism is not exclusive. You can be Confucian, Buddhist and Taoist, and most Chinese were comfortable guiding their lives by all three plus popular beliefs in ghosts and immortals.

[2] These are precisely what philosophical Taoism will oppose very strongly. See the next chapters on Lao-tzu and Chuang-tzu.

involving both ruler and ruled, both superior and subordinate. Each must serve as a role model, each must fulfill their role determined by their title and social position, and do so with ceremonial rituals of respect. Confucius urged leaders to follow his insights — no one in authority paid any attention to his advice. He then turned his attention to students and taught privately, and eventually three hundred years after his death his ideas came to influence and eventually dominate Chinese politics.

The Period of the Hundred Philosophers (or Hundred Schools) includes the lifetimes of Confucius (551–479 B.C.E.) and Mencius (ca. 372-289 B.C.E.), the two thinkers who provided the backbone of Confucianism. They both stressed social morality, the necessity to develop one's innate humanness and benevolence, and they believed it could be best accomplished by mastering ceremonial interaction and participating with others in the world as though all of our social interactions were sacred. We need to have the proper role models, an appreciation for the past and for classic literature, and we need to put the welfare of the group ahead of personal profit or advantage. The ideal person realized an obligation to help others, both socially and politically.

However, the Age of the Hundred Philosophers was not just Confucianism. It was also the age of philosophical Taoism and the period of the law and order philosophy of Han-fei-tzu (d. 233 B.C.E.) whose Legalist philosophical and political ideas were adopted by the ruler of the Ch'in kingdom, and came to dominate the Ch'in dynasty.

After the period of the Hundred Philosophers, the seven remaining kingdoms were reduced to three, and then the king of Ch'in defeated the remaining realms using the philosopher Han-fei-tzu's philosophy of law and order, and established the Ch'in dynasty, the first unified central kingdom in five hundred years. However, the Ch'in[3] dynasty did not last long, and was replaced by the Han (202 B.C.E. - 220 C.E.) dynasty. It is during the Han Dynasty that Confucianism finally gained influence over Chinese politics, and that influence continued on in the twelfth century in Neo-Confucianism, which dominated China until the early twentieth century.

THE EARLY CHINESE DYNASTIES (early dates are approximate)

HSIA (c. 2205-1766 BCE).
SHANG (c. 1766-1122 B.C.E.).
    Capital established in modern Honan in 1401 B.C.E.
CHOU/ZHOU (c. 1122-249 B.C.E.). Central authority disappeared 771 B.C.E.
    King Wen, King Wu, Duke Chou.
  Interstate warfare after 771 B.C.E.
    Spring and Autumn Period 722-481 B.C.E.
      Confucius 551-479 BCE
    Warring States period 403-221 B.C.E.
Ch'in/QIN (221-207 B.C.E.)
    Ch'in-shih Huang-ti, the first Emperor unified all China 221 B.C.E.
    Legalism adopted as official state policy.
    Burning of the books 213 B.C.E.
    Central control and bureaucratic administration over China.
HAN (202 B.C.E.-220 C.E.)

---

[3] We get our word "China" from "Ch'in," the name of the Ch'in dynasty.

15.2 CONFUCIUS: THE RITUALIZATION OF LIFE

Popular religion in China continued to be strongly influenced by the shamanistic belief that there are two realms which make up reality, one the human realm which is physical, and a second shadowy spiritual realm inhabited by forces which overlap with our world, and which can be contacted by means of rituals, prayers, sacrifices, and by means of the altered states of consciousness achieved by the shaman. The ordinary people felt that the spirit realm could bring healing, good fortune, or ill-fortune. The belief that supernatural forces, gods, ghosts, demons, and departed ancestors constantly interacted with our world was pretty much assumed to be true by the majority of Chinese. The writings of the more elite Confucians show less interest in these beliefs.[4] The Confucians do share the idea of Tao as a primal source, one unifying power permeating the universe, as in this quotation from a Confucian art connoisseur:

Furthermore looking at the things made by heaven and earth
One may find that one spirit causes all transformations.
This moving power influences in a mysterious way
All objects and gives them their fitness.
No one knows what it is, yet it is something natural.[5]

This quotation may strike us as religious, but note that Tao, the pathway of nature, is natural, not supernatural. Confucius himself had no interest in traditional religious beliefs including divination and sacrifice to gods, and no interest in shamans or people who claimed to be able to communicate with the spirit realm. If the realm of gods and spirits is considered important to religion, then Confucius is not particularly religious. For example, Confucius does not employ religious sanctions, never claims to have supernatural authority for his teachings, and there is no discernable religious structure at all in his system. He advised his students to respect the gods, but keep them at a distance.

A follower of Confucius, Tzu Lu, asked Confucius about the worship of heavenly beings (*shen*), and ghosts and spirits (*kuei/guei*) in this world. In the Confucian *Analects* 6:2/11:11 Confucius replies:

"We don't yet know how to serve our fellow men, how can we know about serving the spirits?"
"What about death?" was the next question. Confucius said: "We don't know yet about life, how can we know about death?"[6]

Confucianism is primarily practical ethical teachings grounded in the family and applied to the social/political life (political ideology). The Way (Tao) which Confucius teaches and follows is about choosing and following the pathway which brings harmony with the Tao and harmony in life. In the sayings of Confucius, there is no mention of souls or life after death, no belief in immortality.

Moral behavior is respected by the gods, but morality is not based on divinities. Confucian morality is neither about the commands of gods, nor is it about the threat of punishment if we disobey. For the Confucians, humans and gods are a part of the natural world, and the very nature of the world provides guidance for how human beings ought to live. We should study the past because the sages of the ancient past had discovered how humans ought to live in

---

[4] Ch. 74 of the *Shih chi* (Classic of History) recounts that the Confucian Hsun-tzu "detested the policies of a corrupt age, with misruling princes of doomed states coming one after another, who instead of pursuing the Great Way busied themselves with shamans and trusted in omens . . ." in A. C. Graham, *Disputers of the Tao* (LaSalle, IL: Open Court, 1989), p. 237.

[5] George Rowley, *Principles of Chinese Painting: Revised Edition* (Princeton NJ: Princeton University Press, 1974), p. 5.

[6] The *Analects of Confucius*, translated in de Bary, Chan and Watson, *Sources of Chinese Tradition*, Volume 1 (New York: Columbia University Press, 1960), p. 29.

social groups, which puts us in harmony with the patterns of the universe. Your virtuous deeds or your writings might be remembered after death, and this was the only immortality possible.[7]

Is Confucianism religion or philosophy?

Although Confucianism is described as a religion, it is one of the most secular of world religions.[8] Westerners tend to see the sacred realm as separate and apart from our everyday world. In China, the realm of human activity is the locus of the sacred. It is the human community which provides the sacred aspects of life, not some super-natural transcendental realm. It is ritual which makes the everyday human interaction into something sacred. Confucianism does stress rituals and ceremony, something which Westerners tend to associate with religion.

For Confucius, formal rituals make our lives better, make human interaction harmonious, and are essential to shaping moral character. Long after Confucius had died, in the later popular folk religion temples were built for the veneration of Confucius. However, in the early centuries of Confucianism the temples were memorial monuments of respect and remembrance (like the statue of Abraham Lincoln in Washington D.C.) and not religious institutions in any other sense.[9] Confucianism is a perfect example of the difficulty in classifying an Asian thought system as either religion or philosophy.

Unlike the Western philosopher's concern with the nature of ultimate reality, or the use of language to capture and ensure objective truth, Confucius wants us to use words appropriately, to stand by our words, to be trustworthy in what we say. If you are a politician, then there are expectations of how the bearer of the title "mayor" or "police officer" should speak, should behave, and should be treated.

The Confucians ask "how should we behave," not "what is true?" The purpose of Confucian thought is to become a better person, a Superior Person. If we want to be a better person, the question is what pathway (Tao) should we follow, what trail if followed leads to being a better person. The Chinese vision of what Chinese philosophers are doing is better described by gradual moral self-cultivation than the Western philosopher's desire to seek clarity about what we believe to be true about the world.

· The ideal Confucian was a family man, a gentleman, aesthetically sensitive, well-read, with a sense of compromise to deal with opposing perspectives. We might describe Confucianism as primarily a practical political, social and moral philosophy, with religious dimensions. Confucianism becomes associated with the professional well-educated political administrators. Although Confucius was disinterested in the realm of spirits, he was very interested in what makes for a good life. What pathway should we choose if we want a good life, and a harmonious world? Confucians seem to think that there was one, and only one, pathway that one should follow, and it was grounded in

---

[7] Confucians quoted the *Spring and Autumn Annals* which said one continued to live on by words, deeds, and people remembering what one had written down. "When these are not abandoned with time, it may be called immortality." Wing-tsit Chan, *A Source Book in Chinese Philosophy* (Princeton, NJ: Princeton University, 1963), p. 13. From the *Spring and Autumn Annals*, Tso Chuang, Duke Hsiang, 24th year.

[8] In personal life choices, Confucianism is not very religious although it is certainly true that many among the later generations of Confucians were concerned with magic divination. But there are strongly religious dimensions to political Confucianism. Wendi Adamek writes, "Confucian scholars have frequently argued that the normative Confucian-Legalist style of governance developed in the Han was a political philosophy, not a religion. The practical business of government was nevertheless a highly ritualized affair and for the Confucian official careful attention to etiquette, maintenance of parents and ancestors, civil service, and nobless oblige were in effect a religious vocation. Moreover, at the heart of the Chinese polity lay the imperial cult with its calendar of sacrifices honoring ancestors and patron deities. . . . Han state-cult icons carried much weight even in apparently Buddhist-oriented regimes; for example, though the Northern Wei court was imbued with Buddhist devotionalism, Emperor Xiaowen also instituted the first official Confucian temple." Wendi L. Adamek, *The Mystique of Transmission* (New York: Columbia University, 2007), p. 99.

[9] These would be like statues of famous people like George Washington or Johann Sebastian Bach.

patterns of Nature as discovered by ancient sages. Confucianism came to dominate all of Chinese life, in politics, in social, moral, and some aspects of religious life.

15.3 CONFUCIUS: BIOGRAPHICAL REMARKS

Historically, the lifetime of Confucius (551–479 B.C.E.) was the sixth century B.C.E. and it was a time of civil war and chaos. The central authority of the Chou/Zhou (pronounced like "Jo-oh") dynasty had disintegrated two hundred years before, and China was continually undergoing economic changes, military imbalances, and wars between competing kingdoms to establish a new emperor. The world was in disorder and the ancient harmony so much stressed in the previous Chou dynasty was no longer visible in Chinese civilization. Life was difficult, and the energy of thinkers of the time was focused on the question, how can one bring about a well-ordered harmonious society? What pathway should we follow? Many of the great Chinese philosophers wrestled with this problem, including the man Western people call Confucius.

K'ung-fu-tzu/Kongfuzi (551–479 B.C.E.)

Confucius is not a Chinese name at all. Rather, it is an attempt by Roman Catholic Jesuit priests (who had traveled to China to convert the Chinese to Christianity) to use Latin to render the Chinese name K'ung-fu-tzu (Kongfuzi).[10] K'ung-fu-tzu (more commonly known as K'ung-tzu or Kongzi) lived between 551–479 B.C.E. which means that he died at age 72. In modern times his birthday is celebrated on September 28 and is known as Teacher's Day.

Confucius was born in the Kingdom of Lu about three hundred and fifty miles southeast of modern Beijing (Peking) to a teen-aged mother who was the concubine of a 70-year old man who had been a famous warrior, and who already had two wives.[11] A later legend would claim that the virgin mother of Confucius had a dream that she had sex with a divinity, and when she woke up, she found herself pregnant. Confucius's father died when Confucius was only three years old, and the child and his young mother were thrown out of the family compound, disowned by his father's two wives and families. Mother and child were horribly poor, barely surviving. The young boy had an insatiable drive for knowledge, which his mother nurtured. He was not yet out of his teens when his mother died, leaving Confucius alone, an illegitimate impoverished orphan, who had the misfortune of being unusually tall. It was said that he towered over others in the village.

At age nineteen, he married, fathered one son and possibly two daughters, and worked as an overseer for a nobleman, but he wanted to be a scholar. He was talented and he studied hard. Confucius belonged to a group of able ambitious men who could claim a famous father, but had no inherited lands or money to live upon. One avenue available for such people was to became scholars who wandered from state to state, selling their services to the highest bidder. These scholars might teach history, archery, mathematics, music, or rituals. In fact, the Chinese name for the school of Confucius is *Ju-chia/Rujia*, School of Scholars.

We know that Confucius earned his living as a minor bureaucrat (tradition says that he was a clerk in Memorial Temple for Duke of Chou), and later led ceremonies for a local community village temple. One thing seems quite sure. Confucius studied and practiced ceremonial rituals, and became an expert in ancient rituals which went back to before the time the Chou dynasty collapsed. Those rituals were the tools of the professional political administrators, who came after Confucius, and who became influential in the court system. Year after year Confucius tried to obtain a position whereby he might influence rulers, but had no success. We know that in his personal life, Confucius was

---

[10] This Latin version of the Chinese name was created by the Roman Catholic Jesuit priest Matteo Ricci (1552-1610).

[11] There are many legends about Confucius. If you wish more information on Confucius and his influence, you can consult Michael Nylan and Thomas Wilson, *Lives of Confucius: Civilization's Greatest Sage Through the Ages* (New York: Harmony Books: 2010) or Peimin Ni, *Confucius: The Man and the Way of Gongfu* (Lanham, MD: Rowman & Littlefield, 2016).

not self-centered because he is always described as ready to learn from others, and appreciate what other people could do and accomplish.

In 501 B.C.E., when Confucius was fifty years old, he obtained a position as an advisor to the young ruler of the kingdom of Lu, and based on his understanding of the past and the current political situation, he tried to convince the actual rulers to reform their practices and adopt his solutions to bring about harmony, but no one listened to him. He resigned after five years.

According to tradition, at age sixty he was a private teacher who traveled widely, accompanied by a group of students, whom he trained in ancient rituals which were stressed in the Chinese government rituals, and who also studied the ideas of Confucius about ruling and about proper human interactions.

Confucius said: "Having only coarse food to eat, plain water to drink, and a bent arm for a pillow, one can still find happiness therein. Riches and honor acquired by unrighteous means are to me as drifting clouds."[12]

In 484 B.C.E., when he was sixty-seven, Confucius returned to the state of Lu hoping for a high government post which could give him one last chance to fulfill his vision of influencing the political world. He did not get the position, so he retired from political life and devoted the remaining years of his life to training students in what it means to be properly human, and how to live in a manner which will restore order and harmony in the state and in the family. Confucius' own evaluation of himself is told in this passage (*Lunyu* 7:10):

The governor of She asked Zilu about Confucius, but Zilu found nothing to say. The Master said to Zilu: "Why did you not respond: 'He is a man who, in his passion for study, forgets to eat; and in his joy upon acquiring knowledge, forgets his worries. He does not sense the approach of old age.'"

Legends say that there were over 3,000 people who had studied with Confucius during his lifetime, but only seventy-two of them were close to his heart. As he faced the end of his life, his students and followers were all he had. Confucius had been separated from his wife for decades, and his daughter was married and long gone. We do not know the details, but his son had disappointed Confucius.

Confucius passed away in 479 B.C.E. at age 72.[13] He died, perceiving himself to have been a failure who exerted no lasting influence upon China's rulers. However, three hundred years after his death, his ideas would begin to exert a profound influence upon China and then S.E. Asia, including Korea and Japan. Over the centuries the students would trace their lineage connection with the master, and they created a chart of each teacher who had studied with Confucius and his students. When combined with the tradition of reverence for ancestors (filial piety), the teaching lineage became exceptionally important, not just for Confucians, but also for Taoists and even Chinese Buddhists.

Historians are certain that as a young man Confucius had become an expert in ancient traditional rituals in honor of the Chou ruler's ancestors. His own personal interest in traditional rituals would become an important element in his solution to bring about harmony in society. Confucius looked back three hundred years in the past to the Golden Age of the Chou Dynasty, which was believed to be a perfect world ruled by virtuous rulers, and Confucius wished to imitate it in his own time as an important key to harmony. Confucius was sure that by studying the sages of remote antiquity and the achievements of these long-dead rulers, he had rediscovered the secret which enabled them to rule in a manner that brought about peace and order to civilization.

The basic principle was simple: look to the past for the solution to China's chaos. Confucius saw himself as one who could preserve and perpetuate a venerable ancient tradition, and one who shared knowledge of the Way of Nature, the Tao.

---

[12] The *Analects* VII:15, in deBary, Chan, Watson, *Sources of Chinese Tradition*, p. 20.

[13] See Peimin Ni, *Confucius: The Man and the Way of Gongfu* (Lanham: MD: Rowman & Littlefield, 2016).

15.4 METAPHYSICS: QUESTIONS ABOUT THE NATURE OF REALITY

Like the other Chinese thinkers, Confucius was quite practical, that is, he was not concerned with abstract theories, ideas, or concepts like the nature of absolute reality, the nature of truth, or origins of the world, and was not concerned with the supernatural realm. In general, the Chinese did not ask questions about creator gods. It did not occur to Confucius that a single divine being might have created all of reality. Confucius was not a monotheist. The Chinese thought it obvious that one could never get something from nothing. Thus there must always have been matter.

In general, Chinese thinkers assumed that we shared the world with spiritual beings, but the domain of humans (the earth), the domain of animals (nature), and the domain of spirits (heavens) are interconnected and are not separate realms. The world that we know originated in an earlier state of undifferentiated simplicity, a pregnant chaotic unity. No Chinese thinker ever believed that the universe was created out of nothing by some omnipotent deity. The questions that Chinese thinkers asked were questions like "What is the Way (Tao)?" "How can we know the Way?" or "How should we live in order to achieve harmony with the Way?"

Confucius is not seeking something that transcends this world, and never assumes that there exists something more real than what appears to our senses. Instead, he is seeking to live in harmony with the Way of the Sage Kings of the past. He is seeking knowledge of the Tao, the Way that we should live, knowledge of how we should organize our family, community and government to bring it in accord with the Way of Heaven,[14] and ultimately, how to relate Heaven and Earth. The Way of the Sage-Kings of the past reverberates harmoniously with the source of Heaven and Earth, and we must not deviate from the Way. Nature itself provides guidance for how humans ought to live.

Confucianism will stress respect and love for one's family as the proper building block for social, moral, and political harmony. It will stress knowledge and precision in social interaction to bring about harmony in the family and the state. We must honor and respect each other in our behavior. You should work to perfect yourself, and then gradually extend what you'd achieved to your family and then the community. In the public realm, Confucianism will stress taking action, jumping in and volunteering for public office in order to bring virtue into the government as well as pass laws which will bring about a better world by bringing it into alignment with the ancient ways of the Sage-Kings. The government must rule the world in such a way that citizens can live in harmony.

The Confucian pathway leads straight to the goal of political and social harmony, grounded in a mythic understanding of the Chou dynasty of the past and the desire to maintain consistency with the past. Although Confucius himself stressed flexibility, in later centuries when Confucianism came to dominate the court, the scholarly inflexible and politically powerful Confucians tended to be quite certain about right and wrong and rigid about what constitutes propriety.[15] Confucians in positions of power attempted to understand the Tao/reality using educational authority, requiring all to memorize and study the words of the rulers and sages of the past. The Confucians occupied a Chinese world which always was hierarchical: a good citizen must be subordinate to parents, and subordinate to those in power above him or her.

It is important to realize that during his lifetime, Confucius was only one of dozens of thinkers and was not especially important. In fact, as pointed out before, Confucianism was not particularly influential in Chinese government until 300 years after his death.

---

[14] We must be careful not to read Western Christian ideas into the Chinese use of the "Way of Heaven." Heaven is an impersonal moral force which responds to the ruler, not an all-powerful deity who created the world and loves humans best of all.

[15] Unlike Western religions, Confucianism did not try to control people's reproductive choices or how they use their sexual organs. However, they did want to regulate family interaction and social interaction, using role models and shame-based social condemnation.

15.5 THE CONFUCIAN *ANALECTS*

Many westerners have heard about the sayings of Confucius, which in Chinese is known as the *Lun Yü* (Conversations, Dialogues). In English these are known as the *Analects*, which is from the Greek, meaning "Things Gathered." The *Analects of Confucius* is a collected gathering of miscellaneous disconnected sayings and teachings attributed to Master K'ung-fu-tzu. Confucius did not write any of these; it is the memories of students and tradition. It is believed that his grandson had a hand in compiling the aphorisms and dialogues of Confucius. In the version we know, it has 20 chapters and is composed of approximately 12,700 Chinese characters. The earliest version in existence is from about the first century C.E., probably five-hundred years after his death.

15.6 THE CONFUCIAN PROBLEM:
HOW TO INSTALL ORDER & HARMONY AMONG HUMAN BEINGS?
HOW TO BRING ABOUT A WELL-ORDERED SOCIETY?

Confucius lived when China was separate principalities warring with their neighbors. It was not a well-ordered society, and there was little harmony during this period. Central authority had been gone for two-hundred years. The order and harmony of the Chou dynasty had been lost. Why? What went wrong? What actions or decisions had been made which led to the period of the warring independent kingdoms? How to fix it? Confucius believed he had found the answer to this problem, and that he knew how to restore order and harmony in the family, the community, and the government. His solution looked to the past.

The Chinese had many legends of the Sage-Emperors who ruled during the ancient Shang (c. 1766–1122 B.C.E.) and Chou (c. 1122–771 B.C.E.) dynasties. The Chinese (and Confucius) believed that the rulers of the Shang and Chou dynasties ruled with virtue, not power, not fear, not military force. Virtuous rulers inspired virtuous ministers and bureaucrats, who in turn served as role models for local mayors and the citizens. The Sage-Kings Yao and Shun and the early rulers of the Chou/Zhou dynasty were believed to have presided over a Golden Age.

Confucius had special veneration for the Duke of Chou/Zhou, who ruled as regent until his nephew came of age, and then the Duke voluntarily returned the kingdom to the youth, instead of pushing the nephew aside and claiming it for himself. The Duke symbolized the ideal virtuous ruler who genuinely put the welfare of his subjects ahead of personal advantage. Confucius believed that we can return to the well-ordered society based on the golden age of the past if we recover and relearn social ceremonial ritual interactions discovered by and taught by the ancient sage-kings. In addition, we must practice benevolent love grounded in the family, gradually develop our sense of moral righteousness, study history, and master other moral concepts which are embedded in the way of nature.

LI: CEREMONIAL INTERACTION

Confucius's answer to the problem of instilling order and harmony among human beings was a rather simple insight. An important element of order and harmony is the proper civilized and polite interaction between humans. This involves *li*, one of the most important concepts in Confucius's thought.

Li can be translated by such terms as ceremony, ritual, custom, rules of propriety, manners, rites, moral norms, moral laws, religious practices, decorum, social rules, good manners and etiquette. Each of these should be thought of as genuine manners, ritual practiced with genuine devotion, and not conventional social rules performed as mere ceremony or pretense. *Li* is proper behavior with our fellows in all the wide variety of social circumstances. Because no single English phrase can adequately capture all the various dimensions of this key concept, we will use the Chinese term *li* in the following discussion of ceremonial or ritual interaction.[16]

Originally, *li* referred to the ritual sacrifices performed for the gods which included sacred rites of hospitality, with emphasis upon ancestral rituals (which constituted the heart of ancient popular Chinese religion). Confucius enlarged the idea of *li* from rituals pertaining to the sacred realm of the ancestors, expanding it to actions which are ritually sacred and performed with deep seriousness and respect. In the *Analects* VIII:2 we find:

Courtesy without *li* becomes tiresome. Cautiousness without *li* becomes timidity, daring becomes insubordination, frankness becomes effrontery.[17]

Confucius expanded *li* beyond rituals to the gods, to include all human activities, so that all human interaction could be understood as related to the sacred. It is important to note that the Chinese court has always been profoundly ceremonial, and Chinese civilization has put a great deal of stress on rituals and ceremonial interaction. Confucius warns us not to mistake going through the motions of ceremony for a genuineness of spirit:

Lin Fang asked about the fundamental principle of *li* (rites). Confucius replied: "You are asking an important question! In rites at large, it is always better to be too simple than too lavish. In funeral rites, it is more important to have the real sentiment of sorrow than minute attention to observances."[18]

Li are the sacred patterns by which a human being should regulate his or her life; *li* itself is the guide to all aspects of human interaction. Every social interaction ought to utilize the demeanor we have when we ritually interact with ancestors and deities, which is to say that every act takes on a sacred aura of mystery and seriousness. Each ceremonial action requires an appropriate attitude of genuine reverence. For the Chinese, those who master *li* cultivate the correct attitude in everything they do, whether it be bowing to another person, saying "yes" or "no," or interacting with spouse, with children, with friends, with parents, or with those who rule. *Li* is "good form." *Li* will produce social cohesion.

Confucian Rituals are Not About the Gods

In the West, religious rituals are a vertical relationship; a human being on the bottom looks up to a powerful divine being overhead and the rituals are directed upwards, in an attempt to establish or strengthen a closer relationship with divinities, in an attempt to get the gods to do favors. This is not so for Confucius. He recommends we maintain distance between spirits and humans.

Fan Ch'ih asked about wisdom. Confucius said: "Devote yourself earnestly to the duties due to men, and respect spiritual beings, but keep them at a distance—this may be called wisdom."[19]

For Confucius, the point of ritual is not to interact with the gods above us. The heavenly divinities are invited to state and community rituals where oxen and sheep were sacrificed, but rituals are not really for the benefit of gods. Rather rituals relate one person to another person in a horizontal manner; rituals relate one human being to another

---

[16] We should note that a characteristic of the Chinese language is the fact that many quite different Chinese characters with quite different meanings will have the same pronunciation, and so will be written in English using the same letters. For example, *li* does mean "ceremonial interaction," but there are many other Chinese ideograms also written in English as *li*, such as the Neo-Confucian ideal of "principle" or "perfect pattern." As a measure of distance, a *li* is approximately 1890 feet, a little over a third of a mile. See chapter 21 for a discussion of *li* as ultimate principle.

[17] The *Analects* VIII:2, in de Bary, Chan, Watson, *Sources of Chinese Tradition*, Vol. 1 (New York: Columbia University Press, 1960), p. 29.

[18] The *Analects* III:4; *ibid.*, p. 29.

[19] The *Analects* VI:20, *ibid.*, p. 29.

human being as co-participants in the ritual called life. We perform rituals to produce harmony with the fellow human beings who surround us and who are essential if we are to have a good life. This is especially true in the daily ceremonial interactions we share with one another.

Li Avoids Conflict and Produces Harmony

Ceremonial interaction, or *li*, is the foundation of moral development. *Li* is saying and doing what is right, in the proper manner, at the proper time, and this is to follow the Tao/Dao. What Confucius realized is that properly performed *li* will avoid conflict, provide for harmony, and preserve existing harmony. If I say "I'm sorry," or "please pass the salt," this lessens negative tensions and makes us both players in the game of ceremonial rituals. If I shake hands with you, or bow, I am treating you with appropriate respect and engaging in a ritual which means that we are beginning a harmonious and friendly interaction. If two people are on the verge of physical violence, bowing or shaking hands reduces that threat. If we are in a pleasant relationship, the proper polite ceremonial rituals ensure that the harmony is preserved and endures. In a world of conflict, ceremonial ritual interaction lessens conflict and encourages harmony. A person who masters and follows *li* will create no discord, and instead will be good and virtuous. Similarly, a state ordered by *li* will be harmonious and peaceful.

Confucius said: "If a ruler can administer his state with *li* and courtesy—then what difficulty will he have? If he cannot administer it with *li* and courtesy, what has he to do with *li*?"[20]

China has always been a socially hierarchical world with many levels of power and status, and *li* can be quite complicated. Learning these varied ceremonial exchanges begins at home and then gradually we develop our grace and elegance in the performance of *li*. It can take decades to learn all the variety of socially acceptable ritual interactions and master them so well that they become second nature.

In our modern world, consider that there are proper ways for us to deal with our father, our mother, our son, or our daughter, and the same behavior appropriate for one is not appropriate for the other. You speak differently with your employer than with your best friend. You behave differently when encountering a king, an emperor, or a president, than you do when encountering person standing in line hoping for a free meal. You behave differently at a funeral than you do at a wedding, differently at church than you might at a bachelor party or an all-night movie marathon with friends. You behave differently if you are the entertainer before the audience, or a member of the audience. You behave differently when you are gift giving than you might if you are requesting a gift. You behave differently towards your brother if he is asking for a favor, or if you are asking him for a favor.

Li: The Five Confucian Relationships

There are five fundamental superior-subordinate hierarchies which we must consider when we ceremonially interact with people. These are called the Five Relationships: ruler and ruled; father and son; elder brother and younger brother; husband and wife. The fifth relationship of friend to friend is the one that is closest to being on the same level, with the elder friend having a slight edge of superiority. We can note that three of these five are within the family.

Every time we interact with people in these relationships, the act takes on a religious character, an aura of mystery and seriousness, but it must be the genuine inner attitude we would devote to ancestors or spirits/gods. Through the eyes of Confucians, all of life becomes part of an enormous ceremonial ritual, and that is true for everything we do.

As was pointed out previously, Confucius redefined a more ancient meaning for *li*. *Li* is no longer ritual devotion to ancestors or gods; supernatural beings are not the focus of *li*. It is social interaction among the living which is the focus of all the rituals of *li*. *Li* begins by referring to things sacred and religious and is expanded to include all

---

[20] The *Analects* IV:13, *ibid.*, p. 29.

activities — so that everything could be understood as ultimate, as sacred. Confucianism is the teaching of *li*. Confucianism is the ritual religion.

JEN/REN: BENEVOLENCE AND HUMANENESS

Jen/ren[21] was discussed more often by Confucius than any of the other central Confucian concepts. *Jen/ren* is the supreme virtue which connects human beings together, stressing morality as the fundamental human relationship. It is difficult to translate *jen* but these are the English words which scholars have suggested best capture its sense: benevolence, humaneness, brotherly love, humanity, love, human-heartedness, goodness, human-goodness, human kindness and human fellowship.

What is Human Nature?

Jen is the measure of individual character; it is the excellence of human nature. *Jen* is what makes us a human being. When a follower asked Confucius about the meaning of *jen*, Confucius said: "Love your fellow human beings."[22] According to Confucius, *jen* is a natural expression of mankind; it is what sets you apart from and makes you superior to animals. To be a person who encouraged and developed *jen* was the goal of Confucian self-cultivation. *Jen/ren* is a **seed** which when cultivated will grow into adult benevolence. This seed needs to be cultivated by proper activity. The person of *jen* will be conscientious towards one's self, altruistic towards others, and loyal to the proper superior person.

Jen is the seed of and foundation for all particular virtues; *jen* is the moral character which enables humans to perfect themselves as human beings. Confucius urges you to perfect yourself gradually, and then you can extend yourself to others so they can perfect themselves.

Chung-kung asked about *jen*. The Master said, "When abroad behave as though you were receiving an important guest. When employing the services of the common people behave as though you were officiating at an important sacrifice. Do not impose on others what you yourself do not desire. In this way you will be free from ill will whether in a state or in a noble family."[23]

The observant reader will note that the principle that westerners call the Golden Rule is there in the Confucian *Analects*. The person of *jen* will treat others the way he or she wants to be treated, that is, treated appropriately according to the relationship between people. This is reciprocity. In addition, loyalty to oneself and to one's superiors were both essential to a fully mature *jen/ren*.

LI is the EXTERNAL EXPRESSION OF *JEN/REN*.

Jen (benevolence) is a state of being; it is your essence. You were born with the seed of *jen*. On the other hand, ceremonial interaction, *li*, is not inborn; we learn and master *li* gradually as we develop, grow and mature. *Li*, ceremonial politeness, is the unique human activity which expresses this *jen*. Ceremonial interaction, or propriety, is the proper way of expressing *jen*.

We are not born with fully-developed wisdom, with compassion, with humaneness. We are not born with a sense of shame, with a natural inclination to respond with courtesy, and we are not born with a sense of right and

---

[21] In the Wade-Giles system this is *jen*, and in Pinyin it is *ren*. In English it would be pronounced something like "wren."

[22] The *Analects* XII:22, *ibid.*, p. 26.

[23] The *Analects* XII:2, D. C. Lau, *Confucius: The Analects* (Penguin Books, 1979).

wrong. We must cultivate these, and they all grow out of the seed of *jen*. We must practice these virtues until they become second nature. We learn *li* which cultivates our *jen* and our basic seed of kindness, *jen*, is developed. We develop the seed of our potential humanity, our *jen*, by learning and then mastering *li*; and someone who did not learn *li* was someone who would never have an opportunity to become fully and completely human.

In his old age, when Confucius felt he had finally achieved harmony with Nature, he did it by internalizing his response to the will of Heaven. Then, whatever he spontaneously desired was also the moral thing to do. Wandering where he will and responding naturally, Confucius could do what he wished without breaking any moral rules.

We must not overlook the fact that Chinese society and Chinese government were ritually-based institutions to a degree which exceeds that which most readers of this book might be familiar with. The stress on proper protocol was extreme. There was a proper way to say and do just about everything. Especially in the royal courts, *li* was essential.

Confucius was an expert in ancient *li* and he taught these ceremonies to his students. A student of Confucius would be an expert in protocol, in ceremonial interactions, and such a person had skills which were useful to governmental institutions, large and small. In other words, students of Confucius had developed special skills that were useful to the ruling elite, skills which could make those Confucian students employable and influential.

During the later Han dynasty (202 B.C.E.–220 C.E.), when the Confucian ideas came to dominate Chinese political life (as Confucius had intended), the combination of *jen* and *li* had long-term political implications most likely not foreseen by Confucius. *Jen* and *li* combined turned into a powerful instrument of conservative policy.

Confucius wanted a government of people who were naturally harmonious and virtuous. However, for the politically powerful Confucians in court, there was one and only one correct way to be virtuous. In the mind of the Confucian, etiquette, politeness, and social interaction are not conventional and are not relative to one's society. *Li* were established by the greatest of sages and *li* reflected the cosmic order, they reflect reality. The *li* are absolute, and cannot be modified or changed.

The Confucians were certain that a land whose people followed Chinese *li* was a civilized country whereas a land whose people did not follow Chinese *li* was uncivilized and barbaric. *Li* were turned into a list of rules and then laws governing social and political situations. Thus, *li* were used to resist social change; the Confucian thought system became a supporter of rigid social rules and then rigid laws governing everyone in every social situation.

TE/DE: The Virtue of the Sage

Confucius believed that the Sage-Kings who ruled during the Golden Age of the past were in a special position of centrality between Heaven and Earth, and so had ruled with moral excellence and virtue, not with guile, military power or armies. Because rulers were virtuous, everyone lived together in harmony and peacefully, families were ordered and lived in harmony, and the world was perfectly virtuous.

Confucius said: "If a ruler himself is upright, all will go well without orders. But if he himself is not upright, even though he gives orders they will not be obeyed."[24]

Confucius taught that what made this harmonious world possible was the Sage-king rulers who possessed the quality of *te/de*, a kind of virtue, a sacred power inherent in the sage who is in harmony with the Heavens and the Tao. The rulers of the Chou/Zhou dynasty claimed that they had the right to rule because Heaven (*t'ien/tian*) recognized their outstanding virtue (*te/de*) and awarded them the mandate and right to rule.

Te/De is Not Just Moral Virtue

The English term "virtue" strongly suggests simple morality, but there is a related meaning to the term "virtue" that is not strictly moral. In English we can speak about the "virtue of this car is that it gets over forty miles to the

---

[24] The *Analects* XIII:6, de Bary, et. al. *ibid.*, p. 32.

gallon of gasoline," or "the virtue of aloe vera is that it will help heal your sunburn" or "the virtue of this toothpaste is that it will eliminate tooth decay."

Te/de is a virtue in the sense of being a positive beneficial force. We might begin to capture the sense of *te/de* by such phrases as sacred beneficial personal force, spiritual moral energy which affects others for the better, or even similar to moral charisma.[25] *Te/de* is an inner quality of character which is powerfully effective in influencing others for the better. For the Confucian, *te/de* is achieved as a consequence of the ruler mastering *li*, and achieving harmony with the social and political Tao. It is an efficacy for changing others simply by being in their presence. One exerts influence in the sense a genuinely virtuous human being will be a role model that others naturally seek to emulate. In the presence of the moral excellence in the character of a sage, things resolve and improve. Harmonious order results simply because of the *te* energy, simply because the virtuous sage exists. Each of us must work to cultivate virtue.

15.7   THE CONFUCIAN SAGE, THE GLORIFICATION OF THE PAST, and REFORMING GOVERNMENT

For Confucius, an important element in reestablishing order and harmony in the world is realizing that the ruler must rule with moral persuasion, with virtue (*te/de*), by personal example, and not by force, laws and punishment. The way to restore harmony was to have rulers who ruled wisely, with benevolence, and who could serve as role models for all those below. The individual and the society should develop harmoniously, and not the individual at the expense of the society/political order.

> Confucius said: "Lead the people by laws and regulate them by penalties, and the people will try to keep out of jail, but will have no sense of shame. Lead the people by virtue [*te/de*] and restrain them by the rules of *li*, and the people will have a sense of shame, and moreover will become good."[26]

Confucius believed that all of this was simply returning to the way things used to be in the Golden Age, when the sages understood the Way of Heaven. The Confucians tell a story of Yao, the virtuous Sage-King in the Golden Age of the past, who abdicated the throne and offered it to the person best qualified to rule, the sage Shun. Yao selflessly did what was best for all, and did not put himself ahead of the group. Confucians thought that the ancient sages had everything all worked out. We humans have deviated from the sages in the past, but it is not too late to study them and learn their lessons.

Confucius Claims Not to be an Innovator

For the Confucians, to the extent that a theory deviated from the practices of the past, to that extent it was in error. New theories of how to rule and how to behave are bad because they deviate from the ideal past. We should not impose new rules. We do not need new rules because we have the guides handed on down from the Sage-Kings of the past, and these Sage-Kings had everything figured out correctly. The Sage-Kings had deep insight into the Tao/Dao and the way of the past was perfect. Thus, Confucius claimed that he himself was not innovating, but merely pointing out how things were done in the Golden Age.

---

[25] Brook Ziporyn suggests "noncoercive persuasiveness" in his *Zhuangzi* (Indianapolis: Hackett Publishing, 2004), p. 214.

[26] The *Analects* II:3 in de Bary, *ibid.*, p. 32.

I have transmitted what was taught to me without making up anything of my own. I have been faithful to, and loved the Ancients.[27]

What Confucius believed he had transmitted was the Way (Tao/Dao) of the rulers of the Chou (c. 1122–771 B.C.E.) dynasty. The power of the sages of the Golden Past can serve as inspiration for the proper conduct of today's leaders, and even the ordinary Confucian follower. To instill order and harmony among men, it was necessary to return to the principles of the past, the Chou dynasty.

The Master said: "He who rules by virtue [te/de] is like the [north] pole star, which remains unmoving in its mansion while all the other stars revolve respectfully around it" (Analects 2.1).[28]

As we can see, the Confucians assumed that the influence flows from top downward; that if the leaders could be encouraged to be more sage-like, then the people would also rectify themselves by following the models established by the rulers. The kings can lead, and the people will follow, voluntarily participating in the social structure. This idea came to dominate Chinese civilization.

Confucius is advocating that scholars trained in ritual, social skills and arts should run the government, although they had no training in what was necessary to run a government bureaucracy. Confucius seems to have assumed that a person who had developed their *jen* and *li* (benevolence and ceremonial excellence) would serve as superior role models for the other bureaucrats, and could learn the details of running a huge bureaucracy while on the job, or could delegate the responsibilities to underlings.

Untrained scholars and practical bureaucrats make up two realms: the Confucian world where everything is ideal, and the everyday practical business of running the state. However, the ideal political person cannot live only in the perfect world of ideas; he must accommodate the realities of the world. This created a serious tension for Confucian ministers between practical and ideal.

In fulfilling his commitment to humane public service and political leadership in dynasty after dynasty, the Confucian was able to contribute a rational ethos, a standard of service, and a continuity of experience to the government of China such as no other state in human history has enjoyed. Yet in that very attempt he stood exposed, both as keeper of the Chinese social conscience and custodian of its institutions, to the inevitable shortcomings of the system. For him to live by his principles required both idealism and compromise, both firmness and flexibility. His record would never be anything but mixed, since his achievements would never match his aspirations.[29]

15.8 THE SAGE AND THE SUPERIOR PERSON

The ultimate goal for a cultivated Confucian was to be a sage. The Confucians analyzed human beings into several different groups, and what separates them from one another is their degree of moral perfection. The person of the most developed moral perfection is the sage. The sage can never make a mistake in any moral affair. The sage is perfect in human goodness and benevolence (*jen/ren*) and is perfectly comfortable in all situations, always saying and doing the correct thing (the sage has mastered *li*). The sage is perfect in *jen* and perfect in *li*. Harmonious order results

---

[27] Arthur Waley, *The Analects of Confucius* (Everyman's Library, 1938), VII:1, p. 123

[28] Simon Leys, *The Analects of Confucius* (New York: W. W. Norton, 1997), p. 6.

[29] Wm. Theodore DeBary, "Introduction" in *The Unfolding of Neo-Confucianism* (New York: Columbia University Press, 1975), p. 3.

simply because the sage is present in the countrywide. Simply by being a sage, a person of excellent virtue, *te/de*, without exerting any activity, the tensions resolve and the citizens improve.

Achieving the status of a sage is not impossible, just exceptionally rare. Every one of us has the potential to achieve sagehood. But it is not easy; to attain that high status is almost impossible. Confucius denied that he is a sage. Although sagehood is rare and difficult, there is a slightly lower stage of goodness that is attainable by all of us and for which we should strive. That is the *chun-tzu/junzi*, the Superior Person.

CHUN-TZU/JUNZI: THE SUPERIOR/IDEAL PERSON

The ultimate goal for the Confucians was to become a sage, but this was so extraordinarily rare and exceptionally difficult that it was not practical. There was another goal that was achievable and striving for that goal would also bring about harmony with human beings and with nature. That goal is to be a person of virtue. It is appropriate that each of us must aspire to wisdom, to compassion, to nobility, and to be noble is to be a true gentleman, or a superior person. In the *Analects* VII:26 Confucius says that he has never met a sage, and "I cannot hope to meet a sage. I would be content if only I could meet a Superior Person."[30] The goal that is achievable by each of us is to become a *chun-tzu/junzi*, or "Noble Person," "Superior Person," "Ideal Person," or "True Gentleman."

The two Chinese characters *chun* and *tzu* literally refer to the "Son of a Ruler," that is, a male of privilege derived from the hereditary feudal aristocracy. This was a member of the aristocracy who held a position of respect and honor because of his birth into a noble family. Confucius redefined the term *chun-tzu/junzi* from "aristocratic person in a position of honor because of family/birth" to "true gentleman," a noble person, a virtuous person, a person honored because of his character, someone who guided his life by the proper order embodied in the Tao of the ancients. For Confucius, those who were *chun-tzu* were honored because of the virtuous way the lived their life, because of their character, not their birth. We can imagine someone of noble birth who behaves quite abominably, someone who is not a "true gentleman." Confucius is struggling against entrenched power of the hereditary nobility with this concept. Instead of a hereditary elite, Confucius substitutes the notion of an elite based upon virtue, culture, talent, competence, and moral merit.[31]

The *chun-tzu/junzi* is not an egoless saint. The *chun-tzu/junzi* is trying hard to be virtuous but is not perfectly selfless and altruistic. The Superior Person strikes a balance between the desires which benefit the self on the one hand, and selfless altruism on the other. A true gentleman should not be dominated by selfish desires. Ideally, the superior person values desires which contribute to the well-being of the group. The *chun-tzu* is concerned about the common good, and therefore, he would seek public office to serve others.

> The unthinking man accepted things as they were. The "noble man" accepted his responsibility consciously to transform himself and the world in accordance with the Heavenly norms that constituted both his conscience and his natural endowment and potentiality.[32]

How should a Superior Person behave if he is to be a contributing member of the social world? Politically, the Confucian Superior Person was expected to seek government service to serve the people, and once in a position of power the Superior Person must speak the truth to the ruler. In China (and elsewhere), to speak truth to power is very dangerous; that most certainly took courage. To tell the ruler something that he does not wish to hear could result in the death of the scholar. However, Confucius says that the Confucian scholar must do just that: "To see what is just

---

[30] The author's translation from the *Lunyu*, ch. VII:26.

[31] Simon Leys, *Analects of Confucius* (New York: Norton, 1997), p. 105

[32] Wm. Theodore deBary, *The Unfolding of Neo-Confucianism*, p. 9.

and right and not do it, is cowardly" (*Analects* II, 24). A person of *jen* (benevolence) must possess courage, but mere courage alone is not *jen*. A soldier may be very courageous, but still have little benevolence, or compassion.[33]

The superior man is not a sage (a sage is a person of perfect *jen* who perfectly embodies *li* and the highest possible virtues), but is a step below a sage and a step above an ordinary person. The Superior Person can and does make mistakes (the sage does not), but the Superior Person learns from his mistakes, and does not repeat mistakes. Superior Persons make mistakes, but do not give up; they learn from their mistakes and use them to figure out the morally correct solution to the problem. Every day the *chun-tzu* becomes a little more virtuous. The Superior Person is not concerned with profit; he behaves in a way that puts him in accord with the Tao.

> Do not worry if you are without a position; worry lest you do not deserve a position. Do not worry if you are not famous; worry lest you do not deserve to be famous.[34]

> Confucius said: "The *chun-tzu* occupies himself with the Tao and not with his livelihood. One may attend to farming, and yet may sometimes go hungry. One may attend to learning and yet [you] may be rewarded with emolument. What a Superior Person is anxious about is the Tao and not poverty."[35]

A Superior Person would simply state the truth and not argue or contend: ideally, the truth would be stated without concern for the consequences to himself. A Superior Person was not a narrow specialist in a technical art or craft. The Superior Person enjoyed an education in all the liberal arts. He consciously strived to cultivate the virtues within himself; he tried to become refined, cultured, and virtuous.

A cultivated and refined human being has knowledge of the proper ceremonial interaction with every person, according to his or her station in life. This guaranteed that society will be harmonious and orderly, because treating people according to the rules of *li* maintains the hierarchy essential for a well-ordered society (embedded in the cosmic principle of Tao/Dao). Although in Chinese culture there is always a relationship of superior and inferior, there is also the virtue of justice — all persons are treated justly according to their station in life. The *chun-tzu* requites good and evil with justice; he also loves good and hates evil.

"The superior man wants to be slow and careful in his use of words, but diligent and prompt in actions" (*Analects* IV, 24). A superior person will have a deep sense of responsibility towards promoting the welfare of one's immediate family, one's extended family, one's village, one's country, and promoting the welfare of the clan ancestors.

To summarize, a superior person will study the classics in search of wisdom and will study ancient history, and become a virtuous and refined person with the skill of a poet. He will work tirelessly to secure a position in the government, from which he can work to make the community a better place. He will be loyal to his superiors and will not abuse his position of authority. A superior person should be someone we can rely upon to be honest, to keep promises, to be trustworthy. The superior person will be fair, but for the Confucians that meant that he will treat others justly according to their relative position in the social hierarchy, and will always use good manners (*li*) and will be considerate. A superior person will not give up easily when obstacles are placed in his path, and will be brave even when his own life is threatened by those in authority who are not virtuous. He will persevere, will exemplify the virtue of moral discernment (*i*) and can be relied upon to do what is decent and proper (the virtue of *i* is discussed in the next section).

Confucius said: "The way of the *chun-tzu* is threefold. I myself have not been able to attain any of

---

[33] Indeed, Ch'in-shih Huang-ti/Qinshi huangdi (259–210 B.C.E.), the first Emperor of Ch'in dynasty, was so annoyed with scholars who disagreed with his practices that he had over four-hundred court scholars buried alive.

[34] The *Analects* IV:14 in Simon Leys, *op. cit.,* p. 16.

[35] The *Analects* XV:31 in de Bary, *et. al., op. cit.,* p. 31 [XV:32].

them. Being benevolent (*jen*) he has no anxieties; being wise, he has no perplexities; being brave, he has no fear." Tzu Kung said: "But, Master, that is your own way."[36]

15.9   THE CONFUCIAN VIRTUES

The Confucian Virtue of *I* (or *YI*)[37]

The virtue of *i* (also written *yi*) is a natural ability to recognize what is right, what is just, and includes being morally responsible, or righteous. *I* is a sort of moral discernment. For Confucius, *i* provides the standard of correct behavior toward fellow humans. "The Superior Person considers *i* to be essential" (*Analects* XV:17). *I* is recognizing and doing what is right, fitting, proper, decent; what one would expect under the circumstances and actions which are in order. It is one's duty.

The English terms "morality" or "righteousness" would be misleading, because in the Confucian world, our moral obligations are tightly connected to our social relations, and can vary depending on degree of closeness of personal relationship. *I* is not related to a divine law grounded in the commands of a divinity; rather it behaving in a morally responsible manner, it is a sense of obligation about what is appropriate, and is intimately bound up with social relations. Thus our *i* [moral duty] towards a parent can be quite different from our *i* towards a stranger, or towards a ruler.

The Person of *i* Does What Is Right, Not What Is Profitable

When one cultivates the virtue of *i*, one has an interior moral compass. "The Superior Person, in the world, is not for or against anything; he follows only the virtue of *i*." (*Analects* IV:10). Thus, *i* allows us to discriminate between moral goodness and what is morally not-good. This ability is natural, similar to our ability to distinguish sweet from sour.

Confucius warns his students not to be self-centered, not to be concerned with personal advantage. For the Confucian, the most important thing is doing what is right, not doing what is profitable. "The *chun-tzu* understands what is morally responsible [the virtue of *i*]. The inferior man understands what is profitable." (IV.16).[38] When one does what is fitting and correct, one considers what benefits others and not just what benefits oneself.

The Confucians teach us not to be ego-centered, not look out for one's self alone—the *chun-tzu* is striving to be above egotism. When you ask "what's in it for me?" you undermine cooperation, and lose your connectedness with the rest of humanity.

Filial Piety: Have the Proper Attitude of Respect for Elders

Confucius felt that society needs to rediscover the virtue of **filial piety** (*hsiao/xiao*). As we have seen, in popular Chinese religion all the way back to the Chou and Shang dynasties, respectful attitudes towards one's elders and reverential ancestral rituals in honor of departed ancestors were virtually synonymous with religion in ancient China. In popular Chinese religion, it was believed that an ancestor could influence a descendent's fortune, and could reward and punish a descendent's behavior (just like spirits, gods, and goddesses). Customs for proper behavior and

---

[36] The *Analects* XIV:30, in de Bary, op. cit., p. 31; modified by the author.

[37] In Chinese, *i* or *yi* is to be pronounced like the name of the English letter "e". Similarly the classic Chinese *I Ching* (Classic Book of Changes) should be pronounced "E Jing."

[38] The *Analects* IV:16, in de Bary, *ibid.*, p. 31; modified by the author.

rituals for departed ancestors became very strong. Ancestors were an important part of the everyday life of almost every Chinese–another result is that the family and the clan became extremely important in Chinese society.

A man who respects his parents, family and elders would hardly be inclined to show disrespect for superiors. A man who is not inclined to disrespect superiors will not generate disorder. A Superior Person works at the source, the root. Once the root is secured, the Tao/Dao unfolds. Filial piety towards parents and elders and respect for family is the root of *jen*.[39]

A son who does not treat his father and mother morally and with respect is missing something basic to being human. If you cannot respect your own parents, then how can you respect civil and social authorities? Such a person will be a very poor citizen, and poor citizens make for a lack of harmony in civilization. The Confucians advise us to be a good family member, to respect parents and grandparents. We are advised to put our relationships with parents and siblings into proper order.

One begins by acting benevolently towards one's own family, and then naturally one will begin to behave benevolently towards neighbors, and then, gradually the benevolence will expand outwardly to community members. Some thinkers call this "graded love," that is, loving those who are closest to us, our immediate family, and then slowly expanding the circle of loving kindness to include neighbors and fellow villagers.

Personal Morality is Grounded in Love for Family

Filial piety (*hsiao/xiao*) and parental love are natural and spontaneous emotions, not something we feel because of abstract moral principles. From earliest childhood, almost all of us will grow up feeling love for our parents and siblings. A child who is brought up well will grow up to be a virtuous human being. Abstract rules of politeness (*li*) alone are not the foundation for personal morality. Family is the foundation for personal morality.

The basis is the natural attachment and emotional bond that grows between family members. For the Confucians, a healthy and moral society is not ultimately founded on moral principles and a rational (Kantian) grasp of one's duties but on the feelings that emerge within families. . . . The Confucian true person is one who has well cultivated his or her emotional roots and will therefore always naturally do what is appropriate and have no need to look for certain abstract principles or external authorities for guidance.[40]

Because parents devoted much of their lives to raising their children, children were expected to feel strong parental love, but more than that, the children had an unconditional duty of obedience to parents, and should have unquestioned respect for parents (whether by their behavior the parents deserved it or not). Parents have authority, but they also have obligations; children are not just mere possessions but share these duties and obligations, which includes a strong obligation to respect and reverence their parents, grandparents, and ancestors.

Confucius strongly encouraged the traditional observation of three years of mourning after a parent has died. It was expected that following the loss of a parent, for three years a truly Superior Person should not enjoy food, should not play or enjoy music, should not enjoy sexual embraces with his wife, and should dress in plain white and act in obvious mourning.[41] In the *Analects*, Confucius is challenged on this by his student Yu who asserts that one year of mourning should be enough, because otherwise the crops will wither if they remain uncultivated for three years, music

---

[39] *Analects* I:2. Author's translation. This is a Confucian disciple speaking, not Confucius himself.

[40] Hans-Georg Moeller, *The Moral Fool: A Case for Amorality* (New York: Columbia University Press, 2009), p. 9. Moeller refers us to *Analects* 1.2, translated above.

[41] In the Chinese tradition, a funeral is observed by wearing white colored clothing. White connotes simplicity, plainness, and by extension, inexpensive, even cheap, and unbecoming. White hemp clothing implied that the child was so overwhelmed with grief that she or he had no concern for fashion, no concern with looking good, no concern for appearance.

skills will atrophy and disappear if no one plays music for three years, and one's use of appropriate ceremonial behavior will become rusty from non-use. Confucius responds that if the student is comfortable mourning for only one year, then that is what he should do. However, when the student leaves, Confucius confides to his students: "What lack of benevolence in Yu. Only when a child is three years old does it leave its parent's arms. The three years mourning is the universal observance in the world. And Yu—did he not enjoy the loving care of his parents for three years?"[42] For Confucius, traditional ritualistic mourning guides behavior which reflects a continuing family sentiment expressed appropriately, deepening harmony among the family and the community.

The Rectification of Names Guides Social Behavior

The term "names" as it is used in the phrase "rectification of names" refers to role titles and job descriptions. To rectify names is to make the expectations associated with the title of your social role match your actual behavior. Names are labels such as "friend," "professor," "mayor," "firefighter," "president," "brother," "father," "son," and so forth. These are not just names; they are social roles. There are responsibilities and proper behavior for each of these—to be a father is not just to be a biological father; rather, to be a genuine father is to behave like a father should. If your job is that of teacher, then you must be prepared and you should teach well—and if you do not, then you should not be called a "teacher." If your social role at the moment is that of a student, then you also have responsibilities. If you are a ruler, then you should behave wisely, with humanity (benevolence) and a sense of responsibility towards the common people, and if you do not do this, then even though you are sitting on the throne, you're not really a ruler.

It is clear how Confucius intends this to apply to the serious business of politics and the lack of harmony in the state. If your job is that of governor of a province, then you should govern for the benefit of the people, and if you govern for your own personal profit, then you are not properly performing the job of governor and so you are not really a governor.

The application is far broader than just politics. It applies to all of us, for we all play numerous roles daily. Unless people live up to their "names," their roles or job titles (including father, mother, son, daughter, friend, etc.) then we cannot have confidence that they will do what is appropriate to their station or role. The harmony in the family will falter if the parents do not behave properly, if children behave disrespectfully towards parents and towards siblings. The harmony in the community will be damaged if the local leaders do not perform their job as their titles indicate they should.

Here the *chun-tzu/junzi*, Superior Person, behaves properly and fulfills his numerous social roles politely and correctly. A Superior Person is trustworthy in what he says, and behaves properly for his role in society. This is the standard interpretation of this quotation from Confucius:

> Let the ruler be a ruler,
> the subject a subject,
> the father a father,
> the son a son. (XII.11).

When the ruler behaves as a proper ruler should, when the subjects behave appropriately for a subject, when a father acts as a good and conscientious father, and the son treats his father with respect, the world will have "rectified names" and it will be a better place for all of us.

---

[42] The *Analects* XVII:21, in deBary, *et. al.*, p. 28. It is typical of the Confucians to assume that their practices are built into the nature of reality, and therefore must be uniform throughout every civilized nation in the world. So, if they encounter a country with different social practices, a country that does not have three-years of official mourning, then that country must be uncivilized and inferior. This is precisely what the Confucians thought of Europeans when they first encountered them.

15.10 STUDY THE CLASSIC BOOKS

As an expert in ancient ceremonies and rituals, Confucius believed that the Sage-Kings of the Shang (c. 1766–1122 B.C.E.) and Chou (c. 1122–771 B.C.E.) dynasties had observed nature carefully and recognized the one and only proper way to rule and that the subjects responded to their rule in a way which brought about peace and harmony. In his own day, Confucius felt that people of his era had forgotten the Way of the Sages of the glorious past; the people living in the present time period of chaos and mistrust are ignorant of their past, and our ignorance is at least partly responsible for the present-day problems.

The sages of the past are not merely names lost in history. When you carefully study history, you recognize that these legendary rulers are appropriate role models. You are cut off from an important source of morality if you do not understand the sages of the past, and you are more likely to engage in immoral activity. You and I lose the ability to live a moral life if we have the wrong role models to base our behavior upon. Our models/heroes should be those who exemplified a virtuous life, the virtuous sages of the past like the Duke of Chou who ruled as regent and then returned the kingdom to his nephew when the child became of age.

Society is damaged if the people in power and authority who are our role models are not virtuous. Role models should be worthy humans, and not just people whom the media has elevated to a position of media prominence. Role models should be people famous for the moral quality of their lives, and not be famous just because they are wealthy businessmen, or be famous just because they are brave generals, and most certainly not because they are talented entertainers, not because their face appears on movie screens or television series, and certainly not because they are superior athletes. Our ability to have a peaceful life is weakened if we do not model our behavior on the moral lives of the sages of the past.

In our personal behavior, we must understand and return to that time in the past when the rulers ruled because of their virtue and the mayors and governors and even ordinary people modeled themselves on the rulers, and so they too were all virtuous.

15.11 THE STATUS OF WOMEN

The Chinese understanding of reality as a flowing shifting back and forth between two dynamic principles, *yang* and *yin,* had a profound effect on the Confucian understanding of the value of a female child, and the proper role of women in Chinese society. The *yang* was heaven, and *yin* is the earth. The *yang* is the active, bright, rational, and logical. The *yin* was passive, cool, intuitive, and creative. Since the *yin* was the feminine principle, the proper role for a woman was determined by her *yin* status: passive servitude. Heaven is superior to earth. The *yang* male is heaven, so the male is superior, the woman is the subordinate, and her duty is submission.

In her childhood, a woman was dependent upon her father; when married, she joined her husband's family and was dependent upon and obedient to her husband; when widowed and old, she should be dependent upon her sons. A female child was not an asset to the family. A marriage would be arranged for each daughter, and the girl's family would have to pay a dowery to the groom's family, and the daughter would then serve her new family and would not be available to help support her parents in their old age. On the other hand, a son brings not only a wife, but a female helper into the family, who brings a dowery with her. The daughter-in-law becomes a member of her husband's family, and will be there to help support her in-laws as they age. Besides helping her new family with her labor, the wife's duty is to provide her husband and his family with sons. For this reason, female children were not as valued as male offspring. Sadly, occasionally baby daughters might be left alongside the road, or eliminated.[43] Later, when Chinese

---

[43] There has been a deadly bias against female children due to many factors, including kinship systems, old-age support expectations, and property relations. Confucians did not condone female infanticide, but the Confucian stress on filial piety as the province of male children created problems for poorer families. The problem is on-going in Asian/Confucian societies where a family can know the sex of the foetus,

Buddhist monasteries were established for women, a baby girl could be left outside the gate of the monastery, where she would be raised by the nuns and become a nun herself when she grew older.

In Confucian China, the ideal Chinese woman should be obedient to the proper dominant male: her father, husband, and sons. These are the "Three Obediences."[44] Traditionally a Chinese woman would walk slightly behind her husband, and open the door for him. In modern Asian society it was not uncommon for the wife to act as the chauffeur for her husband, who sits in the back seat of the car.

Although the status of women may not be as high as the male, this does not mean that a woman is powerless. In fact, Chinese women had a substantial amount of power in the family. Women were expected to handle the income and expenses of the family. The wife would control the purse strings and could put her husband on a budget or an allowance. Women were considered essential for maintaining proper order and contentment in the family (if these were missing, it was her fault). She was not only responsible for her own moral character, but responsible for the moral character of her husband as well. Clearly, in actual fact this would require courage and personal strength.

The *yin* was creative, which is to say, creating life, and so the most important value of a woman was her ability to have sons—the duty of a son was to have progeny to perform the proper rituals for his parents, his grandparents, and for the seven generations of ancestors before them. If a wife did not fulfill her sacred duty, did not produce sons, if he could afford it the husband could also have a second or third wife, or a concubine, but adopting a son (or adopting a son-in-law) was also a possibility. The status of a wife came from her sons; beyond that, women were not considered to have great value. Ordinarily women were not educated, and because of the ancestor genealogy cult, chastity before marriage was essential, as was marital fidelity.[45] Marriages were arranged, and it was not uncommon for a bride to meet her husband for the first time on the day of their wedding.

If for some reason a woman did not marry because she refused, or for some other reason, about the only positions available to her was as a nun in a Buddhist monastery, a courtesan or a concubine. These various roles became discussed publically in the later Sung Dynasty (960-1279) and following eras.[46]

15.12 RELIGION IN CONFUCIANISM

Although in Western minds Confucianism is categorized as a religion, it certainly counts as one of the most secular of world religions. Confucianism does not resemble Western Christianity and elements like belief and faith are irrelevant. There is a complete lack of what we might call theological speculation in the *Analects* of Confucius. Confucius does not discuss life after death, pretty much ignores the gods (*shen*) and pays no attention to the parts of

---

and abort it if the foetus is female. Because of sex-selective abortions, in 2010 China, the birth rate was 118 males for every 100 females born. In a society which is unbalanced like this, sociologists predict severe problems. A book which provides an excellent historical overview of the problem is Michelle T. King, *Between Birth and Death: Female Infanticide in Nineteenth-Century China* (Stanford, CA: Stanford University Press, 2014). There are good journal articles on this topic. For example, Monica Das Gupta and Li Shuzhuo, "Gender Bias in China, South Korea and India 1920-1990: Effects of War, Famine and Fertility Decline," *Development and Change*, 30, no. 3 (July 1999): 619-652. See also Monica Das Gupta, "Family Systems, Political Systems, and Asia's Missing Girls: The Construction of Gender Bias and Its Unraveling," *Asian Population Studies*, 6, no. 2 (2010): 123-152.

[44] From the appendices to the *I Ching* (Book of Changes), discussed in Willard G. Oxtoby, ed., *World Religions: Eastern Traditions*, pp. 380-381.

[45] As you might expect, fidelity in marriage was not essential for the husband, only the wife.

[46] Beverly Bossler, *Courtesans, Concubines, and the Cult of Female Fidelity* (Cambridge, MA: Harvard-Yenching Institute, 2016).

the human essence which popular religion believed might exist after the body died (the *hun* and the *p'o*).[47] Laurence Thompson notes that "The Chinese religion conspicuously lacked the central concept of the ever-brooding presence of Almighty God, continuously attending to the sins and virtues of every individual, swift to save or damn, requiring submission, belief, faith, and adoration."[48]

One element which the West identifies as religious is sacred ritual. In ancient China, the rulers had a double responsibility: to maintain good order in society, and to produce good order in the universe by the proper observation of heavenly rituals. In fact, it was believed that religious ritual and war were the two most important affairs of state.[49]

Without doubt Confucius was an expert in family propriety and courtly rituals, and thus he valued the performance of all rituals (especially the human interactive sorts of rituals and filial piety) but seems to ignore the more obviously Heaven centered rituals which have a more overtly religious character. As you recall, Confucius advised his students to be honest in their personal conduct and not worry about the spirits, gods, or other spiritual beings.

Fan Ch'ih asked about wisdom. Confucius said: "Devote yourself earnestly to the duties due to men, and respect spiritual beings, but keep them at a distance—this may be called wisdom."[50]

According to the *Spring and Autumn Annals*, a Confucian classic which tradition says was edited by Confucius, there is no real life after death. It is possible to speak of someone being immortal, but this is a metaphor, not an actual state of continuing life. The only real immortality is simply being remembered by succeeding generations. One can be immortal because one is so virtuous that succeeding generations tell stories of one's virtue and repeat the stories long after you have died. The Sage-Kings of the Chou dynasty have this sort of immortality. We might consider the stories of the virtue of George Washington, or the virtue of Abraham Lincoln, as examples of this sort of immortality.

A second way to be immortal is to be remembered because your actions changed history. This would include people like the great Sage-Kings, Alexander the Great, Henry the Eighth, but also people like Adolph Hitler and Joseph Stalin. Similarly, biographical tales found in history books is another sort of immortality.

A third way to be immortal is to have written a book which is read and re-read generation after generation, century after century. The *Analects* of Confucius and the other Confucian classics provides Confucius with this sort of immortality. Of course authors such as William Shakespeare, Fyodor Dostoyevsky and Mark Twain have also achieved this kind of immortality. "When these are not abandoned with time, it may be called immortality."[51]

Although Confucius himself had little concern with the more supernatural aspects of popular religion, with his stress on the Mandate of Heaven, later Confucianism supported the worship of heaven and the cult of reverence for departed ancestors. In fact, much of the Little Tradition popular religion became incorporated into the Confucian system. Ritual ceremony was the heart of the Chinese court. The Confucians asserted that the rules of propriety and polite social interaction (*li*) arose at the same time that Heaven and Earth arose; they are built into the nature of reality.[52]

---

[47] The words of Confucius about what we think of as religion are collected in the section "Religious Sentiment" in Wm.Theodore de Bary, ed., *Sources of Chinese Tradition*, Vol. I (New York: Columbia University Press, 1960), pp. 29–30.

[48] Laurence G. Thompson, *Chinese Religion: An Introduction* (Belmont, CA: Dickinson, 1969), p. 9.

[49] Laurence G. Thompson, *The Chinese Way in Religion*, p. 5, p. 30.

[50] The *Analects* VI:20, de Bary ed., *Sources of Chinese Tradition*, Vol. I, p. 29.

[51] Tso's Commentary on the Spring and Autumn Annals, Tso Chuang, Duke Hsiang, 24th year, translated by Wing-tsit Chan, *A Source Book in Chinese Philosophy*, p. 13.

[52] Laurence G. Thompson, *The Chinese Way of Religion*, p. 22.

The great rituals performed by the ruler magically changed the world, and that attitude toward *li* reveal that there were supernatural powers, gods, and the honoring of Heaven, earth, and imperial ancestors were understood literally. Family rituals in honor of departed ancestors accepted supernatural aspects of the parts of the *yin-yang* soul ascending to the heavens, and this too was understood to be Confucianism. Later in history Confucius himself became the center of a cult which treated him as a deity, with a story of his miraculous birth (his virgin mother dreamed she was visited by a divinity and woke up the next morning to find herself pregnant) and temples were built in honor of Confucius. Sacrifices were made to Confucius, especially by the class of scholars who saw Confucius as their inspiration and patron deity. In mainland China these cults disappeared with the end of imperial rule, but there remain temples to Confucius in Taiwan.

15.13 CONFUCIANISM: THE GUIDE TO LIFE IN CHINA

As we have seen, Confucius wanted to create an environment in which people would naturally be in harmony with the Tao and in harmony with one another, and be virtuous. The problem was "How to instill order and harmony in the family and in society?" and the Confucian solution to the problem was in self-cultivation and in the necessity of those in power to act as responsible role models for their subordinates. As we have seen, two key concepts for Confucius are harmony and order. Order in the family, order in the community, and order in the state.[53]

Basing himself upon the legends of the Golden Age of the Chou/Zhou dynasty, Confucius believed that the ancient Sage-Kings had achieved a wise insight into the nature of reality, insight into the Tao/Dao, and the resulting insight revealed to them the one proper life pathway to bring about order and harmony.

For the Confucians, harmony with the Way/Tao is not culturally relative. The virtues of Confucianism were built into nature, and should be the same for every cultured human being in every civilization. The Confucians were certain that leaders in non-Chinese cultures would have discovered the identical Confucian virtues, if they were wise enough. That these leaders and these cultures did not have the same Confucian practices was evidence of their lack of wisdom, and hence their inferiority.

Harmony with the Tao/Dao results from proper ceremonial interaction, from *li*. *Li* is absolute because it is the result of the sage's wise understanding of the Tao, which the sage then applied to human society. Thus *li* is timeless (proper behavior is always the same) and it is objective (it does not matter how you feel about *li*; propriety is independent of our likes and dislikes). We gradually cultivate the seed of our natural benevolence (*jen*) when we learn the appropriate ceremonial interaction for each situation and each relationship. We express our benevolence using *li*. When we learn *li* and use it, we also cultivate *jen* and the result is harmony.

The Horizontal Dimension of Confucius's Solution

The Confucian desire to solve the problem of the lack of harmony and order in Chinese civilization is grounded in *li*, and ceremonial interaction has two dimensions: a horizontal dimension (the personal solution), and a vertical dimension (the political solution).

The horizontal dimension deals with turning ourselves into a superior person, which in turn affects our neighbors and our fellow community members. This is extending our personal virtue horizontally into our fellows

---

[53] It is worth noting that nowhere in Confucian thought do we find anything like the concept of personal freedom. The Chinese certainly wanted national freedom, that is, they wanted China to be free from external control, such as being free from the dominion of the foreign Mongols of the north. However, political freedom, the right to choose one's own representatives, to participate in the political discussions, to have a fair trial, were not discussed by Confucianism. Individual freedom, the freedom to live as one wished as long as one does not harm another, seems to have been a goal only for the philosophical Taoists; otherwise it seems to have been tolerated by the Confucians but not extolled as a desirable virtue. It is difficult to find any ancient civilization anywhere in the world which valued the freedom to live as one wishes (as it was valued in the American Declaration of Independence which declares the right to life, liberty, and the pursuit of happiness).

and the community we share with them (personal and social morality with extended family and peers). The vertical dimension is about above and below, up and down. It is ruler-to-ruled, or human-to-heaven (superior to subordinate; superior role models influence those who are subordinate). For ordinary people, the horizontal dimension begins with a person's own heart or mind. If you can get your own self in order, then you extend that positive influence to your immediate family, and then extended family, and from that, everything else follows.

Thus the horizontal dimension corresponds to the personal solution to the lack of order and harmony. When your own heart and mind are in order, you then extend that horizontally to one's immediate family, one's extended family, and then to the neighborhood. Confucius believed that the potential to be a good human is inborn; it is the seed of benevolence, or *jen/ren*. That seed is rooted in love for parents and siblings.

Respect and love for parents and extended family members may be basic and very important, but one cannot construct a well-ordered society which is "in accord with the Way" on love for family members alone. Hans-Georg Moller explains:

> Obviously, a society can not be built on [familial] love alone. The Confucians were well aware that, unlike in the Christian model, it is not natural to love everyone. One normally loves one's spouse, one's parents, one's children, but not all others. To envision a society functioning on the basis of mutual love is quite unrealistic. . . . a family can function on the basis of love (instead of morality), but a larger society cannot. . . . A society needs to establish some rules and social mechanisms that prevent, for instance, the stealing of sheep [an example used by Confucius]. The tool that basically all complex societies have developed for dealing with such cases—outside the family—is neither love nor morality, but the law. The law deals more coherently, more consequently, and even more rationally than morality with anything that is regarded as a crime in a society.[54]

The Confucian classic called the *Ta Hsueh* (Great Learning) summarizes the process:

> The ancients . . . wishing to cultivate their persons, they would first rectify their minds. Wishing to rectify their minds, they would first seek sincerity in their thoughts. Wishing for sincerity in their thoughts, they would first extend their knowledge. The extension of knowledge lay in the investigation of things.
> For only when things are investigated is knowledge extended; only when knowledge is extended are thoughts sincere; only when thoughts are sincere are minds rectified; only when minds are rectified are our persons cultivated; only when our persons are cultivated are our families regulated; only when families are regulated are states well governed; and only when states are well-governed is there peace in the world.
> From the emperor down to the common people, all, without exception, must consider cultivation of the individual character as the root.[55]

If you can cultivate those natural virtues within yourself, you will act lovingly and morally toward those closest to you, and then extend that morality towards extended family, then towards neighbors, and using ceremonial ritual interaction, *li*, one can extend harmony towards all human beings and have a well-ordered society. By following courtesy and propriety, *li*, there will be no social problems. By cultivating benevolence, *jen*, and mastering *li*, man can perfect himself, perfect his society, achieve happiness.

---

[54] Moller, *op. cit.*, p. 9.

[55] The "Great Learning" or *Ta Hsueh*, translated in de Bary, Chan, Watson, *Sources of Chinese Tradition*, p. 115.

CHAPTER 15: CONFUCIANISM

The Vertical Dimension of Confucius's Solution

As discussed above, the horizontal dimension of Confucius's solution involved fellow human beings who share a world with us, our neighbors and peers who we treat with proper respect. However, the vertical dimension reflects the superior-subordinate assumptions of Chinese society, extended into politics. The Chinese believed that there is almost always a superior and a subordinate in every relationship. They also believed that we all naturally seek and follow our superiors as role models, as in the family and in the political realm as well. If those at the top of the pyramid of authority and power cultivate their own wisdom and virtue (te/de), the second tier of governing officials will respect and follow the example set by the superiors, and take the superiors as their natural role model. The next level of people in the countryside will respect and take their superiors as role models. As a result the entire population will work to emulate those who we respect and admire. Thus role models and laws provide the vertical dimension, that is, the political solution.

The Chinese classic *Book of Li* (*Li chi*) provides additional quotations from Confucius, and in this quote, we can see that the ultimate goal is an ideal state in this world, not some world after we die:

> When the Great Way was practiced [during the Chou dynasty], the world was shared by all alike. The worthy and the able were promoted to office and men practiced good faith and lived in affection. Therefore they did not regard as parents only their own parents, or as sons only their own sons. The aged found a fitting close to their lives, the robust their proper employment; the young were provided with an upbringing and the widow and the widower, the orphaned and the sick, with proper care. Men had their tasks and women their hearths. They hated to see goods lying about in waste, yet they did not hoard them for themselves; they dislike the thought that their energies were not fully used, yet they used them not for private ends. Therefore all evil plotting was prevented and thieves and rebels did not arise, so that people could leave their outer gates unbolted. This was the age of Grand Unity.[56]

15.14 CONFUCIANISM FOLLOWING THE DEATH OF CONFUCIUS

It is likely that when K'ung-fu-tzu died in 470 B.C.E., he considered his plans to reform the ruling elite and bring about a well-ordered society to have failed. None of the kingdoms were persuaded to put his ideas into practice, and following his death his immediate students were no more successful in convincing rulers to adopt their plan of ruling by virtuous example. Confucius's plans for developing a peaceful and harmonious way of life did not change the civil strife decimating China. Contending states still made war on one another. Governments still remained under the control of military warlords who ruled by power and terror, not virtuous example. None of these seemed interested in the pathway of the sage, and none seemed interested in developing the practical wisdom of the sage which allows the sage to rule by virtuous example.

Gradually, however, followers of Confucianism studied hard and sought out political power because anyone seeking to be a *chun-tzu/junzi* (Superior Person) would extend himself to benefit others by seeking government service. In addition, their knowledge of and mastery of ancient ceremonies and rituals were useful skills to the ruling elite, for whom ritual was essential to governing, and eventually Confucian scholars came to hold important political positions in contending states.

By about 300 B.C.E., at least some rulers were seeking advice from scholars and philosophers. Socially, scholars and philosophers had high social status (unlike the military who had low status), and royal courts which supported

---

[56] DeBary, Chan, Watson, *Sources of Chinese Tradition*, Volume I (New York: Columbia University Press, 1960), p. 176.

scholars and intellectuals were considered refined and cultured. One of those scholars was Meng-tzu/Mengzi, known to us as Mencius.

15.15 MENCIUS

In China, the importance of Meng-tzu/Mengzi (ca. 372–289 B.C.E.), better known in English as Mencius, was second only to that of Confucius. Meng-tzu was born about a hundred years after Confucius died, and thus never knew the master personally. Mencius venerated Confucius as the wisest of all the sages. Mencius further developed the ideas of Master Confucius and thus Mencius' writings became a building block of the later Confucian tradition. Mencius studied with a student of Confucius's grandson, Tzu Ssu. The life of Mencius, the teacher, echoed that of Confucius, inasmuch as Mencius also traveled from court to court, trying to convince feudal lords to put the teachings of Confucius into practice. Mencius lived at approximately the same time period as the Taoist Chuang-tzu/Zhuangzi (see chapter 17 in this book), and it is possible that some of his ideas were a reaction to the Taoism current in his area.

There were now only six kingdoms left in China, and they were locked in battle to see which would become supreme; some fought merely to survive. Mencius did not have any better success than Confucius had in convincing warlords to take up the pathway of the sage; his advice was perceived as irrelevant and impractical. It is likely that he thought of himself as a failure. After his death, the followers of Mencius collected their memories of his ideas in a book which bears his name, *The Mencius* or *Meng-tzu/Mengzi*.

Meng-tzu was not a blind follower of Confucius. He did not merely parrot the teachings of Confucius: he added to them. He believed that Confucius was correct about everything, but he did feel that some of the later followers had misunderstood the teachings of the master. Rather than disagree with Confucius himself, Mencius offered some of his own logical interpretations of main Confucian doctrines.

Mencius On the Mandate of Heaven

We have already seen that the Chinese rulers claimed to have the authority to rule because Heaven recognized their extensive virtue and Heaven granted their family the Mandate of Heaven (*t'ien-ming*).[57] For Confucius this meant that the rulers ought to be exemplars of Confucian virtues and serve as role models, instead of being self-centered and mostly concerned with themselves.

Mencius was much more concerned about the details of material conditions essential for happiness than Confucius. According to Mencius, the ruler had a responsibility to ensure that the people had adequate living conditions, including land reform. Rulers should rule for the benefit of the people. Mencius wrote: "The people come first; the altars of the earth and grain come afterwards; the ruler comes last."[58]

Mencius placed more stress on the abstract notion of Heaven than Confucius did, and emphasized human nature as the source of human morality, and emphasized the impersonal force of Heaven as the natural source of

---

[57] This may strike the perceptive reader as similar to the European doctrine of the divine right of kings to rule, that god had given the king's family the right to rule. The difference is that in China, Heaven can revoke the authority to rule with natural catastrophes.

[58] Mencius, 7B:14. Wing-tsit Chan, *A Source Book in Chinese Philosophy* (Princeton, NJ: Princeton University Press, 1963), p. 81. Another translation: ". . . the people rank the highest, the spirits of land and grain come next, and the ruler counts the least" (de Bary, *Sources of Chinese Tradition*, Vol. 1, *op. cit.*, p. 96).

morality.[59] Mencius believed that Heaven monitors the socio-political world of human beings to ensure that it resonates with the larger rhythms of a universe functioning in natural harmony with Confucian moral principles.[60] Heaven is thus a providential moral force that intervenes in human history. This myth held that whenever a ruler became tyrannical or otherwise morally unfit to exercise rule, heaven would display its disfavor by manifesting ominous portents like earthquakes, floods, and other natural disasters. If the situation became critical enough, heaven would withdraw its mandate, disorder would increase, and the political order would fall into chaos.

From this stress on Heaven and the fact that the ruler drew his right to rule from Heaven's recognition of his virtue, Mencius logically concluded that if the king were not virtuous, and were to become tyrannical, to rule with no consideration for justice and virtue, or became morally unfit to rule, then that must mean that Heaven would withdraw its mandate which gives the ruler the authority to rule. We would know that Heaven no longer gave its mandate to the ruling family because disorder would increase, and the political order would fall into chaos. If the ruler continued to rule badly, heaven would display its disfavor by manifesting natural disasters, floods, famines, or earthquakes. If the ruler loses the Mandate of Heaven, then he has lost the authority to rule. If he continues to try to rule without the proper authority, the ruler is not a true ruler,[61] the subjects have the right to remove him and install a new ruler. What Mencius is now offering is a doctrine of justified revolution.

The doctrine of Rectification of Names plays a role here. If the ruler is not behaving like a genuine ruler, and has lost the Mandate of Heaven, then he is not really a ruler. In that case, this would not be a rebellion against a true ruler. If the ruler is killed in the course of the revolt, the rebels have not killed a genuine ruler because the person sitting on the throne no longer had the right to rule, had lost the Mandate of Heaven. In revolting, the subjects are merely following the will of Heaven, to put someone in control who does rule by virtue. It is unlikely that Confucius himself would have endorsed the claim that the people have the right to eliminate their rulers who had been selected by Heaven.

Human Nature

For Mencius, morality is an innate aspect of the Tao, the Way of Heaven, but it is also innate to human beings who are also a part of nature. Being moral is not about following social and moral rules. Heaven does not give us moral rules; morality is not external to human nature. The sage is intuitively and innately moral. The sage practices self-cultivation and self-transformation and gains a practical expertise in what is moral such that morality is the natural reaction of the sage to whatever event is occurring. However, being a sage is not easy. The goal that is within reach is the Superior Person, or *chun-tzu/junzi*. Mencius was especially concerned with working out the details of the ethical life for the *chun-tzu/junzi*, or the Superior-Ideal Person. He developed a systematic ethical system, grounded in human nature.

The question "What is human nature?" became an important issue debated among the various schools of Chinese thought during the lifetime of Mencius. Unlike the Confucians, we shall see that the philosophical Taoists did not seem to think that conventional morality was a natural outcome of inborn inclinations of human nature.

---

[59] Chinese Buddhists disagreed, and pointed out that if heaven were the source of all things, then the heavens are also the source of bad fortune and disaster, the pain, injustice and misery that humans experience. Bad things happen to good people, and heaven does not send punishment on those lacking in moral conduct. Virtuous people live in poverty, and sometimes even those who are most benevolent (*jen*) die when young.

[60] See Herlee Creel, *The Origins of Statecraft in China*, volume 1, chapter 5, "The Mandate of Heaven," (Chicago: University of Chicago Press, 1970), pp. 81-100.

[61] Remember the Confucian doctrine of rectification of names; if the king misuses his power and oppress the people, then his behavior does not match his "name" (or job title) and so he is not a genuine ruler. Heaven has revoked his mandate to rule.

Taoists argued that humans came into this world without inborn moral guides, that human nature was neither innately good nor innately evil, but rather was morally neutral. Sadly enough, Confucius did not say much about human nature, so later Confucians debated the topic without being able to quote the master. Is the human nature which we all share fundamentally moral, fundamentally good, neutral, or fundamentally flawed (ego-centered, evil)? Is human nature good or evil? When a baby is born, is its nature fundamentally good, is it neutral, or is it stained, selfish, or evil?

Mencius addresses this problem head-on. Mencius asserts that goodness is not something independent of human nature. Disagreeing with the Taoists, Mencius argues that we are born good, that morality is grounded in our mind, grounded in human nature.[62] We have an inborn tendency to do good, to be good. Each of us has the potential to be a sage because we are born with the natural human inclination to be a sage. We are born with that seed of benevolence, that potentiality. We are born good. Mencius was sure that childhood innocence is fundamentally good, and we will grow into good adults if we are not twisted by those around us, by the environment, by society. Mencius said:

> The tendency of human nature to do good is like that of water to flow downward. There is no man who does not tend to do good; there is no water that does not flow downward. Now you may strike water and make it splash over your forehead, or you may even force it up the hills. But is this in the nature of water? It is of course due to the force of circumstances. Similarly, man may be brought to do evil, and that is because the same is done to his nature.[63]

However, this seed, this innate tendency or inclination towards morality needs to be cultivated to mature properly. Basic human goodness is grounded in the seed of benevolence, *jen/ren*: it needs to be nurtured and channeled into appropriate paths. This is done by learning and mastering proper social rituals, *li*. It is because we are innately good that we respond to those people who are good. This is why when an emperor rules by virtue, he will be followed by the people and will make the entire empire more humane. An emperor who rules by military might does not attain the respect and admiration of the people, and thus cannot rule with the same authority.

Mencius realized that human beings had natural appetites for food and sex, but since we shared these with the animals, these were not what made us uniquely human.[64] The animals do not have the innate moral propensities that humans have. He argued that every human is innately moral because we are born with Four Seeds of (1) mercy or compassion, (2) shame, (3) respect or courtesy, and (4) a sense of right and wrong. When these seeds are cultivated, they have the potential to develop into the Four Virtues of *jen* (benevolence), *i* (righteousness), *li* (propriety), and wisdom. The source of morality is the human mind.

> When left to follow its natural feelings, human nature will do good. This is why I say it is good. If it becomes evil, it is not the fault of man's original capability. The sense of mercy is found in all men; the sense of shame is found in all men; the sense of respect is found in all men; the sense of right and wrong is found in all men. The sense of mercy constitutes humanity [*jen*]; the sense of shame constitutes righteousness [*i*]; the sense of respect constitutes decorum [*li*]; the sense of right and wrong constitutes wisdom [*chih/zhi*]. Humanity, righteousness, decorum, and wisdom are not something instilled into us from without; they are inherent in our nature.[65]

---

[62] A thousand years later Chinese Buddhists will argue for the innate purity of mind, arguing that every human is born with the intrinsically awakened nature of a Buddha, which they called "Buddha-nature."

[63] The *Mencius* VI A:2, in de Bary, Chan, Watson, *Sources of Chinese Tradition*, p. 89.

[64] It is interesting to note that the Greek philosopher Aristotle argued that the good life for a human must be connected to something unique to humans, and pleasure was not unique to humans because animals enjoy pleasures as well.

[65] The *Mencius*, VI A:6, *ibid.*, p. 90.

How can Mencius account for the fact that so many people grow into very nasty adults? Mencius argues that selfish desire can override the natural inclinations of the seeds; the seed of mercy, or compassion is fragile and needs to be cultivated with determination and be used—otherwise it can become lost. Evil[66] comes from what Mencius calls the "ensnarement of the heart" by desires we share with animals, so nourish the heart/mind[67] and do not let it get trapped by animal pleasures or self-centered desires. What makes us different from the animals is the thinking aspect of our heart, or mind (*hsin*), which is unique to us.[68] The thinking part of the mind is what allows us to become sages. This innate tendency needs to be cultivated to mature properly.

For Mencius, the natural order of harmony is found in Tao, and is visible in the patterns of Nature/Tao, but we human beings are also part of the pattern of Nature, so that natural harmony can also be experienced in the depths of human goodness. Each of us has the potential to be a sage because we are born with that potentiality.

Therefore, we follow the teachings of Confucius because it is our deepest nature to do so. As a result of following Confucius, we develop those natural tendencies and we bring to perfection our own innate natural tendencies and potentialities. We become fully and truly human. When brought to perfection we exemplify all these virtues and are a Confucian sage. Education is cultivating a spontaneous tendency to be good.

Although Meng-tzu/Mencius never had any position of political power, his ideas of innate human goodness came to dominate the school of Confucianism, and helped to shape later Neo-Confucianism (1,500 years later), discussed in chapter 21.

15.16 HSUN-TZU/XUNZI: THE SCHOOL OF LAW

Like Meng-tzu, the philosopher Hsun-tzu/Xunzi (ca. 312–238 B.C.E.) was also a Confucian, but with a quite different interpretation of the teachings of Master Confucius. Hsun-tzu/Xunzi was active about fifty years later than Meng-tzu, and disagreed with Mencius. He did not think that human nature naturally inclined us towards goodness.

Hsun-tzu seems to have felt that the optimism of Confucius and Mencius concerning human nature was unjustified. He agreed with Meng-tzu on many basic items: he agreed that it is possible to be a sage, that the basic Confucian virtues are the key to a good life, that we are capable of mastering the virtues, that scholarship is important, and that studying the ceremonial rites (*li*) taught to us by the sages of the past was useful. Like Mencius, Hsun-tzu was a follower of Confucius and thought that Confucius was correct about everything.

Hsun-tzu/Xunzi was a high official in the states of Ch'i and Ch'u, and the teacher of two very significant philosophers, Han Fei Tzu and the Ch'in prime minister Li Ssu, whose Legalistic ideas helped the king of Ch'in/Qin overcome all the other kingdoms and establish himself as the first Emperor of all China.

During Hsun-tzu's lifetime the ruler of the Ch'in/Qin kingdom had defeated four of the six neighboring kingdoms and was embarking on the final conquest of the remaining kingdoms to establish himself as the founder of a new royal dynasty. The Ch'in ruler succeeded in 221 B.C.E., nineteen years after Hsun-tzu died. The followers of Hsun-tzu collected his writings, and their memories of his teachings, in a book of thirty-two sections entitled the *Hsun-tzu*.

---

[66] See Franklin Perkins, *Heaven and Earth Are Not Humane: The Problem of Evil in Classical Chinese Philosophy* (Indiana University Press, 2014)

[67] The Chinese character *hsin* denotes both the emotion-filled heart and the abstract mind, and is translated by both terms depending on context.

[68] Aristotle argued that we share sensual desires with the animals, and that the key to a good life must be found in what is uniquely human. The Greek philosophers like Plato and Aristotle also thought that rationality was the unique and essential aspect of a human being. Whether Mencius's idea of "thinking" was the same as Greek concept of *nous* or reason, is a topic for further study.

Compared to Mencius, Hsun-tzu/Xunzi took a rather modern naturalistic view of the supernatural beliefs of the age. He criticized the superstitions of the common people and the popular religion of the time, including belief in divination and fortune telling, uncritical acceptance of magic tricks and miracles, and omens. Chinese stories were full of miracles performed by priests and shamans. Hsun-tzu argued that stories of miracles were nothing more than exaggerations and skillful trickery. He advocated a view of the world that was entirely rational and he asserted that supernatural beliefs were just ignorance. The world is made of natural objects, and there is nothing that transcends the natural realm, nothing supernatural. We can understand nature using empirical investigation. The well-educated *chun-tzu* (Superior Person) uses reason to deal with the world, whereas the common people believe in superstitious beliefs involving magic, good fortune and misfortune.

> You pray for rain and its rains. Why? For no particular reason, I say. It is just as though you had not prayed for rain and it rained anyway.... You consult the arts of divination before making a decision on some important matter. But it is not as though you could hope to accomplish anything by such ceremonies. They are done merely for ornament. Hence the Superior Person regards them as ornaments, but the common people regard them as supernatural.[69]

No Life After Death

Hsun-tzu felt that an educated Confucian scholar would realize that there is no life after death: "Birth is the beginning of a human being, death is his end."[70] He clearly states that rituals in honor of ancestors do not interact with the ancestors, and the ancestors do not influence their descendants after their death. Funeral rites express the grief of the living, but the dead do not continue to live on in a heavenly realm.[71] We ought to do the funeral rites for ancestors, as Confucius said, but not because the rituals have anything to do with ancestors. "The rites of the dead can be performed only once for each individual, and never again. They are the last occasion upon which the subject may fully express respect for his ruler, the son may express respect for his parents."[72]

Heaven

T'ien/Tian (Heaven) is neither a supernatural force nor a divinity. Heaven is the name we give to the sum total of all natural phenomenon and Heaven does not approve or disapprove of human political activity. Heaven does not give the emperor a right to rule, Heaven does not send down blessings, nor does Heaven send natural disasters like earthquakes as portents. There is no supernatural realm of gods, ghosts, and spirits.

> Always, when people [claim to] see ghosts, it is at time when they are aroused and excited, and they make their judgments in moments when their faculties are confused and blinded. At such times they affirm that what exists does not exist, or that what does not exist exists, and then they consider the matter settled.[73]

---

[69] Burton Watson, *Hsun-tzu: Basic Writings* (Columbia, 1963), p. 85. Modified by the author.

[70] *Ibid.*, ch. 19, p. 96.

[71] In general the Confucian scholars had little respect for popular religion and supernatural beliefs which they regarded as superstition appropriate only for the uneducated.

[72] The *Hsun-tzu/Xunzi*, ch. 19, Burton Watson, *Hsun-tzu: Basic Writings*, p. 97.

[73] The *Hsun-tzu/Xunzi*, ch. 21, Burton Watson, p. 135, modified by JeeLoo Liu, *op. cit.*, p. 91.

CHAPTER 15: CONFUCIANISM

Human Nature

Although Hsun-tzu had much in common with Meng-tzu, he vigorously disagreed with Meng-tzu about human nature. Meng-tzu thought that human beings are fundamentally good. Hsun-tzu wrote numerous essays, including one entitled "Our Nature is Bad." In this essay, Hsun-tzu argued that human beings are not innately good; rather they are filled with desires and are innately selfish.

> All man's desire to become good is because his nature is bad. The meagre wishes to be ample; the ugly to be beautiful; the constricted to have scope; the poor to be rich, the lowly to be noble; what you lack within you have to seek outside.[74]

Hsun-tzu was a Confucian; but he thought that Meng-tzu had completely misunderstood what Confucius meant. Mencius had gotten it all wrong.

> Mencius says: "The reason man is ready to learn is that his nature is originally good." I reply: "This is not so. This is due to a lack of knowledge about the original nature of man and of understanding the distinction between what is natural and what is acquired."[75]

Hsun-tzu asserts that our essential nature is bad; we have to use artificial means to overcome our innate selfishness and force goodness on our nature.

> Man's nature is evil; goodness is the result of conscious activity. The nature of man is such that he is born with a fondness for profit. . . . Therefore, man must first be transformed by the instructions of a teacher and guided by ritual principles . . . It is obvious . . . that man's nature is evil, and that his goodness is the result of conscious activity.[76]

We can see that Hsun-tzu believes that both Confucius and Mencius are correct when they assert that *li* (ceremonial interactions) are essential to creating a social system which can produce good people who can live together in harmony, and a well-ordered country. Mencius believed that *li* was a natural expression of human nature. Hsun-tzu disagreed. For Hsun-tzu, *li* is essential because *li* provides us with an artificial formal system, a deliberate effort to control jealousy, hatred, and our other naturally evil inclinations. The rules of proper ceremonial interaction, the *li*, can give us a guide to action when our selfishness dominates and we are not sure what to do. *Li* is the product of culture, and culture is designed to override our natural self-centeredness. *Li* forces us to straighten ourselves out, the way we can force bent wood to become straight with steaming and bending.[77] With sufficient thought, education and training, an ordinary person can become a sage. We are not innately good, but with education and *li* we are disciplining an otherwise spontaneous tendency to disorder.[78]

Since people are fundamentally selfish, they will always ask "what's in it for me?" and once we realize this, we can utilize innate selfishness to control people. Hsun-tzu argues that the sages of the ancient past did not discover

---

[74] Hsun-tzu translated by A. C. Graham in his *Disputers of the Tao* (LaSalle, IL: Open Court, 1989), p. 248.

[75] The *Hsun-tzu* in de Bary, Chan, Watson, *op. cit.*, p. 105.

[76] Burton Watson, *Hsun-tzu: Basic Writings*, p. 157.

[77] The Chinese character for "true" and "correct" is also the same character as "straight," "straighten," and "to make straight."

[78] A. C. Graham, *op. cit.*, p. 250.

morality rooted in nature. Rather, they invented morality as something useful, as early humans invented tools and utensils as useful. The sages created a useful yet artificial method of morality. They imposed *li* and moral standards as clever means to allow us to live together without harming and stealing from one another, to turn naturally selfish people into good humans.

Hsun-tzu argues that our human nature is grounded in self-centered desires, and if those desires are not controlled, anarchy and strife will result. We are born ego-centered and evil, but goodness (sagehood) arises because we are rational, because we think critically and we consciously control our desires. We need proper education to learn to overcome our natural self-centered desires. It is difficult, but it is possible. The sages used their intelligence to figure out how to redirect our natural selfishness and shape it into goodness. Learning *li* can reshape us into good humans. Transform yourself by following Confucius' teachings, model your behavior on the sages of the past, learn the *li* (created by conscious human effort to curb desires), and we will have a good populace and a good government.

Legalism

Han-fei-tzu and Li Ssu, two students of Hsun-tzu, extended the ideas of Hsun-tzu into a political philosophy called Legalism. Knowing that people always ask "what is profitable to me?" provides us with a psychological tool we can use to manipulate and control them: reward people when they do what we want; punish people when they do not do what we want. If we apply this to governing the nation, we get a law-and-order approach which assumes that because each person is self-centered, we cannot trust them to do what is best for the group or for society as a whole, but we can control them using a "carrot and stick" or "reward and punish" approach to governing.

15.17 HAN FEI-TZU: LEGALISM

Han Fei-tzu (ca. 280–233 B.C.E.) was alive at the end of the Period of Warring States and died just before the Ch'in ruler defeated all other kingdoms. Han Fei-tzu was related to the royal family of the kingdom of Han (one of the few remaining independent kingdoms) and was a student of the Confucian philosopher Hsun-tzu/Xunzi. Although Han Fei-tzu was a student of the Confucian Hsun-tzu, he went on to disagree with Confucianism. He created a new philosophy called Legalism which disagreed with the basic claims of Confucius.

He was a very intelligent and a very precise author who composed many essays. None of the rulers in Han were interested in his ideas, and because he was not successful in his own state of Han, he promoted his ideas in the other kingdoms of the era of the Warring States. Like the majority of Chinese thinkers, Han-fei-tzu focused on the art of ruling. The focus of the "Law and Order" ideas of Legalism is on mechanisms of controlling the ordinary people, not for the benefit of the people. Instead, control people for the benefit of the ruler.

The state is not to serve the people; the people exist to serve the state.

Han Fei -tzu argued that it is the duty of the people to obey the ruler. This is his advice to the emperor:
I submit that man's duty in life is to serve his prince and nourish his parents, . . . I further submit that it is man's duty, in all that he teaches, to promote loyalty and good faith and the Legal Constitution.[79]

Han Fei-tzu was a very pragmatic thinker who had little interest in abstract theories. His focus was on practicality and administrative efficiency. Han Fei-tzu does not defend the common people; his perspective is from the ruler and his advice is how the ruler can become unchallenged and how the state can run smoothly as a well-regulated totalitarian empire. Power should be placed in the hands of a single ruler and that ruler must exert absolute and total centralized control. The value of a citizen was his possible use to the ruler. The emperor was not to be a role

---

[79] Translated by Arthur Waley, *The Way and Its Power* (London: George Allen & Unwin, 1968), p. 43.

model; the emperor was an absolute monarch who needed to use fear and force to compel citizens to become strong, disciplined, and submissive to the laws. The emperor had no use for the Confucian virtues of *jen* (benevolence), or *li* (ceremonial interaction), or *i* (righteousness).

Han Fei-tzu did accept the analysis of human nature of his teacher, Hsun-tzu/Xunzi, that by nature human beings are selfish and evil. If human beings are fundamentally selfish, or bad, then the state can use that knowledge to control the people for the betterment of the state. However, Han Fei-tzu did not think that people could be transformed into moral beings.

People cannot be reformed; they can only be controlled.

The primary motivation for human actions and choices is profit and self-interest. Everyone who earns a living is always wondering how they can make more profit, looking for ways to maximize their economic well-being. We put our own advantage first, ahead of the possible benefits for others. Because we always ask "what's in it for me?," the state can use this to control us. We human beings are self-centered by nature. Being self-centered, we try to maximize our own profit and we try to avoid situations that will produce painful consequences for our selves.

Legalism demonstrates how to control the population with sanctions, with rewards and punishments. If you do what the state expects, you will be rewarded. That is a powerful motivation to obey. If you do not do what the state expects, you will be punished. That is a powerful motivation not to disobey. Legalism advocated that the state should make up a detailed list of laws that explain the duties and responsibilities of all its officers and citizens. Anyone who did something that the government did not want was to be severely punished. Punishments included being tatooed, being mutilated (cut off one's nose, for example), and death. Those who fulfilled their duties which the state deemed beneficial to the well-being of the state, would be generously rewarded.

Intellectual ideas that were not useful to the state were to be censored and outlawed. Books which disagreed with Legalism were to be burned. Scholars who advocated ideas that the state did not find useful were to be punished or executed. The people would obey, live frugal and obedient lives, and all their activities would be for the betterment of the ruler and the state.

Legalism is the basis of the Ch'in/Qin Dynasty

This Legalist philosophy of Hsun-tzu provided the platform for the final unification of China during the period of the Warring States. Li Ssu/Li Si, who became the prime minister of the kingdom of Ch'in (Qin) around 240 B.C.E., followed Legalist ideas to their logical conclusion. Using the Legalist techniques of Li Ssu, the Ch'in ruler defeated all contending states and consolidated his power over all northern China.

The king of Ch'in was impressed by Legalistic ideas, and invited Han Fei-tzu to his court. The prime minister, Li Ssu, was also a Legalist. Li Ssu knew that Han Fei-tzu was an exceptionally bright and able thinker. Li Ssu felt his six-year tenure as the single most important adviser to the king to be threatened. To eliminate his perceived rival, he accused Han Fei-tzu of being a Han loyalist and an enemy of the court of Ch'in. The Ch'in emperor imprisoned Han Fei-tzu instead of honoring him at the court. It is said that Li Ssu poisoned Han Fei-tzu before the emperor could realize that Han Fei-tzu was not an enemy Han-state spy, but rather was a gifted philosopher and a shrewd politician.

15.18 THE CH'IN/QIN UNIFICATION OF CHINA

Li-ssu was the adviser to the king of the state of Ch'in. He was also a scholar, statesman, and Legalist follower of Hsun-tzu (Xunzi) who advocated extreme and ruthless techniques to control everyone: reward them when they do their job, punish them when they do not live up to their job description. Li Ssu wanted a state where everyone followed the letter of the law in every detail; no creative responses were desired. If you did less than expected of your job description, you were punished. If you did more than expected of your job description, you were punished. No one was allowed to take any initiative; the rule was "follow orders" and nothing else.

Legalist techniques of Li Ssu were used to consolidate the Ch'in army and to control the conscripts. With these steps in place, the Ch'in ruler defeated all contending states and consolidated his power over all northern China. In 221 B.C.E., the Ch'in ruler became Ch'in-shih Huang-ti/Qinshi Huangdi (First Soverign Exalted Ruler of the Ch'in dynasty). He only lived to age 49 (259–210 B.C.E.). The totalitarian state of Ch'in was ruthless and extremely effective under the rule of the Ch'in Emperor.

Li Ssu became the prime minister to the new emperor of China and Legalism became the official orthodox philosophical system to guide all of China. Following the advice of Li Ssu, the new emperor of all northern China ordered the wholesale destruction of all non-practical and non-technical books, and the destruction of any books which did not agree with the Legalist philosophy. These included the Confucian texts and Taoist texts. Li Ssu encouraged the emperor to abolish all feudal ranks and privileges, and disarm all citizens. Many Chinese were strongly opposed to the ruthless Ch'in domination, and Li Ssu responded by terrorizing, torturing, or killing all who disagreed.

The new Ch'in emperor used Legalism to produce profound changes in Chinese society. The bureaucracy was centralized in a way never seen before in Chinese dynasties. The government standardized wheel-axle size for carts, thereby standardizing the roads and allowing carts and wagons to pass one another in villages and highways. The Ch'in also standardized the Chinese written language for the first time. The people were mobilized under the direction of the government and a vast network of canals and roads built. The Great Wall of China began construction under the leadership of the Ch'in-shih Huang-ti to protect northern China against the predation of the nomadic tribes that were always a danger to northern communities. The Great Wall project also served to keep huge numbers of citizen-workers busy and unable to revolt.

The emperor had envisioned living for centuries, but the reign of the Ch'in (Qin) emperor lasted only fourteen years. After a few years of ingesting longevity potions created by religious Taoist priests, his behavior became more and more irrational, and he became weaker and weaker. Following the death of the ruler (at age 49), the Ch'in dynasty collapsed about 207 B.C.E.

15.19 CONFUCIANISM IN THE HAN DYNASTY (202 BCE–220 CE)

Five years of chaos followed the collapse of the Ch'in dynasty, and after several years of war, a new emperor proclaimed himself founder of a new dynasty, called the Han (202 B.C.E.–220 C.E.). Although the rigid Legalist policies of the previous dynasty were discredited and officially rejected, the Han dynasty continued most of the policies of the previous Ch'in. They continued to centralize, to enforce uniform standards and encourage established traditions in politics and in culture. The followers of Confucius achieved some positions of importance in the Han court, and the ideas of Confucius began to exert a greater influence over court ministers and scholars.

For Confucian scholars at court, the past of the Chou dynasty was the Golden Age, and so they wanted to return to the ways of the ancient past. Consequently, innovation was not valued or prized. To maintain order and harmony, rigid uniformity was imposed by the Confucians echoing the practices of the previous Ch'in dynasty. Officially the government rejected Legalism,[80] and the combination of Confucian and Taoist governing resulted in political stability and economic prosperity for almost four-hundred years. During this period there were many scientific advances including the discovery of steel. Paper was invented during Han (about 100 C.E.) although printing using movable type in China would not occur for nearly five hundred years (the Chinese had moveable type 700 years before Gutenberg in the West).

During the Han dynasty, especially under the influence of Confucians in government, the Chinese literary classics were consolidated and it should surprise no one that the corpus of classic texts were the texts especially valued

---

[80] Although Legalism was officially discredited, and no one ever openly advocated Legalist techniques in following dynasties, later regimes often did make use of Legalist methods which were perceived to be very effective even if they were also associated with evil oppression.

by the Confucians. Later the first national university was founded, and serious history and bibliography was also started during Han dynasty.

15.20 THE FIVE CLASSICS and the FOUR BOOKS

In addition to the *Analects* of Confucius, the most important of the classical literature was the Five Classics. In later centuries four additional books were also accorded the status of classics.

These Five Classics were studied by every educated Chinese person after the Han in the third century C.E. After 125 B.C.E. the texts were the basis for examinations in the imperial college, and later in the T'ang dynasty they were the basis for the Civil Service Examinations.[81] Anyone who wanted to be employed by the government, a highly valued occupation which provided good pay and high status, had to memorize these texts and interpret them in the official Confucian manner. At one time legend said that Confucius edited the classics, but modern scholarship reveals that Confucius did not do so. However, it is clear that Confucian scholars have extensively modified and edited these texts.

The Five Classics

The Shu Ching/Shujing (Classic Book of History)
> A collection of historical documents, mostly speeches, and accounts of principles of government.

The Shih Ching/Shijing (Classic Book of Poetry, Songs or Odes)
> 305 "folk songs" from over a thousand years of Shang dynasty poetry dealing with love, courtship, hunting, dancing, and banquet songs. According to legends, originally it was 3,000 poems, but Confucius was said to have edited it down to the 305 best removing those which were too sexually explicit (scholars doubt that Confucius had anything to do with editing it).

The I Ching/Yijing (Book of Changes).
> A manual of divination based on symbolic interpretation of eight trigrams and sixty-four hexagrams made of straight lines (*yang*) and broken lines (*yin*). Later, commentaries were added which provided metaphysical interpretations and cryptic references to nature.

The Ch'un Chiu/Chunqiu (Spring and Autumn Annals)
> History of and tales about the kingdom of Lu between 722-481 B.C.E, where Confucius was born in 551 B.C.E.

The Li Chi/Liji (Records of Ceremonies, Rituals, or Rites).
> Rules for court behavior, etiquette for nobility, dancing, music, funerals, reverence for ancestors, imperial sacrifices and archery contests, which has been modified by later Confucian practices.

At one time there was also a classic Book of Music, but the text is lost.

The Four Books

Later in Chinese history, another group of four Confucian books was raised to the status of canonical texts. They are the Four Books, which during the Sung/Song dynasty, were grouped together as a counterbalance to the philosophical writings of the Buddhists and the Taoists/Daoists. These were the essential texts of Neo-Confucianism (discussed in chapter 21).

---

[81] The beginnings of the civil service system can be traced to 595 C.E., during the Sui dynasty (589-618). This later developed into a fully functioning imperial examination system in the T'ang and Sung dynasties. This survived in China until 1905.

Lun-Yü (Analects of Confucius)
Meng Tzu (Mencius)
Chung Yung (Doctrine and Practice of the Mean)[82]
Ta Hsueh (Great Learning, Highest Possible Cultivation)

15.21 THE ECLIPSE OF CONFUCIANISM

Toward the end of the Han dynasty, about 200 C.E., the dynasty was ruled by weak and selfish rulers who put their own pleasures ahead of the needs of the people. Han rulers paid no attention to ruling the state and ignored proper courtly rituals. The empire was suffering.

In addition, there were also barbarian invasions from the north and following military success in the north repelling the invaders, the Chinese military revolted, took over the government and a period of disunity lasted for approximately 350 years (221–589 C.E.). Much of the Han had been ruled by Confucian principles, and with the failure of the Han rulers to rule justly and fairly, Confucian ideas were perceived as ineffective, and so there was a return to Taoist theories of rulership. This was also the time when Buddhism began to have political influence, and Chinese intellectuals utilized Taoism combined with the appeal of Indian Buddhism to rule, and for a while Confucianism retreated into the background.

During the later Sui dynasty (589–618) and T'ang dynasty (618–906 C.E.) Confucianism regained much of its importance, but never completely dominated Chinese thought as it had in the past until the advent of Neo-Confucianism in the eleventh century. During the Sui, T'ang, and early Sung (960–1279) dynasties, Taoism and Buddhism came to exert great influence over the rulers and ministers.

Ultimately Confucianism retained its hold on government by the clever strategy of using civil service examinations to pick those who could serve in the government and administration. The idea of civil service examinations was good: find the smartest and best educated to run the government offices. However, the topics that the three levels of civil service exams covered were determined by the Confucians. To pass even the first level the student had to memorize the *Analects* of Confucius, the *Meng-tzu* of Mencius, the *Ta-hsueh* (Great Learning) and innumerable commentaries which were always based on Meng-tzu/Mencius's interpretation of Confucius.[83] To successfully pass all three levels required a student to devote his entire education to Confucian texts and Confucian ideas. Anyone suggesting ideas not in conformity with official Confucius and official Mencius did not pass their examinations and did not work in the government. Those who passed all three levels were brought into the government as district magistrates, and if they showed skill in administration, they could go further up the ladder of success.

Of course, if one's family were wealthy and one's father was already in the government, this helped considerably. As a result, the civil service exams guaranteed that those who ruled China were good Confucians, and tended to guarantee that they came from the wealthy and elite families of China. An unintended consequence of this is that the more abstract Confucian ideas and Confucian philosophy remained primarily in the very well-educated elite upper classes. These people were more sophisticated and tended to look down upon the popular religious beliefs of the peasants as superstition. Among the lower classes, the sources for the popular Chinese religious beliefs in gods, heavens

---

[82] See Andrew Plaks, *Ta Hsueh and Chung Yung: The Highest Order of Cultivation and on the Practice of the Mean* (New York: Penguin, 2004).

[83] Until the middle of the twentieth century, the Chinese understood education to be memorization. Every Chinese scholar would have had all the great texts memorized, and the official interpretations of each passage memorized. By merely uttering a few words, fellow scholars would have known which text was being quoted, and what the full meaning was of the quotation. Much of Chinese scholarly writing involved extensive quotations and the assumption was that the reader would know the name of the text being quoted, and all the allusions contained in the quotation. This was not plagarism because there was no attempt to deceive; the reader had the source already memorized.

and hells, were shamanistic folk religion, religious Taoism, and later, devotional Buddhism.

Chinese religions were not exclusive.

Unlike religions in the West, none of the Chinese religions were exclusive. It was common for people to be Confucians in their family interactions and formal social obligations or occupation, to be a philosophical Taoist when attempting to satisfy the artistic and poetic inclinations, to use religious Taoism to contact spirits and to extend one's life span, and to be a Buddhist when it came to questions about the meaning of existence, and the ultimate meaning of life and death.

Later in the Sung/Song dynasty, new forms of Confucianism came to dominate the Chinese court, and the Chinese intellectual life. This continued until the early twentieth century, when the Chinese correctly perceived that their Confucian educational system was completely unable to deal with the economic and military aggression of Western powers. The Chinese Communist government tried to eliminate Confucianism, Taoism, and Buddhism. However, in more recent decades there has been a resurgence of Confucian ideas in mainland China.[84]

15.22 SUMMARY OF THE CHAPTER

The single most important thinker in the history of China was Master K'ung-fu-tzu, or Confucius. The problem that Confucius attempted to solve was to restore order and harmony in the era of chaos and strife that followed the collapse of central authority in China. K'ung-fu-tzu believed that harmony could be achieved if the ruling classes cultivated a handful of virtues. By cultivating these virtues, the best educated and the rulers would become Superior Persons (possibly even sages), and then they can act as role models which would inspire the ordinary people to behave similarly. It would not be necessary for the rulers to compel the people to obey. The people would cultivate the same virtues, and in the process we would find political, social, and personal harmony.

The keys to order and harmony were just a few of these virtues: development of heartfelt and polite ceremonial interaction (*li*), benevolence (*jen*), moral responsibility or righteousness (*i*), and proper love and respect for family, especially elders and ancestors (filial piety) which also included loving one's siblings.

Ceremonial interaction (*li*) encourages us to realize that we all are participants in the sacred ritual called life. The proper degree of ceremonial interaction also includes the respect and reverence due to our parents and our departed ancestors. We treat our family members with love and with ceremonial correctness, and then extend that practice outwardly to members of the community and the kingdom. As we treat each person with the proper degree of ceremonial correctness, our own humanity (*jen/ren*) grows and develops, and we move from being an ordinary human being to becoming a *chun-tzu/junzi*, or a Superior Person. Although the highest achievement in human goodness belongs to the sage who has perfect moral charismatic virtue or *te/de*, and although the potential to sagehood belongs to each of us, the sage's realization of perfect *jen* and perfect *li* are beyond the reach of almost all of us. As a result our behavior becomes rectified, that is, we behave appropriately for whatever role we are assuming at the moment, whether it be king, father, brother, friend, teacher, or warrior.

As Confucianism became more important over the centuries, students who sought a role in politics scrambled to establish themselves as part of a lineage of teacher-students which could trace its origins back to Confucius himself. One's teacher became the ancestor, and the students created charts showing themselves belonging to this ancestral lineage. Being connected to the Confucian line of teachers gave the student status and respectability.

Mencius, who lived about a hundred years after the death of Confucius, extended the ideas of Confucius and asserted that we are all born fundamentally good, and if we practice the teachings of Confucius, we will fully develop

---

[84] See Kenneth J. Hammond and Jeffrey L. Richey, *The Sage Returns: The Confucian Revival in Contemporary China* (State University of New York Press, 2015).

our humanity and hold the keys to a good life. Mencius also pointed out that kings rule because Heaven recognizes their virtue, but also means that when the rulers no longer are exemplars of virtue, the people have the right to revolt and remove them from office. A king who does not behave in a kingly manner is not a true king. If we cultivate benevolence (*jen/ren*) and learn the proper ceremonial ways to interact with one another, we will have a world of peace and harmony.

The other Confucian of this era was Hsun-tzu/Hsunzi (a contemporary of Mencius), who agreed with Mencius that the teachings of Confucius were the key to a good life, but he arrived at that conclusion from diametrically opposite assumptions. Hsun-tzu believed that we humans are innately selfish, always looking out for our own advantage or profit, and that we had no natural inclination to be compassionate or kindly to others. If we follow our human nature, society is doomed. Hsun-tzu believed that Confucius taught a way to escape the dreary outlook of continuous civil war. The way to escape was to overcome our innate selfishness by cultivating benevolence, *jen/ren*, and to deal with others in a way that allows for justice. We do that by mastering ceremonial rituals that override our ego-centeredness. Thus, Confucius teaches us how to overcome our evil innate nature and by following Confucius, we can have a society in peace where we are all in harmony with ourselves and with Nature.

Han Fei-tzu and Li Ssu were students of Hsun-tzu who took his ideas of the basic selfishness of human beings, and employed them in the service of a ruthless totalitarian regime that ultimately conquered all of China. The Legalist philosophy advocated blind following of instructions: reward those who obey, punish those who do not. These Legalist ideas of Han Fei-tzu and Li Ssu were later regarded as harshly oppressive and exploitative and became synonymous with evil for all Chinese thinkers after the Ch'in dynasty. Confucian ideas continued to influence China from the Han dynasty until the twentieth century in China. The Confucian civil service examination system guaranteed that Confucian ideas and presuppositions would dominate at all levels of government until 1912.

Confucianism did support many features of Chinese civilization which modern times tend to find undesirable. For example, the Confucian endorsement of a patriarchal hierarchy puts males always in the superior position, whether father, husbands, or rulers. The subordinate, the young and women are to obey, to perform their Confucian and other social duties with proper submission. Women were always subordinate, determined by their *yin* nature. A woman's duty is to bear sons, and if she does not fulfill this duty, the husband has the right to additional wives. In traditional Confucianism, women are to obey. The civil service examination system guaranteed that the wealthy and the powerful would control the government, for only the wealthy and powerful could afford the extended education required to pass the three levels of examinations.

However, the positive aspects of Confucianism are obvious in other ways. For example, that we should treat fellow humans politely, with ritual courtesy and respect, and we should always respect our parents and elders. In the political realm Confucius instructs his students that rulers should rule by virtue, not military power. Ministers must be courageous and speak truth to power, telling the ruler "you are wrong" even if such speech might cost the minister his own life.

15.23 TECHNICAL TERMS

Confucius   K'ung-fu-tzu/Kongfuzi
Ch'in-shih Huang-ti/Qinshi Huangdi

Han-fei-tzu/Hanfeizi
Hsun-tzu/Xunzi
Li Ssu/Li Si
Mencius   Meng-tzu/Mengzi

i/yi   rightness, fittingness, appropriateness (pronounced like English "e").

CHAPTER 15: CONFUCIANISM

jen/ren	benevolence, humanity, human-heartedness, compassion, etc. ("wren")
li	ceremonial ritual interaction, rites, decorum, manners, etc.
te/de	virtue; the positive charisma that some people have to influence others (pronounced "duh").
yang	the high, active, bright aspect of the flow of the Tao/Dao
yin	the low, passive, obscure aspect of the flow of the Tao/Dao

Chou/Zhou dynasty, and the Duke of Chou
Ch'in/Qin dynasty
rectification of names

Age of the Hundred Philosophers
Han dynasty
filial piety (reverence for parents, ancestors)

15.24 QUESTIONS FOR FURTHER DISCUSSION

(1) Chinese Confucianism is considered one of the world's major religions, but Confucius had little interest in gods, no belief in life after death, and advised his students to focus on humans and not upon spirits. Despite this, Confucianism places great stress upon rituals. Considering this, should Confucian thought be described as a religion, as a philosophy, or something else?

(2) It might be instructive for the student to list and consider the main virtues of Chinese Confucianism, and then compare them with the main virtues of the Western Christian religions (faith, hope, obedience, chastity, and others). The lists are interestingly different. Why are the moral virtues of one civilization so different from those of another?

(3) Western governments want a well-ordered society of peaceful citizens. What means and methods does Western civilization utilize to accomplish these goals? Is there anything Western governments might learn from the study of Confucius or Mencius?

(4) Ceremonial courtesy is essential to Confucianism. Is there anything equivalent to that in Western civilization? Should there be?

(5) Confucian ideals were the Sage and the Superior Person. How do people in the West visualize the ideal person? Do we have anything equivalent in the West? Who are the heroes in Western civilization? Is a Christian saint like a Confucian sage or superior person? Is our ideal person someone who is morally perfect?

(6) The Chinese believed that reverence for the past and the rulers of the past was essential for a good government. In the USA we talk about the intentions of the "original founders" and perhaps imagine a Golden Age where the presidents and senators governed with virtue for the common good. Is this similar to what the Confucians are doing?

(7) The Chinese virtue of *I* (or "righteousness") is recognizing and doing what is right, fitting, proper, and decent. It allows us to discriminate between moral goodness and what is morally not-good. The Chinese thought that nature provided us with the ability to make this distinction. Is this similar to conscience in the West? How is it different?

(8)   The Chinese Confucians believed that it is human nature to follow role models, and so we need role models who we can emulate. To emulate an ideal person will help us to become good human beings. Who are the dominant role models (or "heroes") in Western culture? Do these Western role models help us to be moral citizens and superior persons?

(9)   Mencius argued for the conclusion that at birth, human nature is basically good. Hsun-tzu argued that humans by nature are self-centered and evil. What is the view of modern psychology? Contemporary anthropology? The Christian religion (are humans born fundamentally good, or are we all stained with some sort of sin)?

(10)   The Legalist philosophy was about manipulating and controlling the population. The Legalists believed that we are all ego-centered and seek our own benefit, advantage or profit as most important. If so, we can all be manipulated by threats to hurt us, or promises to reward us. What do you think, can we be controlled by laws promising rewards and punishments? Would it be more effective to speak politely to people and explain that their behavior was morally wrong? Would that work? Is there an option in between these two extremes?

SELECTED BIBLIOGRAPHY

The Classic Chinese Confucian Texts

Ames, Roger T., *The Analects of Confucius* (New York: Ballantine Books, 1999)

Chan Wing-tsit, *A Source Book in Chinese Philosophy* (Princeton, NJ: Princeton University Press, 1963)

de Bary, Theodore, W. T. Chan and Burton Watson, *Sources of Chinese Tradition*, 2 volumes (New York: Columbia University Press, 1960)

Fingarette, Herbert, *Confucius: The Secular as Sacred* (New York: Harper & Row, 1972; reprinted Waveland Press, 1998)

Fung Yu-lan, *A History of Chinese Philosophy*, two volumes, tr. by Derk Bodde, (Princeton, NJ: Princeton University Press, 1952–1953).

Graham, Angus C., *Disputers of the Tao* (LaSalle, IL: Open Court, 1989)

Ivanhoe, Philip J., and Bryan Van Norden, eds., *Readings in Classical Chinese Philosophy* (Indianapolis: Hackett, 2005)

Lau, D. C., *Confucius: The Analects* (New York: Penguin Books, 1979)

Leys, Simon, *The Analects of Confucius* (New York: W. W. Norton, 1997)

Ni, Peimin, *Confucius: The Man and the Way of Gongfu* (New York: Rowman & Littlefield, 2016)

Nylan, Michael, and Thomas Wilson, *Lives of Confucius: Civilization's Greatest Sage Through the Ages* (Harmony Books: 2010)

Waley, Arthur, *The Analects of Confucius*, (New York: Allen & Unwin, 1938; also Random House/Modern Library, 1938)

Waley, Arthur, *Three Ways of Thought in Ancient China* (New York: Doubleday, 1956)

Chinese Thought During the Confucian Era

Adamek, Wendi L., *The Mystique of Transmission* (New York: Columbia University, 2007) The primary focus of this book is Chinese Buddhism during the T'ang and Sung dynasties.

Bell, Daniel A., *China's New Confucianism: Politics and Everyday Life in a Changing Society* (Princeton, NJ: Princeton University Press, 2010)

Bell, Daniel A. and Hahm, Chaibong, eds., *Confucianism for the Modern World* (London: Cambridge University Press,

2003).

Chan Wing-tsit, *A Source Book in Chinese Philosophy* (Princeton, NJ: Princeton University Press, 1963)

de Bary, Theodore, W. T. Chan and Burton Watson, *Sources of Chinese Tradition*, 2 volumes (New York: Columbia University Press, 1960)

Ebrey, Patricia, *The Cambridge Illustrated History of China* (London: Cambridge University Press, 2010)

Fingarette, Herbert, *Confucius: The Secular as Sacred* (Waveland Press, 1998)

Fung Yu-lan, *A History of Chinese Philosophy*, two volumes, tr. by Derk Bodde, (Princeton, NJ: Princeton University Press, 1952–1953).

Goldin, Paul R., *After Confucius: Studies in Early Chinese Philosophy* (Honolulu: University of Hawaii Press, 2005)

Goldin, Paul R., *Confucianism* (Berkeley, CA: University of California, 2011)

Graham, Angus C., *Disputers of the Tao* (LaSalle, IL: Open Court, 1989)

Hammond, Kenneth J. and Jeffrey L. Richey, *The Sage Returns: The Confucian Revival in Contemporary China* (NY: State University of New York Press, 2015)

Ivanhoe, Philip J., and Bryan Van Norden, eds., *Readings in Classical Chinese Philosophy* (Hackett, 2005)

King, Michelle T., *Between Birth and Death: Female Infanticide in Nineteenth-Century China* (Stanford, CA: Stanford University Press, 2014)

Lagerway, John, and Marc Kalinowski, eds., *Early Chinese Religion: Part One: Shang Through Han* (1250 BC -220 AD) (Leiden & Boston: Brill, 2011)

Lagerway, John, and Lu Pengzhi, eds., *Early Chinese Religion: Part Two: The Period of Division* (220 AD -529 AD) (Leiden & Boston: Brill, 2010)

Li Feng, *Early China: A Social and Cultural History* (New York: Cambridge University Press, 2013)

Munro, Donald, *The Concept of Man in Early China* (Stanford, CA: Stanford Univ. Press, 1969)

Needham, Joseph, *Science and Civilization in China*, Vol. II (London: Cambridge University Press, 1956)

Ni, Peimin, *Confucius: The Man and the Way of Gongfu* (Londond & New York: Rowman & Littlefield, 2016)

Nivison, David and Bryan Van Norden, *The Ways of Confucianism: Investigations in Chinese Philosophy* (Open Court, 1996)

Nylan, Michael, and Thomas Wilson, *Lives of Confucius: Civilization's Greatest Sage Through the Ages* (Harmony Books: 2010)

Perkins, Franklin, *Heaven and Earth Are Not Humane: The Problem of Evil in Classical Chinese Philosophy* (Indiana University Press, 2014)

Shun, Kwong-Loi & David Wong, eds., *Confucian Ethics: A Comparative Study of Self, Autonomy and Community* (New York: Cambridge, 2004)

Van Norden, Bryan W., *Introduction to Classical Chinese Philosophy* (Cambridge: Hackett Publishing, 2011)

Waley, Arthur, *Three Ways of Thought in Ancient China* (New York: Doubleday, 1956)

Wang, Robin R., *Yinyang: The Way of Heaven and Earth in Chinese Thought and Culture* (London: Cambridge, 2012)

CHAPTER 16: PHILOSOPHICAL TAOISM: *Tao Te Ching*

16.1 OVERVIEW OF THE CHAPTER

道 There are a cluster of interestingly different traditions which can be described by the same English term "Taoism/Daoism."[1] Following standard Western practice, there are two umbrella groupings we can use to distinguish these, while still recognizing the diversity implicit in the term "Taoism." In Chinese they are *Tao-chia/Daojia* (philosophical Taoism, literally the "School of Tao/Dao") and *Tao-chiao/Daojiao* (religious Taoism, literally the "Teaching of Tao/Dao").[2]

This chapter discusses the School of Tao, *Tao-chia*, the philosophical and contemplative form of Taoism. This could be described as the form of Taoism associated with the well-educated and valued for its literary and poetic ideas. This form of Taoism explores the root of both heaven and earth, and is interested in how humans are related to all reality. The Taoist wanted to know how to regain harmony with the source of nature, heaven, and earth. To achieve harmony, the Taoists will stress the emulation of role models from nature,[3] such as water, and related ideas about spontaneity and the practice of *wu-wei* or non-action, as the method to return to the Tao, the sacred ultimate. Philosophical Taoism, such as found in the Taoist classic text the *Tao Te Ching*, shows no interest in gods, demons, rituals, liturgies, miracles, church authorities or clergy.

The second form of Taoism, *Tao-chiao/Daojiao*, or "Religious Taoism," is the form which stresses the gods, utilizes rituals and clergy, stresses trained priests controlling spirits, relying on magical spells and charms, learning practical exercises to cure illness, and esoteric practices, and mixing and consuming unusual substances which might produce longevity and even immortality. Unlike philosophical Taoism, religious Taoism is profoundly shamanistic, that is, it has special persons who deal with the realm of spirits, who focus their concern with gods, rituals, longevity potions, liturgies, and over time this tradition of religious Taoism developed a well-established powerful priesthood. Religious Taoists treat the author of the *Tao Te Ching*, Lao-tzu/Laozi, as a heavenly god and rituals are performed in his honor. The compendium of religious Taoist scriptures also includes the *Tao Te Ching* and many other Taoist works. Ritually based religious Taoism was organized in the first century of the common era.

Poets, painters, musicians, and philosophers cultivated the philosophical School of Tao *Tao-chia* Taoism, but it is Religious Taoism that exerted the most influence upon popular Chinese folk religion. Religious Taoism is discussed in chapter 18.

---

[1] As was pointed out previously, the term TAO is the Wade-Giles romanization of the Chinese character and both Wade and Giles intended that the knowledgeable reader would realize that the letter "T" with an apostrophe mean to pronounce the letter with the air coming out of your mouth with force, so it will sound like a "T" in English. However, "T" without an apostrophe was an unaspirated "T" and thus to be pronounced closer to the English letter "D," or DAO. The Pinyin romanization simply writes it as Dao.

[2] The scholar Isabelle Robinet has argued that Taoism has always been religious. See Isabelle Robinet, *Taoism: Growth of a Religion* (Stanford, CA., Stanford University Press, 1997), trans. Phyllis Brooks. This is the view of contemporary sects of religious Taoism. See also Julian Pas, *The A to Z of Taoism* (Scarecrow Press, 2006).

[3] When discussing natural processes like wind, rain, and water flowing downward, we use the term "nature" with a lower-case "n". When discussing the underlying source of the regularity of the seasons, the metaphysical source of natural processes, this is "Nature" with a capital "n", which is also a synonym for Tao/Dao.

THE CHINESE DYNASTIES RELEVANT TO TAOISM

CHOU/ZHOU (c. 1122-771 BCE).
        Interstate warfare after 771 BCE.
        Spring and Autumn Period 722-481 BCE.
            Confucius born 551 BCE
        Warring States period 403-221 BCE.
            Chuang-tzu born
CH'IN/QIN (221-207 BCE): China is truly unified under one ruler
        Legalism adopted as official state policy.
        Burning of the books which disagreed with Legalism.
        Central control and bureaucratic administration over China.

HAN (202 B.C.E.-220 C.E.)
        Confucianism comes to dominate the political world.
        Philosophical and religious Taoism gain political importance.
        Buddhism enters China around 50 C.E.
THREE KINGDOMS (220-265 C.E.)
        China partitioned into three.
        Confucian influence wanes; Buddhist influence growing.
TSIN (265-420 C.E.)
        China beomes Northern (non-Chinese rulers) and Southern (Chinese rulers)
SUI (589-618 C.E.)
T'ANG/TANG (618-906 C.E.)
FIVE DYNASTIES (907-960)
SUNG/SONG (960-1279)

16.2 HISTORICAL BACKGROUND

Traditionally, philosophical Taoism/Daoism is treated as approximately contemporary with Confucianism, and it is very reasonable to assume that the fundamental ideas of the world-view we call "Taoism" also developed during the same Warring States period (following the collapse of the Chou in 771 B.C.E.) of social and political chaos. Although the issues that concerned the Confucians were the same issues which concern the *Tao-chia* Taoists (How can one return to order and harmony? How can one live safely in a world of political oppression and savage and unpredictable violence? How should we live?), there were other concerns as well: a nature philosophy exploring the origin of the cosmos and all the things in the world. There must be a root which accounts for how the world came into being. There were several names suggested for this root: Tao/Dao, the Great Oneness which engenders duality, the primordial Constancy before time. This origin is vague, obscure, deeper than deep, and nameless. Even assigning a term like "energy" (*ch'i/qi*) or "God" (*shen*) misses the mark.

Our understanding of philosophical Taoism/Daoism is distorted if we consider it in isolation. Taoism makes most sense when contrasted with its traditional counter-balance, Confucianism. Philosophical Taoism is at least partly a reaction to the Confucian way of looking at the world, but it is not a complete rejection of all Confucian assumptions. Traditionally, Confucianism has been associated with the ambitious aristocratic male who follows the Confucian path of government service, whereas the philosophical Taoist is someone less success-oriented, less assertive, less concerned with power and control; someone who was not satisfied with the self-confident political certainty of the Confucian scholars in the imperial court.

Confucius argues that we need to cultivate our *jen/ren* (benevolence) and gradually master *li* (ceremonial interaction), and combine that with reverence for ancestors and respect for history and then model our behavior upon the Sage-Kings of the past. Philosophical Taoism/Daoism represents the side of Chinese civilization which is less insistent upon proper propriety, and social respectability. Philosophical Taoism presents itself as more spontaneous, more creative, more intuitive, more eccentric and decidedly more unconventional.

Unlike the Confucians, philosophical Taoists trust in spontaneity—they do not fear that spontaneity will lead to social chaos and disorder. In contrast Confucianism represents the moralistic, the official, the stable and the respectable. For Confucianism, there is a correct way to say and do everything (*li*) and there is little flexibility allowed. People who are spontaneous might say or do anything and so are perceived as a threat to stability and order.

Confucius believed that if we do not follow the ancient rules of proper ceremonial interaction, society will break down into disorder. The Taoists do not reject politeness, but they do reject slavish obedience to *jen* and *li*; and they do not look to Chou Sage-Kings of the ancient past for the key to harmony. Confucians want to direct and control human behavior. The philosophical Taoists rejected this. The Taoists thought that the authoritarian system of Confucius is not discovered in nature, as Confucius claimed. Rather, Confucianism is simply the product of an individual human's viewpoint (Confucius, the Chou dynasty rulers), and Confucian social rituals are merely conventional and traditional. They were neither embedded in nature nor absolute.

To appreciate the insights of *Tao-chia/Daojia* philosophical Taoism, one needed to be able to read, to be able to appreciate poetry and poetic visions, yet to be someone who perceived Confucianism as too confining and rigid. Often philosophical Taoism appealed to those who thought of themselves as creative people, like artists, scholars poets, and musicians. They often tended to be an older segment of the population. However, not all Chinese who studied *Tao-chia* were counter-culture. Many Chinese read philosophical Taoism to gain insights in how to rule the nation using Taoist techniques of non-action.[4]

The most important names associated with philosophical Taoism are Lao-tzu (Laozi in Pinyin romanization) and Chuang-tzu (in Pinyin, Zhuangzi[5]) but the names of Lieh-tzu and Huai-nan-tzu also belong to the list of important Taoists. The 139 B.C.E. text entitled the *Huai-nan Tzu* is a compendium of Taoist ideas putting stress on Taoist cosmology, the physiological basis of human psychology and self-cultivation.[6] The Taoist *Lieh-tzu*[7] is much later than the other three.

In this chapter we will examine Lao-tzu and in the next chapter we will discuss Chuang-tzu. They are the two representatives of philosophical Taoism, as contained in their two great books, the *Tao Te Ching/Daodejing* and the *Chuang-tzu/Zhuangzi*. The two books share a common world view, but are quite different in many interesting ways. We will explore the basic ideas, the commonalities and the differences in this chapter and the next chapter.

---

[4] Note that neither Confucianism nor Taoism/Daoism tried to control scientific discoveries or tried to limit the teachings of science. They accepted Chinese creation myths as stories but did not try to defend them as facts. Traditional Chinese religion did not attempt to control medical technologies like birth control and contraception. For political reasons and to control unchecked population growth, contemporary China has attempted to limit the number of children allowed to a family to just one child, and more recently modified the policy to allow for two children per family under certain conditions.

[5] Chuang-tzu/Zhuangzi is intended to be pronounced something like Jwang-zu.

[6] Charles LeBlanc, *Hui Nan Tzu: Philosophical Synthesis in Early Han Thought* (Hong Kong: Hong Kong University Press, 1985).

[7] A. C. Graham, *The Book of Lieh-tzu* (London: John Murray, 1960), reprinted by the Columbia University Press in 1990.

16.3 CONTRASTING PHILOSOPHICAL TAOISM AND CONFUCIANISM

A convenient device for discussing philosophical Taoism/Daoism is to contrast it with official state-supported Confucianism. The two share a common world-view, agreeing about the flowing Tao, the interaction of *yin* and *yang*, and the need for achieving harmony. They agree in having little interest in the supernatural.

❧

The Taoist and Confucian tend to have rather different ways of thinking about the world. We have seen that Confucius and Confucianism concentrate on taking action following prescribed courses of social conduct, making things better by imposing satisfactory role models, using persuasion combined with the force and power of law, and Confucians focus on human ceremonial interactions and political interaction as essential for maintaining harmony within society and with the Tao/Dao.

❧

Philosophical Taoism/Daoism does not focus on making things happen, and is not particularly concerned with social ritual or social roles. Instead, the concentration in philosophical Taoism is upon the natural path, the pathway of letting things alone, not interfering, and stressing harmony with Nature (Tao). The assumption is that if we are in harmony with Nature, we will also be in harmony with our fellow human beings who belong to Nature and are a part of Nature. The Confucians asserted that their rules and rituals are absolute and grounded in nature. For the philosophical Taoist, Confucian morality and rituals are interesting aspects of human behavior, but they are grounded in conventional human interactions and do not reflect nature and they are not absolute.

❧

The Confucian side tends to look for definite right and wrong answers but the Taoist side allows for many answers in the nebulous area between right and wrong. Confucianism tends towards an either/or world of black or white; the Taoist abides in a realm of shades of grey. Unlike solid Confucian models, the Taoist models are more fluid, more like water, which cannot be so easily grasped. Confucian thinking tends to be logical, precise, exact, specific, and consistent, but the focus is narrow and tends to be rigid. These are typical *yang* characteristics. Taoist thinking tends to be metaphorical, approximate, diffuse, poetic, humorous, playful, and comfortable dealing with contradiction. These are more typical of *yin*.

❧

Confucian thinking tends to focus on differences, separations, and boundaries which clearly demarcate edges; Taoists are more comfortable with vagueness and ambiguity. Life for the Taoists is subjective shifting perspectives, but for the Confucian there are fixed objective values which apply to everyone. The Taoist is comfortable with the oblique and obscure; Confucians are more direct and literal.

❧

The Taoist takes the spontaneity of the child as a primary image, but the Confucian role models are dignified and serious Sage-Kings of the past who rule with virtue. The Taoist encourages childlike wonder, but the Confucian exhorts us to grow up and act more soberly.

❧

For the Taoist, the sage acts spontaneously yet is thoroughly un-self-centered, and because of this, the sage does not take credit for what is accomplished; the Confucian values formal ritual and ceremonial recognition. The Taoists say it is not the straight path that is most fulfilling, but the meandering byways, the bent and crooked way where we can flourish. Humans become refreshed by becoming more sensitive to nature, more appreciative of clouds and trees, rivers and mountains. This relaxed Taoist attitude is captured in this poem by Li Po/Li Bo (701–762):

You ask me why should I stay in this blue mountain.
I smile but do not answer. O, my mind is at ease!
Peach blossoms and flowing streams pass away without trace.

How different from the mundane world![8]

❖

The Taoist values the counter-culture aesthetic life, but the Confucian prefers the practical life, a political life with measurable goals and social recognition. The Taoist sees the world through the eyes of poetic appreciation, whereas the Confucian sees the world with an eye to improve it by returning it to the glorious past.[9]

16.4 THE LITERATURE OF PHILOSOPHICAL TAOISM

The earliest texts of philosophical Taoism appeared about the same era as the *Analects* of Confucius, perhaps 400 B.C.E.[10] The two classic Taoist texts are the *Tao Te Ching (Daodejing)* and the *Chuang-tzu (Zhuangzi)* which are thought to date between the fifth century B.C.E. and the third century B.C.E.[11] The *Tao Te Ching* stressed the art of living one's life by living in accord with natural rhythms and ruling the empire by exerting the least effort. On the other hand the *Chuang-tzu* gives no advice on how to rule, but instead treats the business of running the country as a burden to be avoided.

Historically, in the earliest fourth and third centuries B.C.E. there never was a Taoist School in the same way there was an organized school of Confucianism and Legalism. The model for Confucianism was a lineage of teachers and students, running from one generation to the next like a string of pearls. In the early centuries, the philosophical Taoists did not have such schools. Instead there were separate and independent texts and teachers like Lao-tzu and Chuang-tzu who were exploring ways of achieving harmony with nature.

It was about 200 C.E. when philosophical Taoism became especially popular among some of the well-educated literati class. The distinctive attitude of appreciation of spontaneity common to the *Tao Te Ching* and *Chuang-tzu* attracted the attention of those who were becoming disillusioned with Han dynasty (202 B.C.E.–220 C.E.) politics and unhappy with the inflexibility of Confucianism. There was a movement away from rigid Confucian virtues towards a celebration of the individual, the liberated sage who is free in his choices and unconventional in his behavior. This became known as "Dark Learning" Taoism, the Taoism focused on the unfathomable mystery of existence. The appeal of this form of Taoism tended to be toward the well-educated, the literati, the painters, poets and philosophers.

"Dark Learning" Taoism[12]

A continuation of philosophical Taoism, called "Neo-Taoism" or "Dark Learning," or "Learning of the Mysterious [Tao]," enjoyed political and philosophical vogue among the disillusioned cultured elite of the third and fourth centuries during the Common Era. This would be an alternative to, or a corrective to, the Confucian

---

[8] Chang Chung-yuan, *Creativity and Taoism: A Study of Chinese Philosophy, Art, and Poetry* (New York: Julian Press, 1963, reprinted Harper Colophon Books, 1970; and again by Jessica Kingsley, Publishers, Philadelphia PA: 2011), p. 90. Li Po/Libo is also known as Li Pai/Libai, who along with Tu Fu/Dufu (712–770) are regarded as the two greatest poets in Chinese history.

[9] A part of this structure was inspired by the list in Angus C. Graham, *Disputers of the Tao* (LaSalle, IL: Open Court, 1989), p. 223.

[10] Several ancient texts contain very brief quotations which may have come from classic Taoist texts, although these quotes may have been incorporated into the classic Taoist texts at a later period.

[11] The text certainly existed in some form in the early fourth century B.C.E. Archaeologists discovered lengthy sections of the *Tao Te Ching* in a tomb which dates back to about 300 B.C.E. There is an excellent translation and study of several ancient versions from about 200 B.C.E. done by Robert G. Henricks, *Lao-tzu Te-Tao Ching: A New Translation Based on the Recently Discovered Ma-wang-tui Texts* (New York: Ballantine Books, 1989). For more recent discoveries, consult Wang Zhongjian, *Daoism Excavated: Cosmos and Humanity in Early Manuscripts* (St. Petersburg, FL: Three Pines Press, 2015). This is a volume from the Peking University Center for Taoist Studies.

[12] In Chinese the term "dark" suggests profound, mysterious, and so dark and deep that we cannot get to the bottom.

enterprise.[13] Thus the literature of Taoism includes the two most important Dark Learning commentaries,[14] which are Wang Pi's/Wangbi's (226–249 C.E.) commentary on the *Lao-tzu*, and Kuo-hsiang's/Guoshang's (d. 312 C.E.) commentary on the *Chuang-tzu*.[15] Many well-educated Chinese studied and memorized the *Tao Te Ching* and the *Chuang-tzu*, and studied the numerous commentaries.

Dark Learning, or Mysterious Learning, tended towards a poetic celebration of the individual, a celebration of personal freedom. Many of the Dark Learning thinkers were concerned with politics, and especially with governing by spontaneity and non-purposive action. For these, Dark Learning was practical and not mere metaphysical speculation.[16] They were concerned with morals, with laws, and proper social behavior, mostly within a Taoist framework. Some of these folk were reclusive and concerned with artistic integrity.

The abstract and poetic ideas of Dark Learning were restricted to members of the scholar-official class which included the creative painters, poets, musicians and philosophers. The behavior of many of the Dark Learning followers was refined yet playful, and even inebriated. Dark Learning Taoists engaged one another in abstract discussions about existence and non-existence. Some very fine poetry and black-ink paintings were created which used Taoist-inspired metaphors tightly connected to mountains, rivers, clouds, and Taoist mystics and immortals hidden in those cloud-covered mountains.

Philosophical Taoism After the Fifth Century

Finally, although the direct influence of philosophical Taoism declined after the fifth century of the Common Era, the teachings and attitudes continued to exert a profound influence on Chinese civilization and Chinese art forms. Even though there may not have been a philosophical teaching school or direct lineage of Taoist philosophers (the way there was for the Confucians), the Taoist texts are classics of great literature, and as such were read and studied by following generations of literati. Taoist celebration of the unusual and the free exerted influence on generations of artists and poets. The ideas also persisted because much of the attitudes and sayings of philosophical Taoism were appreciated by and incorporated into later forms of Chinese Buddhism, especially the Ch'an/Chan (Zen) sect. Some scholars have suggested that it is likely that the later ninth and tenth century Chinese Ch'an Buddhist paradoxical dialogues (*wen-ta* or *wenda*) may have been inspired by "Dark Learning" poetic exchanges.

16.5 LAO-TZU/LAOZI: THE OFFICIAL FOUNDER OF TAOISM

老
Lao

Although Lao-tzu (Laozi in Pinyin romanization) is called the founder of Taoism and treated as the author of the classic Taoist text, the *Tao Te Ching* (*Daodejing* in Pinyin), there are questions about these claims. The Chinese character "Lao" means "old" or "ancient," and in this use "tzu" is an honorific meaning "honored teacher." Thus "Lao-tzu" is ambiguous. Lao-tzu literally means "Old Philosopher," "Old Philosophers," or "Old Teacher," or even "Philosophers of Olden Times." Thus "Lao-tzu" might be some person's actual name, or a title or even a reference to teachers in the past, i.e., "teachers from the olden days."

---

[13] "Dark Learning" Taoism, and the Seven Sages of the Bamboo Grove, are also discussed in the next chapter, section 17.10, which deals with the book entitled the *Chuang-tzu* and with later developments in philosophical Taoism and political Taoism.

[14] The first several chapters of this book deals with much of this: Alan K. L. Chan, Yuet-Keung Lo, eds. *Philosophy and Religion in Early Medieval China* (Albany: State University of New York Press, 2010).

[15] Ariane Rump and Wing-tsit Chan, *Commentary on the **Lao-tzu** by Wang Pi* (Honolulu: University Press of Hawaii, 1979): Monographs of the Society for Asian and Comparative Philosophy, no. 6. See also Paul J. Lin, *A Translation of Lao-tzu's **Tao Te Ching** and Wang Pi's Commentary* (Ann Arbor: University of Michigan Papers in Chinese Studies, 1977).

[16] More details are in Alan K. L. Chan, Yuet-Keung Lo, eds., *Philosophy and Religion in Early Medieval China*.

In other words, a book entitled "Lao-tzu" could just as well be a collection of traditional teachings, sayings, and proverbs quoted from various teachers in antiquity. The book known as the *Tao Te Ching* is also know simply as the *Lao-tzu.*

So, was the *Tao Te Ching* the work of one special philosopher named Lao-tzu, or was the *Tao Te Ching* an anthology of ancient teachings and ancient wisdom from several old sages of the past, none of whose names are known presently? If so, the title might be translated correctly as the "Classic of the Old Ones." If the *Lao-tzu* was the work of one person, it is clear that later editors revised and added to the original text. In its present form most of the *Tao Te Ching* may be by one person who is collecting and quoting some ancient sayings and proverbs, but it is clear that it is a book of personal realization and at the same time it is a book of political thought designed to exert a practical influence on social and political theory, especially opposed to Confucian ideas.

Whether or not the book was the work of one person, or an anthology, and whether or not it was composed in the fifth century or third century B.C.E., it is clear that the *Tao Te Ching* is a short book of poetically expressed philosophical insights traditionally ascribed to a person known as Lao-tzu/Laozi.

The biography of Lao-tzu

Although there are some biographical records supplying dates and events in the life of Confucius (551–479 B.C.E.), there are no real biographical records for Lao-tzu. In the first century B.C.E. the great Chinese historian Ssu-ma Ch'ien/Sima Qian (145–79? B.C.E.) searched the imperial library in an attempt to find a biography of the famous author Lao-tzu. In China, almost everyone of any importance had a biographical record. But to the royal historian's astonishment, no biography of Lao-tzu could be found anywhere in any library. After much careful research, biographies were found for several separate individuals, including one person named Li Erh and another biography for someone named Lao Tan/Laodan. Neither biography has any mention of Taoism or the *Tao Te Ching.* Nevertheless, the historian provided these life stories to produce the biography of Lao-tzu as requested by the emperor.

This biography states that Lao-tzu was a royal archivist in the Chou state in the fourth century B.C.E. Although the Lao Tan/Laodan biography made no mention of him authoring any books, Ssu-ma Ch'ien reasoned that Laodan *might* be the same person as Lao-tzu, and so Lao Tan's biography was identified with the author of the *Tao Te Ching.*[17] The combined biography states that Lao-tzu's family name was Li, his personal name was Erh, his public name was Tan/Dan, he was born in the southern kingdom of Ch'u and was an archivist/librarian in the royal library.

According to a legend summarized by the royal historian, at one time Confucius himself consulted Lao-tzu on matters of sages of the past, and ancient propriety and ritual and Lao-tzu replied:

"Those whom you talk about are dead and their bones have decayed. Only their words have remained … Get rid of the arrogance of yours, all those desires, that self-sufficient air, that overweening zeal; all of that is of no use to your true person. That is all I can say to you."

Confucius came away from this encounter in shock, saying: "Creatures that run can be trapped in nets. Those that can swim can be caught in wicker traps. Those that fly can be hit with arrows. But the dragon is beyond my knowledge; it ascends into heaven on the clouds and the wind. Today I have met Lao-tzu and he is like the dragon."[18]

---

[17] The biography is found in the Classic of History (*Shih Chi*), and is discussed by Angus C. Graham in "The Origins of the Legend of Lao Tan" in Arthur Wright, ed., *Studies in Chinese Philosophy and Philosophical Literature* (Albany: State University of New York, 1990). Wang Zhongjian indicates that there is an association with the name Laodan and the Taoist tradition in brief snippets of the *Tao Te Ching* which may extend back to perhaps 500 B.C.E. See Wang, *Taoism Excavated, op. cit.,* p. 3.

[18] The Chinese text for the author's translations of the *Tao Te Ching* is that of Han-shan Te-ching/Hanshan dejing (1546–1620), *Lao-tzu Tao te ching Han-shan chieh* ("Han-shan's Explanation of the *Tao Te Ching*) (Taipei, Taiwan: Shin Wen Hua Yin Shu Kuan, 1973), p. 39. A useful Japanese translation was Fukunaga, Mitsuji, *Rōshi* ("Lao-tzu"), (Tokyo: Asahi Shinbunsha, 1968). Many of the Chinese translations in this book were done during the course of numerous graduate seminars under the tutelage of Professor Chang Chung-yuan, to whom the author is deeply grateful.

If Confucius did go to Lao-tzu for advice, in a hierarchical Chinese civilization which associates wisdom with the elderly, Confucius could never ask advice of someone younger than himself. Such an encounter would be possible only if Lao-tzu were older than Confucius, and since Confucius was born in 552/551 B.C.E, it seemed appropriate to assign a date of around 571 B.C.E. to Lao-tzu.

In the absence of any reliable historical records, we will rely on legends. Legends say the old philosopher Lao-tzu was famous as one of the wisest men in all of China. At an advanced age he retired from his position in the royal library and rode on the back of an ox to the mountain pass, where the gatekeeper asked him to write down his wisdom.
    As he reached the pass, the pass-keeper Yin-hsi said, "You are about to retire. Please try your best to write a book for me." Thereupon Lao-tzu wrote a book in two parts, expounding the ideas of the Tao/Dao and *Te/De* in over five thousand characters and then departed. No one knew how he died."[19]

Thus, the story is that Lao-tzu composed the *Tao Te Ching*, left it with the gatekeeper, and rode his ox off into the west.[20] Although it is by no means settled, in the pages that follow, we'll refer to Lao-tzu as the author of the *Tao Te Ching*.

16.6 *THE TAO TE CHING*

The influence of the *Tao Te Ching/Daodejing* upon China has been enduring, and in modern times the book has demonstrated a great appeal to many in the West. It is claimed that this book has been translated into other languages more frequently than any other book except for the Christian Bible.[21] There are 81[22] poems or chapters, none longer than one page.
    The title, *Tao Te Ching*, can be translated as the Classic (*ching/jing*) which deals with the Path (Tao) or the Way (Tao) and its Virtue, Attainment, Potency or Power (*Te/De*). There is no philosopher or thinker named in the book, not even Lao-tzu himself. Traditionally, the *Tao Te Ching* is in two parts: the first part (chapters 1-37) is the Tao section; the second part is the classic of *Te/De* (chapters 38-81).
    The *Tao Te Ching* does not present a coherent philosophical doctrine, neither does it present a logical analysis of Tao, *yin*, and *yang* and our place in nature. It does not present any orderly system of explanation. It does not define key terms.

The primary audience for the *Tao Te Ching* was well-educated people with political and military power, but the text does not provide explicit directions on how the country should be governed. Instead the text shares the vision of those things which embody the Tao, which follow the natural course of the Tao. One intuited insight is followed by another, without arguments connecting the assertions.
    The parallel passages are condensed and aphoristic, and not argumentative. The stress is not on logic and rationality, but rather on intuition and insight. The text uses sayings, proverbs, metaphors and analogies. Meanings

---

[19] Han-shan Te-ching/Hanshan Dejing, *ibid.*("Han-shan's Explanation of the *Tao Te Ching*), pp. 39-40.

[20] In popular Chinese religion, to "go west" was to die; a popular legend was that there was a magical paradise in the west filled with wonders of the afterlife. As we shall see, after Buddhism came to China, some Taoists/Daoists believed that Lao-tzu went west to India to convert Indian "barbarians" to the wisdom of Taoism. These Taoists claim that his teachings to Indian barbarians became known as "Buddhism."

[21] The earliest translation of the text was into Latin in 1788.

[22] The earliest versions of the text did not have numbered chapters. In Chinese numerology, the number 81 has special significance as both 9x9 and 3x3x3x3, and it is very likely that later editors imposed the 81-chapter structure on the text.

are hinted at, and not made explicit. The passages are so brief as to be enigmatic, and many different meanings can be read into the short verses.[23] The *Tao Te Ching* certainly does include ancient sayings and proverbs, but it is more than that.

The form is poetic and intuitive, probably as an aid to memorization and recitation. The author of the *Tao Te Ching* suggests that "The wise sages of the past behaved this way [and by implication you should too]," or "The Tao is this way, and the sage conducts himself in harmony with this way." The book stresses the patterns and rhythms of nature, and sets these up as models for human beings. The book encourages us to understand simple things deeply.

The Chinese text doesn't make reference to historical events, or provide a context for the sayings and verses. As such, each reader has to supply the background, and in this manner the *Tao Te Ching* is more like a canvas upon which the translator cannot help but project her or his own interpretation and understanding. The obscure wisdom of the text must be augmented by the wisdom of the reader (and translator).

The *Tao Te Ching* certainly goes against our ordinary assumptions about the world and politics. The book encourages us to prefer what seems to be the lesser good. We should prefer weakness over strength, prefer the crooked and bent over the straight, prefer the soft over the hard, the cool over the hot, the passive over the active, the feminine *yin* over the masculine *yang*.

However, these preferences are not a strategy of accepting defeat with grace. Instead, the book teaches that weakness itself is a kind of strength, that to yield is a strategy for success, the soft overcomes the hard, passivity is better at achieving goals than aggression, and other such guides. The *Tao Te Ching* teaches how to win by losing, how to conquer by yielding.

Criticisms of Confucianism

There are many passages which are critical of ideas associated with Confucianism, and this suggests that at least parts of the book were composed after the time of Confucius, perhaps sometime between 400 and 250 B.C.E. The Confucians preach reverent imitation of the ancient kings and Sage-rulers to cultivate respectability and virtue (*te/de*) and tell us to pay scrupulous attention to ritual. Ceremonially regulated social interaction (*li*) is the key to sacred harmony and political peace.

The *Tao Te Ching* advocates spontaneity instead of formality. It advises us to be natural and live our lives in harmony with the grand patterns of Tao/Dao. We humans are a part of the patterns of Nature, we belong to Nature (Tao), so a truly human existence involves living as naturally as the rest of Nature's creations live.

In Confucianism, artificial human-centered rituals and ceremonies (*li*) rule one's life—rules and regulations, decisions about what is appropriate in this situation, and what is appropriate behavior towards that person who stands in a certain social relationship with me. Knowing one's place in the social hierarchy is essential. The Confucian formulates rigid codes and tries to impose them upon all humans. Not so for the Taoist.

Taoists do not think that we need a list of duties and responsibilities (*li*). If anything, this overwhelms and destroys our spontaneous and natural human feelings. The sort of human ritualized society advocated by the Confucians leads us away from natural patterns and rhythms until we are unable to resonate in harmony with Nature any longer.

It is precisely making these kinds of divisions, separations, and decisions which gets us out of touch with the flowing processes of nature. The best life is a simple life, where one gradually gives up being judgmental, gives up trying to be too clever, too calculating in one's response to the world. Instead, become attuned to the natural processes of

---

[23] It is very likely that for the original authors and their intended audience, the text was not as obscure or enigmatic. Much of the impenetrability of the text may be due to time and the fact that we do not speak the same language or live in the same time period. If the student would like to attempt her own translation of the text, there is an interesting book on the *Tao Te Ching* which provides all Chinese characters and their meanings in English for each verse. See Jonathan Star, *Tao Te Ching: The Definitive Edition* (New York: Jeremy Tarcher and Penguin, 2001).

birth, fertility, growth, decay, and death—respond to the cosmic rhythm. It is only after we have lost our harmony with the Tao that people begin to discuss Confucian virtues. Chapter 18 of the *Tao Te Ching* explains:

道、
可
道、
非
常
道。
名、
可
名
非
常
名。
無
名
天
地
之
始。
有
名
萬
物
之
母。

> The Great Tao rejected,
> [only then] we have [Confucian] doctrines of
> benevolence (*jen*) and righteousness (*i*).
> Wisdom and knowledge are discarded,
> [then] we have great hypocrites.
> When the six basic human relationships are not in harmony,
> [only then] we have [people who advocate] filial piety and family love.
> When the country is disordered,
> [only then do] we have loyal patriots/ministers.[24]

For Lao-tzu, Confucian virtues arise when things are in disorder but even when we follow these artificial virtues the world does not get better. Behaviors which are ceremonial are human-centered, self-righteous, self-centered approaches which contribute to the problems. Such behavior will not put us in harmony with Tao. The *Tao Te Ching* urges us to look at the model provided by Nature itself (Tao). Lessen the ego and respond to the natural processes of birth, growth, decay, and death.

Key Concept: The Tao

The very first Chinese character of the *Tao Te Ching* text is **Tao**. The standard rendering of Tao into English is "the Way," "path," or a "pathway," and even "a method" when it is used with the martial arts (i.e. Judo, the gentle way). The art of Chinese calligraphy is the "Way of the brush."

The term Tao/Dao can be rendered more abstractly as a chaotic oneness, an abstract principle, as the pattern of all patterns (of nature), but it also includes the sense of the root, the mother, the matrix or source out of which reality arises. Tao gives birth. Thus Tao is the natural path, the pathway that Nature itself takes. This also includes natural paths of human social behavior.

The goal of most Chinese thinkers is harmony. The Confucians think that humans achieve harmony with Tao by practicing ceremonial rituals and studying history. To the Confucians, Tao was relatively clear and knowable, approached best by learning patterns in social and ritual behavior. Scholarship and learning were an indispensable means of knowing the Tao.

The philosophical Taoist/Daoist disagrees. The *Tao Te Ching* says that the ever-shifting pattern of the Way cannot be formulated in any scholarly definitions or statements. Tao is the infinite indefinable possibility underlying everything. The very first chapter of the *Tao Te Ching* begins with the Chinese character **Tao**:

> The Tao that can be called Tao is not the Tao itself.
> The name which can be named is not the name itself.
> The nameless is the source of Heaven and Earth.
> The named is the mother of all the ten thousand things.[25]

According to the *Tao Te Ching*, "Tao" is the name we give to the unitary source, the ground, the ultimate, the

---

[24] Han-shan Te-ching, *op. cit.* chapter 18, page 72.

[25] *Ibid.*, page 51.

totality, the patterns,[26] but that source itself cannot be captured by words or concepts. Tao is the infinite undefined possibility, it is all the potentiality of all the flowing energies of the world. Tao is prior to all verbal formulations, prior to all categories of thought, prior to differentiation; thus it cannot be defined, categorized, differentiated, summarized, described, or encapsulated in any book or list. This ultimate pattern of reality, this principle of unity, is so complex, so deep, so hidden and mysterious that no one could ever understand it completely.

However, the goal of the Taoist is NOT to try to understand Tao. It is not to describe Tao. It is to be in spontaneous harmony with Tao. To be one with Tao is to reconcile with life, to achieve unity with the source of all.

As the single source, origin, and mother of the original duality of Heaven and Earth, (or *yang* and *yin*), the Tao itself is the source of all concepts, and thus it is deeper than concepts or labels can penetrate. Hence the Tao is nameless. You or I can utter the sound "Tao/Dao" and we can write the word down on paper, but that does not mean either of us is able to grasp and comprehend that which is the source and origin of all dualities. Once we begin the process of naming, we discriminate and distinguish, and out of this process arises all that exists, which the Chinese poetically refer to as the ten thousand things. Tao is the state of one-ness prior to all separation, underlying all duality (even prior to god, says Lao-tzu).

> Tao is empty,
> Use it, it is never filled to overflowing.
> So deep! Bottomless, the source of all things.
>
> . . .
> Deeply existing –
> I do not know whose child it is.
> It existed even before God.[27]

Tao is the Source

Tao is the nameless source of all things, that which underlies and is the source of the fundamental dualities of thought, both Existence and Non-existence, Heaven and Earth, *yang* and *yin*. Tao is the One, the mother, and is natural, spontaneous, nameless, and indescribable (for it is the ultimate pattern behind all thought, and thus thinking cannot get back to its pre-conceptual source). The Tao is creative, the creative impulse which is Nature and which flows through all Nature, which we tap into, whether we consider ourselves creative artists or not.[28]

The Tao cannot be defined in words, but we cannot help but be aware that things around us are connected, and inter-connected. Although we can recognize that the universe is one vast interdependent system, it does not follow that humans can comprehend all the interconnections. We can feel it, but not conceptualize it. We can respond intuitively, but it will not fit into any of our categories, and we cannot explain it.

> There was some thing, undifferentiated yet complete,
> Which existed before Heaven and Earth.
> Silent! Solitary! Empty!
> Dependent upon nothing, unchanging.

---

[26] Think of the pattern of water in a creek as it flows by, or the pattern smoke makes as it rises into the evening sky. No words can describe these simple and completely natural patterns.

[27] Han-shan Te-ching, *op. cit.*, ch. 4, p. 56.

[28] Later Buddhists thought that if the Tao/Dao was the source of all "under heaven," the source of life and death, then it was also the source of sagehood and ignorance, the source of fortune and misfortune and disaster. The Tao was not only the source of good things, but must also be the source of all the bad things.

It acts everywhere yet it is never exhausted.
It might be regarded as the mother of all under heaven.
I do not know its name, but merely call it "Tao."[29]

The true name for the ultimate root-source we have been discussing is not really "Tao." The Chinese character pronounced "Tao/Dao" is merely black marks on paper, a symbol. "Tao" is a **sound** that human beings make, a noise which is intended to draw our attention to whatever pattern underlies what we call reality, to the ultimate, the totality, that which is prior to all categories, prior to differentiation, that out of which all opposites arise, that which is so deep that it cannot be categorized, differentiated, summarized, or described.

From this it follows that it would be incorrect to describe Tao as "good," or as "evil." Tao is deeper than both, it is the source of opposites, it is what good and evil share in common, it is what existence and non-existence share in common. The philosophical Taoists, and Chinese thinkers in general, never saw this world as a battlefield between warring forces of good and evil (this perspective is typical of Persian religions and those later Middle Eastern religions influenced by Persian religions). Good, or health, is when the pattern of Tao is balanced; evil, or illness, is an imbalance of *yin* and *yang*. For the philosophical Taoists, evil is when ego-centered human beings have interfered with natural patterns and thrown things out of balance.[30]

For the Chinese of long ago, Nature (Tao) is not different from human beings and is not apart from human beings. The universe is more like us than we realize; we are a part of the grand symphony which is reality— we are not the audience at a concert, but rather we are the musicians, the players. Nature is our home and we belong here.

Chuang-tzu makes the point in chapter 22:
Tung Kuo Tzu asked Chuang Tzu: "Where is this which you call Tao?"
"Everywhere," Chuang Tzu replied.
"Where specifically?" insisted Tung Kuo Tzu.
"It is in the ant," Chuang-tzu answered.
"How can it be so low?"
"It is in the earthenware tiles."
"Still worse."
"It is in excrement."
To this Tung Kuo Tzu did not answer.[31]

We humans are not observers of Nature; **we are Nature**. Just like every plant and every animal, we humans are born, grow strong, grow old, and then pass on. We are Nature. To achieve fulfillment as a human being, one must be in tune with, in accord with Nature, which is the flow from *yin* to *yang* and back again.[32] You cannot know Tao intellectually in specific things, but you can experience it. Chapter 32 of the *Tao Te Ching* says:

---

[29] Han-shan Te-ching, *op. cit.*, chapter 25, p. 81. Compare Robert G. Henricks: *Lao-tzu: Te-Tao Ching* (New York: Ballantine Books, 1989), ch. 25, p. 77.

[30] However, it is true that the religious Taoists tended to identify the masculine *yang* with good and the feminine *yin* with the negative things of life.

[31] Chang Chung-yuan, *Creativity and Taoism: A Study of Chinese Philosophy, Art, and Poetry*, p. 34. This essential book on Taoism has been reprinted: Chang Chung-yuan, *Creativity and Taoism* (Philadelphia: Jessica Kingsley Publishers, 2011).

[32] As noted in a previous chapter, modern China is Marxist and closer to the common Western view of humans battling to control nature. See Judith Shapiro, *Mao's War Against Nature: Politics and the Environment in Revolutionary China* (Cambridge University Press, 2001).

> Tao: constant, nameless.
> Although simple and slight,
> No one and no thing under heaven can dominate it.[33]

Chapter 56 of the *Tao Te Ching* states:

> The one who knows does not speak
> The one who speaks does not know.[34]

It may be true that "The one who knows does not speak," but this is not because Tao is some sort of special knowledge which must be kept secret from outsiders. Rather, whatever words you utter are merely drawing attention to that which lies behind and beyond words. The words are not the reality; whatever Tao is, no words can capture or describe it adequately. Symbolically, your words are pointing at the original constant Tao which is the source of all, and when people confuse words with reality, whatever words are uttered will be profoundly inadequate, misleading, and wrong. Knowing that, the Taoist sage smiles broadly and remains silent. The Taoist sage knows that whatever he or she says, it cannot help but be misleading and incorrect. So, the sage does not speak.

Tao is Not A Divinity or God

As the reader will have noticed, for philosophical Taoism (*Tao-chia, Daojia*), Tao is not male, is not a father, is not a divinity, is not any sort of god. Tao does not issue commands, does not engender miracles to influence human history, and does not relate to individual people. All that exists is part of an ever-changing self-generating spiritual process but that process is not the result of a creative purposive God. In the West, the divinity is a monarch, a ruler, a commander, a military warlord, the architect, and the building contractor who makes the universe by intelligent planning, a creator external to nature who, out of non-existence, creates the very building blocks of reality, and a symbolic father. This divinity of Western religions demands adoration, rewards faith, and punishes pride and sin. This divinity demands submission, requires faith, and adoration. None of these images applies to Tao.

As noted in chapter 13, Tao/Dao is free from action, thought, feeling and desire. Tao does not respond to devotion or rituals, does not answer prayers, or have favorites. Tao has no goals or purposes. There is no special relationship between Tao and humanity, as there is between humans and the divinity in the West. In fact, according to the Taoist/Daoist philosopher Chuang-tzu/Zhuangzi, a lump of manure is as close to Tao as human beings are. The Tao does not create things out of nothing. In fact, the Chinese never had a creator divinity and firmly rejected the hypothesis that things could ever come from nothing.

The religious form of Taoism/Daoism (*Tao-chiao, Daojiao*) is quite different. There are gods who respond to devotion, rituals, and who answer prayers if sufficient sacrifices are performed. This is discussed in chapter 19.

Tao is Maternal, not Paternal

For the Taoist and Chinese thinkers in general, Tao is thought of as a matrix of creativity, a mother who gives birth. Tao is not a father who creates out of nothingness using incomprehensible powers. Tao is not a personal being who loves human beings best of all. Tao does not create human beings to be special. No one is saved by belief in Tao. Tao cannot answer prayers. Tao is devoid of action, thought, feeling and desire; it is non-purposive. Tao cannot be obeyed or disobeyed—Tao is simply the pattern of all of nature when it behaves spontaneously. Technically, you cannot disobey Tao (you cannot disobey the law of gravity either). The action of Tao is spring followed by summer, leaves

---

[33] Han-shan Te-ching, *op. cit.*, ch. 32, p. 91.

[34] *Ibid.*, chapter 56, p. 118.

falling from trees in the fall, and water flowing downhill. Tao is the skin wrinkling with age. Tao is just a name for what happens naturally. Tao gives birth to all things. Tao is the great mother out of which all things spring, grow, and develop, and Tao is the great receptacle back into which we all return at death. In chapter 52 we find the opening line:

> All things under heaven had a beginning,
> the mother of all the world.[35]

Tao is the maternal pattern which is the harmony of Nature, wherein all opposites exist in unity.

Key Concept: Yin-Yang

As we discussed in previous chapters, the principle of bipolarity lies at the very roots of the Chinese world-view, and the two poles are called *yin* and *yang*. This pair provides a causal explanation for the world. Why do things change in the regular patterns which are so immediately observable to anyone living in touch with natural rhythms? Look around: the universe cycles between poles of *yin* (covered by clouds; dark, hidden, secret, cool) and *yang* (bright and shinny; light, open, warm).

Summertime is bright, warm, and the period of active growth of plants–it is *yang*. Winter is dark and cold, and the time of dormant plants–it is *yin*. *Yin* might be ascendent for a while, but then it will go into decline and be replaced by *yang*. Nothing is completely *yin* or completely *yang*, all things are a flowing swinging movement between the two poles. Reversal is inevitable.

The Chinese world-view assumed that there would always be resonances as things swung back and forth. The world can be explained using these two principles of *yin* and *yang*. We know earth and heaven, cold and hot, dark and light, stillness and motion, receptive and aggressive, passive and active. We know north and south, east and west. The Chinese then explored the world using these fundamental categories, and found resonances with tastes and smells, colors, vibrating musical notes, calender symbols, numbers, planets, and even bodily organs.

Chinese poetry and art utilize many symbols for these two poles. The color red, stallions, dragons, the rooster, horned beasts, jade, mountains, summer, and south are primarily *yang*. The color black, water, valleys, winter, north, the vase, a peach, peony, fish and chrysanthemum are images where *yin* predominates. Vertical lines and shapes are *yang*; horizontal lines and shapes are *yin*. A solid line is *yang*; a broken line is *yin*. Hills are *yang*, and valleys are *yin*. A dragon in swirling clouds symbolizes the harmony of *yang* and *yin*. Heaven is *yang*, earth is *yin*, and humans (and especially the emperor) are the mediating harmony between Heaven and earth. Smoke and clouds are *yin*. A favorite theme in Chinese landscapes is the mountain peaks lost among the clouds, symbolizing the dynamic harmony of *yang* and *yin*. A circle is a *yang* symbol, and a square is a *yin* symbol. Chinese coins and mirrors often utilize the square within a circle motif.

In the roots of Western civilization, the Greek thinkers thought that the world was made of four basic elements (earth, air, fire, water) which were at war with one another. In the Judeo-Christian model, the dual poles are seen as principles of opposition. Light is at war with darkness. Pleasure is opposed to pain; wealth is opposed to poverty. Spirituality is opposed to physicality. Sacred is at war with secular. Positive is to be cultivated, and negative is to be destroyed. Cultivate the former, be rid of the later.

The philosophical Taoists (and the Confucians) would have trouble making sense of these Western oppositions. The image of nature as strife was not the model the Chinese used. The Chinese never saw the world as a battleground between humans and nature. We are not at war with Nature and we could never conquer Nature. It is not a matter of just trusting Nature; ultimately it is realizing that oneself and Nature are one and the same process, the process which we call Tao. The Tao is the unity of opposites, the Way wherein all opposites are harmonized and reconciled. The inner experience of this is opening the door to a life lived fully in the here and now. It is the key to

---

[35] *Ibid.*, ch. 52, p. 112

creative artistic expression as well.[36]

Yin and *yang* are not at war with each other, but are interdependent aspects of one and the same flowing system of Tao. Daylight, the sun in the sky (*yang*), is not at war with night time or the moon (*yin*). Sweet is not at war with sour. The physical is not at war with the spiritual. They alternate and define one another. This bipolarity can be applied to humans with male as predominantly *yang* (open, active, aggressive, logical, hard) and the feminine as predominantly *yin* (hidden, passive, yielding, intuitive, soft).

Each is essential, each necessary; they are mutually interdependent. The two alternate and act together in complete harmony, not strife. *Yin* and *yang* are poles of cosmic energy: *yang* (positive) and *yin* (negative). This is a bipolar duality which implies a hidden underlying unity, that unity out of which both *yin* and *yang* arise. Tao is the source and is that which *yin* and *yang* have in common.

Chapter 28:

> The one who knows the male, yet maintains the female,
> Becomes the channel of the world.
> Becoming the channel of the world,
> one will not be separated from *te* (the virtue of Tao)
> and returns to the state of a young child.
> Knowing the white, yet maintaining the black,
> Become the pattern of the world.
> Become the pattern of the world,
> And the constant *te* (virtue of the Tao) will not falter.
> Returning to the state without limit.
> Know glory, sustain humility.
> Become the valley of the world,
> Becoming the valley of the world,
> and *te* will prevail.
> Return to the simplicity of the uncarved block.[37]

The entire universe is a moving system alternating, reversing. Chapter 40 makes this clear:

> Reversal is the activity of Tao.
> Yielding is the practice of Tao.
> All things originate from being.
> Being originates from non-being.[38]

This alternation of *yin* and *yang* is also a strategy for success. This strategy is often expressed in paradox: to be weak is a kind of strength; to seek power is to lose it; to strive to go to the front is to find oneself at the back.

16.7 PRIMARY MODELS OF THE TAO TO EMULATE

---

[36] As mentioned previously, a masterful exploration of this aspect of the Tao is Chang Chung-yuan, *Creativity and Taoism: A Study of Chinese Philosophy, Art, and Poetry.*

[37] Han-shan Te-ching, *op. cit.*, ch. 28, p. 86.

[38] Han-shan Te-ching, *op. cit.*, ch. 40, p. 101. Here "non-being" is the deeper indescribable source of the pair of ordinary "existence" and "non-existence."

The importance of role models is crucial to understanding the Chinese civilization. Every Confucian is taught to think in terms of superior and subordinate, and believes that we should model our behavior on the proper superior role models. The philosophical Taoists also thought in terms of role models. The difference is that the role models for the Confucians are not the role models for Taoists.

For the Taoists we should not model our behavior on artificial human activities, such as rituals and ceremonies. We need models that are deeper, more primordial, more natural. The cultured civilized practices of Confucian *li* (ceremonial rituals) make it impossible for us to be natural, to be ourselves. The innocence of a young child is symbolic of human nature before we were trained to slavishly follow Confucian ceremonial rules which makes genuine spontaneity impossible. We can emulate natural processes like flowing water, bending bamboo, swirling clouds, and take these sorts of things for our role models.

WATER

For the Taoist, water is a role model which we ought to emulate because water takes the shape of its container, because it is essentially indeterminate and formless. Water flows and shifts directions in a spontaneous reaction to the changing conditions of the landscape. Do not think of water as a still lake or puddle. Water flows continually and is made up of ever-changing ripples and currents. To emulate water is to be fluid, to be flexible, to adapt to new situations effortlessly, quickly, as water adapts to the shape of its container.

Water is apparently the weakest and humblest of all things, always seeking the lowest position. It should be obvious that water is a powerful *yin* image. Water is soft and weak, yet the power of water comes precisely from this fact; it wears away mountains, carves mile-deep canyons.

In the same way that water seeks the lowest spot, human beings too should be humble, not pushing themselves forward; that is a genuine source of strength. Do not disdain the low places in life, and do not seek for recognition and honors. This is explained in many different chapters. Consider chapter 8:

> The highest good is to be like water.
> The good of water is that it is beneficial to all things,
> yet it does not contend with any of them.
> It occupies the lowest places which men dislike,
> but this is what it makes it close to the Tao.[39]

> This same idea is clarified in chapter 78:
> Nothing in the world is weaker and more yielding than water.
> But when attacking the hard and strong
> Nothing can conquer so easily.
> Weak overcomes strong.
> Soft overcomes hard.
> Everyone knows this,
> Yet we find it so difficult to live by it.[40]

THE SMALL CHILD or INFANT

Before it has been taught the rules of society, a small child is a moving force of creative energy, and at the same time it is also a classic model of innocence. The child is innocent of Confucian *li* and the rules of propriety. The child

---

[39] Han-shan Te-ching, *op. cit.*, ch. 8, pp. 59-60.

[40] *Ibid.*, ch. 78, pp. 145-146.

sees everything fresh, without preconceptions of how things ought to be.[41] This innocence is the source of a great creativity and provides a strength which contrasts with its physical weakness. The child can scream all day long without getting hoarse. People do not scheme against a child, but only against the strong and powerful. Children do not yet know artificial human ceremonial interaction, which means they are natural and spontaneous.

A small child is not anxious about tomorrow, and is not concerned with what tomorrow will bring. The child sleeps trusting that her mother will be there whenever needed, and the child trusts that everything will take care of itself. The image of the child is utilized throughout the *Tao Te Ching*. Consider this verse in chapter 49:

> The Sage doesn't have a fixed mind[42];
> The Sage takes the minds of the people as his own.
> That which is good I make more good;
> That which is not good I also make more good.
> The virtue of goodness.
> Trustworthy people I trust,
> Untrustworthy people I also trust.
> The virtue of trust.
>
> . . .
>
> But in the world Sages are childlike.[43]

The child image is also found in chapter 55:

> To be filled with the power and virtue of Tao (*te*) is to be like a child.
>
> . . .
>
> Bones weak, muscles soft,
> But its grasp is strong.
> It does not yet know the union of male and female,
> But its sex is perfectly developed,
> It's vital essence is complete.
> It can scream all day and not get hoarse,
> Its inner harmony is at its peak.[44]

Chapter 76 asserts:

> At birth people are supple and weak,
> They die hard and stiff.
> The ten thousand plants and trees
> Are supple and soft when born,
> And die withered and sere.
> The hard, stiff and strong
> Are the companions of death;

---

[41] Many of the greatest artistic creators in the West have been described as having maintained a child-like curiosity, a child-like openness, all their life.

[42] Remember that "mind" in Chinese is the same character as the one for "heart" and so includes emotions and feelings, and not just pure intellectual consciousness..

[43] Han-shan Te-ching, *op. cit.*, chapter 49, p. 109.

[44] *Ibid.*, chapter 55, pp. 116-117.

The soft and weak are the companions of life.[45]

THE UNCARVED BLOCK, a model for SIMPLICITY

Chapter 28 of the *Tao Te Ching* advises us to "Return to the uncarved block." Imagine that you are a sculptor who works in wood. In your studio you accumulate several medium-sized logs with the bark, branches, and leaves still on them. You look at a log wondering what you will carve out of that uncarved block of wood. Because it has not yet been carved, it can be shaped into a myriad different forms. It is raw potential with few limitations.

Once carved it is no longer in its natural state. When uncarved, it is not artificial but just raw material, and hence, the natural state of things. Applied to humans, a human is like an uncarved block when that human's mind is simple, plain, sincere, spontaneous, un-tooled Nature. This is the original condition of one's mind, before rules, regulations, and human cultural brainwashing turned you and me into a terribly conditioned, un-natural, un-free, non-spontaneous person.

We humans tend to be one sort of person to our friends, a different person to our parents, and a different person to our children. We are afraid to let others see us without wearing different masks. We hide our feelings, our natural reactions. To emulate the uncarved block is to drop masks and trust yourself.

Consider what chapter 19 says:
    Behold simplicity; embrace the uncarved block.
    Selfishness dwindles; desires fade.[46]

The uncarved block is simple, yet it has the potentiality to become almost anything from a carved duck, a statue of the Buddha, a Venus, or a doorstop. Once carved, it has lost its potentiality; it becomes rigid and fixed. Something fixed and rigid has lost its potentiality, and has become narrowed and limited to just one thing. All that is left is for it to break, to be destroyed. Humans do not want to be fixed and rigid and carved; we should be flexible and our minds should be like the uncarved block.

Chapter 37 relates the uncarved block to non-action:
    Tao endures free from unnatural action (*wu-wei*),
    Yet nothing is left undone.
    If kings and lords could possess it,
    All the ten-thousand things would transform themselves.
    Although transformed, they still desire to create;
    I quiet them through nameless[47] simplicity of the uncarved block.
    With nameless simplicity one is freed of desire.
    Being free from desire is equanimity,
    And everything under heaven settles of itself [48]

---

[45] *Ibid.*, chapter 76, p. 144.

[46] *Ibid.*, chapter 19, p. 73.

[47] The "nameless" is what cannot be captured by names, words, or concepts.

[48] Han-shan Te-ching, *op. cit.*, chapter 37, p. 96.

CHAPTER 16: THE *TAO TE CHING*

EMULATE THE VIRTUE OF THE FEMININE CONSCIOUSNESS (*yin*)

In both East and West, when we think about nature, we think in terms of "Mother Nature," the source, the mother of all things. There is a cluster of characteristics which are stereotypes associated with the feminine including weak and submissive; yet at the same time we can easily associate characteristics such as strength and creativity with the feminine. In China, in addition to creativity the feminine consciousness is associated with other *yin* characteristics like tranquility, non-aggression, gentleness, receptivity, intuition and subtlety. The feminine *yin* is also a profound mystery.

> The spirit of the valley never dies.
> It is called the Mysterious Female.
> The entrance to the Mysterious Female
> Is called the source of Heaven and Earth.
> Use it, for it is never exhausted.[49]

In China, the male is associated with action, aggression, competition, domination, and power. These are *yang* traits. The female is associated with being submissive and being passive. The Taoist notices that even though a woman is not supposed to be aggressive and should not take the initiative, she is still able to accomplish her goals; she can act indirectly, act without assertive action. She can bring things about without imposing her will directly.

Creation and Procreation

The feminine is associated with the creative source of life, fertility, and creativity in general. Western culture has tended to associate procreation as something physical and sexual (and for many in the West, the sexual is bad, is at war with the spirit), and thus Western people view procreation as opposed to the spiritual. In the West, unlike procreation, *creation* is non-physical, is spiritual, it is the activity of the gods, and the great artists. In general, Western people do not associate sexual procreation with spiritual creation. Yet, for the Taoists, giving birth to a child is one of the most fundamental acts of all creation. Physical procreation is not inferior to the metaphysical, spiritual, or artistic creation. Conception, gestation, childbirth are symbolic of the deepest creative impulse.[50]

The imagery associated with *yin* is cool, dark, moist, concave, and it is clear why this would be associated with birth. The idea is to recognize the creative power of the feminine, beyond the obvious and apparent female characteristics; all human beings, both men and women, should incorporate these *yin* qualities into their own lifestyles in order to become more at one with the flow of the Tao.

The philosophical Taoists seem to think that the Confucian stress upon the *yang* at the expense of *yin* brings about an unhealthy balance in human beings, and especially in males. To over-stress the *yang* as Confucians do, is to minimize the *yin*, the feminine. As a result, males are weaker in the emotional skills of nurturing, weaker in the ability to respond intuitively to nature and will have lessened empathy for fellow humans. Males will have lessened sensitivity, and caring. Yet, these *yin*-aspects of the personality (male or female) are healthy aspects of a well-balanced human being. Chapter 10 suggests:

> Give birth and nourish,
> Give birth and yet not be possessive.
> Act upon things but do not depend upon them,

---

[49] *Ibid.*, chapter 6, p. 58.

[50] This topic is discussed at greater length in Marta Weigle, *Creation & Procreation* (University of Pennsylvania Press, 1989).

To be the ruler but do not rule.
This is called dark profound powerful virtue of Tao (*te*).[51]

In chapter 61 we find:
In stillness and tranquility,
The female constantly overcomes the male,
In stillness and tranquility,
Takes the lower place.
Thus a great nation
Lowers itself before the small nation,
And wins over a small one.
A small nation
Plays the role of the lower,
And accordingly wins over a great one.[52]

APPRECIATE THE EMPTY

In addition to the four role models discussed above, the philosophical Taoists urge us to learn from the positive potentiality of spaces where there is no matter, empty space, or **emptiness**, that is, the spaces between and around objects.[53] Once again, this is the *yin* contrasted with the *yang* of solid space. Emptiness is not a role model for us to emulate. Rather, the *Tao Te Ching* is encouraging us to appreciate how essential the empty places are.

For Confucians and most of us, areas where there is nothing are of little or no interest. The Confucian values fullness. The Taoist encourages us to understand the value of emptiness. For the Taoist, to be full implies nothing can be added, to be full is to have no room left for change or growth.

It is the emptiness in the wall that allows the light to shine through the window; it is the emptiness in the hallway wall which provides the doorway-access to the classroom. The empty container can be filled with many different things; the full container cannot be used to hold anything else.

A mind filled with certainty has no room for facts with which it disagrees, no room for new knowledge, no room for growth or development resulting from a new perspective. A mind empty of self-centered desires is humble and has no preconceived ideas of how things must be. Such a mind is open to many creative possibilities. A mind without preconceptions can perceive things just as they are. An empty mind is not filled with self-righteousness certainty as to how things must be. To be empty is to allow the possibility of being filled with Tao; to be full is to have no possibilities left.

Chapter 11 says:
Thirty spokes united around the hub make a wheel.
But the wheel's function is possible because of emptiness.[54]
By forming clay we have a utensil,
But the function of the utensil comes from its emptiness.

---

[51] Han-shan Te-ching, *op. cit.*, chapter 10, p. 61.

[52] *Ibid.*, chapter 61, pp. 123–124.

[53] Notice that this is NOT the same as the Madhyamaka Buddhist concept of *svabhava-sunyata*, or "empty of unchanging inner essence" discussed in *Asian Thought: Volume I*, chapter 10.

[54] It is the empty space of the hub which allows the axle to fit, and the wheel to spin.

Doors and windows are cut out to make a room.
Yet the room's utility comes from its emptiness.[55]

Chapter 22 has:
Be humble and you will be complete.
Be bent and you will be straight.
Be empty and you will be filled.
Be well-worn and you will be renewed.
Have little and you will have all you need.
Have much and you will be perplexed.[56]

16.8 METHODS FOR BEING IN ACCORD WITH THE TAO

Wu-wei: the Method of "Non-Action" for Attaining Harmony with the Tao

In Chinese, the character "*wu*" is a negative and means to be without, to be free of, and "*wei*" is to make, to do, to act. Thus, *wu-wei* is usually translated "non-action." But it does not mean sitting down and doing nothing. *Wu-wei* is not the absence of action. *Wu-wei* means "don't push it," "don't try to impose your will on natural processes," or "don't try to force things to happen." Instead, act the way nature does, effortlessly, in the same way the leaves on the trees fall in the winter and return and grow back naturally after wintertime has flowed into spring. To act *wu-wei* is to act the way Tao acts, flowing with the patterns of Nature and not acting contrary to the pattern. To act *wu-wei* is to not act unnaturally. To act *wu-wei* is to respond in an unforced manner, in a way which is effortlessly in harmony with the flowing pattern of Tao.

Instead of making, forcing, or causing things to happen, the *Tao Te Ching* suggests we **allow** things to happen naturally. *Wu-wei* or "non-action" is the absence of *artificial action*. It means *no unnatural activity*. Nature, or Tao, does not force things to happen, Tao is not an active agent, not a mover, not a maker, not a doer of things. Tao doesn't perform special miracles to make it rain, or snow. Tao operates through spontaneity, simplicity, tranquility, gentleness, and non-action. *Wu-wei* is effortless action. To be in harmony with the Tao is to simplify one's life, not to complicate or accumulate concepts.

Pursue knowledge, gain daily.
Pursue Tao, lose daily.
Lose and again lose,
One attains non-action (*wu-wei*).
Non-action and yet nothing is left undone.[57]

---

[55] Han-shan Te-ching, *op. cit.*, chapter 11, p. 63.

[56] *Ibid.*, chapter 22, p. 78.

[57] *Ibid.*, chapter 48, p. 108.

The Chinese painter Pa-ta Shan-jen (1626-c. 1701) expressed it this way:

When the mind is transparent and pure as if reflected on the mirror-like surface of the water,
there is nothing in the world that you would dislike.
When it is serene as the light breeze in the sunshine,
there will be no one whom you would like to forget.[58]

Wu-wei means you do not impose your will on things to make them into what you want. It means you leave things alone to be the flowing processes that they are. There is no effort behind the falling rain or blowing wind. *Wu-wei* is "effortless action" or "no artificial action." *Wu-wei* is not meddling, not going against the natural pattern or grain of things. The last lines of chapter 3 are: "Practice *wu-wei* and there will be nothing out of order."[59]

Wu-wei is getting self-centeredness out of the process of making choices. We humans try to control things for our own benefit, try to manipulate a world of flowing natural processes to our own advantage. As we lose and again lose, as we gradually lessen the ego and our behavior becomes more natural, more unselfconscious, we gradually become more *wu-wei*.

Confucians tend to exert force in an attempt to control the world and human affairs when Taoists prefer simply letting things alone to take their own natural course. *Wu-wei* is to go along, as nature does. The world arises, things are born, grow and pass away, effortlessly. Taoist *wu-wei* means acting without aggressive or self-centered action. *Wu-wei* means not going against the grain of things, *wu-wei* means flowing with the patterns of nature.

Becoming self-less, one's actions are precisely those of Nature, as any genuinely spontaneous actions will be. *Wu-wei* is achieved by gradually lessening ego-centered mental chatter and as the ego lessens, one becomes identified with Nature (Tao). We can act with *wu-wei* as our guide. For example, when one wants to move a cart, one does not push it sideways. One pushes the cart in the direction the wheels roll, one pushes from behind — that is *wu-wei*. To be *wu-wei* is to respond naturally and intuitively. Chapter 43 of the *Tao Te Ching* explains:

The softest thing in the world
Can overcome the hardest things in the world.
Its nothingness interpenetrates where there is no space.
By this I know the advantages of *wu-wei*.
Teaching without words,
Provides the benefits of *wu-wei*.
Few in this world can come to this.[60]

Wu-wei is the life-style of one who is in harmony with the Tao, and as a result is using the least amount of energy in dealing with things, as a fine athlete uses just exactly the right amount of energy to accomplish the task, not too much.

In chapter 48, Lao-tzu stresses non-interference with the Way using non-action *(wu-wei)* to master and control the world:

To pursue learning is to accumulate knowledge day by day,
To pursue Tao is to let things and thoughts decrease day by day.

---

[58] Chang Chung-yuan, *Creativity and Taoism, op. cit.,* plate 10.

[59] Han-shan Te-ching, *op. cit.,* last line of chapter 3, p. 54.

[60] *Ibid.,* chapter 43, p. 104.

Lose and again lose until finally you arrive at non-action *(wu-wei)*.
Nothing is done *(wu-wei)*, yet nothing is left undone.
You can rule the world by practicing *wu-wei* (letting things go their own way).
By interfering you can never rule anything.[61]

Chapter 2 stresses non-action as the way a Sage will act:
Therefore the Sage manages affairs through *wu-wei*,
And teaches without words.
The ten-thousand things flourish.
Things arise and yet the Sage does not claim to possess them.
Deeds are accomplished yet the Sage does not take credit.
No credit is taken,
And achievements endure.[62]

Wu-wei is one of the enduring teachings of the *Tao Te Ching*.

A Person of *Wu-wei* Naturally Manifests the Virtue of *Te/De*

The Chinese character *te/de* indicates a beneficial quality, an effective power. In English we can use the word "virtue" in the sense of the inherent capacity of a thing to perform well its specific function, as in "the virtue of this car is that it will get excellent mileage and rarely need repairs." Consequently, the Chinese term *te/de* is often translated as efficacy, virtue, influence, power, or moral force.

Te Is Different for Confucians and for Taoists

For the Confucians, *te/de* is the conspicuous and positive moral virtue of the respectable Confucian Sage who is perfect in benevolence *(jen)* and perfect in all ceremonial interactions *(li)*, and the result is an inner quality of character which is powerfully effective in influencing others to behave morally. The Confucian sage acts without seeking what is profitable but does what is required by proper ritual and patterns of morality.

For the philosophical Taoists, *te/de* is more obscure, more mysterious, an inherent and creative force or power which flows from Tao. *Te* is the virtue of Tao and the power that flows from being in perfect harmony with Tao. Discussing the ten-thousand things (all that exists), in chapter 51 we find:

Tao give birth to them and *te/de* rears them,
Matter forms them,
Circumstances complete them.
Thus all the ten-thousand things honor Tao and esteem *te*.
Tao is honored and *te* is esteemed.
No one orders it to be that way;
It happens spontaneously and naturally *(tzu-jan/ziran)*.[63]

---

[61] *Ibid.*, chapter 48, p. 108.

[62] *Ibid.*, chapter 2, p. 53.

[63] *Ibid.*, chapter 51, p. 111. *Tzu-jan/ziran* is discussed in the next section of this chapter.

For human beings, the creative energy of *te* is something human beings manifest when they are in accord with the Tao; it is the vital expression of Tao itself in our everyday life. The person who manifests *te* does not stand out of the crowd yet has a positive energy or power which allows very difficult situations to be handled with the least amount of energy and stress.

According to the philosophical Taoists, this charismatic energy is acquired as we gradually perfect the method of *wu-wei*, and also acquired by attaining a stillness of mind, a lessening of ego. With *te* we become able to do things, to accomplish things which seem quite extraordinary. *Te/de* is an effortless skill for getting things done and influencing others without conscious effort. This is the sort of extraordinary skill that we see with some of the greatest athletes and musicians who perform amazing feats and make it look easy.[64]

> People who really know what they are doing, such as a cook carving an ox, or a carpenter or an angler, do not precede each move by weighing the arguments for different alternatives. They spread attention over the whole situation, let its focus roam freely, forget themselves in their total absorption in the object, and then the trained hand reacts spontaneously with a confidence and precision impossible to anyone who is applying rules and thinking out moves.[65]

The greatest *te* is arises because the Taoist has no anxiety about life, has no self-centered ambitions for power, and does not use aggression to make others obey. The attention of the Taoist is not diverted by ego-centered distractions. The Taoist sage manifests *te* and is not anxious about tomorrow, and is not concerned with what tomorrow will bring. The claim is that the Taoist sage will intuitively respond to the flow and the pattern of Nature, and she trusts that everything will take care of itself.

To **try** to be *te/de* is like trying to force yourself to be spontaneous. The harder you try to be spontaneous, the less spontaneous you are.[66] To try to be a person of *te/de* is like trying to grab onto water—the more tightly you grasp, the less you have.

Criticisms of Confucian Virtue

According to the philosophical Taoists, following a Confucian ritual rule for virtuous behavior is to lose sight of one's authentic virtue, one's natural ability to accomplish effortlessly without going contrary to the flow of Tao. When Confucians tell you how to behave, how to be virtuous (*te/de*), and you *try hard* to be that way, you lose your natural spontaneous connection with Tao and become a pale imitation of genuine effortless virtue (*te/de*).

For the Taoists, the Confucians have confused *respectability* with genuine *virtue*, which is quite different. Confucians try to be respectable; Taoists respond intuitively and spontaneously without trying, without ego involvement. The classic citation explaining the creative effortlessness of genuine *te/de* is found in chapter 38 of the *Tao Te Ching*:

> It is because those of the most excellent virtue (*te/de*) do not strive to excel (*te/de*)
> That they are of the highest virtue (*te/de*).
> And it is because the least excellent do not leave off striving to excel
> That they have no genuine virtue (*te/de*).

---

[64] For the Religious Taoist, the *te* is supernatural, closer to a divine power (like the concept of *siddhi* in Indian religion).

[65] Although this remark is about Chuang-tzu, its insights apply equally well to the *Tao Te Ching*. It is from A. C. Graham, *Chuang Tzu: The Inner Chapters* (London: George Allen & Unwin, 1981), p. 6.

[66] For more on this, read Edward Slingerland, *Trying Not to Try: The Art and Science of Spontaneity* (New York: Oxford University Press, 2007).

Persons of the highest virtue take no action (*wu-wei*),
Nor would they have any motivation to act.[67]

For the person of Tao, *te* is an intuitive awareness and non-conceptual spontaneous reaction to the ever-swirling patterns we call "life."

To be ever aware of the enduring pattern,
Is called the original *te/de*.
Original *te/de* is deep, far-reaching and profound.
All things return
And reach the great harmony.[68]

Tzu-jan (Ziran) or Spontaneous Naturalness

The two character compound *tzu-jan/ziran* (pronounced something like "zu-rahn") can be translated "of-itself-so," "spontaneously so," or "naturally so." Mountains are high of themselves, water flows downhill of itself. When applied to human beings, the closest meaning seems to correspond to **naturally spontaneous**. If *wu-wei* means no-unnatural-action, then *tzu-jan* is the positive expression of the same state: spontaneously natural.

Wu-wei: do not act unnaturally, do not impose one's will on natural processes.
Tzu-jan/ziran: do act naturally, spontaneously, going with the flow.

In the very last lines of chapter 25 we find:
Humans follow the patterns of the earth.
Earth patterns itself after heaven.
Heaven follows Tao.
Tao merely follows its own nature (*tzu-jan/ziran*)[69]

If one is self-centered, practicing to achieve personal benefit, calculating ahead, cleverly manipulating others, scheming to get power, then one is not *tzu-jan*. A person of *tzu-jan* is genuinely spontaneous and egoless. If you are not self-centered and not dominated by ego, you will have no motive to do harm to others. According to Lao-tzu, the sage has no need for moral doctrines along the lines of ceremonial *li* for he or she will simply live spontaneously. If one is truly self-less, what could impel you to steal, lie, or hurt anyone?[70]

Being less ego-centered, even egoless, one cannot be depressed or unhappy, because these occur only when one is standing back from creative action, separated from the world. When you are completely absorbed in your action, when you are not aware of yourself as separate from what you are doing, there is neither happiness nor unhappiness, only total absorption. These sorts of moments of absorbed spontaneity can be among the most creative and fulfilling

---

[67] Han-shan Te-ching, *op. cit.*, chapter 38, p. 97; my translation has profited by the felicitous wording found in Roger T. Ames & David L. Hall, *Dao De Jing: A Philosophical Translation* (New York: Ballantine Books, 2003), p. 135–136

[68] Han-shan Te-ching, *op. cit.*, chapter 65, p. 130.

[69] *Ibid.*, chapter 25, p. 82.

[70] This idea is explained in detail in Hans-Georg Moeller, *The Moral Fool* (Columbia University Press, 2009).

of human experiences.[71] Spontaneity translates to simplicity, or being like water. In chapter 17 we find:

> How much value should we give to words?
> When the work is done,
> Everyone says
> I just acted naturally (*tzu-jan/ziran*).[72]

The Taoist insight with *wu-wei* and *tzu-jan* is that when we are faced with a problem, when we are not sure what to do next, we should trust our own inner nature, and not try to figure things out to the last detail. Sometimes if one just lets go and falls asleep, a possible solution becomes clear. Just act spontaneously, follow your heart. A trained musician who is improvising is often advised to do precisely this. There are no guarantees, but take a chance.

> Sitting quietly, doing nothing,
> Spring comes, and the grass grows of itself.[73]

16.9 THE RELATIONSHIP BETWEEN NATURE AND HUMANS

Note that the philosophical Taoists do not place human beings above nature, or believe that humans have some special place in the scheme of creation. The *Tao Te Ching* makes it clear that Tao has no special affection for human beings, above and beyond other living things. Human beings are not intrinsically more important than all other things (even though egocentrically we humans like to think that the universe likes us best of all).

Tao is Nature, and Tao is Heaven as well. Nature is patterns which occur independently of our preferences, our pleas, and our prayers. Tao is selfless and impersonal; it is Mother Nature, which is the realm of balmy days and scorching drought that can last decades, tropical breezes and hurricanes, gentle showers and tsunamis which wipe out cities and coastlines and kill hundreds of thousands of people living in the path of destruction. Heaven was never a loving protector of human beings. Heaven does not love human beings better than the rest of nature. Anyone who lives in the real world can tell that Heaven is not humane, not benevolent (*jen*). Nature is not good in any human sense of the term.[74]

> Heaven and earth are not artificially benevolent (*jen*);
> To them all things are as straw dogs.[75]

---

[71] Think of moments that are most creative, such as a musician playing with a group or a string quartet. Consider the artist in the midst of creation. Think of athletes totally absorbed by the moment as they excel at their sport.

[72] Han-shan Te-ching, *op. cit.*, chapter 17, p. 71.

[73] Shibayama Zenkei, *Zenrinkushu*, (Kyoto: Nakayama Shobo, 1972), p. 194.

[74] For the Chinese, good and evil are not external to human nature. The sources of both good and evil are found within human nature, not in an omnibenevolent deity. See Franklin Perkins, *Heaven and Earth Are Not Humane: The Problem of Evil in Classical Chinese Philosophy* (Indiana University Press, 2014).

[75] See Burton Watson, *The Complete Works of Chuang Tzu* (New York: Columbia University Press, 1970), pp. 158–159. The above explanation is a paraphrase of Watson's remarks.

The Sage is not artificially benevolent (*jen*);
To him all people are as straw dogs.[76]

The image of straw dogs refers to popular shamanistic religious ceremonies. In the ancient past in China, living animals would be sacrificed. Later, the community ceremony used an effigy, a dog-shape made of straw. The straw dog acted as a scapegoat to draw off evil influences at the sacrifice and the effigy was treated with great reverence. After the sacrifice was completed, the effigy was thrown away. In other words, the straw dog is the center of a religious ritual and treated with exaggerated solemn respect, but when the ritual ceremony is over and everyone has left, the straw dog is simply thrown into the trash. Tao doesn't love humans best; we shine for a while and then are discarded to return to Mother Nature (Tao), to be replaced by succeeding generations.

The Taoist Sage Treats All Things With Equal Respect

As you recall, *jen* (benevolence) is a central Confucian virtue. The Taoists understand the Confucian *jen* to be social respectability, to be an artificial showy benevolence. The Taoist sage is not artificially benevolent, but this does not mean that the sage harms humans. We must recall that for Confucians *jen* is the virtue of gradually extending one's good will first to parents, then family, and then the extended family. The Taoist sage is not *jen* in this way.

The important insight is that the ideal Taoist sage is neutral the same way the Tao is neutral; the sage is not human centered. The Taoist sage does not favor human beings over the other ten-thousand things in the world. The Taoist sage shows no favoritism towards her own species. The Taoist sage is neither cruel nor ruthless, just spontaneous and natural. The sage treats everything with equal respect.

If we treat all things with respect, it is not the case that human beings have been demoted to the level of animals. Rather, in the scale of importance all things have been elevated to the level of humans. All things are treated equally because from the perspective of eternity *all things are of equal worth*. Human beings are not shown favoritism over the other parts of the processes of Nature. Everything is sacred.

In chapter 49 we find:
Those who are good I take as good.
Those who are not good I also take as good.
The virtue (*te*) of goodness is attained (*te*).

Those who are trustworthy I trust.
Those who are untrustworthy I also trust.
The virtue of trustworthiness is attained.[77]

The Taoist sage is naturally virtuous, not artificially respectable or benevolent with favoritism shown to those people who are closest, i.e. family. Because the sage is neutral the way nature is neutral, and in complete harmony with the Tao, what the sage does is effortless and spontaneous, the way the Tao is spontaneous. Being spontaneous, the ego is out of the process of choice. From the Taoist perspective, motivation to do evil is gone. Thus it is that the Taoist sage is not concerned with rules of morality, and does not find them useful.

When one begins to use the categories of "good" and "evil," one is dividing up a world of flowing change into categories which do not correspond to nature. To say something is morally good is to talk about our social lives and what we approve of. If an earthquake brings your house down, it is bad. If the earthquake brings new game into your

---

[76] Han-shan Te-ching, *op. cit.*, chapter 5, p. 57.

[77] *Ibid.*, chapter 49, p. 109. This translation is a bit different from a previous translation in this chapter, reflecting the many ways in which one can render the original Chinese text. In this translation I follow the suggestion that *te* (virtue) can be interchangeable with the similar Chinese character, *te* (grasp, attain).

area and hunting is improved, then it is good. If it brings additional rivers, additional fish and drinking water, then it is good. If it brings flooding, then it is bad. In the next chapter, we will consider the Taoist thinker Chuang-tzu/Zhuangzi, who has much more to say about the limitations of human morality.

16.10 THE EMOTIONAL LIFE OF THE TAOIST SAGE

Chinese thinkers pondered the question of what sort of emotions the ideal sage would have. Some thought that the sage never felt any human emotions at all. For example, the Confucians believed that the sage modeled himself after Heaven, which completely transcends human emotions.

The Taoists did not agree with the Confucians. Wang Pi/Wangbi (226–249 C.E.), the ancient Neo-Taoist commentator upon the *Tao Te Ching*, argued that the Taoist sage does indeed have the five emotions of ordinary people (joy, anger, sorrow, pleasure, love), but what the sage does not have is an ego-centered preference for her or his own kind. When it rains, we all get wet.

The sage is not emotionally entangled with people. The ego is lessened, so the sage never asks "what's in it for me?" or "how can I benefit from this?" The sage is not possessive. The earliest extant commentary on the *Tao Te Ching* is by Wang Pi, and in Wang Pi's biography we find a summary of his understanding of the emotions of the Taoist sage:

> He [Wang Pi] felt that the Sage was richer than ordinary people in insight, and the same as ordinary people in the five passions. Being richer in insight, he is able to experience harmony in communicating with non-being. Having the same five passions as others, he is not lacking in sorrow or delight and is responsive to things. Hence by nature the Sage can respond to things without being burdened by them, and to say that the absence of burden means a lack of responsiveness misses by a long shot.[78]

All things arise from Tao and return to Tao and are of equal worth. The process of Tao is rising and falling, alternation and return. At the appropriate time, things can be elevated to the superior position (*yang*) and be important. Following that at some later time, things will be at the low point of the process (*yin*), and unimportant (like a straw dog). These poles of value/valuelessness simply alternate.

> The one who knows honor yet sustains disgrace,
> Becomes the valley of all things under heaven,
> And as such *te* [virtue] will endure.
> Return to the simplicity of the uncarved block.[79]

In modern times we humans have insulated ourselves from the natural processes around us. We live crowded in cities separated from nature and separated from each other. We no longer grow our own food, cut our own firewood, or carry our water in buckets from our well. We give birth and pass away in hospitals hidden away from everyday life. We continue to create new technology, and talk about how much time we have saved. Each new development in technology has further alienated us from our home, alienated us from the natural world around us, and has made us dependent upon our machinery.

The *Tao Te Ching* suggests that from the very beginning humans have always been a part of nature, and returning to our original unity with nature is the key to a good life. Ultimate human contentment cannot result from creating unnatural principles and rules with no analogues in the patterns of nature as the Confucians want to do.

---

[78] Translated by Paul J. Lin, *A Translation of Lao-tzu's Tao Te Ching and Wang Pi's Commentary* (Ann Arbor, MI: Michigan Papers in Chinese Studies 30, 1977), p. 152.

[79] Han-shan Te-ching, *op. cit.*, chapter 28, p. 86.

We can try to make machines that will make nature work the way we want it to, but in fact we do not understand the complexity of the world and when we attempt to change natural things like the course of rivers, our changes generate unintended consequences resulting in greater chaos. The Taoist would say that we cannot change nature to work the way we want it to. Nature is our home and our selves, but Nature does not belong just to human beings; Nature does not give us special favors. Everything under heaven is treated equally; we all experience rain, drought, or earthquake. It is all the same. We must lessen the ego and return to our original harmony with the flowing patterns of nature.

16.11 THE RETURN TO ORIGINS

All of us are rooted in the same place where the heavens and the earth originate, that is, we are rooted in the Tao, the constant unitary chaos which underlies all. We cannot escape Tao. Everywhere we go is Nature. Everything we do is the action of nature. Every thing we do is "nature naturing." According to the philosophical Taoists, with Confucianism we lose the original spontaneity of our natural behavior and try to develop artificial virtues (*te/de*) like benevolence (*jen*) and artificial rules of morality, like ceremonial rituals (*li*). In trying to be respectable, in worrying about what others think of us, we lose our connection with the source. The *Tao Te Ching* encourages us to revert to the original state of Nature, the pattern which is Tao.

The Taoist seeks to return to his or her own roots, to return to a primal indeterminate flowing Tao. Tao is not static; nature is a rhythmic pulsation, continual change and transformation, processes of birth, growth, decay, and dying. There is continuity in the ever-shifting movement from one pole to its opposite. The pendulum swings back and forth, to one extreme of *yang*, but then the motion reverses direction, and swings to the other extreme, *yin*. That pattern is what we call Tao. The pattern is always reversing, returning, and the ultimate return is to the Tao, to the Mother or source, which is deeper than any determinate concept that any of us could have.

> *Reversal* is the motion of Tao,
> And *weakness* is its function.
> All things under heaven arise from determinate Existence,
> and Existence arises from indeterminate Non-Existence (*wu*).[80]

If we focus only on one end of the spectrum, we do not notice that every pole arises together with its opposite. Concave entails convex. The good entails the not-so-good. Honor is impossible unless there is also disgrace. Light depends upon darkness. Darkness depends upon light. If we lose one, we lose both. We cannot have birth unless we have death. Strength entails weakness. Laws entail law-breakers. Success entails failure. The Tao is a dynamic process swinging back and forth. Our job is not to hold onto the one we like and reject the other. The wise Taoist sage responds to the universal rhythm, and taps her feet along with the swinging beat of nature. From the Taoist perspective, there is a swinging back and forth, an alternating *yang* and a *yin* to everything.

> Know the male yet keep to the female . . .
> Know the white yet keep to the black . . .[81]

---

[80] *Ibid.*, chapter 40, p. 101.

[81] *Ibid.*, chapter 28, p. 86.

We already know how to accomplish this return. Just let go. Practice non-action (*wu-wei*). Try to not-try.[82] As you gradually develop your own *te/de* ("graceful virtue") you respond effortlessly to Nature. Do not try to impose your ego-centered will on the world. Respond to the world, participate in the natural processes, but let it be. Practice non-interference with all that exists naturally under heaven. This is the key to a good life. This is how things get done or accomplished — yet no one claims credit.

16.12 THE ULTIMATE LIFESTYLE ACCORDING TO LAO-TZU

For the *Tao Te Ching*, the ultimate goal is to return to nature, live a simple life growing your own food, and re-experience the child-like joy to be discovered in all the processes of nature. Lao-tzu recommends a life apart from the large city, recommending instead a rural grouping where the people live more intuitively, responding to the alternating patterns of the seasons. The ideal life for Lao-tzu is an agricultural and rustic village life.

Without going out of the door, one knows the whole world.
Without peeping out of the window, one sees the Heavenly Tao.
The further one goes, the less one knows.
Thus the Sage does not go about, yet is aware.
The Sage doesn't look around, yet understands.
He does not act and yet he achieves.[83]

The ideal for a Taoist was to be left alone to enjoy life free from the artificial complexity of rules of human-centered politics and culture, thereby preserving one's inner integrity. The way to achieve harmony with the Tao is to reduce self-centered desires and get back into the pattern and flow of the natural patterns of Tao. Leave things to themselves, without unnatural interference and human-centered artificial efforts; leave things in their natural state.[84] This could be achieved by retreating to the countryside, living frugally with few desires, spending one's days in contemplation of the wondrous interacting patterns that make up Nature (Tao). You will grow your own food and trade with your neighbors (note that Taoists were not vegetarians). You'll enjoy poetry and wine. You will not use more than you need, and you won't need much.

In chapter 80, the *Tao Te Ching* portrays the simple life of the person who lives in accord with the Tao:

There's a small kingdom with few people.
Although there are many different labor-saving devices, they are not used.
The people regard death as serious and no one wants to move afar.
They have boats and carriages but no one ever rides in them.
Even though they have weapons and armor, no one uses them.

---

[82] This felicitous phrase comes from Edward Slingerland, *Trying Not to Try: The Art and Science of Spontaneity* (New York: Oxford University Press, 2007)

[83] Han-shan Te-ching, *op. cit.*, chapter 47, pp. 107–108.

[84] This ideal was exemplified in the lives of the so-called Seven Sages of the Bamboo Grove, exponents of "Dark Learning" philosophical Taoism discussed earlier in this chapter, and then discussed again in section 17.9 ("Philosophical Taoism During Later Dynasties") of the next chapter on Chuang-tzu.

Moreover, the people return to the ancient ways which predate counting and writing.[85]
They enjoy their food, decorate their clothes, are comfortable in their homes, and enjoy uncomplicated lives.
Neighboring states may be close enough to be in sight,
Close enough to hear the sounds of barking dogs and crowing roosters,
Still, the people will grow old and die without traveling back and forth.[86]

16.13 POLITICAL ADVICE IN THE TAO TE CHING

As was pointed out earlier, the *Tao Te Ching* does contain advice for how to rule a kingdom. Almost every classic Chinese text is concerned with the "art of ruling," and the *Tao Te Ching* is no exception. Many of the verses and chapters of the *Tao Te Ching* can be interpreted either personally or politically; some are explicitly political. Chapters 57 through 61, 65, 74 and 75 are specifically focused on suggestions for proper governing the kingdom according to Taoist insights. In particular, the concern is with how can an ordinary person survive in a world where rulers of kingdoms are untrustworthy, rulers lie to themselves and lie to the people constantly, turn on and destroy those who advise them, and break treaties when it is advantageous to do so. In this world, armies march and destroy. As was pointed out before, the *Tao Te Ching* rejects the Confucian solutions, but what does it offer in its place?

> If one desires to govern the world and tries to do so,
> I see that he cannot succeed.
> The world is a spiritual thing and should not be manipulated.
> One who manipulates the kingdom damages it,
> To grasp it is to lose it.[87]

If Confucianism is a *yang* masculine, controlling, aggressive and logical approach, the Taoists offer a mirror image, a less aggressive gentler *yin* approach. The Taoists are not advocating the elimination of a ruler, or eliminating the king. For the Taoists, the best ruler is the one who rules least. Chapter 17 explains this.

> The best ruler is one whose subjects barely know he exists;
> The next is one to whom they feel close and praise;
> The next is one whom they fear;
> The lowest is one whom they despise.
> When the ruler's trust is wanting,
>   there will be no trust in him.
> Cautious,
>   he values his words.
> When his work is completed, and his affairs finished,
>   the common people say,

---

[85] The Chinese character describes cords with knots in them. Knotted cords are a very ancient technique used to keep track of larger numbers without the necessity of having words or names for large numbers.

[86] Han-shan Te-ching, *op. cit.*, chapter 80, pp. 147–148.

[87] *Ibid.*, chapter 29, p. 87.

CHAPTER 16: THE *TAO TE CHING*

"It happened of its own accord."[88]

When the ruler stands out, he is a burden on the state. For the Taoist, it is effortless and egoless sincerity of the ruler that flows from harmony with the Tao that is important, not persuasive eloquence and clever manipulation of the perceptions of the citizens. What is needed to rule the kingdom is not aggressive military power, not public relations to spin events in such a way that they will appeal to the majority, or at least appeal to the politician's base (those who approve of the policies). The ruler should not try to be impressive, should not push himself to the forefront. A Taoist Sage-ruler calls so little attention to himself that people think things are just going well naturally, all by themselves. The ruler who is a Taoist Sage acquires the power (*te/de*) of ruling without being known to rule and without making things happen. Chapter 10 explains:

Can you love the people and govern the land, with non-action (*wu-wei*)?[89]
. . .
Rear things, nourish things,
Rear them, but do not take possession of them,
To act upon things but not to manage them;
Be chief among them, but not to master them.
This is called the profound power and virtue of Tao (*te/de*)[90]

In chapter 65, the *Tao Te Ching* adds:

To govern the nation using excessive cleverness and concepts is to do it harm.
Not to use cleverness and concepts in governing the nation is good fortune.
To know both of these two is to know the standard.
To be ever aware of the enduring standard is called the original excellent virtue (*te/de*).
That original excellent virtue is deep, profound, and far reaching.
With it all things reverse and reach the great harmony [of the Tao].[91]

Whoever the author of the *Tao Te Ching* was, the only political model he had was that of an absolute monarch, the king or emperor. All of China's philosophical systems believed that an all-powerful ruler was the only possibility, and that the ruler must strive to be a sage. However they did not agree about what constitutes sagehood.

For the Taoists, the sage-ruler is one who lives his life in harmony with the mysterious principle underlying all of reality, i.e., Tao. The emperor does not need to impose his will upon the world, does not need to act (*wu-wei*), but instead should exude the spiritual power of *te* which will influence the lives of all those around him (on this point the Confucians agreed). This spiritual power of *te* is developed by the emperor's *wu-wei*, no-artificial-action (on this the Confucians disagreed).

The power of *te* is the key to happiness and a good life. When the *te* of the emperor exists, there is no need for

---

[88] *Ibid.*, chapter 17, p. 71. My translation was enriched by reading those of Victor Maier, *Tao Te Ching* (New York: Bantam Books, 1990), ch. 17, p. 79, Arthur Waley, *The Way and Its Power* (London: George Allen & Unwin, 1968), p. 164, and Michael LaFargue, *The Tao of the Tao Te Ching* (New York: State University of New York Press, 1992, p. 118).

[89] The Han-shan Te-ching text reads this as *wu-wei*, i.e. "Govern through non-action," but other texts have *wu-shih* "not-know" which could be translated "govern and yet remain unknown" or perhaps "and be free of cunning" or "while being free from knowledge." Han-shan Te-ching, *op. cit.*, chapter 10, p. 61.

[90] *Ibid.*, chapter 10, p. 61.

[91] *Ibid.*, chapter 65, p. 130.

many laws to coerce people to follow rules (no need for Confucian *li*). When one is *wu-wei*, one is in accord with the ever creative ever flowing Tao, and from this *te* naturally develops.

The *Tao Te Ching* devotes ch. 30, 31, and 69 to the use of military means to dominate the world. Chapter 30 asserts:

> He who assists the ruler by means of Tao
> Does not dominate the world with military means;
> For such things surely rebound back to the doer.
> Wherever armies are, thorns and brambles grow.
> After a great army is raised and marched,
> A year of deprivation and famine follows.
> Thus a good general achieves his purpose and then stops;
> He does not presume to dominate by means of his prowess and power.
> He fulfils his purpose and does not glory in what he has done;
> He fulfils his purpose and does not boast of what he has done;
> He fulfils his purpose, but only as a step that was unavoidable.
> He fulfils his purpose, but without violence;
> Things reach their peak and then grow old.[92]
> This [violence] is contrary to Tao,
> and what is contrary to Tao will soon perish.[93]

Chapter 31 follows the train of thought.

> Fine weapons are instruments of ill-omen,
> So they are not the instruments of a genuinely Superior Person (*chun-tzu*).
> He uses them only when he cannot avoid it.
> He values most the calm and the peaceful
> And does not take joy in conquest and victory.
> To take joy in conquest is to delight in the slaughter of men.
> He who takes joy in killing men will never attain what he wants most out of the world.[94]

Note "He uses [fine weapons] only when it is unavoidable." Lao-tzu is not a pacifist. A person or a community should defend itself when attacked, and the Taoist sage and ruler will take up arms when there is no way to avoid it, but the Taoist sage does not initiate violence.

Not only is Lao-tzu opposed to aggressive wars instigated by politicians for territorial expansion, political advantage and personal purposes, he is also against the Confucian and Legalist practices of making laws and rules to govern every situation. The more laws the politicians and lawyers pass, the more law-breakers will be created. The sage who rules will keep things simple, so simple that the governed will not realize that there are laws at all.

In chapter 57 we find an extended explanation of how to rule.

---

[92] A reference to the *yin* and *yang*; what goes up must fall down again.

[93] Han-shan Te-ching, *op. cit.*, chapter 30, pp. 88–89.

[94] *Ibid.*, chapter 31, pp. 89–90.

Govern the kingdom with rectitude,
And fight wars with surprise tactics.[95]
Rule the country by leaving things alone (non-action, *wu-wei*).
How do I know that it is so?
By this.
The more prohibitions and restrictions in the world,
The poorer the people will be.
The more sharp implements there are,
The more troubled everything will be.
The more scheming and cunning craftsmen there are,
The more complications will arise.
The more laws and orders are promulgated,
The more thieves and bandits there are.

Therefore the Sage says:
I am free from action (*wu-wei*) and yet the people change of themselves.
I love tranquility and yet the people become correct of themselves.
I am free from activity yet the people become prosperous of themselves.
I am free from desires and yet the people of themselves return to the state of the primordial simplicity
of the uncarved block.[96]

A classic admonition about ruling is the opening line of chapter 60 which advises us to govern a big country as you would cook a small fish. If the cook frequently turns the fish over and meddles with it, the fish falls apart. If the cook moves the fish only once, it remains intact. The ruler is the cook. The less turning, pushing and prodding in the process of ruling, the better.

For the Taoist, the discords and contradictions we find in any community can be dissolved by *te* which is a power that can benefit without harming. One cannot intellectually plan out the use of *te/de* to accomplish this; the ruler must be *wu-wei* and by non-interference allow the creative beneficial *te/de* to work its effects. "Yet through his actions which are free from activity, all things are duly regulated."[97]

The *Tao Te Ching* does not value abstract book learning, does not value teachings of artificial benevolence (*jen*) and trying to appear respectable with appeals to duty and rigid morality (*i*). By the time the Confucian begins to preach about benevolence (*jen*), ritual propriety (*li*) and righteousness or morality (*i*), things are already out of control. For the Taoist, ritual ceremonial behavior (*li*) is merely a human contrivance invented to deal with problems that were created in the past by too much meddling, like a band-aid applied *after* the injury has occurred. We must return to the simpler ways of the past. Chapter 75 states:

People are starving because their officials tax them too much.
That is why they starve.
The people are difficult to keep in order because their superiors interfere.

---

[95] Arthur Waley renders this as an old maxim: [An old saying goes:] 'Kingdoms can only be governed if rules are kept; Battles can only be won if rules are broken.' Arthur Waley, *The Way and Its Power* (London: GeorgeAllen & Unwin, 1968), ch. 57, p. 211.

[96] Han-shan Te-ching, *op. cit.*, chapter 57, p. 119.

[97] *Ibid.*, ch. 3, p. 15.

This is why the people are difficult to keep in order.[98]

Philosophical Taoism did have an influence over several great emperors. One emperor was the Han dynasty ruler Wen Ti/Wendi (179–157 B.C.E.) who applied political doctrines of the *Tao Te Ching/Daodejing* to the governing of the empire. Prior Chinese law required punishments which mutilated the body, including cutting off of limbs, hands, legs, ears, nose, and other body parts. Han Wen-ti abolished mutilating punishments. He abolished the law that decreed that an entire family could be exterminated for the crime of one of its members. He minimized taxation, and in fact, reduced, and at one time abolished, the land tax. He attempted a gentle policy of friendship, gifts, and trade with the barbarians on the northern borders. He tried to follow the advice of the *Tao Te Ching* and interfere in the affairs of his people as little as possible. Perhaps as a result, China became more prosperous than it had been for many centuries.[99]

16.14 SUMMARY OF THE CHAPTER

In this chapter we have discussed one of the enduring contributions of China to world spiritual pathways. The philosophical Taoists like Lao-tzu and Chuang-tzu share a vision of the world which is peaceful, but a vision of the world wherein human laws and social sanctions may be useful on occasion but are not so very important. The goal is an egoless feeling of being at home everywhere, a sense of full and complete participation in every moment, a sense of playful interaction with the varying patterns of *yin* and *yang* which constitute Tao.

The philosophical Taoists do not think humans are different from nature; we are nature and as natural as all the other living things on our planet. Heavenly beings such as gods and spirits may exist but they too are natural and play no role in spirituality. The spiritual life is right before us; simply stop separating yourself from the world and break free from the self-imposed prison of rules, concepts, ideas, and words which provide a defective roadmap for how to live. To be at harmony with the Tao is to be at peace.

There may have existed a philosopher named Lao-tzu who may have been born around 500 B.C.E., but we cannot be sure. However, we have ideas presented in the *Tao Te Ching/Daodejing*, ideas which are vague, broad, and suggestive of mysterious depths which we have to plumb on our own. The *Tao Te Ching* offers advice to politicians on the ideal ruler, but the contemporary appeal of the book tends towards the more personal. We need to become as appreciative of the empty as we are of the full. The goal of becoming more like the small child, more *yin*-like, more like an uncarved block, and more like water, provide role models profoundly different from the Confucian role models. To be in accord with the Tao is to manifest *te/de*, the virtue or power that makes life into an effortless ramble. If we can let go of our plans and goals and become more *wu-wei*, the process of non-action slowly transforms us until we become more spontaneous, or *tzu-jan/ziran*. Such a person is in harmony with the flow of the Tao.

Section 17.9 of the next chapter discusses suggestions for how to apply philosophical Taoism to one's daily life in contemporary times.

---

[98] Han-shan Te-ching, *op. cit.*, chapter 75, pp. 142–143.

[99] Holmes Welch, *op. cit.*, p. 104.

16.15 TECHNICAL TERMS

Chuang-tzu/Zhuangzi
Lao-tzu/Laozi

Tao	The Way, the Pathway, the road, mother Nature, the source.
Tao-chia/Taojia	Philosophical Taoism, the "School of Tao."
Tao-chiao/Taojiao	Religious Taoism, the "Teaching of Tao."

Tao Te Ching/Daodejing	The Classic of the Way and Its Power and Virtue
te/de	Virtue; graceful and effortless virtue; positive potentiality to influence others for the better.
tzu-jan/ziran	Spontaneity, naturalness, literally "of itself so."

wu-wei/wuwei	Non-action, no unnatural action, spontaneous activity.

yin/yang	The feminine and the masculine, passive and active, cool and hot, valley and mountain, etc. The alternation of the two constitute the Tao.

16.16 QUESTIONS FOR FURTHER DISCUSSION

(1)   The Taoism of Lao-tzu is often criticized as being too passive, even lazy. Is it possible to be too active, too aggressive? Should Lao-tzu be seen as too passive, or trying to make the Chinese Confucians less aggressive?

(2)   Some have criticized Lao-tzu for offering little to help us make moral decisions. Taoist scholars have suggested that every household taught Confucian morality to its children, so Lao-tzu is attempting to bring some balance into existing Confucian morality, and not just arguing to dump all moral considerations. Others have questioned the value of morality, assuming that when we are spontaneous without being ego-centered, we'll do what is best. Where do you stand on this issue?

(3)   Politically the Taoists say that the best ruler is the one where the citizens do not even know that there is a ruler. Taoists want the government to do very little interfering in the lives of its citizens. This is not just our politically conservative idea of a smaller government. The Taoists would not have the government impose any moral behavior on its citizens, and would reject all government meddling in our personal and medical concerns. It would also reject government attempts to regulate our behavior when it came to drugs, sexual preferences and lifestyle choices. Could a Taoist sort of government actually work in a Western society? Are there any political groups whose vision is similar to that of the *Tao Te Ching*?

(4)   How do you see the world, in stark contrasts of black and white, good and evil? Or do you tend to see the world as shades of grey, without rigid separations and distinctions? Are you a Confucian, or a Taoist?

(5)   The Taoist idea of *wu-wei* has a standard translation as "non-action." Does this mean that we should retreat from life, lie down on a hammock, close our eyes and do nothing?

(6)   The Taoists argue that Chinese society placed too much emphasis on the *yang* aspect of life, and we should bring things back into balance by re-emphasizing the *yin*. Is Western society in balance? What do you think?

SELECTED BIBLIOGRAPHY

The range of translations and secondary material on the *Tao Te Ching* is truly enormous. These are only a few titles to get you started.

Translations of the *Tao Te Ching*

Aldiss, Stephen and Stanley Lombardo, *Tao Te Ching* (Cambridge: Hackett, 1993)

Chan, Wing-tsit, *The Way of Lao Tzu* (Indianapolis: Bobbs-Merrill, 1963).

Chang, Chung-yuan, *Tao: A New Way of Thinking: A Translation of the Tao Te Ching with an Introduction and Commentaries* (New York: Harper & Row, 1975)

Chen Ku-ying, *Lao Tzu: Text, Notes, and Comments* (San Francisco: Chinese Materials Center, Inc., 1977), translated and adapted by Rhett Young and Roger T. Ames.

English, Jane and Gia-fu Feng, *Tao Te Ching* (New York: Vintage Books, 1973)

Hendricks, Robert G., *Lao-Tzu: Te-Tao Ching* (New York: Ballantine Books, 1989)

Ivanhoe, Philip J., *The Daodejing of Laozi* (Cambridge: Hackett Publishing, 2003)

LaFargue, Michael, *The Tao of the Tao Te Ching* (New York: State University of New York Press, 1992)

Lau, D. C., *Lao Tzu: The Tao Te Ching* (Baltimore: Penguin Books, 1963)

Lynn, Richard John, *The Classic of the Way and Virtue: A New Translation of the Tao-te-Ching of Laozi as Interpreted by Wang Bi* (N.Y.: Columbia University Press, 1999)

Mair, Victor, *Tao Te Ching: The Classic Book of Integrity and the Way* (New York: Bantam Books, 1990)

Mitchell, Stephen, *Tao Te Ching* (New York: Harper & Row, 1988)

Roberts, Moss, *Dao De Jing: The Book of the Way* (Berkeley, Ca: University of California Press, 2002)

Star, Jonathan, *Tao Te Ching* (New York: Penguin Classics/Jonathan Tarcher, 2003)

Waley, Arthur, *The Way and Its Power: A Study of the Tao Te Ching and its place in Chinese Thought* (London: George Allen & Unwin, 1968)

Explorations and Studies of the *Tao Te Ching*

Chang, Chung-yuan, *Creativity and Taoism: A Study of Chinese Philosophy, Art and Poetry* (New York: Harper Colophon, 1970)

Chang, Chung-yuan, *Tao: A New Way of Thinking* (New York: Harper Colophon, 1975)

Hymes, Robert, *Way and Byway: Taoism, Local Religion, and Models of Divinity in Sung and Modern China* (Berkeley: University of California, 2002)

Lagerway, John, and Marc Kalinowski, eds., *Early Chinese Religion: Part One: Shang Through Han (1250 BC -220 AD)* (Leiden & Boston: Brill, 2011)

Lagerway, John, and Lu Pengzhi, eds., *Early Chinese Religion: Part Two: The Period of Division (220 AD -529 AD)* (Leiden & Boston: Brill, 2010)

Slingerland, Edward, *Effortless Action: Wu-wei As Conceptual Metaphor and Spiritual Ideal in Early China* (New York: Crown Books, 2014)

_____, *Trying Not to Try: The Art and Science of Spontaneity* (New York: Oxford University Press, 2007)

Smith, D. Howard, *The Wisdom of the Taoists* (New York: New Directions, 1980)

Watts, Alan, *Tao: The Watercourse Way* (New York: Pantheon Books, 1975)

Wang, Zhonglian, *Daoism Excavated: Cosmos and Humanity in Early Manuscripts* (FL: Three Pines Press, 2015)

Van Norden, Bryan W., *Introduction to Classical Chinese Philosophy* (Cambridge: Hackett Publishing, 2011)

CHAPTER 16: THE *TAO TE CHING*

CHAPTER 17: PHILOSOPHICAL TAOISM:
The *Chuang-tzu/Zhuangzi*

17.1 OVERVIEW OF THE CHAPTER

As discussed previously, scholars have distinguished two related yet interestingly different clusters of Taoist traditions: *Tao-chia/Daojia* (philosophical Taoism, literally the "School of Tao") and *Tao-chiao/Daojiao* (religious Taoism, literally the "Teaching of Tao"). The philosophical and contemplative form of Taoism shows no interest in gods, rituals, confessions, blessings, curses, magical healing, liturgies, or clergy. It shows little interest in extending one's life span hundreds or thousands of years. These shamanistic themes were the primary concerns of religious Taoism. However, the religious Taoists do include the writings of the philosophical Taoists Chuang-tzu/Zhuangzi and Lao-tzu/Laozi as part of their collection of sacred books.[1]

The philosophical School of Tao, *Tao-chia* Taoism, was cultivated by Chinese poets, painters, musicians, and philosophers, but primarily this appealed to the literate, to the Grand Tradition, not Little Tradition. The influence upon popular Chinese folk religion is found mostly in the *Tao-chiao* or "Religious Taoism." We will discuss Religious Taoism in the next chapter.

In this chapter we will examine the Chinese philosopher Chuang-tzu (in Pinyin, Zhuangzi[2]), the second great representative of philosophical Taoism, and his ideas contained in the book which tradition has entitled the *Chuang-tzu/Zhuangzi*. This and the *Tao Te Ching/Daodejing* share a common world view, but are quite different in many interesting ways. Whereas the *Tao Te Ching* offers positive advice to rulers on how to rule well, the *Chuang-tzu* considers politics absurd, foolish, and to be avoided. For each of us, the important issues are the creative spirit as it develops during the continuum of birth, growth, development, and death. Birth and death are part of the same seamless flowing process called Tao, and both are to be accepted with equanimity.

Chuang-tzu's ideas are not for the immature who have yet to experience the real problems of life. He is not encouraging us to be impulsive and reckless. Chuang-tzu's philosophy is for those who are mature, those who know the Confucian rules, who have lived in a society where they have met the expectations of others both socially and morally. Once we have learned these roles and have fulfilled them, we are now in a position to better understand our real role in life. Our mature perspective allows us to see past the immediate concerns of society and family, to see what is really important.

---

[1] The religious Taoists interpreted the collected sayings of Chuang-tzu/Zhuangzi rather differently than the literati tradition. For the religious Taoists, Chuang-tzu/Zhuangzi is a disciple of Lord Lao-tzu/Laozi, and Lord Lao-tzu/Laozi is regarded as a divinity who taught the worship of the deeply mysterious Tao/Dao.

[2] The name Chuang-tzu/Zhuangzi is intended to be pronounced something like Jwang-zu.

CHINESE DYNASTIES RELEVANT TO TAOISM

CHOU/ZHOU (c. 1122-771 BCE).
       Interstate warfare after 771 BCE.
       Spring and Autumn Period 722-481 BCE.
          Life of Confucius (551-479BCE)
          Perhaps the life of Lao-tzu (b. 571 maybe)
       Warring States period 403-221 BCE.
          Mencius (Meng-tzu/Mengzi) (ca. 372-289 B.C.E.)
          Chuang-tzu (ca. 369-286 B.C.E.)
CH'IN/QIN (221-207 B.C.E.)
       Ch'in-shih Huang-ti/Qinshi Huangdi unifies China under his rule
       Legalism adopted as official state policy.
       Burning of the books which disagreed with Legalism.
       Central control and bureaucratic administration over China.

HAN (202 B.C.E. - 220 C.E.)
       Confucianism comes to dominate the political world.
       Philosophical and religious Taoism gain political importance.
       Buddhism enters China around 50 C.E.

THREE KINGDOMS (220-265 C.E.)
       China partitioned into three.
       "Dark Learning" philosophical Taoism and the Seven Sages of the Bamboo Grove.
       Confucian influence wanes; Buddhist influence growing.
TSIN (265-420 C.E.)
       China divided between North (non-Chinese rulers) and South (Chinese rulers)
SUI (589-618 C.E.)
T'ANG/TANG (618-906 C.E.)
FIVE DYNASTIES (907-960)
SUNG/SONG (960-1279)

17.2 CHUANG-TZU CONTINUES THE TAOIST TRADITION

The *Chuang-tzu* can be reliably dated to about two centuries after Confucius, that is, to around 300 B.C.E. However, it is possible that some portions of the *Chuang-tzu* might be earlier than some editorial changes found in the *Tao Te Ching* (discussed in the previous chapter).

Unlike the problem of whether Lao-tzu was a real person, or merely "teachers of the ancient past," we can be fairly certain that the a human being named Chuang-tzu did live in the time period of the fourth and third centuries B.C.E., and was the author of much of a book that bears his name, the *Chuang-tzu*. It is true that not all of the contents of the *Chuang-tzu* are the words of the man himself, nevertheless the first seven chapters are considered to be reliable indicators of the world-view of the philosopher Chuang-tzu.

The author of the *Chuang-tzu* was a master of the Chinese language who wrote in a unique style, as well as a gifted poet, a penetrating philosopher, and a free and easy spirit. His writing is not dry, academic, or scholarly. Chuang-tzu was a creative writer cleverly using sophisticated literary devices such as parallel rhyming structures, but within that structure we find fantasy, humor and satire.

CHAPTER 17: THE *CHUANG-TZU*

Chuang-tzu was very much a product of his historical era, in the sense that his time period was the Warring States period (approximately 475–221 B.C.E.), the same time-frame that produced the problems that Confucius and other Chinese thinkers were trying to resolve: how can we restore order and harmony with our fellow humans, and within the state? We saw that like the *Analects* of Confucius, the Taoist classic *Tao Te Ching* also offered political solutions as well as personal solutions to the turmoil. Chuang-tzu lived during this period of military and political upheaval, and he too is clearly concerned with harmony, but has no interest in politics.

The perspective of Chuang-tzu will be that of the exuberantly creative person for whom the process of artistic creation is enhanced by experiencing harmony with the flowing Tao, and in the process, a mental state of tranquil exhilaration results. The key to harmony will be internal and not the stifling rules of Confucian social morality. Instead, the goal will be creativity, the creativity of the changing universe — and you and I can be in harmony with that creative energy.

17.3 THE LIFE OF CHUANG-TZU

Although we do not have precise dates for Master Chuang there is a biographical entry in the *Historical Records of Ssu-ma Ch'ien/Sima Qian* (c. 145–c. 89? B.C.E.). Whether this biographical entry is accurate is a matter of discussion among scholars. A popular date for Chuang-tzu is 369–286 B.C.E. although it is perhaps too precise. That would make him roughly contemporary with Mencius (Meng-tzu/Mengzi ca. 372–289 B.C.E.) who was the most important follower of Confucius.[3] During this period China was still separate independent kingdoms at war with one another, and the final unification of China under the ruthless Ch'in/Qin ruler would not occur until sixty years after Chuang-tzu died.

Chuang-tzu/Zhuangzi lived in the south of China in what is known as Ho-nan province today. He was married and had children. He had no use for politics or rulers, and rejected the Confucian stress on propriety, or sacred performance of society's customs (*li*). Like Lao-tzu, Chuang-tzu finds the Confucian preoccupation with ceremonial interaction (*li*) to be narrow and the claim that there is an absolutely correct way to interact with other humans to be arbitrary.

Chuang-tzu appears to have been a non-conformist who had no interest in being socially respectable or in serving in the government. According to his biography, King Wei of Ch'u (339–329 B.C.E.) sent messengers and costly gifts to Chuang-tzu and invited him to become Prime Minister. Chuang-tzu replied "I would rather disport myself to my own enjoyment in the mire than be a slave to the ruler of a state. I will never take office. Thus I shall remain free to follow my own inclinations."[4]

17.4 THE BOOK ENTITLED *CHUANG-TZU*

We do not know what title Chuang-tzu might have given to his book, but it was quite common in China for books to be known by the names of their authors. Thus the *Tao Te Ching* is also popularly known as the *Lao-tzu* and this book is entitled the *Chuang-tzu*.

It seems very probable that the first seven chapters of the book entitled the *Chuang-tzu* are the work of a single person with a bold and unique style, and a very distinct personality.[5] The early chapters are filled with imaginative

---

[3] We should note that Mencius is not mentioned by name in the *Chuang-tzu* and Mencius never mentions Chuang-tzu in his writings.

[4] Fung Yu-lan, *A History of Chinese Philosophy*, *Vol. I* (Princeton, NJ: Princeton University Press, 1952), p. 221. The entire passage is translated in Brook Ziporyn, *Zhuangzi: The Essential Writings* (Indianapolis: Hackett Publishing Company, 2009), p. vii.

[5] See Harold Roth, "Who Compiled the *Chuang Tzu*?" in Henry Rosemont Jr., ed., *Chinese Texts and Philosophical Contexts* (LaSalle, IL: Open Court, 1991) pp. 79–128.

stories, outrageous fables, very unusual characters, and fantasy. Chuang-tzu was as much a jester as well as a philosopher. Chuang-tzu's personal name was Chuang Chou/Zhuang Zhou, and one of the most famous of all the fables in the *Chuang-tzu* is this one from the end of the second chapter, "Discussing the Equality of Things":

> Once Chuang Chou dreamt he was a butterfly, a butterfly flitting and fluttering around, happy with himself and doing as he pleased. He didn't know he was Chuang Chou. Suddenly he woke up and there he was, solid and unmistakable Chuang Chou. But he didn't know if he was Chuang Chou who had dreamt he was a butterfly, or a butterfly dreaming he was Chuang Chou. Between Chuang Chou and a butterfly there must be *some* distinction! This is called the Transformation of Things.[6]

The early chapters of the *Chuang-tzu* are a succession of brilliant and original essays which belong to the philosophical tradition associated with Lao-tzu, and inspired many of the greatest Chinese thinkers in succeeding centuries. The Taoist scholar Herlee Creel writes: "The *Chuang-tzu* is in my estimation the finest philosophical work known to me, in any language. Its authors included some of the keenest minds that the world has known."[7]

The *Chuang-tzu* in the form of 33 chapters that we know started out as a much longer text, compiled and then abridged and given chapter titles by the Neo-Taoist thinker, Kuo Hsiang/Guo Xiang (d. 312 C.E.).[8] Sadly, the longer original text is now totally lost, and Kuo Hsiang's shorter text is the only one we have today. The shorter Kuo Hsiang version of the book has three sections:
(1) the Inner Chapters, composed of seven chapters generally agreed upon as having been written by Chuang-tzu himself.
(2) The Outer Chapters (chapters 8–22), which reflect the personality of Chuang-tzu and may have extended sections written by him or written by his immediate followers.[9]
(3) The Miscellaneous or Mixed Chapters (chapters 23–33), some of which were probably written by later followers of the Taoist school, and other miscellaneous chapters most of which were not composed by a Taoist. Whether the third portion of the books has any integral connection with the Inner chapters and the Outer chapters is a matter of disagreement among scholars.

According to A. C. Graham, who devoted most of his scholarly life to the study of and translation of the *Chuang-tzu*, in the Inner Chapters we find,
> . . . contrasting yet reconciled strands, irreverent humour and awe at the mystery and holiness of everything, intuitiveness and subtle, elliptical flights of intellect, human warmth and inhuman personality, folkiness and sophistication, fantastic unworldly raptures and down-to-earth observation, a vitality at its highest intensity in the rhythms of the language which celebrates death, an effortless mastery of words and a contempt for the inadequacy of words, an invulnerable confidence and a bottomless scepticism.[10]

---

[6] Burton Watson, *The Complete Works of Chuang Tzu* (NY: Columbia University Press, 1970), p. 49.

[7] Herlee G. Creel, *What is Taoism?* (Chicago: University of Chicago Press, 1970) , p. 55.

[8] Much of our understanding of the meaning of the *Chuang-tzu* comes from the edited text, which means that we are not on solid ground when we stress the chapter order or chapter titles as giving us an important insight into Chuang-tzu. The editor, Kuo Hsiang, was a member of the Neo-Taoist "Dark Learning" movement described at the end of this chapter.

[9] Precisely which sections of the Outer chapters are by Chuang-tzu himself and which are written by other authors is discussed and summarized in Harold Roth, "Who Compiled the *Chuang Tzu*?" in Henry Rosemont Jr., ed., *op. cit,* p. 81.

[10] A. C. Graham, *Chuang Tzu: The Inner Chapters*, p. 4.

CHAPTER 17: THE *CHUANG-TZU*

Chuang-tzu often exaggerates for effect, utilizing images which are absurd and fantastic. He creates strongly philosophical dialogues between characters with strangely descriptive names and these characters inhabit a universe of myth and fable quite unlike the one the rest of us inhabit. For example, in chapter 22 we find this parable:

> Knowledge journeyed northward . . . and met Do-Nothing-and-Say-Nothing. Of him Knowledge asked: "How must we think in order to come to a knowledge of Tao? How is it approached? How do we pursue and attain it?" Do-Nothing-and-Say-Nothing answered not a word because he could not. Knowledge then traveled southward . . . and met All-in-Extremes and put the identical question to him. "I know," All-in-Extremes answered. And he started to tell him but immediately forgot what it was he was going to say.
> Knowledge then went to the Yellow Emperor and put his questions to him. The Yellow Emperor replied: "Tao may be known by no thoughts, no reflections. It may be approached by resting in nothingness, by following nothing, pursuing nothing. . . . The Sage teaches a doctrine which does not find expression in words."[11]

With a passage like the one above, it is quickly evident that we cannot read Chuang-tzu as though he were a contemporary Western philosopher seeking clarity in what we think to be true, and providing logically strong arguments in support of conclusions. For Chuang-tzu, logical arguments are both a useful tool and an obstacle — an obstacle because they can imprison us within the limits of words, concepts, and doctrines if we take these too seriously. Neither does the text resemble the sort of writings Westerners associate with religious scripture, because the author never claims that he is speaking to gods, or for the gods, although he does suggest that those who are truly in harmony with Nature[12] can accomplish what appear to be extraordinary feats.

The goal of Chuang-tzu is persuasive. It is personal transformation, not compelling arguments or expressions of faith. Chuang-tzu invites us to let go, to freely move between various perspectives, to enjoy fluttering between certainty and uncertainty, to recognize that the difference between dreaming and waking is not so important, and that life is not to be held onto tightly, and death is not to be feared. The use of metaphor and analogies in the *Chuang-tzu* also allows us to provide several different interpretations of the meanings. The richness and complexity of Chuang-tzu can only be hinted at in a brief summary, such as this chapter attempts.[13] A. C. Graham describes Chuang-tzu as a unique individual who has an absolutely fearless eye for reality:

> . . . rather than rebelling against conventional modes of thinking, he seems free of them by birthright. In the landscape which he shows us, things somehow do not have the relative importance which we are accustomed to assign to them. It is as though he finds in animals and trees as much significance as in people; within the human sphere, beggars, cripples and freaks are seen quite without pity and with as much interest and respect as princes and sages, and death with the same equanimity as life.[14]

---

[11] Chang Chung-yuan, *Creativity and Taoism: A Study of Chinese Philosophy, Art, and Poetry* (New York: Julian Press, 1963), p. 42. Reprinted by Jessica Kingsley Books, 2011.

[12] As in the previous chapter, when the word "Nature" denotes the grand pattern of all patterns, or the Tao, it is capitalized. When we are referring to natural phenomenon like wind, rain, and seasons, the term is written using a lower case "n."

[13] Any student who finds something interesting in the brief snippets of Chuang-tzu discussed in this chapter is strongly advised to dip into the original book of *Chuang-tzu* and the literature on Chuang-tzu, listed in the bibliography at the end of this chapter.

[14] A. C. Graham, *Chuang-tzu: The Inner Chapters*, p. 4.

CHAPTER 17: THE *CHUANG-TZU*

Chuang-tzu takes a playful approach to everything, including himself. In fact, humor is one of the defining characteristics of the *Chuang-tzu*. Using exaggeration and humorous fable as tools Chuang-tzu is able to discuss some of the most troubling issues in human lives, especially death, a topic that many of us are very uncomfortable discussing. Chuang-tzu points out how we can flourish in a world where there is nothing to hold on to, how we can have a good life in a world that is dangerous and confusing.

Chuang-tzu is skilled at logical thinking but he uses logic to show the limitations of logic. He follows the logical implications of a position until it yields absurdity. Thinking logically is not the key to the most important features of a good life; certainly logic will not put one in accord with the flow of Tao. When discussing topics with logicians, nothing is more powerful than to use logic to demonstrate that the positions of logicians are more illogical than they realized. Chuang-tzu uses logic in precisely this way.

The *Chuang-tzu* is an anthology of brief dialogues, glorious stories, fables, and unusual allegories, many of which wander into the realms of myth and the fantastic. His very keen analytical mind generates parables, encased in paradoxes. Things are exaggerated and extraordinary characters are treated as completely ordinary. For example, the opening chapter of the *Chuang-tzu* tells this story:

> In the bald and barren north, there is a dark sea, the Lake of Heaven. In it is a fish which is several thousand *li* across, and no one knows how long. His name is K'un. There is also a bird there, named P'eng, with a back like Mount T'ai and wings like clouds filling the sky. He beats the whirlwind, leaps into the air, and rises up ninety thousand *li* [approximately 30,000 miles], cutting through the clouds and mist, shouldering the blue sky, and then he turns his eyes south and prepares to journey to the southern darkness.
>
> The little quail laughs at him, saying, "Where does he think *he's* going? I give a great leap and fly up, but I never get more than ten or twelve yards before I come down fluttering among the weeds and brambles. And that's the best kind of flying anyway! Where does he think *he's* going?" Such is the difference between big and little.[15]

One way to read this story is to recognize that those of limited perspective are unable to comprehend the broader picture available to those with the big picture. The fish and the bird are huge, arise out of the subterranean darkness of the Lake of Heaven, and fly into the southern darkness, but are unafraid of the darkness, which is the darkness of the unconscious, the darkness of creativity and liberating insight. The P'eng bird and K'un fish properly fulfills its capacity; their absolute freedom is identical. There is much more to the world than is realized by people who are wearing cultural blinders, who only see what they've been conditioned to see. If you want to know about the universe overhead, do not ask a frog trapped at the bottom of a well.

There is another perspective available for this story. You might think that it is better to be the huge P'eng bird than the small quail, but this is a mistake. The large P'eng bird can fly ninety thousand *li* without effort because by nature the bird is so big. The small quail can fly ten or twelve yards, because by nature it is a quail. The behavior of the quail is perfect, for a quail. The behavior of the P'eng bird is perfect, for a large P'eng bird. Each thing fulfills its own nature; each affair fulfills its own possibilities. Each creature should be content to be what it is, and not to strive to become what it is not. If you are a brick, no amount of polishing can transform you into a mirror.

To fulfill your own natural capacity is to lose your self-imposed obstructions. There is no one proper height to fly, or proper size to be. Yet the small things do not realize that, and do not allow for the possibility of other viewpoints and standpoints besides their own; they want to impose their own small limitations on everything. It is equally a mistake for big things to look with pity upon the small. This is illustrated by this section from chapter VIII:

> The duck's legs are short, but if we try to lengthen them, the duck will feel pain. The crane's legs are long, but if we try to cut off a portion of them, the crane will feel grief. Therefore we are not to

---

[15] Burton Watson, *The Complete Works of Chuang Tzu*, p. 31. This is the second version of the story; in the first the fish becomes the bird. The distance of one *li* is approximately one-third of a mile. In Chinese myth, 90,000 *li* is the distance between heaven and earth.

amputate what is by nature long, nor to lengthen what is by nature short.[16]

You and I should seek to discover our own nature, and not seek to be what we are not. We must not be trapped by or limited by the expectations of society, family, or friends. We can soar above the limited perspective of the Confucian with his rigid system of rules and we can see that life is an effortless ramble, as long as we follow our own nature.

Chuang-tzu stressed the idea of achieving harmony with the flow of the Tao which results in the maximum of creative freedom in every aspect of our spiritual lives. Chuang-tzu advises his readers that what is most valuable is artistic creativity and spiritual integrity. Be free, be unfettered — but the freedom he is talking about is not political freedom, which would be concerned with the right to vote, to choose one's representatives, the right to be treated fairly by the government, its officials, and its court system. Chuang-tzu seems to have no interest in that. What Chuang-tzu is interested in is individual freedom. But, individual freedom does not mean following momentary impulses, or whims, and doing things to shock and scandalize our neighbors.

Chuang-tzu valued the personal freedom that comes when you peel back social conditioning and find your true self, which he called the True Person (*chen-jen*).[17] Then you think what you will, speak freely, and follow your profession or chosen lifestyle, in the midst of the freedom to roam where one's will takes one. The True Person acts spontaneously, responds egolessly, and is without contrivance. The most important element of individual freedom in Chuang-tzu is the inner freedom which results from perfect harmony with that creative power that accompanies harmony with Tao.

The World is in Continual Change

For Chuang-tzu, reality is just a natural and spontaneous process of transition and continual change. With the flow of *yin* and *yang*, we can see that everything is always changing. Change normally makes us nervous and anxious; Chuang-tzu wants us to celebrate the ever-changing and find the changeless in the midst of continuing transformation. Chuang-tzu suggests that we should be more like a small child who has no expectations as to what ought to happen; the child takes delight in whatever happens.

Notions of "should" and "ought" are not found in nature, and not found in the minds of those who are childlike and at home in the universe. "Should" and "ought" are the domain of the Confucian who knows precisely how one should speak, how one should respond, how one should dress, how one ought to behave (*li*, ceremonial interaction). Chuang-tzu is opposed to those who teach ceremonial respectability or propriety (*li*) and showy benevolence (*jen*) and rigid righteousness (*i*).

To live fully and naturally, we must allow ourselves to resonate to the ongoing rhythm, to the flowing pattern. When we are completely absorbed in the moment, we are in harmony with the Tao and we lose anxieties, worries vanish, and we make no conscious distinction between "self" and "other."

"All Things Are One"

Perhaps one of the most famous quotations which expresses this perfectly is found in chapter 2 of the *Chuang-*

---

[16] *Ibid.*, chapter 8, "Webbed Toes," pp. 99–100.

[17] Later religious Taoism will reinterpret this idea of the *chen-jen/zhenren* to be a fully-developed realized human being who has transcended this world and attained his status because of rigorous discipline and mastery of arcane religious Taoist texts. The Chinese Buddhist teacher Lin-chi (d. 866 C.E.) will borrow this philosophical Taoist term and make it one of the key technical terms of his teachings.

tzu. Chuang-tzu says: "Heaven and earth came into being with me together, and with me, all things are one."[18]
What could this mean? Let us examine this and its implications. We use concepts to distinguish and discriminate one thing from another, to separate *yin* from *yang.* Remember that the Tao is understood to be deeper than our dualities, deeper than Heaven and Earth. Chuang-tzu is referring to what is underlying our opposites. How are we related to what is common to *yin* and *yang*, to heaven and earth, to inside and outside? Is it that they support and condition each other, is it that all things are mutually interdependent? Or, having made such a claim, does Chuang-tzu really think all things are one? The complete quotations clarifies the issues. First, Chuang-tzu writes:

"[H]eaven and earth were born together with me and the myriad things and I are one."

but then in the very next sentence he follows it with:

Now that we are one, can I still say anything? Now that I have called us one, did I succeed in not saying something? One and the saying make two, two and one make three. Proceeding from here even an expert calculator cannot get to the end of it, much less a plain man.[19]

Is the statement "all things are one" a true statement? Clearly Chuang-tzu recognizes that the claim that "all things are one" produces nonsense when we treat it as an accurate description and draw implications. If we understand it as metaphor, or as poetry, does it make better sense? Perhaps Chuang-tzu's point is that this sort of writing is useful, and we should not try to impose categories of "true" and "false" or "correct" and "incorrect" when we engage in dialogue with others, without realizing that there are numerous other perspectives available.

17.5 MAJOR THEMES IN THE INNER CHAPTERS

The major themes of the *Chuang-tzu* include
(1) The "free and easy wandering" of the Sage or "True Person" grounded in Tao.
(2) Scorning wealth and political recognition.
(3) Rejection of logic as a useful tool to attain happiness or freedom.
(4) Artistic creativity results from Tao.
(5) The relativity of things and distinctions.
(6) It is impossible to pass certain judgment on truth or goodness
(7) Equanimity towards death because it is an aspect of the universal process of Tao.

FREE AND EASY WANDERING

The Chinese title of the very first chapter in the *Chuang-tzu* is entitled *Hsiao yao yu. Hsiao* ("roaming," "dissolving"), *yao* ("far") and *yu* ("unrestrained flow of banner in wind," "fish swimming playfully"). There are numerous attempts to render this three-character Chinese title into English, among them:
Free and Easy Wandering [Burton Watson],

---

[18] Fung Yu-lan, *A History of Chinese Philosophy, Vol. 1*, p. 244; Burton Watson, *The Complete Works of Chuang Tzu*, ch. 2, p. 43; A. C. Graham, *Chuang Tzu: The Inner Chapters*, ch. 2, p. 56. This is echoed in numerous later Chinese thinkers, including the Neo-Confucian thinker Wang Yang-ming (1472-1529).

[19] Author's translation from the *Chuang-tzu yin-te/Zhungzi yindi* (The Harvard-Yenching Institute Concordance to the Chuang-tzu, Taipei reprint, 1966), chapter 2, page 5, lines 52-54.

CHAPTER 17: THE *CHUANG-TZU*

Going Rambling Without A Destination [Arthur F. Wright],
Happy Wandering [Feng & English],
Roaming in Absolute Freedom [Chang Chung-yuan],
Wandering Where You Will [Martin Palmer],
Soaring and Roaming (Kuang-ming Wu),
Wandering Far and Unfettered (Brook Ziporyn).

Each translation of *Hsiao yao yu* is trying to capture the sense of unhurried movement, playful, relaxed, spontaneous, going nowhere special. In the process, everywhere we wander becomes special. Chuang-tzu invites us to engage in carefree meandering every moment of our life. The idea of "Free and Easy Wandering" can be understood as the Taoist Sage, or "True Person," or "Perfected Person" as Chuang-tzu calls him, freeing herself or himself from self-centeredness, from ego which separates us from our surroundings. The Perfected Person is free from amassing accomplishments and is free from concern with fame. With ego-centeredness diminished, worry about the future fades. With these disruptive and uncomfortable parts of our personality minimized, we can then wander freely wherever we go. Here is Chuang-tzu's description of the True Person, the Perfect Man or True Man:

The True Man of ancient times knew nothing of leaving life, knew nothing of hating death. He emerged without delight; he went back in without a fuss. He came briskly, he went briskly, and that was all. He didn't forget where he began; he didn't try to find out where he would end. He received something and took pleasure in it; he forgot about it and handed it back again. This is what I call not using the mind to repel the Way, not using Man to help out Heaven. This is what I call the True Man.[20]

A human life is a journey from birth to death, a journey which arises out of Tao/Nature and then returns back to Tao. It is a journey which can be a free and effortless ramble in an ever-changing realm of Tao, if we can return back to the flowing patterns of our own nature. Such a person is at home everywhere, for our home is wherever we are at the moment. We ramble free from the social expectations of others. We ramble spontaneously, we respond to whatever appears before us, without ego-centeredness.

The Taoist life will have its share of unhappiness and suffering, but these experiences are made worse by our failure to understand life. Misery and unhappiness are not to be removed by fighting against them; let them be, let them dissolve by simplifying and not interfering (*wu-wei*). It is an even more miserable life for one who does not allow herself to be free, who is afraid to soar, to roam, who is not at home everywhere. Chuang-tzu advises you to trust your deepest inner nature which is naturally in accord with Tao. When your understanding is clear, your movements are natural, spontaneous, and effortless, and also appropriate.

Our ability to discriminate and conceptualize is a powerful tool, but it also allows us to create rules and rigid patterns of behavior and this is what puts us out of touch with the interactive patterns which are Tao. Confucian rules and ideas of how civilized people ought to behave are the cause of many of our problems. According to the *Chuang-tzu*, social order, control from above, hierarchies of superior and subordinate, are what's wrong with the world. We tend to be absorbed in our own business, to be locked into the perspective of our neighbors and friends, our society; we focus on our own benefit and advantage, and we do not pay enough attention to the patterns which are Nature.

The freedom that Chuang-tzu values transcends not only society's expectations, but even transcends the limitations of our own expectations. Return to your true self, which is perfect and complete in itself. Contraries and differentiations are transcended. To be genuinely free from good and evil is not for good to conquer evil, or for evil to be destroyed. The entire dichotomy has to be recognized as grounded in perspectives none of which are ultimate or absolute, and then you are free and have attained Tao.

---

[20] Burton Watson, *The Complete Works of Chuang Tzu*, ch. 6, p. 78. Note the reference to the *chen-jen*, the True Person.

CHAPTER 17: THE *CHUANG-TZU*

In chapter 1 of *Chuang-tzu*, the logician Hui Shih/Huishi[21] is critical of Chuang-tzu. Hui Shih chides his friend Chuang-tzu for being selfish, and compares him to a large but useless tree:

> I have a great tree, people call it the tree-of-heaven. Its trunk is too knobbly and bumpy to measure with the inked line, its branches are too curly and crooked to fit compasses or L-square. Stand it up in the road and a carpenter wouldn't give it a glance. Now this talk of yours [like the tree] is big but useless, dismissed by everyone alike.

Chuang-tzu replies:

> Now if you have a great tree and think it's a pity it's so useless, why not plant it in the realm of Nothing whatever, in the wilds which spread out nowhere, and go roaming away to do nothing at its side, ramble around and fall asleep in its shade?
> > Spared by the axe
> > No thing will harm it.
> > If you're no use at all,
> > Who'll come to bother you?[22]

Chuang-tzu agrees that by Confucian standards his philosophy is not useful or important because it is not useful for impressing others with one's virtue, and it is entirely useless for the central task of ruling. In fact, Chuang-tzu is indifferent to the task of ruling. Nevertheless, he rejects the perspective of Hui Shih. He invites Hui Shih to consider the situation from a new perspective, a higher point of view. Hui Shih's social and political expectations are simply conventional, and in the grand scheme, they are unimportant and have always been unimportant. From the higher perspective, the journey of life becomes a carefree and effortless ramble for one in accord with the Tao.

As pointed out previously, Chuang-tzu's Taoism is not for reckless immature youth who have not learned from the vicissitudes of life. It is not for those who are foolishly impulsive. Instead his thought is directed to those whose minds who are mature, who have grown up knowing the Confucian rules, who have lived in a society where they have met the expectations of others both socially and morally. Once we have learned these roles and have fulfilled them, we are now in a position to better understand our real role in life. Our mature perspective allows us to see past the concerns of society and family, to see what is really important.

Chuang-tzu is inviting us to let go of our socially determined roles and social expectations, and instead enjoy life where everything around us is astonishing, everything is fantastic, and we inhabit a world to be explored in a carefree meandering way. See the world through the eyes of a child, and every thing you see, hear, touch, or taste is amazing. If you can wander freely and easily, without contrivance, you can smile at the world. Your creative response to nature is laughter, imagination, and creativity. When one has the perspective of the Tao, one's life is an effortless ramble. One is not trapped by desires for worldly success and fame, things which have no natural stopping point.

On the other hand, one does not try to escape from this world. Instead one soars above the restricted viewpoints of the world to find a universe which is restless, flowing, changing, pulsating with spiritual freedom, and it is our home, to wander in freely from birth to death.

---

[21] A study of Chuang-tzu's friend Hui Shih is found in chapter IX, "Hui Shih, K'ung-Sun Lung and the Other Dialecticians," in Fung Yu-lan, *A History of Chinese Philosophy: Volume I* (Princeton, NJ: Princeton University Press, 1952).

[22] A. C. Graham, *Chuang-tzu: The Inner Chapters*, p. 47.

CHAPTER 17: THE *CHUANG-TZU*

SCORNING WEALTH AND POLITICAL POSITION

The Confucians tell a story of Yao, the Sage-King in the Golden Age of the past, who abdicated the throne and offered it to the person best qualified to rule, the sage Shun. However, Chuang-tzu imagines that Yao offered it to someone else before he offered it to Shun. In chapter 1 of the *Chuang-tzu*, Chuang-tzu tells the story of Yao first offering the empire to the Taoist recluse and sage Hsu Yu/Xuyu. Chuang-tzu imagines the Emperor Yao saying to Hsu Yu, "If you took the throne, the world would be well ordered. I go on occupying it, but all I can see are my failings. I beg to turn the world over to you."

The Taoist hermit Hsu Yu replies: "You govern the world and the world is already well governed. Now if I take your place, will I be doing it for a name? But name is only the guest of reality — will I be doing it so I can play the part of a guest? When the tailor bird builds her nest in the deep wood, she uses no more than one branch. When the mole drinks at the river, he takes no more than a bellyful. Go home and forget the matter, my lord. I have no use for the rulership of the world."[23]

Do you want to be famous? Do you seek power? Do you want everyone to look up to you because you are so very important? In China, as in most of the world, it was through politics that one could achieve these goals. In chapter 17 of the *Chuang-tzu*, "Autumn Floods," the author tells a story about a minor god of a great river (who is conceitedly proud of his immensity). The minor god engages in a dialogue with the lord of the much larger North Sea. When the river god realizes how the immense North Sea absorbs his own river and remains unaffected, his pride evaporates. The great river was not so very big when compared to the ocean. But, the Lord of the North Sea, even though he is much much larger, is not filled with pride at his own immensity. Chuang-tzu then puts these words into the mouth of the Lord of the North Sea:

I take my place with heaven and earth and receive breath from the *yin* and *yang*. I sit here between heaven and earth as a little stone or a little tree sits on a huge mountain. Since I can see my own smallness, what reason would I have to pride myself?[24]

If the deity who is the immense North Sea can see his own smallness, how much less should we be seeking some sort of cosmic importance. Should we be proud of ourselves? Chuang-tzu's conclusion is *not* that we humans are unimportant or worthless. "Therefore great wisdom observes both far and near, and for that reason recognizes small without considering it paltry, recognizes large without considering it unwieldy, for it knows that there is no end to the weighing of things."[25]

REJECTION OF LOGIC AS BEING OF ULTIMATE VALUE

In his dialogues, Chuang-tzu argues that using logic, we can support almost any position whatsoever, politically conservative or liberal, carnivore, vegetarian or vegan, and so forth. Logic is a tool we use to convince others of our own position, but logic is not a tool for revealing reality. Politicians you agree with use logic to argue for positions you agree with. But politicians you disagree with use logic to argue for positions that you disagree with. Using logic, one can argue for capital punishment or against it. One can argue for same-sex marriage, or against it. One can argue for war, or against war. Using logic, we can generate paradoxical descriptions of reality. Logic does tell us when our

---

[23] Chapter 1 of Chuang-tzu, in Burton Watson, *The Complete Works of Chuang Tzu*, pp. 32–33. See also A. C. Graham, *Chuang Tzu: The Inner Chapters*, p. 45.

[24] Burton Watson, *The Complete Works of Chuang Tzu*, p. 176.

[25] *Ibid.*, pp. 176–177.

conclusions follow from our premises, but our premises are tied to our language and our cultural presuppositions. Using logic to arrive at conclusions does not produce some sort of absolute truth independent of language and culture. Logic is built upon manipulating language and categories, and categories are human mechanisms we use to make conceptual sense out of the world. But reality itself is neither rational nor irrational. It simply is.

There are no puzzles or paradoxes in nature; puzzles and paradoxes appear only in our human descriptions of nature. Paradoxes arise as a consequence of the categories we attempt to use to describe reality. We mistakenly assume that we have accurate categories, but there are no entirely accurate categories. We mistakenly assume our logical categories contain and describe reality accurately. The realm of concepts is the mind; it is not the world. Chuang-tzu wants us to dissolve our rigid categories by which we build our concept of reality. Logic is useful, but we cannot use logic to prove those things that are most important for a good life. For the Taoist, it is completely natural intuitive spontaneity that provides a good life, not logic.

Language and categories are useful; but we must be careful not to assume that they correspond one-to-one with reality. Use words to indicate, to point at what you want to convey, but do not fall into the trap of assuming that you have described the way things truly are. To make this point, with some typical Chuang-tzu humor, we find:

> The fish trap exists because of the fish; once you've gotten the fish, you can forget the trap. The rabbit snare exists because of the rabbit; once you've gotten the rabbit, you can forget the snare. Words exist because of meanings; once you've gotten the meaning, you can forget the words. Where can I find a man who has forgotten words so I can have a word with him?[26]

Spontaneity: *tzu-jan/ziran*

Tzu-jan/ziran is acting spontaneously natural, without artifice or contrivance. For Chuang-tzu/Zhuangzi and the Taoists in general, we human beings are simply a natural part of the great flowing process the Chinese call Tao. Nature (Tao) does not force anything to happen. Nature is just the process of things happening. The course of the Tao is *tzu-jan/ziran*, which is spontaneity, acting without artificial action (*wu-wei*).

We humans have the ability to reason and discriminate, and that is a useful skill if one is engaged in activities requiring weighing and measuring, if one is building a tower, a home, or a bridge. But, we humans use this ability inappropriately when we separate ourselves from nature and discriminate in an effort to force things to go the way we want them to go, the way we think they ought to go, and in this way we no longer act spontaneously. Spontaneity is acting the way water acts: water does not decide to flow downhill; it simply flows. Similarly a human is *tzu-jan/ziran* (spontaneously natural) if the person acts as freely as water flows.

I lose that spontaneity when I discriminate between value judgments and concepts, and then act as though the abstract discriminations I have made actually existed in the world. If I see one thing as beautiful, then I also have to see other things as ugly. The moment I assume that my conceptual discriminations correspond to reality or Nature, I have lost my way in the flow. In nature, things simply exist and move with the great flowing pattern. Beautiful and ugly are human constructs and have no correlation in nature.

ARTISTIC CREATIVITY FLOWS FROM HARMONY WITH TAO

The *Chuang-tzu* book has been popular among poets and painters for its stress upon unity of Tao leading to the freeing of the artist from society's social constrictions, encouraging spontaneity and creativity. Nature is constantly creating and we humans are not separate from Nature. We humans are also creative, but our creativity has been blocked by artificial social constructs. "To be free from the confusion of external conditions, to be rid of the

---

[26] Burton Watson, *Chuang Tzu: Basic Writings*, Ch. 26, "External Things," page 140.

perplexities of life, is to be fully charged with primordial creativity, is to attain Tao."[27]

If we are fundamentally the same stuff as Tao, then the creativity of Nature which is displayed everywhere we look, is our creativity as well. Nature creates effortlessly, egolessly, spring comes and the grass grows of itself. As Tao, we humans can create effortlessly and egolessly as well. When we perceive the world "from the inside" so to speak, as someone who is unaware of herself as separate from what is seen, we inhabit the wholeness of everything, we enter into the wholeness and are unified with the deep underlying harmony of the movement of *yin* to *yang*, and back again. The musician who becomes one with her instrument and one with the music has achieved this creative harmony. This harmony is the Tao itself. To be in the flow of the Tao is to be as creative as any human can be.

RELATIVITY OF THINGS AND DISTINCTIONS

Chuang-tzu and his friends realized that the names we give to things are conventional. We use the English word "dog" to name that canine that goes on all fours and barks, but we could just as well have used some other sound to pick out that animal, perhaps "chien" or "inu." Anything might be called by any sound whatsoever.

Names are central to language and concepts. We use names to make distinctions, and yet anything might be called by any sound. Chuang-tzu's thinking goes beyond the mere fact that names are conventional. The sound "dog" is relative to a culture and relative to social agreement. Chuang-tzu asks whether there is anything not relative to culture and society, whether anything exists independently of other things, whether anything has intrinsic existence. Chuang-tzu concludes that nothing exists as a thing apart from the many relationships it has with other things. All things are mutually dependent, not self-sufficient or uncaused.

> Wisdom consists in perceiving that opposites, far from being sequestered in their exclusive individuality, ceaselessly modify and communicate with each other. The one never transpires but in response to the other, and all reality is nothing more than this process of reciprocal engendering. Art and wisdom consist, then, in allowing oneself to be led from one extreme to the other, intervening as little as possible, in order to benefit fully from the logic — inherent in the real — constituted in this dynamic of reversal.[28]

Nature simply is what it is, and does what it does. For Chuang-tzu, distinctions exist only in the human mind, and are relative to human purposes. Good, bad, should, should-not, right, wrong, ought, ought-not, up, down, this, not-this — all are relative and useful for some purposes, but have no intrinsic value. These are not absolute values built into the nature of reality, the way Confucians believed. These opposites of good and evil have their meaning only because they are paired. If you have right, you must have wrong — they are paired like up and down, like concave and convex.

For Chuang-tzu, in the search for a good life there are no absolutes. There is no single perspective which is objective and universal. What is best for one is not necessarily best for all. We humans are not all the same. You are aware that what is a good life for one person is not a good life for another. The best occupation for your father or your mother, your brother or your sister, is not necessarily the best occupation for you. Our desires differ, and our temperaments differ. The circumstances of my father's life and my mother's life are not the circumstances of my life. These vary vastly from one time and place to another, and we recognize that a great deal of variation is inevitable.

Chuang-tzu argues that what we value in our lives is relative. No values are objective, none are absolute. Some people will value a life spent working with machinery, some working with the earth, and some will value a life spent in dancing, making music, or even quiet careful thinking or contemplating the first principles of reality. Some value

---

[27] Chang Chung-yuan, *Creativity and Taoism: A Study of Chinese Philosophy, Art, and Poetry* (New York: Julian Press, 1963), p. 67.

[28] Francois Jullien, *In Praise of Blandness: Proceeding from Chinese Thought and Aesthetics*, translated by Paula M. Varsano (New York: Zone Books, 2004), pp. 42–43.

a life spent in quiet meditation. One lifestyle that is attractive to you can be repellent to others. Chuang-tzu's advice: lessen the ego, try to go with the flow naturally and spontaneously, and do not be so judgmental of the choices of others.

When we are fully in the moment, we lose our sense of separateness, we become one with the flowing energies that comprise the Tao. It is from that perspective that all judgments are relative to one another. All things are equally flowing manifestations of Tao. Dreaming and waking are not fundamentally separate. Yesterday and tomorrow are equally free and flowing, with no strict demarcation between them. The Tao is in the heavens above, but it is equally in the animal excrement beneath our feet. Nature is flowing forces, and we need to maintain an equal balance shifting between the various extremes (the way a surfer or skateboarder stays in balance by shifting from side to side). We are what happens spontaneously (*tzu-jan/ziran*) and in harmony with the flowing Tao.

Is Taoism Better Than Confucianism?

Is it better to be a wandering Taoist Sage or a conforming Confucian gentleman? Because Chuang-tzu is so obviously critical of the Confucian approach to life, he must think it is better to be a Taoist sage. But, aren't these both "equally flowing manifestations of Tao"? How can one be better than the other? Is one to be preferred? It would seem that Chuang-tzu would hold that the problem with the Confucian choice is that it is limited by the assumption that there is only one perspective; all who disagree are wrong. The spontaneous choice of the Taoist sage is not attached to any perspective and more naturally in accord with the Tao, and it is from that higher perspective that it is to be preferred.

The fundamental ethical principle of Chuang-tzu can be summarized as "To be happy put yourself into spontaneous accord with the flow of the Tao and then act naturally." But how can we do that?

We are trapped by superficial thinking if we look for happiness in socially approved goals such as fame, fortune, recognition for our political acumen, or any of the various lifestyles which are determined by officially approved culture. Happiness is not the result of changing the external world to match our desires. Rather, happiness is grounded in the wisdom and quietude which lies underneath one's superficial conceptual mind, underneath conceptual thought, and logical reasoning.

THE PIVOT/AXIS/HINGE OF THE TAO

In chapter 2, Chuang-tzu considers distinctions, and takes as an example the relationship between "this" and "that." We have a tendency to identify something as "this" and something else as "that," without recognizing that the identity of things depends upon one's perspective. Things shift depending upon the point of view. If something is close to me, I'll call it "this"; if it is over there on the other side of the room, I'll call it "that." If I change my location, "this" becomes "that," and "that" becomes "this." If I am in the middle, in between, it is no longer relevant to distinguish "this" from "that," and then things are no longer either "this" or "that."[29]

Affirmation arises from negation, and negation from affirmation. Therefore, the sage disregards all distinctions and takes his point of view from Heaven. The "this" is also "that," and the "that" is also "this." "This" has its right and wrong, and "that" also has its right and wrong. Is there really a distinction between "this" and "that"?[30]

So, in fact, does he still have a "this" and "that"? Or does he in fact no longer have a "this" and

---

[29] The "this" versus "that" discussion seems intended to refute a previous discussion of this topic by the logician Kung-sun Lung in his "Discussion of Names and Actualities."

[30] Chang Chung-yuan, *Creativity and Taoism*, op. cit., p. 36.

"that"? A state in which "this" and "that" no longer find their opposites is called the hinge or axis of the Tao. When the hinge is fitted into the socket, it can respond endlessly. Its right then is a single endlessness and its wrong too is a single endlessness. So, I say, the best thing to use is clarity.[31]

The Chinese character translated "clarity" appears throughout the *Chuang-tzu*. The Chinese graph, pronounced *ming*, is a combination of the two separate ideograms for the sun and the moon, the brightest things in our world (until quite recently). The meaning is "bright," "illumination," "brilliant," and as used by Chuang-tzu this seems to suggest "illuminative understanding," "illuminated discernment," and "clarity." Some even translate *ming* as "enlightenment." To see things from the pivot or axis of the Tao is illumination, it is to use clarity, to be enlightened.

The axis of the Way, or the hinge of the Tao, is the metaphorical pivot around which the universe revolves, and it is the perspective of the Taoist sage. The axis is the center of the Tao, the center around which Tao swirls. Consider the face of a clock. From the 3 o'clock edge of the circle that is the clock face, "this" is next to me and "that" is on the opposite 9 o'clock position of the circle's diameter. However, when we make our way to the center of the circle, "this" and "that" are no longer in opposition; we respond freely to both. Either can be "this" or "that." The sage does not prefer "this" over "that." Now imagine the circle to be a sphere; the perspectives within the sphere are endless. The center of the sphere is where all the possibilities are available, and from the perspective of the center, terms like "correct" or "incorrect" would make no sense.

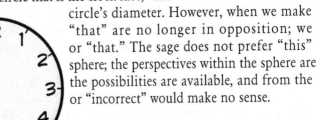

What we need to recognize is that when we strongly affirm "yes, this," it has the potential to generate a strong denial, "no, that." Denial follows affirmation — they are in no way absolute; they are co-relative, or co-dependent. "This" can become "that," and from a different perspective, "right" becomes "wrong." Our side has "freedom fighters," but their side has "terrorists." Your religion is "sacred" and "true," but their religion is "demonic," or "evil." The creation story of your faith is "fact," the creation story of their religion is "myth," the miracles described in the sacred texts of your religion actually happened, but the miracles described in another's sacred text never happened. Your favorite political group has the "truth," but their side is perhaps "mistaken," perhaps "dummies," certainly "wrong" or perhaps "bullheaded."

Instead of taking sides, the sage takes the viewpoint of Chuang-tzu's butterfly, the viewpoint from the center. From the perspective of eternity, the battle of "this" vs. "that" is not so important. All opposites are generated out of the common field which is Tao; thus all opposites are mutually supporting. This is realized by applying *ming*,[32] that is, applying illuminative discernment, clarity, or illumination. The pivot is the center of the opposites; it is the center of transformation, the center of the arising of things, and the center from which the *yin* and *yang* alternate. The center of a circle with radius of infinity is nowhere and everywhere.[33]

The Impossibility of Passing Judgment on Certain Truth or Good

Chuang-tzu discusses the topic of discriminating right from wrong in a clever dialogue in chapter 2:

---

[31] Burton Watson, *The Complete Works of Chuang Tzu*, chapter 2, p. 40.

[32] Chad Hanson suggests "a plurality of natural perspectives" as well as "discerning" and "understanding the guiding perspectives of others" for *ming* in his technical article on Chuang-tzu/Zhuangzi for the internet Stanford Encyclopedia of Philosophy, http://plato.stanford.edu/entries/zhuangzi/.

[33] This passage is discussed in Kuang-ming Wu, *The Butterfly As Companion: Meditations on the First Three Chapters of the Chuang-tzu* (NY: State University of New York Press, 1990), pp. 193-195.

Nieh Ch'ueh asked Wang Ni: "Do you know what all things agree in calling right?"

"How would I know that?" said Wang Ni.

"Do you know that you don't know it?"

"How would I know that?"

"Then do things know nothing?"

"How would I know that? However, suppose I try saying something. What way do I have of knowing that if I say I know something I don't really not know it? Or what way do I have of knowing that if I say I don't know something I don't really in fact know it? Now let me ask *you* some questions. If a man sleeps in a damp place, his back aches and he ends up half paralyzed, but is this true of a loach or eel? If he lives in a tree, he is terrified and shakes with fright, but is this true of a monkey? Of these three creatures, then, which one knows the proper place to live? . . . Men claim that Mao-ch'iang and Lady Li were beautiful, but if fish saw them they would dive to the bottom of the stream, if birds saw them they would fly away, and if deer saw them they would break into a run. Of these four, which knows how to fix the standard of beauty for the world? The way I see it, the rules of [Confucian] benevolence and righteousness and the paths of right and wrong are all hopelessly snarled and jumbled. How could I know anything about such discriminations?"[34]

Chuang-tzu is telling us that there are no objective standards independent of nature that we can use to measure things. We can agree that this box weighs 30 pounds, but disagree as to whether it is heavy or not heavy. Some find spiders terrifying; others find them interesting. These sorts of human judgments are not determined through rational processes.

From the perspective of Nature, things are neither right nor wrong. The lion which chases us is not evil or immoral; it is simply behaving naturally.[35] We do not argue that the tree that is merely 30 feet in height is wrong, and the 90-foot tree is right. We do not argue that the chirping of this bird is right, and the chirping of that bird is wrong. Morality is invoked only when there is some social moral rule which covers a situation, morality is not in nature. It is only our human **descriptions** of reality that involve morality, that involve right and wrong, and arguments about who is right and who is wrong are pointless. Discriminations between right and wrong are not illusory; rather knowledge of right and wrong, and social relationships are relative to the participants or observers, according to Chuang-tzu.

Chapter 2, "Discussing the Equality of Things," provides an extended discussion which concludes that right and wrong cannot be settled by argument.

Suppose that you argue with me. If you beat me, instead of my beating you, are you necessarily right and am I necessarily wrong? Or, if I beat you and not you me, am I necessarily right and are you necessarily wrong? Is the one of us right and the other wrong? Or are both of us right and both of us wrong? Both of us cannot come to a mutual and common understanding, and others are all in the dark. Whom shall I ask to settle this dispute? I may ask someone who agrees with you; but since he agrees with you, how can he settle it? I may ask someone who agrees with me; but since he agrees with me, how can he settle it? I may ask someone who differs from both you and me; but since he differs from both you and me, how can he settle it? I may ask someone who agrees with both you and me; but since he agrees with both you and me, how can he settle it? In this way, you and I and others would all be unable to come to a mutual and common understanding; should we wait for still another person?[36]

---

[34] Burton Watson, *The Complete Works of Chuang Tzu*, chapter 2, pp. 45–46.

[35] For more on this, see Franklin Perkins, *Heaven and Earth Are Not Humane: The Problem of Evil in Classical Chinese Philosophy* (Bloomington, IN: Indiana University Press, 2014).

[36] Fung Yu-lang, *A History of Chinese Philosophy, op. cit.*, p. 231.

Consider that with two people, either they agree or disagree. If they agree, there is no problem and they will call that "knowledge." The question is how are we to proceed if they disagree?

If they disagree, they ask a third party which of them is correct. If the third party agrees with (1), he says (1) is right; if the third party agrees with (2), he says (2) is correct; it is also possible that the third party will offer another entirely different alternative. We have not really settled the issue. How to proceed?

So, we can ask a fourth person -- either she agrees with (1) or (2) already -- and thus his/her opinion cannot settle the issue, or else he/she has still another viewpoint, which does not settle the argument. Chuang-tzu is not claiming that there is no such thing as knowledge. Rather, Chuang-tzu concludes that what we call knowledge is just knowledge of relations.[37]

"Three In the Morning"

Knowledge of the world is based upon distinctions we impose upon reality, distinctions which are relative; knowledge is expressed by terms which are relative to each other. Thus our knowledge cannot help but be relative; knowing this, we should not be bound by this relative knowledge, nor mistakenly take it for absolute certain knowledge (such as the certainty we can achieve with mathematical relationships). Use language, make distinctions, but never assume that your judgments about the world are certainly true. There is no absolute standard, judge, or law, by which we can establish absolute certain knowledge of the world. Things are just relative to our concepts and distinctions: why wear ourselves out by trying to make them into anything else? Chuang-tzu deals with dogmatic assertions about what is right in his famous fable of "Three In The Morning" which encourages us to "walk two roads":

> But to wear out your brain trying to make things into one without realizing that they are all the same — this is called "three in the morning." What do I mean by "three in the morning"? When the monkey trainer was handing out acorns he said, "You get three in the morning and four at night." This made all the monkeys furious. "Well, then," he said, "you get four in the morning and three at night." The monkeys were all delighted. There was no change in the reality behind the words, and yet the monkeys responded with joy and anger. Let them, if they want to. So the sage harmonizes with both right and wrong and rests in Heaven the Equalizer. This is called walking two roads.[38]

The monkeys are obsessed with the right way to do things and the wrong way to do things; they stress the correctness of how things ought to be. The trainer, who is a sage, realizes this, and instead of insisting that one way is better than another, or even pointing out to the monkeys that the two are equivalent, the sage "harmonizes with both right and wrong and rests in Heaven." The Taoist sage affirms both choices, like the monkey trainer. The sage doesn't get taken in by "three in the morning" which is equivalent to a dogmatic assertion that things can only be one way and no other way. Instead the sage harmonizes with both right and wrong and takes the position of the center of a circle whose radius is infinity. This is what Chuang-tzu called "walking two roads."

---

[37] Our modern notions of empirical knowledge which is repeatable and testable (scientific knowledge) did not yet exist in the West or in China. Western philosophers distinguish opinion from knowledge by authority, and although we do not have complete certainty even when there is a consensus of agreement among genuine authorities, it is considered reasonable to accept their conclusion. Even claims about empirical knowledge (things we know by seeing, hearing, touching, tasting, and smelling) can be understood to be relative. Consider: "I can see that building is tall." Chuang-tzu would answer, "Compared to what?"

[38] Burton Watson, *The Complete Works of Chuang Tzu*, chapter 2, p. 41.

17.6 METHODS TO ACHIEVE UNITY WITH THE TAO

We will discuss three methods found in the *Chuang-tzu* which are supposed to result in a person maximizing their innate creativity by experiencing harmony with the flow of Nature (Tao):

(1) To not be trapped by labels or concepts, or to be free-from-concepts (*wu-nien/wu-nian*), which is to have a mind that functions like a mirror.

(2) Mind-fasting and sitting in forgetfulness; stilling the incessant chattering of mind and achieving insight.

(3) To be "clear as the morning."

WU-NIEN (WUNIAN)

Wu-nien/wunian translated literally means "no thought" or "to be free from thinking."[39] This does not mean to make one's mind blank, *Wu-nien* means not to be carried away by thought in the process of thought. It means not to be trapped by names, by concepts, by arbitrary and conventional discriminations. A person of *wu-nien* sees things from more than one narrow perspective, sees things as a part of a single flowing organic whole, not individual items separate from one another. The ones who are trapped by *nien* (discriminative thinking) are the ones who use concepts to separate things into arbitrary, distinct compartments and assume that reality corresponds to these distinctions the person has just made. This is what passes for knowledge in the Confucian world, which does make such distinctions. Not to be trapped by concepts is to see the many possible pathways or perspectives possible on almost any issue. Next, we lessen the hold of the ego, because it is the ego which pushes us to assert "My view is correct; your view is wrong." Thus *wu-nien* means something like "free from being trapped by discriminative thinking while thinking."

When any person is totally and completely absorbed in what they are doing, they can be said to have forgotten the self. Such a person is lost in the moment. The subjective result is a state of tranquility, of quiet delight in all things equally. When you are totally focused upon a task (hitting a baseball, playing a musical instrument, absorbed in the setting sun or a swirling waterfall), discriminations and distinctions are irrelevant. This is the mind of *wu-nien*. The mind in such a state is tranquil and accepts what is; at that moment no anxiety or adversity touches such a mind. Acting effortlessly (*wu-wei*) with the flow of things, amazing feats of artistry and craftsmanship could be accomplished.

The Sage's Mind Functions LIKE A MIRROR

When we are no longer trapped by concepts (*wu-nien/wunian*), we can be said to have a mind like a mirror. A quality mirror simply reflects what is before it without distortion. When we have a mind like a mirror we are aware of what is before us, and we do not distort what we experience. For most people, unexamined assumptions, confusion, prejudice and bias distort perceptions. A mind like a mirror simply reflects events without categorizing, reinterpreting, distorting or holding onto them. For the mind like a mirror, the world is seen with a joy and acceptance of things without attachment to them. Such a mind is not greedy or possessive. Chapter 7 of the *Chuang-tzu* sounds much like the *Tao Te Ching* in the following passage:

Do not be an embodier of fame;

do not be a storehouse of schemes;

do not be an undertaker of projects;

do not be a proprietor of wisdom.

Embody to the fullest what has no end and wander where there is no trail.

---

[39] *Wu-nien/wunian*, "free from thought," will become important in the later Ch'an Buddhist traditions of China. See chapter 21.

Hold on to all that you have received from Heaven but do not think you have gotten anything.
Be empty, that is all.
The Perfect Man uses his mind like a mirror -
going after nothing, welcoming nothing, responding but not storing.
Therefore he can win out over things and not hurt himself.[40]

An American Buddhist student expresses the experience of mind-like-a-mirror as:

. . . reflecting the universe just as it is — in its totality, excluding nothing. It reflects all things in the universe in an equal way, just like a mirror. A mirror does not reflect only the beautiful and not the ugly, or only the colorful and not the drab, or only the rich and not the poor. It reflects everything, just as it is. It also reflects each thing in its uniqueness, each thing being what it is uniquely. The mirrorlike enlightened mind is able to respond appropriately to what it reflects.[41]

The Chinese poet seems to express the same idea of reflection as creativity:
The wild geese fly across the long sky above.
Their image is reflected upon the chilly water below.
The geese do not mean to cast their image on the water;
Nor does the water mean to hold the image of the geese.[42]

FASTING OF THE MIND

In chapter 4, "In the world of men," Chuang-tzu describes a technique which can be translated literally as "mind-fasting." Chuang-tzu creates an imaginary dialogue between Confucius and a disciple to explain the meaning of the term. The disciple seems to achieve an understanding which penetrates so deeply that he loses awareness of duality, an understanding which penetrates to the core of his existence.

The dialogue begins when the student, Yen Hui, calls on Confucius and asks permission to travel to the kingdom of Wei and set the murderous ruler on a correct path. Confucius inquires how he intends to accomplish this, since the king is as likely to execute Yen Hui as to listen to him. Yen Hui says that he will be ". . . punctilious and impartial, diligent and single-minded." Confucius laughs and says "Oh no, that's no good at all!"

Yen Hui keeps offering new strategies and for each strategy Confucius points out that being virtuous, moral, upright, sincere, benevolent and ceremonially proper is not enough. Finally Yen Hui runs out of strategies, and asks Confucius what to do. Confucius tells him that he must fast, but he does not mean avoiding meat or rich foods. Rather he must practice a fasting of the mind.

Yen Hui asks, what is "fasting of the mind?"
Confucius: "Maintain the unity of your will. Cease to listen with the ear, but listen with the mind. Cease to listen with the mind, but listen with the spirit [*ch'i/qi*]. The function of the ear is limited to hearing; the function of the mind is limited to forming images and ideas. As to the spirit [*ch'i/qi*], it is an emptiness responsive to all things. Tao abides in emptiness and emptiness is the fast of mind."[43]

---

[40] Burton Watson, *Chuang-tzu*, chapter 7, "Fit for Emperors and Kings", pp. 94-95.

[41] Elaine MacInnes, *The Flowing Bridge: Guidance on Beginning Zen Koans* (Boston: Wisdom, 2007), p. 23.

[42] Chang Chung-yuan, *op. cit.*, p. 57. This poem is frequently quoted in Ch'an Buddhist collections.

[43] Han-shan Te-ching, *op. cit.*, chapter 4, p. 15 of chuan 3.

Yen Hui said, "Before I heard this, I was certain that I was Hui. But now that I have heard it, there is no more Hui. Can this be called emptiness?"

"That's all there is to it," said Confucius."[44]

In other words, Yen Hui's insight is recognizing that . . . "The only obstacle which keeps me from practicing the fast of the mind lies in my self. As soon as I come to practice it, I realize that there has never been my self at all. Is this what you mean by emptiness?" "Exactly," said Confucius. "That is all there is to it! . . ."[45]

"Fasting of the mind" seems to be describing an egoless mind open to all things, perceiving things without adding distortion, bias, or prejudice (a mind like a mirror), and being so totally absorbed in the present that one is no longer aware of the ultimate distinction between subject and object. Chuang-tzu, the author of this imaginary dialogue, called this "emptiness of mind." Reality is flowing Tao, not separate individuals trapped in conceptual schemas trying to impose their will upon fellow humans and upon the world.

A good life is not the automatic result of wealth, or power, or social recognition. These are superficial values, related as "this" is to "that." One must understand that the same situation can been seen from a variety of perspectives. One person's fame ("this") is another person's suffering ("that"). For one person, wealth means the loss of the affection of spouse and children; for another, it enables those in need to find food, education, or a roof over their heads. Chuang-tzu suggests that a genuine good life is grounded in the quiet tranquility which lies underneath one's superficial conceptual mind. The realization of a good life is to be sought inside, by "fasting the mind."

STEEPED IN FORGETTING, or SITTING IN FORGETFULNESS

Another central concept in the Chuang-tzu is *tso-wang*, literally the Chinese characters for "to sit" and "forget." This might suggest something like the idea of repression in Freudian psychotherapy, but this is not what Chuang-tzu means. Indeed there is forgetting, but it is not uncomfortable or painful memories that one forgets. Rather, one forgets one's own ego and forgets one's sense of separateness from the world.[46] When we achieve being steeped in forgetfulness, dichotomies and differences no longer trap us. When your mind is so tranquil that you respond authentically to all that happens, without distortion, then one becomes one with the flow of the Tao. This is the state of mind of people we consider extraordinarily skilled, people like the great musician, athlete, or artisan.

In chapter 6 of the *Chuang-tzu*, the author creates another imaginary dialogue between Confucius and his disciple Yen Hui. Yen Hui tells Confucius that he is making progress; Confucius asks in what way:

"I have forgotten the Confucian virtues of benevolence [*jen*] and righteousness [*yi*]."

"Not enough," Confucius says.

"I have forgotten ceremonial rites [*li*] and music."

"That's good. But you still haven't got it."

"I am *steeped in forgetting*."

---

[44] Burton Watson, *The Complete Works of Chuang Tzu*, pp. 54–58. The same passage is translated slightly differently in A. C. Graham, *Chuang Tzu: The Inner Chapters*, pp. 66–68.

[45] John Wu, *The Golden Age of Zen* (New York: Doubleday Image, 1996), p. 39 and p. 41

[46] Livia Kohn, *Sitting in Oblivion: The Heart of Taoist Meditation* (Three Pines Press, 2010). This is understood as going into a deep trance, as "sitting in absorption" and might be an early form of seated meditation before Buddhism entered China. Professor Kohn traces the history of meditation (in the period nearly a thousand years after Chuang-tzu) in the later religious and philosophical Taoist traditions in this volume.

Confucius: "Explain what you mean by that."

"I have dropped the body and limbs and discarded intelligence and consciousness. Freed from the body and knowledge, I have become one with the Great Thoroughfare. This is what I mean by sitting in forgetfulness."

Confucius: "To be one with the Infinite is to have no more likes and preferences. To be thoroughly transformed is to have no more fixations. In this you have gone ahead of me. Let me follow in your steps."[47]

CLEAR AS THE MORNING

Chapter 6 of the *Chuang-tzu*, the author provides another interesting dialogue between a Taoist teacher, the elderly Woman Crookback, and Nan-po Tzu-k'uei/Nanbo Zikui. Nan-po Tzu-k'uei inquires of the Woman Crookback why she looks so young and fresh, and she tells him it is because she has heard the Tao, the Way. Intrigued, Nan-po Tzu-k'uei said to Chu Nu [Woman Crookback]: "Can one grasp and understand the Tao?"

Goodness, how could that be? Anyway, you aren't the person to do it. Pu-liang Yi had the ability to be a sage but not the Tao of a sage. I thought I would try to teach him and see if I could really get anywhere near to making him a sage. It's easier to explain the Tao of a sage to someone who has the talent of a sage, you know. I explained for three days, and after that he became detached from all the things under heaven.

Then I watched and guided him for seven days before he was detached from things sensual and material. I kept at him for nine days more, and after that he was detached from holding onto life. Only when one has been detached from the clinging to life can one be as *clear as the morning*.

After he had put life outside himself, he was able to achieve the *brightness of dawn*, and when he had achieved the brightness of dawn, he could see his own aloneness.

After he had seen his own aloneness, he could do away with past and present, and after he had done away with past and present, he was able to enter where there is no life and no death.[48]

When a person has attained the brightness of dawn, this is awakening insight. Ego is lost, at least temporarily. She is "in the zone." Such a person effortlessly adapts to the flowing patterns, accepting all and welcoming all, equal to all tasks. Is such a person oblivious to the world, lost in absorption, or is such a person open to the world without ego or judgment? Chuang-tzu never makes this clear.

17.7 EQUANIMITY TOWARDS DEATH

It is in the attitude toward death that we see how very different Chuang-tzu is from the many forms of religious Taoism. Chuang-tzu's attitude towards death is also profoundly different from his contemporary religious Taoists, and quite different from the common Western religious perspective. It has been said of western people that we all want to go to heaven, but no one wants to die. Religious Taoists seem frightened of death and want to extend

---

[47] Han-shan Te-ching/Hanshan dejing (1546–1620), *Lao-tzu Tao te ching Han-shan chieh* (Han-shan's Explanation of the *Tao Te Ching*) (Taipei, Taiwan: Shin Wen Hua Yin Shu Kuan, 1973), pp. 59–60.

[48] This translation is from the *Chuang-tzu yin-te/Zhungzi yindi* (The Harvard-Yenching Institute Concordance to the Chuang-tzu, Taipei reprint, 1966), pp. 16.36–17.41. An interestingly different translation is Brook Ziporyn, *Zhuangzi* (Indianapolis: Hackett Publishing, 2004), pp. 44–45.

life, want to achieve longevity and achieve something approaching immortality. Although Chuang-tzu does not deny the existence of immortals, or criticize the immortals, he seems to find their goal uninteresting.[49]

The *Chuang-tzu* finds death as natural as life. We can recognize this if only we will look around and pay attention to nature. Every bird, every tree, every squirrel, and every earthworm is born out of nature, grows, dies, and returns to nature. We could understand spring as the death of winter, but we are not unhappy about it. We could understand autumn as the death of summer, but normally we do not perceive it as a bad thing. Spring follows winter, autumn follows summer, and death follows birth. We could think of sunrise as the death of night, but we do not perceive it as a bad thing. It is due to human ego, human self-centeredness, and the fact that we have lost our sense of identity with Nature that we hope we will be exempt from this universal process.

For we humans to fear death and cling to life is to misunderstand profoundly the world and our place in it. There is always the swinging back and forth from the two extremes of *yin* and *yang*, and then a return. Yet the common origin for both extremes (i.e., birth and death) is the Tao itself. We are participants in the process whereby all things arise out of Tao and eventually return to Tao.

To return to the Tao is not to die and then live in heaven, or to die and be punished in a hell. For Chuang-tzu, there is neither reward nor judgment after death. The Taoists live within the alternation of *yin* and *yang*, and Chuang-tzu is fearless in his willingness to see that to embrace life requires us to embrace death as well. The alternation of life and death continues to cycle along, and both are the universal process of nature. We all enjoy sitting on a beach and watching a beautiful sunset. Sunset is the termination of and transformation of daytime, and can be enjoyed as such. If you are going to enjoy your life, you must also enjoy your death, for the two are equally important. Several passages in chapter 6 of the *Chuang-tzu* make this clear:

> The Great Clod [Nature, Tao] burdens me with form, labors me with life, eases me in old age, and rests me in death. So if I think well of my life, for the same reason I must think well of my death.[50]

and in this passage:

> . . . the human form has ten thousand changes that never come to an end. Your joys, then, must be uncountable. Therefore, the sage wanders in the realm where things cannot get away from him, and all are preserved. He delights in early death; he delights in old age; he delights in the beginning; he delights in the end.[51]

In the last story in chapter three, Chuang-tzu imagines the death of the great Lao-tzu. Lao-tzu's students and friends wail and cry. One follower, Ch'in Shih/Qin Shi went in, but chides those students of Lao-tzu who respond to his death with sadness and tears. He tells them, **In coming when he did, the Master was on time; in departing when he did, the Master was on course, and sadness and joy cannot find a way in.**[52]

> Your master [Lao Tzu] happened to come because it was his time, and he happened to leave because things follow along. If you are content with the time and willing to follow along, then grief and joy

---

[49] In the *Chuang-tzu* there are two extended references to immortals, one in chapter 11 and the other in chapter 12. Because these references are not in the Inner Chapters which are actually by Chuang-tzu, it is possible that these reflect interest in the immortals among later philosophical Taoists.

[50] Burton Watson, *The Complete Works of Chuang Tzu*, ch. 6, p. 80.

[51] *Ibid.*, p. 81

[52] Angus Graham's felicitous line from chapter 3 in his *Chuang-tzu: The Inner Chapters*, p. 65.

have no way to enter in. In the old days, this was called being freed from the bonds of the gods.[53]

The Tao is the pulsation of *yin* and *yang*, it is the swinging between birth and death, and Taoist wisdom is simply riding the flowing motion between the two poles; to prefer one and reject the other is a waste of energy (none of your tears will make any difference), and a falsification of the nature of reality.[54]

In chapter 6:39 of the *Chuang-tzu*, Taoist master Yu falls seriously ill, but responds to the ongoing transformation of life into death with both curiosity and with humor.

"My, my! So that which makes all things is making me all crookedy like this . . .".
"I don't resent it. I received life because the time had come; I will lose it because it is time to follow the order of things as they pass on. Be content in this time and find your place in this process, and then neither sorrow nor joy can touch you. . . .
Dying, he says, "Shoo, get back! Don't disturb the process of change!"

. . .

"Who can climb up to heaven and wander in the mists, roam the infinite, and forget life forever and forever?"[55]

As theoretical as this sounds, the concern with death takes a very personal turn in chapter 18. Hui-tzu/Huizi, a very close friend of Chuang-tzu, comes to help Chuang-tzu deal with his grief following the death of his wife.

Hui-tzu came to console him, but Chuang-tzu was sitting, legs akimbo, bashing a battered tub and singing.
Hui-tzu said: "You lived as man and wife, she reared your children. At her death surely the least you should be doing is to be on the verge of weeping, rather than banging the tub and singing: this is not right!"
Chuang-tzu said, "Certainly not. When she first died, I certainly mourned just like everyone else! However, I then thought back to her birth and to the very roots of her being, before she was born. Indeed, not just before she was born but before the time when her body was created. Not just before her body was created but before the very origin of her life's breath. Out of all of this, through the wonderful mystery of change she was given her life's breath. Her life's breath wrought a transformation and she had a body. Her body wrought a transformation and she was born. Now there is yet another transformation and she is dead. She is like the four seasons in the way that spring, summer, autumn and winter follow each other. She is now at peace, lying in her chamber, but if I were to sob and cry it would certainly appear that I could not comprehend the ways of destiny. This is why I stopped."[56]

---

[53] Burton Watson, *op. cit.*, ch. 3, pp. 52–53. The Chinese language has nothing resembling a capital letter, and the Chinese character can be translated "God" as Watson does, but more in keeping with traditional Chinese thought, this would be the divinities in heaven.

[54] In the *Rubiyat of Omar Khyam*, we find "The moving finger writes, and having writ, moves on, and all thy piety and wit cannot lure it back to cancel half a line, nor all thy tears wash out a word of it."

[55] To clarify the attitude towards death and dying, I have modified and omitted portions of the Burton Watson translation with reference to the *Chuang-tzu yin-te/Zhungzi yindi* (The Harvard-Yenching Institute Concordance to the Chuang-tzu), pp. 17–20. Burton Watson, *op. cit.*, ch. 6, pp. 80–84. The last line in Watson's elegant translation comes from a separate dialogue between three friends.

[56] Martin Palmer, *The Book of Chuang Tzu* (New York: Penguin ARKANA, 1996), introduction, p. xvii, from ch. 18.

The Taoist wisdom of Chuang-tzu involves creative egoless involvement in the continuing transformations of the Tao. There is no fear of death because one is creatively involved in every moment of life. No biases, no prejudices. When one is focused on the moment, there is no room for anxiety, for fear. Labels and concepts do not matter when one is engrossed in an activity (in this case, the activity of living).

Words point to reality, but no one assumes that words capture perfectly the way things are. Most of our social values are relative to our situation and our environment. There are no absolutes in Chuang-tzu's world-view. We wander freely enjoying our life, ignoring the painful pursuit of wealth and fame. Although logic is useful for solving math problems, or practical problems with automobiles and computers, it will not help you create an artistic masterpiece or provide you a key to ride the constantly transforming waves of *yin* and *yang*.

17.8 PHILOSOPHICAL TAOISM DURING LATER DYNASTIES

Towards the end of the second century in the common era (200 C.E.), the Confucian-dominated Han dynasty was ruled by weak and selfish rulers, and as a result, the empire suffered. There were political upheavals as well, with barbarian invasions from the north; military leaders took over and a period of disunity lasted for approximately 350 years (221–589 C.E.) until the Sui dynasty was able to impose order.

Confucian ideas were no longer perceived as the only possibilities, and many people turned more to Taoist ideas about life and politics. During this time period Indian Buddhism was growing in importance in China and Chinese Buddhist scholars began to have an influence upon the government, and ultimately, Chinese Buddhist priests began to exert influence over the government in the same manner Taoist priests and Confucians had in the past. Political Taoism combined with the appeal of Indian Buddhism pushed Confucianism into less prominence than it used to have. During Sui dynasty (589–618 C.E.) and T'ang dynasty (618–906 C.E.), Confucianism became more important but would not regain its luster as the single most important intellectual force for philosophy and theology for another 500 years. During the Sui and the T'ang dynasties, Taoism and Buddhism tended toward the greatest importance.

New forms of Taoism: DARK LEARNING

The Taoist classics include some of the greatest Chinese literature, masterpieces of wit and imagination. The world-view of Lao-tzu and Chuang-tzu has had a profound appeal to the most creative elements of Chinese society, the artists, philosophers, poets, and musicians, even though the great mass of Chinese did not find themselves attracted by the abstract primary principle of patterns of change of the universe (Tao). For this reason the philosophical ideas of the Taoists were primarily an upper-class phenomenon, which appealed especially to those with an aesthetic appreciation of life and nature.

Many of the philosophical Taoists (*Tao-chia/Daojia*) were literati or intellectuals who were disappointed with the feuding and corrupt kingdoms, and tried to find an aesthetically and creatively satisfying simple life far from the political realms. During the third century C.E., scholars, poets, musicians and painters who disdained official positions would gather together to enjoy one another's company. These scholars tended to focus their energies on the Taoism of Lao-tzu and Chuang-tzu.

The Seven Sages of the Bamboo Grove

One famous development in philosophical Taoism was the "Pure Talk" of the Seven Sages of the Bamboo Grove, a loose knit collection of third and fourth century officials who had shaken off the restraints of Confucianism, and became free spirits who sought an unconventional and carefree way of life. Although many of the "Dark Learning"

148

CHAPTER 17: THE *CHUANG-TZU*

Taoists focused on using Taoist ideas to rule the country, this group of Seven Sages sought to transcend the chaos of the the political realms. They detached themselves from their rigid social roles, and instead celebrated personal freedom and individualism: writing poetry, playing the Chinese *ch'in* (like a lute or a Japanese *koto*), and drinking wine until they reached a "glorious indifference to the world and intimacy with Tao."[57] Over an extended period of decades, the seven sages gathered together for "pure conversation" discussing just the philosophical ideas with no practical application, discussing the mysterious and profound dark reality which is the Tao/Way.

The group of scholars and musicians shared negative attitudes towards social authority. Included among the Dark Learning scholars were Wang Pi/Wangbi (225–249 C.E.) and Kuo Hsiang/Guo Xiang (d. 312 C.E.) who wrote early commentaries on the *Tao Te Ching* and the *Chuang-tzu*.[58] Another famous member of this group, Liu Ling (231–300 C.E.), used to have his servant follow him about, with a flask of wine in one hand and a shovel in the other. It was said that the wine was in case he wanted a drink, and the shovel was to bury him wherever he fell. Liu Ling preferred to remain natural and unclothed in his home, and when people came to visit him and were shocked at the absence of clothing, he would tell them: "I take heaven and earth for my pillars and roof, and the rooms of my house for my pants and coat. What are you gentlemen doing in my pants?"[59]

The great epoch of Taoist influence and power lasted from about 200 B.C.E. to 600 C.E. (i.e., the Han Dynasty through the chaotic period of the Six Dynasties). Much of the greatest Chinese nature poetry is Taoist in inspiration and imagery. Even when philosophical Taoism became less influential as an independent movement, the Ch'an school of Buddhism incorporated many of its aesthetic attitudes, ideas and insights, and Taoism lived on artistically and creatively within Chinese Ch'an Buddhism.

17.9 APPLYING THE FUNDAMENTAL INSIGHTS OF PHILOSOPHICAL TAOISM

Although the Taoism of Lao-tzu and Chuang-tzu might seem far removed from our modern lives, there are insights of the *Tao Te Ching* and the *Chuang-tzu* which might apply to our lives in the modern world.[60] In the hurried world of most of us, many human beings have lost touch with nature, lost touch with running streams and trees and the stars overhead at night. What does nature sound like? What does nature smell like? It is not jackhammers and auto exhausts. It is difficult to be a Taoist sage in a world of asphalt and bricks. The Taoist suggests that having lost touch with nature, we find that our lives do not go smoothly, things are not comfortable; we are anxious, we are unhappy. We are in a hurry and cannot find time to relax our minds. We are not at peace with ourselves and we experience social conflict. The chaos and misery of armed conflict will follow. Here is a summary of the main points of Taoism which might apply to our world.[61]

[57] David Howard Smith, *Wisdom of the Taoists* (New York: New Directions, 1980), p. 23.

[58] These commentaries are dealt with in the first several chapters of Alan K. L. Chan, Yuet-Keung Lo, eds. *Philosophy and Religion in Early Medieval China* (Albany: State University of New York Press, 2010).

[59] Holmes Welch, *Taoism: The Parting of the Way, Revised edition*, pp. 124–125; Richard B. Mather, trans., *Liu I-ch'ing, Shih-shuo Hsin-yu: A New Account of Tales of the World* (Minneapolis: University of Minnesota Press, 1976), p. 374.

[60] Many of these Taoist ideas are echoed in some modern psychology. See Abraham Maslow, *The Farther Reaches of Human Nature* (New York: Penguin, 1993). pp. 61–71; also many of the books by Alexander Lowen on what he called "Bio-Energetics."

[61] The student might consult Sam Crane, *Life, Liberty, and the Pursuit of Tao: Ancient Chinese Thought in Modern American Life* (London: Wiley Blackwell, 2013).

CHAPTER 17: THE *CHUANG-TZU*

FIRST INSIGHT: knowing the facts of science, economics and history are important, but they are not sufficient to provide a good life. There are other factors which are also valuable guides to life. One of these factors is an appreciation for the world we inhabit, the realm of nature. Western society is one which has completely lost touch with nature's rhythms; we have even lost touch with our own bodily rhythms.

We do live in nature (although this might remain unnoticed if we live in large urban areas), and there are patterns in life and patterns in nature including the seasonal changes. These patterns are internal as well; they include the patterns of your own body, patterns of breathing, heartbeat rhythms, rhythms of walking and running. There are the patterns of awake and sleep. Find the rhythms of your own life, and harmonize these with the patterns of nature. When the rhythms of your life are not harmonized with the rhythms of your own body and nature, inner turmoil is created.

When your ignore your own rhythms and try to live in accordance with externally imposed rhythms (the clock, the job, or your class schedule), it is like living on a treadmill, running just to keep up; the personal meaning goes out of one's life. The Taoist path is to take a deep breath, quiet down, and pay genuine attention to the sights, sounds, and smells of the natural realm. The minute we think we know how something ought to turn out, we structure the situation that way instead of allowing it to turn out naturally. We human beings need to learn to be less aggressive, to learn to leave things alone.

SECOND INSIGHT: live fully in the present. Do not spend all of your efforts thinking about how things will be in the future, planning how great things will be when you finally leave home after you graduate, after you're married, after you get your new car, after you retire . . . Do not sit in class daydreaming about how great the future will be. When you start putting your energies into the future, you miss your actual life. The only life you have got is here-and-now, and nowhere else. You must not treat the present merely as a means toward some future end. Live fully in the **now**, which is all there is to your life, and all there can be. Be fully present even for the sad and painful things; along with the good things, these are our life.

THIRD INSIGHT: we do need to become less serious and more like the happy child we once were (the uncarved block and the innocence of the small child). Be more natural, more spontaneous, be more open and less judgmental. Be more receptive to the way things are and do not demand that things work out the way you want them to. Do not demand that the present must correspond to your desires, wishes, or expectations, or the desires and expectations of your political or religious group. Do not be taken in by fads, fashions, dogmas, habits, "shoulds" or "oughts." And, just like a child, when you are hungry, that is when you should eat, and when you are tired, that is when you should sleep. Too many of us are unable to even feel when we should eat and when we should sleep. We eat when we are not hungry; we try to sleep when we are not tired; when we are tired, we cannot sleep.

FOURTH INSIGHT: Be free to be who and what you are, without fear. For the Taoist, what we might call the "true self" is deeper than social conditioning, it is not ego-centered, is not bigoted, but it is buried deeply out of sight. With so much social conditioning since earliest childhood, it can take much effort to reveal the deeper self. You need to lose and again lose, to simplify, until all that is left is the spontaneous true self.[62] When you have found your true nature, you can be free of what others may think. Drop your masks, drop your efforts to be what other people want you to be, drop your efforts to impress others, to influence others, to please others, to be loved, to win applause. Become less judgmental of others, but especially less judgmental of your own person. Free yourself from your own fears. Worry less about what others think; be less ego-centered ("sitting in forgetfulness"). Shyness and lack of self-confidence will fade. Find something that you can become totally absorbed in. When you are absorbed in what you are doing, you will not be self-conscious, you will be less critical of your self, and free to be yourself. Become fully functioning, letting your abilities and capacities flow without trying (*wu-wei*) too hard, behaving thoughtlessly (*wu-nien*).

---

[62] The ancient world never heard of abnormal psychology, never heard of biological problems with the brain, and thought we could be trusted in our deepest selves. Clearly the Taoist would not want a sociopathic personality to act spontaneously.

17.10 SUMMARY OF THE CHAPTER

In this chapter we have discussed one of the enduring contributions of China to spiritual pathways. Chuang-tzu is a philosophical Taoist like Lao-tzu. The two of them share a vision of the world in which everything is in harmony, but a vision of the world wherein human laws and social sanctions are not so very important. The world is our home, not a temporary place we are visiting. We belong to this world. We are part of nature.

The goal of the follower of Chuang-tzu is an egoless feeling of being at home everywhere, a sense of full and complete participation in every moment, a sense of playful interaction with the varying patterns of *yin* and *yang* which constitute Tao. The philosophical Taoists do not think humans are different from Nature (Tao); we humans are Nature and as natural as all the other living things on our planet. Heavenly beings such as gods and spirits may exist but they too are natural and play no special role in spirituality. The gods are little more than powerful bureaucrats.

The spiritual life is right before us; simply stop separating yourself from the world and break free from the prison of rules, concepts, ideas, and words which provide a defective roadmap for how to live. To be at harmony with the Tao is to be serenely at peace.

Chuang-tzu/Zhuangzi certainly knows many of the sayings of the *Tao Te Ching*, and shares the goals of *wu-wei* ("non-action"), *tzu-jan* ("spontaneity"), *te* (the natural power of the Tao), and the desirability of being in harmony with the Tao, but the *Chuang-tzu* goes off into different territory. Chuang-tzu has no interest in advising a ruler how to rule. Chuang-tzu's advice is return to the countryside where you can truly follow your heart, dance, play an instrument, or go fishing!

When we escape the trap of a strictly human-based perspective, we realize that the useless is useful; the ugly is as valuable as the beautiful, the silences and rests are as important as the musical notes. One person's misfortune is another's fortune. If one can see the world from the center, from the axis of Tao, then one achieves a perspective which is not limited by claims of what is true vs. what is false. If each person offers her own narrow perspective on reality, then the ideal view is the one that soars above each individual perspective. From the perspective of the sage, all things are equally what-they-are. The beautiful mountain is not better than the small hill; each simply is. We need to be a fully active participant in a world where everything is best, and then we will not be trapped by discriminations, distinctions, and concepts. This is the state of *wu-nien*, to be free from concepts.

17.12 TECHNICAL TERMS

Chuang-tzu/Zhuangzi   Lao-tzu/Laozi

Tao	The Way, the Pathway, mother Nature, the source.
Tao-chia/Taojia	Philosophical Taoism, the "School of Tao."
Tao-chiao/Taojiao	Religious Taoism, the "Teaching of Tao."

Tao Te Ching/Daodejing	The Classic of the Way and Its Power and Virtue
te/de	Virtue; positive potentiality to influence others for the better.
tzu-jan/ziran	Spontaneity, naturalness, literally "of itself so."

wu-nien/wunian	To be free from thinking, free from concepts, literally "no-mind."
wu-wei/wuwei	No unnatural action, spontaneous activity, literally "non-action."

yin/yang	The feminine and the masculine, passive and active. The alternation of the two constitute the

Tao.

17.13 QUESTIONS FOR FURTHER DISCUSSION

(1) On what issues do the *Tao Te Ching* agree with the *Chuang-tzu*, and on what issues do the two Taoist classics disagree? Do they agree on politics? Do they agree on the ideal life of a sage? Do they agree on artistic creativity? Do they agree on life and death?

(2) Chuang-tzu's attitudes towards what is important in life, and what is not important in life, seem to be very different from most people living in the Western world. What is most important for a good life, according to Chuang-tzu?

(3) One of the most famous stories from Chinese thought is Chuang-tzu's dreaming that he was a butterfly. What do you think was Chuang-tzu's point when he told this story [can there be more than one answer]?

(4) Thinking logically is very important if one is repairing an automobile, or trying to analyze an illness from the symptoms. However, is logic equally useful in choosing a mate? Should we do a cost-benefit analysis in choosing our friends?

(5) Chuang-tzu seems to be advocating an unstructured freely roaming lifestyle of spontaneity. However, many people are very uncomfortable without some sort of a structure to their life. In fact, some people require structure. Where do you stand on this issue? Which appeals to you?

(6) The Confucians say that we are not serious enough about our lives, and must become more serious in social relationships if we want a life of harmony. The Taoists say we are too serious about our lives, and must relax and respond intuitively in our social relationships which puts us in harmony with Nature. Where do you stand on this issue?

(7) Someone who perceives the world as a battle between absolute good and absolute evil, would probably reject Chuang-tzu's analysis of good and evil. For Chuang-tzu, good and evil are related like "this" and "that," so that an action that is good from one perspective (build a dam to ensure water supplies) can be bad from another (disrupt the ecosystem and cause species to become extinct). Chuang-tzu seems to be advocating that we recognize how much our value judgments are affected by our perspectives. What is your reaction to Chuang-tzu's position?

SELECTED BIBLIOGRAPHY

Philosophical Taoism: Translations of the *Chuang-tzu*

English, Jane and Gia-fu Feng, *Chuang Tsu: Inner Chapters* (New York: Vintage Books, 1974)
Graham, Angus C., *Chuang-tzu: The Seven Inner Chapters and Other Writings* (London: George Allen & Unwin, 1981).
Mair, Victor H., *Wandering on the Way: Early Taoist Tales and Parables of Chuang Tzu* (New York: Bantam Books, 1994)
Merton, Thomas, *The Way of Chuang Tzu* (New York: New Directions, 1965)

CHAPTER 17: THE *CHUANG-TZU*

Ming, Chang Wai, *The Book of Chuang Tzu* (New York: The Penguin Group, 2007)

Martin Palmer, *The Book of Chuang Tzu* ( )

Roth, Harold D., "A Companion to Angus C. Graham's *Chuang Tzu: The Inner Chapters*" (Monograph of the Society for Asian and Comparative Philosophy, 2003)

Watson, Burton, *Chuang Tzu: Basic Writings* (New York: Columbia University Press, 1964)

Watson, Burton, *The Complete Writings of Chuang Tzu* (New York: Columbia, 1968)

Ziporyn, Brook, *Zhuangzi: The Essential Writings* (New York: Columbia University, 2006).

Philosophical Taoism: Studies of the *Chuang-tzu*

Allinson, Robert E., *Chuang-Tzu For Spiritual Transformation* (New York: State University of New York Press, 1989)

Chan, Alan K. L., Yuet-Keung Lo, eds. *Philosophy and Religion in Early Medieval China* (Albany: State University of New York Press, 2010)

Chang Chung-yuan, *Creativity and Taoism: A Study of Chinese Philosophy, Art, and Poetry* (New York: Julian Press, 1963). Reprinted by Jessica Kingsley Books, 2011.

Cook, Scott, *Hiding the World In The World: Uneven Discourses on the Zhuangzi* (New York: State University of New York Press, 2003)

Coutinho, Steve, *Zhuangzi and Early Chinese Philosophy* (Burlington, VT: Ashgate, 2005)

Creel, Herlee G., *What is Taoism?* (Chicago IL: University of Chicago Press, 1970)

Fung, Yu-lan, *A History of Chinese Philosophy: Volume I* (Princeton, NJ: Princeton University Press, 1952)

Jullien, Francois, *In Praise of Blandness: Proceeding from Chinese Thought and Aesthetics*, translated by Paula M. Varsano (New York: Zone Books, 2004)

Kjellberg, Paul and Philip J. Ivanhoe, eds., *Essays on Skepticism, Relativism, and Ethics in the Zhuangzi* (New York: State University of New York Press, 1996)

Klein, Esther, "Were there 'Inner Chapters' in the Warring States? A New Examination of Evidence about the Zhuangzi," *T'oung Pao* 96 (2011): 299-369.

Kohn, Livia, *Sitting in Oblivion: The Heart of Taoist Meditation* (Three Pines Press, 2010). Taoist meditation as practiced by later traditions of religious Taoism.

Kohn, Livia, *Zhuangzi: Text and Context* (Three Pines Press, 2014) Professor Kohn presents the Chuang-tzu/Zhuangzi book as seen through the eyes of the religious Taoist traditions.

Mair, Victor H., ed. *Experimental Essays on Chuang-tzu* (Honolulu: University of Hawaii Press, 1983)

Mair, Victor H., *Wandering on the Way: Early Taoist Tales and Parables of Chuang Tzu* (New York: Bantam Books, 1994)

Moeller, Hans-Georg, *Taoism Explained: From the Dream of the Butterfly to the Fishnet Allegory* (Chicago: Open Court, 2004)

Martin Palmer, with Elizabeth Breuilly, *The Book of Chuang Tzu* (New York: Arkana Penguin Books, 1996)

Rosemont Jr., Henry, ed., *Chinese Texts and Philosophical Contexts* (LaSalle, Illinois: Open Court, 1991)

Roth, Harold D., "A Companion to Angus C. Graham's *Chuang Tzu: The Inner Chapters*" (Monograph of the Society for Asian and Comparative Philosophy, 2003)

Roth, Harold D., *Original Tao: Inward Training and the Foundations of Taoist Mysticism* (New York: Columbia University Press, 1999)

Roth, Harold D., "Who Compiled the *Chuang Tzu*?" in Henry Rosemont Jr., ed., *Chinese Texts and Philosophical Contexts* (LaSalle, Illinois: Open Court, 1991)

Slingerland, Edward, *Effortless Action: Wu-wei As Conceptual Metaphor and Spiritual Ideal in Early China* (New York: Crown Books, 2014)

Slingerland, Edward, *Trying Not to Try: The Art and Science of Spontaneity* (New York: Oxford University Press, 2007)

Smith, David Howard, *Wisdom of the Taoists* (New York: New Directions, 1980)

Watson, Burton, *The Complete Writings of Chuang Tzu* (New York: Columbia, 1968)

Welch, Holmes, *Taoism: The Parting of the Way, Revised edition* (Beacon Press, 1971)

Wu, Kuang-Ming, *The Butterfly as Companion: Meditations on the First Three Chapters of the Chuang-tzu* (New York: State

University of New York Press, 1990)

Wu Kuang-Ming, *Chuang Tzu: World Philosopher at Play* (New York: Crossroads Publishing Company and Scholar's Press, 1982).

See also:

Lagerway, John, and Marc Kalinowski, eds., *Early Chinese Religion: Part One: Shang Through Han* (1250 BC -220 AD) (Leiden & Boston: Brill, 2011)

Lagerway, John, and Lu Pengzhi, eds., *Early Chinese Religion: Part Two: The Period of Division* (220 AD -529 AD) (Leiden & Boston: Brill, 2010)

Perkins, Franklin, *Heaven and Earth Are Not Humane: The Problem of Evil in Classical Chinese Philosophy* (Indiana University Press, 2014)

Van Norden, Bryan W., *Introduction to Classical Chinese Philosophy* (Cambridge: Hackett Publishing, 2011)

Han-shan Te-ching (1546–1620), *Lao-tzu Tao-te-ching Han-shan chieh* ("Han-shan's Explanation of the *Lao-tzu Tao-te-ching*"), Taipei, Taiwan: Shin Wen Hua Yin Shu Kuan, 1973. This volume also includes Han-shan's explication of the *Chuang-tzu* text as well.

Internet article:

Hanson, Chad, "Zhuangzi" in the Stanford Encyclopedia of Philosophy, http://plato.stanford.edu/entries/zhuangzi/

CHAPTER 18: RELIGIOUS TAOISM

18.1 OVERVIEW OF THE CHAPTER

In the previous chapters, we discussed Confucianism and *Tao-chia*, the philosophical variety of Chinese Taoism. Both Confucianism and philosophical Taoism belong to the Grand Tradition, the realm of the well-educated, the political leaders, the literati, the elite artists, musicians and poets. These aspects of Taoism were abstract, theoretical, and poetical. When it comes to the ordinary folk in China, these Grand Tradition forms were not quite as important.

Popular Chinese folk religion tends towards shamanism, spirits and gods, and magical rituals and ceremonies with which we can interact with spirits and gods. The majority of the people draw upon a wide variety of religious practices and apart from monks or priests, very few people in China were exclusively followers of Confucius, or exclusively Taoists, or exclusively Buddhists. Popular Little Tradition religion of the people has been a creative and ever-changing mixture of Confucianism, Taoism, Buddhism, reverence for ancestors and heavenly beings, myths of sacred beings and great emperors of the past, myths of recluse immortals, all combined with local and regional beliefs and shamanistic practices which focus upon local gods. Popular Chinese religious attitudes draw upon the common tales and myths, and the common community practices.

Although many of these thought-systems did affect the Chinese world-view, the widely varying cluster of beliefs and practices which we call religious Taoism (*Tao-chiao*) is a singularly important element influencing popular Chinese religion. Although there never was a single unified church of religious Taoism, "... [religious] Taoism appears as a force which orders and gives theological meaning to the religion of the Chinese people. ... The Taoist is himself a devout believer in the religion of the Chinese people, and as such performs a role in the community of expert in religious affairs."[1] Taoist priests would claim to be possessed by spirits, and speak with and for these beings in parallel realms.

In the second century C.E., religious Taoism elevated Lao-tzu to the status of a god, understanding him as a miraculous savior and the head of a church and a political movement. The religious Taoists were very practical. They were involved in all aspects of Chinese religious life, including performing community rituals designed to control spirits, bring the blessings of heaven, and cure illnesses (illness was often believed to be caused by spirits residing in certain areas of the human body). Religious Taoism is the basis for most of what is called traditional Chinese medicine. In general, religious Taoism has been heavily oriented towards rituals: sacraments; ritual initiations; purification rituals; ordination rituals; a major ritual for the annual renewal of the cycle of life (after Buddhism entered China, many Buddhist rituals were incorporated into ritual religious Taoism).

One of the defining characteristics of religious Taoism is the search for personal longevity, even immortality. Clearly, being healthy is relevant to longevity. However, longevity meant much more than just being healthy. The religious Taoists asserted that performing their rituals and following their practices offered the possibility of living healthily in this very body for hundreds of years. Taoist immortality was both physical and spiritual. To accomplish this, the religious Taoists used different techniques including alchemy, physical forms of exercise, and meditative introspection.

Priests would drive evil spirits out of the body, thereby improving health. In addition, sexual exercises were

---

[1] Michael Saso, *Taoism and the Rite of Cosmic Renewal* (Washington State University Press, 1972), p. 1.

utilized, breathing exercises were used, physical stretching and bending were used, and esoteric mixtures and combinations of herbs and 'medicines' were also ingested. Religious Taoists ate concoctions made of ingredients composed of stuff like cranes, tortoises, cicadas, butterflies, pine, cinnabar, and gold dust.

Some in China avoided society and sought life in the mountains as Taoist hermits, or sought inner peace with various devices including physical exercises and herbs, minerals and other 'medicines.' It is not surprising that many Chinese desired to find a paradise where everything was peaceful and beautiful, and where the inhabitants lived exceptionally long and satisfying lives. These desires are what religious Taoism claims to satisfy, and this is much of the appeal of religious Taoism.

Popular Chinese religion is an interesting intermixture of Confucianism, Buddhism, literary and philosophical Taoism, and the great cluster of practices we call religious Taoism, set against a background of insecurity and violence. We need to understand each of these if we wish to understand the basic ideas of Chinese thought.[2]

CHINESE DYNASTIES DISCUSSED IN THIS CHAPTER

Shang Dynasty c. 1600 – 1100 BCE
Chou/Zhou dynasty c. 1122 – 771 BCE
Period of Disunity 769 – 202 BCE
Ch'in/Qin (221 BCE – 207 BCE)
   (Legalists/Law & Order)
Han dynasty 202 BCE – 220 C.E.
   Southern & Northern Dynasties (420–589)
Sui (590–618 C.E.)
T'ang/Tang (618–906 C.E.)
   Five Dynasties (907–960)
Sung/Song (960–1279)
Yuan (1280–1368)
Ming (1368–1644)
Ch'ing/Ching (1644–1912)

18.2 THE TWO FORMS OF TAOISM

In the previous two chapters we discussed the two dominant thinkers of *Tao-chia/Daojia*, the philosophical forms of Taoism, and the two classic texts associated with these sages, the *Tao Te Ching* and the *Chuang-tzu*.[3] In this chapter, we will discuss the wide-ranging cluster of beliefs and practices which have been traditionally associated with

---

[2] As pointed out in a previous chapter, the scholar Isabelle Robinet denies that these are two separable forms of Taoism, and sees the so-called "religious" Taoist practices as techniques employed by the so-called "philosophers" that lead to the mystical experiences and to ecstasy as depicted in philosophical Taoist texts. Isabelle Robinet, *Taoism: Growth of a Religion* (Stanford University Press, 1997).

[3] Much of *philosophical* Taoism was unsatisfactory for those who wanted a meaningful connection to the spirits and gods. Tao is not a divine personal being who loves human beings and cares for them. No one's life is improved by belief in Tao and Tao does not respond to prayers or sacrifices. Tao is passive, devoid of action, thought, feeling and desires. Tao cannot be obeyed or disobeyed — Tao is the pattern of all of nature when it behaves spontaneously. In contrast to this, *religious* Taoism offers spirits and gods who interact with us, who respond to prayers and sacrifices, and can be bribed with gifts, and who can be manipulated by shamans with esoteric knowledge.

non-philosophical Taoism, *Tao-chiao/Daojiao*, or religious Taoism.[4]

The term "Religious Taoism" is misleading, because there never was a single group of people to whom the label could be applied. There never was a supreme leader or pope for these groups. There were scriptures, but there was no holy scripture to which all looked upon with reverence. The term "religious Taoism" applies to a broad range of practices, and applies to numerous diverse groups of people. Speaking very generally, religious Taoism encompassed several different groups of teachers including those who specialized in magic, in fortune telling and healing, and also teachers who claimed to hold the secret to long life, or even immortality.[5] Actually there are many forms of non-philosophical Taoism, which intermix and overlap.

In this chapter we will explore a few of the most important ideas of these different streams. The defining characteristic of the majority of these forms is the shamanistic belief that someone with the proper esoteric knowledge can mediate between the human realm and the invisible realm of spirits and demons, and using that proper knowledge, the religious Taoist can provide protection and numerous benefits. Primary among these benefits is the ability to extend one's life, often by exorcizing demons, although there was political and monastic Taoism as well. Major forms of religious Taoism continue even into modern China, especially in Hong Kong and Taiwan. In contemporary Taiwan, scholars distinguish five orders of religious Taoists among the Taoist priesthood.[6]

We must also stress the fact that this chapter is a simple overview. The topics discussed in this chapter (and indeed, in each chapter in the book) are much more complex than they appear in a simple overview. The actual practices and symbols involved in religious Taoism are the study of a lifetime, and all we can do here is indicate the important features.

Much of the material discussed in this chapter on religious Taoism is esoteric, it is secret, and should not be discussed by anyone other than the serious student of the priest who has spent a lifetime mastering the techniques and systems of symbols. Scholars believe that much of esoteric religious Taoism has borrowed from Chinese Tantric Buddhist thought originating in India. For example, there are Taoist "thunder-magic" sects which have borrowed heavily from Vajrayana Tantric Buddhism.[7] Other forms of Buddhism influenced religious Taoism with the important concepts of the bodhisattva ideal of universal liberation of all beings, not merely salvation for one's own ancestors. Buddhist burial practices and rituals also had a great influence on popular religion in China.

The Texts of Religious Taoism

The *Tao-tsang/Daozang* is the major collection of documents of religious Taoism, but was first compiled after 1442, and collected together over a thousand disparate essays and scriptures. The religious Taoist texts were not like

---

[4] As mentioned before, the scholar Isabelle Robinet (*Taoism: Growth of a Religion*, op. cit., trans. Phyllis Brooks) has argued that what we refer to as "religious Taoism" is simply not separable from philosophical Taoism, and that Taoism has always been a religion. Others see later religious *Tao-chiao/Daojiao* Taoists adopting quotes from the *Tao Te Ching* and the *Chuang-tzu* and interpreting them using religious exegesis. Chinese Buddhists seem to have believed there were at least two forms of Taoism. In 637 C.E., Buddhists pointed out to the Taoist emperor that Lao-tzu wore ordinary garb, not Taoist priestly robes and turbans, did not have disciples or a "school" of followers, did not establish or visit temples, did not try to control spirits, and that the ideas of religious Taoist priests had no real relationship with the actual teachings of Lao-tzu.

[5] Eva Wong, *The Shambhala Guide to Taoism* (Boston: Shambhala, 1997), p. 32.

[6] See Michael Saso, *Taoism and the Rite of Cosmic Renewal*, chapter 5: Five Kinds of Taoism.

[7] Michael Saso, *The Teachings of Taoist Master Chuang* (New Haven: Yale University Press, 1978), pp. 7-13. The Tantric Thunder Magic Taoist sect is Hua-shan Taoism, using exorcism and purification rituals to oppose evil "Taoists of the Left" who use their power to cause harm. Those sympathetic to Chinese esoteric religious Taoist thought explain the similarity between Indian Tantric rituals and religious Taoism by claiming that Chinese esoteric ideas influenced Indian Tantric Buddhism, and not vice versa.

Confucian texts.

It includes the works of philosophers like Laozi and Zhuangzi, pharmacopoeias, the oldest Chinese work on medicine, lives of the saints, long ritual texts larded with sympathetic magic, imaginary geographies, dietary and hygienic prescriptions, anthologies of hymns, speculations on hexagrams in the *Book of Change*, guides to meditation techniques, alchemical texts, and collections of moral precepts.[8]

The texts of religious Taoism were not intended for ordinary folk to read, or even for the well-educated. The religious Taoist texts claimed to reveal cosmic secrets to priests who had special training, and each priest would have had teachers who could uncover the esoteric meanings hidden in the obscure language.[9] These were texts filled with secret knowledge and magical formulas, completely unlike the texts associated with philosophical Taoism, texts like the *Lao-tzu* and the *Chuang-tzu*.

Of course these non-philosophical Taoists were perfectly aware of the Confucian classic texts, and shared most of the Confucian assumptions about reality and about society. Chinese family structure and Chinese morality were grounded in Confucian thought. The majority of the common people did not think of themselves as Taoists in opposition to Confucians. All Chinese shared Confucian and Taoist perspectives. The religious Taoists we discuss in this chapter placed greater stress on specific religious Taoist approaches, but for most Chinese, Taoism was a supplement to Confucianism and not opposed to Confucianism.

Goals of Non-philosophical Religious Taoism

The many different goals of non-philosophical religious Taoism help us to understand some of the ways that non-philosophical Taoism functioned in popular Chinese religion. Achieving those goals often involve *te/de* (which we previously translated as "virtue" or "positive potentiality" in the context of Confucianism), which for the religious Taoist is a kind of power of the Tao/Dao, the supernatural power to transform reality. The religious Taoist goals included the following:

Extend one's life well beyond ordinary limits; "long life without aging."
Become a Taoist immortal by achieving union with transcendent Tao.
Obtain good fortune,[10] make money, achieve fame and acquire power.
Cure illness, obtain healing powers, win blessings, expel demons.
Perform funeral and burial rituals for the dead.
Perform rites for seasonal renewal of village which can bring forth a new beginning as spring is a renewal of nature following a cold winter.
Bring blessings on one's village, or social groups, or individuals, using magic.
Establish a Taoist theocracy, a government run by Taoist religious leaders who could return the country to the Golden Age.
Obtain salvation for those who have died and are being punished in purgatories or hells (important only after

---

[8] Isabelle Robinet, *Taoism: Growth of a Religion*, p. xii.

[9] As noted, the collection of religious Taoist texts is a huge storehouse of over a thousand documents, containing books of magical spells, visions, advice on diet and hygiene, metaphysical claims about reality or cosmology, explanations of how to absorb energy to extend life, ritual texts and collections of alchemical speculations. Very little of this material has been studied or translated.

[10] In China, "good fortune" is symbolized by the swastika symbol (the cross with four ends bent at right angles to rotate clockwise). It is a symbol of the four directions, and later, represents the number ten-thousand or "uncountably many." The swastika symbol in China is used to wish someone ten-thousand years of good fortune. The same symbol was used by the ancient Greeks, Celts, ancient India, Native Americans, and Anglo-Saxons, and was popular in the USA prior to WW II.

Buddhism came to China).

In Chinese communities, individuals and groups would hire shamanistic Taoist priests who claimed to be able to control spirits in supernatural realms who will do one's bidding. These religious Taoist priests claimed to provide benefits to the person who hired them, but some of the priests also claimed to be able to do black magic, that is, to be able to harm others with magic spells, invoking and controlling malevolent spirits with the popular esoteric ritual knowledge of a Taoist priest, preserved by a family or clan and taught to the priest by his father.

The central imperial government was most often controlled by Confucians, who had privilege and power, and many of whom treated popular Chinese religion as lowly superstitions fit for peasants. Thus institutional forms of religious Taoism were a means for the people to express their resentment and anger at the Confucian elite, and to meet the religious needs of the common folk in local communities.

18.3 TYPES OF RELIGIOUS TAOISM

As mentioned before, there is no single religious tradition which comprises religious Taoism. There are many varieties of religious Taoism, and they are interwoven and intertwine. A person might be involved in only one of these, or many of these forms. Some Taoists separated themselves from community life and lived in mountains and monasteries, following unusual diets and mastering what appears to be meditation and concentration. Some priests married and lived among the people and performed rituals for the benefit of individuals and the community. These operated outside the boundaries of institutional Taoism.

Many scholars believe that during the second century B.C.E., several of these separate strands began to congeal into something which many scholars refer to as "religious Taoism." The main themes of religious Taoism were fully developed and solidified by the first half of the fourth century C.E.

Religious Taoism is essentially connected with popular Chinese religions. Although there is a body of common doctrines available to the masses (involving the *yin*, the *yang*, and the five processes of wood, metal, earth, water and fire), most of religious Taoism's forms involve esoteric knowledge, that is, they contain secret knowledge which is intentionally kept from outsiders.

Speaking broadly, we might distinguish between several interwoven strands that comprise non-philosophical Taoism:

(1) Institutional Non-military Political religious Taoism;
(2) Military Political Taoism,
(3) Communal Shamanistic Taoism;
(4) Alchemical Taoism;
(5) Monastic Taoism influenced by Buddhism;
(6) Philosophical inspirations where Taoist priests interpreted Lao-tzu and Chuang-tzu as supporting the longevity goals of religious Taoism.

(1) Institutional Non-military Political Taoism

There are forms of religious Taoism which are institutional and political, which originally developed in the first half of the second century C.E.[11] Many scholars date the beginnings of "religious Taoism" with the appearance

---

[11] A succinct summary of the varied texts of religious Taoism can be found in Terry Bilhartz, *Sacred Words: A Source Book on the Great Religions of the World* (New York: McGraw-Hill, 2006), pp. 274–277.

of the Heavenly Master or Celestial Master sect, around 200 C.E. This group developed church-like organizations encouraging a Taoist theocracy, and stressed correct performance of rituals and literary study of Taoist classic texts. These Taoists believed that spirits could be controlled by proper knowledge of secret rituals. Some of these rituals can cure illnesses. The goal for the religious Taoist practitioner is to empty and purify the inner self, to bring about union with the Tao and become an immortal.

In popular Chinese religion, high mountains with multiple peaks and grottos were often sacred places because they were the homes of spirits and immortals, and potential sources of power. The mountain peaks were lost in the clouds and awe-inspiring. It was believed that in remote mountain landscapes one could find the secrets to the elixirs of life. Deities and powerful spirits were believed to dwell in these peaks. These wild mountains were beyond the edges of urban and even rural lives. On a mountain side one might find a cave, or a hut, or a hermitage (and these are important features in Chinese and Japanese landscape paintings). A wandering pilgrim could retreat to the cold mountains to write poetry, to commune with nature. In the mountains one might find harmony and surcease from suffering. One could also ask for blessings, or seek out gods or powerful wizards.

In China there were unusual, eccentric recluses, who lived in caves, huts or hermitages deep in these mountains. They were thought to possess mysterious powers to control and manipulate demonic forces. These strange men were similar to the dangerous wizards in the Western traditions, powerful sorcerers of whom we must be very wary. These wizards were often believed to be Taoist immortals who could reveal secrets of healing and even immortality, but these wizards could be gruff and cantankerous, or worse. So, for the Taoist priest to achieve the secrets of immortality, a priest must become a highly trained specialist who has learned difficult and dangerous secrets from strange, ascetic, unkempt teachers. The mountain recluse does not give up his secrets easily; the hermit instructs the student only when the student has passed tests and the teacher is certain that the student is ready.[12]

The search for longevity and health did play a role in institutional Taoism, but was only one aspect of institutional political Taoism. The Taoist priests of institutional Taoism were well-educated, were quite solemn in performing their rituals, and often cultivated inner techniques of quiet meditation and peacefulness.

The Celestial Master Tradition (Five Bushels Sect) is the earliest institutional form of religious Taoism. It developed in the second century C.E. in south Western China. It was started by charismatic leaders who functioned as both military leaders and magical healers. The founder, Chang Tao Ling/Zhang Daoling, claimed that the divine Lord Lao-tzu/Laozi[13] had appeared to him in 142 C.E. and made him a Heavenly Master and told him to make the world better. Lord Lao-tzu instructed Chang Tao-ling to improve people's respect for what is correct, and stop them from worshiping evil influences.[14]

The idea was to create a perfect world, going all the way back to China's Golden Age when everyone would again live in harmony with themselves and nature. These groups wanted to eliminate the emperor and the ruling aristocracy, and replace them with an autonomous state ruled by shamanistic Taoist priests who served Lao-tzu and other gods.

To join the Heavenly Master or Celestial Master sect, the person had to contribute five pecks (or bushels) of rice; thus the sect was often called the Five Bushel Sect, or the Five Peck Sect (a peck of rice was about 7 kilograms or 15½ pounds). The rituals of the Five Bushel Sect focused upon faith healing and miraculous events, and stressed doing good works and avoiding evil behavior. The Celestial Master sect is also known as the Cheng-I (Orthodox One) sect and the Meng-wei (Auspicious Alliance) order.

---

[12] These sorts of stories are not unique to religious Taoism. Magic and folklore can play a role in Buddhism as well. Buddhist masters were often thought to be mysterious and possessed of supernatural powers. A few were famous for living the life of a recluse in the mountains, like the famous T'ang dynasty poet Han-shan ("Cold Mountain").

[13] Lao-tzu/Laozi was deified officially in 166 C.E. The royal family of the T'ang era (618–907) claimed to be descended from Lao-tzu.

[14] Terry F. Kleeman, *Celestial Masters: History and Ritual in Early Daoist Communities* (Cambridge, MA: Harvard-Yenching Institute, 2016).

CHAPTER 18: RELIGIOUS TAOISM

The founder claimed to have made the elixir of immortality, and stressed use of talismans to deal with spirit forces including gods, immortals and other celestial beings. The founder wrote books, converted people, and was immensely popular. He claimed to know ways to control higher spirits who could be summoned when he invoked their special rituals. He opposed sacrificing live animals to the various divinities (*shen*), and substituted offerings of cooked vegetables.

He taught his followers that the problems of our world, including human weakness and sickness were caused by offenses against gods in heavens, earthly spirits, and underworld spirits, and that one had to confess one's misdeeds to spirits in the heavens, the spirits who share our lives on the earth, and the spirits in the underworld, in order to get better. Priests of the Heavenly Master sect took care of this process. One's detailed confession was written on three pieces of paper. One piece was buried in the earth. The second was put on a mountain top (heavens). The third was put into a river (underworld). Thus the spirit-world was informed of the sincere desire to repent. The Heavenly Master priests were well-educated and borrowed this three-paper confession structure in imitation of the court system of the earlier Han (202 B.C.E. – 220 C.E.) empire, where scribes of the royal court sent documents, memorials, and rescripts through the spiritual bureaucracies of the heavens, earth, and underworld.

The text called the *Yellow Court Canon*[15] is source for many important elements of the Heavenly Master sect. Leadership within the sect became hereditary. Male and female members of the community would assist the leaders. Women could be priests, but were kept from the higher levels of the institution. The Heavenly Master sect was particularly important in southern China and continued in various forms until the present. After China under Chairman Mao outlawed the sect, they moved their headquarters to Taiwan.

(2) Military Political Taoism

The Ling-pao/Lingbao form of political Taoism became so well organized and so powerful that it nearly overthrew the Han dynasty in an attempt to establish a Taoist theocracy, a country ruled by Taoist priests who were inspired by the divine Lao-tzu/Laozi. Like all the other religious traditions in China, this Taoist group presupposes the rule of an absolute monarch who seeks to enact his will through an elaborate bureaucratic apparatus. In the early centuries, the Ling-pao/Lingbao sect of non-philosophical Taoism was begun as political and revolutionary secret society attempting to overthrow the state and the emperor, and replace it with a Taoist absolute monarch.

The Ling-pao sect was similar in many ways to the Celestial Master sect. The main difference is that Ling-pao Taoism actually engaged in military battles with the government in an attempt to overthrow the emperor and set up a new ruling elite for the kingdom. The Ling-pao leaders claimed that the emperor and his Confucian advisors had neglected the proper balance of *yin* and *yang* and were not acting properly in accord with the flowing seasons, and as such they were losing their right to rule.

The Ling-pao rebellion is called the T'ai-p'ing/Taiping (Great Peace) rebellion, which is also associated with the later rebels called the Yellow Turbans, named for the color of the bandanas the followers wore on their heads. The Yellow Turbans wanted the country to be governed in accord with the religious Taoist ideas. They wanted to eliminate the Confucian state and return to their Taoist idea of an ideal government, while the world waits for the arrival of the Great Peace. Obviously the Confucian rulers did not initiate the desired government, and the result was the Great Peace or Yellow Turban revolt (184–215 C.E.) in the eastern provinces, which almost succeeded in overthrowing the weakening Han dynasty (202 B.C.E.–220 C.E.). Eventually the Ling-pao movement came to control eight Chinese provinces.

These religious Taoist groups were not merely concerned with military matters and revolution. The followers also desired longevity, they cultivated the inner practices to develop health and drive out spirits, and had very special diets. They practiced fasting and prayer, and group confessions to achieve healing. They stressed purification rites and rituals, to attain original harmony with the Tao. Following these esoteric practices could lead to longevity, and possibly

---

[15] The *Yellow Court Canon* involves lists of spirits and gods who inhabit the human body, which could be made visible using meditative techniques. The goal of the text was immortality. The text is supposed to have been written by a female Taoist adept in the third century C.E. The text is discussed in more detail later in this chapter.

even immortality. Belief in a Taoist messiah became an inspiration for numerous secret societies which threatened the government and stability of the state, and is one of the reasons that modern Chinese political leaders are so suspicious of organized religion.

Perceiving these T'ai-p'ing/Taiping Taoists as a serious threat, the government obliterated the Way of Great Peace group in a complete massacre. After the Yellow Turban revolt was quashed by the Han troops, religious Taoism in general became less focused upon rebellion and battle, and put more energy into inward means for developing religious goals rather than political goals.

Institutional forms of political Taoism focused on spirituality and alchemy, and practical goals such as having religious Taoist advisors to the rulers in the government. Over the centuries the political Ling-pao and Yellow Turban groups became more socially acceptable and came to dominate popular Chinese religion.[16] By mid fourth-century, the Ling-pao rites of renewal and burial adapted the rival Heavenly Master ritual of exteriorizing the spirits and the sending off of documents to the three realms as an essential part of its public liturgy.[17] By the sixth century C.E., the two religious Taoist traditions were united in ritual practice.

(3) Communal Taoism and Shamanistic Taoism

Political Taoism overlaps with the next form, Communal Shamanistic Taoism, the aspect of Taoism which served the needs of local communities. These village Taoists are not priests in Taoist temples, but are local healers, the shamans who healed using herbal cures and who communicated with the realms of spirits.

After lengthy preparation including diet and rituals, the shaman could be possessed by a spirit, and slip into a spiritual frenzy. The shaman is believed to be a conduit for a spirit, and can compel the spirit to perform work for humans. A shaman could exorcize demons who caused illness or bad luck from the head, heart, or abdomen. The shaman could determine which days were lucky or unlucky (astrology and numerology[18]). A shaman would be consulted to determine auspicious locations for graves, or (later on) auspicious locations for one's home (feng-shui, or geomancy). Shamans were thought to be able to divine the future by reading one's face, by studying the date of one's birth (year, month, day, time of birth), and by studying the apparently random motion of falling sticks and coins. Horoscopes were also used; a shaman would determine the birth-date of the owner of a home to find the correct orientation for the owner's bed, and using the date the home was completed, the shaman could determine if there was a conflict between owner and home. The same ideas could be applied to prospective marital partners, to see if there was a potential conflict. A shaman could use the special secret Taoist written script to write out a talisman or charm which could protect the client from harm and misfortune.

Local Taoist shamans were believed to be able to control spirits for the benefit of the person who paid, or even send out evil spirits to harm those the client wished to harm. These sorts of shamans were not attached to any institutional temples. They taught and practiced ancient Chinese medical practices, including an early form of acupuncture (steel needles did not exist yet) and ch'i-kung/qi-gong[19] (breathing and stretching exercises). Chinese medicine envisioned the yin and yang energies circulating invisible life-energy (ch'i/qi) via invisible channels, and the knowledgeable priest could remove blockages in the energy channels, and this can also include removing blockages

---

[16] An excellent study of this topic is Rolf A. Stein, "Religious Taoism and Popular Religion from the Second to the Seventh Centuries" in Holmes Welch and Anna Seidel, eds., *Facets of Taoism: Essays in Chinese Religion* (New Haven: Yale University Press, 1979), pp. 53–82.

[17] Michael Saso, "Buddhist and Taoist Notions of Transcendence," in Michael Saso and David W. Chappell, eds., *Buddhist and Taoist Studies I* (Honolulu: University Press of Hawaii, 1972), p. 8.

[18] In Chinese popular religion, the number 4 is unlucky because it is pronounced the same way the Chinese word for "death" is pronounced (shih/shi). The number 8 is lucky because its pronunciation, pa/ba, sounds like fa, "luck." The number 9 (jiu) is especially lucky because it is pronounced like the word "longevity." Obviously, 9 x 9 is incredibly more auspicious.

[19] Ch'i/qi is the life energy, the life-breath, and kung/gong is skill or technique.

which obstruct one's understanding of the true self, to lessen conditioned thinking. Some Taoist priests perform rituals only for the living, and other priests also perform rituals for the dead.

Although later institutional Taoism might utilize shamanism, scholars separate out the forms of Taoism of mediums who were possessed by spirits from the original institutional forms of religions Taoism.[20]

(4) Alchemical Taoism

Religious Taoism includes numerous methods and techniques to extend one's life, or cure illness. Long before institutional religious Taoism, there were alchemist-magicians (*fang-shih*/*fangshi*) who claimed that their ability to manipulate the five basic processes (five elements: metal, wood, earth, fire, and water) was so advanced that they had discovered methods for extending life, or possibly had produced an elixir that bestowed immortality upon those who consumed it. When applied to China, the term "alchemy" denotes those proto-scientists who believed that the universe was composed of the five fundamental processes of metal, wood, earth, fire, and water, who attempted to turn lead into gold, and who spent most of their time concocting miraculous remedies, poisons, and magic potions. The main purpose of these herbs and spices was to produce a Grand Elixir of Immortality, which, if ingested, would extend life greatly, or perhaps forever.

All the forms of alchemical Taoism which involved external chemical or botanical manipulations to achieve their ends are called **Outer Alchemy**. There was another form of alchemy, that which utilized natural internal bodily processes to achieve health or extend life. This form is **Inner Alchemy**. Many inner alchemical techniques involved meditation, physical exercise, aerobics, gymnastics, stretching, control of breathing, and even sexual practices. We will discuss this aspect in more detail later in this chapter.

(5) Monastic Taoism.

Monastic Taoism[21] appears in China only after the Buddhists had established monastic organizations, and Taoist monasteries seem to have borrowed Buddhist structures, rites, rituals, liturgy (Taoist rituals include chanting Buddhist Sanskrit texts which are incomprehensible in Chinese) and Buddhist meditation interpreted as special techniques which extend life span. The earliest forms of temple (Mao-shan) monastic Taoism were primarily meditative and introspective, but later the private meditations were replaced by popular public rituals.

It has been suggested that Taoist monastic institutions may have arisen after Taoists saw the results of patronage given by the emperor and wealthy families to Buddhist monasteries. As a result of patronage, the Buddhists accumulated land, wealth, and power. In addition to inspiring monastic religious Taoist temples, Buddhism influenced other aspects of religious non-philosophical Taoism. Taoists developed complex burial rituals, many aspects of which were borrowed from Buddhist rituals. The Taoists also valued the idea of universal salvation, that is, it is not only for the benefit of one's ancestors that one should perform rituals. There had been no idea of karma prior to Buddhism entering China, but Taoists came to adopt the idea that karmic continuity continues as life-cycle after life-cycle is suffered through. The Taoists also accepted that a person is reborn in one of six Karmic Destinies: Hells; Hungry ghost; Animal; Demon; Human; Celestial Being.

The great majority of Chinese never really understood the Buddhist idea that there was no permanent soul, nothing unchanging in a human (no essence), no *atman* (*anatman*), and so they imagined that a small part of a human spirit, some sort of a luminous soul (called the *hun* or *shen*) underwent the journey to these various destinations.

---

[20] Michael Saso, *The Teachings of Taoist Master Chuang*, footnote 11, page 270. "In Master Chuang's opinion the historians who consider possessed mediums or *wu* (sometimes called shamans) to be predecessors of orthodox Taoism are in error. Medium possession is allowed by the popular or local Shen-hsiao orders and the Lu Shan Redhead Taoists, but not by the classical orders . . ."

[21] The Mao-shan order of religious Taoism is monastic, but also stresses literary skills and cultivation of inner alchemy for self-perfection. For more details, see Isabelle Robinet, *Taoist Meditation: The Mao-Shan Tradition of Great Purity* (New York: State University of New York, 1993), and Livia Kohn and Robin Wang, eds., *Internal Alchemy* (New Mexico: Three Pines Press, 2009).

Chinese Buddhist priests earned a living caring for the luminous souls of the deceased by offering sacrifices, and performing funerals to help those who had not yet succeeded in achieving union with the Tao when they died. Borrowing more from Buddhism, religious Taoists encouraged the Taoist monk to be humble, selfless, and uninterested in wealth or fame,[22] and they utilized such things as *mantras* (chanted phrases of power), *mudra* (hand positions with special meanings) and Taoists also practiced building *mandala* (the rectangular-circular Buddhist diagrams which became very important in religious Taoism).

(6) Philosophical Taoism Influences Upon Religious Taoism

We will discuss the influence of the *Tao Te Ching* and the *Chuang-tzu* on religious Taoism at the end of this chapter.

18.4 THE NUMEROUS STRANDS OF RELIGIOUS TAOISM

Religious Taoism became a central lynchpin of the popular religion in China, with the majority of people taking part in collective ceremonies through which their evil misdeeds were washed away and a happy destiny prepared in the other world, and with the Taoist priests, magicians or adepts following secret rituals combined with physical techniques to "nourish the vital principle" (*ch'i/qi*) in order to obtain an extended life in this body and an exalted rank within the hierarchy of the immortals.

COMMUNAL TAOISM AND SHAMANISTIC TAOISM

There are many myths about Taoist hermits who practiced their magical craft as recluses, and it was believed that Taoist immortals lived deep in the mountains or else on magical islands off the coast. Although they may have started as ordinary human wanderers or pilgrims, ultimately they became Taoist immortals who were more than human. The problem was that Taoist immortals did not interact with ordinary humans. However, local communities had religious and medical needs as well, none of which were met by state Confucianism or by Taoist hermits (who were of no use to the community). It was the religious Taoist adepts who met these needs. They were the village healers or shamans, who cured problems by communicating with spirit realms.

After days of arduous preparation, the shaman claimed to be able to manipulate spirits to perform work for humans. A shaman might even be possessed by the demon. If a demon had caused injury, bad luck, or illness, a shaman could exorcize demons, for a fee. The shaman could determine which days were lucky and which were unlucky (astrology and numerology) for travel, for business, for wars, for weddings, and even for funerals.

Shamans were able to control spirits for the benefit of the person who paid, or even harm others on behalf of those who paid. A shaman was not attached to any Taoist institutional temple and thus was different from a priest associated with a Taoist temple line.

Over the centuries, forms of shamanistic Taoism combined with institutional Taoism and, further influenced by Buddhism, developed into a hereditary priesthood. The Chinese cultural stress on genealogy and lineage came to influence shamanistic Taoism. Each priest learned his magic arts from his father or other family members. These forms of religious Taoism claimed Lao-tzu as the patron divinity of their magic and alchemy and concocted genealogical lineage charts which connected them with Lao-tzu himself.

---

[22] Such goals are the common heritage of Confucianism and Chinese thought in general.

CHAPTER 18: RELIGIOUS TAOISM

Taoist priests provided certain kinds of rites and ceremonies for the community: rites of exorcism; rites of purification; funeral rites; burial services; communal sacrifices to local spirits of soil and grain. Buddhism was the inspiration for many of these rites. Often the priests employed Buddhist *mantras*, Buddhist esoteric hand positions (called *mudras*), and Buddhist rituals.[23]

Non-philosophical religious Taoism was almost synonymous with popular folk religion. It was the primary source of religious beliefs for the great masses of people, and it continues to permeate everyday lives of the Chinese, in mythology, in legend, and in popular belief. Many of what Western people think of as traditional Chinese medical practices originated in religious Taoism. Everyday Chinese would live their lives by divination, magic, Taoist medicine, and they devoutly believed in immortals, gods, and heavenly palaces. After Buddhism became popular, religious Taoism added beliefs about karma and reincarnation, and believed in ten hells of punishment which one will traverse one after another, paying for misdeeds.

Unless you can become an immortal, you will go to these hellish realms after your death — everyone will pay for misdeeds, and everyone performs misdeeds. Taoist hells are located in the west, and there are ten divisions, each with its own king. Like the heavenly realms, the hells of popular religion are organized into a vast bureaucracy in the same manner as traditional Chinese government. After traversing all ten hellish destinations, people meet "Mother Meng," and she gives the persons the "Tea of Forgetfulness," so they will not remember what happened when they return to earth.

If the principles of Chinese religion can be expressed in a clear and succinct manner, one can say that the purpose of the prayers, rituals, and other activities of the system is to win the blessing associated with *Yang* [heavens and immortals] and suppress the evil forces belonging to *Yin* [the earth, the demons or evil spirits who harm us]. In the minds of the men and women of the community, the power of good and evil, *Yang* and *Yin*, are personified into world after world and layer after layer of spirits, good and evil. The highest spirits, residents in heaven, are associated with life and blessing. The spirits who rule the visible world, such as the god of the hearth and the lord of the soil, watch over the good and evil deeds of men, reporting them to the heavenly rulers for reward or punishment. The demons of the underworld, both orphan souls and the spirits of men who died a death by violence, cause harm to men through sickness, calamity and misfortune. Men and women of the visible world handle the spirits much as they handle the visible magistrates of the central government. The gods are banqueted and rewarded, thus building relationships of reciprocal obligation. Demons and spirits are given paper money as bribes, much as one buys political favor and influence.[24]

GEOMANCY (*Feng-shui*)

The Chinese emperor was associated with the north star, and thus the throne room had to be oriented north-south, and the throne always had to place the emperor in the northern end of the building. In the centuries before the compass, this was a very specialized task which the religious Taoist priests worked hard to master. Later in Chinese history, a shaman would be consulted to determine auspicious locations for graves. More recently, Taoist priests would be consulted on auspicious locations for one's home (*feng-shui*, or geomancy).

The science of geomancy studies the currents of the subtle energy of the Tao which permeate all landscapes with their hills, rocks, trees and rivers. In the management of actual terrain the Taoist idea was that the currents present in the earth since ancient times should always be preserved. When a well

---

[23] A very important ritual is described in detail in the book by Michael R. Saso, *Taoism and the Rite of Cosmic Renewal*.

[24] Michael Saso, *Taoism and the Rite of Cosmic Renewal*, pp. 13–14.

was to be sunk, or a grave, house or road made, skilled diviners were called in to work out the correct locations and paths, to avoid 'disturbing the sleeping dragon', as the common expression puts it.[25]

Feng-shui literally is "wind and waters" and incorporates beliefs that certain compass orientations, certain ratios, and other elements of architectural design were magically auspicious or magically inauspicious. For example, it is believed that both northeast and southwest are inauspicious directions, for they lack heavenly and earthly essences. It was believed that Chinese homes should face south, where the *yang* is most vital (just as the emperor faces south while seated on the throne). Chinese temples utilized the same orientations. Contemporary scholarly research has revealed that many *feng-shui* beliefs and practices in China and the West are not ancient, but quite recent.

THE SEARCH FOR IMMORTALITY

The search for immortality is a theme found in all civilizations and belief in some pill, food, magic fountain or elixir to extend life is found in cultures everywhere. In the West there are people willing to sell us shark fins, or some special yogurt, or sell us a mattress with magnets sewn into the lining, and many put their faith in science to make a magic pill. Of course, many in the pseudo-science world are happy to sell gullible people a pill claimed to cure all ills.

In China, belief in the possibility of immortality usually involves the belief in actual immortal beings (*hsien*). Using special diets, secret recipe books involving herbs (pine needles, melon seeds, roots, and fungus) and wines, physical and meditative exercises, and ingesting drugs made of mineral substances, they believed it was possible to achieve the goal of immortality.

According to popular legends, some immortals lived in a green-and-gold paradise in the west, filled with beautiful trees and ornate pavilions. Some joined the Heavenly Court where they rode on cranes or dragons. Immortals in the heavens can return to earth,[26] but some immortals live only on the earth, perhaps in caves, in deep woods, remote mountains, or may live on magical islands offshore.

Religious Taoists believe that one can extend the life in one's physical body for centuries, but at some point an immortal might shed his or her physical body (die), but the immortal can continue on as a spiritual force in the heavens. Immortals who share our world possess magical powers, including invisibility, the power to fly, the power to bring skeletons back to life, to raise spirit-armies, to eat boiled stones, and even perform successful major surgery.[27]

THE MAGICAL ISLES OF P'ENG-LAI

The magic islands of P'eng-lai are part of ancient Chinese mythology, and became the preoccupation of royalty in much the same way the obsessive search for the Christian Holy Grail became important to European royalty. The P'eng-lai islands are the magic isles of the immortals, floating free in the bottomless sea, secured to the heads of five giant tortoises while ten more tortoises stand guard and wait their turn to support the isles. These magical islands are places where the serious Taoist adept could find plants and minerals which conferred immortality. P'eng-lai mountains are not the only magical islands in Chinese legends but they are the most famous.

The actual beginnings of the cult of the Magical Islands are lost in obscurity. We know that a hundred years before Ch'in-shih Huang-ti/Qinshihuangdi (259–210 B.C.E) became the first Emperor of a unified China, Duke Wei of the kingdom of Ch'i (357–320 B.C.E.) sent out ships to search for the magic isles of P'eng-lai where immortals lived. A hundred years later the founder of the Ch'in dynasty repeatedly traveled to the coast and stood on the sea shore

---

[25] Philip Rawson and Laszlo Legeza, *Tao: The Eastern Philosophy of Time and Change* (London: Thames & Hudson, Ltd., 1973), p. 18.

[26] Borrowing the idea of rebirth from the Buddhists, religious Taoists believed that the author of the *Tao Te Ching*, Lao-tzu/Laozi (a divine immortal), was continually being reborn each generation. Many religious Taoist leaders claimed to be incarnations of Lao-tzu.

[27] Rawson and Legeza, *op. cit.*, p. 23.

searching for the magical islands. Later, during the Han dynasty, the Han Emperor Wu-ti/Wudi (141-87 B.C.E.) sent a large group of explorers to the east China sea with instructions to find the home of the immortals and bring back the elixir of eternal life.

The P'eng-lai mountainous isles are the home of many beings including the Eight Immortals. On the island of immortals, homes are made of gold and silver, and birds and animals are all white. Pearl and coral trees grow in profusion. Flowers all have a sweet flavor. The beings who inhabit the islands drink water from the fountain of life, and live in ease and pleasure.

These islands of the immortals were quite different from ordinary islands that sailors encounter. Since the magic islands were not rooted to the ocean bottom, they floated and that meant that they did not remain in the same place so they could not be charted on any map. They could be blown farther out to sea or closer to the coast. It was possible for human beings to reach these magical islands, but very difficult. At certain times of the year they were not too far off the coast, and standing on the beach one could just barely see them and even get to them in the right sort of weather.

There was a good reason why so very few humans ever seemed to get to those islands. When humans got too close, the winds could blow the humans back, or blow the islands away. In some cases, the islands could simply flip over, inverted in the water, so that to the ship passing by they seemed to be just small flat uninteresting islands.

If a human being could make his way to those islands, it might be possible to talk the immortals into sharing their secrets, and the result was either a greatly extended and healthy life, or even the possibility of putting a complete end to death.[28] Because of this, any person claiming to have visited the islands stood to make a great fortune in the courts of wealthy lords and rulers. From time to time elderly gentlemen presented themselves at court, claiming to be six or seven hundred years old, and claiming to possess the secret of immortality. Some were believed and had very good lives at court, at least until the lords and rulers began to doubt their veracity.

The Chinese believed in heavenly beings, and combined the stories of (a) the heavenly deities, *shen* and (b) the humans who became immortals, the *hsien*. The Taoist immortals became celestial officials who governed the world from Heaven. Although born as human beings, they won magic powers and prolonged life through various practices, usually described as hygiene. Their life breath, their *ch'i* (energy of life, breath, vital spiritual essence), could become pure via these hygiene practices, and as a result they acquired immunity to fire and water, could ride the wind, and became nearly immortal. A human being who found the islands of the immortals and got the favors of the immortals, could learn how to attain the same skills and powers.

As we have seen, the educated Confucians of the literati class tended to minimize aspects of popular religion involving supernatural powers and beings, and some even denied the possibility of life after death. The Confucian scholars and officials ignored or tolerated these popular religious beliefs as long as they did not threaten the power of the Confucian elite. However, when certain forms of political Taoism became powerful enough to be a genuine threat to the power of the Confucians, the Confucian-dominated government forcibly suppressed political Taoism. Later in Chinese history, when religious Taoism came to dominate during the reigns of specific emperors, the rulers were persuaded to persecute Buddhism which was a threat to Taoist political power.

18.5 TAOIST ALCHEMY TO ACHIEVE IMMORTALITY

There are two types of Taoist Alchemy: Outer Alchemy and Inner Alchemy. **Outer Alchemy** involves manipulation of herbs, wines, minerals and other substances in order to convert base substances into gold, and if ingested, perhaps to confer immortality. **Inner Alchemy** seeks a long life without growing old and the goal is achieved by "hygiene," that is, interior methods of purification, breathing, exercise, stretching, and so forth. The goal is to return

---

[28] Holmes Welch, *Taoism: The Parting of the Way, Revised Edition* (Boston: Beacon Press, 1965), p. 97.

to the state of youth in the same way that nature goes from winter (old age) to spring (youth) and renews itself yearly. If humans could renew their life forces yearly, this would be immortality or close to it. The ideal was the small child, even the infant within the mother's womb.

Outer Alchemy to Obtain Longevity

Outer Alchemy involves chemical manipulation of the Five Processes or Five Elements[29]: **wood, metal, fire, water, earth**. The Yin-Yang school argued that these five interact in repeating cycles, and understanding their complex interactions would help explain what was going to happen next in the world. Many medical and divination practices drew on these ideas about which elements are compatible and which are incompatible, and how they correspond to colors and bodily organs.[30] For example, water is compatible with wood but incompatible with fire. The most important aspect of doing chemical manipulations was the search for immortality using external chemical manipulation (outer alchemy).

The Importance of Gold to Alchemy

Gold has always been important for alchemists, because gold does not rust or tarnish. Gold resists the aging process that is so evident in other metals which do rust. Rusting is a metaphor for growing old. Searching for an element which would turn lead into gold (alchemy) is also a metaphor for taking the decaying mortal human being and transmuting one's essence so that one becomes renewed and immortal. Because the gold color was associated with not growing old, gold-colored yellow minerals were important in alchemical manipulations. Also from ancient times the color red was the color of life and eternity, so certain red chemical compounds were highly valued. External alchemists were confident that certain special herbs, chemicals and drugs, when properly prepared and ingested, conferred life without end; these were elixirs of immortality.[31] These ingredients were often believed to be found in the remote mountains which Taoists considered sacred, and certainly reflects the tendency to understand mountains as the crystallization of basic energies. These mountains have been known as sacred places to the Taoists for centuries (scholars describe mountain worship as an aspect of popular Chinese religion).

Techniques of Outer Alchemy

There were three aspects of alchemical Taoism which constitute Outer Alchemy. The first aspect did not involve ingesting anything. It was believed that utensils for dining and eating made of that gold would have a beneficial effect. Eating from such utensils would increase the emperor's *ch'i* (vital energy, life breath essence). Jade was also associated with both purity and immortality, and in funerals jade could be used on a dead body to keep the negative *p'o* soul from returning to do mischief in this world.

The second way that substances could extend life was by ingesting medicinal fortified wines and herbs, but

---

[29] This ancient belief is sometimes attributed to Chou Yan/Zouyan (ca. 325 B.C.E.)

[30] The Taoists developed a complex set of correlations with these five. For example, wood is correlated with the liver, with a sour taste, with the color green, with the east, with springtime and with the eye. Fire is associated with the heart, with a bitter taste, with the color red, with the south, with the summertime, and with the tongue. The metal gold is associated with the lungs, with a metallic taste, with the color white, with the west, with autumn time, and with the nose. These were even correlated with nine stars.

[31] Many of the European explorers of the 1600s were searching for the fountain of youth.

most important were the magical substances, especially cinnabar[32] (red mercuric sulfide), which alchemists tried to turn into gold. The alchemists sought to discover or create substances or drugs (which they called "medicines") which could be classified into three categories: (1) the best are drugs which provide immortality; (2) second best are drugs which prolong life; (3) also valuable are drugs which cure illness. Some ingredients were from creatures that enjoy long lives, like the crane, the tortoise, and pine trees (pine needles). The drugs were usually made of cinnabar, gold, silver, five mushrooms, jade, mica, pearls, malachite, sulphur, saltpeter, and the gold-colored yellow mineral, orpiment.[33] This was not a simple process. These herbs and minerals needed to be gathered during the correct time of the day and year, with the help and support of the spirits. Evil forces could obstruct the successful gathering of these substances. Taoist priests and shamans could supply charms and talismans to protect against malign forces, and also used magic dances to deal with supernatural forces.

The primary goal was create the elixir of immortality, but even if the drug failed to confer immortality, at least it could cure illnesses and prolong life while keeping one's vitality high. Those who practiced outer alchemy believed that it offered the promise of genuine immortality; they also believed that the natural techniques of inner alchemy could only provide a lengthened life span, but not immortality. Sadly, when put to the test, they did not work. Emperor Kao-tsung (who reigned 618–626 C.E.) was in failing health, and asked the Taoist alchemist Liu to prepare an elixir to improve his health. The emperor asked Liu to drink first, which he did, and which resulted in the alchemist's death.[34]

Can a Human Live Forever in this Physical Body?

Generally, religious Taoists did not think that a physical human body could live forever. Genuine immortality was only partially in this very body; when the immortal felt like it was time to move on, it was believed that the immortal could actually shed his body and live permanently as a heavenly deity or heavenly official. In the centuries following Buddhist influences, this would include rebirth in a heavenly realm or paradise. Although ingesting magical potions or elixirs (such as Powder of Liquified Gold, Dragon Foetus, Jade Essence,[35] and Gold Elixir) could result in the death of the physical body, many Taoists sought to lengthen their productive lives in this body and in this world. They wanted a long and vital life without illness or death.

It was believed that males were predominantly *yang* in their nature, and the symptoms of aging, infirmity, and ultimately, death were the result of the *yang* element in the male becoming depleted. To achieve health and long life, the goal was to accumulate *yang* and not lose it, and then restore the human body to the primordial state in which *yin* and *yang* are so closely embraced that they are indistinguishable.

Scholarly Confucian View of Immortality

The elite Confucian scholars tended to look down upon this entire immortality enterprise as superstitious nonsense. As you recall, in Confucianism immortality is not survival of an individual. The three ways in which a human can become immortal involved people remembering the individual: (a) people continuing to tell stories about

---

[32] Cinnabar appears in royal burials of the Shang dynasty (1600–1100 B.C.E.) and so was a sacred mineral since ancient times. Cinnabar describes both red mercury sulfide (HgS), and the opaque reddish-orange colored pigment called vermilion, the common ore of mercury derived from powdered cinnabar. Like all mercury compounds it is toxic. Vermilion is the traditional red pigment of Chinese art. On a Chinese scroll one sees the small circular or rectangular name stamp of the artist or calligrapher, printed with a red cinnabar paste, and vermilion (or cinnabar) is the pigment used in Chinese red lacquer. Cinnabar-red was the color of life and eternity.

[33] Orpiment is arsenic trisulfide.

[34] Stanley Weinstein, *Buddhism Under the T'ang* (Cambridge University Press, 1987), p. 36.

[35] The dragon was a powerful *yang* symbol, and Chinese alchemists treated jade as congealed dragon semen, and thus the essence of Heaven, and *yang* energy.

one's virtue long after one's death, (b) stories of one's accomplishments survive in the history books long after one's death; (c) one's writings survive (such as the *Analects* of Confucius, or the *Tao Te Ching*). "When, although a long time has passed, [one or more of these three] has not been forgotten, we may speak of [a deceased person's] immortality."[36]

Chinese Buddhist View of Immortality

Later, Chinese Buddhists often claimed that some Buddhist practices might extend one's life, but that immortality was not the goal of a true Buddhist. The immediate goal was to be a bodhisattva, but the ultimate goal of a bodhisattva was to achieve buddhahood, nirvana, or sagehood, not immortality in this body or in a heavenly realm. Thus the Chinese Buddhists were dismissive of the religious Taoist focus on immortality.

18.6 "PILLS OF IMMORTALITY"

Ch'in-shih Huang-ti: The Ch'in/Qin Dynasty (221–206 B.C.E.)

The Period of Disunity following the collapse of the central authority of the Chou dynasty in 771 B.C.E. resulted in centuries of civil war, political decay and destruction. China broke into several smaller kingdoms and wars between them continued on until 221 B.C.E. when the ruler of the Ch'in kingdom finally defeated the sole remaining kingdom of Chu, and as a result the Ch'in king established himself as the first emperor of a unified China. The man who managed to accomplish this for the first time is the First Emperor of the Ch'in/Qin Dynasty, Ch'in-shih Huang-ti/Qinshi Huangdi (259–210 B.C.E), who became very interested in extending his life.

After the new Ch'in ruler became the one supreme emperor, alchemist-magicians flocked to the emperor's court from the northern areas. They persuaded Ch'in-shih Huang-ti to adopt the Five Processes theory and their alchemical ideas. His dynasty, the Ch'in, was represented by the element water, and the color black. The Ch'in had destroyed the Chou Dynasty, which represented fire and red, and we all know that water is the destroyer of fire. In fact, after the Ch'in dynasty collapsed, it was replaced by the Han dynasty, which was associated with earth because earth can blockade the flow of water.

The alchemist-magicians persuaded Ch'in-shih Huang-ti to equip expeditions of ships to search for the P'eng-lai magic islands. One expedition is believed to have carried 3,000 young men and virginal young women as well as the seeds of the five grains and artisans of every kind. The Ch'in emperor used to make trips to the northern coasts, and stand on the beach hoping for a glimpse of the magical islands of P'eng-lai. He believed that giant fish, far out to sea, were blocking his view.

Meanwhile, court alchemist-magicians developed potions made of cinnabar (mercuric sulfide), which since ancient times was associated with life-giving properties. The Ch'in court magicians thought that when properly purified and eaten, it can produce immortality. It is very likely that Ch'in-shih Huang-ti ingested the mercury-cinnabar elixir because his behavior became more and more paranoid and erratic. Today, we know what mercury poisoning does to the brain. Recognizing how dangerously irrational the ruler had become, the most powerful of the imperial alchemists, Magician Lu, fled the court. Ch'in-shih Huang-ti was so annoyed when the alchemist he relied upon ran away, that he ordered the execution of nearly five-hundred remaining alchemist-magicians and scholars in his court.

Two years later, he was standing on the beach, with a large bow in his hands trying to shoot an immensely

---

[36] Tso's Commentary on the Spring and Autumn Annals, Tso Chuan, Duke Hsiang, 24th year. See Wing-tsit Chan, *A Source Book in Chinese Philosophy*, p. 13.

large fish which he imagined was barring the way to the magic islands. He became progressively more and more ill and finally died at age 47 while on one of his many expeditions away from the capital.

Han Dynasty (202 B.C.E.–220 C.E.) Cult of Immortality

Following the death of Ch'in-shih Huang-ti in 210 B.C.E., rebellion broke out against the surviving Ch'in family, and after several years of battle, a new dynasty began, known as the Han, which lasted more than four-hundred years (202 B.C.E. - 220 C.E.). The first emperor of the Han was supposed to have succeeded to the throne by following Taoist strategies.

There were many discoveries and inventions during the Han period. After about ten years of inactivity, new construction was begun again on the Great Wall (started by the Ch'in emperor) and the protection provided by the wall was extended. Paper was invented during Han about 100 C.E. The period of the Han dynasty was a time of relative stability and prosperity because the nomadic barbarians in the north were restrained by the Great Wall. During this time a national university was founded and the Chinese concern with recording a bibliography for every important person in Chinese civilization was started during Han dynasty. The first official Chinese historian, Ssu-ma Ch'ien/Sima Qian (145-90 B.C.E.) was appointed.

Emperor Wu-Ti/Wudi (156–87 B.C.E.)

The cult of the immortals as heavenly divinities was becoming important once again during the Han dynasty. In the court of the Han ruler Wu-ti/Wudi, an alchemist-magician claimed that he himself had been to P'eng-lai islands of the immortals, and that he too was now an immortal. He claimed to be familiar with events that had happened in the distant past, but in ministering to the emperor Wu Ti/Wudi, the alchemist stressed the elixir and the *hsien* immortals themselves. Instead of just inhabitants of the Isles of Immortality, the alchemist-magician explained that immortals acquired magic powers like invisibility, which we could learn from them. Wu-ti surrounded himself with alchemist-magicians and established rituals in honor of Taoist immortal spirits who in later centuries were worshiped as divinities by religious Taoists.

The royal alchemist had a special diet which included avoiding grains, claiming that this aided in immortality. He convinced Han emperor Wu-ti to seek for longevity by transmuting cinnabar into gold. The transmuted cinnabar is not to be eaten; rather first it is made into utensils, dishes and other cooking kinds of vessels. Eating from these kinds of vessels conveys longevity, not immortality. However, having achieved longevity, one can live long enough to see and learn the deeper secrets of the *hsien* immortals on the magic isles of P'eng-lai. The emperor also practiced special breathing and concentration exercises as well. It is reported that after devoting so much time and energy to the struggle for immortality, the emperor finally concluded that "If we are temperate in our diet and use medicine, we make our illnesses few. That is all we can attain to."[37]

18.7 TECHNIQUES OF INNER ALCHEMY

Inner Alchemy (*neidan* or *neigong*) is the second technique used to free the body from impurities, and thus make it fit for becoming immortal (perpetuation of the physical body).[38] It is methods for inner purification. The

[37] Quoted by Martin Palmer in Kwok Man Ho, Joanne O'Brien, *The Eight Immortals of Taoism* (New York: Meridian Books, 1991), p. 16.

[38] There are several books on inner alchemy published recently. Consider Livia Kohn and Robin Wang, eds., *Internal Alchemy* (New Mexico: Three Pines Press, 2009). One book written by a believer and practitioner is Damo Mitchell, *Daoist Nei Gong: The Philosophical Art of Change* (Singing Dragon, 2011). A more advanced text is Wang Mu, *Foundations of Internal Alchemy: The Taoist Practice of Neidan*, translated by Fabrizio Pregadio (Golden Elixir Press, 2011).

physical body was conceived of as a shifting locus of flowing energies, not self-contained and not independent of the external world. The religious Taoists believed that energies of the world and the energies of the human body share the same flow and must be interconnected. The inner currents of energy are frequently studied and mapped in Taoist works. The same currents (which are invisible to all except for Taoist adepts) are the focus of what later became acupuncture and acupressure.

The Yellow Court Canon

One of the most important sources for freeing the body of impurities and inner cultivation is the third or fourth century C.E. text entitled the *Yellow Court Canon*.[39] The "Yellow Court" is the religious Taoist's name for an invisible source of life in the body, an empty void at the microcosmic center of a human being. The alchemical Taoists thought of the Yellow Court as a hollow center which, though having no precise physical location, is a place from which the source of life works invisibly. The first step to prepare the body for immortality is casting out the many guardian spirits and evil demons that dwell within the body.[40] A human body has what Taoist medicine describes as three fields of cinnabar which are focal points for assembling the spirits: (1) the *ni-wan*[41] palace in the brain (called the Red Palace, which corresponds to Heaven); (2) the heart behind the solar plexus (which corresponds to earth); (3) the cinnabar field in the lower abdomen below the navel (which corresponds to the watery underworld).[42]

Cultivation of purity of spirit, and circulation of spiritual breath-energy of life (*ch'i/qi*) within the microcosmic empty center is the way to eternal life. It was believed that the evil demons who inhabit the body cause illnesses and attack the body's vitality. The spirits in the brain attack the eyes and cause mental disturbances and illnesses; the demons of the heart region cause problems with the stomach and intestines; the lowest cause kidney and blood ailments. Traditional Chinese medicine believed that the demons who inhabit the body desire their freedom, but can be freed only by the death of their host body, so these demons desire to kill their host as quickly as possible.

The religious Taoists believe that the Yellow Court is an empty center where the spirits and phenomenal elements cannot penetrate. An inner alchemy Taoist attempts to contain and preserve the principles of life (primordial breath, primordial spirit, and seminal essence) in the Yellow Court, and closing the exit and entrance to this empty center within the person thereby preserving the very basic principle of life. One expels the myriads of evil spirits and congeals one's vital breath, *ch'i/qi*, and in the process, immortality is within reach.

It is obvious that breathing exercises would be fundamental to these goals. There is a large lore of breathing techniques analyzing some breaths as beneficial, some as malevolent, and others neutral. To breathe the way an embryo breathes in its mother's womb was a basic goal for religious Taoists. The life breath, *ch'i*, must be retained if one is to live a long time. So, holding one's breath for a long time must be a part of an adept's practice. Also, certain foods cause gas which can be lost at the other end of the gastrointestinal tract. These foods are to be avoided as well because to lose gas is also to lose life-breath.

The three fields described above are also relevant for breathing exercises. It was believed that an adept could force the life-breath to circulate below the heart, inside the intestines, and just below the stomach, and in the process

---

[39] The *Yellow Court Canon* involves lists of spirits and gods who inhabit the human body, which could be made visible using meditative techniques. The goal of the text was immortality. The text is supposed to have been written by a female Taoist adept in the third or fourth century C.E. The Yellow Court Canon should not be confused with an entirely different text with a similar title, i.e., the Yellow Emperor's medical treatise. See Ilza Veith, *The Yellow Emperor's Classic of Internal Medicine* (Berkeley: University of California Press, 1966) and Ni Maoshing, *The Yellow Emperor's Classic of Medicine* (New York: Shambhala, 1995).

[40] Michael Saso, "Buddhist and Taoist Notions of Transcendence," in Michael Saso and David W. Chappell, eds., *Buddhist and Taoist Studies I* (Honolulu: University Press of Hawaii, 1972), p. 14.

[41] The Buddhist influence upon popular Taoism is evident when we note that *ni-wan* is an early Chinese transliteration of the Sanskrit term "Nirvana" which would be pronounced Nir-van. Michael Saso, *op. cit.*, p. 15.

[42] Saso, "Buddhist and Taoist Notions of Transcendence," *op. cit.*, p. 14.

the breath could nourish the entire body. Physical exercises, with the body facing the proper direction, could aid the process. The ever-moving *yin* force could be balanced with the *yang* force, and health encouraged.[43]

Meditation to "Guard the One"

By the sixth century C.E., religious Taoists had developed a meditation technique they called "Preserving the One," or "Guarding the One."[44] Religious Taoists saw the human body as a microcosmic counterpart to the full universe itself, with the human skull corresponding to the vault of heaven, the eyes corresponding to the sun and the moon, the veins corresponding to the rivers of the world, etc. Our body is filled with thousands and thousands of gods charged with protecting our organs, joints, and bodily parts from the attacks of evil spirits (these attacks explained illness and early death). If there were thousands of gods within us, how can we help them to protect us? The answer is that religious Taoist medicine claimed that there was a supreme deity, the Supreme One, who dwells in our bodies and who supervises all the smaller gods within us. We should "Guard the One," which was a meditative visualization technique intended to provide prolonged life, and possibly, even immortality.[45]

The Return

An important idea in philosophical Taoism of Lao-tzu is the idea of **returning**, in the sense that the alternating movement of *yin* to *yang* and back again, is found everywhere in nature. The religious Taoist alchemists believed that the human body has *yin* blood vessel and *yang* blood vessel, and these two are the way in which the upper and lower parts of the body communicate. Taoist alchemists believed that male human beings were predominantly *yang*, and that females were predominantly *yin*. Popular Chinese medicine believed that at birth a male is filled with primordial *yang* energy, but as life goes on the *yin* increases and the *yang* is depleted, leading to loss of vitality and ultimately to death. In other words, males slowly lose their *yang* essence, and this loss causes them to grow old and die.

This religious Taoist medical model for how life works raised questions about how to slow the process of dying. Perhaps techniques could be devised so that the *yang* male vital essence could be held in, retained, and thus the male could stay alive and vital. Another possibility is that perhaps one can ride the swinging pendulum and **return** to youth.

Lao-tzu, Chuang-tzu and the philosophical Taoists urged us to become one with the flowing Tao. Nature renews itself each year; Nature is reborn every spring, and almost every eastern and Western religion has major holidays in March or April celebrating rebirth and a new life. Religious Taoists reasoned that we humans are nature, and so can imitate nature and be reborn each year, and thereby become immortal as well.

METHODS TO REPLENISH THE *Yang* AND EXTEND ONE'S LIFE SPAN

If we believe that every male child is born with a fixed amount of *yang* energy, and that illness and death exist because males slowly lose their *yang* vital essence, then this suggests that males should be careful in how they expend

---

[43] Additional sources on these techniques are Lu K'uan Yu (Charles Luk), *Taoist Yoga: Alchemy and Immortality* (New York: Samuel Weiser, 1970), and Luk's *The Secrets of Chinese Meditation* (New York: Samuel Weiser, 1964). See also Thomas Cleary, *Taoist Classics, Volume 2* (New York: Shambhala, 2003).

[44] This term appears in the later outer chapters of the *Chuang-tzu* which religious Taoists are fond of quoting: "I guard this unity (*shou-i*), abide in this harmony, and therefore I have kept myself alive for twelve hundred years, and never has my body suffered any decay." *Chuang-tzu*, ch. 11, Burton Watson, *Complete Works*, p. 120.

[45] Isabelle Robinet discusses "Preserving the One" and the "Supreme One" in her book, *Taoism: Growth of a Religion*, tr. by Phyllis Brooks. See also Isabelle Robinet, *Taoist Meditation*, and also Henri Maspero, *Taoism and Chinese Religion* (Amherst: University of Massachussets Press, 1981), pp. 272–283, where "guarding the one" is discussed under the Chinese terms *shou-yi*.

their *yang* vital essence. Religious Taoism slowly devised several techniques that they believed might conserve the finite male *yang* energy.

Ritual Sunbathing

Males can expose their naked body to sunlight (sunlight is *yang*, moonlight is *yin*). It would follow that if males exposed their bodies to sunlight to replenish the *yang* element which is slowly becoming depleted, then females should expose their bodies to moonlight for the same reason.

Dietary Techniques

Religious Taoists developed unusual medical ideas about which foods were healthy and which were not, and somehow came to believe that the immortals had a diet which involved drinking only morning dew and never eating the five grains. The five grains are rice, millet, wheat, barley, and beans — but lists vary.[46] Certain herbs were recommended, and others were forbidden.[47] These medical dietary practices were supplemented with breathing exercises and physical stretching and aerobics.

Respiratory Techniques: *qigong*

Respiratory techniques involving breath control were believed to contribute to extending one's lifetime. If adults are trying to return back to the stage of childhood, then the ultimate child is the embryo in the womb. The religious Taoists had ideas about how an embryo breathed: keep inhalation and exhalation as quiet and smooth as possible and hold the breath as long as possible.[48] The embryo in her mother's body does not breathe air at all; the Taoists imagined that for nine months the embryo had oxygen in its lungs but breathed internally by circulating the breath without exhaling. Similarly the Taoist should try to circulate the breath internally throughout the body without actually inhaling or exhaling air. The texts describe the breath circulating in the body from one's head to one's toes, and back again. This is referred to as *ch'i-kung/qigong*, the technique of using breathing techniques which religious Taoists believed could massage the internal organs and keep them healthy and resistant to illness.[49]

It was believed that proper breathing would ensure proper blood circulation, which was essential to the balance of *yin* and *yang*. As noted before, traditional Chinese medicine tended to see most illnesses as due to spirits and demons, as well as improper circulation of *ch'i/qi* (life breath energy) throughout the body, and poor blood circulation. Some of the techniques to ensure health involve quiet sitting with very slow breathing, while focusing one's attention on the area below one's navel, which would quiet bodily stresses and bring about serenity. Other *ch'i-kung/qigong* techniques are much more active and involve slow rhythmic motions of hand and body. In other words, the breathing techniques were supplemented with physical stretching exercises, resembling modern aerobics in slow motion.

---

[46] A recent book on a Taoist diet is Livia Kohn, *Taoist Dietetics*: *Food for Immortality* (New Mexico: Three Pines Press, 2010).

[47] Joseph Needham, *Science and Civilization in China* II, (London: Cambridge University Press, 1991), pp. 146-152. This incredible series on China has been reprinted several times.

[48] See Chang Chung-yuan, *Creativity and Taoism*, ch. 4, for details on this aspect.

[49] There are a great many books written on *ch'i-kung/qigong* by Western authors, although most of their authors learned *qigong* from other Western authors and often the methods taught or described are not ancient practices from classic inner alchemy Taoism.

CHAPTER 18: RELIGIOUS TAOISM

Aerobics and Gymnastics

Aerobics and gymnastic techniques involved stretching, extending and contracting the body and the limbs. The popular medical model in China was based on the idea that the *ch'i* (vital life essence, life force) needed to flow freely throughout the body, and if someone were ill, it must be because there were energy blockages obstructing the free flow. The religious Taoists developed exercises used to relax the breath and clear the external obstacles of the body so that the *ch'i* energy can flow freely. Virtually all the popular Traditional Chinese medical exercise techniques developed from this aspect. The aerobic techniques also became combined with military aspects of later religious Taoism and became fighting styles (*kung-fu/gongfu*) etc. and fighting systems[50] including those where the warrior used bare hands and did not use swords, spears, or other weapons.

Sexual Hygiene

Once we are aware of the presuppositions of Chinese culture that the basic motion of all reality is an alternating sequence of the negative and positive forces, of *yin* (the feminine) and *yang* (the masculine), it is quite natural for the Taoists to assume that there was a close correlation between human sexual relations and the *yin-yang* operation of the entire universe. The Chinese believed that when aroused, both male and female produce powerful sexual energies, and manipulating those sexual energies was a form of self-cultivation which can affect health and longevity. The primordial union of *yin* and *yang* in the Tao is re-enacted when sexual relations between male and female bring about harmony of *yang* and *yin* and could aid one in the search for immortality.[51]

Since *yang* corresponds to male, then the energy of *yang* can be identified with semen and especially with the process of male ejaculation during sexual activity. Popular traditional Chinese medicine believed that when the semen (*yang*) is discharged, the male body strains to replace it, and the raw materials are taken out of the blood stream, which in order to replenish itself withdraws precious elements from every part of the body, especially the liver, kidney, spleen, and brain. This weakens the male and shortens his lifespan.

Sexual Intercourse is Potentially Deadly

Popular religious Taoist medicine believes that the activity of male ejaculation is destructively unhealthy and hurries illness and aging. Taoist practitioners believed that every male was born with a fixed amount of *yang* life-force or energy. When a male had totally depleted his finite amount of *yang*, at that point there was no way to replace or replenish it, and death would result. If a male did not understand this, and engaged in sexual activities without the proper knowledge and proper techniques to conserve semen, he was hastening his own death.

Popular Chinese religion believed that there could be several benefits from sexual intercourse including extending the life of a male if the sexual act is performed correctly (to be explained below). Sexual intercourse could also be used for preventing illness or a means to healing. Chinese Taoists developed a detailed typology of sexual behavior, such that different positions during sex were regarded as having the ability to prevent illness, increase vital life energy (*ch'i*), decrease stress, and speed healing.

Some Taoist sexual practices were done in public; some Taoists proposed that one man should have intercourse

---

[50] Popular legends connect the empty-handed *kung-fu/gongfu* fighting styles with the sixth century Chinese Buddhist monk, Bodhidharma, who spent three days at the Shao-lin monastery around 525 C.E. However, scholars find no evidence whatsoever that Bodhidharma knew or practiced any fighting style or any physical exercises, and there is no evidence for the weaponless fighting styles of *kung-fu* prior to the fifteenth century in the Shao-lin temple.

[51] It is interesting to note that in India, Tantric Hinduism and Tantric Buddhism put great amount of thought and analysis of the process of sexual intercourse, but never associated this with exchanging sexual energies which could lengthen one's life, or promote health. These are discussed in *Asian Thought*, Volume I, in the chapters on Tantric Hinduism, section 5.7, and chapter 11, Tantric Buddhism.

with 1200 girls aged 16–17 to attain immortality. An example of sex as a means to health was the classic prescription to have sex nine times daily for nine days.[52]

If a man has sex to orgasm and ejaculation, then by emitting his *yang* essence, he was losing his vital life essence (*ch'i*) and was hastening his own death. Religious Taoists believed that women were trying to steal the man's seed to propagate male weakness, to drain men of their vital energy.

However, it was just the opposite if the man could have sexual relations without having an orgasm. It was believed that a man could obtain *yang* energy from the breasts of his partner, but the most powerful energy occurred when the female partner experienced an orgasm; she was emitting *yang* energy which could be absorbed by the male sex organ. If the male did not ejaculate, then he did not lose his own *yang* and in fact acquired even more energy absorbed from his partner.

Popular Chinese medicine believed that a woman has inexhaustible resources of *yang* or "blood-energy" to give to a man, but her fluid energy is easily exhausted, so if she experiences numerous separate sexual encounters with her partner on the same day, she cannot continue to emit *yang* energy. An extended encounter is more useful to a man than several separate couplings.

Thus, the man must have sex with as many different women as possible without losing his own *yang* energy. It would follow that having sex with as many women as possible and providing as many orgasms for the women as possible since this was understood as the woman transferring some of her *yang* energy to the male, which would extend a man's life. In addition, popular Taoist medicine believed that monogamy has adverse effects on the quality of the woman's emissions.

For religious Taoists, sex was a ritual, carefully choreographed to achieve the desired responses. Ideally, the man's sexual partner should also be a Taoist skilled in the complexities of sexual techniques; it was considered inappropriate for the man to profit from the sexual act at the woman's expense. The woman would then become an object to be used by males for increasing the male life span. Nevertheless, if she did not have an orgasm, her emissions would not be released, and then this would not nourish the male.

Chinese sex manuals place great emphasis upon techniques for prolonging intercourse. Since the man wanted to absorb as much of the woman's *yang* emissions as possible, in one encounter, the more orgasms he could provide the better, and consequently the religious Taoist sex treatises place stress upon techniques for pleasing the woman.

There were many other sexual techniques. An example of this concerns what to do if the male were so aroused that he experiences unintended ejaculation. In that case, the male was taught not to allow the semen to leave his body. He accomplished this by tightly pinching the base of the penis. By keeping semen within his body, Chinese alchemists believed the semen could be transformed into *ch'i* energy. Here is a modern explanation of this process:

> Taoist alchemy forsakes the worldly way of life by preventing the generative force which produces the generative fluid from following its ordinary course which satisfies sexual desire and procreates offspring. As soon as this force moves to find its usual outlet, it is turned back and then driven by the inner fire, kindled by regulated breathing, into the microcosmic orbit for sublimation. This orbit begins at the base of the spine, called the first gate, rising in the backbone to the second gate between the kidneys and then to the back of the head, called the third gate, before reaching the brain (*ni wan*). It then descends down the face, chest and abdomen to return to where it rose and so completes a full circuit.[53]

---

[52] The number 9 is a lucky and important number in China. The Chinese pronunciation of "nine," *chiu/jiu* sounds like the Chinese character for longevity, enduring and lasting; nine times nine must be even luckier! The *Tao Te Ching* was later broken into 81 chapters.

[53] Lu K'uan Yu, *Taoist Yoga: Alchemy and Immortality* (New York: Samuel Weiser, 1970), p. xii. Note that the brain experience, *ni wan*, referred to in this quote is in fact the Chinese for the Buddhist term "Nirvana."

Traditional Chinese medicine envisioned the semen directed upwards within the body, up the spinal column, to rejuvenate the upper parts of the body with *yang* energies (the Chinese medical model was in error: modern biology reveals that what actually happened was that the semen was merely forced into the bladder).

When we remember the importance placed on children, and especially male children, we can see that it is essential that the husband engage in sexual relations to impregnate his wife or concubine. However, the only reason for a male to ejaculate was to have children; at all other times, the semen was to be retained in the body. If you wanted to have children, Chinese numerology played an important role (odd numbers are *yang*/male, while even numbers are *yin*/female). Having intercourse on the first three odd-numbered days after menstruation would produce a boy, while having sex on the first three even-numbered days after menstruation would produce a girl.

> Of all the ten-thousand things created by heaven, man is the most precious. Of all the things that make man proper, none can be compared to sexual intercourse. It is modeled after heaven and takes its pattern by earth, it regulates Yin and rules Yang. Those who understand its significance can nurture their nature and prolong their years.[54]

Once we realize the Chinese attitudes towards the union of *yin* and *yang*, and how semen loss is destructive we can understand why the Chinese view male masturbation as losing one's life energy (semen) and thus unhealthy. On the other hand, same-sex male relations exchanges *yang* but do not lose it, so it is not as bad as masturbation. Same-sex relations between women and female masturbation is condoned for the female has an unlimited number of orgasms.

18.8 THE HAN DYNASTY RELIGIOUS WORLD-VIEW

During the Han dynasty (202 B.C.E.–220 C.E.), China traded with Rome (Roman gold and silver exchanged for Chinese textiles, spices and silks), an also traded with India along the Silk Route of central Asia. It was during the Han period when Confucian bureaucrats and their stress on *li* (rituals and ceremony) began to take on more of a semi-religious role. Government work included numerous state cult rituals and court ceremonial activities as well. We know that Confucius himself loved *li*, the ancient rituals. These were found everywhere in government work.

There was no independent religious priesthood in China, and the Confucian bureaucrats with their mastery of ceremony and ritual fulfilled many of the roles that organized state religion would fulfill. The later Han embraced Confucianism because it offered a semi-religious way of ensuring cultural harmony and unity, without the harsh military controls utilized by the previous Ch'in dynasty and the Ch'in stress on the reward and punishment philosophy of Legalism, the school of *fa* (law).

The ideas of the cosmic polarities of *yin* and *yang* (being and non-being, heaven and earth, male and female) permeated into all areas of life. In popular religions, Confucianism and Taoism came to intermix. The Chinese people tended to be Confucian in their families, in ethics, and in state rituals; to be philosophical Taoists in art, music and poetry; to be religious Taoists in the interaction of spirit realms and human realms including sexuality, exorcisms and medicine. Later, during the Sui and T'ang dynasties the Chinese populace would incorporate Buddhist beliefs and practices as well into popular religion.

---

[54] Akira Ishihara, *et. al*, *The Tao of Sex: A Translation of the Twenty-Eighth Section of the Essence of Medical Prescriptions* (Integral Publications, 1989), p. 156.

CHAPTER 18: RELIGIOUS TAOISM

In general, the better educated Confucians tended to have a rather negative attitude towards the unquestioning reliance on gods and demons to explain health and luck, and the uneducated folk ritual and devotional attitudes towards spirits that was typical of the popular religion. The attitude of literati towards what they regarded as superstition varied from limited affirmation and acceptance of a parallel realm filled with spirits, to complete rejection of everything supernatural. There were a few aspects that were important for both the elite and the popular, including reverence for ancestors, filial piety, and the rituals built into hierarchical social relationships by Confucian *li* (ceremonial interaction). Confucian officials would occasionally have to deal with infestations of ghosts or other demonic forces, and preside over rituals of exorcism. Government officials would carry out rituals at temples of state-approved gods, to benefit the well-being of the emperor and the empire.[55]

Over the centuries, the elite members of the Han aristocracy appropriated more and more wealth and found clever ways to shield it from taxation. Poor people, tenant farmers, and small landholders came to bear more and more the burden of financing the government. As a result there developed social, economic, and religious frustrations.

The Confucian bureaucrats (Superior Persons, *chun-tzu/junzi*) performed rituals for cosmic harmony based upon study of Confucian classics, but these abstract political rituals did not satisfy popular religious longings. Popular religion needed deities who responded to pleas and prayers, and most Chinese were illiterate, and could not read or study the classics. Good fortune did not seem available to those outside the circle of privilege and power. For this illiterate group, rituals at local temples and hiring a shaman were their religious options. There was no way for the non-wealthy non-aristocracy to gain access to the power and privileges of Confucian elite, since it took lots of money and leisure to study to pass the Civil Service exams and get a lucrative job with the government. Meanwhile, the imperial royal family was more interested in pleasures than it was in ruling justly, and these all combined to produce great unrest and anger among the common people toward the end of the Han dynasty.

The Great Wall was not a perfect barrier to the clever nomads of northern China; the barbarians gained strength and begin attacking again. The government was not able to fight them off, and by 220 C.E., the Han dynasty fell to non-Chinese invaders. Three hundred years of invasions and civil war followed (220-589 C.E.).

The cultural homeland of Han civilization, northern China, was under continuous attack. Northern China was again separate kingdoms with no central authority. Many of these kingdoms were ruled by non-Chinese northerners. Many Han Chinese families escaped into the central and southern parts of China. Chinese intellectuals and civil servants fled south where they preserved northern Han Chinese culture and bureaucracy in their new homes in central and southern China. South China was stimulated socially and economically as a result. In the non-Chinese northern lands the country went through what is called Sixteen Kingdoms. There were brief dynasties in the south called the Period of the Six Dynasties.

With the period of unrest and change, the demand for cultural and political uniformity was relaxed and great diversity of thought and religion resulted. It was no longer necessary to conform. Religious Taoism regained its power again and Buddhism also took hold in China in the court and among the people. Religious Taoism/Daoism was established as state religion during the period 424-452 C.E. As a result, in 446 Taoists/Daoists in court persuaded the emperor to persecute the foreign religion of Buddhism, a persecution which lasted for six years. This period of separate kingdoms and disunity persisted until 581 C.E.

China is Reunited in the Sui Dynasty

Finally, once again China was reunited under one emperor and one dynasty: the Sui (581-617). China remained unified under the following T'ang dynasty (617-907). Patronage of Taoism/Daoism continued even during the T'ang/Tang dynasty because the T'ang imperial family considered itself descendants of Lao-tzu, who at this time,

---

[55] See Judith Boltz, "Not by the Seal of Office Alone" in *Religion and Society in T'ang and Sung China*, ed. by Patricia Buckley Ebrey and Peter Gregory (Honolulu: University of Hawai'i Press, 1993).

was considered a deity. Religious Taoist masters mixed potions which rulers imbibed; some died as a result.[56]

Taoist religious monasteries were constructed, modeled along the lines of the Buddhist monasteries already populating China. Like Buddhism, Taoists established a hierarchical church organization which issued certificates of ordination to priests, monks, and nuns, for a fee. Spirit-summoning rituals were practiced in the imperial court. In the eighth century, by imperial decree, the *Tao Te Ching* was officially declared a basic literary and religious classic text. On and off in following centuries and dynasties, Taoism/Daoism was patronized by emperors of the T'ang/Tang and Sung/Song.

18.9 SUMMARY OF THE CHAPTER

We have seen that religious Taoism is a complex phenomenon, made up of numerous separate groups with overlapping practices and beliefs. The Yin-Yang and Five Process world view came to dominate all aspects of Chinese life, and these were essential to religious Taoism as well. Some religious Taoism was political and revolutionary. Other aspects turned into a hereditary priesthood, some of whom were shamans trained in methods to control spirits for the benefit of the populace, and others who practiced in monasteries. Techniques of inner and outer alchemy to extend one's life were used in varying degrees by religious Taoists. Religious Taoist beliefs about immortals and the islands of the immortals came to permeate popular Chinese religion and mythology.

Religious Taoist goals of achieving immortality, or at least attaining a long life with few illnesses, was believed to be possible by engaging in external practices like eating the correct magical foods like dew, gold dust and mercury, or cooking one's food in gold utensils. In addition, it was thought that by proper stretching and focused movements, by proper breathing practices, and by special sexual activities, males could extend their life and avoid illness. These ideas have continued to affect popular Chinese medicine into the modern era.

Traditional Chinese medicine is based on the *yin-yang* imagery and the idea of an invisible undetectable flowing *ch'i* energy. With these assumptions, much of religious Taoist imagery becomes understandable.

18.10 TECHNICAL TERMS

ch'i/qi   vital energy, life breath essence

feng-shui   geomancy, belief in invisible yet powerful currents that flow in nature

The Yellow Court   Outer Alchemy   Inner Alchemy

18.11 QUESTIONS FOR FURTHER DISCUSSION

(1)   Think about the general goals of Religious Taoism. How many of them do you share? How many of them does our culture share? Do you have goals not on the list? Do Western religions share goals with non-philosophical Taoism?

---

[56] See Stanley Weinstein, *Buddhism Under the T'ang* (Cambridge University Press, 1987), esp. p. 36, p. 115, p. 135.

(2)   There are people in the West who offer *feng-shui* services, as though it were a form of interior decoration. What are the metaphysical assumptions of *feng-shui* and what were the goals of *feng-shui* practitioners?

(3)   For both Western alchemy and Chinese alchemy, gold has been a very important substance. But its importance was not its yellow shiny beauty or its cost per ounce. Why was gold so important to alchemy?

(4)   The image of the swastika is profoundly negative in Western civilization since the Nazi appropriation of the symbol. It means hate-filled genocide and racist attitudes. What does the swastika symbolize in traditional Chinese religion? The image is also found in India and in native American religious symbols. What does it mean there?

(5)   Religious Taoist understanding of human sexuality is profoundly different from Western attitudes and Western science. Does it seem that patriarchal attitudes dominate these religious sexual practices which are supposed to lead to a long life, and even immortality?

SELECTED BIBLIOGRAPHY

Popular Religious Taoism

Blofeld, John, *Beyond the Gods: Buddhist and Taoist Mysticism* (New York: E.P. Dutton & Co., 1974)

Blofeld, John, *The Secret and Sublime: Taoist Mysteries and Magic* (New York: E.P. Dutton & Co., 1973)

Bokenkamp, Stephen R., *Ancestors and Anxiety: Daoism and the Birth of Rebirth in China* (Berkeley: University of California, 2009) Author traces development of the Indic idea of rebirth into Chinese Taoism and popular religion.

Chappell, David W., and Michael Saso, eds., *Buddhist and Taoist Studies I* (Honolulu: University Press of Hawaii, 1972)

Chappell, David, *Buddhist and Taoist Studies II: Buddhist and Taoist Practice in Medieval Chinese Society* (Honolulu: University Press of Hawai'i, 1987)

Cleary, Thomas, *Taoist Classics, Volume 2* (New York: Shambhala, 2003)

Girardot, N. J., *Myth and Meaning in Early Taoism* (Berkeley: University of California Press, 1983).

Hansen, Chad, *A Daoist Theory of Chinese Thought* (New York: Oxford University Press, 1992)

Hymes, Robert, *Way and Byway: Taoism, Local Religion, and Models of Divinity in Sung and Modern China* (Berkeley: University of California, 2002)

Ishihara, Akira, *et. al, The Tao of Sex: A Translation of the Twenty-Eighth Section of the Essence of Medical Prescriptions* (Integral Publications, 1989)

Kaltenmark, Max, *Lao Tzu and Taoism* (Stanford, CA: Stanford University Press, 1969)

Kohn, Livia, *Daoism and Chinese Culture* (Magdalena, NM: Three Pines Press: 2001)

_____, *Sitting in Oblivion: The Heart of Taoist Meditation* (New Mexico: Three Pines Press, 2010). Taoist meditation as practiced by later traditions of religious Taoism.

_____, *Zhuangzi: Text and Context* (New Mexico: Three Pines Press, 2014) Professor Kohn presents the Chuang-tzu/Zhuangzi book as seen through the eyes of the religious Taoist traditions.

Kohn, Livia, and Robin Wang, eds., *Internal Alchemy* (New Mexico: Three Pines Press, 2009)

Kirkland, Russell, *Taoism: The Enduring Tradition* (New York: Routledge, 2004)

Luk, Charles (Lu K'uan Yu), *Taoist Yoga: Alchemy and Immortality* (New York: Samuel Weiser, 1970)

_____, *The Secrets of Chinese Meditation* (New York: Samuel Weiser, 1964)

Maspero, Henri, tr. by Frank Kierman, Jr., *Taoism and Chinese Religion* (Amherst, Mass.: University of Massachusetts Press, 1981)

Mitchell, Damo, *Daoist Nei Gong: The Philosophical Art of Change* (Singing Dragon, 2011)

Moeller, Hans-Georg, *Daoism Explained: From the Dream of the Butterfly to the Fishnet Allegory* (Chicago: Open Court, 2004)

Moeller, Hans-Georg, *The Moral Fool: A Case for Amorality* (New York: Columbia University Press, 2009) Although this book argues that moral categories are unnecessary at best, it draws upon philosophical Taoism for many of its insights and arguments.

Needham, Joseph, *Science and Civilization in China* II, (London: Cambridge University Press, 1991)

Ni Maoshing, *The Yellow Emperor's Classic of Medicine* (New York: Shambhala, 1995)

Palmer, Martin, in Kwok Man Ho, Joanne O'Brien, *The Eight Immortals of Taoism* (New York: Meridian Books, 1991)

Rawson, Philip, and Laszlo Legeza, *Tao: The Eastern Philosophy of Time and Change* (London: Thames & Hudson, Ltd., 1973)

Robinet, Isabelle, *Taoism: Growth of a Religion* (Stanford, CA., Stanford University Press, 1997), trans. Phyllis Brooks

Robinet, Isabelle, *Taoist Meditation: The Mao-Shan Tradition of Great Purity* (New York: State University of New York, 1993)

Roth, Harold, *Original Tao: Inward Training and the Foundations of Taoist Mysticism* (New York: Columbia University Press, 2004)

Saso, Michael, *The Teachings of Taoist Master Chuang* (New Haven: Yale University Press, 1978)

_____, *Taoism and the Rite of Cosmic Renewal* (Washington State University Press, 1972)

_____, "Buddhist and Taoist Notions of Transcendence," in Michael Saso and David W. Chappell, eds., *Buddhist and Taoist Studies I* (Honolulu: University Press of Hawaii, 1972)

Schipper, Kristofer, *The Taoist Body* (Berkeley: University of California, 1993) An overview stressing the unity of shamanism, religious Taoism, and philosophical Taoism.

Veith, Ilza, *The Yellow Emperor's Classic of Internal Medicine* (Berkeley: University of California Press, 1966)

Wang, Mu, *Foundations of Internal Alchemy: The Taoist Practice of Neidan*, translated by Fabrizio Pregadio (Golden Elixir Press, 2011)

Welch, Holmes *Taoism: The Parting of the Way*: Revised Edition (Boston: Beacon Press, 1965)

Welch, Holmes and Anna Seidel, *Facets of Taoism* (New Haven: Yale University Press, 1979)

Wong, Eva, *Taoism: A complete introduction to the history, philosophy and practice* (Boston: Shambhala, 1997)

See also:

Lagerway, John, and Marc Kalinowski, eds., *Early Chinese Religion: Part One: Shang Through Han* (1250 BC -220 AD) (Leiden & Boston: Brill, 2011)

Lagerway, John, and Lu Pengzhi, eds., *Early Chinese Religion: Part Two: The Period of Division* (220 AD -529 AD) (Leiden & Boston: Brill, 2010)

CHAPTER 19: BUDDHISM COMES TO CHINA

19.1 OVERVIEW OF THE CHAPTER

About two thousand years ago, Buddhists from India and Central Asian kingdoms were engaged in trade with the Chinese, and in the process Chinese became aware of Indian forms of Buddhism. These strange practices and ideas began to intrigue some Chinese thinkers. The civilization of China was fully the intellectual equal of that of India, and for five-hundred years systems like Confucianism, philosophical Taoism, and other schools had exerted profound political influence as well as intellectual stimulation for the well-educated Chinese literati. Why then did Chinese feel an attraction to Indian Buddhism?

Indian Buddhism had many things to offer to the Chinese: the Indians practiced elaborate rituals and rites which had strong appeal to Confucians and non-philosophical Taoists; Indian Buddhism offered careful analyses of life after death; it had a very sophisticated philosophical system and precise logical argumentation; it offered supernatural figures (buddhas and bodhisattvas) with supernatural and magical powers who might protect a ruler and a kingdom from harm. Buddhist monks practiced Indian forms of astrology, did miraculous magic to convert leaders, and chanted magical incantations. It offered meditation exercises which seemed similar to religious Taoist breathing exercises to extend one's life. It seemed to have something for everyone.

Some aspects of Indian Buddhism were offensive to many Chinese. The Chinese considered the emperor to be in charge of everything, and had great difficulty with the Indian idea that any religious practitioners should be free from political control. For most of their history Buddhist temples in China were under the control of imperial bureaus and officials, who tried to regulate who could be ordained as a monk and controlled where temples could be built, and named the abbots of monastic institutions. Imperial representatives provided gifts and financial support which was necessary for Buddhism to grow and develop.

Expecting Buddhist institutions to be under the control of the imperial court was not the only area of conflict. The Chinese were uncomfortable with the apparent pessimism of *duhkha* (suffering, dissatisfaction), they considered begging to be demeaning, considered it insulting when monks and nuns were expected to shave their hair, found the stress upon monastic celibacy to be an assault on Confucian family structures, and did not like the implications of the doctrines of karma and rebirth.

The earliest forms of Buddhism in China were tightly connected to Indian practices and scholastic Indian Buddhist texts, but by the sixth century C.E., some Chinese Buddhists had the self-confidence based in personal experiences to give their own answers to key questions, and the result was the evolution of new forms of Buddhism, forms that had never existed in India. After 500 C.E. along with the earlier forms, there were four basic traditions of Chinese Buddhism which were in their stages of early development, and over the next five hundred years, these would become schools which would produce new insights and practices that had never been seen in India.

CHINESE DYNASTIES REFERRED TO IN THIS CHAPTER

CH'IN/QIN (221-207 B.C.E.)
HAN (202 B.C.E. - 220 C.E.)
             Buddhism enters China around 50 C.E.
 SUI (590-618 C.E.)
 T'ANG/TANG (618-906 C.E.)
 FIVE DYNASTIES (907-960)
 SUNG/SONG (960-1279)
 YUAN (1280-1368)
 MING (1368-1644)
 CH'ING/CHING (1644-1912)
 REPUBLIC (1912 -
      Republic of China (1912-1949)
      People's Republic of China (Mao) (1949-)

19.2 FROM INDIA TO CHINA

A quick look at a map of India reveals that north India is bounded by the tallest mountains in the world, the Himalayan mountain ranges. There was no easy way to go from India directly to China. Trade routes did develop, but it was a long, dangerous, and arduous journey. The most important overland trade route from India to China was called the Silk Road, which went from China to the Mediterranean. From India to China, the trail covered thousands of miles, winding through plains and steppes, through searing deserts, deep canyons and frozen mountains. It was possible to go from India to China via the sea, but a journey around south-east Asia was no less dangerous or shorter. A third way to get from India to China involved some land-routes connecting the area of South-east Asia to Vietnam and then to China.

We do not have a precise date for the introduction of Buddhism to China, but it seems clear that Buddhism was beginning to have influence in the Chinese royal court some time between 50 B.C.E. and 65 C.E.[1] This would be almost 500 years after the death of the Buddha, and corresponds to a time when northern India was in the early stages of Mahayana Buddhism, including the ideas of the bodhisattva and the Madhyamaka *sunyata* (empty of unchanging substance) ideas grounded in the *Prajnaparamita* (Perfection of Wisdom) literature. In China, this period corresponds to the middle of the Han Dynasty (202 B.C.E.-220 C.E.).

Of the three possible routes from India to China (Silk Route, seafaring merchant ships, land routes through South-East Asia), it seems clear that the most important source was the Silk Road. Spices and other valuables traveled from northern India to be exchanged for silks and other Chinese items. The terminus of the Silk Route was the Chinese capital city of Xian (also known as Ch'ang-an), the center of government and the focus for Confucian and Taoist scholars and ministers. Indian traders, accompanied by Buddhist merchants and monks, were doing business

---

[1] There are some references that suggest that there may have been earlier contact. There is a tale of a non-Chinese magician with a staff and begging bowl visiting the court of the kingdom of Yen in 317 B.C.E. although some scholars discount this story. There is a possibility that a Buddhist visited the Ch'in court around 220 B.C.E. If true, neither had lasting consequences.

in the capital city of northern China. Thus, Buddhism spread to China along the trade routes with northwestern India (primarily Mahayana areas) and central Asia.[2]

During the earliest decades, Buddhism was a religion practiced by non-Chinese foreigners seeking business opportunities in China. None of the Chinese religions were monotheistic or exclusive, so gods from other cultures were not a problem to the Chinese. When traders from two cultures interact, it is good business for each side to treat the other's gods with respect. Business opportunities arose for those who could recognize their own deities had much in common with those local gods of the other culture.

Two small Buddhist monasteries were established in the capital of Xian/Ch'ang-an in the early decades of the 1st century C.E. Also there were centers of religious activity along the trade routes, but these centers also functioned as hostels, warehouses, and banking centers for foreign traders from India and Persia. The buildings and compounds had to be sturdy to resist bandits, but over the centuries Buddhist monasteries grew in these locations and adapted to became Chinese institutions. Once having traveled successfully to China, these monks from Indic regions faced the problems of how to earn their livelihood, how to get native Chinese speaking scholars to understand them (which involved problems of translation into Chinese), and then adapting Buddhism to fit the Chinese presuppositions and world-view. To facilitate understanding, new Chinese terms had to be created to translate Sanskrit Buddhist technical terms, or old Chinese terms had to be re-purposed, reused and redefined.

Positive Features of Indian Buddhism

There were many features of Indian Buddhism which appealed to the Chinese. Buddhists employed elaborate rituals, and rituals were the heart of Confucianism and the royal court. Buddhism taught breathing exercises and meditation, offered complex philosophies, and in the search for nirvana, the Buddhists were withdrawing from the world (which echoed behavior of Taoist hermits and immortals).

Buddhist practitioners, especially the Tantric Buddhist teachers who came to China, were thought to have supernatural powers, and the ability to do magic, control spirits who controlled the weather, read minds, fly through the air, and they claimed to have skill in divination (fortune-telling). There are many tales of Indian Buddhist masters performing miracles before kings and their courts. Miracles were used as a tool to demonstrate the efficacy of buddhas and bodhisattvas, and were a powerful instrument for conversion. Miracles included people praying to particular bodhisattvas and then being healed or rescued, people describing the Buddhist afterlife after Buddhist monks miraculously raised them from the dead, and numerous wonders performed by monks and nuns with special spiritual powers. Indeed, monks with the apparent ability to perform miraculous feats impressed many more people than those monks who were experts in abstract Buddhist thought or solitary meditation.[3] Later, Chinese Buddhist monks were assumed to be skilled in controlling and exorcizing demons and curing the sick, powers believed to be derived from meditative prowess and from chanting Buddhist sutras.

It was the Mahayana forms of Buddhism which came to dominate in China. The appeal of Mahayana for many tended to be devotional, not philosophical. Over the centuries, the study of Buddhist philosophy and the analysis of Buddhist texts was not an important part of being a Buddhist monk in China. In general, Buddhism was understood to be a magical process and tool for protecting the state and generating good karma (merit) as a supernatural reward. The more substantial the gifts given to the Buddhist community of monks, the more substantial the karmic payback would be. In many respects, the activities of Buddhist monks often resembled the shamanistic side of religious Taoism/Daoism, with mediums and exorcists.

---

[2] It should be noted that Buddhism was not the only religion to spread along the Silk Route. We know that the Persian religions of Zoroastrianism and Manicheanism used that route, and that Assyrian Nestorian Christianity and Islam also sent missionaries along the Silk Route.

[3] An excellent study of this miracle-working aspect of fifth century popular Chinese Buddhism is the translation by Robert Ford Campany, *Signs from the Unseen Realm: Buddhist Miracle Tales from Early Medieval China* (Honolulu: University of Hawai'i Press, 2012).

CHAPTER 19: BUDDHISM COMES TO CHINA

Rituals, sacrifices, and chanting were the popular activities. An important practice was the performance of rituals for the dead, conducting offerings and sacrificial ceremonies designed to help one's ancestors get out of hellish realms.[4] Buddhist monks would pray to various buddhas on behalf of themselves or on behalf of those who made generous donations to the monasteries. Monks would perform rituals to bestow blessings and long life for the same generous donors. When someone was ill and the doctors were not able to effect a cure, the family would get priests to pray to the buddhas (and the gods), but they would also seek help from religious Taoist shamans.

When Buddhism entered China, China was already home to a vigorous cultural civilization with a long and rich tradition of philosophy and religion, and the Chinese believed in the superiority of their own traditions of Confucianism and Taoism/Daoism. Everyone in China grew up with Confucianism, which was primarily concerned with personal relationships, politics, and society, and also with the place of human beings in the cosmos. Philosophical Taoism was for the elite, and it tended to focus primarily on cosmic matters, and only secondarily on politics and society. Religious Taoism was popular Chinese religion, and it focused on spirits, local gods, shamans, health and immortality. These three systems of thought complemented each other.

This Chinese belief in the natural superiority of their own indigenous traditions over foreign ideas made for tension with Buddhism. Controversies did arise, and either Chinese attitudes had to change, or Indian Buddhism in China had to change. Both occurred.

It is quite extraordinary that Buddhism was able to have such a profound influence upon China. The indigenous Chinese religious traditions were long and venerable, they were the result of centuries of native traditions of literacy, of philosophical and religious traditions based upon sacred texts (especially the Confucian classics and the Taoist classics), of political and institutional ideals correlated with large-scale patterns of social organization.

19.3 BUDDHIST SCRIPTURES ARE TRANSLATED

An important concern for early Buddhism in China was the translation of the Sanskrit Indian Buddhist scriptures (*sutras*) into Chinese. The Chinese could not read Sanskrit, and did not have any understanding of the historical complexity of Indian Buddhist history. The Chinese did not know about the diverging Theravada[5] and Mahayana traditions and their accompanying literature which spanned nearly a thousand years.[6] The Mahayana texts translated into Chinese were critical of what they called "Hinayana" and the Chinese accepted these criticisms as fact. They did not understand that Conservative Buddhist texts could have been composed five hundred years before the later Mahayana texts. They did not realize that Buddhism had splintered into divergent sectarian traditions in India, and that *sutras* accepted by one group were rejected by another. When an Indian sacred text (*sutra*) began "The Buddha said . . ." the Chinese assumed that the words were the actual words of the Buddha. Chinese Buddhists believed that each and every sutra from India was the actual words of the Buddha.

This belief produced serious problems for Chinese Buddhists when they studied the Indian texts translated into

---

[4] Many scholars have pointed out that China did not have a concept of afterlife hells until after Buddhism came into China in the middle of the Han dynasty (202 B.C.E. - 220 C.E.).

[5] A recent book which provides a valuable scholarly overview of the creation of the numerous Chinese Buddhist collections of texts is Jiang Wu and Lucille Chia, eds., *Spreading Buddha's Word in East Asia: The Formation and Transformation of the Chinese Buddhist Canon* (New York: Columbia University Press, 2015).

[6] Some of what are believed to be the most accurate translations into Chinese were accomplished in the early decade of the 400s of the common era, nine-hundred years after the death of the Buddha. Translations continued until approximately the year 1000 C.E., the end of the T'ang dynasty. In addition, several Chinese sutras attributed to the Buddha are known to have been composed and created in China, such as the *Perfect Awakening Sutra*, the *Vajrasamadhi*, and commentaries like the *Awakening of Faith*.

CHAPTER 19: BUDDHISM COMES TO CHINA

Chinese. Theravada Buddhism had the *arhat* as a goal (the follower of the Buddha who put an end to suffering and achieved nirvana), but Mahayana sutras rejected the *arhat* calling this an inferior and selfish goal. Some scriptures said that everyone had the potential to be a buddha, but other texts denied this. Some sutras claimed that the ultimate understanding was insight into emptiness (*sunyata*), whereas others said that the ultimate was Buddha-nature, and yet others insisted it was mind or consciousness. Theravada texts did not agree with Mahayana sutras, and the Mahayana sutras from different Mahayana schools contradicted one another. Tantric Buddhist texts minimized the achievements of the Mahayana. The Chinese did not understand any of these aspects; they only knew that the sutras did not always agree with one another. Attempts to resolve this problem was one of the several factors that led to a distinctly Chinese version of Buddhism.

Indian Buddhist Terminology

The metaphysical concepts of Indian Buddhism, like nirvana, *bodhi* (awakening), karma, dharma, *samsara* (the cycle of birth-and-death) or *pratityasamutpada* (dependent co-arising) had no equivalents in Chinese thought and no words in Chinese which carried these meanings. The Chinese did not know Indian thought or Sanskrit. These terms had to be rendered into Chinese in order for a Chinese person to make any sense of them. The problem was that educated Chinese came to Buddhist texts with Confucian and Taoist presuppositions, and could only understand Indian Buddhism through those Confucian and Taoist perspectives. A Chinese Buddhist's understanding of these ideas came from reading translations into Chinese using Confucian and Taoist equivalents. Confucianism had little interest in questions about the ultimate nature of reality, but philosophical Taoism did have a vocabulary of terms dealing with the ultimate reality, Tao, *yin* and *yang*, a vocabulary of negation (*wu*, emptiness, *wu-wei*, non-action, *wu-nien*, no-thought) and a lively interest in a flowing reality and our inability to describe it (a dominant feature of the Taoist text, the *Chuang-tzu*).

Many of the earliest translators of Buddhist sutras into Chinese had been students of Taoism/Daoism, so they utilized "Dark Learning" Chinese Neo-Taoist terminology to render Indian concepts. Taoist texts advocated letting go of possessions and adopting a simple life of solitude, making these Taoists more comfortable with monastic Buddhism.

Indian Buddhist texts were written in Sanskrit, but almost no Chinese Buddhist monks could read Sanskrit, so no one could tell when Chinese translations using Taoist terms had distorted the original Buddhist ideas. For example, the Sanskrit phrase "the Buddha achieved awakening (*bodhi*)," the Chinese translated as "the Buddha attained the Tao." As a result, Chinese readers of Buddhist texts received the impression that Indian Buddhism was a complex variation of Taoism, and that a buddha was a sage as envisioned by Confucius or Taoists.

Buddhist Magic and Miracles

The attraction of Buddhism for the Chinese went beyond Buddhist texts. They were also interested in Buddhist magic, and were fascinated by the physical meditative and breathing techniques of the Buddhists, which the Chinese interpreted as related to religious Taoist longevity exercises. The earliest Buddhist missionaries emphasized occult meditation and ritual, and the Chinese were interested in these things because of their similar importance in religious Taoism, and Confucians rites. Buddhist rituals in honor of various buddhas and bodhisattvas made sense in the shamanistic assumptions of China, because these were treated as important gods and people performed rituals in honor of buddhas and bodhisattvas in order to bring down blessings, to help them, their families, or their communities.

Important aspects of Buddhism felt familiar to the Chinese because they resembled features of philosophical and religious Taoism. Magical aspects of Indian Tantric Buddhism had parallels in Chinese shamanism. In fact, all of this made it easier for Chinese to adopt Buddhism.

Buddhism taught the restraint of the senses and non-attachment, which resonated with both Confucians and Taoists. Buddhist meditation and focused concentration exercises also were a practical means for self-control

(Confucianism) and self-restraint. In addition, the wide variety of Buddhist meditative practices contributed to and enriched religious Taoism and its search for long life, and the highly speculative and analytic Buddhist philosophy enriched Taoist philosophy.[7]

19.4 CONFUCIAN OBJECTIONS TO EARLY INDIAN BUDDHISM

There was a problem. Although Chinese businessmen were open to Indian gods, the politically powerful Chinese scholars in the court put great value on their ethical and philosophical religious traditions founded by Confucius and Lao-tzu, and Buddhism was a foreign religion. Should the court and its scholars allow Buddhism to flourish in China, or should it be condemned and outlawed?

Many of the traditional Chinese in the court were opposed to Buddhism, claiming that Buddhist doctrines were un-Chinese, and therefore they had to be wrong, or at least of no value to a Chinese person. There is no question that many Indian Buddhist practices and doctrines were decidedly un-Chinese. The Chinese were uncomfortable with *duhkha*, with monks who begged, with monks and nuns shaving their hair, with men leaving home and family, with monastic celibacy, and with the doctrine of karma and rebirth.

The Indian doctrine of *duhkha* (frustration, dissatisfaction, suffering) was perceived as excessively pessimistic, because Chinese life during the early centuries of the Han dynasty (202 B.C.E.–220 C.E.) was going smoothly. In addition, Buddhist monks in India were expected to beg for their meals, but no religion in China practiced begging. For the Chinese, begging was demeaning.

Buddhists did not teach the virtue of reverence for ancestors, but filial devotion was essential to the Chinese world view. One of the most important Buddhist virtues is loving compassion for all living things, and over the centuries Chinese Buddhism came to put particular stress on compassion towards one's parents in addition to compassion for others, kindness and generosity. The Confucians approved of the Buddhist virtue of loving kindness (which seemed similar to the Confucian virtue of benevolence, *jen*), and they approved of special affection for one's family, and reverence for elders and ancestors. Chinese Buddhism came to stress these same aspects. Indian Buddhism also stressed kindness to non-human life forms, and the attitudes of Chinese society towards farm animals was slowly influenced by and transformed by this view.

Monasteries caused a problem as well. There was nothing in traditional China resembling monastic institutions. This too was decidedly un-Chinese. When a Chinese young man entered a monastery, his family was abandoned. The centrally important relationship of parent and child was damaged, even severed. In a Buddhist monastery, one's family became fellow monks and nuns.

In India, ascetic beggars and Buddhist monastics alike renounced their homes, their families, their social worlds, and embarked on an odyssey of escape from bondage to the continuing cycle of birth-and-death.[8] This attitude was intolerable to the Chinese, for whom family was the most important element in social relationships. To escape from family ties was shameful; family ties were the foundation of Confucianism and Chinese society. To turn one's back on one's family was the behavior of a criminal who fled the household because he had brought shame on his family lineage. Even joining a Buddhist monastery was a rejection of the family.

---

[7] Many early Buddhist texts tended to focus on distinctly Chinese Taoist concerns, such as correspondence between the directions, planets, mountains, mythic emperors, elements, and organs of the body. For more on this, see Wendi Adamek, *The Mystique of Transmission* (New York: Columbia University, 2007), p. 85.

[8] Later forms of Indian Mahayana Buddhism argued that all things were empty of essence, and to "escape from" was an error in understanding. Wisdom and liberation were to comprehend that there was no ultimate difference between nirvana and samsara, and this is how one can escape from mistaken conceptual construction and achieve liberation. This world *is* nirvana when understood correctly.

CHAPTER 19: BUDDHISM COMES TO CHINA

Celibate monks and nuns were another blow to the heart of the Confucian world-view. Celibate monks and nuns meant that there would be no grandchildren to perform essential family rites and ceremonies. There would be no grandchildren to care for the elderly, or take over work on the farms. The virtue of filial piety was one of the core concepts of Chinese civilization. The Confucian thinker Meng-tzu (Mencius) had written in IV-A 26:1, "There are three ways in which one may be unfilial, of which the worst is to have no heir." Having no heir was horrifying to those Chinese who knew that sons and grandchildren were essential to care for the parents in their old age, and the Chinese believed that sons and grandsons were essential to perform the rituals to ensure that one's life would continue in the heavenly realms. Celibacy for monks and nuns was an attack on filial piety and family values, the heart of Confucianism. In traditional China, the value of a woman was in her ability to bear sons. Chinese tradition valued male descendants above all else.

The tension between filial piety and celibate monks and nuns was dealt with by having new Buddhist rituals performed in monasteries to benefit *all* departed ancestors residing in heavenly realms. This way, even if the son who entered a monastery had no children, essential rituals were still being performed in the monastery to benefit all ancestors. This was an important accommodation of Indian Buddhism to the Chinese world-view. In later centuries the Confucians criticized Buddhist monks as morally corrupt (many Chinese joined Buddhist monasteries to escape from taxes and to get an easy life, and there were many tales of immoral monks). The same criticisms related to the state support of Buddhism, and the fact that popular Buddhism promised good karmic rewards if people contributed money to Buddhist groups. This did bring in many huge donations.

As we discussed in a previous chapter, in general Chinese thinkers were not much concerned with details about the possibility of an afterlife, and had only rather vague concepts of a heavenly life after death, but the majority did believe that the *yang* part of the human essence would live after the death of the physical body in a pale shadowy afterlife in a heavenly realm, closely related to the human realm. Chinese thought did not focus on life after death; instead the Chinese were much more human-centered than their Indian counterparts, and Chinese thinkers concentrated their energies on this world and this life. Buddhists taught not only heavens but also and hells, and rebirth — and neither hells nor rebirth were compatible with human-centered Confucianism or native Chinese religions.[9]

Buddhist monks incorporated popular religious folk beliefs and superstitions into their sermons, which made Buddhism more palatable to the Chinese. Chinese Buddhism developed elaborate funeral ceremonies, which fit in with Confucian reverence for ancestors (filial piety). The Buddhists were able to explain the cycle of birth and death so it seemed compatible with Chinese beliefs in ancestors in heaven, and ghosts and spirits.

However, the details of Indian Buddhist belief in a continuous cycle of rebirth (*samsara*) did not fit in with Confucian heavenly realms inhabited by ancestors, and the possibility that one's ancestors might return in the next life as a mule pulling a plow, or a dog, or the pork or chicken meat served at dinner, offended the Chinese reverence for ancestors. Slowly, Chinese Buddhists came to accept rebirth, but it was not quite identical with the Indian view.

The two ideas that ancestors live on in heavenly realms and interact with descendants, and the idea that each of us is reborn in many different destinations (heaven, human, animal, ghost, hells) were quite vague and it seemed possible to hold both simultaneously as long as one did not think about it too hard, or investigate it too closely. The Chinese affirmed this life and affirmed the value of this world. Many Chinese Buddhist thinkers were comfortable with the interpretation that each of us is reborn countless times in this very life, that rebirth is a metaphor, not something that happens after one dies.

Yet another feature of Indian Buddhism was offensive to Confucians. Buddhist monks and nuns would shave their heads, but Confucians asserted that one's body and one's hair were a gift from one's parents and shaving that hair off was an insult and ungrateful response to that gift. This remained a problem for over a thousand years.

---

[9] As was noted previously, pre-Buddhist Chinese religion did not have hells, but as a result of Buddhist teachings, it became possible for the departed to live in a hellish existence and not just a heavenly life.

CHAPTER 19: BUDDHISM COMES TO CHINA

Finally, in India, Buddhist monks left society and Indian society treated these mendicants as especially sacred individuals who had gone beyond society and transcended all the rules and regulations of society. In India, Buddhist monks were no longer members of society. Indian Buddhist monks did not work. They were non-productive. They were above traditional social roles, and were not expected to treat a ruler or politician with special reverence. But no one in China shared this view. Buddhist monasticism challenged the sacred character of the emperor and the fact that he was the connection to Heaven, and he was needed to maintain the proper harmony between heaven and earth. It was a traditional assumption among Chinese thinkers to regard all under heaven as subservient to the emperor. Of course, that must include Buddhist monks as well.

The Chinese Buddhist monks had read about the traditions in India, and so Chinese Buddhist monks insisted that they were not subject to the emperor, and so they would not bow to the emperor. Traditional Confucian political thinkers were both horrified and offended by this. In 340 C.E. a debate occurred on the topic. An uneasy compromise was eventually worked out that allowed monks not to bow. This was changed temporarily in the eighth century.[10]

The Chinese world view did not allow for monastic institutions to exist as an autonomous social body outside of secular authority. The emperor ruled all by the grace of heaven, he had a special bond with heaven which made everything under heaven subject to his authority. He had the mandate of heaven which meant he was essential for proper harmony in the world, which most certainly must include the religious realms as well as the socio-political realms.[11] In India, the monastic institutions were thought to transcend this world into a separate and higher realm, but the Chinese did not share this view. Peter N. Gregory remarks that the ". . . this-worldly orientation of Chinese civilization saw little distinction between sacred and profane. Rather than viewing the religious life as a separate and higher norm, the Chinese have tended, instead, to invest the secular with religious meaning."[12]

The Confucian scholars and literati who had devoted their lives to memorizing and interpreting Confucian classics found it difficult to accept the idea that any philosophical wisdom of value might originate from outside of classical China. For the Confucians, people in India were barbarians because they did not know or practice *li* (ceremonial ritual interactions). There was one way to deal with the difficulty. Some Chinese remembered that when Lao-tzu left China he went "into the west," and India was a land located in the west. Perhaps Lao-tzu traveled west until he arrived in India and, once there, he taught the Buddha. Another possibility is that Lao-tzu was the same person as the Buddha and therefore Lao-tzu himself was the teacher of the barbarians of India. Either way Buddhism would not be foreign. Indian Buddhism could be thought of as "degenerate Taoism" with some useful features added.

Religious Taoism was of great importance in the royal courts, and this group also supported the idea that Indian Buddhism was degenerate Taoism. If the teachings of the Buddha were actually Indian Buddhism-Taoism, then it had to be a degeneration of Lao-tzu's teachings because Buddhism in India did not make any contributions to the religious Taoist obsessive search for an elixir of immortality. It seemed that Buddhist meditation might be interpreted as exercises to extend life, but in fact, Indian Buddhists seemed to have no interest in becoming immortal or extending their life span. The ultimate goal of the Chinese Buddhist monk or nun was awakening or nirvana, and having an extra long life span was of no interest to a buddha or a bodhisattva. This certainly disappointed religious Taoists.

---

[10] In 733, during the rein of Emperor Hsuan-tsung/Xuanzong, a decree was issued requiring monks and nuns to pay obeisance to the emperor. However, twenty-five years later the clergy was again exempted from paying obeisance to their parents and the emperor. For more on this see Stanley Weinstein, *Buddhism Under the T'ang* (Cambridge University Press, 1987), pp. 34–35.

[11] A book which deals with Confucian criticisms of Buddhism in China and Korea is Charles A. Muller, tr., *Korea's Great Buddhist-Confucian Debate* (Honolulu: University of Hawai'i Press, 2015).

[12] Peter N. Gregory, *Tsung-mi and the Sinification of Buddhism*, p. 107. As was remarked in the introduction to *Asian Thought*, the notion of a separate religious realm apart from politics and economics is a recent Western phenomenon. "Separation of Church and State" is not shared by the majority of the world's cultures now, or in the past, for whom what we think of as "religion" was definitely a part of governing.

CHAPTER 19: BUDDHISM COMES TO CHINA

19.5 POST-HAN DEVELOPMENTS

The Han dynasty ended in 220 C.E., and in the process of overthrowing the Han royal family, civil strife, civil war, and internal divisions began that were to last for more than three hundred years until 581 C.E. when China was once again unified under central authority. In the early Han when everything was fine, Buddhism was perceived as overly pessimistic with its stress on suffering, on *duhkha*, but this changed with the collapse of the Han.

As a result of civil strife, political chaos and war, there was misery everywhere throughout China. In addition to the famines caused by wars, and the heavy taxes paid to support the military, there were natural disasters as well including floods and droughts. Social disorder and civil war after the fall of the Han dynasty encouraged people to find both political Confucianism and political Taoism to be flawed and ineffective. Neither were able to solve the problems of China. The Buddhist doctrine of *duhkha* was no longer perceived as excessive; life in China was decidedly unsatisfactory and miserable.

The Buddhist explanation of karma as the cause of much of the misery made sense to many Chinese, who added Buddhist ideas to their Confucian and Taoist beliefs. Popular Buddhism promised that if people did good deeds (good karma), then good consequences would ensue including a future life of happiness. In addition, if politicians and leaders did bad things, we could be certain that their bad karma would earn them a very painful existence in Buddhist hells.[13]

After the Han, although a few Buddhist monks did come to China from India, almost all Buddhist monks in China were Chinese. These Chinese Buddhist monks knew no Sanskrit, were raised in traditional Chinese Confucian families, and they did not give up their popular religious beliefs when they became Buddhist monks. Chinese Buddhism could not help but absorb the presuppositions of the Chinese. In fact, Chinese Buddhist monks often incorporated Chinese shamanistic folk-religion into Buddhism, and talked of supernatural powers and miracles. In other words, Buddhism was becoming more and more Chinese with each passing century.

Following the collapse of the central authority of the Han dynasty, northern China was a battlefield between northern Han Chinese, armies of Turks, Tibetans, and Mongols who struggled to dominate northern China. With central Han rulers gone, non-Chinese ruled in the north of China and their courts were open to scholars and teachers and religions traditions from India. Buddhism was patronized by petty warlords of northern China, but still considered a foreign religion ignored by the majority of Chinese.

During the early period, the majority of the forms of Buddhism in China were tightly tied to various Indian Buddhist books, both sutras and scholarly commentaries. Similar to the way modern Christians quote from their sacred texts to support various positions they take (even contradictory positions have been supported by the same quote), the Chinese considered a discussion settled when one monk or another could produce a quotation from a Buddhist book which supported their understanding. A similar approach in the West during the Middle Ages is described by the term scholasticism.[14]

Buddhist monks stressed the magical powers of the many buddhas, comparing them to Chinese immortals, gods, and other spiritual beings. Buddhas were interpreted to be divinities. Non-violence was an essential part of

---

[13] As noted above, China before Buddhism did not have hells, but as a result of Buddhist teachings, the oppressed in China could be certain that those wealthy and powerful clans and politicians causing them such misery would suffer in hellish realms no matter how many rituals were done in their honor by their sons.

[14] Early Buddhist 'schools' in China tended to be based on very academic Indian Buddhist commentaries. For example, the Chinese Ti-lun tradition was based on Bodhiruci's translation of Vasubandhu's *Dasabhumikabhyasya*. The She-lun was based on Paramartha's translation of *Mahayanasamgraha*. The San-lun was based on three treatises written by the Madhyamika philosopher Nagarjuna. These traditions slowly disappeared during the Sui (590–618) dynasty and were replaced by the Ch'an, Hua-yen, T'ien-t'ai and Pure Land schools, discussed in the next chapter.

Buddhist ethics, and it was clear that all buddhas valued peace. As a result, almost every court of every separate kingdom offered support for Buddhism because they believed that heavenly buddhas and bodhisattvas would protect the state allowing for peace. In exchange for the protection provided by Buddhist spirits and gods, the government provided funds to create and support different monasteries and learning institutions. Tax money paid for books, statues and for the support of monks and scholars.

Confucian political advisors objected for several reasons. The Confucians in the government were worried by growing Buddhist influence in the political realm, especially since the majority of courtly advisors were Confucians and they would lose influence if Buddhists gained influence. Also Confucians believed that the teachings of Confucius should be used to guide the state, not ideas from Indian Buddhism.

Buddhism in the North of China is Elite and Scholarly

In the north of China, Buddhist monks focused their efforts on converting the politically powerful rulers and nobility. A central religious duty of Chinese Buddhist monks was to conduct rituals for the protection of and prosperity of the state, for the health of the rulers, and to produce benefits for particular individuals. The Chinese perceived these as *li* (ceremonial rites) and as powerful magic, and felt that this was a good thing.

In the early years of the fifth century, with royal financial help, scholarly monks established translation bureaus in the north to produce new and more accurate translations into Chinese from the Sanskrit originals. One of the most important of these translators was the monk Kumarajiva (344-c. 413) who knew Sanskrit well, but whose Chinese was not very elegant, and Kumarajiva had several very skilled Chinese assistants, including a great philosopher named Seng Chao/Seng Zhao (374-414). Rulers believed that they earned good karma if they funded these translation institutes, but it also gave the state some control over the spread of Buddhist ideas.

Because of the support of rulers in the north of China, Chinese forms of Buddhism came to be influential in the court and many Buddhist monks achieved positions as religious advisors, military advisors, diplomatic couriers and ministers, and even took over administrative roles. Many Chinese Buddhists of the time seemed to feel a duty to promote Buddhism to a status equal to that of state-supported Confucianism and Taoism. The Buddhists in the north felt that Buddhism should be a state religion, like Confucianism and Taoism.

Buddhism in the south of China is not narrowly focused on scholarship

The situation in the south, where central governmental authority was not as relevant, produced forms of Buddhism with broader appeal, appealing to individual farmers, and forms of Buddhism which stressed monastic and cultural aspects. In the south, numerous monks contributed to scholarship and made efforts to reconcile Buddhism and Confucianism. The political intrigues and squabbles in the northern capital cities were not relevant to Buddhism in the south, which tended to be mostly independent of the major temple structures in the north. In southern China, the gentry class dominated, and the forms of Buddhism which flourished appealed mostly to this group.

19.6 BUDDHISM DURING THE SUI (590–618 C.E.) DYNASTY

Although many Chinese monks attempted to travel to India to bring back new Buddhist scriptures, the journey was extraordinarily difficult and dangerous, and a great many perished making the trip. It required several years of travel just to get to India, and several more to return home (one famous pilgrim required fifteen years to make the round trip). The travel required the monk to carry money, which was very likely to be stolen by brigands and thieves. After the sixth century C.E., travel along the silk trade route became so extremely dangerous that few people used the Silk Route any more. Bandits would not only rob the caravans, but also kill the merchants and their guards. Some of the water-holes and oases along the route had provided food, water, and protection in the past, but now these too came under attack by small armies of well-armed bandits, and with the oases gone and the protection they offered gone, travel became almost impossible.

The connection between India and China was growing weaker and weaker.

In the past there had been numerous thriving communities along the Silk Road which drew their livelihood from the traveling merchants. Some of these areas also had been centers of Buddhist practices and learning. These were now ghost-towns. Buddhism in China was basically cut off from Indian influence, and this was another factor which encouraged the development of new forms of Chinese Buddhism.

By the early sixth century, Buddhism had been in China for over 400 years and there were many Chinese with deep and profound understanding of Buddhism. There were now great Chinese monks who spoke with confidence and authority and insight; they began to guide Buddhism in China into new forms. These people had a deepened Chinese appreciation of Indian Buddhist concepts, and they no longer interpreted Buddhism as a variant of Taoism. These individuals were quite confident of their own understanding, and slowly new understandings of important Buddhist ideas developed.

Chinese Buddhist Sects Organize Around Specific Sutras

With the connection with India severed, Chinese interest was focused on the Indian Buddhist sutras as the best sources for understanding Buddhism. However, lacking any understanding of the fact that different sutras were composed at different times and were affiliated with different schools of Indian Buddhism, the Chinese teachers instead picked specific sutras which were relevant to their own religious needs, and based their teaching on these sutras.

For this reason Chinese Buddhism of the Sui and T'ang eras tended to develop around specific groups of sutras and commentaries. The previously translated Indian Conservative Buddhist texts slowly faded from attention, but the Mahayana texts with their bodhisattvas became more important, with entire sects in China devoted to specific Mahayana sets of scriptures. However, as noted previously, the Mahayana sutras contradicted one another because the Indian original texts were sectarian. In the process of dealing with conflicting positions, particular monks would stake out one set of texts as the ultimate authority, and other monks would choose different texts as the ultimate authority. The result was different groups of Chinese Buddhism developed. In the process Indian Buddhism in China was transformed.

By the late 400s and early 500s in China, several non-Indian Chinese forms of Buddhism were taking shape. In the Sui dynasty (590–618 C.E.), and later in the T'ang (618–907), these forms of Buddhism became completely Chinese. All the monks and nuns were raised in Chinese Confucian families and shared the traditional Chinese world-view, so Chinese culture influenced Buddhism profoundly. On the other hand, Buddhism began to influence Chinese culture as well. Buddhist ideas, Buddhist rituals, and philosophy and divinities began to change and enrich Chinese culture. As Buddhist influences permeated Chinese civilization, Chinese poetry, ink painting, and sculpture were infused with a new creative spirit, which went on to full development during the T'ang and later southern Sung dynasty.

19.7 BUDDHISM BECOMES UNIQUELY CHINESE

In the process of becoming uniquely Chinese, Buddhism in China dropped many of the basic assumptions of Indian religions and replaced them with Chinese understandings of the same situations. There were many assumptions and presuppositions of Indian Buddhism which the Chinese simply did not share.

CHAPTER 19: BUDDHISM COMES TO CHINA

Fixed Social Status is not Important

One Indian assumption which the Chinese did not share would be the Indian cultural assumption of fixed social status due to karma (where one's occupational caste was religiously ordained and unchangeable). In India, one's situation in this life was the proper result of one's prior choices and actions in previous lives, and one deserved the status one was born into; therefore it was immoral and ignorant to try to change one's social or occupational position. In India, one worked hard in this life to gain good karmic merits which would allow one to be reborn in a more spiritually satisfying life in the next cycle of life. Buddhism arose in a religious world-view which held these assumptions. The Chinese simply ignored most of this. By the time of the Han dynasty, the Chinese believed that one's social status was flexible; that even the poorest farmer's son could, by means of talent and scholarship, improve his station and rise to the position of advisor to the emperor.

Purity and Defilement are not Important

In general, Indian religious culture was obsessively concerned with purity and defilement, concepts tied to the Hindu caste system but also spiritually important. Social group contamination and individual pollution have been important concepts in India since the earliest times. It is believed that people can become polluted by what they eat or drink, and by what they touch. Some humans are permanently impure. That is, they have ritual pollution attached to them by virtue of their birth, and because of their contamination, they must be avoided by the upper castes. Others are only temporarily impure and can be purified by rituals performed by Brahmin priests. The Chinese simply did not share that presupposition. For some Indian Buddhists, one could make spiritual progress by austerities and self-purification. In China, some religious Taoists sought an extra long life using austerities and purification, but this was not for the purpose of achieving awakening or sagehood. In general, the Chinese simply did not share the Indian presupposition that spiritual progress was dependent upon spiritual self-purification and eliminating contamination.

Sagehood Does Not Depend Upon Morality

In Indian Buddhism, to achieve nirvana required morality, mental discipline, and wisdom (these three are cornerstones of the Noble Eightfold Path). Indian Buddhism placed great stress on morality as a necessary condition for the attainment of nirvana. For the Chinese, the goal was to become a sage. Thus, liberation or enlightenment was sagehood. In Chinese thought, sagehood was not dependent on moral status; awakening was about wisdom and discipline, but not linked so tightly to moral uprightness. Every Chinese family learned morality at home in the context of Confucianism. They knew that they had to strive to be a Superior Person (*chun-tzu/junzi*), or even a sage. As a result, the Indian Buddhist moral teachings were mostly redundant and unnecessary in Chinese culture.

Philosophical Taoism also had an influence on Buddhism, and we know that the Taoist understanding of virtue and morality was fundamentally different from the Indian view. In addition, Taoists rejected many of the Confucian ideas. For the Taoist, Confucian morality caused us to deviate from our essential intrinsic nature and is the cause of chaos. For the Taoist, to be truly good was to be spontaneous and in harmony with the flowing Tao.

The Chinese considered a sage to be equivalent to a buddha, and a buddha to be a variant of a Chinese sage. Thus ancient Chinese models of spiritual perfection came to influence Chinese understandings of the goal of Buddhism. For the Taoists, the sage was playful, was spontaneous, unconventional, was in accord with the flowing Tao, "... but who might still have a family, life an ordinary life, enjoy catching fish and eating them with a jug of good wine."[15] The poetry of Lao-tzu's *Tao Te Ching* advised that the sage was in harmony with Tao, and to achieve the Tao does not require any moral or intellectual preparation.

Pursue knowledge, gain daily.
Pursue Tao, lose daily.

---

[15] Francis Cook, *Sounds of Valley Streams* (New York: State University of New York, 1989), page 6.

> Lose and again lose,
> One attains non-action (*wu-wei*).
> Non-action and yet nothing is left undone.[16]

To "lose day by day" does not take many lifetimes of moral practices to achieve. The practice of "losing day by day" is cultivating *wu-wei* (taking no unnatural or artificial actions). To cultivate *wu-wei* is to avoid behavior which went counter to the moving and alternating *yin*-to-*yang* pattern which constitutes the Tao.

It Does not Take Lifetimes to Achieve Sagehood and the Process is not Gradual

One question which did arise in Indian Buddhism was the question of whether awakening was a slow and gradual process, or whether it was abrupt, or sudden. What was a minor issue in Indian thought became of immense importance in China. The Taoists seemed most comfortable with the idea that Taoist illumination was sudden, and perhaps this influenced Chinese Buddhism in general. After substantial debate, Chinese Buddhism concluded that enlightenment was not a gradual ladder-like step-by-step process, with the student being 10% awakened, then 20% awakened, and so forth. Rather, the awakening experience is abrupt, is sudden, and this implies that awakening does not have to be preceded by lengthy preparatory stages of moral and cognitive self-purification. However, further cultivation may be necessary after the abrupt awakening experience to deepen it.

Monasteries Become Self-Supporting

The monastic institution was also changed by Chinese assumptions about the world. Chinese Buddhist monks grew up with Confucian ethics, and this offered no respect for those who did not work. Reacting to this, Chinese Buddhist monasteries became self-supporting, using the manual labor of the monks and nuns as training devices. In India forest monks were mendicants and even monastic monks begged. Not in China. Note also that Chinese did not have the tradition of mendicancy which the Indians may have had since the time of the Indus Valley civilization. As noted previously, these newly re-conceptualized Chinese Buddhist monasteries also adopted rituals for the benefit of departed ancestors in response to the concern about the celibacy of monks and nuns.

Buddhist Priests Participate in the Political Realm

Another change to Buddhism has already been noted. In India, in theory Buddhist monks lived away from society and politics. Like the historical Buddha, Indian Buddhist priests could give advice to rulers if asked, but did not accept positions in the government. The situation was different in China. The Chinese respected scholars and scholarship, and even Buddhist scholars had a high social standing, higher than the military. In China, many Buddhist clergy became a part of official Chinese government, with famous teachers invited to preach in the capital and given honors, titles, and gifts. Most of these monks were excellent scholars and were admired for their learning. As a result of this interchange, it was not uncommon for monks to take on many official functions, as advisors and couriers, and some became a part of the official bureaucracy as ministers. In fact many Chinese Buddhist monks sought out imperial recognition and favors.

Not all Chinese Buddhists approved of this. Some Chinese Buddhist monks considered involvement with politics a perversion of basic Buddhist ideals, and thought that Buddhism should avoid places of power. These Buddhists preferred a life spent in meditation in a search for sudden awakening, and many of the greatest of the Buddhist monasteries were established in the south of China, deep in the mountains, far from politics and commerce.

---

[16] Author's translation from chapter 48 of the *Tao Te Ching*; Han-shan Te-ching, *op. cit.*, p. 108.

CHAPTER 19: BUDDHISM COMES TO CHINA

19.8 SUMMARY OF THE CHAPTER

We have seen that Indian forms of Buddhism came into China during the Han dynasty (202 B.C.E.–220 C.E.). Northern forms of Chinese Buddhism had more interest in and support from the rulers and the courts, and tended toward elite scholarship. Southern forms of Buddhism tended to be less concerned with imperial patronage, and had more appeal to the common folk. Kings and courts sponsored the translation of Indian Buddhist texts, and paid for Buddhist monasteries to be erected and statues of buddhas and bodhisattvas to be carved. Although both Theravada and Mahayana texts were translated, Mahayana ideas captivated the Chinese and the earlier Conservative Theravada texts faded in importance until Chinese Buddhists simply no longer paid attention to the earlier traditions. Until the sixth century C.E. Buddhism in China was primarily in a period of importation, and assimilation.

Confucians were critical of many features of Buddhism: Buddhist monks were supposed to beg, but China had no tradition of begging; Buddhist monks and nuns were to shave their heads, but the Chinese regarded that as an insult to one's parents; Buddhist monks and nuns lived in monasteries which were supposed to be supported by householders, but the Chinese felt that a person who did not work was lazy; Confucius did not teach Buddhism, so Buddhism was a foreign religion and must be useless to China and wrong; Buddhist monks and nuns were celibate, but this meant that there would be no grandchildren to do the sacred rituals required to keep ancestors in heavenly realms; rebirth meant that one's ancestors could return as horses or mules, which were worked very hard, or pigs, or chickens which a family might eat, but this also horrified Confucians; Buddhists regarded themselves as beyond the authority of the Chinese Emperor and political system, but Confucians believed that the Emperor ruled everything "under heaven."

Then between the sixth and eighth centuries (the Sui dynasty), conflicting Indian sutras provided the impetus for Buddhists in China to expound on their own understanding, and Buddhism flowered and became the most creative thought system in China, influencing philosophy, religion, poetry and all the arts. Great Chinese teachers arose and their ideas became the foundation for new schools of Buddhism which had no actual antecedents in India. Uniquely Chinese schools of Buddhism were the result, and from then on, the Chinese rarely sought new ideas from India. Buddhism was now a part of the fabric of Chinese civilization.

19.9 KEY CONCEPTS AND IMPORTANT TECHNICAL TERMS

Kumarajiva — important translator of Buddhist texts into Chinese

Seng Chao/Seng Zhou — an assistant to Kumarajiva and a very important Chinese Buddhist thinker

dharma — in Indian Buddhism, the teachings of the Buddha
duhkha — frustration, dissatisfaction, misery, suffering

karma — the natural pattern whereby each moral deed has consequences which resemble that deed

Nirvana — the blowing out of the flames of anger, hatred, self-centered attachments, and ignorance

pratityasamutpada — dependent co-arising; the insight of the Buddha that all things are interconnected and interdependent

samsara — the cycle of birth and death
sutras — the scriptures which contain the teachings of the Buddha

Tao — the Way, the pattern of all reality, the source, the foundation.

CHAPTER 19: BUDDHISM COMES TO CHINA

yin   the feminine, intuitive, cool, dark and mysterious aspect of Tao
yang   the masculine, aggressive, logical, and bright aspect of Tao

Han dynasty	Sui dynasty	T'ang dynasty
The Silk Road	translation institutes	introduction of Buddhism into China

19.9 QUESTIONS FOR FURTHER DISCUSSION

(1)   Indian Buddhist religion was brought to China by merchants who traveled along the Silk Route. Are there other religions that were spread by priests accompanying merchants along trade routes?

(2)   It has been claimed that all religions must change over time, and must change when a religion moves to a different culture; if the religion will not change, it will die out. This has been observed as Indian Buddhism became Chinese Buddhism. The Chinese Buddhists would claim that the essence of Buddhism was preserved, and the cultural accretions were discarded. Here's a question: how can we tell which beliefs and practices are the essence, and which are superficial? Western Christianity also changed as it went from one culture to another. How can one determine which practices and beliefs are essential, and which are not? For example, is covering one's head in a church or temple essential, or socially conventional? Is the use of Latin as a liturgical language essential, or socially conventional? Is kneeling essential or conventional?

(3)   Which practices of Indian Buddhism bothered the Chinese Confucians? Were those changed? Which survived and which did not survive?

(4)   Which practices of Indian Buddhism were approved of by the Chinese Confucians? Were there any changes in Buddhism to allow for these practices?

(5)   One thing which attracted the Chinese to Buddhism was the many Indian monks who seemed to be able to perform miracles. For westerners, which sort of persons exert the most influence for religion? Is it those who seem to be peaceful and wise, or is it those who seem able to perform miracles such as curing the sick or exorcizing demons, or is it those who are intellectually skilled in explanation of texts and concepts?

SELECTED BIBLIOGRAPHY

Chinese Buddhism

Balazs, Etienne, *Chinese Civilization and Bureaucracy* (1964).
Beckwith, Christopher I., *Empires of the Silk Road: A History of Central Eurasia from the Bronze Age to the Present* (Princeton, NJ: Princeton University Press, 2009).
Campany, Robert Ford, *Signs from the Unseen Realm: Buddhist Miracle Tales from Early Medieval China* (Honolulu: University of Hawai'i Press, 2012)
Chappell, David, *Buddhist and Taoist Studies II: Buddhist and Taoist Practice in Medieval Chinese Society* (1987).

CHAPTER 19: BUDDHISM COMES TO CHINA

Cook, Francis, *Sounds of Valley Streams* (1985).

Ch'en, Kenneth, *Buddhism in China: A Historical Survey* (Princeton, NJ: Princeton Univ. Press, 1964).

Fung, Yu-lan, *History of Chinese Philosophy: The Period of Classical Learning*, Vol. II (Princeton, NJ: Princeton University Press, 1953)

Ge Zhaoguang, tr. by Michael S. Duke and Josephine Chiu-Duke, *An Intellectual History of China, Volume 1* (Leiden & Boston: Brill, 2014)

Lagerway, John, and Lu Pengzhi, eds., *Early Chinese Religion: Part Two: The Period of Division* (220 AD -529 AD) (Leiden & Boston: Brill, 2010)

Liebenthal, Walter, "The Immortality of the Soul in Chinese Thought," *Monumenta Nipponica* 8 (1952), pp. 327-397.

Loewe, Michael, *Everyday Life in Early Imperial China* (1968).

Nattier, Jan, *Once Upon a Future Time: Studies in a Buddhist Philosophy of Decline* (Berkeley: Asian Humanities Press, 1991)

Pachow, W., "Buddhism and Its Relation to Chinese Religions," *Chinese Buddhism* (1980).

_____, "Lao Tzu and Gautama Buddha," *Chinese Buddhism* (1980).

Robinson, Richard, *Early Madhyamika in India and China* (1967).

Saso, Michael and David Chappell, *Buddhist and Taoist Studies* I (1977).

Takakusu, J., *The Essentials of Buddhist Philosophy* (Greenwood Press, 1956).

Yü Ying-shih, "Life and Immortality in the Mind of Han China," *Harvard Journal of Oriental Studies* 25 (1964–1965), pp. 80-122.

Visvader, John and W. Doub, "The Problem of Desire and Emotions in Taoism and Ch'an," in *Early Ch'an in China and Tibet*, Whalen Lai and Lewis Lancaster, eds. (1983).

Weinstein, Stanley, *Buddhism Under the T'ang* (Cambridge University Press, 2008)

Wright, Arthur, *Buddhism in Chinese History* (1959)

Wu, Jiang, and Lucille Chia, eds., *Spreading Buddha's Word in East Asia: The Formation and Transformation of the Chinese Buddhist Canon* (New York: Columbia University Press, 2015)

Zürcher, Erik, *The Buddhist Conquest of China: The Spread and Adaptation of Buddhism in Early Medieval China*, 2 volumes (Leiden: Brill, 1959).

Zürcher, Erik, edited by Jonathan A. Silk, *Buddhism in China: Collected Papers of Erik Zurcher* (Leiden & Boston: Brill, 2014)

CHAPTER 20: DEVELOPMENT OF BUDDHISM IN CHINA

20.1 OVERVIEW OF THE CHAPTER

In the first centuries after the introduction of Buddhism to China (about 50 B.C.E.) Chinese monks tried to establish traditional Indian forms of Buddhism but almost none of those Indian schools survived into the Sui dynasty (590-618 C.E.). By the beginning of the Sui dynasty, things had changed. Many Chinese Buddhists felt confident in their understanding of Indian Buddhism and its doctrines. These Chinese Buddhist monks no longer felt that they simply had to quote Indian texts to justify their positions. They reinterpreted these texts to suit their own understanding. In addition, at least some Chinese teachers seemed to be genuine sages, even enlightened, and their authority was taken seriously.

Even in India there was no central authority for Buddhists, there was no one who could declare one view orthodox and the opposite view heretical. In the same way that forms of Buddhism developed along different lines in India, so too Chinese Buddhists were free to develop Buddhism in uniquely Chinese ways, embedding it in uniquely Chinese assumptions about religion and the world.

Several new forms of Chinese Buddhism arose which were not merely a continuation of Indian Buddhist schools. These new Buddhist traditions used terms and ideas and methods of expression which had never existed in India. These new uniquely Chinese forms of Buddhism were the Pure Land, the T'ien-t'ai/Tiantai, the Hua-yen/Huayan, and the Ch'an/Chan traditions. The T'ien-t'ai and Hua-yen developed Buddhist philosophical insights in a Chinese context, making them uniquely Chinese. The Ch'an schools developed new methods unique to itself, including the puzzling question called a *koan* (ko-an).

In this chapter we'll consider the historical and philosophical development of the first three of these schools: the Chinese Pure Land form of Buddhism; the T'ien-t'ai; the Hua-yen tradition. The fourth school of uniquely Chinese Buddhism, the Ch'an, will be considered in the next chapter.

CHINESE DYNASTIES RELEVANT TO CHINESE BUDDHISM

HAN (202 B.C.E. - 220 C.E.)
> Buddhism enters China between 50 B.C.E. and 50 C.E.

SUI (590-618 C.E.)
> Chinese Buddhists become confident and new schools arise.

T'ANG/TANG (618-906 C.E.)
> The great flowering of Chinese Buddhism which influenced philosophy and art.

SUNG/SONG (960-1279)

20.2 HISTORICAL BACKGROUND

We have seen that due to the ongoing social disorder after the fall of the Han dynasty in 220 C.E., many Chinese lost confidence in traditional answers and turned away from both social Confucianism and religious Taoism because neither seemed able to solve the problems of China. Buddhism was slowly expanding into China during this time of disorder, and Buddhist teachings of *duhkha* (misery, suffering) were now perceived as an accurate depiction of the reality of life in China. In the north, Buddhist monks who were admired for their learning, their philosophical acumen, and their magical powers, were assimilated into local governments and became advisors, couriers, and even ministers, making them part of the official bureaucracy.[1] Chinese Buddhists were Chinese, which means that their model of the ideal relationship between state and religion was that of Confucian power in the royal court. These monks wanted to elevate Buddhism to a position of importance equal to state-supported Confucianism and Taoism.

20.3 THE BUDDHIST FLOWERING UNDER THE SUI AND T'ANG

Following more than three hundred years of war and misery after the collapse of the Han dynasty, China once again came under one central ruler. A Northern Chinese general was able to control all of the north, and founded the Sui (590-618 C.E.) dynasty. He went on to conquer the south as well, unifying China for the first time since the fall of the Han in 220 C.E. In the Sui court, Taoism was given official recognition and Lao-tzu honored, and treated as a deity. The new Sui ruler wanted to establish the sanction and authority of Heaven (*t'ien-ming/tianming*) giving him the right to rule, and so Confucianism was selectively revived because the Confucians were the experts in the ancient rites and rituals which were used to lend legitimacy to the new Sui dynasty and reestablish a connection with the Han dynasty. Confucianism was no longer the central political philosophy in court because it was believed that the fall of the Han dynasty had shown that Confucian ideas for social and political control were not as effective as previously believed.

During the previous five centuries, Chinese Buddhism had developed as well. Chinese monks were confident of their understanding of Buddhism, and this allowed the more creative Chinese monks to break free from the Indian models and express themselves in uniquely Chinese ways. Several problems in Chinese Buddhism had arisen which required solution, and the attempt to resolve these questions provided a uniquely Chinese understanding of Buddhism.

Long before the Sui dynasty, Chinese Buddhist teachers had recognized that the various Buddhist texts attributed to the Buddha did not always agree with one another. This was a problem. If a Buddhist text came to China from India, the Chinese believed the sutra was completely authentic. After all, each Buddhist sutra began "Thus I heard . . ." and therefore must have been the words of the Buddha. So, then, why would the Buddha contradict himself? Why did the Buddha teach conservative Theravada Buddhism only to reject it with Mahayana teachings? Why did the Buddha teach that all things are empty of unchanging essence (*svabhava-sunyata*), but also teach that the mind was not empty (Yogacara Buddhist texts)? Why did the Buddha teach that some people could never become enlightened buddhas (Yogacara texts), but also teach that everyone has the Buddha-nature?

Modern students of Buddhism recognize that the Indian sutras were composed by different groups over a period of nearly a thousand years, but the Chinese did not know this. Chinese Buddhists believed that every sutra was authentic. They were forced to solve this problem without any knowledge of the development of contending schools

---

[1] An excellent detailed scholarly analysis of this topic is the two-volume classic by Eric Zürcher, *The Buddhist Conquest of China: The Spread and Adaptation of Buddhism in Early Medieval China* (Leiden, Netherlands: E. J. Brill, 1959).

belonging to the conservative Theravada and more liberal Mahayana Buddhist traditions in India.

One strategy for dealing with this problem was that Chinese Buddhist monks began to focus their energies upon specific Indian Buddhist texts which appealed to them, and Chinese schools of Buddhism developed around these texts. They studied the *Lotus sutra*, the *Avatamsaka sutra*, the *Perfection of Wisdom sutras*, the Mahayana *Nirvana sutra*, various Madhyamaka essays of Nagarjuna and others. In an attempt to explain and account for the differences in the various Mahayana sutras, monks came up with some philosophically profound doctrines which were instrumental in creating schools of Chinese Buddhism that had never existed in India or Southeast Asia.

During the Sui (589-618) and T'ang (618-907) dynasties, Buddhist philosophy, ritual, and iconography began to influence Chinese culture profoundly. Chinese arts, especially brush painting and sculpture, were infused with a new spirit and energy, producing early masterpieces, many of which have been excavated from tombs and studied by archaeologists, and others which still survive in the Buddhist cave paintings and sculpture of Northern China.[2] In addition several forms of Buddhism enjoyed support from the state and the common people, and many different Buddhist groups, which focused on specific scriptures, flourished. Chinese rulers and wealthy merchants supported Buddhist activity, and new Buddhist sects sprang up in the capital cities of Ch'ang-an and Lo-yang.

Elite Buddhism and Popular Buddhism

During these early centuries of the Sui (581-619 C.E.) and T'ang (618-906 C.E.) dynasties, Buddhism slowly separated into two loosely distinguished forms: the scholarly or elite, and the popular devotional. There were several scholarly forms of Mahayana Buddhism which tended to have more appeal for the intellectually elite upper classes, and popular devotional forms of Buddhism which appealed to the less philosophically-inclined people. The elite highly literate form, the Grand Tradition Buddhism, appealed to those who had the time and support to study in cloistered monasteries, or those who were so well-educated that the metaphysical and philosophical texts and insights of Buddhism appealed to them; these tended to be the literati scholars and members of the aristocracy. However, the aristocracy were politically powerful members of the government, and the imperial government exerted a great deal of control over these forms of Buddhism, including managing the Buddhist hierarchy and assigning Buddhist monks to particular temples. The court also attempted to limit the number of ordained monks and nuns, and to limit the size of the various temples and monastic institutions.

Popular devotional forms of Buddhism generally had more appeal to the common people who were illiterate, and made less use of meditation, philosophy, and less use of aspects like "emptiness" (*sunyata*) which required education or intellectual sophistication. Popular Buddhism tended to rely on faith, incantations, various healing miracles, talismans and rituals. The Chinese, like most people throughout human history, were mainly concerned with how supernatural powers could help them, their families, and their communities in their daily struggles. The most common way to enlist these powers was to appeal to gods at local temples. For most Chinese, the various buddhas were just more gods. We know from the voluminous biographical accounts of famous Buddhist teachers in Chinese history that in addition to monks skilled in meditation, monastic discipline, and translators, there were monks who were thought able to perform magic with the aid of spirits, monks who overcame and exorcized demons, monks who cured illnesses, monks who controlled the weather, and other miracle workers. There are legends of monks who created manifestations, or appeared with changed bodies.

Lives of the monks in Buddhist monasteries

Buddhist monasteries flourished during this time, but it was not always because the monks desired to pursue Buddhist nirvana. The monastic life offered safety from labor gangs and military conscription, and because monasteries were exempt from taxes, the monks could enjoy a relatively easy life supported by governmental tax money. Some

---

[2] A profusely illustrated book dealing with this topic is James C. Y. Watt, *China: Dawn of a Golden Age, 200-750 AD* (New Haven, Yale University Press and the Metropolitan Museum of Art, 2004), especially the Angela F. Howard article, "Buddhist Art in China."

monastic institutions and monks became quite wealthy and engaged in affairs which seem contrary to the codes of Buddhist life.[3] The monastery also offered a quiet contemplative atmosphere, where one could cultivate scholarly and aesthetic pursuits safe from the uncertainties of political life.

The great majority of Buddhist monks did not study Buddhist philosophy. They would memorize the precepts, and they would memorize and chant scriptures, but not discuss their meaning. They would perform rituals for the dead, conduct offerings and sacrificial ceremonies designed to help ancestors get out of hellish realms. They would pray to various buddhas on behalf of themselves or on behalf of those who made contributions to the monasteries. Monks would perform rituals to bestow blessings and long life for the generous donors. When someone was ill and the doctors were not able to effect a cure, the family would get priests to pray to the buddhas (and the gods), but they would also seek help from religious Taoist shamans. In the monasteries there were daily morning and evening services, there was ringing of the bell and the ritual drumming, there was daily work cleaning the monastery and working in the fields growing vegetables. There was cleaning the kitchen and the lavatory. Some monks were needed to cook, and other monks washed clothes of those fellow monks who were ill or elderly. Of course, monks would also perform repentance rituals. Time to study philosophy and meditate was not easily available. Monks didn't study the sutras; they simply memorized and chanted them as magical words of power. Monks who could teach Buddhist concepts to the other monks were very rare, and those who could teach members of the public were even more rare.

Monasteries were constructed for women as well. Buddhist monasteries carried an appeal to women beyond the appeal of Buddhist religious doctrines. There were few options for women in China other than marriage, and to become a Buddhist nun opened up at least a few new choices other than marriage. Monks and nuns were freed from arranged marriages, freed from Confucian *li* ceremonial and ritual responsibilities, and free from strictly defined family roles. In China, Buddhist nuns were not taught to read or write, and normally did not study philosophy or texts; rather they carried on social work.

20.4 THE SCHOOLS OF CHINESE BUDDHISM

By the sixth century, many Chinese Buddhist monks were confident that they understood Buddhist texts on their own terms, and most no longer felt it necessary to travel along the dangerous Silk Route to India to procure new Buddhist sutras. Some Buddhist teachers had great reputations for their wisdom, and they seemed to have achieved deep and profound levels of understanding. Buddhist teachers often disagreed with one another, but there was no central Chinese Buddhist authority with the power to declare one view correct and another mistaken. Rather, the issues were debated, quite often in the capital city and even in the royal throne room with the emperor as the judge declaring the winner.

Slowly the Chinese Buddhists evolved technical terms that reflected Chinese presuppositions, technical terms which had no analog in the Indian Buddhist sutras or commentaries. Chinese Buddhists argued about whether Buddhist awakening happens suddenly or all-at-once, or whether it happens through a process of gradual self-realization. They wondered how the Buddha and bodhisattva were related to the Tao. Chinese thinkers tended to think using categories of opposites such as *yin* vs. *yang*, intuition vs. progressive exercises, abrupt vs. gradual, universality vs. particularity, time vs. timelessness, form vs. formlessness, and substance (what-a-thing-is) vs. function (what-a-thing-does). These dualities played a role in how these disagreements among sects were formulated, and resolved.

---

[3] See Stanley Weinstein, *Buddhism Under the T'ang* (Cambridge: Cambridge University Press, 1987), pp. 50ff.

CHAPTER 20: CHINESE BUDDHISM

The result was several uniquely Chinese forms of Buddhism. Between about 450–700 C.E., indigenous forms of Chinese Buddhism gradually arose, and slowly separated out:[4]

Pure Land (Ching-t'u/Jingtu) (in Japanese, Jodo)
T'ien-t'ai (Tiantai) (in Japanese, Tendai);
Hua-yen (Huayan) (in Japanese, Kegon);
Ch'an (Chan) (in Japanese, Zen).

For a while there was a Chinese Tantric Buddhist tradition called the Chen-yen (*mantra*) school, which had power and patronage for about a hundred years, but did not endure with any strength as a unique tradition. However, during the initial period while it was still flourishing in China, Chen-yen was transplanted to Japan where it became known as Shingon and became a dominant form of Japanese Buddhism.

In China, the newer Buddhist groups tended to base themselves upon a small cluster of texts which had special meaning to their founders. The Pure Land followers relied on the three Pure Land sutras; the T'ien-t'ai/Tiantai tradition put the most value on the *Lotus* (*Saddharmapundarika*) sutra and the writings of Nagarjuna; the Hua-yen school took inspiration from the Sanskrit *Avatamsaka sutra* (which in Chinese is the *Hua-yen sutra*). The Ch'an/Chan schools quoted freely from numerous texts, especially the *Prajna-paramita sutras* ("Perfection of Wisdom") and Buddha-nature texts, but in general Ch'an came to assert that relying on scriptures was an error because no sutra could possibly contain the highest truth which the Buddha experienced under the Bodhi tree. The Chen-yen, or Mantra school, tended to rely on secret Tantric texts, esoteric rituals, *mandalas*, incantations, mantras, chants, and pageantry. The two enduring and important of these Chinese Buddhist traditions was the Pure Land school, and the Ch'an school (which will be discussed in the next chapter).

20.5 PURE LAND BUDDHISM

We have already seen that when the Han dynasty ended in 220 C.E., China went from relative stability to apparently never-ending civil war, and the political chaos caused misery everywhere in China that lasted for almost four hundred years until the Sui dynasty in 581 C.E. War causes taxes to be raised, and when the military requisitions great amounts of food for the army, famine in the countryside results. During this time there were natural disasters as well including floods and droughts. Neither Confucian political ideas nor Taoist philosophical or alchemical practices, or military solutions worked to solve the problems of China. The Buddhist doctrine of *duhkha* (misery, frustration, unhappiness) was now understood to be an accurate description of life in China. The world was filled with suffering at every turn. Something was terribly wrong somewhere. The Pure Land form of Indian Buddhism seemed to offer an explanation, and the promise of a solution.

In the chapter on Indian Buddhism in *Asian Thought*, Volume I, we noted that about the first century C.E. in India, the general tendency in Indian religion was moving towards ritual and especially *bhakti*, personal loving devotion focused on *devas* and Buddhas. The Indian Pure Land form of devotional Mahayana Buddhism began as a movement about the end of the first century C.E. in northern India.

---

[4] In the interests of simplicity, in these chapters the author is treating the different traditions as sects or schools which were clearly separated. However during the T'ang/Tang dynasty, monks of many different affiliations lived under the same monastery roof, and to think that there existed clearly separated traditions with names like "Chan" or "Pure Land" is anachronistic. Such groups focused around sutras or teacher-lineages and were very slow to think of themselves as a separate school. "The relationships between T'ien-t'ai, Vinaya, Pure Land and Ch'an in the Nan-yueh region were extraordinarily interwoven and cannot be simply disentangled. The cross-allegiances, cross-pollination and debates were multi-layered . . ." in John Jorgensen, *Inventing Hui-neng, the Sixth Patriarch* (Leiden and Boston: Brill, 2005), p. 436. An extremely thorough analysis of this topic can be found in Stanley Weinstein, *Buddhism Under the T'ang*.

CHAPTER 20: CHINESE BUDDHISM

Pure Land Buddhism in India

Among the many Mahayana Sanskrit texts in Indian Buddhism, there were a couple of Pure Land sutras, but Pure Land was not a form of popular devotional Buddhism. In India, Pure Land was mostly an elite monastic meditation technique involving visualization exercises. Monks would sit and visualize the pure land paradise (*sukhavati* in Sanskrit) and the celestial buddha who presided over it, Amitabha. In addition to practicing the visualization of Amitabha Buddha as a meditative technique, the monks also used to chant the name of the Buddha as a *mantra*. Many reported religious visions of the buddha of the Pure Land, which was regarded as confirmation of the effectiveness of their religious visualization exercises.

We have seen that the bodhisattva (in Mahayana forms of Buddhism) was a being who spent uncountably many lifetimes on the path leading to buddhahood, and in the course of those lifetimes bodhisattvas kept returning to help others, even though the bodhisattva knew how to escape from the cycle of birth and death. In the process of helping living beings, lifetime after lifetime, it was thought that, because of the depth of their compassion, some bodhisattvas had acquired so much merit that they had the power to create a purified realm not in our time and space, and set it aside expressly for the deliverance of sentient beings who express faith in them.

Even those of the lowest spiritual capability can achieve rebirth in the Pure Land because entrance into it depends upon the compassion of the bodhisattva, not the spiritual development of the individual. The ancient celestial Buddha Amitabha, the buddha of longevity and infinite light, emerged as the most popular of these bodhisattvas and stories about Amitabha took form as three sutras.

The Indian Pure Land Sutras

Indian Pure Land Buddhism originates with three *Sukhavati-vyuha* (Sutra of Infinite Light) Pure Land sutras. They tell the story of the Buddha of Infinite Light, Amithabha[5] (who lived in the ancient past long before Siddhartha was born), and of the forty-eight vows[6] he made while still a bodhisattva, working towards buddhahood. The most important is the 18th, where he vows not to achieve buddhahood unless he is assured that any who call upon him with full confidence (which might be at the moment of dying), can be reborn in his Pure Land paradise in the West. That Pure Land has birds singing the Buddhist sutras, and the streets and buildings are made of precious jewels. *Duhkha* (suffering, frustration, misery) will be non-existent in this realm and there are no hells. Having achieved rebirth in the Pure Land, the follower is guaranteed to never fall back into an ordinary existence, and will be able to achieve full enlightenment and nirvana.

All that is required of the devotee is to hold in the mind the name of Amitabha without any distractions. As a result one will have a vision of Amitabha in this very life, and at the moment of death, Amitabha will welcome the devotee and carry her or him over to Amitabha's Pure Land Paradise in the West. No one anywhere could ever be good enough to deserve or earn rebirth in the Pure Land, but being reborn in the Pure Land is not the result of any good behavior, not the result of morality, not the result of performing rituals. One attains the Pure Land, not by one's own powers, but instead by relying on the compassion of and grace of Amitabha. The Pure Land school relies on the egoless compassion of Amitabha Buddha, and his helper, Avalokiteshvara (Ah-va-lo-ki-tesh-va-ra, the Bodhisattva of compassion) who will lead followers to the Pure Land.

PURE LAND BUDDHISM IN CHINA

---

[5] Amitabha is also known by the name Amitayus, "Infinite Life." In Japan he is Amida Buddha.

[6] The story of the sutra is summarized in Alfred Bloom, *Shinran's Gospel of Pure Grace* (Tucon, Arizona: University of Arizona Press, 1965), on pages 1–4. See also Allen A. Andrews, *The Teachings Essential for Rebirth* (Monumenta Nipponica, 1973), pp. 8–11.

CHAPTER 20: CHINESE BUDDHISM

The Chinese Pure Land movement (Ching-t'u/Jingtu), as a popular form of Buddhism, began around the fourth century C.E. Chinese folklore already had a Western Paradise. This Western Paradise was presided over by a Queen Mother of the West, Xi-wang-mu, the wife of the Jade Emperor. She travels by riding on a crane, and lives in a nine-story palace of jade encircled by a golden wall more than a thousand miles long. The Buddhist notion of a Pure Land in the West fit perfectly into existing popular Chinese religion.

THE THREE PERIODS OF THE BUDDHA-DHARMA

The Indian Sanskit *Lotus sutra*, translated into Chinese in 406 by Kumarajiva, had predicted the that the history of Buddhism would eventually divide into Three Periods of the Dharma (Teaching), and Chinese Buddhists took the *Lotus sutra* and the notion of the three ages of the Buddha-dharma quite seriously. This became very important for Chinese Pure Land and the other forms of Chinese Buddhism.

The first is the **Period of the True Dharma** (which lasts about 500 years; thought to end about 50 C.E.). It began with the birth and lifetime of the Buddha, when people would hear of Buddhism, practice it and become awakened easily. The Indian Buddhist texts tell of over a thousand followers, male and female, who attained liberation after hearing the Buddha speak. But, that was not happening in China of the fourth and fifth century or in India. It was obvious that enlightenment is no longer easily available, and it must be because people's abilities have diminished.

The second period is the thousand-year period called the **Period of the Semblance of the Dharma/ Counterfeit (or Quasi-) Dharma** (thought to have started about the time Buddhism entered China, and which would end about 1050 C.E.). In this second period, Buddhism is in its initial stages of decay, and the teachings during this period closely resemble the Buddha's actual teaching, but they have drifted away and are no longer completely authentic. During this time Chinese Buddhist monks were not achieving awakening. The teachings are not quite authentic, human abilities have diminished, and deep understanding is now very rare, or even impossible for some followers.

This is not the end of Buddhism. The teaching in this period resembles genuine Buddhism closely, and awakening is still possible — just very difficult. After all, this second period is the time of great teachers like Nagarjuna who was thought to have been a bodhisattva.

The third and last period is the **Period of the Decay of the Dharma**.[7] These will be the beginning of progressively darker ages for Buddhism, a period of irreversible spiritual decline. With each passing century, human abilities decline more and more. Almost no one will have the discipline, zeal or intelligence to attain enlightenment by his or her own efforts. During this stage the Buddha's enlightenment is so extremely rare that very few people can reasonably hope to achieve it even within tens of thousands of lifetimes. In the Mahayana, genuine buddhahood suggests god-like powers, someone closer to a superhuman deity. None of us can achieve this. We are simply common human beings with no special gifts or skills. The situation is bleak. Nothing will ever get better; it will only get worse. This is the dark ages. Each generation will find life more difficult than the previous generation. How can anyone achieve liberation? Is it hopeless?

The Pure Land answer is that it is not hopeless. We do not need special talent, high intelligence, extraordinary morality or focused meditation and discipline. As related in the Indian Pure Land sutras, Amitabha Buddha has responded to our situation in the dark ages and offers a pathway to liberation suitable for ordinary people.

Call on Amitabha with confidence and complete faith, and one can be reborn in the Western Pure Land where the Buddha is available to teach you personally. Liberation is easily achieved once one has reached the Pure Land of the West. One attains liberation by relying on the divine power of the Buddha of Infinite Light, Amitabha. No one could achieve liberation by himself or herself alone. None of us are good enough to deserve nirvana, none of us are

---

[7] Different Chinese Pure Land teachers assigned different dates for these periods. This concept of a time of decay was an ancient concept in India, referred to as the *Kali-yuga*, which was discussed in *Asian Thought*, Volume I, chapter 5, on devotional Hinduism. The Chinese term for this third period of decay is *mofa*, and in Japanese it is *mappo*.

smart enough or focused enough to achieve it on their own. But, in Pure Land Buddhism, the Pure Land is a gift which can be obtained by simply asking, with genuine faith.

Amitabha Buddha (Omito-fo in Chinese) presides over the Pure Land and is assisted by the bodhisattva Avalokiteshvara/Avalokitesvara, who in China is known as Kuan-yin/Guanyin. Amitabha Buddha is the central divinity, and Avalokiteshvara is the mediator who brings compassion and grace to the faithful, to those who respond by chanting the name of Amitabha in deep sincere devotion. All one needs is faith, and chanting the name of Amitabha. The bodhisattva Kuan-yin remains important in modern Chinese folk religion, where most are not aware of the details of her ancient Buddhist origins.[8]

THE PURE LAND MANTRA

The Chinese Pure Land tradition traces its origins to the Buddhist monk Hui-yuan (334–417) who experienced an ecstatic vision of Amitabha's Pure Land using his own visualization meditative practices. The second important Pure Land monk is T'an-luan (476–542), who remembered the 18th vow of Amitabha Buddha, that "all beings who think even once (or one moment) on the Buddha, sincerely and with faith, when they hear the Buddha's name, will be reborn in that Pure Land."

T'an-luan popularized chanting the name of Amitabha as a way to concentrate one's attention on the Buddha, sincerely and with faith. This is known as the Amitabha *mantra*, also called the *nien-fo*[9] *mantra*, which is a devotional practice suitable to the poorest and least educated householder or farmer. The practice is simple: continually chant the name of Amitabha Buddha, out loud or silently. In Chinese, the Sanskrit name Amitabha is pronounced Omito. The Chinese character "fo" means Buddha. Thus "Amitabha Buddha" is Omitofo.

This *nien-fo mantra* is just reciting the Chinese name of the Buddha: **na-mo o-mi-to fo** (in Japan they chant **namu amida butsu**). The literal meaning is "homage to Amitabha Buddha" but it is not the meaning that is important. It is the focus, the spirit and sincerity with which the *mantra* is recited. The devotee recites the *mantra*, often accompanied by running rosary-like strung beads between the fingers with each repetition. With the *nien-fo*, Buddhism does not require leaving home and entering a monastery, and Buddhism does not require any literary or philosophical skills. This practice does not require cross-legged sitting in focused meditation. The *nien-fo* makes devotional Buddhism available to everyone under any conditions. The Buddhist heavenly Pure Land is available to everyone who asks. It is during the early 600s that Pure Land monks began to preach the Pure Land ideas to common people, who responded with enthusiasm.

Shan-tao/Shandao (613–681), considered the Third Chinese Patriarch of Pure Land, was the one who systematized Pure Land thought and brought it to a high peak of development in China. Shan-tao seemed to have a intense awareness of his own spiritual failings, his tendency towards error and his own inadequacy to achieve any of the lofty Buddhist goals using his own ability. For Shan-tao, the Pure Land offered a chance for even an inadequate person like himself to achieve liberation, and he responded with profound gratitude. In his writings, Shan-tao described five ways for the follower of Pure Land Buddhism to practice Buddhism which included uttering the name of Amitabha Buddha and chanting Pure Land sutras.

SELF-POWER AND OTHER-POWER

The Pure Land tradition allows us to draw a distinction between two approaches to Buddhism, Self-Power and

---

[8] There is a medieval legend about princess Miao-shan, whose parents killed her to prevent her from joining a monastery and becoming a nun. Kuan-yin/Guanyin is often associated with Miao-shan in popular Chinese religion.

[9] *Nien-fo* means "thinking of Buddha," "Buddha invocation," or "keeping the Buddha in one's mind," and in Japanese it is pronounced *nembutsu*.

CHAPTER 20: CHINESE BUDDHISM

Other-Power.[10] Other-Power describes those Buddhist schools which rely on a buddha, bodhisattva, or savior external to one's self. Self-Power describes those Buddhist schools which asserted that each individual has the power and ability to extinguish the poisons of anger, ego-centered craving and possessiveness, and ignorance, and attain the goal of liberation, using discipline, meditation, concentration, and relying on the self-liberating power of one's own mind. In general, the Pure Land teachers argued that Buddhists in the First Period of the Dharma might have had enough ability (Self Power) to achieve Nirvana, but we are no longer in that first period.

Pure Land Buddhism considers it fundamentally egocentric and arrogant to believe that any individual, living during the second Period of the Semblance or Counterfeit Dharma (or the third period), using her own ability (power), could purify herself or himself to the degree that he could become a buddha. There is no practice (self-power) whatsoever which a living sentient being can perform which will bring awakening or the certainty of liberation. We know that we live in the third period of the Decay of the Dharma, when no humans are good enough to achieve awakening and nirvana on their own.

The Pure Land practice is not for those people who are morally good, self-confident, and filled with spiritual energy. Rather, the Pure Land recitation of *nien-fo* is intended for those who are filled with lust and passion, those who are wicked, those are feel inadequate, those who know they could **never deserve** rebirth in a heavenly paradise.

The spiritual strength of Other-Power Buddhism is giving up ego. The Pure Land follower gives up self-centered overconfidence. The follower knows that nothing he or she could ever do could bring about liberation. We cannot rely on our own efforts. We are not worthy. All of us are too imperfect. We cannot be proud (ego) of our spiritual attainments, because we recognize that we have no spiritual attainments and no possibility of ever attaining anything on our own. By putting complete faith in the power of the buddha or bodhisattva to bring one to liberation, we lose the ego-centered self. We do not need to be perfect; we merely need to have confidence in the vow and the compassion of Amitabha Buddha.

Pure Land teaches that one may be reborn in the Pure Land without extinguishing human passions, and once in the Pure Land, one can work to eliminate *duhkha* and attain nirvana without hindrances. The constant recitation of *mantras* is an important tool of liberation. The Pure Land monk Tao-ch'o/Daocho (562–645) is reported to have recited the title of the Pure Land sutra 70,000 times a day, and argued that Pure Land approach was the only suitable means of salvation in this degenerate age.

Where is the Pure Land?

There is another rather sophisticated way to conceptualize the Pure Land, and some Chinese Pure Land teachers encouraged us to realize that the Pure Land was not an external paradise to which one traveled after death. Rather, the Pure Land might be understood as nowhere other than your own mind, and it is the death of the ego which gets us to the Pure Land. The Amitabha Buddha whose name you chanted, and his Western Paradise was within, not somewhere you go after you die. The Amitabha Buddha that you visualized was no other than the innate purity of your own mind. Dying refers to the death of self-centered craving or possessive desires, which is the death of ego-centeredness. Thus, some Pure Land practice identifies one's own mind with the Buddha, or at least one realizes that the two were not ultimately different.

Pure Land Survives the 845 Persecution of Buddhism

Although the Pure Land ideas were popular among the common people, the Buddhist elite in the capital cities ignored the devotional teachings. This changed in 845. In 845 there was an imperial persecution of Buddhism, resulting in the destruction of the major temples associated with scholars in the capital and the major cities in the north, and

---

[10] This is especially important in Japanese forms of Buddhism.

withdrawal of government assistance to Buddhist monasteries and temples, but this had little effect upon those who recited the *nienfo*. Following the 845 persecution, Pure Land remained strong. In the following centuries Pure Land continued to appeal to Buddhists in China, who were seeking not only liberation but also seeking a divine power that will respond to their needs and answer their prayers.

Kuan-yin/Guanyin is the mediator between the divine Amitabha and the unworthy masses. As the incarnation of mercy and love, in the Chinese form of Kuan-yin, the iconography is clearly female. Kuan-yin is a patron for many in China. Women wanting to become pregnant pray to Kuan-yin, who becomes a "giver of children." Some icons of Kuan-yin portray her holding a child.

Pure Land Buddhism is the form of East Asian Buddhism closest to what Western people think about when they think of "religion." Amitabha/Omito is clearly a divine being filled with compassion and the positive power of grace to bring all to paradise. Amitabha also has a helper, an intermediary who answers prayers and lovingly dispenses salvation. That is the Bodhisattva Kuan-yin/Guanyin.

However, these have little resemblance to the gods of Western religion. Amitabha is not a creator deity. Amitabha neither rewards nor punishes anyone, but dispenses loving compassion to all, without exception. The Pure Land does not have a hell and does not use heaven or hell as reward or punishment.[11] All who ask with sincerity are guaranteed to be reborn in the Western Paradise. No one is kept out.

20.6 THE TIANTAI/T'IEN-T'AI SCHOOL

The T'ien-t'ai/Tiantai school of Buddhism is named for the Heavenly Terrace mountain (T'ien-t'ai shan) in southeastern China, which was the home temple of the founder, Chih-i/Zhiyi (538–597). Chih-i (pronounced something like "Jur-e") devoted his life to meditation and to writing about meditation, but he also wrote about numerous philosophical topics as well. He was regarded very highly by the Sui Dynasty (589–618) royal court and received imperial patronage.

Chih-i's influence was immense. It is believed that Chih-i came up with the basic "Four Vows" which are taken and chanted by almost all Asian Buddhists, and many Western Buddhists as well. These vows define and clarify the Mahayana bodhisattva pathway. They are:

Sentient beings are uncountably many, I vow to free them all.
Egoistic desires are inexhaustible; I vow to end them all.
The Buddha-dharma (teaching) is without limit; I vow to master it all.
The Buddha's Way is unsurpassable; I vow to attain it.[12]

T'ien-t'ai Genealogies

Perhaps because of the stress on filial piety and ancestor rituals, the Chinese often constructed detailed genealogies of master-disciple relationships to prove a contemporary teacher's ideas were correct and thus the teacher had the right to teach. Every important Confucian teacher could produce a teacher-student genealogy to connect his teachings to a student of Confucius himself. Taoists had genealogies to connect them to Lao-tzu himself. Similarly,

---

[11] Buddhism has hells as one of the five karmic destinations, but one earns the trip to hell by one's own deeds. Buddhist hells are temporary, not permanent.

[12] These vows are essential to Chinese Buddhism, and to Japanese Buddhism as well. They are chanted daily in Ch'an and Zen monasteries.

the T'ien-t'ai school devised an elaborate (but historically inaccurate) teacher-student genealogy which connected the Buddha to the great philosopher Nagarjuna, and then a genealogy which connected Nagarjuna to Chih-i of the T'ien-t'ai monastery. In the Chinese mind, that genealogy gave special legitimacy and status to the T'ien-t'ai school. Inspired by this, other Buddhist schools began to improvise fictional genealogies which connected them to the Buddha as well.

The *Lotus Sutra*

Although the T'ien-t'ai school considered the *Lotus sutra* (*Saddharmapundarika sutra*) to be their fundamental text, the T'ien-t'ai school was troubled by the fact that the Buddhist sutras from India were so contradictory, yet each claimed to be the word of the historical Buddha. How could one sage offer so many different teachings, and give incompatible answers to questions about doctrine? Was there any way to reconcile the diversity of Buddhist teachings, each attributed to the same Buddha?

The Five Stages of the Buddha's Teachings[13]

The T'ien-t'ai tradition solved the problem without having to reject any Buddhist sutra, and without having to analyze the authenticity of any Buddhist scripture. First of all, they asserted each and every text was the actual words of the Buddha, even though the texts did contradict one another. The T'ien-t'ai reasoned that the texts did not always agree because the Buddhist sutras are records of teachings which the Buddha delivered to many different audiences at different stages of his life. The Buddha simplified his teachings for some students, yet gave other students the full teaching. For example, a math teacher will teach 3rd grade arithmetic at a very different level than a university professor teaching advanced calculus. T'ien-t'ai claims that when we understand the historical context and audience, the apparent contradictions will fade away. In addition, even the simplest individual sutras can be understood to have at least two levels of meaning, a simpler and obvious teaching and then a way of understanding that teaching which revealed deeper truths hidden and not obvious to the ordinary reader.[14]

The T'ien-t'ai Five Stage Analysis

(1) Immediately after his awakening the Buddha revealed the full content of his experience to his students. They promptly wrote down everything he said, and we know it as the *Avatamsaka* (Flower Garland, Hua-yen) sutra.

(2) However, the great majority of the students could not understand what they had written down, so the Buddha then offered them a much simpler teaching suitable for those of inferior ability, including the Four Noble Truths, the Noble Eightfold Path, and dependent co-arising (*pratityasamutpada*). This is the teaching he gave to the conservative Theravada (or Hinayana)[15] monks. Following those teachings, they eliminated their own suffering and became *arhats* and (according to Chih-i) selfishly left the cycle of birth-and-death (*samsara*) without helping others lessen their own suffering.

(3) However, some of the monks were capable of deeper levels of understanding, so then the Buddha taught the third

---

[13] The fully worked out system of Five Periods and Eight Teachings is the work of the T'ian-t'ai monk Chan-jan (711–782).

[14] Buddhist monks were thus freed to write extravagant interpretations of the hidden meanings in Buddhist texts, and the levels of symbolism they found could be quite astonishing.

[15] The *Lotus* which originated in India uses insults to refer to the pre-Mahayana conservative Buddhists, and constantly refers to them as arrogant yet ignorant students who are members of the Hina-yana, the "Inferior Vehicle" of Buddhism. Of course no Buddhist ever thought of herself as belonging to the "Inferior Vehicle" or holding an inferior teaching. The term "Hinayana" is insulting but early Western scholars did not realize this, so the term appears in books written in English and refers to what we have called early "conservative Buddhism."

CHAPTER 20: CHINESE BUDDHISM

stage texts. These are the elementary Mahayana doctrines of the bodhisattva who postpones her own entry into nirvana to achieve the more elevated goal of complete buddhahood, and in her continued life cycle after life cycle, she remains and can help all living beings. The great majority of the monks were completely satisfied with these teachings, but some could go beyond, and to these he taught the more advanced Mahayana concepts.

(4) The more philosophically sophisticated Mahayana concepts were taught to students with greater ability. These are the *Prajnaparamita sutras* (the Perfection of Wisdom that carries one over to the other shore).[16] This teaches the insight of *svabhava-sunyata* (empty of unchanging self-nature) expounded by Nagarjuna (explained in section 10.5 of *Asian Thought*, Volume I).

(5) To the very few who mastered emptiness and who were capable and ready, the Buddha then taught the perfect doctrine, the highest doctrine, the single teaching found in the *Lotus sutra* [17] and the Mahayana *Nirvana sutra*,[18] both texts which originated in India. The T'ien-t'ai tradition felt that the *Lotus sutra* unified all the teachings of the Buddhist into a single grand synthesis. Although Buddhist history was analyzed into five different teachings, the final conclusion was that, in actuality, they were really five stages of one teaching. The *Lotus* offers only one teaching expressed in different degrees of difficulty.

One important feature of this T'ien-t'ai theoretical structure is that each and every school of Buddhism is included as "genuine Buddhism," and none are incorrect or wrong, although some are more elementary than others. T'ien-t'ai tried to include all forms of Buddhism within this structure of the Five Teachings, and did not want to exclude any forms. Chih-i, the founder of T'ien-t'ai, made room for each school of Buddhism, and included a universal synthesis of all Buddhist doctrines, while placing its own T'ien-t'ai teachings and the *Lotus* in a position of special importance.[19]

Emptiness and Buddha-nature

In addition to the *Lotus sutra*, the T'ien-t'ai lineage relied heavily upon Nagarjuna's Madhyamaka writings about *svabhava-sunyata*, that is, all things are empty of self-existent unchanging substance (*svabhava*), all things are without of any eternal self-nature. Instead, things arise dependently, are constantly changing, and are empty of any independent existence. All things may be empty of unchanging essence, but they are also real.

Things in the world are real and they do exist, but they do not exist the way we mistakenly believe they exist. Our language and our concepts impose a tendency to see things in the world as enduring and distinct from one another, as not changing (because we mistakenly believe that they possess an essence or substance), instead of realizing it is all flowing change. In mis-perceiving things-in-the-world as substantial and continuing, we are not seeing things as they really are and we experience *duhkha* (frustration, dissatisfaction, suffering).

---

[16] The *Prajna-paramita sutras* taught the emptiness of all *dharmas*, and were the inspiration for Nagarjuna's Madhyamaka school.

[17] It should be clear that as clever as the T'ien-ta'i analysis is, historically speaking it is completely and totally incorrect. Until recent times, no Chinese scholar comprehended the long centuries of development and sectarian nature of Indian Buddhist texts and they did not understand the true complexity of the development of Buddhism in India.

[18] The Mahayana *Nirvana sutra* is a Mahayana retelling of the last days of the Buddha before he died, and as such in China it had the status of the final and ultimate teachings. Contemporary Buddhist scholars assign the Mahayana *Nirvana sutra* to the *Tathagatagarbha* (Buddha-nature) form of Buddhism and scholars do not accept it as a historically accurate text.

[19] Most books which discuss the history of Buddhism in China will discuss the Chinese theory which organizes the variety of Buddhist texts. One book devoted to this topic is Chanju Mun, *The History of Doctrinal Classifications in Chinese Buddhism* (New York: University Press of America, 2005). See also Peter N. Gregory, *Tsung-mi and the Sinification of Buddhism* (Honolulu: University of Hawai'i Press, 2002).

CHAPTER 20: CHINESE BUDDHISM

The T'ien-t'ai teacher Chih-i combined the insight into *sunyata* or emptiness, with the insights of the Mahayana *Nirvana sutra* (a *Tathagathagarba* or buddha-nature) text, which claimed that all beings possess the nature of a buddha. If we all have an innate buddha-nature, then the awakening of the Buddha is within each one of us; there is nothing to seek and nothing to acquire. If we all have the buddha-nature, then all sentient beings are already perfect, they lack nothing. They already **are** what they are searching for, already they are buddhas. Ultimately, all things are empty of essence which means that all are flowing change with nothing essential to separate one from the other. The result is that there is no genuinely absolute distinction between things, not even ultimates like *samsara* and nirvana.

The condition of *samsara* (birth-and-death) does not have some defining substance or inner essence; it is empty of unchanging essence. Nirvana does not have an enduring substance that makes it what it is and separates it from everything else; it too is flowing change. When we are ignorant, we see the world as *samsara* and experience suffering. When we see things as they truly are, we see the world as nirvana and realize our original buddha-nature. Nirvana and *samsara* are simply conventional names intended to draw our attention to various processes of flowing change. It follows that all reality is pure—all things (even mountains and rivers) possess the buddha-nature.

T'ien-t'ai Meditation

The T'ien-t'ai school of Chih-i was not just abstract and philosophical. It put even greater emphasis on the practice of seated meditation (*dhyana*). The T'ien-t'ai school worked out a detailed system of meditation to help the monk to realize the ultimate truths and see things as they truly are, as flowing, as interdependent, as ever-changing. Chih-i wrote exhaustively about the two bed pillars of Buddhist meditation, calm concentration (*shamatha*) and insight (*vipassana*). Concentration involves exercises to pacify and bring to a stop the ordinary wandering consciousness so we can focus without being distracted. The second aspect of meditation, insight, is seeing the nature of reality and realizing that all things do exist in what T'ien-t'ai calls the One Mind or the Absolute Mind. As its basic tools, Tendai utilized the two practices of seated focused concentration, or cross-legged mediation, and liberating wisdom or insight. Finally, the influential idea of the age of the "Decay of the Teaching" or "Decay of the Dharma" appears in the *Lotus* sutra, and plays a role in T'ien-t'ai thought.

The Triple Truth of T'ien-t'ai

To say that all things are *svabhava-sunyata*, empty of unchanging essence, does not mean that things do not exist. Based on a quote from a text by the Indian philosopher Nagarjuna, T'ien-t'ai's Chih-i says that there is a Triple Truth involving conventional existence, absolute existence, and a middle ground:
  (1) all things are empty of unchanging essence, yet
  (2) at the same time things do exist, albeit temporarily and provisionally.
  (3) the third truth is the truth that transcends both emptiness and temporariness.[20]

The first of the truths is absolute, it is emptiness. The second includes the conventional, the provisional, the relative existence of things. The third truth, the truth of the Middle, asserts that the relatively real realm that we inhabit, and

---

[20] The "Triple Truth" seems to arise from a mistranslation of a verse by Nagarjuna:
> We state that whatever is dependent arising, that is emptiness.
> That is dependent upon convention. That itself is the middle path.

Nagarjuna's Sanskrit verse explains the identity of two truths: dependent arising, emptiness, and their identity which was the Middle Way. The Sanskrit was translated into Chinese, and the Chinese T'ien-t'ai school understood to be teaching three separate and distinct truths: emptiness; dependent origination (the conventional); the highest truth which transcends both, i.e., the Middle Way. The quote is from chapter 24, verse 18, discussed in chapter 10 of Volume 1 of *Asian Thought*. This translation is from David Kalupahana, *Nagarjuna: The Philosophy of the Middle Way* (New York: State University Press of New York, 1986), pp. 339–341. Compare this with Jay Garfield, *The Fundamental Wisdom of the Middle Way* (New York: Oxford University Press, 1995), pp. 304–308.

the realm of emptiness which Buddhas perceive, as taught by Nagarjuna, are identical. This third truth reconciles the relative and the absolute.

One can realize the emptiness of all things, realize that each thing lacks an essential unchanging essence, and so nothing has any essence or enduring existence. One knows that things exist only temporarily. When the student has combined both, she or he has achieved freedom from *samsara*.

T'ien-t'ai Fades in China

The profoundly philosophical T'ien-t'ai school was quite academic and scholarly and required the extensive support of the government and wealthy donors to pay for its libraries, its foods, its ink and paper, and the other needs of monastic scholars. The government subsidy stopped with the 845 C.E. imperial persecution of Buddhism, the major temples were destroyed, the monks driven out, and the library's valuables confiscated by the government. Entire monastic libraries of scholarly T'ien-t'ai commentaries and sutras were burned. T'ien-t'ai was nearly destroyed as a result. There was a revival of the T'ien-t'ai school in the tenth century Sung dynasty although the revival tended to be strong only in a few regions in China. After 845, in the late T'ang (618–906 C.E.) and Sung (960–1279) dynasty eras, it was the Ch'an or meditation school of Buddhism which dominated Chinese Buddhism.

20.7 THE HUAYAN/HUA-YEN BASED ON THE *AVATAMSAKA SUTRA*

Many scholars consider the Hua-yen/Huayan school to be the highest achievement of Buddhist metaphysical thought in China, and argue that it may well rank with the highest development of Mahayana Buddhist philosophy anywhere in the history of Buddhism. Its vision is vast, abstract and poetic. Some describe it as "mystical." It is also quite different from most Indian forms of the Mahayana.

As an overview, we can describe Hua-yen as combining

(a) the idea that at birth all beings possess the fundamentally good[21] intrinsically awakened Buddha-nature (*Tathagatagarbha*) with
(b) the *Prajnaparamita* assertion that all things are empty of unchanging inner essence, *sunyata*.

Of course, it is the Indian Madhyamika thinker Nagarjuna (c. 100–200 C.E.) who explicitly described the emptiness of all forms. Hua-yen philosophy then takes that pair of ideas and extends it in ways that no one in India thought of.[22]

The Chinese Hua-yen tradition took its name from the Indian sutra that is central to its teachings, the *Avatamsaka sutra* (Hua-yen sutra, Flower Garland sutra)[23] which the Chinese regarded as the most complete expression

---

[21] This Buddhist claim resonated with Confucians and especially followers of Mencius, who, eight hundred years before, argued that human beings are born fundamentally good.

[22] There are several good books on Hua-yen. Certainly one of the very best which concerns itself with the philosophy of Hua-yen is Francis H. Cook, *Hua-yen Buddhism: The Jewel Net of Indra* (University Park, Pennsylvania: Pennsylvania State University Press, 1977). See also Robert Gimello, *et.al.*, eds., *Avatamsaka Buddhism in East Asia: Hua-yen, Kegon, Flower Ornament Scripture* (Otto Harrassowitz Verlag, 2012), and the more historical volume, Imre Hamar, ed., *Reflecting Mirrors: Perspectives on Huayan Buddhism* (Otto Harrassowitz Verlag, 2007).

[23] This sutra is translated in full in Thomas Cleary, *Flower Ornament Scripture* (New York: Shambhala 1993).

of the Buddha's teaching,[24] the sutra which contains the awakened Buddha's deepest insights stressing complete harmony and interpenetration among all phenomena.

The initial Indian Sanskrit *Avatamsaka sutra* was considerably shorter than the Chinese version of the text which the Hua-yen school uses, and which was first translated in 420 C.E. The later Chinese version is not only much larger than any Indian version, but it is clear that Chinese Buddhists have added large portions to this sutra. The Chinese text is filled with elements which are atypical of Indian Buddhism, but very typical of Chinese Buddhist concerns.

There never was any tradition of *Avatamsaka*/Hua-yen Buddhism in India. Hua-yen Buddhism is a uniquely Chinese form of Buddhism. The Chinese Hua-yen scholars did not use the entire *Avatamsaka sutra*, but only portions which they found useful. In addition, many of the most important assertions and conclusions of Hua-yen Buddhism are not found anywhere in the *Avatamsaka* sutra itself. Chinese Hua-yen Buddhism is not merely an explication of an Indian sutra, but rather it is a complex set of Chinese philosophical insights into the nature of reality which drew an initial inspiration from one version of the *Avatamsaka sutra* (*Hua-yen sutra*).

The Hua-yen Insight into Causation

The Hua-yen insight into causation involves each and every element of reality (called *dharmas*) and envisions each point of the realm of all *dharmas* as connected to and influenced by every other point. Hua-yen agrees that all *dharmas* are empty of self-existing inner essence (*svabhava-sunyata*). Hua-yen also considers the relationship between particularity and universality. The fundamental insight is the **unimpeded mutual inter-penetration of all particularities**. Each and every item which we think of as a "thing" is merely an interdependent interconnected flowing process, interacting with every other process.

The harmonious interplay between each particular *dharma* (empty of enduring inner essence) or particularity, and the harmonious interpenetration between particularity and universality reveals a luminous universe, simultaneously free of limitations of space and time, yet also remaining our own everyday world. The basic image the Hua-yen thinkers used to explicate these ideas is referred to as the **Net of Indra**.

Indra's Net

Imagine a fishing net made of rope, laid flat and extending infinitely in two dimensions. Now imagine that each intersection in the net has a rope extending vertically outwards, into the third-dimension. Layer after layer of nets extend up and out, infinitely. Each point is the intersection of an x-axis, a y-axis, and a z-axis. Each intersecting point is then imagined as a gem, a cut and polished diamond which reflects every point that surrounds it. But in reflecting the point above and below, each of those above and below points already reflect the points above it, and to its left and right. In other words, ultimately each intersection contains and reflects every other point. It is a three-dimensional ocean of gems, each individual gem reflecting and containing the content of all the others. A change anywhere is reflected everywhere.

Indra's Net is a metaphor for the universe which we inhabit. Everything in the *dharma*-realm is interconnected. Hua-yen causality is not just a flowing from past to present to future. Causality extends timelessly in all directions. Anything that happens anywhere is reflected and affects every other point. We are familiar with the concept that a stone thrown into a pond ultimately moves every molecule of water in the pond. Ultimately a change anywhere effects

---

[24] This later first or second century C.E. Mahayana sutra portrays itself as the teachings of the Buddha immediately following his awakening under the Bodhi-tree. Actually it is a compilation of smaller Mahayana texts composed probably three or four-hundred years after the death of the Buddha. The Chinese accepted each Indian sutra at face value and wholeheartedly and enthusiastically accepted the sutra's claim that it was the true story of the content of the Buddha's awakening. This is similar to contemporary Christians who accept each passage in the Gospels as word-for-word the sayings of Jesus, whereas scholars knowledgeable in the history and development of the various gospel texts are much less certain.

changes everywhere.

Every point in Indra's Net is dependent upon every other point, the content of each point arises from the complex of conditions, which means that things lack an inherent nature, they are empty of *svabhava*. Everything is empty of self-existence.

The T'ien-t'ai philosopher Chih-i would add that things are real, but lack a self-nature. Hua-yen takes a different attitude: because things lack an inherent self-existent nature, they cannot be considered to be *ultimately* real, but all things share the fact that they are without independent existence.

Consider the Western analysis of the redness of a red beach ball. Western philosophers have argued that the color red does not exist in the external world, but redness arises dependent upon white light shining upon an object, dependent upon the object itself absorbing most of the light but reflecting back light in a narrow band of frequency, and finally the redness depends upon human sense-organs (eyes) being sensitive to light within that narrow band. Redness does not exist out in the world any more than intoxication exists in fermented grape juice. Redness arises in the interdependent process of perception and would not exist without human minds to perceive the light. Without eyes, the world would simply be waves of light in different frequencies, but no colors.

Similarly, for Hua-yen Buddhism, all the things we perceive in the world do not exist independently of human minds. Can we get out of our minds to perceive the world as it is independent of human minds? No. It is not possible. All the characteristics we perceive when we have experiences are the effect of our minds. The world does not possess phenomenal characteristics that we think it does; the entire world we experience is mind-dependent and thus all things have no underlying self-existent substratum, no true existence, no true reality which could be perceived.[25]

Is This World an Illusion?

The *Avatamsaka sutra* states:

> Living beings and lands, all things there are in all times, in the same way, without exception, all are illusory. Making illusory forms of men and women, elephants, horses, cattle, and sheep, houses, ponds, springs, and such, gardens, groves, flowers and fruits, illusory things have no awareness and also have no abode. Ultimately of the character of nullity, they only appear according to imagination.[26]

The Hua-yen thinker and patriarch Fa-tsang/Fazang (643–712) comments:
[W]hatever there is in the world is only the creation of one mind; outside of mind there is not a single thing that can be apprehended . . . It means that all discriminations come only from one's own mind. There has never been any environment outside the mind which could be an object of mind.[27]

Are the Hua-yen philosophers asserting that the world is lacking any objective reality? The Hua-yen passages certainly seem to be rejecting the reality of the world. The problem is that the term "unreal" or "illusory" is being used in a different sense than we use it in English. For us, "illusory" means something like a mirage or a hallucination. The authors of the *Avatamsaka* sutra were born in India, and in India, the belief was that things which are real have the eternal unchanging essence; hence anything which changes is not ultimately real. For Hindus, anything which depends on causes and conditions and lacks an unchanging substance could not be truly real. The Indian Buddhist authors are

---

[25] The influence of Indian Yogacara/Yogachara is clear in this analysis. See Volume I of *Asian Thought*, ch. 10.

[26] Thomas Cleary, trans., *The Flower Ornament Scripture: A Translation of the Avatamsaka Sutra* (Boston, MA: Shambhala Publications, 1993), ch. 20, p. 452.

[27] "Cultivation of Contemplation of the Inner Meaning of the Hua-yan," Thomas Cleary, *Entry into the Inconceivable: An Introduction to Hua-yen Buddhism* (Honolulu, HI: University of Hawaii Press, 1983), p. 165.

using "unreal" in this second sense, the sense that things lack unchanging inner substance (*svabhava*) and do depend on causes and conditions. This allows us to read these Hua-yen passages, and not see it as asserting that the things are all unreal. Francis Cook writes:

> The doctrine of *sunyata* [emptiness] is, stated in the most direct way, a denial of the independent existence of any thing. . . . Thus, the emptiness doctrine should not be understood as a naive rejection of the material world as pure illusion; it indeed recognizes the existence of the natural world but denies that it has any duration or independent being. In fact, being is rejected in favor of a constant, never-fully-completed becoming.[28]

The famous Chinese Hua-yen thinker Chih-yen/Zhiyan (602–668) explains what he means when he says there is no separate objective realm outside the mind.

> Good or bad is according to the operation of the mind—which is why it is called creation by the operation of the mind. Since there is no separate objective realm outside of mind, we say "only mind." If it operates harmoniously, it is called nirvana; therefore the scripture says, "Mind makes the Buddhas." If it operates perversely it is birth-and-death; there the scripture says, "The triple world is illusory — it is only made by one mind." . . . Purity and impurity are both only mind; therefore apart from mind there is nothing else. Hence the *Lankavatara* scripture says, "Outside mind there is no objective realm, no illusory views of sense data."[29]

What would the universe be like if no one were observing it? There would be vibrations of the air, but without ear-drums, there wouldn't be sounds. There wouldn't be colors, only light waves of different frequencies; without eyes and brain-processes to translate wave-lengths of varying frequency, colors do not exist. Without minds, there wouldn't be flavors, smells, good or bad, pleasant or unpleasant. Meaning would not exist. Therefore, the world we inhabit, filled with odors, colors, sounds, pleasant experiences and unpleasant experiences, is the world created by minds.

The Interdependent Realms of *Li* and *Shih*

The relationship between particularity and universality is of concern to Hua-yen thinkers. The particular is the marble statue of the Greek goddess Venus, or the cat sitting in my lap. The universal is what all pieces of marble share or have in common, or what universal characteristic all felines share, i.e., catness or cathood.

The Universal (*li*)

The Hua-yen discussed this relationship between universality and particularity in terms of the interpenetration of *li* and *shih/shi*. There are many quite different Chinese characters all of which are pronounced *li*. We have discussed the Confucian *li* which is translated "propriety" or "ceremonial interaction." The Hua-yen term is a very different Chinese character, also pronounced *li*, which originally denoted the flowing natural patterns one can discern in a piece

---

[28] Francis Cook, "Causation in the Chinese Hua-yen Tradition," *Journal of Chinese Philosophy* 1979, Vol. 6, No. 4, pp. 368–369. Diacritical marks have been omitted.

[29] "The Mysterious Gates of the Unitary Vehicle of the Hua-yen by Chih-yen," Thomas Cleary, *Entry into the Inconceivable: An Introduction to Hua-yen Buddhism*, p. 145.

of quality jade. So this Chinese character pronounced *li* is referring to an organic pattern.[30]

The Hua-yen philosophers use *li* to mean pattern, or basic principle, including the basic principle of *svabhava-sunyata* (empty of self-existent essence). The realm of *li* is the abstract realm of universals or principles, including abstract things like shape, form, and even the principles which constitute the laws of nature.[31] The *li* are abstract but also describe universal properties. As such, Hua-yen thinkers consider *li* as equivalent to *sunyata*, emptiness.

The Particular (*shih*)

Contrasted with the universal (the abstract *li*) is the Chinese character *shih/shi*, which means something like phenomena, particularities, actualities, events, the basic stuff that we perceive and makes up the world of human experience. The *shih* are the stuff of the world which we perceive; *shih* are **not** the tiny atom-like particles that make up the world (we cannot perceive those). In India, dharmas are the smallest elements of existence; in China, *shih* are not atom-sized dharmas; rather they are the perceivables, the sights, the sounds, the smells. *Shih* is the phenomenal world of human experience. A dog is *shih*, a cat is *shih*, and so is a chair or eyeglasses.

The Four-fold Relationship Between *Li* (the Universal) and *Shih* (the Particular)

Hua-yen thinkers relate *li* (emptiness, the nature of reality, ultimate principles, sacred ultimate), and *shih* (perceivable particularities), in the following four-fold relationship:
(1)   The realm of *shih*: individual events, appearances, particularity.
(2)   The world of *li*: universality, formless emptiness, reality.
(3)   The realm of *li* and *shih* completely interfused, interdependent, identified. The truth that each particular is interpenetrating with the abstract essence.
(4)   The realm of *shih* and *shih*, where each particularity is perfectly unimpeded and mutually identified with each other particularity. The truth that each perceptible is interpenetrating with every other particular (Indra's Net).

The Treatise on the Golden Lion

The classic explanation that all phenomena are simultaneously the same, yet different, is found in the *Treatise on the Golden Lion* by Hua-yen philosopher and patriarch, Fa-tsang/Fazang (643–712). It tells of the time that Fa-tsang tried to explain the idea of the fourfold relationship of *li* and *shih* to the royal court. For an example which people could see and understand, he used an exquisitely detailed statue of a lion, made of pure gold. If we focus on the fact that it is gold and it is priceless, then our attention is on the universal and the real (the *li*), the gold itself. In that case we do not pay attention to the particular lion shape (*shih*) that the golden statue takes.

Nevertheless, we can admire the marvelous artistry of the artist who shaped that raw material into the beautiful lion that is utterly realistic. The statue is so beautifully created that each hair is a lion-hair; each eye is a lion-eye, each paw is a lion-paw. When we wonder at the statue's details (*shih*), then we do not pay attention to the fact that it is pure gold (*li*). Yet apart from the gold there is no lion to be found. When we are lost in admiration at the solid life-like creation, both the abstract form and the universal reality of gold-ness disappear from our consciousness.

The physical particular statue in the lion-shape is the *shih*, and the gold is the universal, the real, the *li*. There is no particular lion-form without the gold; but the gold itself must have some particular form in order to exist. Gold

---

[30] An excellent exploration of this concept can be found in Brook Ziporyn, *Ironies of Oneness and Difference: Coherence in Early Chinese Thought; Prolegomena to the Study of Li* (New York: SUNY, 2013), and his companion volume, *Beyond Oneness and Difference: Li and Coherence in Chinese Buddhist Thought and Its Antecedents* (New York: SUNY, 2014)

[31] Later Neo-Confucians will place great stress on this same character of *li* or pattern, understanding it to refer to ultimate Principle, Ultimate Reason, or even Heavenly Reason. Neo-Confucianism is discussed in chapter 22 of this volume (Vol. 2) of *Asian Thought*.

itself is independent of the lion-shape. The lion-shape is independent of the gold. The gold is not the lion, the lion-form is not the gold, but the existence of each depends upon the other. The dichotomy between ultimate reality (gold), and particular appearance (the lion-shape), disappears. The Hua-yen philosopher Fa-tsang explains it as follows:

> If we look at the lion [as lion], there is only the lion and no gold. This means that the lion is manifest while the gold is hidden. If we look at the gold, there is only the gold and no lion. This means that the gold is manifest and the lion is hidden. If we look at them both, then both are manifest and both hidden . . . The gold and the lion may be hidden or manifest, one or many, definitely pure or definitely mixed, powerful or powerless, the one or the other. . . . Principle [*li*, the gold] and fact [*shih*, the lion-form] appear together and are completely compatible with each other. They do not obstruct each other's peaceful existence, and thus the subtle and the minute are accomplished. . . . In each of the lion's eyes, ears, limbs, joints, and in each and every hair, there is the golden lion. . . Thus in each and every hair there are an infinite number of lions, and, in addition all the single hairs, together with their infinite number of lions, in turn enter into a single hair. In this way, the geometric progression is infinite, like the jewels of Celestial Lord Indra's net.[32]

Hua-yen Buddhism was not purely philosophy to the exclusion of practice. Monks in Hua-yen monasteries practiced seated meditation as a way to achieve a deeper intuition into the interdependent interpenetrating dharma-realms described by Hua-yen thinkers based on the *Avatamsaka sutra*.

Until 840 Hua-yen was the most highly regarded metaphysical and philosophical school of Chinese Buddhism. Prior to 840 both the Hua-yen and T'ien-t'ai were active in the courts and received a great deal of financial support from the government. The best monks of these schools were superb scholars, and in China, scholars were esteemed. Intellectual and artistic achievements were honored, and many of these monks received the respect and prestige that had been accorded to the old Confucian literati. They had become intellectual leaders of Chinese civilization and thought.

However, the 845 persecution of Buddhism weakened all those northern China Buddhist groups which depended upon and thrived under imperial patronage, including T'ien-t'ai, Hua-yen, and the Tantric followers of the esoteric teachings called Chen-yen. Although there was somewhat of a revival of T'ien-t'ai later in the Sung dynasty with patronage by literati scholars, the Hua-yen never did recover as an independent school. However, later Ch'an teachers incorporated much of Hua-yen into Ch'an Buddhist teachings.

20.8 ESOTERIC CHEN-YEN BUDDHISM

In the early 700s, several teachers in China gained popularity for their esoteric or Tantric-dominated consecration rituals and magical incantations. These ritually-dominated currents of Indian Buddhism seem to have been brought to China by the Indian monk Vajrabodhi (671–741). Vajrabodhi came to China in 719, and his principal student, Amoghavajra is treated as the founder of the Chen-yen Buddhist lineage in China.[33] The practitioners became

---

[32] Wing-tsit Chan, *A Source Book in Chinese Philosophy* (Princeton, NJ: Princeton University Press, 1963), pp. 411–412.

[33] An important follower of Amoghavajra was the monk Hui-kuo (746–805), who was the teacher of the Japanese monk Kukai (774–835). Kukai studied in China and then when he returned from China, he asserted that he brought a special secret Chen-yen teaching to Japan, where it is called Shingon. In Japan, Shingon Buddhism became exceptionally important and politically powerful lineage tradition, or "school," whereas in China there were many teachers who used Tantric methods but it is unclear if they thought of themselves as teachers in a distinctly separate lineage of esoteric Buddhism. If it ever was a separate school in China, Tantric Buddhism quickly faded. See Robert H. Sharf: *Coming to Terms with Chinese Buddhism* (Honolulu: University of Hawai'i Press, 2002), Appendix 1: "On Esoteric Buddhism in China,"

famous for their magical abilities: the biographies of these T'ang dynasty teachers "revel in accounts of their miraculous powers: they subjugate demons, summon dragons, make rain, quell storms, avert calamity, and even raise the dead."[34]

The Chinese called this form of Buddhism "Chen-yen," two Chinese characters which literally mean "true word." This was a Chinese attempt to capture the meaning of the Indian Sanskrit term *mantra*. As we have seen before, a chanted *mantra* is a word or phrase containing magical power, and believed to capture an insight that cannot be expressed in ordinary language. The Chen-yen school understood a *mantra* to be an ideal conceived in a buddha's mind but not expressible in words.

In previous chapters in Volume 1 of *Asian Thought*, we have discussed Tantric Hinduism, esoteric Indian Buddhism, and Tibetan forms of Tantric Buddhism. Drawing on Indian Tantric forms of Buddhism, Chinese Chen-yen followers understood themselves as possessing a higher doctrine which transcended all Conservative (pre-Mahayana) and Mahayana doctrines, transcending anything which could be expressed in words. As with other sutras which had been translated into Chinese, the Chinese tended to accept the claims written in the Tantric Buddhist sutras as genuinely the words and teachings of the Buddha.

Techniques of Chen-yen Chinese Buddhism

The basic techniques of Chen-yen Buddhism are complex secret rituals, chanted invocations of *mantra* and *dharani* ("incantation," short magical phrases to avert evil and bring about blessings), fortune-telling or divination, magic, *mandala* images, elaborate consecration rituals, symbolic finger manipulations (*mudra*), and other skillful devices (*upaya*) to symbolically illustrate the highest truth.

The Chen-yen teachers also used visualization of Buddhist gods in meditative exercises. As a result of these secret practices, hidden from outsiders, Chen-yen practitioners believed that they could develop magical powers such as the power to control celestial forces. Chen-yen monks utilized words and phrases of power (*mantras*), which they believed would increase the supernormal powers (*siddhi*) developed by their difficult spiritual practices. They also thought that these difficult spiritual practices provided a shortcut to the ultimate goal of Buddhism for those who were sufficiently prepared.

The Chinese Confucians in court and Chinese civilization in general valued ceremonial rituals and considered them to be essential to an effective government. They also were prepared to accept claims of magical powers, for similar claims were made by religious Taoist teachers who were popular at court. Like its Indian counterpart, Chen-yen used secret and elaborate rituals, which fascinated many Chinese. Certain temples in the Chinese capital became richly decorated centers for the performance of complex rituals which made use of secret hand gestures, brilliant colors, music, and drama.

Chen-yen also used chanted *mantras*. It was believed that spiritual goals could be achieved by such chanting, but one may also gain worldly goals and the properly chanted phrases could provide protection from danger. Instead of philosophical analysis and focused meditation, the tendency in Chen-yen was for richly ceremonial rituals, forms of magic, and secret teachings to become the secret but speedy Buddha way to awakening.

The Chinese already believed that immortals, sages and alchemists could possess magical powers via religious Taoist secret practices. Consequently, a major attraction of Chen-yen Buddhism was the belief of the Chinese that Chen-yen Buddhists were wizard-like masters who really did acquire supernormal powers by their complex and secret ritual practices. They were believed to be genuine miracle-workers, and court aristocrats thought that Chen-yen monks

pp. 263–278)

[34] Robert H. Sharf, *op. cit.*, p. 269.

could manipulate the world using their magical powers.[35] In the Chinese biographical literature there are many tales of extraordinary miracles enacted by these Tantric adepts. Their powers could bring blessings to someone who paid for the performance of rituals. These powers could bring disaster on one's enemy, or the enemies of the state. These powers could be used to predict disaster and avert catastrophe. These rituals could control the weather and banish demons.[36] These powers even reached to the departed, and could affect their karmic fate. There are stories of Tantric rituals used to raise the dead.[37]

The belief that Tantric Buddhist priests could perform elaborate rituals and secret incantations which would lead to divine protection for the state became important for some T'ang dynasty emperors. It was thought that the ritual invocations from some esoteric Buddhist sutras could provide protection from rebellions, foreign invasions, and other disasters. In the year 765, the emperor of China sought the divine help from various buddhas in courtly rituals he sponsored.[38]

The Buddhist sutras which justify and teach these sorts of esoteric Buddhist devices are usually preached by a great cosmic sun Buddha whose name is Vairocana,[39] or Mahavairocana ("Great Sun"). A basic text of Chen-yen is the *Mahavairocana sutra*, the sutra of the Great Sun Buddha. For Chen-yen, the historical Buddha, Siddhartha Gotama, was merely one of many manifestations of the eternal Great Sun Buddha. However, after penetrating deeply into the Chen-yen insights, the student comes to the personal realization that the Sun-Buddha, Mahavairocana, is *sunyata* (empty of eternally existing essence) and Chen-yen interprets *sunyata* as the ontological basis for existence, the source of *yin* and *yang*, or the source of *pratityasamutpada* (dependent co-arising).

The Great Sun Buddha, Mahavairocana, is not only emptiness, but it is also the Buddha-nature inherent in all things. Mahavairochana is the third and cosmic body of the Buddha, the *Dharmakaya*,[40] the ultimate nature of reality and the ultimate truth. However, the student must come to the deep and profound realization that Mahavairocana does not exist apart from the mind.

Mantras are a means to unite one with Mahavairocana. By chanting these, and reciting and meditating upon these, one can achieve awakening. Even the title of a sutra can be a *mantra*. The Chen-yen sect puts great stress on esoteric symbolic and iconographic representations of truth. Chen-yen believes that certain hand positions (*mudra*) have powers.

Although teachers who focused only on Chen-yen rituals were popular for a while, their lineage seems to have endured for only a little more than a century in China (it was weakened after the 845 persecution and further weakened after 890). Nevertheless, supernatural elements associated with Tantric Buddhism survived from the Tang dynasty (618–906) into the next dynasty, the Sung (960–1279), and were often incorporated into other Chinese schools of

---

[35] Prominent religious Taoist priests in the royal court and imperial throne room had made similar claims in the past, so it was easy to accept Tantric Buddhist claims of supernormal powers.

[36] A book devoted to East Asian Tantric Buddhism is Richard Payne, ed., *Tantric Buddhism in East Asia* (Boston: Wisdom Publications, 2005).

[37] Chou Yi-liang, "Tantrism in China," *Harvard Journal of Asiatic Studies* 8 (3–4), 1945, pp. 241–332.

[38] The influence of esoteric Buddhism in the Chinese imperial court is documented in Stanley Weinstein, *Buddhism Under the T'ang*, p. 77ff.

[39] The Sanskrit "c" is pronounced "ch," so Vai-ro-cana is pronounced "Vai-RO-cha-na."

[40] The three bodies of the Buddha were discussed in *Asian Thought* Volume 1, chapters 9 and 10 on Indian Mahayana Buddhism. These are the physical body (*nirmanakaya*) the Buddha used in teaching his followers, the bliss-body (*sambhogakaya*) which the Buddha uses talking to bodhisattvas and visiting their heavenly realms, and the ultimate body (*dharmakaya*). Chinese Buddhists will adopt this, but offer many different interpretations of what these mean.

Buddhism. The numerous *mantras* (chanted phrases of power), *dharani* (brief memorized phrases of power),[41] prayers, magical hand gestures, and Tantric texts lived on in many popular Buddhist rituals and in Buddhist art.

20.9 BUDDHISM IN THE NORTHERN CAPITAL

Although weakened by the 755 C.E. An Lu-Shan Rebellion and the battles which decimated the capital, the scholarly Buddhist schools remained centered in the two Chinese capital cities in the north because they depended upon the emperor and his court to support their academic endeavors, and to supply their need for food, bedding, a quiet place to study, a well-stocked library, paper, ink, and other necessities. These monks associated with the wealthy and those who were from politically powerful families and clans.

Because the monks and scholars interacted with the aristocrats and political realm of the court, they were expected to perform elaborate and costly Buddhist rituals serving needs of the state and wealthy aristocracy. Many of the monks from these scholarly monasteries were talented in the aesthetic realm as well, and used arts, including architecture, sculpture and painting to enhance impact of rituals and deepen and reshape the aesthetic culture of China. All of this would change following the persecution of Buddhism in the year 845 C.E. Apparently a significant number of Buddhist monks were seeking an easy life but were uneducated in Buddhism, and some were ex-convicts, some carried on with mistresses and prostitutes, owned slaves, and became wealthy.[42] These facts were used as an excuse to attempt to eliminate Buddhism from China. The 845 persecution resulted in dismantling more than 4,600 monasteries, defrocking over 260,000 monks and nuns, the destruction of more than 40,000 chapels and hermitages, and the confiscation of fertile and taxable land from monasteries.[43]

Although severely weakened by the 845 persecution of Buddhism, an esoteric Buddhist lineage was further weakened when another rebellion in 878-882 destroyed the books and the monasteries.[44] The academic monasteries of the scholarly schools in the north were decimated, and in the later Sung dynasty (960-1279), two traditions of Chinese Buddhism would dominate (although there was a resurgence of T'ien-t'ai during this period). One of the two dominant systems was the Pure Land school, which was discussed above. The other was the Ch'an school, which will be discussed in the next chapter. These two schools exerted the most influence upon later Chinese society, Chinese thought, poetry, and all forms of art.

20.10 SUMMARY OF THE CHAPTER

There were four schools of Buddhism which developed in China, inspired by Indian Buddhist texts and concepts, but which had never existed independently in India. These schools had their beginnings in the fourth and fifth centuries in China, and achieved their highest development in the later Sui (590-618) and T'ang (618-906) dynasties. The devotional Pure Land school of Chinese Buddhism based itself on the story of the Bodhisattva Amitabha, who vowed to create a Pure Land in the West, where anyone who asks could be guaranteed to get there after death. Rebirth in the Western Paradise was assured for those who asked. Whether that Pure Land was in the practitioner's own mind, or whether it was actually off in the west, nirvana was certain.

The T'ien-t'ai school was inspired by several different Sanskrit commentaries, where the ideas of Madhyamaka

---

[41] For more details on *dharani*, see Buswell and Lopez, eds., *The Princeton Dictionary of Buddhism*, pp. 241-242.

[42] Stanley Weinstein, *Buddhism Under the T'ang* (Cambridge University Press, 1987), p. 119.

[43] *Ibid.*, p. 134.

[44] *Ibid.*, pp. 147-149.

philosophy and Nagarjuna were combined with novel elements of the *Lotus* sutra to produce a philosophical vision quite different from that of the Indian Madhyamaka. The Chinese T'ien-t'ai practitioners also put great stress on the analysis of focused meditation, and produced many volumes of writings on focused concentration. It is a combination of insight and wisdom, and meditation.

The Hua-yen school took its original inspiration from Nagarjuna's emptiness philosophy plus a particular Indian sutra called the *Avatamsaka* (Hua-yen sutra in Chinese) but utilized only parts of the sutra and shaped the ideas into something uniquely Chinese. The metaphysical insight of Indra's net, as explained in the *Treatise on the Golden Lion*, explicates the interpenetration of all particulars with all universals, and the ultimate interdependence of each particular upon every other particular. These ideas brought Buddhist thought to new heights of metaphysical speculation.

The Chen-yen ("true word" or *mantra*) teachings came into China in the early decades of the eighth century, and the earliest teachers were carrying on Tantric traditions current in Indian Buddhism. Using secret and elaborate rituals, and chanted phrases of power, it was believed that worldly goals could be achieved, and protection from danger was possible. Temples and monasteries became richly decorated intentionally making use of all the arts, including painting, music, and sculpture. Instead of meditation, the tendency was for these theatrical richly ceremonial rituals themselves to become the way to buddhahood. Esoteric Buddhism was severely weakened in China after a rebellion in 878–882 destroyed the books and the monasteries.

20.11 TECHNICAL TERMS

T'ien-t'ai (Heavenly Terrace)   School of Chinese Buddhism.
Hua-yen (Flower Ornament)   School of Chinese Buddhism.
Pure Land (Ching-t'u/Jingdu)   School of Chinese Buddhism.
Chen-yen (mantra)   Buddhist teachers who focused on magical chants and rituals (Tantra).

Sui dynasty   Buddhism develops during the Sui dynasty.
T'ang dynasty   Buddhism flowers in the T'ang dynasty.

Avatamsaka sutra (Hua-yen sutra)   Hua-yen text.
Lotus sutra   T'ien-t'ai text.
Prajna-paramita sutras (Perfection of Wisdom) Teaches emptiness.

Amitabha Buddha   Buddha of the Western Paradise, the Pure Land.
Nien-fo/nianfo   Chanted mantra, an invocation of Amitabha Buddha.

Indra's Net   Hua-yen analogy for the universe.
li and *shih*   Universality and particularity in Hua-yen thought.
The Three Periods of the Dharma (Teachings)

20.12 QUESTIONS FOR FURTHER DISCUSSION

(1)   An enduring question for world religions is what elements of the religion are its essence and cannot be changed, and what elements are cultural and can be changed. Indian Buddhism changed in China, and apparently some elements of Indian Buddhism were perceived to be cultural baggage, but not essential.

Question: how can we tell which elements of a religion are its living core, and which elements can change as the religion moves from culture to culture?

(2)   Hua-yen Buddhism wrestles with the question of how individual perceivable particulars (*shih*) are related to abstract universals (*li*). Explain the Hua-yen problem, and the solution. How is a particular chair related to "chair-ness," the universal feature which all chairs share in common?

(3)   Pure Land Buddhism says that not one of us is self-disciplined enough, or good enough, to achieve nirvana using our own abilities. However, we can get to a heavenly realm by the grace of the Buddha of the Western Paradise, Amitabha. Are there any parallels to this in Western religious traditions?

(4)   Chinese Buddhists accepted every word of the Indian Buddhist sutras as the actual words uttered by the Buddha himself. The T'ien-t'ai school did its best to explain how the same person could advocate contradictory positions. What was the T'ien-t'ai solution?

(5)   Many contemporary Buddhists in China are very comfortable with science, not considering it a rival but rather exploring their own Buddhist concepts of human origins, the status of humans, human consciousness, ethics, and self-cultivation. Similar attitudes have been noticed in Western Buddhists as well. What do you expect would account for this?

(6)   Buddhist scholars are aware that the various Buddhist sutras were composed over a long time, and most are not the actual words of the historical Buddha. Is there any parallel in Western biblical scholarship. Do biblical scholars agree that all the four Gospels were actually written by Matthew, Mark, Luke, and John? Are there passages in the Gospels which tell the same story in two or more different and incompatible ways?

SELECTED BIBLIOGRAPHY

Chan, Wing-tsit, *A Source Book in Chinese Philosophy* (Princeton, NJ: Princeton University Press, 1963)

Hammerstrom, Erik J., *The Science of Chinese Buddhism: Early Twentieth-Century Engagements* (New York: Columbia University Press, 2015). An excellent exploration of contemporary Chinese Buddhists and their appreciation of science and the interconnection between Buddhist theories of consciousness and reality.

Lagerway, John, ed., *Modern Chinese Religion I* (960–1368), 2 vols. (Leiden: E. J. Brill, 2015)

Takakusu, J., *The Essentials of Buddhist Philosophy*, (Greenwood Press, 1956).

Watt, James C. Y., *China: Dawn of a Golden Age, 200-750 AD* (New Haven, CT: Yale University Press and the Metropolitan Museum of Art, 2004)

Weinstein, Stanley, *Buddhism Under the T'ang* (MA: Cambridge University Press, 2008)

Welch, Holmes, *The Practice of Chinese Buddhism: 1900-1950* (Cambridge: Harvard University Press, 1967)

Wu, Jiang, and Lucille Chia, eds., *Spreading Buddha's Word in East Asia: The Formation and Transformation of the Chinese Buddhist Canon* (New York: Columbia University Press, 2015)

Zürcher, Eric, *The Buddhist Conquest of China: The Spread and Adaptation of Buddhism in Early Medieval China* (Leiden, Netherlands, E. J. Brill, 1959)

T'ien-t'ai Buddhism

CHAPTER 20: CHINESE BUDDHISM

Chappell, David and M. Ichishima (tr.), *T'ien-t'ai Buddhism* (Honolulu: University Press of Hawaii, 1984)

Chen, Jinhua, *Legend and Legitimation: The Formation of Tendai Esoteric Buddhism in Japan.*

Donner, Neal, "Chih-i's Meditation on Evil," *Buddhist and Taoist Studies II* (1987).

Fung, Yu-lan, *History of Chinese Philosophy*, Vol. II (Princeton University Press, 1953), pp. 360–386.

Hurvitz, Leon, *Chih-i (538-597), Melanges chinois et bouddhique* Vol. 12 (Bruxelles: 1960–1962)

Luk, Charles, *The Secrets of Chinese Meditation* (New York: Samuel Weiser, Inc., 1964), ch. 4.

Mun, Chanju, *The History of Doctrinal Classifications in Chinese Buddhism* (New York: University Press of America, 2005)

Swanson, Paul, James A. Heisig, David Chappell, *Foundations of T'ien-t'ai Philosophy: The Flowering of the Two Truths Theory in Chinese Buddhism* (Asian Humanities Press, 1989).

Ziporyn, Brook, *Being and Ambiguity: Philosophical Experiments with Tiantai Buddhism* (Indiana University Press, 2016)

_____, *Ironies of Oneness and Difference: Coherence in Early Chinese Thought; Prolegomena to the Study of Li* (SUNY series in Chinese Philosophy and Culture, 2013)

_____, *Beyond Oneness and Difference: Li and Coherence in Chinese Buddhist Thought and Its Antecedents* (SUNY Series in Chinese Philosophy and Culture, 2014)

Hua-yen

Cook, Francis H., *Hua-yen Buddhism: The Jewel Net of Indra* (University Park, Pa.: Pennsylvania State University Press, 1977)

Chang, C. C., *The Buddhist Teaching of Totality* (University Park, Pa.: Pennsylvania State University Press, 1971).

Cleary, Thomas, *Entry Into the Inconceivable: An Introduction to Hua-yen Buddhism* (1983).

Cleary, Thomas, tr., *Entry Into the Realm of Reality (The Gandavyuha, the Final Book of the Avatamsaka Sutra): The Text (1987); The Guide by Li Tongxuan* (Boston: Shambhala, 1989).

_____, *The Flower Ornament Scripture: A Translation of the Avatamsaka Sutra* (Boston, MA: Shambhala Publications, 1993)

DeBary, W. T., ed., *The Buddhist Tradition in India, China and Japan*

Gimello, Robert, *et. al.*, eds., *Avatamsaka Buddhism in East Asia: Hua-yen, Kegon, Flower Ornament Scripture* (Otto Harrassowitz Verlag, 2012)

Gimello, Robert, and Peter Gregory, *Studies in Ch'an and Hua-yen* (Honolulu: University Press of Hawai'i, 1983).

Gregory, Peter N., *Tsung-mi and the Sinification of Buddhism* (Honolulu: University of Hawai'i Press, 2002)

Hamar, Imre, ed., *Reflecting Mirrors: Perspectives on Huayan Buddhism* (Otto Harrassowitz Verlag, 2007)

Odin, Steve, *Process Metaphysics and Hua-yen Buddhism* (New York: State University Press of New York, 1982)

Takakusu, J., *The Essentials of Buddhist Philosophy* (Greenwood Press, 1956)

Suzuki, D. T., *Essays in Zen Buddhism*, 3rd Series, Ch. 1, 2, 4.

Ziporyn, Brook, *Ironies of Oneness and Difference: Coherence in Early Chinese Thought; Prolegomena to the Study of Li* (SUNY series in Chinese Philosophy and Culture, 2013)

_____, *Beyond Oneness and Difference: Li and Coherence in Chinese Buddhist Thought and Its Antecedents* (SUNY Series in Chinese Philosophy and Culture, 2014)

Pure Land Buddhism

Andrews, Allen A., *The Teachings Essential for Rebirth* (Monumenta Nipponica, 1973)

Bloom, Alfred, *Shinran's Gospel of Pure Grace* (Tucson, AZ: University of Arizona Press, 1965, 1973)

_____, *Living in Amida's Universal Vow* (World Wisdom, 2004)

Blum, Mark, *The Origins and Development of Pure Land Buddhism* (New York: Oxford University Press, 2002)

Foard, J., and M. Solomon, eds., *The Pure Land Tradition* (Berkeley: Buddhist-Studies Series, vol. 3, 1997)

Hirota, Dennis, *Toward a Contemporary Understanding of Pure Land Buddhism* (New York: SUNY, 2000)

Hsiao Ching-fen, *The Life and Teachings of T'an-luan* (1967).

Hurvitz, Leon, "Chu-hung's One Mind of Pure Land and Ch'an Buddhism," in deBary, ed., *Self and Society in Ming Thought* (1970), pp. 451-482.

Okusa, Yejitsu, S. Yamabe, Tada Kanai, eds., *In the Name of the Amida Buddha: Classic Writings from the Pure Land Sect of Buddhism* ( )

Payne, Richard K., and Kenneth Tanaka, eds., *Approaching the Land of Bliss: Religious Praxis in the Cult of Amitabha* (Honolulu: University of Hawai'i Press, 2005)

Reichelt, K.L., *Truth and Tradition in Chinese Buddhism*, pp. 127–170.

Takakusu, J., *The Essentials of Buddhist Philosophy* (Greenwood Press, 1956)

Lagerway, John and Marc Kalinowski, eds., *Early Chinese Religion: Part One: Shang Through Han* (1250 BC -220 AD) (Leiden & Boston: Brill, 2011)

Lagerway, John and Lu Pengzhi, eds., *Early Chinese Religion: Part Two: The Period of Division* (220 AD -529 AD) (Leiden & Boston: Brill, 2010)

CHAPTER 21: *CH'AN* BUDDHISM

21.1 OVERVIEW OF THE CHAPTER

In this chapter we shall discuss one of the most important schools of Chinese Buddhism, the Ch'an tradition. The Ch'an tradition is not only important in the history of China; it has a significant presence in the West as well.

The Chinese character pronounced as *Ch'an* (in Wade-Giles romanization), or *Chan* (in Pinyin romanization), is a Chinese attempt to capture the sound of the Sanskrit term *dhyana* (focused meditation, pronounced dhya-an). For this reason sometimes Ch'an is called the Meditation School of Chinese Buddhism.

Ch'an began in China around the sixth century, and several centuries later, Ch'an was carried to Korea, and then to Japan, where it was known as Zen. The period in Chinese history where Ch'an was of major cultural and religious influence was roughly from 700 to 1500 C.E.

Ch'an will develop several unusual techniques to help students recognize that their own basic human nature is the same as the nature of an enlightened buddha, and insight into that human nature puts one on the path to awakening. Certainly, the Ch'an practitioner will use focused concentration, or *dhyana*-meditation to allow us to discover the awareness that we truly are, the same awareness which constitutes the awakening experience of the Buddha. One of the most distinctive and unique skillful devices of Ch'an is the *koan* (ko-an), a brief dialogue or anecdote of encounters from Ch'an history which the teacher presents to the Ch'an student as a question, as an obstacle or challenge, and ultimately as a tool to bring about a spiritual breakthrough.

The basic insight of Ch'an seems to be that the spiritual realm or sacred ultimate reality is not somewhere other than the flowing here-and-now. When one lives deeply and fully in the present, deeply aware of who we truly are, *just that* is the ultimate truth. Whether coming or going, one is at home.

As we shall see, the classic Ch'an teachers do not have any lists of doctrines which one must accept, or teachings to memorize or believe. Reading about Ch'an Buddhism, we encounter countless dialogues and stories attributed to ancient respected teachers, or Ch'an "masters." We will share many of these with you in this chapter. We have seen this same preference for anecdotes in the writings of the Taoist Chuang-tzu/Zhuangzi. In fact, the influence of philosophical Taoism on Ch'an is clear.

If Ch'an Buddhism were a philosophy in the way that the West understands the term, then Ch'an would be explicating the basic concepts of reality, which is called ontology or metaphysics. Although Chinese Buddhism accepts the Buddhist insight that all things are in flowing change, in endless interaction, and are empty of enduring substances (*sunyata*), the Ch'an teachers urge us to find out for ourselves, and are often portrayed as preferring not to explain. If Ch'an were a philosophy, it would be concerned with the nature of the self and limitations of knowledge (epistemology). Although Ch'an does think we misunderstand the nature of the self and of reality, and that this ignorance is a major cause of our emotional dissatisfaction, the Ch'an teachers tend not to explain. If Ch'an were a philosophy, it would be concerned with an analysis of human nature, and would offer an explication of concepts such as emotional obstacles (*klesa*) and origins of self-centeredness. Ch'an doesn't do this. Ch'an does accept the Indian Buddhist analysis of human nature as empty of anything like an unchanging enduring soul (*atman*), and somehow human nature involves some kind of inner awareness they call "Buddha-nature" but doesn't explain. If Ch'an were a philosophy, it would offer an analysis of the foundations of moral behavior (ethics). Ch'an treats morality as embedded in Nature (Tao), and moral injunctions as puzzles to be resolved, not rules to be followed blindly.

225

CHAPTER 21: CH'AN BUDDHISM

Like Confucianism and religious Taoism, Ch'an does practice rituals and chanting, and seems to think that some sounds possess power (mantras). Ch'an teachers will talk about buddhas and bodhisattvas, although quite often these are treated as metaphors for our own true self. The Ch'an literature has tales of monks burning statues of the Buddha on a cold night, and some Ch'an art depicts Ch'an teachers tearing up the sacred texts, or laughing uproariously at a sacred book whose pages are all blank. This sort of behavior is iconoclastic, which westerners tend to associate with anti-religion.

The general field of Ch'an and Zen studies is already immense and still growing. No single chapter of a book could be more than a brief overview.[1]

CHINESE DYNASTIES RELEVANT TO CH'AN BUDDHISM

HAN (202 B.C.E. - 220 C.E.)
        Buddhism enters China between 50 B.C.E. and 50 C.E.
    Three Kingdoms (221–265 C.E.)
    Six Dynasties (265–580 C.E.)
        Bodhidharma (d. 525?)
SUI (590–618 C.E.)
T'ANG/TANG (618–906 C.E.)
        Hui-neng, the Sixth Patriarch (638–713)
        Ho-tse Shen-hui, student of Hui-neng (684–758)
        The Great Persecution of 845
        Lin-chi (810? – 866)
SUNG/SONG (960–1279)
YUAN (1280–1368)
MING (1368–1644)
        Ch'an and Pure Land Buddhism combine
CH'ING/CHING (1644–1912)

21.2 INTRODUCTORY REMARKS

In early Indian Buddhism the stress tended to be upon a lonely process of self-cultivation by which the forest monk practiced the Noble Eightfold Path of morality, mental discipline, and wisdom, also mastered levels of meditative accomplishment, lessened self-centered grasping and possessiveness, and finally lessened *duhkha* (misery, suffering, frustration, dissatisfaction) or perhaps even eliminated *duhkha* from his life. The goal was nirvana which was the cessation of misery and suffering, and escape from the cycle of birth-and-death (*samsara*). The Chinese Ch'an model is interestingly different. For Ch'an, the goal becomes insight into one's nature, which can produce an abrupt euphoric insight experience, known in the West as *satori*. Spiritual advancement occurs in the context of a student-teacher interaction, during which process the mind of the student and the teacher are thought to be in harmony.

Ch'an Buddhism in China is a complex phenomenon. Like the great majority of Asian thought systems, there is no central authority that can dictate to followers how they must behave or what they must believe. Of course there are rules for monks in monasteries, but there has never been a single central authority for Ch'an ideas, and different

---

[1] Of course, this is true for each topic in this book.

CHAPTER 21: CH'AN BUDDHISM

Ch'an teachers place stress on different aspects. We might begin by describing Ch'an as a creative Chinese development of and confluence of many strands which we have previously discussed in this book, including:

(1)   the world-view and paradoxical language typical of the Indian *Prajna-paramita* (Perfection of Wisdom) texts as explained in the Madhyamaka **emptiness** tradition associated with Nagarjuna (no unchanging self-existent substances or essences anywhere);

(2)   the Buddha-Nature (*Tathagathagarbha*) ideas of the Mahayana that everyone has the potential of buddhahood;

(3)   the Indian Buddhist "consciousness-only" Yogachara ideas which argue that consciousness creates much or all of the reality we live in, and that we are confused about the nature of reality;

(4)   cross-legged meditation practices (*dhyana*),

(5)   the insights of philosophical Taoism, especially the humorous attitudes of the easy-going *Chuang-tzu*, and the philosophical Taoist dialogues found in "Pure-Talk Taoism."

(6)   Confucianism and Confucian morality is incorporated into Ch'an.

What the Ch'an traditions have done with these various threads is to produce something interestingly different from its sources, but something quite comfortable for many Chinese. Since the apparent goal of Ch'an is to live fully in reality, many Ch'an teachers are portrayed as having a preference for pointing to reality, insisting that their students recognize what is right before their eyes. These teachers put less stress on providing concepts to be explicated. This does present a problem for scholarly conceptual analysis.

The Ch'an school encouraged disciplined creativity in all areas of artistic endeavor. Ch'an enriched Chinese arts and the art of Korea and Japan as well. It influenced black-ink painting, calligraphy, poetry (the Japanese *haiku* is a Ch'an form), garden design, tea ceremony, aspects of music (the *shakuhachi* bamboo flute is especially associated with Zen), the martial arts, and other aspects of Asian cultural life such as the *Noh* drama in Japan.

21.3 TWO APPROACHES TO THE ACADEMIC STUDY OF CH'AN

Some Western scholars contrast a traditional (or "idealistic," "romantic" or even "mythological") approach to Ch'an/Chan with a more critical approach which stresses a historical and cultural analysis as the foundation of an accurate understanding of the school.[2] From the 1920s until almost 1970, the less historically rigorous romantic approach to Ch'an dominated in the West.[3] However, starting in the 1960s significant numbers of Western students traveled to Japan or Korea to study in traditional monasteries, and as these scholars gained fluency in ancient classical Chinese, Korean and Japanese languages, and combined this linguistic fluency with authentic historical sources about the school, a rather different picture began to emerge. For those Western students who gained fluency in Japanese, the

---

[2] These same two approaches are found in the study of most religions, including all aspects of Hinduism and Christianity. For example, in popular Christianity Jesus is born in a *manger*, yet Christian scholars who know the ancient language well tell us that *manger* is a mistranslation. Also Christian scholars are certain that Jesus was **not** born on December 25th and not even born in wintertime. Christian theologians have written many dozens of books from a critical perspective searching for historical truth and rejecting legends.

[3] The Zen scholar Steven Heine has written a book on these two perspectives of traditional Zen vs. critical Zen: *Zen Skin, Zen Marrow* (London: Oxford University Press, 2008). The late Ch'an scholar John McRae, utilizing some of the best contemporary Japanese scholarship, is one of many who advocate a critical and historical approach to Ch'an and Zen historical studies. For example, see his *Seeing Through Zen* (Berkeley, CA: University of California Press, 2003).

world of Japanese scholarship revealed that in the West there has been a major confusion of myth and reality.[4] For example, the traditional description of the history of early Ch'an is regarded as fascinating, instructive, but at best misleading, and at worst false in almost every detail.

Traditional romantic Ch'an portrays Ch'an Buddhism as an unbroken line of perfectly awakened teachers beginning with the Buddha, the identical awakening experience for each generation transmitted by apparently irrational dialogues and bizarre questions. Romantic Ch'an portrays Ch'an teachers as uniformly opposed to the academic study of Buddhist sacred texts, as extolling creative spontaneity and minimizing the value of Buddhist rituals and prayer, as not treating statues of the Buddha with serious reverence, as being iconoclastic, as a school relying only on one's own abilities (contrasted with schools which rely on the salvific powers of buddhas and bodhisattvas), as avoiding political entanglements with the royal court, and as "free-and-easy wanderers" in the style of the Taoist *Chuang-tzu*.

There is no question that written records from the eleventh century do portray many Ch'an teachers of the earlier T'ang/Tang (618-906 C.E.) and Sung/Song (960-1279) dynasties in precisely this way, but more recent scholarship has revealed that the great majority of Ch'an teachers carefully studied Buddhist scriptures and treated the texts with special reverence as sacred, and they practiced chanting and other religious rituals faithfully,[5] lived in monasteries where their lives were carefully regulated, took on the duties comparable to a community parish priest, and many important teachers even cultivated relationships with the magistrates and the imperial court in order to curry favor and gain fame and power among the aristocracy and the rulers (a common practice among all the various Buddhist groups in China).[6]

Ch'an teachers who interacted with politicians provided rituals which called on the supernatural protection of buddhas, offered worldly benefits to those who paid for ceremonies, chanted phrases of power (*mantras*) for healing, and offered the possibility of salvation after death. Some early Ch'an teachers called on Amitabha Buddha of the Pure Land with faith.

The fact is that scholars believe that many of the irrational dialogues attributed to T'ang/Tang dynasty (618-906 C.E.) Ch'an teachers never occurred in the form in which they have been handed down to us. The common opinion is that in the eleventh and later centuries, the Ch'an chronicles were rewritten by editors to make the various lineages appear to be an unbroken line of teachers, each generation brought to awakening by iconoclastic irrational encounters. The historical tales of Ch'an teachers contain much that is myth. Recent critical historical scholarship provides a more analytic history of Ch'an and Zen, focused on facts, names, dates, and cultural influences.

The emic and mythic history of Ch'an and Zen contains insights which tell us how Ch'an views itself, and its own ideals. The romantic approach to Ch'an is significant, and contains revealing insights but it is important not to confuse it with actual history. This traditional mythical history is a great deal of fun to read about, and this chapter will include much of this approach. However, we would be remiss if we did not supplement it with an etic critical history, if we did not point out the aspects of Ch'an which were not quite as portrayed in the traditional writings. Thus, this chapter will encompass both emic and etic approaches, but will also try to distinguish them.

21.4 THE EARLY HISTORY OF CH'AN

Ch'an is one of the four uniquely Chinese schools which were not a continuation of any Indian lineage or Indian tradition. There was no Ch'an school or Ch'an lineage in India. Despite the legendary history which Ch'an

---

[4] It has also been noted that those students who studied the Japanese writings came away with a distinctly Japanese interpretation of Chinese Buddhism, with Japanese scholars stressing certain aspects of Buddhism in Japan that may not have been stressed in China, such as strong separation between Buddhist sects, and a strong Japanese stress upon teacher-to-teacher lineages.

[5] For a more critical perspective, see Steven Heine, ed., *Zen Ritual: Studies of Zen Buddhist Theory in Practice* (London: Oxford, 2007).

[6] This intermixing of religion and politics is seen in just about every civilization and every religion.

constructed, there was no unbroken line of teachers in India, and no lineage or tradition of Ch'an in India. This does not mean that Ch'an is not Buddhism; rather it means that Ch'an is not a school of <u>Indian</u> Buddhism and never was.

The beginnings of early Ch'an are roughly about the same time as the other enduring schools of Chinese Buddhism, in the post-Han (after 220 C.E.) chaos and the later stability of the early Sui (590–618 C.E.) dynasty. By the early 500s in northern China, there were several small loosely structured groups of monks gathered around isolated teachers, with the focus on the cultivation of seated meditation, but there is no evidence to indicate that they thought of themselves as belonging to a unified tradition calling itself Ch'an. Among those early monks one would include an Indian monk named **Bodhidharma** (in Chinese, P'u-t'i ta-mo/Puti-damo; in Japanese Daruma) and some of his Chinese followers.[7]

By the 600s and 700s, some of those earlier groups had grown into larger collections of monks who focused on meditation, an "East Mountain" group, and an "Ox-head" group, but they did not consider themselves as belonging to an unbroken tradition from India. They did not have any single scripture considered basic for all Ch'an followers, with no single authority, and no uniform agreement on basic doctrines and methods of meditation. There was a great deal of variation.

Ch'an Geneologies

Chinese civilization has always been extremely conscious of genealogical lineages. One reason for the importance of this among Chinese Buddhist teachers is that a genealogy provides a means to connect the Indian roots of Buddhism, connect the Buddha himself, with the teachers of the sixth century in China. This was particularly important for those Chinese Buddhists who were unsettled by the geographical and historical distance that separated them from the India of a thousand years in the past, an ancient India which was the cradle of Buddhism.

Another reason for the importance of genealogy is that in China, a teacher gains legitimacy, respect, and authority when the teacher can produce a lineage connecting himself to a famous sage of the past.[8] The popular Chinese stress on filial piety and reverent respect for one's ancestors helped to shape this attitude, but it was also thought that the student of a student of the master had a better understanding of the teachings than someone who merely read books about the master. Confucian schools traced their lineage back to students of Confucius himself. The same was true for many followers of Lao-tzu and religious Taoism which constructed myth-filled histories for themselves.

The Chinese T'ien-t'ai had already created a fictitious genealogy which connected it to the great Indian sage Nagarjuna and through him to the Buddha. In China, lineage and genealogy guaranteed authenticity of a sage and gave the teacher authority. To compete, Ch'an needed a lineage to connect it with the Buddha, but Ch'an had no direct connections to India. This Chinese need to anchor one's teachings in a lineage could not help but affect Ch'an, and the result was that Ch'an teachers constructed their own genealogy which connected them with India and the Buddha.

Ho-tse Shen-hui is the Author of Many Ch'an Legends and Myths

Around 730 C.E. a Ch'an teacher named Ho-tse Shen-hui[9] (Heze Shenhui, 684–758) gave a series of public

---

[7] For information on the legends and their influence on China, see Andy Ferguson, *Tracking Bodhidharma: A Journey to the Heart of Chinese Culture* (Counterpoint: 2012).

[8] In Western culture, a musician can gain respect if she can show she belongs to a lineage connecting her to a famous composer or performer in the past; an architect can gain status if she studied with a famous architect, a therapist can gain status if she or he studied with a student of Freud, a student of C. G. Jung, and so forth.

[9] Ho-tse Shen-hui (684–758) was a student of Hui-neng (638–713), known as the Sixth Patriarch. After his death Ho-tse Shen-hui was declared the Seventh Patriarch of the Ch'an lineage. However, his importance declined in following decades until he was almost entirely forgotten in Ch'an histories.

talks in which he expounded an imaginary genealogical connection between his school of Chinese Ch'an and the Buddha in India. Inspired by earlier fictional biographies constructed by different groups, Ho-tse Shen-hui explained an imaginary connection between Ch'an and the Buddha himself. Based on his inspired story-telling, a later modified version of the lineage story he made up became the official history of Ch'an according to Ch'an, and is often repeated in modern books dealing with Ch'an.

The Legend of the Flower Sermon of the Buddha

At a large public gathering, Ch'an teacher Ho-tse Shen-hui informed his audience that Ch'an teachings had been taught by the Buddha himself, and that there existed an unbroken lineage of fully awakened teachers connecting the Buddha to Chinese Ch'an teachers and to Ho-tse Shen-hui himself. Each of these teachers carried the full and complete enlightenment of the Buddha, and transmitted the tradition of Ch'an Buddhism to the successor generation, completely and fully.[10] Ho-tse Shen-hui explained that the Ch'an tradition teaches the highest truth of Buddhism and the ultimate truth cannot be captured in words or explained.

The Buddha Holds A Flower

The Indian Madhyamaka claim that the highest teaching cannot be written down led to the myth in which the Buddha himself is the origin of Ch'an. This is called the "Flower Sermon." The story is that one afternoon the Buddha came before the assembled audience, but instead of speaking, the Buddha merely held up a flower and remained silent. After a few moments of confused silence from the audience, one of the listeners, Mahakasyapa,[11] broke into a big smile. Buddha returned the smile and said:

> I have the eye of the true teaching, the heart of Nirvana, the true aspect of non-form, and the ineffable stride of Dharma. It is not expressed by words, but especially transmitted beyond teaching. This teaching I have given to Mahakasyapa.[12]

This story claims that with the lifting of the flower, the Buddha had transmitted the essence of Ch'an itself on to Mahakasyapa. The Buddha did *not* give some *thing* to Mahakasyapa; rather the Buddha acknowledged that Mahakasyapa had seen into and awakened to his own true nature, and understood profound meaning contained in act of the lifting up the flower. The Buddha's smile acknowledged that the spiritual insight of Mahakasyapa was equal to that of the Buddha.

Ho-tse Shen-hui then goes on to explain how successive generations of teachers in India conveyed this profound and liberating teaching process which did not rely upon words or letters. The claim is that Ch'an Buddhism teaches the Highest Truth, or the First Principle of Buddhism, and as every Chinese person knew, the highest sacred truth could never be expressed in language.[13]

---

[10] Ho-tse Shen-hui was *not* the first Ch'an teacher to make this claim; a monk named Fa-ju/Faru (638–689) also made this claim.

[11] Mahakasyapa is celebrated as one of the ten great *arhats* featured in the earliest Buddhist sutras, and the Buddha would often call upon him to preach to the assembly. It is believed that Mahakasyapa was in charge of the Buddhist community after the Buddha died. Mahakasyapa is supposed to have convened the first Buddhist Council wherein the students recited their memories of the teaching, laying down the foundations of the Buddhist sutras. The Ch'an tradition puts Mahakasyapa as the single official successor to the Buddha, and then the *arhat* Ananda as the successor to Mahakasyapa.

[12] This is a later version translated by Nyogen Senzaki in Paul Reps, *Zen Flesh, Zen Bones* (Rutland, Vt.: Charles Tuttle, 1957), p. 95. This story does not appear in any Indian Buddhist work; it appears for the first time in eighth century China.

[13] Recall the opening verse of the first chapter of the *Tao Te Ching*: "The Tao that can be spoken of is not the Tao itself; the name that can be named is not the name itself." Also remember Nagarjuna's Madhyamaka analysis of language, where he argued that not even Buddhist language can adequately capture reality. We should also note that this implies that all those Chinese Buddhist schools which relied on texts

Bodhidharma, the 28th Patriarch

Ho-tse Shen-hui needed something that could connect himself and his teacher, Hui-neng, to that mythical string of awakened teachers who had this special Indian wordless teaching. Some previous Ch'an and T'ien-t'ai Buddhist groups had already created limited genealogies of their teaching lines, and Ho-tse Shen-hui seems to have drawn some of his inspiration from these.

Ho-tse Shen-hui asserted that the Indian monk Bodhidharma was the single official teacher in India with the highest teaching, and Bodhidharma brought the unbroken Ch'an lineage and inexpressible teachings from India to China along the dangerous Silk Road. According to legend, he arrived in China around the year 525 C.E.

During this era, many Buddhist priests taught that making substantial monetary donations to the Buddhist monasteries would bring good karma or "merit" to the donors. The emperor and wealthy patrons understood Buddhism as a magical process and tool for protecting the state and generating good karma as a supernatural reward for supporting Buddhist activities such as:

(1)   performance of rituals focused on Buddha images;
(2)   construction of imposing temples and creation of beautiful statues;
(3)   translation of Sanskrit sacred texts into Chinese.[14]

In both India and China it was believed that a spiritual being like a sage has

Bodhidharma

were inferior to Ch'an.

[14] During this time Chinese Buddhism still relied upon Indian texts (which placed a stress on the written word, and on philosophy), and copying translated sutras by hand (no printing presses would exist in China until the eighth century, and printing presses did not appear in the West until the 1455 Gutenberg bible in the fifteenth century).

a virtuous spiritual energy (which the Chinese called *te/de*[15]), the virtuous power to transform and improve everyone in the vicinity of the sage, and so too Bodhidharma (a Buddhist sage) must have *te/de* which was good for the country. Hearing that a Buddhist sage had come to China, the story is that Emperor Wu (who reigned 502–549) invited Bodhidharma to the court for an audience. Bodhidharma was escorted before the emperor.

> Emperor Wu of the Liang: "Since I came to the throne, I have built countless temples, copied countless *sutras*, and given supplies to countless monks. Is there any merit in this?"
> Bodhidharma: "There is no merit at all."
>
> Wu: "Why is there no merit?"
> Bodhidharma: "All these are only the little deeds of men and gods, a leaking source of rewards, which follow them as the shadow follows the body. Although the shadow may appear to exist, it is not real."
>
> Wu: "What then is true merit?"
> Bodhidharma: "True merit consists in the subtle comprehension of pure wisdom, whose substance is silent and empty. But this kind of merit cannot be pursued according to the ways of the world."
> Wu: "What is the first principle[16] of the sacred Holy doctrine?"
> Bodhidharma: "Vast emptiness with nothing sacred in it!"
> Wu: "Who is it who stands before me?"
> Bodhidharma: "No knowing."[17]

To ask "Who is it who stands before me?" is asking: "Who are you?" A superficial response would be your name, or your job title. But the deeper way to understand the question is to ask "Who are you, truly, deeply?" or "What is your true self?" "What is your deepest nature?"

For Buddhists, what we call the "self" is nothing more than interdependent flowing processes of rapidly changing sense impressions, moods, thoughts, constantly changing yet inter-connected physical processes, and the like. There is no static and unchanging self in the midst of these ever-new succeeding patterns of experience. There is no enduring *atman* (no eternal soul), no immutable continuing ego, no separate *me* which **has** experiences; rather there are just the experiences themselves as each achieves some kind of unity, and then perishes to be replaced by a successor.[18] Thus Bodhidharma's reply "Don't know" or "No knowing" could be understood to be saying "No concepts or ordinary knowledge can answer the question 'Who are you?'" As entertaining as this story is, the more authentic early historical biography of Bodhidharma does not mention an interview with the emperor or tell of any of these events, nor are there any court records of such a meeting.

Ch'an master Ho-tse Shen-hui's imaginative eighth century fiction provided an explanation of how Indian Ch'an was transported onto Chinese soil in the sixth century. Later, Bodhidharma is referred to as the Twenty-eighth

---

[15] Pronounced like a short "duh." This was discussed in previous chapters on Confucianism and philosophical Taoism.

[16] The term "first principle" or "Highest Principle" is the "Highest Truth" of Buddhism, i.e., the content of awakening, the deepest insight, the true nature of Reality.

[17] A shorter version of the story originally appeared in Ho-tse Shen-hui's text *P'u-t'i-ta-mo Nan-tsung ting shih-fei lun*. It is embellished and retold in many later Ch'an sources; it appears as the first case of the Ch'an collection of *koans*, the *Blue Cliff Records* (in Japanese it is the *Heikiganshu* of which there are numerous translations). The version quoted here is a variation of the expanded story told in John Wu, *The Golden Age of Zen* (New York: Doubleday Image, 1996), pp. 34–35.

[18] This is explained in Francis Cook, *Sounds of Valley Streams* (New York: State University of New York Press, 1989), p. 54. Western views of mind and consciousness offer a similar view. For example, see Marvin Minsky, *The Society of Mind* (New York: Simon and Schuster, 1986) and Susan Blackmore, *Consciousness: An Introduction* (New York: Oxford University Press, 2004).

CHAPTER 21: CH'AN BUDDHISM

Ch'an Patriarch in India, and simultaneously the single founding teacher, the First Ch'an Patriarch[19] in China. One of Bodhidharma's students, Hui-k'o, would then become known as the Second Patriarch, the second in the line of founding teachers in China.[20]

Bodhidharma is credited as the author of four stanzas which summarize Ch'an:

> A special tradition outside the Buddhist scriptures.
> No dependence upon words or letters.
> Direct pointing at the essence of a human being.
> Seeing into the deepest part of your nature, attaining Buddhahood.[21]

Calling Ch'an "a special tradition outside the Buddhist scriptures" which does not rely on words or letters, refers to the myth that Ch'an did exist in India even though there is no written mention of Ch'an in any Indian scripture. This is claiming that the Mahayana Buddhist sutras were expositions of Buddhist concepts in written words, but something written down could never be the ultimate truth. The conclusion that we are invited to draw is that Ch'an Buddhism is closer to true Buddhism because it does **not** rely upon sacred scriptures the way the other Chinese schools did.

The third and fourth verses of Bodhidharma's poem are the heart of later Ch'an identity. The third is: "Direct pointing at the essence of a human being." The Ch'an tradition asserts that the great Ch'an teachers of the T'ang (618–906 C.E.) and Sung (960–1279) dynasties did not think it was important that they wear the robes of a monk or nun, were not particularly interested in whether one shaved one's head, were not concerned about abstract Buddhist ideas, and not much interested in texts, rituals, devotional worship or any of the traditional trappings of religion.

This lesson that we are to take from this is that Ch'an considers the essence of Buddhism to be awakening, and the way to achieve that is for the teacher to point directly at the student's Buddha-nature and for the student to become directly aware of his or her own true nature. "Seeing into the deepest part of one's own nature" is to penetrate into the very heart, or essence of the self, and find its true nature. To encounter this is to know Buddha-nature directly. In the language of Ch'an Buddhism, to perceive your self-nature *is* the key to the attainment of buddhahood. "Our original nature is Buddha, and apart from this nature there is no other Buddha."[22]

Separating Legends from Historical Fact

What are the facts about early Ch'an? Modern critical historians agree that there was a monk named Bodhidharma who came to China perhaps as early as 480 C.E., that he did have a student named Hui-k'o/Huike, but in the early biographies of these two monks there is no mention of Ch'an or any Ch'an practices, no mention of an interview with an emperor, no mention of details about Hui-k'o, and nothing resembling the bizarre encounters described in the later tenth and eleventh century Ch'an records and legends.

Despite the entertaining detailed stories in the Ch'an history texts from the eleventh century, there appears

---

[19] The Chinese character means "founding teacher," or "important founding ancestor," but many translators prefer "patriarch" (a term borrowed from Western religions) used in the sense of a high dignitary of the priesthood and a founder of a tradition. The sense of the term can also be captured by "Grand Master."

[20] Steven Heine presents a careful historical analysis of the historical development of different stories about Bodhidharma and Hui-k'o/Huike in his *Zen Skin, Zen Marrow*, pp. 22–25.

[21] This is the author's translation. Historians know that these four stanzas did not appear until hundreds of years after Bodhidharma had died, but they are an excellent summary of the later Ch'an understanding if not Bodhidharma's.

[22] John Wu, *The Golden Age of Zen*, p. 63.

to be no genuine teacher-to-student lineage connecting sixth century Bodhidharma and his student Hui-k'o (in the 500s in China) to the later Ch'an teachers of Ho-tse Shen-hui's time, which is the eighth century (700s). The scholars agree that the historical record reveals that Bodhidharma did not bring a pre-existing Indian tradition of Ch'an into China.[23]

Ho-tse Shen-hui's Version of Ch'an History After Bodhidharma

Ho-tse Shen-hui continued to construct his genealogy story. He went on to claim that after Bodhidharma, there were four consecutive Ch'an founding teachers, or patriarchs in a Chinese lineage. Each inherited the highest and wordless Ch'an teaching. The teachers Ho-tse Shen-hui called the fourth and fifth patriarchs are associated with a group of Buddhists called the East Mountain group. Then Ho-tse Shen-hui adds a sixth name to his list. He names the famous East Mountain teacher Hung-jen/Hongren (602–675) as the fifth patriarch, and Hong-jen's student, Hui-neng (638–713) as the sixth. In fact, Hui-neng was the teacher of Ho-tse Shen-hui, and Ho-tse Shen-hui is the monk who was making up these pseudo-historical connections.[24]

The Legend of the Poetry Contest

A few decades after Ho-tse Shen-hui had argued that his teacher, Hui-neng, was the one and only Sixth Patriarch in all of China, a new legend grew up about Hui-neng, a legend which includes a poetry contest. The story begins in the south of China where an illiterate woodcutter named Hui-neng lived. The twenty-three-year-old Hui-neng had cut some bamboo and happened to overhear someone chant a verse from the *Diamond Sutra* (an important *Prajnaparamita* text), "Let your mind function freely without abiding anywhere or in anything," and this initiated a deep insight experience which led him to seek out a Buddhist teacher. Hui-neng traveled to the north of China and arrived at master Hung-jen's huge monastery. He was accepted as a worker in the monastery kitchen.

Shortly thereafter Hung-jen, the monastery abbot, decided to choose a successor using a poetry contest. The monk who wrote the poem most infused with awakening would become Hung-jen's official successor and be placed in charge. The head monk of Hung-jen/Hongren's monastery was a famous scholar who is supposed to have written the following poem:

> The body is the Bodhi tree [tree of awakening],
> The mind is like a bright mirror standing,
> At all times take care to wipe it,[25]
> Allow no grain of dust to cling.

Cutting Bamboo

The illiterate bamboo-cutting Hui-neng counters the scholar's poem with this:

> Fundamentally the Bodhi tree does not exist,
> The bright mirror is nowhere standing.
> From the very beginning, not one thing,

---

[23] "While the historical origins of Ch'an are still a matter of considerable scholarly debate, Ch'an's diachronic portrayal of its own history is now all but totally debunked." Robert E. Buswell, Jr., *The Formation of Ch'an Ideology in China and Korea* p. 7.

[24] Ho-tse Shen-hui did not make this lineage up entirely on his own. An epitaph from 690 for a monk named Fa-ju/Faru provided the first five names, and Ho-tse Shen-hui added his own teacher's name to the list as the sixth founding teacher or sixth patriarch.

[25] The standard explanation for "To wipe the mind" is to practice meditation, and the dust is a poetic metaphor for ego-centered desires, attachments, possessive attitudes, anger, and ignorance. Quiet the mind and allow no thoughts to remain.

In what place could a grain of dust cling?[26]

The key line is the rather startling third, "from the very beginning, not one thing." This is explained as "From the very beginning, not one thing [exists independently]" or "From the very beginning, not one thing [exists with an immutable essence]." This reflects the Madhyamaka emptiness insight (discussed in chapter 10 of *Asian Thought* Volume 1) that all things are in flowing change and empty of an inner essence or unchanging substance (*svabhava-sunyata*). From the very beginning not one thing exists independently or separately from the world around it. Nothing is self-existing; everything is interacting process in a world of flowing processes. All things (*dharmas*) are empty of *svabhava*, empty of an inner self-existing unchanging essence or substance.[27] From the very beginning, not one independent thing.

According to Ho-tse Shen-hui's fictitious story, the head of the monastery, Hung-jen, acknowledged the depth of the young Hui-neng's understanding, and the illiterate Hui-neng became the successor and the official Sixth Patriarch of Ch'an in China.[28]

Historical Accuracy

It is a fact that there was an eighth century Ch'an teacher named Ho-tse Shen-hui who saw his role in life as a crusading spokesman for a more authentic Ch'an teaching, perhaps in an attempt to propel it to the courtly prominence and recognition that he felt it deserved. As a result of Ho-tse Shen-hui's forceful and popular lectures, the importance of his teacher, Hui-neng, continued to grow, until almost every succeeding Ch'an teacher made sure that he had a genealogical connection with Hui-neng, no matter how tenuous.

Even though most of Ho-tse Shen-hui's historical claims discussed above are false, they are important. These myths about Mahakasyapa and the flower sermon, the myths about Bodhidharma and the Sixth Patriarch (Hui-neng), were absorbed into Ch'an and became a part of the way later Ch'an (and later Zen in Japan, in Europe and in America) understood its own religious tradition. The myths are essential. We cannot understand Ch'an Buddhism if we restrict ourselves to historical facts alone.

One problem which was to plague Ch'an was Ho-tse Shen-hui's claim that a Ch'an patriarch, teacher, or "master" belonged to an unbroken string of fully-awakened masters, which elevates ordinary meditation teachers to the status of fully-awakened perfected buddhas. The problem is that throughout history a "Ch'an master" or "Zen master" in China or Japan was a respected teacher, but the great majority of these were not thought to be fully-awakened perfect buddhas.[29]

---

[26] The author's translation from Nakagawa Michi, *Rokuso dankyo* (*Zen no goroku* vol 4: Tokyo: Chikuma shobo, 1976), p. 27, p. 36. There is a substantial amount of historical scholarship devoted to the authenticity of these poems.

[27] Things are not non-existent, but no thing possesses an immutable inner substance. Things are real and exist, but they are flowing processes. Nothing you see or touch or taste or smell is a container for an inner self-existing essence. Things are empty of *svabhava*. Dharmas themselves are simply changing processes, not unchanging ultimate eternal constituents of reality.

[28] This poetry contest could not have occurred, since historical records indicate that the scholar Shen-hsiu left the monastery of Hung-jen before the young Hui-neng arrived.

[29] The myth of the fully-awakened Ch'an teacher (or *roshi*) was taken seriously by many in the West, although in China, Korea and Japan it was clear to the community that their Buddhist teachers were not even remotely perfect. A Ch'an teacher, or *roshi*, was mostly understood as how an ideal teacher *should* be, but it was understood that a *roshi* often had many flaws. Ch'an teachers were treated with respect, but not more than that. Thus, "respected teacher" would be a reasonable translation of the Japanese *roshi*. If a student accepted the myth that a Ch'an master, a *roshi*, was an enlightened buddha, then the student would believe that his or her teacher could never make a mistake, could never do anything wrong. In *The Guru Papers–Masks of Authoritarian Power* (Frog Books, 1993), the authors Kramer and Alstad write: "the concept of enlightenment, precisely because it is so exalted, almost inevitably lends itself to abuse and corruption. It can be used to justify any behavior, privileges, or excesses, creating an insidious double standard for the superior ones" [footnote 79, p. 378]. Teachers demonstrating un-

CHAPTER 21: CH'AN BUDDHISM

In following centuries, the lineage of Hui-neng (and his student, Ho-tse Shen-hui), came to be called the Southern School of Ch'an, and many followers of the Southern school have been depicted as discarding the excessively scholastic approaches typical of the aristocratic forms of Buddhism (the T'ien-t'ai and the Hua-yen). Despite the romantic perception of Ch'an, Ch'an teachers never did give up the reading of Buddhist sutras. The Mahayana bodhisattva path was also the goal in Ch'an, and in more recent times, Ch'an monks recite the four vows of the bodhisattva daily:

> Sentient beings are numberless; I vow to liberate them all.
> Ego-centered desires are inexhaustible; I vow to put an end to them.
> The teachings of the Buddha (dharma) are boundless; I vow to master them.
> The Buddha's Way is unsurpassable; I vow to attain it.

21.5 HUI-NENG: SUDDEN ENLIGHTENMENT

In the *Platform Sutra*, a text attributed to the Sixth Patriarch, Hui-neng, there is stress on abrupt awakening or **sudden enlightenment**, and by that term it seems to be saying that a profound insight experience (*wu*) does not have to be preceded by lengthy stages of moral and cognitive self-purification. It is a breakthrough moment of understanding, prompted by an abrupt glimpse into one's own buddha-nature. Sudden enlightenment might be understood to be the abrupt and direct insight into the nature of mind, an insight that is not only intellectual but also transformative, a sudden understanding that we are not containers for an inner essence (that we are empty of *atman* or soul) and that all conceptualization is dependent and relative to the changing world around us, or "empty."

A Ch'an student may read many books, listen to many lectures, and sit in meditation for many hours, but not yet have the insight to understand reality or Buddhism — not until he or she has an abrupt insight experience, a sudden awakening. This means that genuine Ch'an study doesn't really **begin** until after the student experiences one or more powerful breakthrough insight experiences which are then followed by an extended process of deepening understanding usually guided by a teacher. This practice of deepening is believed to lessen the negatives in the student's personality and gives the student clearer insight into the way things really are. The authors of the *Platform Sutra* understand Buddhism as being about abrupt awakening, not about conventional piety, not about chanting or praying, and not about having faith in a set of correct propositions.

About two-hundred years after Hui-neng, five styles of Ch'an practice (called the Five Houses) evolved which tinkered with their history so that each lineage could trace its teachings in genealogical fashion to Hui-neng, who is now acknowledged as the one and only true Sixth Patriarch. Over the centuries one of the five incorporated Hua-yen philosophy into its Ch'an teachings. Ultimately, two of the five branches came to prominence: the Lin-chi/Linji line and the Ts'ao-tung/Caodung line.[30]

---

enlightened behavior is not unique to the East; it has been found in many Western religious leaders who have taken advantage of members of their groups. Ignoring the many problematic Western religious teachers, we know there are *gurus* from India, Tibet, China, Korea, and Japan, who have come to this country, and who took advantage of students. Some spiritual teachers were known to have problems with alcohol, some seduced students, some lived lavishly, and did other things which certainly appeared incompatible with the behavior expected by a perfectly awakened sage, a "master." One book on this subject is Michael Downing, *shoes outside the door: desire, devotion, and excess at san francisco zen center* (Washington D.C.: Counterpoint Books, 2001). In addition to Zen groups in Germany and France, a partial list of North American Zen centers that have had trouble, includes the San Francisco Zen Center, Moonspring Hermitage in Surry, Maine, the Los Angeles Zen Center, the Kwan Um School of Zen in Providence R.I., the Toronto Zen Centre, Shasta Abbey in northern California, and the Kanzeon Zen Center in Salt Lake City. Also, in a study of eight cases of student betrayal by Zen teachers in the United States, five involved inappropriate sexual behavior by the teacher. These problems are not unique to Zen or to Asian religions. We are all aware of similar events in Christian churches. Any time that a student idolizes an authoritarian teacher, there is opportunity for abuse and corruption.

[30] Almost any book purporting to provide the history of Ch'an has an explanation of the five styles of Ch'an/Zen lineages. One excellent study and translation is Chang Chung-yuan, *Original Teachings of Ch'an Buddhism* (New York: Vintage Books, 1971). Another book is Thomas

236

CHAPTER 21: CH'AN BUDDHISM

Although challenging dialogues between students and teachers were not typical of the earlier period of Ch'an history, it appears that by the late tenth or early eleventh century intriguing dialogues between brilliant teachers, or between teachers and their students who were provoked to deepened insight, were recreated, recorded, collected and edited in later eras. These dialogues provide the foundation for how Ch'an understood itself for the next thousand years.

21.6 IDEALIZED CH'AN AS PHILOSOPHY

The romantic depiction of Ch'an treats it as a school which rejects the value of studying Buddhist scriptures, stressing immediate and direct experience instead. Scholar Steven Heine writes:

Traditional Ch'an thought was generally expressed in the "sparse words" of minimalist yet evocative verse, often accompanied by eccentric gestures or body language as well as other forms of creative expression. Ch'an masters sought to attain liberation from bondage to inhibiting psychological and social structures in pursuit of spiritual freedom, regardless of ideology.[31]

One could also say that the majority of Ch'an teachers understood Buddhist philosophy as metaphor, not literally. For example, traditional Indian Mahayana Buddhist schools portrayed the Buddha as a heavenly being who chooses to come to earth to teach humans how to lessen suffering. As explained in Volume I of *Asian Thought*, Mahayana Buddhist texts would talk about the three bodies of the Buddha:

(1)   The *dharmakaya*, the first of the three bodies of the Buddha. It is the ultimate body of truth, body of dharma (Buddhist teachings), body of reality, the unconditioned, the absolute, that which is perfectly pure (symbolized by Vairocana Buddha).

(2)   The second of the three bodies of the Buddha is the *sambhogakaya*, the "bliss body" or "reward body," the body visible only to bodhisattvas in which the Buddha experiences the bliss of nirvana (symbolized by Amitabha Buddha).

(3)   The third body is the *nirmanakaya* or the physical body that the Buddha assumed in order to teach, that is, the physical body of Siddhartha (who is also called Shakyamuni Buddha).

Are there really three bodies to the Buddha? One of the greatest of all the Ch'an teachers in T'ang China was named Lin-chi/Linji (born perhaps 810, d. 866 C.E.). Lin-chi tells his students to ignore the supernatural god-like attributes ascribed to buddhas and bodhisattvas. Instead, we should see these statements as symbolic of human behavior, and especially to mind, consciousness, and mental behavior. For example, Lin-chi explains these three bodies of the buddha eliminating anything supernatural, using the metaphor "your own house" for your body and mind:

The pure light in a single thought of yours—this is the dharmakaya buddha within your own house. The nondiscriminating light in a single thought of yours—this is the sambhogakaya buddha within your own house. The nondifferentiating light in a single thought of yours—this is the nirmakaya

---

Cleary, *The Five Houses of Zen* (Shambhala, 1997). For details on the major Ch'an and Zen teachers, see also Nelson Foster and Jack Shoemaker, eds., *The Roaring Stream: A New Zen Reader* (Hopewell, N.J.: The Ecco Press, 1996) or Andy Ferguson, *Zen's Chinese Heritage* (Boston: Wisdom Publications, 2000) which is filled with detailed translations. The most detailed historical treatment is Heinrich Dumoulin, *Zen Buddhism: A History*, Vol. 1, India and China (New York: Macmillan Publishing Company, 1988). As one might expect, the actual details of each of these lineages is more complex than indicated here.

[31] Steven Heine, *Bargainin' For Salvation* (New York: Continuum, 2009), p. 15. The author substituted "Ch'an" where Heine has "Zen."

buddha within your own house. This threefold body is you, listening to my discourse right now before my very eyes.[32]

Did the various buddhas and bodhisattvas exist in the past in the way that Buddhist stories and texts describe? Is the Buddha some sort of ultimate reality which transcends space and time? Do not take these scriptural tales literally, because if you do, you miss the point of them. Lin-chi explains:

> Followers of the Way, if you say that the Buddha is the ultimate, how is it that after eighty years of life the Buddha lay down on his side between the twin sala trees at Kushinagara and died? Where is the Buddha now? We clearly know that his birth and death were not different from ours.[33]

Are buddhas and bodhisattvas godly, supernatural? Buddhas and bodhisattvas are simply our own potentials, our own possibilities. Lin-chi explains:

> There's a bunch of students who seek [the bodhisattva of wisdom] Manjusri on Mount Wutai.[34]
> Wrong from the start! There's no Manjusri on Wutai. Do you want to know Manjusri? Your activity right now, never changing, nowhere faltering—this is the living Manjusri.[35]

"Do Not Explain Too Clearly"

When asked to explain the truths of Buddhism, many Ch'an teachers are portrayed as utilizing *upaya*, the skillful teaching devices of Mahayana Buddhism. The teachers are portrayed as refusing to offer complex philosophical explanations, feeling that such an explanation produces concepts that the students will memorize and hold onto, instead of doing their own thinking for themselves. Life itself is the problem. But it is not an unsolvable problem.

So what does the Ch'an teacher do? The teacher points the student in a useful direction, but the teacher does not provide followers with answers to be recited or memorized. The ideal Ch'an master is skillful in *upaya*, the skillful use of words and body to teach insights of Mahayana Buddhism. The teacher is both a role model and a guide, pointing out the important questions and forcing the student to discover the answers for himself or herself. This is not something for the student to memorize. With the aid of meditation and puzzling questions, the student will practice until there is an abrupt moment of insight. Each student must find the truth for herself, or himself.

> A monk asked, "I have just come to this monastery. I beg you to show me the way to Truth."
> The Master said, "I would rather be crushed to dust. I dare not blind any monk's eye."[36]

Any descriptive answer will provide the monk with a concept to hold to and to use to interpret experience; this is to blind the monk's eye which can see things most clearly when concepts are neither held onto nor pushed away. The monk has everything he needs; he has the buddha-nature. Anything the teacher might say could provide words or concepts for the student to attach himself to, and thereby go farther away from bare realization. The Ch'an teacher

---

[32] Ruth Fuller Sasaki and Thomas Yuho Kirchner, *The Record of Linji* (Honolulu: University of Hawaii Press, 2009), p. 160.

[33] *Ibid.*, p. 223.

[34] Mt. Wutai, a collection of five peaks, located in Shanxi, was regarded as the most sacred of the four sacred Buddhist mountains in China. It was also regarded as the dwelling place of the bodhisattva of wisdom, Manjusri. Chinese Buddhists tended to accept the stories of buddhas and bodhisattvas quite literally, and even the imperial court focused lavish support of the Buddhist temples in the Wu-tai mountain, regarding Manjusri (Wen-shu) as a superior divinity. Esoteric Buddhism performed extravagant rituals in homage to Manjusri. The Ch'an attitude towards divinities tends to be quite different from the popular understanding. Lin-chi is directing his student's attention to the here-and-now, and telling him not to be concerned with rituals and magic. Manjusri is a metaphor, not a god. Manjusri is you.

[35] Sasaki and Kirchner, *ibid.*, p. 202.

[36] Chang Chung-yuan, *The Original Teachings of Ch'an Buddhism*, p. 279.

does not explain this meaning, however. The student must figure it out for himself.

These sorts of collected irrational dialogues are often the result of the student asking a question of the teacher. Sometimes the teacher's reply is clear and obvious, but in other cases the teacher's response seems designed to provide the student nothing to grasp, nothing to conceptualize, no idea to which one could hold onto and believe mistakenly that one conceptually understands ultimate truth.

As portrayed in the eleventh century Ch'an histories, when asked these ultimate questions, the great Ch'an teachers of the eighth and ninth century T'ang era might tell the student to have a cup of tea, to go and wash his dishes, might give a shout, might quote a saying of a master of the previous generations, might improvise a poem or quote a poem, might hit the monk with a stick, or slam a door in the monk's face. The response seems intended to frustrate the student's attempt to reason it out. Sometimes the monk's question is a direct challenge to the teacher, in which case the dialogue becomes a dazzling display of challenge followed by a succession of insights.

Here is an example of an exchange between the student Ku-shan Shen-yen/Gushan Shenyen (863–929) and the Ch'an master Hsueh-feng I-ts'un/Xuefeng Yicun (822–908):

> Ku-shan came to Master Hsueh-feng. The moment Ku-shan entered the monastery gate, master Hsueh-feng grabbed him and said, "What is it?"
> Ku-shan experienced deep insight (*wu, satori*).[37] He lifted up his hands, and waved them.
> Hsueh-feng said, "What principle did you come to understand?"
> Ku-shan said, "How many principles are there?"
> Master Hsueh-feng acknowledged the insight.[38]

On another occasion, master Hsueh-feng was asked what he had learned from his teacher, Te-shan/Deshan (782–865). Hsueh-feng replied: "I went to see him empty-handed and empty-handed I returned."[39]

Not all teachers offer these sorts of responses. Many Ch'an masters provide complex explanations of what Ch'an is all about and what the awakened monk achieves.[40] However, it is the puzzling answers stressed in eleventh century revised histories which are most revered by traditional and contemporary Ch'an followers. Most of the "romantic" scholars of Ch'an agree that the early generations of Ch'an adepts were not trying to get the student to profess faith in a buddha, or to commit themselves to the truth of propositions about Buddhism. The teacher can only point at the truth, and the student must find it for herself or himself. Many understand the Ch'an purpose as helping the student discover the fullness of life in each moment of experience for herself. Ch'an is about doing whatever you are doing fully and completely.

"The First Principle is Inexpressible."

Ch'an dialogues often refer to the "Highest Truth" or the "First Principle" (literally "Number One Principle"). The Highest Truth of Buddhism is the content of awakening and seeing things as they truly are without bias, prejudice

---

[37] See "Central Concepts of Ch'an" in this chapter for an explanation of *wu* or *satori*.

[38] Author's translation from the sayings of Hsu-t'ang Chih-yu (1185–1269), *Hsu-t'ang chih-yu yu-lu*, Taisho 47, page 1025c10–12.

[39] John Wu, *ibid.*, p. 118.

[40] The earliest Bodhidharma text, the teachings of the Ox-head school of Ch'an, the *Platform Sutra of the Sixth Patriarch* and most of the collected writings of Ho-tse Shen-hui are decidedly philosophical and not so paradoxical.

or confusion. The Madhyamaka ideas of the second century Indian philosopher Nagarjuna come into play here. Using logic and philosophical analysis, Nagarjuna argued that the ultimate nature of reality cannot be captured by language, by theories or any intellectual conceptualization. The problem then becomes, how can we express the inexpressible?

A monk asked the Ch'an master, Fayen Wen-i (885-958), "What is the First Principle?"

Fayen answered, "Anything I could tell you would become the second principle."[41]

According to Ch'an and Nagarjuna, no holy scriptures or sutras can really describe the Ultimate, Highest, Number One Truth. The experiential truth is not to be found in concepts, labels, words or letters, not even the words of the Buddha himself.

A monk asked Yun-men (d. 949): "What is the fundamental idea of Buddhism?"

Yun-men: "When spring comes, the grass turns green of itself."[42]

"Spiritual Cultivation Cannot be Cultivated"[43]

The idea of cultivation evokes an image of a garden. One takes a patch of dirt, plants the seeds and then tends the garden, one cultivates the plants and helps them to grow up properly. Spiritual cultivation carries the image of trying to cultivate one's religious nature, to cause awakening to grow where there was no awakening before, where there was only dirt. The problem is that in the Chinese Taoist world view, the sage is **not** someone who developed something new that the sage did not have before. What makes a sage is a completely spontaneous (tzu-jan, "of itself just so") person in total accord with the flow of Tao. Spontaneity cannot be practiced or cultivated. It is action without hesitation. It happens only when you stop trying to cultivate it. To be spontaneous is to lose awareness of one's self and simply be fully present and absorbed in each moment.

To cultivate spirituality is to try to achieve awakening by doing something special in order to attain a special "something" external to ourselves, but Ch'an suggests that true spiritual freedom is not acquired by physical practices whose purpose is to achieve something we lack. Genuine attainment is an abrupt spiritual break-through, a spiritual insight into one's own true nature. There is not something outside ourselves called awakening (or wu) which we were lacking. The great T'ang dynasty Ch'an master Lin-chi says,

In my view, there is no buddha, no sentient beings, no past, no present. That which is attained was already attained — it's not something that requires time. There's nothing to practice or cultivate, nothing to realize, nothing grasped, nothing missing or lost.[44]

Why Practice Ch'an If There is Nothing to Practice?

When Lin-chi/Linji tells us that we are not missing or lacking anything, he does not mean that you have no need of Buddhist practices. Rather, he is telling students that the answers you seek are found within yourself and not outside of yourself. Lin-chi addressed the assembled monks and said, "Those who study the Way these days need to

---

[41] *Transmission of the Lamp*, chüan 24, Taisho 47.589c. The entire section of this brilliant Ch'an master is in Chang Chung-yuan, *Original Teachings of Ch'an Buddhism, op. cit.,* p. 246.

[42] From the *Transmission of the Lamp* translated by Chang Chung-yuan, *op. cit.* p. 292.

[43] Borrowed from Fung Yu-lan, *A History of Chinese Philosophy* , tr. Derk Bodde (Princeton NJ: Princeton University Press, 1953), p. 390.

[44] Author's translation from Akizuki Ryumin, *Rinzai roku* (*Zen no goroku* vol. 10: Tokyo: Chikuma shobo, 1972), p. 61. The student might compare the translation in Burton Watson, *op. cit.,* p. 33, or the translation in Jeffrey L. Broughton, *The Record of Linji* (Oxford University Press, 2013), pp. 44-45.

have confidence in themselves and not go searching for something outside."[45]

To continue seeking for something outside yourself which you think needs to be acquired is to miss the point of the whole Ch'an enterprise. There is nothing to be gained, nothing to understand intellectually — no new knowledge to add to your store of things known (concepts). Instead, there is insight which needs to be deepened. Lin-chi/Linji said to the assembled monks:

> Just get so you can follow along with circumstances and use up your old karma. When the time comes to do so, put on your clothes. If you want to walk, walk. If you want to sit, sit. But never for a moment set your mind on seeking Buddhahood.[46]

Yun-men told the assembled monks:

> When a patch-robed monk sees this staff, he just calls it a staff; when he walks, he just walks; and when he sits, he just sits. In all of this he cannot be stirred.[47]

Lin-chi instructed the monks:

> Don't try to do something special, just act ordinary. You look outside yourselves, going off on side roads hunting for something, trying to get your hands on something. That's a mistake. You keep trying to look for the Buddha, but Buddha is just a name, a word.[48]

The following story is told about the great teacher Ma-tsu/Mazu when he was still a student:

> When Ma-tsu (709–788) dwelt on Mount Heng, he sat in meditation day after day. Master Huai-jang (677–744) came to see him, and asked him what it was that he sought through meditation. Ma-tsu replied that he wished to achieve Buddhahood; whereupon Huai-jang took a piece of brick and began grinding it against a stone. When Ma-tsu asked why he ground the brick thus, Huai-jang answered that he was planning to make it into a mirror. Ma-tsu, surprised, demanded, 'How can you ever make a brick into a mirror by polishing it?' Huai-jang in turn asked, "How can you ever achieve Buddhahood through meditation?"[49]

We can polish a dirty mirror and make it into a clean mirror, and that applies to awakening also. We all possess the buddha-nature, we are innately enlightened, and all the words in the world and all the meditation practice will not give us what we already have.[50] Your mind-mirror is obstructed by anger, ignorance, ego, and possessiveness; polish the

---

[45] Author's translation from sect. 17, Akizuki Ryumin, *Rinzai roku*, p. 74, p. 75.

[46] *Ibid.,* p. 26.

[47] Urs App, *Master Yunmen* (New York: Kodansha International, 1994), paragraph 167, page 169. In Alan Watts' felicitous translation, in *The Way of Zen* (New York: Pantheon, 1957), p. 139, this is: When walking, just walk; When sitting, just sit. Above all, don't wobble.

[48] Watson, *op. cit.* p. 29.

[49] Chuang Chung-yuan, *Original Teachings of Ch'an Buddhism*, p. 131. A longer version is case 139 in Thomas Yuho Kirchner, *Entangling Vines: A Classic Collection of Zen Koans* (Boston: Wisdom Publications, 2013).

[50] This suggests a parallel with the 1939 Hollywood film, *The Wizard of Oz*, where the lion, the tin man, and the scarecrow each discover that they have been searching externally for what they already have had from the beginning.

mirror and find out what you have always been — you have the mind of a buddha, you have the buddha-nature.

Without trying to be a Buddha, you are a Buddha

For Chinese Ch'an, awakening or enlightenment is **not** a blinding new transforming insight which transcends this world of ours. It is not a divine magical experience. Certainly there can be a powerful emotional experience which accompanies the insight. However, what is realized or attained is not some new knowledge or new information which you did not have before; it is not something added to the store of information you possess. What you acquire is a new perspective. With awakening one discovers what one has always had, one discovers one's own pure awareness, one's intrinsic nature, what the Ch'an teachers (and some Mahayana Buddhists) refer to as one's Buddha-nature, or Buddha-mind.

Ch'an philosophy argues that each of us are born with the potential to be a buddha, to be awakened. Consequently, Ch'an training is pointing at your own true nature, trying to get you to see what you have always had. Once you have penetrated to the core or essence ("seen into your own true nature"), you experience things a bit differently most of the time, instead of some of the time. You have transformed yourself, you see things from a new perspective, and there is nothing fantastic or secret about it. Really, there is not anything secret. Just dig past your anger, your ego, your confusion, and be your true self. Zen teacher Suzuki Shunryu said, " . . . try not to achieve anything special. You already have everything in your own pure quality. If you understand this ultimate fact, there is no fear."[51]

Several times we have quoted from Lin-chi/Linji (810?–866 C.E.), recognized as one of the greatest of all the Ch'an teachers in T'ang China. Here's a version of the story of Lin-chi's initial breakthrough experience.

> Lin-chi was a student at Huang-po's temple for three years, and never conversed with Ch'an master Huang-po. At head monk Mu-chou's prompting, Lin-chi finally ventured into the room of the master and asked him about the Highest Truth of Buddhism, and received a blow from the master.
> On Mu-chou's friendly advice, Lin-chi returned to the master a second and a third time, only to have the experience repeated.
> Lin-chi did not understand, and thinking that his failure was due to his own evil karma, he decided to leave the master and monastery.
> Bidding the master [Lin-chi] farewell, Huang-po asked Lin-chi to visit his former disciple, Ta-yu who lived across the valley.
> Lin-chi journeyed to Ta-yu, and Ta-yu said that Huang-po had treated him with considerable kindness, and scolded Lin-chi for his obtuseness.
> With that, Lin-chi was enlightened, and he said, "The Teaching of Huang-po was nothing special."
> Ta-yu said, "You impudent pipsqueak. A minute ago you were asking what your mistakes were, and now you make light of the dharma of Huang-po!"
> Lin-chi then pummeled him three times in the ribs. Ta-yu told him to go back to Huang-po, who was his real teacher.
> When he told Huang-po what happened, Huang-po said, "If Ta-yu were to come to this monastery, I'd give him twenty blows with my stick!"
> Lin-chi replied, "No need to wait for that; here you are!" and slapped the old master in the face.
> Huang-po said, "You madman," and then the two of them went to Huang-po's room and shared

---

[51] Suzuki Shunryu, *Zen Mind Beginner's Mind*, p. 61, p. 132. "Without trying to be Buddha, you are Buddha. This is how we attain enlightenment."

a cup of tea.[52]

Once you have penetrated through the veil of paradoxes and confusion created by your intellectual attempt to enclose the world into some kind of conceptual grid, everything becomes clearer and more simple. Your awareness was always there, but buried under ideas and concepts. You did not gain something in the process of insight; rather, you simplified, you let go. The teaching of Ch'an was "nothing special." Once you have penetrated to the core or essence, you change as a result, and there is nothing fantastic or secret about it. You are not lacking anything. You are not missing something called "awakening," and there is not some important fact you need to memorize. The teachings describing the great Ch'an teacher Lin-chi's lineage makes this very clear:

> . . .no need to arouse the mind to stop evil thoughts, nor arouse the mind to cultivate the Way. . . Nowhere is there either dharma-principle we ought to embrace, nor any Buddha that we ought to strive to obtain. . . . Because outside of our mind itself, there is absolutely not the least little thing of value to be obtained.[53]

"If you meet the Buddha on the road, kill him!"

Ch'an master Lin-chi had a quite shocking dictum which is often quoted by many in the West: "If you meet the Buddha on the road, kill the Buddha!" But the actual words of Lin-chi are more than this. The full quotation is:

> Followers of the Way, if you want to get the kind of understanding that accords with the Dharma, never be misled by others. Whether you're facing inward or facing outward, whatever you meet up with, just kill it! If you meet a buddha, kill the buddha. If you meet a patriarch, kill the patriarch. If you meet an arhat, kill the arhat. . . . Then for the first time you will gain emancipation, will not be entangled with things, will pass freely anywhere you wish to go."[54]

This rather famous quotation from Lin-chi's teaching can be misunderstood. If you see a buddha *outside your own self*, then you are not seeing things as they really are. If you think there is a buddha "over there" and that buddha-person is somehow profoundly and magically different from you, then you are not seeing things as they truly are. You have mistakenly limited yourself and separated yourself from the world. According to Ch'an and the Buddha-nature tradition, your own unsullied awareness, your own pure nature is your own awakening. You are innately awakened. You contain the wisdom of Buddha and you contain the solution to all of your own problems.

In the pursuit of awakening one must let go of the mistaken idea that there is a holy buddha on the road, and there is an ordinary person on the road, and the two are different. See reality as flowing inter-connected processes, without an absolute distinction between self and world. This is how one kills the mistaken separation of yourself from the buddha on the road.

As we have already pointed out, according to Ch'an, when you finally see into your own true nature, you

---

[52] This story was paraphrased from Heinrich Dumoulin, *A History of Zen Buddhism*, 1st edition, p. 119. John Daido Loori tells virtually the identical story in *Two Arrows Meeting in Mid-Air* (Rutland, VT: Charles Tuttle, 1994), pp. 108–112. These differ in many details from the version found in the original Chinese "Record of Lin-chi" (*Lin-chi yu-lu*). For example, see Burton Watson, *The Zen Teachings of Master Lin-chi* (Boston: Shambhala, 1993), pp. 104–106.

[53] Ruth Fuller Sasaki, Yoshitaka Iriya, Dana Fraser, *The Recorded Sayings of Layman P'ang: A Ninth-Century Zen Classic* (New York: Weatherhill, 1971), p. 17, a translation from the Chinese text by Tsung-mi, which is found in Kamata Shigeo, *Zengen shosenshu tojo*, in *Zen no goroku*, vol. 9 (Tokyo: Chikuma shobo, 1971), p. 307.

[54] Burton Watson, *The Zen Teachings of Master Lin-chi*, p. 52.

realize that once you get past misplaced conceptualization, get past social and family conditioning, there is nothing lacking, nothing to be gained, nothing to be achieved. Master Lin-chi says: "Cease from running; look, there is nothing lacking."[55] However, most of us do not know that, or if we've been told, we do not believe it. If the Ch'an teachers are correct, we have the answer within.[56]

If that is so, where should we look? Not outside ourselves. But, what happens? We go to the teacher or to someone claiming to be a spiritual teacher, a "master," or a buddha, we bow down, and we ask them to give us what we seek. This is a mistake. Huang-po, the teacher of Lin-chi, wrote "If you conceive of something called 'a Buddha,' you will be obstructed by a Buddha."[57] So, kill that conception and the obstruction is gone.

The life of the Sage is not different from that of the ordinary person

The attainment of Ch'an insight (*wu/satori*) is not a once-and-for-all transforming insight that catapults an ordinary person to the ultimate of full awakening or enlightenment. Despite the rhetoric of "sudden awakening" as the ultimate beginning of the Buddhist pathway, for beginners there are stages. The beginner's stage is easily understood. It is the way we normally see things, some good, some bad, some beautiful, some ugly. According to the contemporary Chinese Ch'an teacher Sheng Yen,

Chan transcends the ordinary and then returns to the ordinary.... First, one must practice to attain a unified, concentrated state of mind, then cast off this mind and return to the ordinary world. At this stage one is truly liberated and free to roam in the world. To use an analogy, the ordinary mind sees mountains and rivers as mountains and rivers. Next one reaches a state where mountains are no longer mountains and rivers are no longer rivers. This is the mind of non-discrimination. Finally, even this state is transcended and we again see mountains and rivers as part of the ordinary world. This is no-mind but it has embraced the real world.[58]

Once you have achieved the goal of insight, then what do you do? Now that you are an awakened sage, or an enlightened master, do you live differently? Are you now better than the rest of us ordinary humans? Are we ordinary people not pure enough to associate with you? Should the awakened sage walk on purified carpeting so that she or he will not be dirtied by this dusty world?

The Chinese Ch'an teacher Sheng Yen answers the question. The awakened person is not one who has left humanity behind. The awakened person has not entered a transcendental stage called 'Sagehood' or 'Buddha-hood.' Awakened sages are not super-human, they are not semi-divine. In fact, they do the same things they've always done. According to the Ch'an tradition, it is not *what* the person does, but *how* she does it — fully, completely, with less of a self-centered ego which separates us from the world. It is what you do when you are absorbed in the activity.

Monk: "How can I become free from the daily tasks of eating and dressing?"
Mu-chou replies: "Put on your clothes and eat your meal."

---

[55] Suzuki Shunryu, *Zen Mind Beginner's Mind*, p. 34.

[56] Psychotherapist Sheldon B. Kopp is the author of *If You Meet the Buddha On the Road, Kill Him!* (New York: Bantam Books, 1972). The book is described as "While seeking to be taught the Truth the disciple learns only that there is nothing that anyone else can teach him . . . the secret is that there is no secret," and "The most important things that each man must learn no one else can teach him. Once he accepts this disappointment, he will be able to stop depending on the therapist, the guru who turns out to be just another struggling human being."

[57] Author's translation from Huang-po, *Wan Ling Yu-lu – Ch'uan-hsin Fa-yao* (Essentials of Mind Transmission), in Iriya Yoshitaka, *Denshin Hoyo – Enryoroku* (*Zen no goroku* Vol. 8, Tokyo: Chikuma shobo, 1969), p. 102, p. 104. Taisho vol. 48, 384c.

[58] Sheng Yen, "Chan, Meditation, and Mysticism," *Chan Magazine*, Autumn 2010, Volume 30, No. 4, p. 8.

Even if you don't understand, just dress and eat each day anyway.[59]

According to the Ch'an tradition, awakened persons have simplified, have found the mind of shining awareness and attained clarity and insight and a different perspective. Their minds are supposed to be more pliable, less judgmental and less rigid, they are wiser, they are more compassionate, they are less self-centered, they do not harm themselves or others by thought, word, or deed. Such a person who has attained 'nothing' comes back to the city and lives like an ordinary person, but lives life as a sage, lives fully every second.[60]

21.7 CENTRAL CONCEPTS

Awakening According to Ch'an

The goal of Indian Buddhism was nirvana, the cessation of frustration and misery, the cessation of *duhkha*, and when one realized that *duhkha* had stopped, this is *bodhi*, awakening or enlightenment. The Buddha's awakening has nothing to do with a realm which transcends our world. It is the mental state wherein one's *duhkha* has stopped.
Chinese Ch'an has its own understanding and its own terminology. Despite the fact that the fictional Ch'an lineage charts imply that each Chinese master had achieved the identical awakening *bodhi* experience of all the Indian predecessors, the Chinese Ch'an tradition often describe the insight experience by the Chinese character *wu* (a term which the Japanese render into the noun *satori*). The Chinese term *wu*, or *satori*, it is not a once-and-for-all complete and total awakening.[61]

The Ch'an *wu* experience is often translated into English as "enlightenment," but *wu* is not something supernatural, it is not some kind of transcendent elevation of consciousness.[62] *Wu* or *satori* is often identified with the euphoria which comes from a breakthrough insight into the nature of the self or the nature of the world. It is common in Ch'an literature for monks to have several *wu* experiences, each deeper than the previous. They are often described as "seeing one's own true nature," or obtaining a glimpse of one's buddha-nature. The contemporary Chinese Ch'an teacher Sheng Yen explains:

> Buddhism emphasizes the need to practice in order to realize one's own buddha-nature. This does not mean that someone who perceives buddha-nature is no longer subject to vexation. After experiencing buddha-nature for the first time, one still has habits and propensities that can lead to impure thoughts and impure conduct; greed and aversion may still arise. However, one is at least able to see clearly that

---

[59] Chang Chung-yuan, *Original Teachings of Ch'an Buddhism*, p. 92.

[60] The problem with this claim of romantic Ch'an is that there are people who have been acknowledged as a "master" but they have done harm to people and abused their position of authority.

[61] Indian Buddhism refers to the Buddha's experience as complete unexcelled awakening (*samyaksambodhi*). This is not the meaning of *wu* or *satori*.

[62] This felicitous expression came from Hans-Georg Moeller, *The Moral Fool: A Case for Amorality* (New York: Columbia University Press, 2009), p. 57.

one's mind still cannot completely control the arising of vexations.[63]

Insight is not the same as Euphoria

Wu or *satori* seems to be transforming euphoric insight experiences of varying intensity and depth, not a once-and-for-all momentary experience. It is important to realize that *insight* is not identical with *euphoria*; one can have the awakening insight experience without the positive emotional release of tension that comes from understanding clearly. Euphoria is **not** the goal; insight is the goal. Ch'an teachers stress lifelong practice.[64] The Ch'an teacher, Sheng Yen, asserts:

> Most of the great Masters in China developed their enlightenment slowly, that is, their realizations gradually got deeper and deeper. They did not become great Masters overnight. My practice has been like this also. The most startling experience I ever had was when I was twenty-eight years old, but after that time as I went on practicing its not that I had a lot of great colorful experiences, but rather I did feel a gradual deepening process. ... If you just read some general books on Ch'an and you see a story of a person getting enlightened here, and another suddenly getting enlightened there, you'll be completely misled, because you just read the account of their enlightenment without seeing what they had to go through beforehand.[65]

Ch'an Buddhists Are Not Trying To Escape the World

The Chinese Ch'an masters do not seem to have had any interest in escaping from the world, and did not think that the awakened sage transcended or rejected the world of cause and effect. Ch'an Buddhist teachers thought that awakening lessened self-centered perspectives, and resulted in a clearer understanding of the interconnected nature of reality, which is flowing change, and impermanence, and awakening allowed you to live fully in the Tao (which is reality). Enlightenment or awakening does NOT free one from the everyday realm of impermanence; the awakened sage is constantly changing yet fully at home in the flowing changing world where nothing is permanent.

In Ch'an, things such as impermanent phenomena, even death, are not transcended, not evaded, and not denied — rather they are deeply affirmed and accepted, and as a result, cause less stress and pain. Worldly conditions do not vanish for the awakened; the individual does not escape involvement with worldly conditions. Rather, one simply lets go. Freedom is freedom in the midst of causal conditions. This echoes the understanding of the philosophical Taoist text *Chuang-tzu*, discussed in chapter 17 of this volume.

So, the Ch'an insight experience of *wu* (or in Japanese, *satori*) is not the same thing as complete unexcelled awakening in early Indian Buddhism. Ch'an awakening is a glimpse into one's own true nature, but this *wu* was not considered to be the same depth as what Buddhists believe the Buddha achieved under the Bodhi tree.

We must understand that seeing into one's nature, or experiencing enlightenment, does not necessarily mean one is permanently enlightened. Enlightenment is a momentary flash when a person sees his true nature - the nature of no self. According to the Ch'an historical record, there have been

---

[63] Sheng Yen, in *Chan Magazine*, Vol. 26, No. 4, Autumn 2006, p. 9.

[64] The Ch'an tradition has a series of woodblock prints that lay out this gradual process in an artistic way, called the Ten Ox-Herding Pictures. These have been translated several times. Those Ch'an teachers who have a liberating experience and then assume that they have nothing more to learn, can become an ego-centered danger to themselves and their students.

[65] Shen-Yen, *Ch'an Magazine*, vol. 2, no. 4, Spring 1981, page 29.

a few monks who, in one enlightenment experience, became thoroughly enlightened. . . . More often, one enlightenment is not enough.[66]

Do not be trapped by labels and concepts which are merely conventional

When facing difficult questions about life, quite often we humans contemplate how we should respond to a situation, we reason carefully, weigh the options, and then we make a choice and act. Although this process is necessary if one is building a house or constructing a dam, our daily life is not so complicated. Like the Taoists before them, the Ch'an teachers felt that in our everyday lives of farming, walking, talking, and interacting, we must learn to be less egocentric, more spontaneous, and trust ourselves. We need to eliminate the self-centered attitude we have. It is due to that self-centeredness and lack of trust in our own nature that we are confused and we do not see clearly.[67]

"No-mind" and "No-thought"

There are two terms which are important in the Southern Ch'an texts: *wu-hsin* (no-mind) and *wu-nien* (no-thought). To be in a state of "no-mind" (*wu-hsin*) or "no thought" (*wu-nien*) does not mean that we should make our minds blank. Ch'an teachers reject students who sat in meditation and tried to force their minds to be blank.

Rather, being "free from concepts" or "not trapped by our conceptual categories" seems to capture at least some of the meaning.[68] When people are totally absorbed in what they are doing, there is no sense of separation between action and actor. Think of an athlete, a tennis player, a skier, a surfer, someone doing needlepoint or cooking, each focused on the moment. There are no second thoughts, no hesitation, no confusion, no doubt, and both past and future are fading because one is so focused in the moment. When you are so focused, so identified with what you are doing, the ego fades, conceptual categories fade in importance, and all that is left is creative activity. "No-mind" also implies that if you believe you *have* a mind which is some sort of thing, then search for it — you will never find it. What you think of as mind is just the constant flowing of thoughts and impressions. There are thoughts, but no one behind the thoughts doing the thinking.

If you think that *wu-hsin* or *wu-nien* means to sit quietly in meditation trying to use your thinking mind to push thoughts away, you have made a terrible mistake.

> No-thought [*wu-nien*] means not to be defiled by external objects. It is to free thought from external objects and not to arouse thoughts about dharmas. But do not stop thinking about things, nor eliminate all thoughts.[69]

The Ch'an people use a startlingly powerful analogy to point out the error of trying to stop one's thoughts; they say using thought to push away thoughts is like trying to wash away blood with blood.

---

[66] Sheng-Yen, *The Infinite Mirror* (Dharma Drum Publications, 1990), pp. 19–20.

[67] People who are self-conscious often have problems with public speaking, because they worry about what the audience thinks. Those who are less self-conscious can speak more spontaneously with confidence.

[68] An entire book has been written on the subject. D. T. Suzuki, *The Zen Doctrine of 'No-Mind'* (London: Rider & Co., 1949). The Chinese Ch'an scholar Tsung-mi (780–841 C.E.) interpreted the phrase "no mind" to mean that there were no discriminating thoughts such as desire, anger, hatred or other defilements remaining in the mind. The Chinese Taoist philosopher Chuang-tzu put great stress on *wu-nian*. See chapter 17 of this volume.

[69] This is from section 17 of the *Platform Sutra of the Sixth Patriarch*, in the translation of Yanagida Seizan, found in Sasaki and Kirchner, *The Record of Linji*, p. 222. This same passage is translated by Yampolsky, *op. cit.*, p. 51.

Wu-nien is becoming completely absorbed into what one is doing. The mind does not stop for deliberation; the mind is mirror-like (Chuang-tzu). The mind of no-mind, the *wu-hsin* mind of the Ch'an poet or teacher, is captured in the following poem which serves as a metaphor for the idea of reflection as creativity:

The wild geese fly across the long sky above.
Their image is reflected upon the chilly water below.
The geese do not mean to cast their image on the water;
Nor does the water mean to hold the image of the geese.[70]

An early Ch'an treatise on "no-mind" explains: "Is [mind] inside or outside, or somewhere in between? As long as one looks for mind in one of these three locations, one's search will end in failure. Indeed, searching for it anywhere will end in failure. That's exactly why it is known as no-mind."[71]

The idea of *wu-hsin* is expressed in the following quote from *The Record of Lin-chi*:

"When its time to get dressed, put on your clothes . . . Don't have a single thought in your mind about seeking for Buddhahood. . . .
When you want to go, go. When you want to sit, sit. . . .
What do you lack in the way you are functioning right now?
What will you add to where you are?"
"There's nothing equal to wearing clothes and eating food.
Outside of this there are neither Buddhas nor Patriarchs."[72]

An activity is awakened so long as one's awareness is totally absorbed in the action with no sense of separation between the person and the experience; but the next activity becomes unenlightened when one becomes aware of one's self, when ego separates us from experience. If genuine awakening is being totally absorbed with the activity, there must be an ongoing effort to achieve this consciousness in moment after moment of activity and encounter.

21.8 SOME INSIGHTS OF CH'AN

The Stress is on Awakening, not on Creating Good Karma

Many popular Buddhist sects have made their goal success, good karma or good merit, believing that this will ensure fortunate circumstances (i.e., either in this realm, in the next life, or in the Pure Land). Some believe that awakening requires a high degree of asceticism and renunciation; abandoning the householder lifestyle to enter a monastery with few or no creature comforts. Some believe that the Buddha's enlightenment is so extremely rare that very few people can reasonably hope to achieve it within thousands of lives; for these the Buddha's awakening suggests the god-like powers of a superhuman being.

Contrary to all of these, after the ninth and tenth centuries, Ch'an teachers seem to declare the insight of

---

[70] Chang Chung-yuan, *Creativity and Taoism*, p. 57.

[71] From the *Wu-hsin lun*, translation by Urs App, "Treatise on No-Mind," from *Eastern Buddhist*, New Series, Vol. 28, p. 88.

[72] *Rinzai roku* (*Zen no goroku* 10), *op. cit.*, pp. 39ff.

awakening (*wu*) as possible for any one, because we all have the Buddha-nature (the *tathagatagarbha*), although the person must make a serious effort in order to get past his or her own confusion and misconceptions. In classical and traditional Ch'an the emphasis is upon individual awakening, not philosophical understanding. Ch'an has as its goal the deepening experience of liberating insight (*wu*) and it has worked out several techniques to facilitate this realization, techniques which had no corollary in Indian Buddhism. In Ch'an, strenuous and single-minded practice might lead to a burst of insight and comprehension which will transform the way one perceives the world — it results in an awareness where the strong separation between the individual person and the world fades, and wherein concepts are seen merely as conventional, but never ultimate. "The answers to all questions any of us have and will have lie within each one of us."[73] Everyone already has the nature of a Buddha. Everyone already has everything she needs. The only thing to do is to lessen or eliminate false notions and mistaken attitudes. Then the inborn wisdom and compassion appear and function freely. That is the goal of Ch'an.

There is Nothing to Teach

The Buddha-nature sutras (texts) stresses the fact that each of us has "Buddha-nature," or "Buddha-mind," the nature of a buddha and the capacity for awakening up to that potential. We need only to realize what we have always had. All sentient beings are complete and lack nothing — so what is there to teach? and how to teach it? A Ch'an text offers this explanation:

> When the wild birds sing their melodies from the tops of the trees,
> They carry the thoughts of the Patriarch.
> When the mountain flowers are blooming,
> The genuine meaning comes along with their fragrance.[74]

The experience of awakening is waking up to your original nature, what you have always had, or always been. It is awareness, it is being fully present at every moment. You always have this awareness. No one can give this to you; the experience of awakening can only be realized by oneself, personally, and cannot be taught to one or given to one by another person or a savior. A teacher can point but you need to find it for yourself.

Ignorance and Confusion are the Primary Cause of Duhkha

In Indian Buddhism, the obstacles to awakening are three: failures of morality, lack of mental discipline (self-discipline), and conceptual mistakes or lack of wisdom or insight. In Chinese Ch'an Buddhism, the tendency is to find the primary cause of *duhkha* in the third, our ignorance, our failure to see things clearly. Instead of recognizing our own buddha-nature, our consciousness has been focused outwardly, and we misunderstand the world we perceive. We think that the world is made of solid substantial things independent of us, and fail to recognize our world is the interdependent realm of evolving processes. We think of our selves as separate and independent from the world. We have a tendency to over-intellectualize, we analyze, ignorantly we attempt to apply fixed labels to flowing reality, we categorize and conceptualize the flowing reality. This is what stands in the way of realizing our awakened nature. We get trapped by concepts, by words, by names and labels. Ch'an is a reaction against becoming stuck at the intellectual or word level.

---

[73] John Daido Loori, *Two Arrows Meeting in Mid Air*, p. xviii

[74] Chang Chung-yuan, *Creativity and Taoism*, p. 113.

CHAPTER 21: CH'AN BUDDHISM

The universe is vast flowing process, empty of unchanging essence, with no single thing intrinsically holy or intrinsically sacred in it. If the Buddha had written a book, it would be a **description** of the first principle, a description of the highest truth, and not the truth itself (it would be the restaurant menu but not the food). All the works composed by priests of great insight since the Buddha are merely descriptions of the truth. They are a finger pointing at the full moon overhead, but they are not the moon of truth itself (they are the map, but they are not the territory). Ch'an stresses personal experience and insight, not memorizing or having faith in someone else's words.

Do not Describe Your Understanding — Demonstrate It!

If you have that breakthrough insight, that liberating *wu* experience, the Ch'an tradition requires the student to demonstrate insight-understanding. The new understanding is not allowed to be merely theoretical; it must be expressed in action. According to romantic Ch'an, we awaken to our own buddha nature, and in that glimpse we lessen or lose our ego-centeredness, at least temporarily. We have a glimpse of our own true nature. In that state, we are not really separated from nature; we are one with nature. If we have experienced awakening and have developed that insight, we interact with the world realizing that all things are aspects of the same flowing processes. This is not a doctrine to believe in, it is not an article of faith — we must come to know that for ourselves, as clearly as we know that the water we drink is cold.

> When Shui-liao asked him the meaning of Bodhidharma coming to China, the Master [Ma-tsu] kicked him in the chest, knocking him to the ground. This startling response suddenly awakened Shui-liao to the Truth. He rose from the ground laughing and clapping his hands, and shouted, "It is strange indeed! It is strange indeed! Numerous *samadhi* [deep meditative experience] and all subtle truths are revealed in the tip of a single hair—it is thus that I have suddenly realized the Source! He made a deep bow and departed.[75]

There Is No Sacred or Absolute Reality Beyond or Distinct from the World of Change

In early Buddhism the liberating insight of the Buddha was to see the interdependent interconnected nature of reality, *pratityasamutpada* (translated as dependent co-arising). This led to the insight of the three characteristics: (1) impermanence, (2) no *atman*, and (3) *duhkha* (frustration, misery, dissatisfaction, suffering). Ch'an Buddhism also utilizes these insights. These three characteristics apply to tables and chairs, mountains and stars, shoes, ships and sealing wax, but especially it applies to each person.

Each of us arises out of a network of relationships which are continually changing. My character is dependent upon parents, grandparents, childhood, culture, friends, favorite movies, and even the air I breathe and the water I drink. We are conditioned by the books we choose to read, the internet/cable television programs we watch, the games we play, the news sources we read, the political environment, the advertising which engulf us from our earliest years. Our environment is not unchanging and static. My home town changes over the years, the weather changes, the crops change, and everything changes.

The fact that everything changes doesn't mean I have to accept everything and do nothing. Ch'an is not about being passive. Instead, I've got to find my home in this flowing world. I am not going to escape the world. I am an ever-changing interdependent being interacting with a world which is ever-changing and interdependent. I am not independent; ultimately I am not different from the world. The world is not different from me.

This is the insight of *sunyata* (shun-ya-TA, empty of essence) which was the cornerstone of Nagarjuna's Mahayana Buddhism, and Chinese Ch'an Buddhism is inspired by Nagarjuna. In general, the Ch'an teachers tend to be less philosophical when dealing with these Mahayana concepts. Sometimes they just point and invite us to see the interdependent swirling patterns that we think of as a dog or a cat. Dogs do not have an enduring unchanging dog-

---

[75] Chang Chung-yuan, *Original Teachings of Ch'an Buddhism*, p. 134.

essence. Dogs are empty of dog-substance. The dog is one of the myriad ways emptiness appears before me. A Ch'an teacher might say that the world as emptiness eternally and incessantly crystalizes in the form of bird, person, flower, stone, and cloud. What we experience is a focalization or crystallization of emptiness, of interdependent being.[76]

Like the teachings of the *Chuang-tzu* on the unimpeded harmonious unity in all phenomenon, the Ch'an teachers might teach the insight in the form of a humorous dialogue:

> One day a monk came to the monastery. The master asked him whether he had been here before. The answer was "no." The master said: "Have a cup of tea."
> Later, another man who had been there before came to see the master. Again the answer was "Have a cup of tea."
> Thereupon a monk of the monastery asked the master, "How is it that you give the same answer to these two men regardless of differing circumstances? For the one who has been here and the one who has not been here your answer is, 'Have a cup of tea.'"
> The master immediately called the monk's name, saying "Have a cup of tea."[77]

21.9 THE PRACTICE OF CH'AN

For a serious monk who is willing to put his or her energies into Ch'an, the tradition has developed practice-techniques aimed at penetrating past the ego-self and its intellectual constructions. The claim is that our ego separates us from people and the world around us. The ego keeps us from seeing that we are a process in a world of processes. The goal is to transform the ego-centered self into a less ego-centered awareness. According to the romantic forms of Ch'an, the teachers avoid abstractions and refuse to speculate on concepts. The practice of Ch'an will not involve studying sacred scriptures, or memorizing answers or ideas. On the spiritual path you have chosen, you do not need someone else's words; you need to see into your own true nature and find the answers within yourself. The teachers can point, but you need to find your own treasure.

Ch'an Buddhism has inherited the distrust in the ultimate accuracy of language and descriptions, a distrust grounded in the Madhyamaka Buddhism of Nagarjuna, a mistrust expressed in sutras like the *Vimalakirti sutra*, and the playful understanding of language typical of the philosophical Taoist classic, the *Chuang-tzu*. These influences result in some very unusual training methods.

If (as Nagarjuna argued) words and concepts cannot capture or convey the highest truth of awakening, then how can we teach anyone about Ch'an? If we cannot rely on books, sermons, or lectures, then how can a Ch'an teacher teach the student? If the teacher is quiet, the teacher cannot teach. If the teacher speaks, everything said is misleading (at best).

Ch'an Buddhism developed a skillful teaching device (in Sanskrit this Mayhayana skillful teaching device is called an *upaya*) to deal with this conundrum. We'll begin our exploration of Ch'an practice methods with a famous technique of *upaya* never used in India, but born in China and honed to perfection in the Ch'an traditions. It is called a *koan*.

Koan (Kung-an/Gongan) Practice

---

[76] Francis Cook, *Sounds of Valley Streams, op. cit.*, page 25.

[77] Chang Chung-yuan, *Creativity and Taoism*, p. 114.

CHAPTER 21: CH'AN BUDDHISM

Westerners have been fascinated by one of the most important tools of the Ch'an tradition, the *koan*[78] (pronounced ko-an), which literally means a "public case" in the same way a settled point of public law is a legal precedent which can be used to decide current legal cases. With a *koan* we can test our own understanding against the insights of the great teachers of the past.[79]

According to the classic Ch'an texts of the past, a student would ask the Ch'an teacher about awakening, or about ultimate reality, and the teacher responded with words or behavior that appears to defy common sense. Ideally, the teacher displays both wisdom and wit in the interchange. The result is dialogues, anecdotes, or brief sayings which are understood to be especially profound, and difficult to penetrate. In this way the Ch'an teacher of the past is expected to serve as an exemplar of awakened behavior, and the student attempts to put herself or himself into the same state of mind as the teacher of the past.[80]

The popular explanation is that a *koan* is an enigmatic question the teacher asks of the student which requires the student to plumb the depths of the most important issues in life, but which is worded so that logic alone will not provide the connection between question and reply. The student cannot look up an answer in a reference book. The student is able to answer the question only when the student has shifted into a new perspective or many new perspectives, an insight into the self, the world, or the interconnection of self and world and their mutual relativity. Ch'an scholar Steven Heine offers this brief explanation of the traditional *koan* practice:

> … koans are rhetorical devices that use paradox, wordplay, and ambiguity to communicate a message about the maddening quality and inherent limitations of language. The absurdities, contradictions, negations, and double negations, as well as the gestures, demands, and demonstrative behavior that characterize this discourse, point to a direct, unimpeded realization of the true nature of reality liberated from all illusion, pretension, and attachment.[81]

Theoretically, to successfully respond to a *koan* the students must wrestle with the question until a great sense of doubt permeates the mind. In that doubt the students let go of at least some of the socially conditioned and rigid views of themselves and their world. *Koans* seem designed to take us deep into the fabric of the thing we call the "self," the "mind," the thing that is *me*, to reveal the ground which underlies the ego, that which is often called one's buddha-nature.[82] *Koans* are a device to get us to realize our true nature, to realize it by direct experience. Ch'an seems to have little interest in making a list of claims we are asked to believe on faith. "Koans are about manifesting that and actualizing that [nature] in everything we do"[83] A koan requires the student to become familiar with the fragmented perspectives we have of ourselves and the world.

Here is a *koan* (number 47 from the *koan* collection called the *Gateless Gate*) which deals with some of the most

---

[78] In Chinese this is a *kung-an/gongan*, but the Japanese pronunciation *koan* (ko-an) has been used in the West since the 1930s, and appears in English dictionaries. For this reason, even though we are discussing Chinese Ch'an, we will use the Japanese term.

[79] Paraphrasing American Zen teacher Jerry Shishin Wick, *The Book of Equanimity: Illuminating Classic Zen Koans* (Boston: Wisdom Publications, 2005), p. 1.

[80] See Steven Heine and Dale Wright, eds., *The Koan: Texts and Contexts in Zen Buddhism* (London: Oxford University Press, 2000).

[81] Steven Heine, *Opening A Mountain: Koans of the Zen Masters* (New York and London: Oxford University Press, 2002), p. 6. We should note that Dr. Heine considers this description only a partial view of koans which misses other aspects, including supernaturalism, ritualism, and mythological and magical features. These are explained in his book.

[82] In the paragraphs that follow the author's explanation of *koans* will utilize writings of several contemporary native English-speaking American Zen teachers who have gone through the hundreds of *koans* in their practice, and whose answers have been accepted by their teachers. These authors are providing an emic explanation of the *koan*. There are numerous etic studies of the *koan*, including Steven Heine and Dale S. Wright, eds., *The Koan: Texts and Contexts in Zen Buddhism*.

[83] John Daido Loori, *Two Arrows Meeting in Mid Air: The Zen Koan* (Rutland, Vt.: Charles E. Tuttle, 1994), p. xxiv

important of life's questions: how can one gain insight into one's true nature? How should I behave when I am about to die ("when the light of your eyes fails")? Where does one go after death (the elements of your body scatter and then what)?

> The priest Tou-shuai [d. 1091] set up three barriers in order to examine his students:
> "You make your way through the darkness of abandoned grasses in a single-minded search for your self-nature. Now, honored one, where is your nature?"
> "When you have realized your self-nature, you are free of birth and death. When the light of your eyes fails, how are you free?"
> "When you are free of birth and death, you know where to go. When your four elements scatter, where do you go?"[84]

If you have ever personally struggled with the ultimate questions of the meaning of life, and your own life and death, you may have experienced the mass of doubt that the Ch'an tradition believes to be essential to resolving a *koan*.

When master Fa-ch'ang was dying, a squirrel screeched on the roof. "It's just this," he said, "and nothing else."[85]

Resolving a koan

Although we can talk about "solving" or "answering" a *koan*, those who have passed through *koan* study suggest that it might be more correct to say that the student penetrates into the *koan*. The student offers a response which elucidates an issue raised in the *koan*. As such, often the answers do not make sense to someone who has not explored the issue deeply. The reply will be puzzling. For the person with insight into the *koan*, the connection between the question and the student's response is clear.

The student answers the *koan* by being forced to adopt different perspectives, perspectives which give the student some insight into the nature of the self, the nature of the world, and the interaction between self and the world. *Koans* are designed to frustrate our standard, usual way of thinking about the world and our interaction with the world, because our usual way of thinking is constrained, is socially conditioned and socially manipulated.

A *koan* is **not** a paradox, it is **not** something like "when a tree falls in the forest, and no one hears it, does it make a sound or not?" The reason the "tree in the forest" problem is not a *koan* is because it is so easily solved with a bit of logic.[86] On the other hand, *koans* are not easily solved with a bit of logic or even a careful logical analysis. Here is a modern example: "A girl is crossing the street; is she the younger or the older sister?"[87] How does logic help one answer this question without additional information? Another question: "The student whispers into the ear of the

---

[84] Robert Aitkin, *The Gateless Barrier* (Berkeley: North Point Press, 1991), p. 278.

[85] Alan Watts, *The Way of Zen* (New York: Pantheon, 1957), p. 201

[86] In this famous paradox, the term "sound" is used in two different meanings, i.e., ambiguously. "Sound" can mean either (a) molecules in the air are moved and create sound waves, or "sound" could mean (b) vibrating molecules in the form of sound waves strike a human ear. Logically, you tell me which of the two distinct meanings of "sound" you are using when you ask "Does it make a sound or not?" and I can tell you if the falling tree makes a sound. If by "sound" you mean (a), then the answer is "yes, the falling tree causes molecules to move and so makes a sound." If by "sound" you mean (b) then the answer is "no sound waves strike the human ear drum, so there is no sound."

[87] Quoted in Alan Watts, *The Way of Zen* (New York: Pantheon Books, 1957), p. 167. The student is being asked to demonstrate insight into the distinction between "younger" and "older" — is it an absolute distinction?

teacher; what did he whisper?" There is an even shorter one: the teacher asks the student, "What is this?"[88]

"A single hand does not make a clap"

There is a Chinese proverb on the necessity of teamwork: "A single hand does not make a clap." One of the most famous of the *koans* is based on this. We all know the sound of two hands clapping. The *koan* asks, "What is the sound of one hand clapping?" Logically the answer is that there is no sound, but if you answer "no sound," your teacher will not accept your answer. If you use one hand so that your fingertips pat your palm, the movement will not be accepted as an answer.[89]

The purpose of a *koan* is to force the student to cut through the layers of personal and social conditioning since earliest childhood. This is not to jettison the past (which is impossible), but rather see through it with clarity. As a child one might have been told that he was not smart, that she was not pretty, that she or he would never succeed, and the like, and these judgments continue to weigh us down, keeping us from seeing ourselves clearly. We have been conditioned to accept certain presuppositions of our parents, our family, our culture, our religion, our political realm, and these unchallenged assumptions distort our perceptions and keep us from seeing things clearly. Unchallenged assumptions are like biases and prejudices. In the same way a prejudiced person does not think she or he is prejudiced, so too we have assumptions about our self and the world which we do not recognize.

Each time a student sees the point of the *koan* and realizes another perspective, and then responds to it successfully, another layer of conditioning is revealed. You must stop holding onto things, thinking that they will solve your problems; you learn to let go. The *koan* process is gradually peeling back one layer after another.[90]

In traditional Ch'an, the *koan* questions are usually taken from Ch'an dialogues or anecdotes of the past, and when the teacher assigns a *koan* to her student, the teacher is asking the student to demonstrate that he or she understands the point of the question or dialogue. One's understanding is not merely intellectual; the teacher can ask the student to demonstrate understanding. New *koans* continue to appear, sometimes current, sometimes right out of today's news. For example, a Japanese Zen teacher living in Los Angeles might ask: "When you are driving on the freeway, where is your mind?"[91]

---

[88] In a classic Ch'an text, *The Platform Sutra*, Hui-neng asks "What is this?" and the question generates an insight experience in the follower. Stephen Batchelor recounts his attempt to resolve the "What is this?" question, "What is it that lies before the spoken word?" "Irrespective of how suitably enigmatic they seemed, my answers were either trite or predictable. After a while, I simply gave up trying to find an answer. 'What is this?' is an impossible question: it is designed to short-circuit the brain's answer-giving habit and leave you in a state of serene puzzlement." Stephen Batchelor, *Confession of a Buddhist Atheist* (New York: Spiegel & Grau, 2010), p. 64. Strictly speaking, "What is this?" is called a *hua-tou* (a short sentence or phrase) and not a *gong-an/koan*. It is a question that when meditated upon generates a sense of wonderment, a great mass of doubt, which can sometimes lead to insight. Examples of *hua-tou* include "Who is chanting this sutra?" "Who is taking this meal?" "Who is sleeping?" The intellectual answer is "mind," but the teacher wants the student to demonstrate this.

[89] The inspiration for this may lie with case eighteen in the Chinese text *Blue Cliff Records*, where the teacher Hsueh-tou comments, "A single hand does not make random sound." However, this "What is the sound of the one hand?" *koan* originated in Japan with the teacher Hakuin (1686–1769), and was not used in China. This *koan* on the sound of the one hand does not appear in any classic *koan* collection. The teachers in the lineage of the Japanese teacher Hakuin passed this on orally: "Listen to the sound of the Single Hand!" Miura and Sasaki, *Zen Dust, op. cit.*, p. 44.

[90] John Daido Loori, *Two Arrows Meeting in Mid-Air, op. cit.*, p. xxiv

[91] Joshu Sasaki (1907–2014), a Rinzai Zen teacher from Japan who settled in southern California.

CHAPTER 21: CH'AN BUDDHISM

There are many Ch'an *koan* collections, several of which have been translated into English more than once.[92] Here's an example of *koan* 24 from the *Gateless Gate* which invites to student to consider the question of how to explain the direct experience of reality, the ultimate truth, without falling into the trap of concepts (speech) or remaining silent, where no explanation is possible.

"Without speaking, without silence, how can you express the truth?"
Feng-hsueh/Fengxue (896-973) observed, "I always remember spring time in southern China. The birds sing among innumerable kinds of fragrant flowers."[93]

Often, the answer to a *koan* is not in words. It can also be a shout, a nod, a smile, the blinking of an eye, pushing one's foot down on the floor, pointing, hitting your chest with your hand, slamming a door, bowing, or even holding up a flower. Consider this acceptable answer to an informal *koan*:

When Yueh-shan roamed the mountain with Yun-yen, the sword worn by Yueh-shan made a rattling sound. Yun-yen asked him, "Where does this sound come from?" Yueh-shan immediately drew the sword and lifted it as if he were going to split something.[94]

Yueh-shan revealed his Ch'an understanding through physical action, not concepts. A Chinese Ch'an teacher would except the same physical demonstration from you, when you experience insight, when you understand.

The Two Functions of a Koan

Koans function in two different yet related ways:

(1) to initiate some insight, realization or attainment by the student;
(2) to allow the teacher to determine the depth of the student's realization.

(1) Resolving a *koan* can initiate insight.

Trying to answer the question posed by the *koan* can be very frustrating, but ultimately it can initiate or spark a student's spiritual realization. In penetrating or resolving a *koan* the student is forced to see a situation from a different perspective, freeing herself from some of the prior conditioning and assumptions, thereby providing a glimpse of the way things really are and a breakthrough into a deeper understanding. Many of the classic *koan* stories end with the monk obtaining *wu*, *satori*, or insight as a result of the *koan*.

(2) The teacher can use a *koan* to test the depth of the student's understanding.

In theory, if one genuinely awakens to one's own true nature, then one can answer each and every *koan*. "If

---

[92] The two most important and famous are the *Gateless Gate* (*Wu-men kuan* or *Mumonkan*), and the *Blue Cliff Records* (*Pi-yen lu* or *Heikigan roku*), but there are numerous other texts in use, including *The Iron Flute*, *The Book of Equanimity* (also translated as the *Book of Serenity*), *Entangling Vines* and others.

[93] Paul Reps, *Zen Flesh Zen Bones* (Rutland, Vt: Charles Tuttle, 1957), case 24, p. 109. The author has replaced the Japanese rendering of the name with the original Chinese spellings.

[94] Chang Chung-yuan, *Original Teachings of Ch'an Buddhism*, p. 50.

you break through one koan, hundreds and thousands of koan have all been penetrated at once."[95]
     A Ch'an teacher can test the depth of the student's understanding by asking further follow-up *koans* which a student with deep understanding should be able to answer. When the teacher finally comes to a follow-up *koan* that the student cannot answer, the limits of the student's understanding have been reached, and the *koan* process begins again when the teacher assigns a new *koan*.

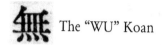 The "WU" Koan

     A *koan* often given to a student as their very first is a reproduction of a dialogue involving one of the great T'ang Ch'an masters, Chao-chou/Zhaozhou (778–897).
     When asked "Does a dog have a Buddha nature?" Chao-chou replied "*Wu.*"[96]

     Although the term "*wu*" normally means "non-" or "non-being," or "free from," here it is understood to be an expression of the awakened mind of Chao-chou. The student works on displaying an understanding of the mind of Chao-chou when he uttered "*wu*" and expressing this insight to his or her teacher.[97] The Ch'an teacher Ta-hui (1089–1163) explains this:

> This one character [*wu*] is the rod by which many false images and ideas are destroyed in their very foundations. To it you should add no judgments about being or non-being, no arguments, no bodily gestures like raising your eyebrows or blinking your eyes. Words have no place here. Neither should you throw this character away into the nothingness of emptiness, or seek it in the comings and goings of the mind, or try to trace its origins in the scriptures. You must only earnestly and continually stir it [this koan] around the clock, sitting or lying, walking or standing, you must give yourself over to it constantly. "Does a dog have the Buddha-nature?" The answer "Wu." Without withdrawing from everyday life, keep trying, keep looking at this koan![98]

     The student wrestles with this *koan*, becoming more and more frustrated and filled with doubts, until finally she or he achieves clarity, and provides an answer which the Ch'an master accepts as insightful. Having approved of the student's answer, there are a cluster of subsidiary questions which follow your successful response to the initial question, to check how many perspectives you have understood. The teacher may ask, "Bring forth the proof of this *wu.*""When you don't say *wu*, what do you say?""The essence of *wu*, what's it like?""The working of *wu*, what's it

---

[95] Shibayama Zenkei, *Zen Comments on the Mumonkan* (New York: Harper & Row, 1974), p. 23.

[96] This *wu* (in Japanese, *mu*) is the negation, the "non-" or "free from" or "without" as in *wu-wei* (non-action) or *wu-nien*, to be free from concepts. It is also "non-being" or "non-existence" as contrasted with "being" or "existence." However, the Ch'an teachers will tell you that you are not to get caught up in the **meaning** of *wu*. According to Buddhist philosophy, all living beings possess the Buddha-nature, but Chao-chou replied *wu*. At this point, the teacher asks "What do **you** say?" In some sense, the interdependent essence-less nature of reality has appeared before you in the form of a dog; how do you express your insight?

[97] Books have been written on this *koan* by students who have mastered the *koan* process. See James Ford and Melissa Blacker, eds., *The Book of MU: Essential Writings on Zen's Most Important Koan* (Boston: Wisdom Publications, 2011). There is also Steven Heine, *Like Cats and Dogs: Contesting the Mu Koan in Zen Buddhism* (New York: Oxford University Press, 2013).

[98] Heinrich Dumoulin, *Zen Buddhism: A History, Vol. 1: India and China* (New York: Macmillan Publishing, 1988), p. 258.

like?""Show me the form of *wu*."[99]

Each of these subsequent questions can probe the depth of the student's understanding, but also can help the student to clarify that original insight, to help the student to cling less and less to her attainment. To answer a *koan*, you must go deep into your own fundamental states of consciousness, through your own layers of conditioning, and arrive at the inexpressible insight which you are compelled to express. The most common explanation for how to probe a *koan* from those who have done so successfully is the following:

> The only way through the koan, no matter what koan, is to be the koan. The only way through a barrier is to be the barrier. If the barrier is fear, the only way to the other side of that barrier of fear is to be that fear. If the barrier is pain, the only way to the other side is to be the pain. When you are the pain, when you are the barrier, the barrier fills the whole universe. The whole relativistic system disappears. When the barrier fills the universe, there's nothing outside it. It includes everything. The world of differentiation disappears. . . . The way to work with any koan, . . . is to be the koan, be the barrier. Don't separate yourself.[100]

The *koan* functions as a special creative device to initiate insight, or to measure the depth of insight. In the Mahayana Buddhist traditions, this sort of technique is referred to as *upaya*, "expedient means" or a special teaching trick. It is clear that the apparent irrationality of the Ch'an *koan* is a sort of *upaya*, a special device to help the student achieve insight.[101]

Zazen or **Dhyana**

As you recall, the Chinese term "Ch'an" is an attempt to capture the sound of the Sanskrit word *dhyana* (dhy-an), a general term which can denote meditative practices, or the one-pointed focused state of mind which results from meditation. The primary Ch'an Buddhist meditative practice is *zazen*, the Japanese two-character phrase that means "to sit" and "meditate," so we might render it as cross-legged meditation, or seated meditation. Although *zazen* (tso-ch'an in Wade-Giles Chinese, zuochan in Pinyin) literally means cross-legged, seated upright meditation, the tradition uses it to mean more than this. Part of *zazen* is allowing the internal chatter or internal conversation going on in the mind to quiet down, allowing the mind to become quieter and more serene, but also to focus, to bring full attention, to bring insight to this very moment.[102]

> In our upright sitting all different kinds of thoughts come up, stay for a while, and disappear. We just let them come up and let them go away, not controlling our mind or preventing thoughts from coming up and passing away, not grasping or chasing after them either.[103]

---

[99] Many different books deal with the first *koan* of the *Gateless Gate*. An extended discussion is found on pages 53-76 of John Daido Loori, *Two Arrows Meeting in Mid-Air*. Several of the follow-up questions are in Kirchner, *Entangling Vines*, pp. 65-67.

[100] John Daido Loori, *Two Arrows Meeting in Mid-Air*, p. 319.

[101] The ability to utilize a skillful teaching device, or *upaya*, is one of the skills of a buddha and bodhisattva. Using *upaya*, buddhas and bodhisattvas can lead people from this shore of *dukkha* to the other shore of nirvana.

[102] Among the excellent books on how to learn *zazen* there is John Buksbazen, *To Forget the Self: An Illustrated Guide to Zen Meditation* (Los Angeles: Zen Center Publications, 1978)

[103] Shohaku Okumura's introductory essay in Tom Wright, Jisho Warner, Shohaku Okumura, translators, *Opening the Hand of Thought: Foundations of Zen Buddhist Practice* (Boston; Wisdom Publications, 2004), p. xviii.

CHAPTER 21: CH'AN BUDDHISM

Some mistakenly believe that the goal of Ch'an meditation is to make the mind blank. This is not correct. Some think of meditation as a "trance." This too is not correct.

Zazen may begin as seated focused concentration to bring one into a full presence of the present moment, but over time it becomes a moment-by-moment, lifelong process of experiencing events fully as they occur. *Zazen* is quiet awareness, paying complete attention, without judging, without comment. It is seeing the causal interconnectedness of the experiences in the present moment.[104]

> . . . we can turn our minds towards those experiences and look at them very very closely without reacting. Just observe them, just allow them to come and go in the field of our awareness. In practice, this is precisely what we do. Whether it is pleasant or not so pleasant, even when pain arises, we just allow it to appear in the field of our awareness.[105]

The Ch'an practice of *zazen* enables you to develop single-pointedness of mind, enabling you to put your mental focus where you want it, and hold it steady. Ideally, *zazen* expands to include all daily activities. At the beginning, *zazen* is just something done for a few hours in the meditation hall or in one's home. Ultimately, however, *zazen* is not just sitting quietly; it expands to include everything we do — it is everything we do in a way that is fully present, completely alert, and aware in that moment.[106] It is full awareness.

> "What is true zazen? When you become you! When you are you, then no matter what you do, that is zazen."[107]

Seated meditation has been a traditional practice in almost all Ch'an monasteries up to the present. Ch'an practitioners are confident that *zazen* is a discipline which facilitates seeing directly into one's flowing self and experiencing full awareness. They say we are lost in a superficial mental arena filled with chatter, ideas, expectations, judgments, prejudices, emotions, and they are in constant flux in our minds. We tend to see things in terms of our own ego, or from the perspectives of our own group, and as a result we do not see what's right in front of our face. Instead we see what we expect to see, or hope to see, or want to see. We do not live in the reality of the ever-changing moment; we are most aware of our concepts of reality. We try to live in a world of concepts, biases, prejudices, and as a result we are ignorant of the way things really are

Ch'an teachers say that seated meditation is something you do to express your Buddha-nature, not something to believe in. In theory, Ch'an meditation is intended to train the practitioner to pay attention, to become aware, to be mindful — and not be deceived by verbal formulas. *Zazen* does not stop when one experiences insight, or *wu/satori*. *Zazen* is a moment-by-moment, lifelong process of experiencing events in the present without the distortions induced by an unexamined cultural conceptual matrix. To the extent that one is able to have *zazen* focused concentration in all experiences, one also continually encounters the experience with an awakened consciousness. In the twelfth century Ch'an teacher Hung-chih/Hongzhi (1091–1157) put great stress on "quiet sitting" (meditating without any mental object to focus upon) as the foundation of Ch'an practice, leading to a "silent illumination," although he was also the

---

[104] One of the best books on this is Hakuyu Taizan Maezumi and Bernard Glassman, *On Zen Practice: Body, Breath, and Mind* (Wisdom Publications, 1999). See also *The Hazy Moon of Enlightenment* (Wisdom, 2007), by the same authors.

[105] Zarko Andricevic, "Acceptance and Appreciation," *Chan Magazine*, Vol. 33, No. 4 (Autumn 2013), p. 18. Mr. Andricevic is one of five dharma-heirs fully authorized to teach in the lineage of the Chinese Ch'an master Sheng yen.

[106] John Daido Loori, *Two Arrows Meeting in Mid-Air*, p. xxvii.

[107] Shunryu Suzuki, *Zen Mind Beginner's Mind*, p. 81.

author of a collection of koans.[108]

Zazen Combined with Koan Practice

The regular practice of seated meditation can ensure that we will not be easily distracted and we can focus our attention and hold it on whatever we are doing. Seated meditation alone, or meditation combined with the great doubt produced by a *koan*, has the potential to trigger *wu* or *satori*, insight into the flowing changing character of one's own nature.

Although not all Ch'an Buddhist schools stress the *koan* technique, the practice of *zazen* and *koan* study are often combined. When your *zazen* practices have developed sufficient concentration, then you are ready to apply it to the resolution of your *koan*.

The Ch'an Teacher

The process by which a respected Ch'an teacher passes on the authority to teach to his or her student is called **transmission**. However, there is much confusion in the West about the transmission process. The Chinese term for a Ch'an teacher is *lao-shih*, and in Japanese it is *roshi*. Most American Ch'an or Zen Buddhist teachers use the Japanese term, *roshi*, to denote the teacher. In English, this is most often rendered "Ch'an master" or "Zen master," but that title is decidedly misleading if we assume that in the Ch'an tradition a *roshi* is a nearly perfect human with some supernatural insight, or that she has achieved anything like the perfect awakening ascribed to the Buddha. Western students have had a tendency to treat Ch'an and Zen teachers as deserving of unquestioning loyalty and obedience because of such imagined perfection.

In Asia, even profoundly unawakened Buddhist priests can be called *roshi*. The title *roshi* is an institutional term which makes no assumptions about the spiritual understanding of a monk. This is similar to the situation within Christian churches. In English, the term "priest" could refer to a leader of a small rural group, but it is equally true that a bishop of the Catholic church (sometimes referred to as a "prince of the church") is also a priest. Similarly, the terms "Reverend" or "Minister" tell us little about the religious accomplishments of the person. The term *roshi* is as much a description of one's status within the Ch'an hierarchy and tradition and as such it can be equivalent to a diploma.[109]

The contemporary Chinese Ch'an teacher Sheng Yen (1930–2009) wrote this about the process of transmission:

Many people feel that transmitting the Dharma is a mysterious, unfathomable phenomenon. But in

---

[108] Hung-chih/Hongzhi collected koans in his *Book of Equanimity* (also known as the *Book of Serenity*). A collection of his poetry is found in Taigen Dan Leighton and Yi Wu, *Cultivating the Empty Field: The Silent Illumination of Zen Master Hongzhi* (Tuttle, 2000).

[109] *Lao-shih* , or the more popular *roshi*, is just "old teacher." There is no precise level of attainment that a monk has to realize to be given the title *roshi*. Most Americans do not realize that in Japan often the title is strictly an institutional position with no level of attainment implied and very little training required. In other cases it can be granted to authorize someone to teach Buddhism to a group, but the most important point is having the group, not having a superior level of realization or attainment. Other times the title is granted for political reasons, for instance the new *roshi* may have good political contacts. There are cases where the title *roshi* was granted via mail. Monks in Asia gave unquestioning obedience to the *roshi* because he was higher up in the temple hierarchy, usually the abbot, not because he was perfect. The title *roshi* is a bit like the title "professor." It can be a courtesy title applied to someone with little understanding and little teaching ability, or apply to a popular well-trained Ph.D., or even apply it to a Nobel Prize winning expert who is a marvelous teacher. Some place a *roshi* on the level of a "stream-entrant" discussed in Volume I of *Asian Thought*, chapter 8. A steam entrant (*srotaapanna*) has eliminated (1) belief in separate *atman*; (2) doubt; (3) unwarranted confidence in vows and rituals [see Buswell and Lopez, *The Princeton Dictionary of Buddhism*, page 854 under *srotaapanna*]. There still remains some ego-centeredness, sensual desire, some anger, and some ignorance. A stream-entrant is not a beginner, and has made great progress but she or he has overcome only three of the ten fetters. According to reports, some American *roshi* have indeed suffered from self-centeredness, acted on sensual desires, and demonstrated inappropriate anger.

fact, since the time of Shakyamuni Buddha up until now in history, transmitting the Dharma is simply a passing on of responsibilities – the responsibility of carrying out the mission of benefitting sentient beings through Buddha-dharma [teachings of the Buddha]. As for this thing called 'enlightenment,' yes, there is such a phenomenon called enlightenment. If people have received Dharma transmission, it does not mean that they have already attained Arhat stage or are thoroughly enlightened. Dharma transmission is **not** contingent on whether the recipient is enlightened or not.[110]

In most American Ch'an groups, we should understand the Ch'an teacher (*roshi*) as a respected teacher, as someone who is ahead of the student on the pathway to buddhahood, and such a person can be very helpful to the student. But this does not mean that a *roshi* is morally perfect or has arrived at the end of the pathway. If one is a serious American Zen student in a training temple where the teacher is expected to have had several deep experiences of insight, the *roshi* (Ch'an teacher) can help a student from getting stuck in the experience, feeling such exhilaration that it results in inflating the student's ego instead of lessening it.

It has been recorded that when a student resolves a *koan*, when the great sensation of doubt is penetrated, it can often bring a shattering yet euphoric experience of *wu* or *satori*, and this might have been the most powerful emotional experience that the student has ever experienced. It is very easy for a student to believe that because the intense experience was so profound, it must have been the ultimate awakening with nothing more to learn. Often this experience is life-changing and results in an intense shifting of perspective. That in turn can generate a spiritual egotism, a mistaken belief that one has achieved the peak of Buddhist experience and henceforth one deserves the deference which Buddhists give to the Buddha himself. If one is not careful, this can result in an ego-centered feeling that "I'm awakened and I'm really spiritual, and all of you should bow down to me!"[111]

The Ch'an *roshi*, having personally gone through that aspect of the Ch'an training, is expected to recognize the potential problem created by euphoric insight and give the student additional exercises, additional *koans* until the student finds one that she or he cannot answer. This is an antidote to spiritual egotism. The teacher pushes the student on until sooner or later the student progresses beyond and insight deepens once again. Ideally, as one's practice moves on, the student can get to the stage where the ego is weakened, or perhaps even experience the great loss of the ego, a self-less state.

A monk brought two potted plants to his Master. 'Drop it,' ordered the Master. The monk dropped one pot. 'Drop it,' again ordered the Master. The monk let the second pot go. 'Drop it,' now roared the Master. The monk stammered: 'But I have nothing more to drop.' 'Then take it away' nodded the Master.[112]

Even dropping what we have, all we have, is not an easy thing. But dropping what has us, our ingrained opinions, views, ideals, our dear burdens that we so hotly and volubly defend – we cannot drop them by an act of will. It is just that which is the rub. We never even dare to look at them

---

[110] Sheng Yen, "Transmission" in *Chan Magazine*, Spring 2009, Volume 29, Number 2, pp. 17-18. Stress on "not" added by the author.

[111] The late Tibetan teacher Chogyam Trungpa (1940–1987) wrote a book on the problem of spiritual training which can result in inflated pride enhancing the student's ego making one more self-centered: *Cutting Through Spiritual Materialism*. (Shambhala: 2002). The Ch'an text *Record of Equanimity* describes three kinds of Ch'an sickness: (1) stuck in the ordinary world; (2) experiencing insight but then continuing to cling to the emotional experience and not letting go; (3) not dwelling inwardly in emptiness or grasping outwardly to things, but clinging to this state of non-dependence as though it were the absolute and ultimate.

[112] This is a variation on case 6 of the *Shūmon kattōshū*. The Chinese Ch'an teacher Sheng-yen recounts the time his teacher kept him moving from room to room, to teach him to let go, to "drop it." Sheng-yen, "On Gong'ans," in *Chan Magazine*, Spring 2013, p. 9.

openly, much less to doubt their validity.[113]

21.10 MAJOR HISTORICAL DEVELOPMENTS IN THE T'ANG (618–906 C.E.)

During the T'ang dynasty, Buddhism became very important in China, and numerous Buddhist monasteries (which were tax exempt) became wealthy. The government and wealthy patrons gave lavishly to the monastic institutions expecting miraculous benefits from transcendent buddhas in return. Many Buddhist teachers became famous, and some even became advisors to rulers and the emperor, giving the monks and their monasteries great political power. Buddhist ritual became state ritual. As a consequence, control of the Buddhist clergy was firmly in the hands of the political establishment. This gave political authorities control over who was allowed to be a monk, and who was promoted within the Buddhist hierarchy. State-supported Buddhism had to compromise with the bureaucrats to ensure and maintain the economic advantages which accrue from government sponsorship.

This worldly and political success of Chinese Buddhism had negative consequences: its influence generated resentment by Confucians and Taoists at court, who regarded Buddhism as both a competitor for political power and a foreign religion. Confucians in court were offended that the emperor supported foreign religions which contradicted Chinese Confucian customs. These factors led to two significant events in the history of Chinese Buddhism, both of which strongly affected Ch'an Buddhism.

The An Lu-shan Rebellion of 755

In the middle of the eighth century, 755 C.E., a powerful northern general named An Lu-shan led his troops in a revolt in an attempt to place himself on the throne. The ensuring civil war plunged the empire into bloody war and confusion for nearly eight years. The major battles occurred in the capital and its vicinity, destroying the grand temple complexes, ultimately resulting in the weakening of the old aristocracy who did their best to escape south as their homes became the battlefield. The major capital cities were in ruins as the emperor and his advisors fled to the south of China. The political structure of imperial China was devastated and for a while there was no central authority to provide patronage or support for the Buddhist monasteries and temples which surrounded the court and the capital city. With imperial and governmental patronage removed and capital temples and monasteries looted and razed, these politically powerful Buddhist groups were weakened.

The Great Persecution of 845 by Taoist Emperor Wu-tsang.

By the middle of the ninth century, five generations after the An Lu-shan rebellion, once again the monastic groups had become powerful and were independent of the government. There were many Buddhist monks who were quite brilliant as teachers, as philosophers, and artists. Buddhism was independent and creative. The problem was that the monasteries were supported lavishly by the wealthy and the powerful. The power and wealth of temples were growing beyond the control of emperor and court officials to keep it in check. Buddhist groups did not pay taxes, and many wealthy landowners were able to shield their taxes using Buddhist temples. The emperor always needed more money and the tax base was diminishing. Also, Buddhist monks were exempt from military service, and were exempt from being impressed into labor gangs. The result was a loss of tax revenues and a loss of ready manpower.

In addition to the financial problems, Confucians and Taoist politicians resented the political power of the Buddhists and insisted that the emperor must do something to diminish or eliminate Buddhist influence in the

---

[113] Roshi Irmgard Schloegl, *The Wisdom of the Zen Masters* (New York: New Directions, 1976), pp. 17–18.

country. It was clear that many young men were joining Buddhist groups to avoid being drafted, but had little interest in meditation or awakening. Some forms of Buddhism were even a threat to imperial rule.[114]

The Confucians in court drew upon a traditional ethnocentric attitude in China, that the Chinese were the most civilized and highly developed nation on earth, and that any system of thought not originating in China was foreign, was not Chinese, and could not really be of any use or value to the Chinese people. This claim had been made often in the past because aspects of Buddhism contradicted Confucian values. Confucians and Chinese in general resented the celibacy of monks which interfered with filial piety, with the duty of the son to carry on the family line so appropriate rituals could be performed to benefit ancestors in heaven, for many generations.

The imperial need for additional revenues became intense. The Confucian and Taoist criticisms of the foreign religion continued, and finally the Emperor Wu-tsang mounted a massive anti-Buddhist persecution in 845 C.E. Thousands of Buddhist temples (especially those closest to the capital cities in the north of China) were destroyed, and the government took over the lands belonging to temples (so they rejoined the tax base). Monks and nuns were forbidden to wear their robes, and were forced to return to the life of a householder or lay person. It became illegal for monks or nuns to shave their head; they were required to let their hair grow long again. It is estimated that at least 250,000 monks and nuns were affected, and many were killed.[115] The government confiscated Buddhist statues which were then melted down for coins, or the metal used for weapons.

After a year the harsh penalties were lifted. However, the persecution had made major changes in China. The Buddhist sects that survived were those which were not based in the areas around the Chinese capital city. Many teachers had gone into hiding in the mountains to avoid the authorities. There were many monastic groups located in the remote mountains far to the south and east, away from imperial power, and these were less affected by the 845 persecution.

Scholars point out that there was a tendency for surviving Buddhist groups to place less emphasis on overly ornate and fancy rituals aimed at transcendent god-like buddhas and bodhisattvas, and to be less concerned with difficult-to-understand philosophy. The Buddhist practices of surviving groups were more easily understood by non-scholarly Chinese and they were relevant to the lives of ordinary Chinese (who lived very differently from those who lived in the capitals).

Following the 845 persecution, two Buddhist sects grew stronger. One was the Pure Land sect, which as we saw in the previous chapter, tended to adopt a simple straight-forward *bhakti* (devotional) approach. All the follower needed to do was recite the name of Amitabha Buddha with faith, and he or she could be assured of rebirth in the Pure Land of the Western Paradise.

The other form of Buddhism which thrived was the Ch'an school. The Ch'an Buddhist groups that survived typically were less concerned with the trappings of conventional religion, so it made little difference to them that they had to shave their heads and put on ordinary clothes, and many of its practitioners had a genuine disdain of political entanglements (sharing the attitude of Chuang-tzu). Ch'an/Chan not only survived the persecution, but later became the dominant form of Buddhism and the most powerful creative and spiritual influence in the growth of Chinese culture in the T'ang and Sung dynasties.

However, although Ch'an dominated, it was not Ch'an alone which survived. The T'ien-t'ai tradition experienced a strong revival later in the Sung dynasty and was supported by rulers and officials. T'ien-t'ai philosophy appealed to many. Even esoteric Chinese Buddhism experienced textual, artistic, and liturgical reinvigoration during

---

[114] There had been a few political uprisings by Buddhists who belonged to the cult of Maitreya, the Buddha of the last (third) period of Buddhism. These Buddhists believed that as the political/social order came to an end, it would lead to the new Buddha and institute a new age of enlightenment.

[115] Denis Twitchett, ed., *The Cambridge History of China: Volume 3 – Sui and T'ang China, 589-906, Part I* (Cambridge: Cambridge University Press, 1979), pp. 666-667.

the Sung.[116]

21.11 CH'AN BUDDHISM FOLLOWING THE T'ANG DYNASTY

The influence of Ch'an Buddhism on culture and philosophy reached its height in the Southern Sung/Song dynasty (1121-1279), and the following Yuan and Ming dynasties, when Ch'an monasteries became the leading centers of Chinese scholarship. There was a tremendous cross-fertilization of philosophical, scholarly, poetic, and artistic pursuits in which Ch'an and Taoist ideas of "naturalness" became the dominant theme. This was the period that Ch'an was transplanted to Japan by the Japanese monks Eisai (1141-1215) and Dogen (1200-1253).

21.12 THE UNIFICATION OF CH'AN AND PURE LAND

By the Sung dynasty (960-1279), the two streams of Lin-chi Ch'an and Ts'ao-tung Ch'an were the dominant schools of Buddhist thought in China, profoundly influencing art, poetry, and philosophy, with most of the other Buddhist groups either incorporated into Ch'an or into the popular religion of magic and superstition. The Lin-chi lineage slowly absorbed the other schools of Ch'an, eventually even absorbing the Ts'ao-tung line. The Chinese love of harmony also influenced Chinese Buddhism, and people began to wonder why there was both Ch'an Buddhism and Pure Land Buddhism; there was only one Buddha. Why were there two main approaches to Buddhism?

By the end of the Ming dynasty (1368-1644), the self-reliant school of Ch'an had combined with the devotional Pure Land in China, and very few purely Ch'an monasteries survived. Ultimately, Buddhist meditation and Buddhist ideas strongly influenced later forms of Confucianism (Neo-Confucianism), and Neo-Confucianism dominated China until the turn of the twentieth century. Finally, following the Communist revolution of 1949, Mao Tse-tung attempted to eliminate Buddhism, Taoism, and Confucianism from China and replace them with Maoism.

The synthesis of the two Chinese Buddhist schools of Ch'an and Pure Land is seen clearly in modern Chinese Buddhism. For example, some Chinese Ch'an Buddhist teachers have come to north America teaching meditation but at the same time utilizing Pure Land chanting. One example of this is found in New York. The teacher Sheng-yen (1930-2009), who was born in mainland China but who went to Taiwan to study Buddhism in 1949, utilized both *koans* and chanting the name of Amitabha. Before his death, Shen-yen authorized several Western students to teach in his traditional lineage. Another example of Chinese Ch'an incorporating Pure Land practices is in California where there is the City of Ten Thousand Buddhas, established in 1974 by Hsuan-hua (1918-1995).

21.13 CH'AN BUDDHISM IN THE WEST

American scholars first heard about Ch'an in its Japanese form of Zen when it was represented in the 1893 World Conference of Religions in Chicago. Scholarly books focused explicitly on Zen have been available in English ever since 1927 when D. T. Suzuki (1870-1966) published the first volume of his trilogy *Essays in Zen Buddhism*. Suzuki's entertaining and intriguing scholarly books fueled much of the interest in Ch'an/Zen in the West. Suzuki wrote about Ch'an from a traditional, personal and rather idealized perspective, and the influential British authors R. H. Blyth (1898-1964) and Alan Watts (1915-1973) continued on the same tradition inspired by Suzuki in their many writings. Suzuki's books remain in print to this day.

In its Japanese form of Zen, this tradition has been very popular in Europe and North America, especially in

---

[116] For more on this, see Albert Welter, *Monks, Rulers, and Literati: The Political Ascendency of Chan Buddhism* (Oxford: Oxford University Press, 2006), p. 16.

the last decades of the twentieth century. Western poets, painters, and writers were intrigued by the Zen forms of Buddhism and one can find many Zen references in American literature, beginning in the 1950s and 1960s (such as Jack Kerouac's 1958 book *Dharma Bums*), in the writings of Peter Mathiessen (b. 1927) and in great American poets such as Gary Snyder (b. 1931) and Allen Ginsberg (1926-1997). The avant-garde composer and artist John Cage (1912-1992) drew heavily upon Zen for his inspirations.[117]

Interest in Ch'an was not merely in literature, poetry, and scholarship.[118] In 1905 a Japanese Zen monk named Nyogen Senzaki (1876-1958) came to the U.S. and fifteen years later opened a meditation center in San Francisco. Later in 1930 a Japanese teacher named Sasaki Shigetsu (1882-1945) established what became the First Zen Institute in New York. He was succeeded by the American-born Ruth Fuller Sasaki (1892-1967), who became a priest and translator in Japan, and facilitated study of Zen in Kyoto for several important future poets and scholars.[119] Contemporary Zen in the USA tended to derive from the Japanese Soto tradition of Suzuki Shunryu, and the Rinzai Zen traditions. The Zen of Maezumi Haku'yu (1931-1995), who established the Zen Center of Los Angeles in 1956, was a combination of Soto and Rinzai (the Sanbo Zen lineages). Pure Rinzai derived from Sasaki Joshu (1907-2014) who came to southern California in 1962 and opened his own Zen training center in 1968. The Soto tradition of Suzuki Shunryu (1904-1971) was established when he founded the Zen Center of San Francisco in the early 1960s. There are numerous American successors to these teachers, both male and female, such as the late Robert Aitkin (1917-2010), Charlotte Joko Beck (1917-2011), Jerry Shishin Wick, Jan Chozen Bays, and Bernard Tetsugen Glassman, and the influence of the Japanese style of Chinese Ch'an has been profound in north America. The Korean Ch'an (Seon) teacher Seung Sahn (1927-2004) established several successful groups and successors.

Only a few Chinese Ch'an teachers have established enduring temples in north America. In the 1960s the large institution called the City of Ten Thousand Buddhas was established by Hsuan Hua (1918-1977). Drawing on Ch'an and Pure Land, Hsuan Hua founded several institutions including the Dharma Realm Buddhist Association, the Dharma Realm Buddhist University, and the Buddhist Text Translation Society. Another important Chinese teacher was Sheng Yen (1930-2009), who came to the U.S.A. in 1977 and founded the New York Chan Meditation Center and the Dharma Drum association.

21.14 THE LAUGHING BUDDHA

If the historical Buddha was born in India and was a thin ascetic, why was he portrayed as fat and as Chinese? The answer is simple. There are many buddhas, not just one buddha. The fat, laughing buddha is *not* Siddhartha Gautama, the founder of Indian Buddhism. The fat and laughing fellow is Pu-tai/Budai (in Japanese, Hotei), which means "a bag made of hemp." He became a popular figure in Ch'an paintings, where he tends to be portrayed as a fat jolly innocent who wanders the world without a care.

In fact, the iconography of the fat laughing Buddha was inspired by this Ch'an Buddhist monk who is thought to have died about 916 C.E. (approximately 1500 years after the historical Buddha). It seems as though several legends coalesced around this happy monk. This monk was a free and easy wanderer who occasionally wrote poems and left them scattered around. Over time the stories of this wandering monk combined and ultimately he became the embodiment of health, happiness, prosperity, good luck and longevity.

---

[117] For example, see Helen Westgeest, *Zen in the Fifties: Interaction in Art between East and West* (Reaktion Books, 1998), Ray Kass and Steven Addiss, *John Cage: Zen Ox-herding Pictures* (New York: George Brazilier, 2009), and Kay Larson, *Where the Heart Beats: John Cage, Zen Buddhism, and the Inner Life of Artists* (New York: Penguin, 2012).

[118] A book which deals with contemporary teachers and their varied teachings is James Ishmael Ford, *Zen Master Who? A Guide to the People and Stories of Zen* (Wisdom, 2006).

[119] Isabel Stirling, *Zen Pioneer: The Life and Works of Ruth Fuller Sasaki* (Counterpoint Books, 2006).

Pu-tai/Budai may have claimed to be an incarnation of the future Buddha Maitreya (Chinese: Mi-lo or Mi-to-lo-fo; Japanese: Miroku). Pu-tai left several enigmatic poems. One poem attributed to him reads:

Mi-lo, true Mi-lo
Reborn innumerable times
From time to time manifested to men
The men of the age do not recognize you

Wherever this wanderer went, he had a large cloth hemp-bag over his shoulder (in Chinese, a "hemp bag" is a *pu-tai* or *budai*, in Japanese *hotei*). Thus he came to be known as Pu-tai ho-shang ("hemp-bag monk"). The legend is that he carried a large bag for begging, and that he stuffed lots of other things into it as well, including toys for children. Artists often depict him surrounded by playful children, echoing the important Chinese stress on a large family with many children. Some sources claim that he carried this bag over his shoulder on a stick as he wandered through the hamlets of rural China.

Iconographers in the tenth century summed up these various elements of happiness in a representation of the fat Laughing Buddha (only a rich person would have enough food to eat and actually get fat), clutching his Buddhist prayer beads in one hand and with a bag (or bar) of gold in the other.

Early sources relate that portraits of Pu-tai were worshiped by people in the belief that Pu-tai was in fact an incarnated form of the Buddha Maitreya. Imported into Japan along with other elements of Chinese Buddhism, Putai was transformed into Hotei, one of the seven gods of good luck. Perhaps we can say that the appeal of the Laughing Buddha is an appeal to enjoy a good life, to enjoy what is around us, and to laugh more often. For more scholarly details, see "The Laughing Buddha" by Ferdinand D. Lessing, Chapter 13 in *The Chinese Way in Religion*, ed. by Laurence G. Thompson, pp. 109–116.

21.15 SUMMARY OF THE CHAPTER

The Ch'an tradition of Buddhism was one of two enduringly important sects of Buddhism in China. Its origins begin in China in the sixth century, at about the same time as the other uniquely Chinese Buddhist sects. The Ch'an tradition created a fictitious genealogy which connected it to the Buddha in India, and this gave it legitimacy in China. The Indian monk Bodhidharma became known as the founding teacher, or first patriarch, even though there is no historical evidence to connect him with the later Ch'an tradition. Long after his death, the teacher named Hui-neng was given the label of "Sixth Patriarch," and even today, every Ch'an tradition in China, Korea, Japan, and the West, traces its lineage to Hui-neng and Bodhidharma.

Especially in the form of Zen, this Buddhist teaching has exerted significant influence on many in Europe and North America, and continues to expand and develop in the West.

The Ch'an tradition asserts that we do not lack some spiritual substance which needs to be sought after, a substance which an enlightened teacher can give us. Rather, each one of us possesses the nature of a Buddha. We are lacking nothing, except insight into our true nature. The Ch'an tradition pushes students to achieve an insight experience, called *wu* (in Chinese) or *satori* (in Japanese). The experience of awakening cannot be given to the student, and cannot be written down. Each student must find it for herself or himself.

The Chinese roots of Ch'an certainly include the philosophical Taoist stress on spontaneity as well as Confucian morality. The Indian philosophical antecedents of Ch'an are clearly in Nagarjuna's emptiness doctrine (*sunyata*), but Mahayana ideas of Buddha-nature and skillful teaching means (*upaya*) are employed as well. Chinese Hua-yen Buddhist philosophy of universal and particular also influenced Ch'an teachings. The Ch'an *koan* is an apparently irrational question-and-answer mechanism intended to spark insight in the mind of the student, but also test the depth of the understanding. Koan study combined with seated meditation (*zazen*) is the dominant means for provoking insight.

One of the enduring figures to come from the Ch'an tradition is the so-called "Laughing Buddha," the jolly fat Ch'an monk who, in popular Chinese religion, was believed to be an incarnation of the Bodhisattva Maitreya. He is known as Pu-tai/Budai (Hotei in Japan) and he brings good luck and happiness.

Following the persecution of Buddhism in 845, the Ch'an school and the Pure Land traditions were the only schools to gain strength and flourish after the persecution lifted. Ch'an developed five slightly different teaching styles, which are called the "Five Houses" but of these five, only two endured into the present. One is the Lin-chi/Linji (Rinzai in Japanese) lineage, and the other is the Ts'ao-tung/Caodung (Soto in Japanese) lineage. These were combined with the Pure Land practices in sixteenth century China, so contemporary Chinese Buddhism is a mixture of both.

21.16 TECHNICAL TERMS

Ch'an
: Chan in Pinyin romanization; this is the Chinese transliteration of the Sanskrit dhyana, or meditation. The Ch'an school is the meditation school.

Hua-yen Buddhism
: An abstract and philosophical school of Chinese Buddhism which focused on the interrelation between the universal (*li*), like gold, and the particular (*shih*), like the statue made out of gold, or the earrings made of gold. This school also utilized meditation. Hua-yen ideas and references can be found in Ch'an koans and other Ch'an literature. Hua-yen was discussed in more detail in the previous chapter.

koan
: An apparently irrational question used as a skillful teaching device (*upaya*). The teacher asks a question which cannot be answered by logic or research. When focusing on the question, often a great doubt occupies the mind of the student. When the student finally understands the issue deeply and glimpses the flowing nature of the self, the result is an insight experience provoked by the koan. The teacher can ask follow-up koans to test the depth of the student's understanding. In theory, each koan which is resolved leads the student into deeper insight and closer to the status of an awakened sage.

satori
: The Japanese term for an insight experience, pronounced *wu* in Chinese.

te/de
: The spiritual virtue possessed by a Sage to influence others for the better. This common Chinese idea was found in Confucius and Confucianism, and in both forms of Taoism.

wu
: the Chinese term often translated as "enlightenment" but perhaps better it is an insight experience often accompanied by a feeling of euphoria; in Japan this is *satori*. This is not the complete and total enlightenment of the Buddha under the Bodhi tree.

wu
: This Chinese character can be translated "non-" or "non-being" or "without," or "no." In Ch'an literature it is often treated as a synonym for *sunyata* ("empty of unchanging essence") or just "emptiness."

zazen
: The Japanese pronounciation for the Chinese *ts'o-ch'an*, literally "seated meditation," which combines meditation to quiet the mind and meditation to gain insight into the flowing interdependent nature of reality. Although the student begins to learn this skill while seated, later on the state of mind is carried on whether walking, running, or lying down.

CHAPTER 21: CH'AN BUDDHISM

NAMES

Bodhidharma   Puti-tamo in Pinyin. A Buddhist monk from India who came to China around 500 C.E. and stressed seated meditation. Long after his death, an 8th century Ch'an monk (Shen-hui) named Bodhidharma as the link connecting the mythic history of Ch'an in India to the Southern Line of Ch'an in China. He is referred to as (1) the first patriarch in China, and (2) the 28th Patriarch in India.

Ho-tse Shen-hui   684–758. Heze Shenhui in Pinyin. He is the student of Hui-neng and the one who made up much of the mythic history of Ch'an.

Hui-neng   The illiterate monk who became known as the Sixth Patriarch of Ch'an. 638–713

TERMS FROM PREVIOUS CHAPTERS

arhat   In early Indian Buddhism, one who follows the pathway of the Buddha and puts an end to *duhkha*, thereby achieving Nirvana.

atman   Sanskrit term for the eternal unchanging inner essence, the "soul."

bodhi   Awakening; the realization that one has put an end to *duhkha* and sees things as they really are.

duhkha   frustration, dissatisfaction, misery and suffering.

sunyata   Sanskrit term meaning "empty," short for *svabhava-sunyata*, "empty of inner unchanging essence."

upaya   In Mahayana Buddhism, this allows us to understand the teaching of the Buddha as skillful teaching devices. In one sutra the Buddha teaches the Four Noble Truths and advocates Theravada. In a Mahayana Buddhist sutra, the Buddha ignores the Four Noble Truths and insults Theravada followers. If the Buddha appears to contradict himself from one sutra to the next, the Mahayana tradition explains that as a teacher, the Buddha had to use simpler language and concepts that the unawakened student could understand. Thus these are skillful teaching devices. In China, the koan can be understood as a skillful device intended to provoke the student to insight into her own true nature.

21.17 QUESTIONS FOR FURTHER DISCUSSION

(1)   We have seen that Ch'an Buddhism, as presented in this chapter, is not quite like most traditional religions. Western scholars have debated whether to call Ch'an a religion, or not. Which features of Ch'an do you consider typical of religions? Which features do you consider atypical of religion?

(2)   What is the "Flower Sermon" of the Buddha? Why does traditional Ch'an Buddhism consider this mythical event important to their tradition?

(3)   Ch'an followers claim to be replicating the awakening experience of the Buddha. They claim that faith is not required, but only the confidence that you yourself can achieve the goal. How is this approach different from the most common Western religions?

(4) You might have seen a popular animated film entitled *Kung-fu Panda* which suggests that the secret ingredient in the soup is obvious if you have insight. The secret on the martial arts scroll is obvious, when you really understand. Do you find any parallels with Ch'an claim, "Without trying to be a Buddha, you are a Buddha"?

(5) If you know a Buddhist teacher whose students treat the teacher as though he or she is morally perfect because the teacher is "awakened," would you do whatever the teacher tells you to do, even if it violates your conscience? Suppose the teacher asks you to perform a sexual act, and you decline. Now suppose the teacher says that your hesitation to obey merely demonstrates your spiritual immaturity or your selfish egotism which you must overcome, then what would you say or do? Suppose this teacher says that the sexual act is just a "skillful means" to help you achieve your spiritual goal. What would you say or do?

(6) Suppose you read a Ch'an teacher who writes that there is nothing to achieve, that there is not much in Ch'an teaching after all. How can this be correct? Doesn't a student work hard and achieve awakening? Discuss.

SELECTED BIBLIOGRAPHY

NOTE: The material on Chinese Ch'an and Japanese Zen is so large that even though the following list is lengthy, it is only a brief list of some of the more relevant sources. For Ch'an and Zen-related books prior to 1991, the student might consult:

Gardner, James L., *Zen Buddhism: A Classified Bibliography* (New York: Random House, 1991)

Basic Resources for the History

Addiss, Stephen, Stanley Lombardo, Judith Roitman, eds., *Zen Sourcebook: Traditional Documents from China, Korea, and Japan* (Cambridge: Hackett Publishing Company, 2008)

Chang Chung-yuan, *Original Teachings of Ch'an Buddhism* (New York: Random House, 1969).

Dumoulin, Heinrich., *Zen Buddhism: A History: Vol 1: India and China* (1990).

_____, *Zen Buddhism: A History: Vol 2: Japan* (1990).

Ferguson, Andy, *Tracking Bodhidharma: A Journey to the Heart of Chinese Culture* (Counterpoint: 2012)

_____, *Zen's Chinese Heritage: The Masters and their Teachings* (Boston: Wisdom Publications, 2000)

Heine, Steven and Dale Wright, *The Zen Canon: Understanding the Classic Texts* (London: Oxford, 2004)

Kapleau, Phillip, *The Three Pillars of Zen* (Beacon Press, 1967)

Lessing, Frederick D., "The Laughing Buddha" chapter 13 in Laurence G. Thompson, ed., *The Chinese Way in Religion*, (Belmont, CA: Dickinson, 1973), pp. 109-116.

Sasaki, Ruth Fuller and Isshu Miura, *Zen Dust: The History of the Koan and Koan Study in Rinzai Zen* (New York: Harcourt Brace, 1966)

Schloegl, Irmgard, *The Wisdom of the Zen Masters* (New York: New Directions, 1976)

Albert Welter, *Monks, Rulers, and Literati: The Political Ascendency of Chan Buddhism* (Oxford: Oxford University Press, 2006)

Wu, John C., *The Golden Age of Zen* (New York: Doubleday Image, 1996)

Practice Oriented Books

Aitkin, Robert, *The Mind of Clover: Essays in Zen Buddhist Ethics* (Berkeley: North Point, 1984)

_____, *Taking the Path of Zen* (San Francisco: North Point Press, 1982)

Beck, Charlotte Joko, *Everyday Zen* (San Francisco: Harper, 1989)

_____, *Nothing Special: Living Zen* (San Francisco: Harper, 1994)

Beck, Charlotte Joko and Ezra Bayda, *Being Zen: Bringing Meditation to Life* (Boston: Shambhala, 2003)

Buksbazen, John Daishin, *To Forget the Self: An Illustrated Guide to Zen Meditation* (Los Angeles: Zen Center Publications, 1978)

Hagen, Steve, *Buddhism is Not What You Think* (San Francisco: Harper, 2003)

_____, *Buddhism Plain and Simple* (New York: Tuttle, 1997)

_____, *How the World Can Be the Way It Is* (Quest Books, 1995)

Katagiri, Dainin, *You Have To Say Something: Manifesting Zen Insight* (Boston: Shambhala, 1998)

Kapleau, Philip, *The Zen of Living and Dying* (Boston: Shambhala, 1998)

Loori, John Daido, *Two Arrows Meeting in Mid-Air* (Rutland, Vt.: Charles Tuttle, 1994)

Maezumi, Haku'yu and Bernard Glassman, *The Hazy Moon of Enlightenment* (Los Angeles, Zen Center Publications, 1978)

_____, *On Zen Practice: Body, Breath, and Mind* (Wisdom Publications, 1999)

Shibayama, Zenkei, *A Flower Does Not Talk: Zen Essays* (Rutland, Vt.: Tuttle, 1970)

Smith, Elihu Genmyo, *everything is the way: Ordinary Mind Zen* (Boston: Shambhala, 2012)

Suzuki, Shunryu, *Zen Mind, Beginner's Mind* (New York: Weatherhill, 1973)

Suzuki, Daisetz T., *The Training of the Zen Buddhist Monk* (New York: University Books, 1965)

Scholarly Studies of Aspects of Ch'an and Zen Buddhism

Adamek, Wendi L., *The Mystique of Transmission: On An Early Chan History and Its Contents* (New York: Columbia University Press, 2007)

Baroni, Helen Josepphine, *Obaku Zen: The Emergence of the Third Sect of Zen in Tokugawa Japan* (Honolulu: University of Hawaii Press, 2000), 280 pages.

Batchelor, Stephen, *The Faith to Doubt: Glimpses of Buddhist Uncertainty* (Berkeley: Parallax Press, 1990).

Buswell, Robert E., *The Formation of Ch'an Ideology in China and Korea* (1989).

Cole, Alan, *fathering your father: the zen of fabrication in tang buddhism* (Berkeley: The University of California Press, 2009)

Ferguson, Andy, *Tracking Bodhidharma: A Journey to the Heart of Chinese Culture* (Counterpoint: 2012)

Gimello, Robert and Peter Gregory, eds., *Studies in Ch'an and Hua-yen* (1983).

Gopfert, Caryl Reimer, *Student Experiences of Betrayal in the Zen Buddhist Teacher/Student Relationship*, Ph.D. dissertation from the Institute of Transpersonal Psychology, 21 March 1999, pp. 273-275.

Hanh Thich Nhat, *The Diamond that Cuts Through Illusion: Commentaries on the Prajnaparamita Diamond Sutra* (Berkeley: Parallax Press, 1992)

Hassan, Steven, *Releasing the Bonds: Empowering People to Think for Themselves* (Freedom of Mind Press, 2000) [This study examines Behaviour Control, Information Control, Thought Control and Emotional Control]

Heine, Steven, *Dogen and the Koan Tradition* (New York: State University Press of New York, 1995)

_____, *Zen Skin, Zen Marrow* (London: Oxford University Press, 2008)

Heine, Steven, ed., *Zen Ritual: Studies of Zen Buddhist Theory in Practice* (London: Oxford, 2007).

James, Simon, *Zen Buddhism and Environmental Ethics* (Burlington, VT: Ashgate, 2005)

Jorgensen, John, *Inventing Hui-neng, the Sixth Patriarch: Hagiography and Biography in Early Ch'an* (Boston and Leiden: Brill, 2005) This is a very technical and scholarly study of early Ch'an.

Kramer, Joel and Alstad, Diana, *The Guru Papers – Masks of Authoritarian Power* (North Atlantic Books, 1993)

Lachs, Stuart, "The Zen Master in America: Dressing the Donkey with Bells and Scarves," paper delivered at the Annual Meeting of the American Academy of Religion, Washington D.C., 18 November 2006, pp. 1-2. Available at www.hsuyun.org.

CHAPTER 21: CH'AN BUDDHISM

Lai, Whalen and Lewis Lancaster, eds., *Early Ch'an in China and Tibet* (Berkeley: Asian Humanities Press, 1983).

McRae, John, *The Northern School and the Formation of Early Ch'an Buddhism* (Honolulu: Univ. Press of Hawaii, 1986).

_____, *Seeing Through Zen* (Berkeley, Ca: University of California Press, 2003)

Schlutter, Morton and Stephen Teiser, *Readings of the Platform Sutra* (New York: Columbia University Press, 2012)

Sorensen, Henrik H., "The History and Practice of Early Ch'an" in Morten Schlutter and Stephen Teiser, *Readings of the Platform Sutra* (New York: Columbia University Press, 2012)

Suzuki, D. T., *Manual of Zen Buddhism* (1935).

_____, *The Zen Doctrine of 'No-Mind'* (London: Rider & Co., 1949).

Sunim, Mu Soeng, *Heart Sutra* (Cumberland, R.I.: Primary Point Press, 1992)

Yu, Chun-fang, *The Renewal of Buddhism in China: Chu-hung and the Late Ming Synthesis* (New York: 1981)

Victoria, Brian, *Zen War Stories* (London: Routledge, 2003)

Waddell, Norman, *Zen Words for the Heart: Hakuin's Commentary on the Heart Sutra* (Boston: Shambhala, 1996)

Watts, Alan, *The Way of Zen* (New York: Pantheon, 1957)

Wright, Tom, Jisho Warner, Shohaku Okamura, translators, *Opening the Hand of Thought: Foundations of Zen Buddhist Practice* (Boston; Wisdom Publications, 2004)

Wu Jiang, *Enlightenment in Dispute: The Reinvention of Chan Buddhism in Seventeenth-Century China* (London: Oxford University Press, 2008)

Zeuschner, Robert, "The Meaning of 'Hinayana' in Northern Ch'an," in *Eastern Buddhist*, vol. 11, no. 1, May 1978.

_____, "On the Understanding of Mind in Northern Ch'an," in *Philosophy East and West*, Vol. 27, No. 1, January 1978.

_____, "The concept of *li-nien* in the Northern Line of Ch'an Buddhism," in Lewis Lancaster and Whalen Lai, eds., *Early Ch'an in China and Tibet* (Berkeley: Asian Humanities Press, 1983).

_____, "Awakening in Northern Ch'an," in David W. Chappell, *Buddhist and Taoist Practice in Medieval Chinese Society* (Honolulu: University of Hawaii Press, 1987)

Translations of Basic Ch'an/Zen Texts

App, Urs, *Master Yunmen: From the Record of the Chan Teacher* (New York: Kodansha, 1994)

Blofeld, John, *The Zen Teaching of Huang Po* (1958).

_____, *The Zen Teaching of Hui Hai* (1962).

Broughton, Jeffrey L., *The Bodhidharma Anthology: The Earliest Records of Zen* (Berkeley: The University of California Press, 1999)

_____, *The Record of Linji: A New Translation of the Linjilu in the Light of Ten Japanese Zen Commentaries* (New York: Oxford University Press, 2012)

Cleary, J. C., *Zen Dawn: Early Zen Texts from Tun Huang* (1986).

_____, *Zibo: The Last Great Zen Master of China* (1989).

Demieville, Paul, *Entretiens de Lin-Tsi* (Paris: Fayard, 1972)

Foster, Nelson and Jack Shoemaker, *The Roaring Stream: A New Zen Reader* (Hopewell, N.J.: The Ecco Press, 1996) (the basic texts of the great Ch'an/Zen masters in China and Japan)

Franck, Frederick, *Zen and Zen Classics: Selections from R. H. Blyth* (New York: Vintage Books, 1978)

Green, James, *The Recorded Sayings of Zen Master Joshu* (Boston: Shambhala, 1998)

Heine, Steven, *Opening A Mountain: Koans of the Zen Masters* (New York and London: Oxford University Press, 2002)

Heine, Steven and Dale Wright, *The Zen Canon: Understanding the Classic Texts* (New York: Oxford, 2004)

Hanh Thich Nhat, *The Diamond that Cuts Through Illusion: Commentaries on the Prajnaparamita Diamond Sutra* (Berkeley: Parallax Press, 1992)

Hoffmann, Yoel, *Radical Zen: The Sayings of Joshu* (Brookline, Ms.: Autumn Press, 1978)

_____, *The Sound of the One Hand* (New York: Basic Books, 1975)

Hori, Victor, *Zen Sand: The Book of Capping Phrases for Koan Practice* (Honolulu: University of Hawaii Press, 2003)

Ives, Christopher and Tokiwa Gishin, *Critical Sermons of the Zen Tradition: Hisamatsu's Talks on Linji* (Honolulu: University Press of Hawaii, 2002)

Leighton, Taigen Dan, and Yi Wu, *Cultivating the Empty Field: The Silent Illumination of Zen Master Hongzhi* (Tuttle, 2000)

Nishiyama, Kosen and John Stevens, trs., *Shobogenzo*, Vol. 1 [Sendai, Japan: Daihokkaikaku, 1975] This is the classic work by the Japanese Zen Buddhist Dogen (b. 1200)

Pine, Red (Bill Porter), *The Diamond Sutra: Text and Commentaries Translated from Sanskrit and Chinese* (New York: Counterpoint, 2001)

_____, *The Zen Teaching of Bodhidharma* (New York: North Point Press, 1987)

Sasaki, Ruth Fuller, *The Record of Lin-Chi* (Kyoto, Japan: The Institute for Zen Studies, 1975).

Sasaki, Ruth Fuller, Isshu Miura, and Dana Fraser, trans., *A Man of Zen: The Recorded Sayings of Layman P'ang* (New York: Weatherhill, 1971)

Sasaki, Ruth Fuller, and Thomas Yuho Kirchner, *The Record of Linji* (Honolulu: University of Hawaii Press, 2009)

Shigematsu, Soiku, *A Zen Forest: Sayings of the Masters* (New York: Weatherhill, 1981)

Shibayama, Zenkei, Shimano Eido, translated by Robert Lewis, *The Book of the Zen Grove: Phrases for Zen Practice*, 2nd edition (Jacksonville: Zen Sangha Press, 1996)

Sunim, Mu Soeng, *Heart Sutra* (Cumberland, R.I.: Primary Point Press, 1992)

Suzuki, D. T., *Manual of Zen Buddhism* (London: Rider & Co., 1935)

_____, *The Zen Doctrine of 'No-Mind'* (London: Rider & Co., 1949)

Waddell, Norman, *Zen Words for the Heart: Hakuin's Commentary on the Heart Sutra* (Boston: Shambhala, 1996)

Watson, Burton, *The Zen Teachings of Master Lin-chi* (Boston: Shambhala, 1993)

Wood, Frances, and Mark Barnard, *The Diamond Sutra: The Story of the World's Earliest Dated Printed Book* (Oxford: The British Library, 2010)

Yamada, Mumon, tr. by Victor Hori, *Lectures on the Ten Oxherding Pictures* (Honolulu: University Press of Hawaii, 2004)

Yampolsky, P. B., *The Platform Sutra of the Sixth Patriarch* (New York: Columbia, 1967).

Zeuschner, Robert, "The *Hsien-tsung chi*: an early Southern Ch'an Text" in *Journal of Chinese Philosophy*, vol. 3, 1976, pp. 299–311.

Ch'an and Zen: *Koan* collections

Aitken, Robert, *The Gateless Barrier: The Wu-men Kuan (Mumonkan)*, (San Francisco: North Point Press, 1981)

Broughton, Jeffrey and Elise Yoko Watanabe, *The Chan Whip Anthology* (New York: Oxford University Press, 2015)

Cleary, Thomas, *Book of Serenity: One Hundred Zen Dialogues* (Boston: Shambhala, 1998)

_____, *Secrets of the Blue Cliff Record: Zen Comments by Hakuin and Tenkei* (Boston: Shambhala, 2000)

_____, *No Barrier: Unlocking the Zen Koan* (New York: Bantam Books, 1993)

_____, *Transmission of Light: Zen in the Art of Enlightenment by Zen Master Keizan* (San Francisco: North Point Press, 1990)

_____, *Unlocking the Zen Koan: A New Translation of the Wumenguan* (Berkeley: North Atlantic Books, 1997) (same as *No Barrier*)

Cleary, Thomas, and J. C. Cleary, *The Blue Cliff Records* (Boulder and London: Shambhala, 1977).

Ford, James, and Melissa Blacker, eds., *The Book of MU: Essential Writings on Zen's Most Important Koan* (Boston: Wisdom Publications, 2011)

Heine, Steven, *Opening A Mountain: Koans of the Zen Masters (Critical Commentary on Sixty Zen Koans)*, (London: Oxford, 2001)

Heine, Steven, and Dale S. Wright, *The Koan: Texts and Contexts in Zen Buddhism* (London: Oxford University Press, 2000)

Hoffmann, Yoel, *The Sound of the One Hand* (New York: Basic Books, 1975) translates answers to several classic *koans*

_____, *Every End Exposed* (Brookline, MASS: Autumn Press, 1977)

Hori, Victor, *Zen Sand: The Book of Capping Phrases for Koan Practice* (Honolulu: University of Hawaii Press, 2003)

Kapleau, Philip, *Straight To the Heart of Zen: Eleven Classic Koans and Their Inner Meanings* (Boston: Shambhala, 2001)

Kirchner, Thomas Yuho, *Entangling Vines: A Classic Collection of Zen Koans* (Boston: Wisdom Publications, 2013)

Low, Albert, *The World: A Gateway: Commentaries on the Mumonkan* (Rutland, Vt.: Charles E. Tuttle, 1995)

Loori, John Daido, *Two Arrows Meeting in Mid Air: The Zen Koan* (Rutland, Vt.: Tuttle, 1994)

Loori, John, and Kazuaki Tanahashi, *The True Dharma Eye: Zen Master Dogen's Three Hundred Koans* (Boston: Shambhala, 2005).

Miura, Isshu and Ruth Fuller Sasaki, *Zen Dust: The History of the Koan and Koan Study in Rinzai Zen* (New York: Harcourt Brace, 1966)

Reps, Paul and Nyogen Senzaki, *Zen Flesh, Zen Bones* (Rutland, VT: Tuttle, 1957)

Senzaki, Nyogen and Ruth Fuller McCandless, *The Iron Flute: 100 Zen Koan* (Rutland, VT: Tuttle, 1961)

Sekida, Katsuki, *Two Zen Classics* (Weatherhill, 1977). Contains the *Blue Cliff Records* and the *Gateless Gate*.

Shibayama, Zenkei, *Zen Comments on the Mumonkan* (New York: Harper & Row, 1974)

Shibayama, Zenkei, Shimano Eido, translated by Robert Lewis, *The Book of the Zen Grove: Phrases for Zen Practice*, 2nd edition (Jacksonville: Zen Sangha Press, 1996)

Shigematsu, Soiku, *A Zen Forest: Sayings of the Masters* (New York: Weatherhill, 1981)

Tanahashi, Kazuaki and John Daido Loori, *The True Dharma Eye: Zen Master Dogen's Three Hundred Koans* (Boston: Shambhala, 2005)

Tarrant, John, *Bring Me the Rhinoceros: and Other Zen Koans to Bring You Joy* (New York: Harmony Books, 2004)

Wick, Gerry Shishin, *The Book of Equanimity: Illuminating Classic Zen Koans* (Boston: Wisdom Publications, 2005)

Zen and the Arts/Creativity

Awakawa, Yasuichi, *Zen Painting* (Tokyo: Kodansha, 1970)

Blyth, R. H., *Zen in English Literature and Oriental Classics* (Dutton, 1960)

Blyth, R. H., *Zen and Zen Classics* (5 volumes) (Tokyo: Hokuseido, 1960–1975)

Chang, Chung-yuan, *Creativity and Taoism* (Julian Press, 1963).

Fontein, Jan and M. Hickman, *Zen: Painting and Calligraphy* (Boston: Museum of Fine Arts, 1970).

Hisamatsu, Shin'ichi, *Zen and the Fine Arts* (Tokyo: Kodansha, 1971)

Iriya, Yoshitaka, "Chinese Poetry and Zen," in *Eastern Buddhist* vol. 6, no. 1, May 1973, pp. 54-67.

Kass, Ray, and Steven Addiss, *John Cage: Zen Ox-herding Pictures* (New York: George Brazilier, 2009)

Larson, Kay, *Where the Heart Beats: John Cage, Zen Buddhism, and the Inner Life of Artists* (New York: Penguin, 2012)

Shimano, Eido Tai and Kogetsu Tani, *Zen Word Zen Calligraphy* (Boston: Shambhala, 1995)

Stirling, Isabel, *Zen Pioneer: The Life and Works of Ruth Fuller Sasaki* (Counterpoint Books, 2006)

Suzuki, D. T., *Zen and Japanese Culture* (New York: Pantheon, 1959)

Watts, Alan, *The Way of Zen* (New York: Pantheon, 1957)

Westgeest, Helen, *Zen in the Fifties: Interaction in Art between East and West* (Reaktion Books, 1998)

Kopp, Sheldon B., *If You Meet the Buddha On the Road, Kill Him!* (New York: Bantam Books, 1972)

Buddhism in Modern China

Bush, R. C., *Religion in Communist China* (1970)

Chan, Wing-tsit, *Religious Trends in Modern China* (New York: Columbia Univ. Press, 1953).

Welch, Holmes, *The Buddhist Revival in China* (Cambridge: Harvard Univ. Press, 1968).

Welch, Holmes, *Buddhism Under Mao* (Cambridge: Harvard Univ. Press, 1972)

Yü Chün-fang, *The Renewal of Buddhism: Chu-hung and the Late Ming Synthesis* (1981).

CHAPTER 22: NEO-CONFUCIAN THOUGHT

22.1 OVERVIEW OF THE CHAPTER

The two related systems we in the West call "Neo-Confucianism" were the political and cultural basis for the Chinese world-view from the thirteenth to the nineteenth centuries. "Neo-Confucianism," or "New Confucianism" was profoundly optimistic, arguing that through self-cultivation human beings could cultivate their unique creative role whereby we could serve the family, serve the state, and unify with Heaven, Earth, and all the ten-thousand things. The focus of Neo-Confucianism was human society and relationships between the individual and society. The religious goal of Neo-Confucianism was to become a genuine sage, a person who loved scholarship and at the same time a cultivated person of integrity, serenity, and mental purity. Such a person would be a perfect advisor to the throne in addition to being an ideal citizen.

This was a movement, both philosophical and spiritual, which brought about a new definition for political orthodoxy, and established new traditions based on Confucius. To be a Neo-Confucian male was to be involved in politics. This meant that he had to adjust himself to the demands of the world, but it should not be at the expense of his sincerity and his humanity (*jen*). This movement developed gradually from the tenth century to the thirteenth century, and then expanded and developed for about six-hundred years until the twentieth century. It was within the last hundred and fifty years that what was left of Neo-Confucianism in China was replaced by Western political models, ultimately Marxism which functioned as a state religion until recent times.

The Chinese referred to this school as *Tao-hsueh / Daoxue* (Learning the Way), and *Li-hsueh*, the **School of *Li***, or the **School of Principle**, where *li* is the Chinese character commonly translated "principle," "manifest patterns" or "rational patterns" which govern and guide the processes of change and growth throughout the universe.[1] *Li* are the underlying structures of that which constitutes ultimate reality. One of the defining characteristics of Neo-Confucianism is the stress on the fundamental concept of "principle" or "pattern" which is *li*.

A later school of Neo-Confucianism called the **School of Mind** achieved prominence in the 1400s and had continuing influence in China and in Japan. In the West, the entire movement of reformulated Confucian philosophy is called "Neo-Confucianism" ("New Confucianism").

---

[1] This Chinese character pronounced *li* meaning "principle" or "pattern" should not be confused with the completely different Chinese character used by Confucius to mean ritual, propriety, respectability or ceremonial interaction (*li*).

CHAPTER 22: NEO-CONFUCIANISM

CHINESE DYNASTIES RELEVANT TO NEO-CONFUCIANISM

206 B.C.E. - 220 C.E.	Han Dynasty
220–265	Three Kingdoms (Wu, Wei, Shu)
265–581	Six Dynasties
581–618	Sui Dynasty
618 - 906	T'ang Dynasty
907–960	Five Dynasties
937–975	Southern T'ang
960–1279	Sung Dynasty
1115–1234	Chin Dynasty
1279–1368	Yuan Dynasty
1368–1644	Ming Dynasty
1644–1912	Ch'ing Dynasty
since 1912	Republic
since 1949	People's Republic

22.2 INTRODUCTION TO NEO-CONFUCIANISM

Chinese thought is generally described as comprised of the Three Traditions of Confucianism, Taoism, and Buddhism. Each of the three traditions of China fulfilled different and somewhat complementary functions. Although Buddhism originated in India, over the many centuries Buddhist thought, beliefs and practices had become firmly entrenched in the daily religious lives of the Chinese and it no longer appeared to be a foreign religion.

Confucian thought, with its stress on governing and family morality, emphasized correct performance of ritual as the foundation of benevolence. This was for those with elite educations and interest in politics and political power and advancement. Confucianism also served as the foundation for family values and the correct performance of one's social roles.

Religious Taoism satisfied the needs of popular folk religion appealing to those Chinese who were interested in shamans, in magic, in alchemy, longevity, and obtaining favors from gods and other supernatural figures. Religious Taoism also was the foundation for traditional Chinese medicine, which understood illness as caused by evil spirits. The more sophisticated Confucian scholars had a tendency to look down on popular Taoism and other aspects of popular religion as superstition.

Confucianism focused on family, on rulers and on society, and religious Taoism focused on magic and longevity. Many aspects of Chinese Buddhism also satisfied the devotional impulses of the people. If one had questions about human nature, the prevalence of suffering, the nature of reality, the meaning of existence, or the relationship between humans and the cosmos, these were all dealt with within the framework of Buddhism. Even though the poetic and philosophical Taoism of Lao-tzu and Chuang-tzu dealt with many of these issues, by the T'ang/Tang (618-906) and Sung/Song (960-1279) dynasties, much of the philosophical Taoism had been absorbed into various Buddhist schools.

Confucianism was still the predominant quasi-religious framework for the cultured and educated upper classes who participated in the Confucian enterprise of ruling and were concerned with the proper relationship between ruler and ruled. Stimulated by Buddhist thought, Neo-Confucianism, a new form of Confucian rationalism, began to flower during the Sung/Song dynasty (960-1279). The Sung/Song dynasty was a dynamic period of creative interaction between the three traditions of Confucianism, Buddhism, and Taoism/Daoism. Philosophers were involved with the court, and debated with one another, offered various interpretations of teachings, and shared their searches for meaning within these three frameworks. In this chapter we will focus almost entirely on the movement called Neo-Confucianism, but we must not forget that Chan and Pure Land Buddhism were also very active, and religious Taoism/Daoism had also support from the royal family and was encouraged.

Where could the well-educated Confucian elite look for new ideas and new answers to their deepest questions? Not in traditional Confucianism which looked to the past for all answers and discouraged innovative thinking. The Confucian upper classes tended to look down on the superstitious popular religion commonly involving shamanism. In general, the interests of well-educated Chinese were not reflected in alchemical and religious Taoism, or the popular belief in buddhas and bodhisattvas as god-like beings who answered prayers, and Buddhist priests who seemed able to perform miracles before admiring crowds. But philosophical Buddhism had a great appeal to those upper class scholars who wrestled with the ultimate questions concerning human beings, nature, the meaning of existence, and the foundation of morality.

Confucians in the court did not like the respect given Buddhism as able to answer these profound spiritual questions. After all, Buddhism was a foreign system of thought, so how could it be of any value to China? The court rivalry brought about scholarly attacks beginning in the ninth century, when a few Confucian thinkers of the T'ang/Tang (618–906) dynasty such as Han Yu (768–824) and his pupil Li Ao (d. ca. 844), criticized Buddhism as unsuitable for the Chinese people, and attempted to offer Confucian solutions to the philosophical problems that had hitherto been the domain of the philosophical Taoists and Buddhists.

The problem was that philosophical Confucianism was about family, governing, and morality, but not about metaphysical questions wrestling with the nature of existence or ultimate reality. Traditional Confucian thought would need to develop a new metaphysical basis which would allow it to become competitive with philosophical Buddhism. The eleventh century Sung/Song (960–1279) dynasty philosopher Chou Tun-I/Zhou Dunyi (1017–1073) recognized that Han Yu and Li Ao had failed to produce an adequate basis to compete successfully with Buddhism, and he worked to produce a metaphysical system of Confucianism. However, his system relied too heavily on Taoist imagery and not enough on Confucius.

Ultimately Confucian scholars like Chu Hsi/Zhu Xi and Wang Yang-ming established a philosophical foundation for Neo-Confucianism, and their two systems came to dominate Chinese thought until the beginning of the twentieth century.

22.3 THE METAPHYSICS OF NEO-CONFUCIANISM

In China, early Neo-Confucianism is the **School of Li**, or the **School of Principle**, where *li* is the Chinese character meaning "principle" or "rational patterns," the underlying patterns which govern and guide the processes of change and growth.[2] *Li* is the deep structure of all that constitutes ultimate reality.[3]

The Confucian thinkers in the School of *Li* could not help but be profoundly influenced by the previous centuries of Chinese Buddhist philosophy. After six-hundred years, Buddhist rituals, meditative practices, and ideas had been important in the court and were taught in temples everywhere. To the Chinese, Buddhism in China felt as traditional as the writings of Confucius and Lao-tzu. However, most elite Confucians did not respect popular religions focused on miracles and divinities. The beliefs of the upper class Confucians tended to be less superstitious. However,

---

[2] As noted before, the Neo-Confucian concept of *li* is completely different from the Chinese character used by Confucians to mean "ritual," "propriety," or "ceremonial interaction." Neo-Confucian *li* is the fundamental principle which underlies all principles.

[3] Brook Ziporyn has investigated the complex development of *li* as "principle" in Brook Ziporyn, *Ironies of Oneness and Difference: Coherence in Early Chinese Thought; Prolegomena to the Study of Li* (New York: State University of New York Press, 2013) and the companion volume, *Beyond Oneness and Difference: Li and Coherence in Chinese Buddhist Thought and Its Antecedents* (New York: SUNY, 2014)

there were many Buddhist thinkers who minimized or paid little attention to miracles and divinities. These teachers, especially those from the Ch'an/Chan groups, had significant support from many of the well-educated literati. Then some Confucian court scholars noticed that even when Buddhism was at its most philosophical and not based in supernatural popular religion, it was still grounded in fundamental concepts like *pratityasamutpada* (dependent co-arising) and *sunyata* (emptiness) which originated in India and were not at all Chinese.

The well-educated upper classes in positions of power were primarily Confucians, certain that Chinese thinkers like Confucius and Mencius must be superior to all others, including Indian scholars. These Confucian scholars had a tendency to conclude that if neither Confucius nor Mencius had discussed concepts such as "emptiness" and "dependent co-arising," then these ideas could not be of any value to China.

As a result, some Confucians in positions of political power began to recognize how many central concepts and ideas the Chinese had accepted from non-Chinese Indian Buddhism, and began the attempt to produce a purely Chinese Confucian world-view completely free from Indian Buddhist ideas, while fully compatible with the sayings of Confucius, and Meng-tzu/Mencius and the Confucian classics. Ideally, the system should not be too dependent upon Taoist thought either.

22.4 OVERVIEW OF NEO-CONFUCIAN TEACHERS

The thinkers who are considered the founders of the Neo-Confucian School of *Li* are the Ch'eng brothers, Ch'eng Hao/Cheng Hao (1032–1085) and Ch'eng I/Cheng Yi (1033–1107). They argued that the proper basis for Confucian thought should be the concept of "pattern," "deep structure" or "principle," that is, *li*. Those philosophers who followed the Ch'eng brothers embraced this step, so the ideas of following centuries can be described as "The School of *Li*" from this point on.

Neo-Confucianism attained a high level of philosophical sophistication in the thirteenth and fourteenth centuries, during the Sung (960–1279) dynasty, the Yuan dynasty (1279–1368), and the Ming dynasty (1368–1644). One of the two most important of all the Neo-Confucian thinkers was Chu Hsi/Zhu Xi (1130–1200). Chu Hsi and his followers recognized that earlier generations of Neo-Confucians had failed in their attempts to take the traditional ceremonial and social Confucianism, and find within it a spiritual and metaphysical basis which could compete with the ideas of Buddhism and philosophical Taoism. Chu Hsi wanted to produce an ideal Confucian sage, not a Taoist sage and not a Buddhist sage.

After Chu Hsi, the second great Neo-Confucian thinker is the scholar, general, and idealist philosopher Wang Yang-ming (1472–1529). Wang Yang-ming rejected many of the key ideas of Chu Hsi, and the result was that he became the founder of the second major branch of Neo-Confucianism, the School of Mind. Wang Yang-ming's focus is on moral values, the mind, and the relationship between knowledge and action. Wang Yang-ming rejected the rigid social conformity demanded by Chu Hsi's philosophy, and instead advocated a gentle non-conformity and spontaneity. The competing Chu Hsi School of *Li* branded the School of Mind as suspiciously close to Ch'an Buddhism.

Tai Chen/Daijen (1723–1777) was the last great Neo-Confucian philosopher. He reacted against the abstract rationalism of Chu Hsi, and the idealism of Wang Yang-ming. Tai Chen feels that the error of the previous Neo-Confucians was an obsessive concern with abstract principles, *li*, instead of focusing on our everyday world. Tai Chen came to emphasize the empirical realm of things we can see, hear, touch, taste, and smell.

As in the earlier centuries, government supported Neo-Confucian thinkers continued to look to the past to find inspiration for the answers to all problems, and continued to believe that all other world civilizations were inferior to China, because every other world civilization lacked Confucian principles.[4]

Certainly, Buddhist and Taoist philosophers responded to these Neo-Confucian assertions and arguments, and there were Confucian thinkers who did not agree with Neo-Confucian dogma, but the power was in the hands of

---

[4] One might note that European cultures tended to devalue other civilizations because these others were not grounded in Christianity.

Confucians at court, and as is common with those in power, they suppressed unwelcome ideas. The established social and political order ensured that ideas that did not agree with Chu Hsi did not expand and propagate. The backward-looking Confucian attitude encouraged by politicians made China ill-prepared to deal with nineteenth century Western interest in dividing up the economic treasures of China.

The last Chinese dynasty fell in 1911, and following that collapse the younger Chinese rejected traditional Neo-Confucian education. Instead, the brightest among the elite Chinese flocked to European and American universities to study science, technology, philosophy, and political systems. Although many Chinese returned from the West with the ideals of democracy, it was the Western philosophy of Marxism which ultimately achieved a military victory over all the other systems including democracy.

22.5 THE HISTORICAL ROOTS OF NEO-CONFUCIANISM

Confucius and Mencius

Obviously, the foundation for Neo-Confucianism is the teachings of Confucius (Kung-fu tzu, Kongzi, 551–479 B.C.E.) and his most important follower, Mencius (Meng-tzu/Mengzi ca. 372–289 B.C.E.). As you recall from chapter fifteen, during the lifetime of Confucius, the school of Confucius was only one of many different systems of thought that arose during the period of social chaos. Confucianism did not come to dominate Chinese political life until the Han dynasty, nearly three hundred years after Confucius died. After the collapse of the Han, both Taoism and Buddhism came to share in political power, but the political influence of Confucianism remained strong.

The Han Dynasty (206 B.C.E. – 220 C.E.)

During the Han dynasty era the country had approximately three-hundred years of harmony and peace. The population had almost doubled in two-hundred years. The economy was improving, and wealth was increasing, although distributed inequitably. The common people were still living in indescribable poverty.

It was during this time period of the Han that Confucius was promoted as the greatest sage who ever lived, and Confucianism became official state policy. If someone wanted to begin a career in the government, which was a source of power, influence, wealth, and status, it required being born into an aristocratic family or, for a select few friends of aristocratic families, skills in scholarship. An early form of imperial civil service examinations began during the Han, but it was often wealthy aristocratic families who put their candidates forward for official positions. To pass successfully, one needed to know a range of topics including military skills as well as memorizing classics of Chinese literature (including the Confucian *Analects*, the *I Ching* or Book of Changes, and other classics). Certain aspects of religious Taoism, the *Yin-Yang* and the Five Element schools were also included in the official world-view of the Han dynasty.

Towards the end of the Han dynasty, the power of the emperor was declining, and with it the power of Confucianism weakened as well. A battle for political power began. Religious Taoist ideas began to re-enter Chinese political life, and philosophical Taoism also offered appeal as people become more open to challenges to Confucian orthodoxy.

The Later Sui (581–618) and T'ang (618–906) Dynasties

As Confucianism came to dominate the royal court, it slowly became quite conservative. As is typical whenever a religious system becomes incorporated into the government, the official religious world-view must support the political status quo. As is so often the case, when a religion becomes identified with the government, no criticism is encouraged and sometimes it is forbidden and punished. Thus, no careful analysis of strengths and weaknesses of Confucianism was encouraged by those who supported and controlled the literati in the court. Correct performance of ancient ritual was more important. Quoting from Confucius, Mencius, and other the Confucian classic books was enough to be able to win a debate. No one in politics or official education was allowed to suggest that there was any possible difficulties, weaknesses, or flaws in the Confucian classics. Later in the Sui dynasty a more rigorous set of civil service exams based on the classics of Confucius and Mencius was inaugurated, and for the first time, the examination system became potentially open to any well-educated male instead of just aristocrats.

Every student mastered the same set of uniform Confucian values which guaranteed a narrow cultural uniformity among those who successfully passed the system to gain influence and power in court. Even the 95% of those who did not pass the exams had learned the same set of philosophical values and carried these into their families and communities. Because during the Sui dynasty the system was open to talented and wealthy students who were not from aristocratic families, it became a new means to gain a position of status and wealth in the court. That examination system guaranteed that talented individuals could gain access to the court, but it also guaranteed that every scholar in a position of influence and power was first and foremost, trained to be a Confucian scholar.

Confucians were taught to memorize the classic books, because they believed that if one could study the past, one could obtain a solution to all social and political problems.[5] The Confucian stress was on loyalty and social conformity. Confucian thinkers were taught to value traditional answers from the past, and as a result creativity was discouraged during the later Sui (581–618) and T'ang (618–906) dynasties when Buddhism dominated Chinese thought. As far as Confucians were concerned, the ancient Sage-Kings of the Chou dynasty, and sages like Confucius and Meng-tzu/Mencius had figured out all that we need to know.

Official Confucianism stressed ethical and political dimensions more than supernatural and religious realms, and so Confucianism became primarily a social and political system although Confucians did stress ritual interaction and Confucians performed priest-like rituals in the courts. Even though culturally elite Confucian scholars tended to reject many aspects of popular religion, some elements of Chinese shamanistic folk-religion also came into play. The person of Confucius was elevated to the level of a spiritual king, a savior of the nation. In fact, Confucius was believed to be a miracle-worker and elevated to a super-human-being ruling a heavenly realm.

New Confucianism will grow in influence at the end of the T'ang (618–906) dynasty, and become dominant during the subsequent Sung dynasty (960–1279). The literary foundation for Neo-Confucian thought was (a) the Four Books, the *Analects* of Confucius, the *Book of Mencius*, the *Great Learning*, and the *Doctrine of the Mean*, and (b) the Five Classics.[6] These texts (especially the Four Books) provided the basic ideas which were drawn upon to provide justification for new and innovative Confucian philosophies. These books came to serve the Neo-Confucians the same way the Buddhist sutras provided the foundation for the Buddhists, and the Taoist classics provided the foundation for later Taoist thought.

Buddhism During the Sui and T'ang

Traditional Confucianism had little interest in metaphysics, the study of the nature of ultimate reality. In contrast, Buddhism dealt with the ultimate fundamental principles of reality (such as *pratityasamutpada*, causality) and from them, derived principles for living and for attaining buddhahood. The Chinese tended to equate buddhahood with the ideal sage of Confucians and Taoists. Although Confucians and Taoists still exerted great political influence, during these dynasties Buddhism was supported by the rulers, Buddhist scholars were invited to court, and Buddhism became the dominant theoretical, religious and philosophical system, becoming most influential from about 650–1200 C.E., during the Sui, T'ang and Sung dynasties. As such it was a serious challenge to Confucian court dominance, both

---

[5] As is quite often the case among Western Christians, a quote from the Christian bible is enough to settle a disagreement. Among Buddhists a quotation from a Buddhist sutra can be taken as settling the final answer. These too are an appeal to the past.

[6] The Five Classics are before the time of Confucius (although legend claims that Confucius himself edited these), and include the *I Ching* (Book of Changes), the *Shu Ching* (Classic of History), the *Shih Ching* (Classic of Poetry), the *Spring and Autumn Annals*, and the *Li Chi* (Classic of Propriety or Rites). Excerpts from the Four Books and these five are found in many anthologies, for example Robert E. Van Voorst, *Anthology of World Scriptures*, 6th ed. (Belmont, CA: Wadsworth/Cengage Learning, 2008).

intellectually and politically.

The Political Weakening of Buddhism in the T'ang Dynasty

In 755 C.E., during the T'ang (618–906), General An Lu-shan led his troops in a revolt. The ensuing series of battles plunged the empire into years of bloody war, the major battles of which occurred in the capital and its vicinity. The most important northern cities were in ruins as the emperor and his advisors fled to the south of China. The politically powerful Buddhist groups in the northern capital area were separated from their patrons who fled south. Monasteries were weakened, and many temples faded from any active role in Chinese Buddhism.

After General An Lu-shan was defeated, and the T'ang/Tang dynasty became restabilized, the governmental support of Buddhism returned and many of the surviving temples acquired additional lands, more wealth, and political influence. However, there was a negative side to all of this. The power and wealth of temples were growing beyond the control of emperor and beyond the ability of court officials to keep it in check. Buddhist groups did not pay taxes, and many wealthy landowners were able to shield their taxes claiming that Buddhist temples owned their farmlands. The emperor always needed more money and the tax base was diminishing. Also, Buddhist monks were exempt from military service, and were exempt from being impressed into labor gangs. Many monks had become indolent and had little or no interest in Buddhist spirituality. The result was a governmental loss of tax revenues and a loss of ready manpower. The imperial need for additional revenues became intense. In the court, Confucian and Taoist advisors and ministers continued their criticisms of Buddhism which they described as a foreign religion which could never be as good as the ideas of native thinkers like Confucius.

HAN YU (768–824) Criticizes Buddhism

Han Yu (768–824) and his pupil Li Ao (d. ca. 844) are the early forerunners of Neo-Confucian thought. Han Yu was one of the early important critics of Buddhism, and religious Taoism. Han Yu argued that Buddhism and Taoism should be outlawed because their philosophies would lead to social anarchy and the end of civilized harmony of the sort promoted by Confucius. Han Yu argued that Buddhists attempted to escape from family responsibilities because they lived in a monastery, whereas all Chinese knew that family and children must come first. The family structure was central to Chinese spiritual life, and the Buddhists undermined the family when children become celibate monastics. Ancestors would be abandoned if Buddhism were adopted. Also Buddhists focused upon the mind and did not put enough emphasis upon Confucian values such as *jen/ren* (human-hearted benevolence) and *li* (ceremonial interaction with fellow humans) and Buddhists rejected family lineage values when they demanded celibacy from monks and nuns. Han Yu complained to the emperor that Buddhists and Taoists were responsible for the political problems of the day.

> But now the followers of Lao-tzu and the Buddha who talk about rectification of the mind ignore this world and their native land and reduce the normal duties required by Heaven to *nothingness*. Following the ideas of Lao-tzu, a son does not have to consider his father as a father, nor does a man have to regard the king as a king. He does not even have to discharge his duties as a subject.[7]

Han-yu's reference to *nothingness* is referring to the Buddhist concept of *svabhava-sunyata* (empty of unchanging essence or substance). As will be typical of most Confucians, Han-yu misunderstands the Buddhist insight of *emptiness* (that nothing possesses an unchanging essence and all is in flowing change) and mistakenly interprets the Buddhists as claiming that all things in the world are nothing, are worthless, and are unreal.

Han-yu's solution to the political problems was to return to the past, return to the ideas of Confucius and Meng-tzu/Mencius. Han Yu says that Mencius was correct that human nature was fundamentally good, and it was possible for a human to perfect both ceremonial propriety, *li*, and human benevolence, *jen*. The court should apply

---

[7] Carsun Chang, *Development of Neo-Confucian Thought* (New Haven: College and University Press, 1963), p. 96.

jen as the cornerstone of governmental activity. Han Yu also argued that the royal court needed to reintroduce the ancient Confucian rituals which had been neglected. Han Yu asserted that neither Buddhists nor Taoists could offer any social or political guidance which could compare to that of Confucius.

Han-yu's criticisms were succinct: society and family must come first, and neither Taoism nor Buddhism puts the family and social group first. Han-yu argues that philosophical Taoists talk about being in harmony with nature but minimize the ceremonial rules of society and governing. Religious Taoists seek alchemical compounds which can provide immortality, which is a personal goal, not social. Buddhists seek to achieve the personal goal of awakening, ignoring social concerns. Buddhists talk of emptiness or nothingness (*sunyata*), while Taoists talk of the "flow of Tao." Such metaphysical speculation gets one away from the practical affairs such as running the country and keeping the family in order and ensuring that the various social relationships are put in proper hierarchical order.

According to Han-yu, Buddhism ignores the most important things in life (politics and family) and is trapped in useless metaphysical speculation about ultimate reality. Buddhist practice is unimportant; what is most important is the practical dimension of Confucian rites and rituals and etiquette (*li*). Han-yu concluded that Buddhism should be outlawed. However, although he rejected Buddhism, Han Yu was not able to offer any Confucian-based system which could compete with it when it came to explaining the nature of reality.

Li Ao (fl. 798)

Li Ao (d. ca. 844), a pupil of Han Yu, continued the attack and criticisms, although he had appreciation for the character and intelligence of some Ch'an Buddhist monks. Nevertheless, he wanted to create a Confucian philosophical system which had practical Confucian principles resting upon a comprehensive philosophical foundation which could equal that of Buddhism.[8] Li Ao asked "what was the meaning of human existence, according to Confucius?" Like the Confucians before him who stress human nature, Li Ao agrees with Mencius that our original nature is basically good. However, we humans allow our feelings to override the seed of goodness, and powerful emotions will lead to the corruption of this original nature. Only Confucian virtues can help us realize our innate goodness. The problem was that the method to control these powerful emotions that Li Ao advocates is calming the mind using cross-legged focused meditation, the same techniques used in the Buddhist Ch'an, Hua-yen and T'ien-t'ai schools. Li Ao seems not to have realized that seated meditation did not originate in Confucian China but cross-legged seated meditation (*dhyana*) had originated in India. In advocating a Ch'an/Zen meditation technique as a way of controlling feelings, Li Ao produced a hybrid of Confucianism and Buddhism.

The Buddhist Persecution of 845 C.E.

As a result of political, social and economic pressures, and the criticisms of Confucians like Han Yu, the Taoist Emperor Wu-tsang mounted a massive anti-Buddhist persecution in 845 C.E. Thousands of Buddhist temples (especially those close to the capital cities in the north of China) were destroyed, and the government took over the lands belonging to temples, and re-distributed the land to small farmers (so the land rejoined the tax base). Government regulations forbade monks and nuns from wearing their Buddhist robes, and they were forced to return to the life of a householder or lay person. It became illegal for monks or nuns to shave their head (Buddhist monks and nuns were the only Chinese with shaven heads); they were required to let their hair grow long again. The government confiscated Buddhist statues the metal of which was then melted down for coins, or used for military purposes like weapons.

Emperor Wu died after a year, and his successor lifted the harsh anti-Buddhist penalties. However, the persecution had seriously affected the scholarly branches located in the major northern capital cities. The monasteries did not get their land back, and no longer had the economic resources or the popularity they had prior to 845. The

---

[8] Carsun Chang, *ibid.*, p. 36.

CHAPTER 22: NEO-CONFUCIANISM

Buddhist sects that survived tended to place less emphasis on ornate rituals and to be less concerned with abstract philosophy, and tended to be more relevant to the lives of ordinary Chinese. Following the persecution of 845, only two Buddhist groups grew stronger: the Pure Land sect, and the Ch'an monasteries in the south and east.

Not all the Confucians in the court accepted that all the truth lay in the past, in the writings of the Confucian classics. Two loyal literati came to the conclusion that the classics were not perfect. Scholar Liu Tsung-yuan (773–819) and fellow scholar Liu Yu-hsi were exiled by the court. This exile forced Liu Tsung-yuan to rethink his life, and as a consequence he wrote to Liu Yu-hsi when they departed for their exiles,

> Faith in the Writings is self-deception,
> Slowly, through experience, you know they are wrong.

This heretical conclusion implies that the Way had to be discovered by the individual, and not found in writings of the past, no matter how much they were revered, and no matter how dangerous it was to express any doubts. This also opened the possibility that the path of the sage might not be restricted to Confucian models, but could possibly include Buddhism.[9] Indeed, many Chinese Buddhist ideas and techniques made their way into what would become Neo-Confucianism.

During this time of cultural stress, the Confucians in court drew upon an ethnocentric attitude common in China. Of all the countries that China had encountered, only India seemed to have a culture that rivaled its own in sophistication and achievement. However, Indian thinkers did not value *jen* and *li*, and did not know the wide variety of Chinese ritual courtesies, and so the Chinese concluded that India was inferior to China, and that the Chinese were the most civilized and highly developed nation on earth, and that any religion not originating in China was foreign, therefore inferior. Because Buddhism was not Chinese, it could not really be of any use or value to the Chinese people. For members of the T'ang Confucian court, Buddhism still carried the stigma of being a foreign religion, even though at this point it had been in China for 800 years. With the weakening of Buddhist influence, the Confucians argued that the royal court must revert to a purely Chinese system of thought.

The ability of T'ang dynasty rulers to control the country had been weakened, and their rule did not last much longer. Military strongmen had gained economic sources of income, and they became more assertive and demanding of additional favors. The emperor in the palace was in conflict with the eunuchs who protected the royal wives and concubines, and their power increased as the power of the emperor decreased. The old aristocratic families saw opportunity as the royal court was weakened, and they sought out additional sources of revenue and political influence. New rebellions were launched by warlords, and peasants rebelled against the landlords, killing the aristocratic families, and rebelled against the harsh taxation imposed by tax collectors and government representatives. In 907 the T'ang dynasty collapsed and China was broken into separate warring states until 960 when the Sung dynasty began.

22.6 NEO-CONFUCIANISM BEGINS IN THE SUNG DYNASTY

In 960 a new Sung/Song dynasty began, unifying China once again, and establishing a new court with a new civil bureaucracy. Talented individuals were recruited, and these educated gentlemen were experts in classical history and literature, but especially were experts in Confucius and Mencius. There were other advisers among the educated elite who were Taoists and Buddhists.

The Confucians were annoyed when Buddhist priests began to accept important roles in the governing of the nation, for they considered the role of advising the ruler to be exclusively for Confucian scholars and Confucian ministers. Many Confucians criticized Buddhism, trying to convince the emperor that because of its foreign origins, it should be outlawed. The difficulty was that Chinese forms of Buddhism flourished in the previous T'ang, and had become a powerful force in philosophy, religion and art.

---

[9] John Jorgensen, *Inventing Hui-neng, the Sixth Patrarch* (Brill, 2005), p. 432.

CHAPTER 22: NEO-CONFUCIANISM

During the Sung (960–1279) dynasty, although Buddhist art flourished and there were many individual brilliant Buddhist masters, the intellectual vitality of Buddhist philosophy was slowly beginning to decline. Buddhists in positions of political power receiving economic patronage were putting more stress on tradition, on quoting from the past, and stressed rituals more than ideas. Buddhism had become more popular and more devotional and Buddhist thinkers had a tendency to become locked into a hierarchy of monastic and political authority that no longer valued original thought or deep personal realization.

Philosophical Taoism of Lao-tzu and Chuang-tzu had faded into an enduring literary tradition, although many of the ideas were still alive within Buddhist thinkers, especially the Ch'an tradition. Religious Taoism was part of the folk traditions of Chinese religion, regarded as mere superstition by most Chinese intellectuals. As a result, by the fourteenth and fifteenth centuries, political Buddhist ministers were replaced by Neo-Confucian ministers whose ideas then dominated Chinese intellectual life until the beginning of the twentieth century.

To achieve a position of undisputed authority, Neo-Confucianism needed a robust philosophical system to replace Buddhism and Taoism. In order to do this, Neo-Confucianism tried to fulfill a number of needs previously met by Buddhism and Taoism. New Confucian thought needed to be intellectually and spiritually stimulating in the same way Buddhism had been. It needed to deal with metaphysical questions about the ultimate nature of reality. Neo-Confucianism was grounded in the firm morality of Confucianism so its ethical foundation was secure.

The Buddhists and the Taoists had stressed individual spiritual awakening over conformity to the group. Neo-Confucianism needed to give meaning to the individual and at the same time provide a framework for relating the individual to the community, to the state and ruler, and to the world at large. Neo-Confucianism needed an ideology which supported the mutual relationship between the individual and the group, and the group and the state. Spiritual and religious experience must also be described and encouraged, but only within a Confucian framework.

Neo-Confucians promoted the idea that the country was in trouble because the performance of very ancient rituals had been neglected. In fact, the Neo-Confucians placed a nearly obsessive stress on Confucian rituals (as did Confucius himself). Ideally, each aspect of the Neo-Confucian philosophical and religious system would interact with every other aspect, in a resonant system of interdependence.

The Creation of a Confucian Philosophical System to Rival that of Buddhism

The beginnings of the Neo-Confucian approach is found at this point in Chinese history. The Confucians recognized the sophistication and complexity of the Buddhist analysis of the world, and sought to create a purely Confucian metaphysical explanation of the universe which could rival the Buddhist analysis in its completeness and its satisfactoriness. Confucians stressed ancient Confucian rituals instead of popular Buddhist rituals, and wanted a system to rival Buddhist religious concerns with the individual, and a system which could provide the intellectual stimulation typical of Buddhist philosophy, but based on Confucius and Mencius.

Confucian scholars needed to find an explanation of the ultimate nature of reality, and the meaning of existence in the world, but an explanation purged of "foreign" Indian Buddhist elements. The problem was that Buddhism had been in China so long that the scholars were really unable to tell which ideas were purely Chinese and which were "foreign." Thus it was that the earliest attempts to return to the teachings of Confucius (Neo-Confucianism) were in fact a synthesis of Confucianism, Taoism, and Buddhism. It was not until after 1500 that the Chinese succeeded in really separating Buddhist-Chinese ideas from purely Chinese concepts.

22.7 CHOU TUN-I / ZHOU DUNYI (1017–1073)

Although not considered a Neo-Confucian, the Sung dynasty philosopher Chou Tun-I/Zhou Dunyi

(1017–1073)[10] would shape the direction that Neo-Confucian thought would take for the next several centuries. He recognized that his Confucian predecessors, Han Yu and Li Ao, had failed to produce a metaphysical system of Confucianism which could compete with the sophisticated philosophy of Buddhism. Chou Tun-I (also known as Chou Lian-tzu/ Zhou Lianzi) was knowledgeable about Taoism and Buddhism, and was able to recognize the weaknesses of his predecessors and worked to construct a more coherent and systematic Confucian philosophy. He was especially concerned with the classic *Book of Changes* (*I Ching*) and tried to incorporate the sixty-four hexagrams into his thought. However, he did not succeed in creating a purely Confucian system.

Chou Tun-I Responds to Taoist Metaphysics

The philosophical Taoists, quoting from poem 40 of the *Tao Te Ching* (*Daodejing*), explained that the ground of being or existence issued from original non-being (*wu*) which was the origin of all that exists ("being").

All things originate from being.
Being originates from non-being.[11]

That original non-being is what the Taoists called the Tao, the infinite indefinable possibility, deeper than the dependent concepts of 'being' and 'non-being.' For Lao-tzu, the original non-being gives rise to the ultimate duality of *yin* and *yang*. These two interact and produce everything else.

Chou Tun-I had a simple argument against this. He argued that no rational human being could think that it was possible to get something from nothing. Not even a god could get something from nothing. If it is impossible to get something from nothing, then there must be some pre-existing source. If Tao is truly non-being, then Tao could not be the source of all things. The ultimate source and origin could not be non-being, but must itself be some thing which is ultimately real. Chou Tun-i called that ultimate source of reality **T'ai-chi/Taiji** (Great Ultimate).

This new idea of T'ai-chi presented a problem, however. Neither Confucius nor Mencius had any concern with the source of all things, or with the concept of a "Great Ultimate." Chou Tun-i ignores the fact that the two most important Confucians never heard of a T'ai-chi, and were both uninterested in a "Great Ultimate."

How does the Great Ultimate give rise to all of reality? Chou Tun-i's answer is that T'ai-chi/Taiji is so filled with creative energy that it moves, and with that movement *yang* (the active male cosmic force) is created. When activity reaches its limit, it becomes tranquil, and through its tranquility *yin* is created. When passivity reaches its limit, it reverses and returns once again to activity, and through their alternation and interaction, the (quasi-sexual) interaction of *yin* and *yang* create the Five Agencies (material principles, elements) of water, fire, wood, metal, and earth. The interaction of these five produce all the "ten-thousand things": this process operates according to an abstract principle (*li*). Anyone who has read Lao-tzu's *Tao Te Ching* would recognize this as essentially a mirror-image of the Taoist world view of reversal, replacing Tao with T'ai-chi, the Great Ultimate. However, there is a major difference between Chou Tun-I and the ideas of the *Tao Te Ching*. According to Lao-tzu, ultimate reality (the Tao) has no special affection for humans. According to the Confucian Chou Tun-i, T'ai-chi/Taiji has a special affection for human beings, and the Great Ultimate gives humans the special gift of *jen/ren* (benevolence) for we humans are the highest manifestation of the union of these five forces. Neither Confucius nor Mencius or any of the other early Confucian thinkers discussed reality in this manner.

The Chinese were certain that human beings are the most intelligent species and Chou Tun-yi asserts that humans and humans alone have received the gifts of superior intelligence and moral principles from the Great Ultimate, T'ai-chi. In addition human beings have *jen* bequeathed them by the Great Ultimate. Confucius had argued that *jen* is the basic element of human nature and we are all born with it. By developing one's innate *jen*, one develops

---

[10] "Chou" and "Zhou" are pronounced "joe" and so his name is "Joe Dun E."

[11] Han-shan, *Lao-tzu Tao te ching Han-shan chieh* ("Han-shan's Explanation of the *Tao Te Ching*) (Taipei, Taiwan: Shin Wen Hua Yin Shu Kuan, 1973), ch. 40, p. 101.

her or his true humanity, but Chou Tun-I adds that one is also perfecting the gift from the Great Ultimate, and the result is a harmony between humans, Heaven and Earth. If one follows Chou Tun-I, humans form a harmony with the universe, which is the goal of Confucianism.

Confucius said that moral principles are grounded in *jen*, or human benevolence and kindness, and from *jen*, ceremonial propriety (*li*), righteousness (*i*), wisdom, and loyalty emerge. In this process, to become a Confucian sage in an innately moral universe, one must be true to these moral principles. Mencius had argued that human nature is the source of morality, that we are born good. Chou Tun-I agrees but adds, "The reason [that] a person must act in accord with the fundamental moral principles is that these constitute one's fundamental nature as produced by the Great Ultimate."[12]

In this way the moral principles of Confucianism are put on a metaphysical foundation by Chou Tun-I. The foundation of reality is also the foundation of ethics. The principle of sagehood is the same principle as the Supreme Ultimate. To be a superior moral human being is the result of understanding the nature of ultimate reality, T'ai-chi/Taiji.

Although this was not a purely Confucian system, it provided the framework for the two thinkers who followed, the Ch'eng brothers. The actual establishment of a Neo-Confucian school of *li* can be said to have begun with the two Ch'eng brothers.

22.8 THE CH'ENG BROTHERS: THE NEO-CONFUCIAN SCHOOL BEGINS
Ch'eng Hao/Cheng Hao (1032–1085) and Ch'eng I/Cheng Yi (1033–1107)

The Ch'eng brothers accept Chou Tun-I's metaphysical explanation of how human nature is related to the universe but found it too Taoist. The Ch'eng brothers wanted a principle which connects all the elements of the universe and which is common to all that exists, whether human beings or Nature.[13] The Ch'eng brothers based their ideas on the same idea that Chou Tun-I had used, the pattern of all patterns, *li*. *Li* was the idea of a "principle" or "the pattern or rational principle which all things must follow."[14] The ideas of the Ch'eng brothers provided the foundation for the two later developments of Neo-Confucian thought, the realistic Neo-Confucian school also called the **School of Li**, or the **School of Principle**, and the idealistic **School of Mind**.

The Principle of *Li*

The Chinese philosophical concept of "principle" or *li* was originally utilized eight-hundred years earlier by the "Dark Learning" Taoist philosopher Wang Pi/Wang Bi (226–249 C.E.) who wrote a key commentary on the *Lao-tzu*. Next, the philosophical Taoist concept of *li* was expanded and further developed by Chinese Hua-yen Buddhist philosophers four centuries later, where *li* was used to mean the abstract realm of universals or principles, including things like shape, form, and even the principles which constitute the laws of nature.[15] *Li* is also synonymous with

[12] John Koller, *Oriental Philosophies*, 2nd edition, p. 310

[13] The two brothers did not agree on everything. Cheng Yi, the younger brother, is thought of as the inspiration for the "realistic" School of *Li* later developed by Chu Hsi (1130–1200). Cheng Hao, the older brother, is an inspiration for the "idealistic" School of Mind, later developed by Wang Yang-ming (1473–1529).

[14] As has been pointed out previously, do not confuse the Chinese character meaning "deep structure" or "pattern" (pronounced *li*) with the completely different Chinese character used by Confucius to mean "ritual," "propriety," or "ceremonial interaction" (*li*).

[15] An excellent exploration of this can be found in Brook Ziporyn, *Ironies of Oneness and Difference: Coherence in Early Chinese Thought; Prolegomena to the Study of Li* (State University of New York, 2013) and the companion volume, *Beyond Oneness and Difference: Li and Coherence in Chinese Buddhist Thought and Its Antecedents* (SUNY, 2014)

highest truth or ultimate reality. There is no plural to Chinese characters, so *li* could be "principle" or "principles."

Li implies numerous underlying structures or principles which work together and interconnect to form the pattern we call reality. These principles include the laws of physics and other laws of nature, but also include the principles which guide human moral conduct. For the Chinese, human social and moral rules and the law of gravity are equally natural, equally guided by *li*. Humans bowing to one another, or humans wearing white at a funeral, are as natural as mountains thrusting upwards and rivers flowing downwards.[16] Each of these can be comprehended by intellectual study. This order or pattern of things is not entirely independent of human beings; humans have an indispensable role in ordering Nature and in regulating themselves. "In differentiating things, man made a difference in the universe. Ordering things, he fulfilled the cosmic order."[17]

Expanding on the Hua-yen Buddhist and the Taoist concepts, the Neo-Confucians tended to use the term *li* in several related ways; most often it tended to mean **"a deep pattern or unifying rational principle describing patterns which things follow."** Like the many laws of nature, there are several specific *li* which govern the myriad phenomena. Yet each of these specific *li* can be reduced to one universal *li* (principle). For example, if we understand the nature of gold, we then understand the underlying reality of a lion statue made of gold, we understand the underlying reality of the earrings made of gold, we understand the jewelry container made of gold. We understand the unifying nature of all of these particularities.

The Ch'eng brothers take *li* or *principle* as the foundation for their system of thought. According to the Ch'eng brothers, the ultimate patterns called *li* are not independent of human beings. *Li* are **rational** principles and patterns. Being rational, they cannot be separated from rational minds, so it must follow that the specific *li* can be found self-contained within our own rational mind. The same principles which underlie the natural order of heaven provide the orderly life for all things "under heaven." This includes human beings. If this is true, then by examining our own inner nature, we can reach a state of realization of the ultimate *li*. To understand the ultimate ordering principle, *li*, is to understand how reality operates. When a human being finds an understanding of *li* within himself, or herself, she has understood the unifying principle (connection) between human beings and Nature. Thus, when you understand *li* you understand your own place in the scheme of things.

METAPHYSICS: The Physical World is Made of *Ch'i/Qi*

What is the ultimate nature of the physical world and physical human beings? Like many of the Confucians before them, the Ch'eng brothers were anti-Buddhist and were trying to purge Buddhist elements from their philosophy. They believed that the Buddhists claimed that the world was unreal, was empty, was nothing. The Ch'eng brothers argue that the Buddhists are mistaken, because what we call reality is made of two things:

(1) unformed physical stuff (*ch'i* in Wade-Giles, *qi* in Pinyin, pronounced something like "chee"), the material forces which make up the real world and the physical nature of humans;[18]
(2) some real and underlying rational principle which imposes pattern and order onto the chaos of raw

---

[16] Because of this, the Confucians thought that their own Confucian rules of politeness were not cultural or conventional, but were universal because they were built into nature. Consequently Confucians in the court felt that any civilization that did not use Confucian rituals must mean that they weren't intelligent or sophisticated enough to figure these out, and so that group must be barbaric and inferior to China. The assumption that Europeans were stupid, barbaric, and inferior turned out to be a major mistake when it came to dealing with Western military power and Western civilization.

[17] de Bary, *Unfolding of Neo-Confucianism, op. cit.*, p. 11.

[18] The uncle of the Ch'eng brothers was Chang Tsai/Zhang Zai (1020-1077) and he emphasized *ch'i/qi* as an explanation for the physical world. When *ch'i* is under the influence of *yang*, it floats and rises upward producing air, clouds, and the empty sky. When *ch'i* is under the influence of *yin*, it condenses and falls, which results in the concrete solid things in our world.

physical stuff.

This distinction that stresses the reality of the world is intended to counteract the Buddhist idea of emptiness.[19] Confucians in the court were scholars who had devoted their lives to the study of and memorization of Confucian classic texts, and most had little concern with Chinese Buddhist ideas. If ideas were not Confucian, they must be of little value. This was especially true when it came to the Buddhist idea of *svabhava-sunyata* (empty of self-existent essence or substance), translated into Chinese as *k'ung/kong* (empty). Confucians saw the character *k'ung/kong* and mistakenly thought that the Buddhists asserted that things are not real.

Confucians believed that morality was grounded in human nature and grounded in the real world. Of course, if things in nature are not real, then this would remove the Confucian basis of morality. Because of this complete misunderstanding, Neo-Confucians would stress the reality of the world and the reality of moral rules, mistakenly claiming Buddhists would deny their reality.[20]

For the Ch'eng brothers, reality starts out as chaotic formless matter, or *ch'i/qi* (a physical vital force that constitutes the substance of physical reality).[21] *Ch'i* is active, and can be thought of as a form of material energy which occupies empty space and can condense or coagulate to produce rocks and mountains, trees and gods, human bodies and the forms of spirits and ghosts. The physical aspect of things is truly real and fundamentally basic—this is what will become essential to the Neo-Confucianism of the Ch'eng brothers.

Principle (*li*) plus Function produces all that Exists

Reality starts out as formless chaotic energetic matter, *ch'i*, and then the deep underlying principle of order, *li*, forms it and organizes it. So, if the same universal principle imposes order upon and forms *ch'i*, why doesn't everything physical all look the same? The answer is that the original principle (*li*) is affected by use or **function**. The unifying perfect principle (*li*) is affected by specific function, and principle plus function acting upon matter (*ch'i*) is the Neo-Confucian explanation for all the different things in the world.[22]

All things have their own individual unique *li* (pattern) but all of these different *li* have a deeper more fundamental underlying nature which renders them essentially one. Gold is one universal element, but gold can function in many ways. There is a commonality to gold coins, gold dishes and cups, gold earrings, a golden needle, a gold ring, gold bracelets, and a statue of a lion made of gold. Their functions are different.

To understand the general pattern or shape of a particular human being leads one to an understanding that all human beings share that common pattern. Thus the *li* of one thing is essentially the same as that of all things. *Li* is one, but its variety of functions means that it manifests itself as many. *Li* in humans can become manifest as hands, as feet, as eyes, as bone, as muscle, as sinew. Their functions all differ, but their essence is the same.[23]

---

[19] When Confucians and Neo-Confucians heard the Chinese word, *k'ung*, used to translate "empty" from the Sanskrit *sunyata*, they interpreted it as "unreal." As we saw before, this is a misunderstanding because for Buddhists things which are empty are real, but real things are *empty* of an unchanging eternal self-existent nature.

[20] Of course, philosophical Buddhism asserts the absence of enduring substances, or emptiness of unchanging essences, but for the Buddhists things are real — real flowing processes.

[21] Note that *ch'i* is not created by a deity; not even a deity can make something come from nothing. Thus *ch'i* has always existed.

[22] The student might find it valuable to compare and contrast the Ch'eng brothers' ideas of *ch'i/qi* and *li*, and those of the Indian Samkhya idea of three basic forces which constitute physical reality, *prakriti*, which then are upset and evolve by the nearness of a non-physical principle, *purusha*.

[23] Is there some similarity with the modern biological idea of stem cells which can develop into the various functions of the physical body?

CHAPTER 22: NEO-CONFUCIANISM

Moral Principles Are Not Absolute

There is more to *li* than just the patterns and principles of physical processes, and laws of nature. What about moral principles? The Ch'eng brothers explain that the *li* are also the foundation for all moral laws; both universal and particular. In the same way there is a unifying principle to all reality, there must be some unifying moral principle which unifies human society and human relations. However, although the unifying moral principles are identical, they do depend upon circumstances or function, and so moral behavior is not identical for everyone.[24] We have what a thing is (a human), and then we have what the thing does, the function (a warrior, a teacher, a mother, a child, a tax collector, a ruler). Specific behavior will depend upon the function, so moral behavior is adapted to individual circumstances.[25] The function of a mother and child relationship is quite different from the circumstances of the function of an executioner and a condemned prisoner.

Li Are Part of Nature

Li do not have a supernatural origin. This ultimate principle is not imposed externally upon matter by a god, by divinities or by any other source; rather *li* is the natural or spontaneous tendency of every thing in the universe. We humans are a part of the universe, not separate from these principles and patterns. The image behind *li* is a universe which is like a plant; the source is organic, it is natural. We see the natural tendency of a tree to grow upwards, of a child to crawl and then walk.

Since every thing possesses *li* as a spontaneous tendency, one may understand *li* by investigating individual things. This can include reading books, studying history, examining oneself, or even examining a blade of grass, seeing that it is both universal and unique. Yes, it is a unique one-of-a-kind blade of grass, but the same blade of grass shares the universal called greenness, and it shares the universal of being a plant which it shares with all other plants.

If we want to understand the more important idea of *li*, we must not be distracted by specific individual features, for these are the product of use or function acting upon principle, acting on *li*. We must be able to think abstractly, to focus on and conceptually extract the universal principle which is common to all things. We need to train ourselves to look past the differing functions of golden objects, and see the gold which is common to them all.

Theories of Spiritual Cultivation.

The Ch'eng brothers draw upon the key Confucian virtue of *jen/ren* (benevolence, humanity) to explicate the relationship of human beings to the universe as a totality. The Chinese assumption was that human beings are a natural part of the universe and not separate from non-human things; all are composed of *ch'i*. The original state of human beings is union with the universe. This unity becomes lost through the assertion of the individual ego. The goal of spiritual cultivation is to destroy the artificial barriers created by the ego, and return to an original state of unity. With the ego lessened, altruism emerges naturally.

> The man of *ren* takes Heaven and Earth as being one with himself. To him nothing is not himself. Having recognized them as himself, what cannot he do for them?[26]

---

[24] A valuable philosophical treatment of the Ch'eng brothers which analyzes Ch'eng responses to Western ethical problems is Yong Huang, *Why Be Moral? Learning from the Neo-Confucian Cheng Brothers* (New York: SUNY Press, 2014).

[25] Students familiar with Plato's theory of Forms (*eidos*) and the Form of the Good may feel a sense of familiarity with *li*. Those who know Thomas Aquinas's distinction of the eternal law, the plan in the mind of God, will also see similarities. However, gods play no role in the Chinese understanding of the origin of *li*. Gods are as much a product of *li* as plants and mountains, and in this sense belong to the natural world.

[26] Cheng Hao quoted in Laurence C. Wu, *Fundamentals of Chinese Philosophy* (New York: University Press of America, 1986), p. 240.

To cultivate *jen/ren* (human hearted benevolence) is to establish a connection between the human realm and the same underlying reality and foundation of all the universe. In their essence, human beings are a part of the universe and not ultimately different from it. Our humanity, our *jen*, is the natural expression of the ultimate principle, ultimate *li*. We contain within ourselves the same universal principle which structures all reality.

Jen/ren (benevolence) is the foundation virtue, the principle which can be applied to all human beings. *Jen* is a universal principle which is the essence of humans, in much the same way *li* is the universal principle which is the essence of reality. Because *jen* is essentially within the human sphere, it is analogous to *li* (principle) which is the essence of the universe. *Li* gives organization and structure to external reality, as *jen* structures the moral life of a human. The particular moral situation is "Do not kill John Clayton," but the more universal principle which underlies the first is "Do not kill."

The student of Confucianism must first comprehend *jen*, for the man of *jen* is one with the essential principle of all things. Ceremonial interaction or propriety, righteousness (*yi*), wisdom, and faithful loyalty are all manifestations of *jen*. Recognizing this, and cultivating it with sincerity and earnestness is all that a human being needs to do. This is not just knowledge obtained by reading books; to cultivate our humanity a person must actually experience *jen* as his or her deepest nature. Although we are born pure, tranquil, and fundamentally good, we have accumulated many bad habits over the years. It is only because the bad habits of the past are not removed that one must cultivate one's own mind.

The School of *Li* can be said to have begun with the younger brother, Ch'eng I more than with his brother, Ch'eng Hao. But there was still a question which neither of the Ch'eng brothers could adequately explain. Why do innately good beings develop such bad habits that can turn us into evil human beings? These ideas and problems set the background for the greatest of all the Neo-Confucian thinkers, Chu Hsi/Zhu Xi.

In the early centuries, the ideas of the Ch'eng brothers were criticized by other Confucian thinkers. It was only later that their ideas become accepted as a rigid orthodoxy immune to criticism.

22.9 CHU HSI/ZHU XI (1130–1200)

Chu Hsi/Zhu Xi [pronounced "Jew-shi"], who lived during the Southern Sung era (1127-1279), is one of the two most important of all the Neo-Confucian thinkers. Chu Hsi (1130-1200) accepted a rational basis for the ultimate principles (hence he was a rationalist) and he drew upon and synthesized almost all the elements of previous thinkers into a single coherent philosophy. Chu Hsi is second only to the two founders, Confucius and Mencius, in terms of his importance to Chinese Confucianism. Chu Hsi's School of *Li* (*Li hsueh*) dominated China from 1313 on. His Neo-Confucian philosophical system was incorporated into the civil service examination system and it remained the official orthodox interpretation of Confucianism until the early 1900s.

A contemporary of Chu Hsi was the Confucian thinker Lu Chiu-yuan (1139-1193) who disagreed with Chu Hsi. Lu Chiu-yuan stressed the mind and awareness, not matter, as fundamental to reality. Lu's philosophy was called the "School of Mind" (*Hsin hsueh*) in contrast with Chu Hsi's "School of *Li*" (*Li hsueh*).

Initially Chu Hsi was attracted to Buddhist thought and there are Buddhist allusions in his writings, and Buddhist practices in his life. However, perhaps from reading the works of the Ch'eng brothers, his interest shifted to Confucianism. Chu Hsi's writings gave a new direction and a deeper philosophical foundation to Neo-Confucian thought. Chu Hsi seems to have thought that the lengthy tradition of Confucian scholars and their commentaries on the ancient classical texts of Confucius and Mencius, have obscured the original meaning of these great sages of antiquity. He urged scholars to return to the original texts, and not to focus so much on a thousand years of commentary texts.

CHAPTER 22: NEO-CONFUCIANISM

There Are Many Different *Li*

Chu Hsi accepts the idea that the physical material force *ch'i/qi* coagulates and condenses to form physical objects in the world. But if everything in our world is made out of the very same basic stuff, why are stones so different from humans, and why are humans so different from trees?[27] Chu Hsi's conclusion is that different things have different principles of organization, different *li*. There is a *li* principle of organization for humans, and a different *li* for trees, and when *ch'i* condenses under the influence or pattern of the human *li*, then we get a human. When *ch'i* condenses under the influence of the tree *li* or the rock *li*, then we get trees or rocks.

The *li* function like a blueprint which structures and organizes the physical matter into different forms. Depending upon the blueprint, lumber can become a home, a boat, a cabinet or bookcase, a temple, or a palace.[28] The blueprints (*li*) are eternal and will continue to exist even if every human, tree, boat, or palace all disappear. To investigate the nature of reality is to investigate the various *li* which organize and give individual shape and direction to all things. This abstract process of study can lead to discoveries and inventions, but the *li* or patterns of these discoveries and inventions existed before the inventor. The abstract form or *li* of a digital computer has always existed even though it was not realized until recently. Humans do not create out of nothing; rather they discover these *li* and apply them.

The Importance of Education in the Thought of Chu Hsi

Chu Hsi seems to have felt that the previous Neo-Confucian thinkers had received gifts, status and patronage from the rulers and court ministers, and this led to problems. People with status and power often try to institute top-down changes to produce an ideal world, but Chu Hsi felt that these people were too idealistic, too doctrinaire, and lacked the practical experience required to make changes in the world.

Instead, Chu Hsi came up with a new vision of human fulfillment within a Confucian paradigm, grounded in **education**. Ideally a Neo-Confucian should not focus only on public service; he should have a life-long pursuit of scholarship and book learning as well as an extensive knowledge of art, of calligraphy, of lyric poetry and the ability to appreciate these. These produce a contemplative spirit and moral cultivation, the result of a quality education.

For Chu Hsi and the Neo-Confucians that expanded vision of human fulfillment was achievable only through an ordered pattern of education and growth — regulating in almost fanatical detail every aspect of one's personal and social life — food, dress, living arrangements, daily routine, family and community life, and so on. Though usually justified by some scriptural reference, these minute prescriptions derived from no prevailing convention or established norm.[29]

To produce a noble person, a student needed rigid social and family rules to control his personal life, supported by a structured education with graded difficulties of texts intended to produce social and moral discipline, both prerequisites for growth and maturation as a superior person. Respect for knowledge and a thirst for education was essential if one were to make progress in politics and personally. As one's advanced philosophical training develops, ideally the way of the sages becomes clear and meaningful, and within reach. It might even include an epiphany or illumination experience. Chu Hsi helped compile an anthology of quotations from the sages of the past intended to

---

[27] This is similar to the question that arises when we assert that everything in the universe is made out of the same elements described in the chemical table of elements. How is it that oxygen, carbon, hydrogen, nitrogen, potassium, iron, and sodium etc. can combine to produce a a dog, a cat or a sentient human being? Contemporary neurobiologists have answered this question with DNA. Of course, Chu Hsi is arguing that there is something like DNA for rocks and iron, not just living things.

[28] In this sense Chu Hsi's system of philosophy resembles the Forms (*eidos*) of the Greek philosopher Plato.

[29] Wm. Theodore deBary, *The Unfolding of Neo-Confucianism, op. cit.*, p. 8.

advance self-cultivation. That text is entitled *Reflections on Things at Hand*[30] and was intended to help those at the lower levels of their education.[31]

Chu Hsi Advocates "Quiet Sitting"

It is interesting to note that in his personal life, Chu Hsi described himself as devoting "half the day to book-learning and half to quiet-sitting."[32] The "quiet sitting" of Chu Hsi seems not to be different from Indian Buddhist focused meditation, or *dhyana*. There is no evidence of any early Confucian practicing seated meditation. The practice of cross-legged quiet sitting did not appear in China until after Indian Buddhism came to China.[33] By the time of Chu Hsi, meditation had been in China for a thousand years, and its non-Chinese non-traditional roots were not recognized or were not considered a problem. The daily practice of quiet meditation became an official part of the Chu Hsi orthodoxy. Chu Hsi saw meditation as a means of moral training and a manifestation of moral seriousness.

The extent to which this practice became established in 'orthodox' Ch'eng–Chu schools whenever Neo-Confucianism spread in China, Japan, and Korea is only one indication of its pervasive influence and decisive character. Few important thinkers of the early Ming [1368–1644] were untouched by it.[34]

The goal for the Neo-Confucian remains sagehood, and we see that a classic image of a Neo-Confucian sage is someone exercising mind-control and sitting in the posture of cross-legged meditation.

Quiet sitting is a spiritual exercise in self-discipline and the epitome of self-cultivation, but in a sense it shifts the balance between public service and intellectual cultivation into a new direction: quiet sitting is centered on the self, not centered on society or the group. Unlike ritual and ceremonial interaction, quiet sitting is done in isolation and not in interaction with others. Thus, although Chu Hsi puts great stress on public education, the state of mental equanimity produced by quiet sitting was shifting the focus in Neo-Confucianism away from society and politics onto one's own mind.

Chu Hsi On the Problem of Good and Evil

The Chinese Buddhists had argued that all things (including human nature) are empty of an unchanging inner essence, and so nothing was inherently good or inherently evil. Morality was what lessened suffering, which meant that much of it was traditional and conventional, not eternally or absolutely correct. If the Buddhists were right, that made the traditional norms of Confucianism relative, not absolute as the Confucians had argued. Chu Hsi needed to provide a basis for reaffirming the absolute moral values of his Confucian ancestors. He also inherited a related problem from Confucius and Mencius.

If morality is grounded in human nature, and we are born good, the problem Chu Hsi needs to explain is

---

[30] See Daniel K. Gardner, *Learning to Be a Sage: Selections from the "Conversations of Master Chu, Arranged Topically" by Chu Hsi* (Berkeley, CA: University of California Press, 1990).

[31] Along with the basic Four Books (Confucian *Analects*, the *Meng-tzu*, the *Great Learning*, the *Doctrine of the Mean*), Chu Hsi's added *The Lower Education, Reflections on Things at Hand*, and *Outline and Digest of the General Mirror for Aid in Government* (a scholarly general history). These were the basic texts of the curriculum of the later Chu Hsi educational system.

[32] de Bary, *Unfolding of Neo-Confucianism, op. cit.*, p. 14.

[33] Some have claimed that the philosophical Taoists may have practiced some sort of focused concentration, based on very vague statements in the *Tao Te Ching* and *Chuang-tzu*. Later Taoist traditions used meditation, but the earliest clear statements are after the arrival of Indian Buddhism into China.

[34] deBary, *op. cit.*, p. 17.

why so many humans do so many evil things. This is the problem of the origin of evil. The Neo-Confucians assert that all humans are born with a human nature in common. This is the human *li*. If humans are born fundamentally good, as Mencius asserted, why do some people grow into good humans, or even sages, and others turn into perpetrators of monstrous evil deeds? Why do some control their passions, and others experience passions which lead them to evil choices?[35] Almost fifteen hundred years earlier, Mencius had attempted to explain it as deficiencies in family upbringing and culture which teach us bad habits. Chu Hsi provides a different explanation drawing upon the Supreme Ultimate and how it is interrelated with human beings.

After much consideration, Chu Hsi concludes that the problem is not with the *li* of human nature. The *li* of human nature is the ideal pattern, it is the way a human being ought to be, it is good. *Li* is moral value, and it is truth. So the problem cannot lie with the ultimate principle, ultimate *li*. *Li* which is *jen/ren* (benevolent) is always complete. The organizing principles of human nature are always complete, but it must be some other thing which obscures, distorts or clouds our original nature.

A century earlier the Ch'eng brothers had argued that humans are made of two things: a universal human nature (abstract *li*) and physical matter-energy (*ch'i*). Chu Hsi reasoned that if evil cannot be due to *li*, then it must be due to the physical matter *ch'i/qi* which makes each human unique, different from one another.

Li: Abstract and Perfect But *Ch'i* is also Human Nature

We can think of the organizing principle, *li*, as like the blueprint of a house. When we examine the blueprint, every corner is 90° and every window is perfect. The blueprint is perfect. But then construction begins and the contractors and builders get busy, and when they finish, the final physical house has doors which stick and windows that will not close tightly. In theory, in the blueprint, the house is perfect, but once the principle is embodied in real lumber and real plaster, the actual house is never as perfect as the theoretical house.

A similar analogy works for Chu Hsi. He argues that it is because of the impediments of *ch'i* (material force, the matter that provides form and shape), that the innate goodness of *li* is unable to manifest itself in its entirety. *Li* is the ideal, it is the pattern of how a thing ought to be if it were perfect. The difficulty is that the perfect principle can become manifest only to the extent that it is permitted by the limits imposed by our physical body, by *ch'i*. *Ch'i* is where self-centeredness originates, and is where evil arises from.

Human nature is perfect in *li*, but it is given material form by *ch'i/qi*, and that's why there is evil in our world. It is up to our heart/mind to control these problems generated by the physical matter. The ideal pattern of human nature is *jen/ren* (benevolence, human goodness) which by itself is good, but *jen* adapted to different individual human forms becomes confused and mixed, such that *jen* is corrupted by mater.[36]

Ch'i, matter, substance, vital energy or material force, is obscure, muddy, opaque, or impure, but it can be made purer, or cleaner. People whose *ch'i/qi* is more pure are naturally wise and comfortable with life, and naturally attracted to the good. Those who receive (from Nature) impure *ch'i* have it within them to become evil human beings. Feelings and passions belong to *ch'i* and these passions obscure the original goodness of our human nature. So, by principle, by nature, we are good, but when our abstract nature takes specific physical human form, the material-energy *ch'i* corrupts us in different degrees, some more pure, some less pure. Evil arises from our physical nature, and different people have different degrees of purity. Our heart/mind (*hsin*) has the task of governing both our pure nature but also our material feelings. The mind is supposed to control nature and feelings, but it is difficult to overcome natural

---

[35] No Chinese (or Indian) thinker ever thought that the issue was related to human free will. Free will is a Judeo-Christian religious concept used to explain why humans no longer inhabit the Garden of Eden. Western philosophers find the concept quite problematic generating theories of the Libertarians (free will is uncaused acts), Determinism (every act is caused so there is no free will), and Soft Determinism (an act is free if your own desires are among the causes of the act).

[36] The Chinese Buddhists solved the problem in a similar manner. They asserted that every human was born with the Buddha-nature, but the clouds of ignorance, confusion, anger, hatred, ill-will, and ego-centered craving obscured that Buddha-nature from us, hiding it, and so we did not realize our own true nature.

physical desires and self-centeredness.

The sage is the person who has a gift from Heaven. The sage receives *ch'i* in its purity, without it being "too impure." Chu Hsi believes that the sages of the Golden Age two- or three-thousand years ago were born with naturally pure *ch'i*, but in the time of Chu Hsi (1130–1200) human *ch'i* has become muddy and impure and so we must work hard to purify our *ch'i*.[37]

Chu Hsi seems to argue that because the individual organizing pattern (*li*) of human nature is ideal and perfect, and because all *li* are perfect, therefore they can be identified with each other. If two things are identical because both are perfect, then they must also be identical with each other.[38] The principle of human nature is identified with perfect principle or *li*; which means that human nature is identical with the ideal pattern of humans, of earth, and of heaven. This is the Supreme Ultimate principle which unifies all of the universe. *Li* is the T'ai-chi/Taiji. T'ai-chi is the source of both *li* and *ch'i*. Chu Hsi identifies mind with the basic nature of humankind, and this is already identified with *li*, which in turn is the Supreme Ultimate.[39]

The Supreme Ultimate

What can we say about the nature of the Supreme Ultimate? It is not a separate being, not a divinity, not a person or a supernatural force. T'ai-chi is just the impersonal absolute, the abstract underlying principle or structure that makes all the ten-thousand things take on coherent forms. T'ai-chi is the underlying structure of unity. Is this Supreme Ultimate one or is it many? There are many different *li*, a pattern for tree, for rock, for mountain, for dog, and for human. Yet all of these are contained in the Supreme Ultimate. Chu Hsi claims that individual things contain the Supreme Ultimate in its entirety. How is this possible? Chu Hsi gives us a rather poetical solution:

> But one Supreme Ultimate exists, which is received by the individuals of all things. This one Supreme Ultimate is received by each individual in its entirety and undivided. It is like the moon shining in the heavens, of which, though it is reflected in rivers and lakes and thus is everywhere visible, we would not therefore say that it is divided.[40]

Jen is Mind, *Jen* is the Supreme Ultimate

According to Confucius, and Chu Hsi, *jen/ren* (human kindness, benevolence) is the foundation of all virtues and is our essential human nature. The mind is also our essential human nature. If two things are both identical to a third, then the two must be identical. So, it follows that *jen* (benevolence) is the same as our mind. Yet *jen* is identical with the underlying principle of all reality. In that case, *jen* is the same as the Supreme Ultimate as well!

How to realize one's *jen*? This is asking "how do we discover our true nature?" The Neo-Confucian answer: practice sincerity, humility, benevolence, kindness, ritual courtesy, quiet meditation, and find the pure and calm mind within. Then one will experience love (*jen*) for all human beings (paraphrasing Confucius). The fundamental moral

---

[37] There remains the question of why *ch'i* should change and degrade over time. The Buddhists claimed that things got worse because we were far from the time when the Buddha lived among us. Remember that Chinese T'ien-t'ai and the Pure Land Buddhists had previously argued that in the past, in the time of Buddhas, people were pure and could achieve awakening by their own efforts. Now, in the current world, we were in the last stages of the *dharma* and human nature was corrupt. No one could achieve awakening by herself; for the followers of the Pure Land school, we all need to pray to the Buddha of the Pure Land and receive the gift of the Western Paradise. This idea that things go from good to chaos also relates to the Indian Hindu idea of *Kali Yuga* at the end of time.

[38] Consider, if the "law of gravity" is a law of nature, and "the law of the expansion of gases" is a law of nature, are the two laws identical with each other?

[39] John Koller, *Oriental Philosophies*, 2nd. ed., p. 319.

[40] Ch. 94 of Chu Hsi, translated by Laurence C. Wu, *op. cit.*, p. 244. The allusion to the single moon reflected in many pools of water is a well-known Buddhist analogy.

principle of the human mind, *jen*, is identified with the Supreme Ultimate; it follows that human morality is part of the very essence of the cosmic order. Morality is not conventional; it is grounded in reality. For Chu Hsi, the path leading to the realization of one's true nature is the investigation of things.

The Investigation of Things

The basic principle for Chu Hsi is the "investigation of things." To investigate things is an academic scholarly practice. But one needs a mind to investigate anything! Since investigation is possible only through the mind, and the mind is identified with the foundation of morality, therefore to think is also to practice moral conduct. One can also investigate the actual functioning of these abstract principles, *li*, in our everyday lives, and when we find ourselves deviating from our innate goodness, we can straighten ourselves out. Mencius had said that our human goodness can slip away if it is not cultivated properly. Chu Hsi agrees: through self-perfection and self-cultivation we can preserve our innate goodness — not allowing it to slip away.[41]

"To investigate things" certainly included investigating the ancient classics of the Confucians, including the *Analects* and the *Book of Mencius* and the *Great Learning* (*Ta Hsueh*). Scholarly learning in the tradition of a Confucian education becomes the Neo-Confucian backbone for how to grasp the innate goodness of each human being.

Li in itself is perfect principle and is completely good. It loses its perfection as soon as it becomes actualized within *ch'i*. *Ch'i* obstructs and corrupts the manifestation of *li*. This corruption gives rise to the human passions, which cause evil.[42] The cure lies in self-cultivation, having a sincere attitude in one's mind and developing intellectual knowledge about the self and the world. Education and intellectual skill is the foundation of moral development. Morality depends on the intellect. In addition, self-cultivation of one's moral nature is deepened by meditation.

After Chu Hsi

Chu Hsi died in 1200. The Neo-Confucian scholars in following centuries seemed to be happy simply parroting and quoting Chu Hsi, and creative thought was discouraged. There was only one official Confucian position, Chu Hsi's "School of *Li*" (*Li hsueh*), and it should never be questioned. The scholars in the court were certain that their School of *Li* had all the answers, and the Chinese civilization was superior to every other civilization in the world.

In the early 1400s, Chinese trading and exploration ships sailed from Beijing to India and beyond, and Chinese merchants involved in ocean trading became quite wealthy and they learned a lot about non-Chinese customs and culture, and found value in these. The Neo-Confucian officials at court were horrified at the thought that there might be value in non-Confucian cultures. They argued that all non-Chinese were barbarians and a bad influence on Confucian values. They asserted that Chinese had nothing to learn from any non-Chinese persons or cultures. The court Confucians discouraged the emperor from further ocean-going exploration, and the huge armada of trading ships was abandoned. This was a century before Christopher Columbus set sail on his voyage of exploration.

Similarly, Neo-Confucian court officials who protected state orthodoxy simplified Chu Hsi, adopted only the simplified Chu Hsi school's analysis of ancient Confucian classics, and refocused the civil service examination system on the Chu Hsi line of philosophers. During the process the more spiritual dimension of Chu Hsi's work was lost, and critical analysis of the basic claims and assumptions of Chu Hsi was discouraged. For these less creative court scholars, Chu Hsi was about examining and investigating universal principles, and abstractions dominated the school. Chu Hsi's concern with moral behavior had been overlooked or minimized. Thus, the more practical dimension of Chu Hsi's

---

[41] John Koller, *Oriental Philosophies*, 2nd. ed., p. 319.

[42] Several Middle Eastern pre-Christian religions claimed that spirit or mind is pure and that matter is evil and at war with spirit. The physical body is matter. Physical pleasures arise from the physical body. The Manicheans concluded that all sex is evil and having children is also evil for it is a victory for physical matter. An attitude of perceiving sexual relations as passionate and evil had an influence on early Christianity. However, the Chinese did not find sexuality to be evil.

thought became reduced to theoretical principles.

22.10 WANG YANG-MING (1472–1529)

The second great Neo-Confucian thinker is the Ming dynasty scholar, general, and idealist philosopher Wang Shou-jen/Wang Shouren, better known as Wang Yang-ming (1472–1529). His philosophy drew heavily on an earlier contemporary of Chu Hsi named Lu Chiu-yuan/Lu Jiuyuan (1139–1193) who three-hundred years earlier was known as the founder of the "School of Mind" (*Hsin hsueh*). Drawing on key ideas from Lu Chiu-yuan, Wang Yang-ming expanded those ideas and ultimately provided support for a rather different Neo-Confucian tradition called the "School of Mind." Wang Yang-ming argued that knowledge and action are one and the same. If one had genuine knowledge, acting on that knowledge would occur spontaneously with no hesitation. Action could not be separated from the knowing. To know the good was to act spontaneously on that knowledge. In this he was opposed to Chu Hsi's orthodox "School of *Li*" or School of Principle which treated gaining knowledge as a kind of ongoing cultivation that, when completed, could lead to and guide action. For the school of Chu Hsi, knowledge was theoretical and not practical. One could have knowledge and not act on that knowledge. Wang Yang-ming disagreed. He argued for the unification of knowledge and action. If action was not spontaneous and instantaneous, then one cannot be said to have knowledge.

If Chu Hsi came to represent the more socially conservative branch of Neo-Confucianism, Wang Yang-ming was the court liberal who challenged the Confucian orthodoxy. Wang Yang-ming was a scholar in the court, and when pressed into military service became a very successful general in the army as well. The students of Wang Yang-ming tended to be more socially rebellious thinkers who challenged traditions and valued spontaneity. These gained importance in the court for a while and were a counter-balance to the orthodox followers of Chu Hsi who wanted rigid social regulation where everything was orderly and predictable.

The Background of Wang Yang-ming

Wang Yang-ming started out as a good Confucian, studying and mastering the writings of Confucius, Mencius and Neo-Confucians including Chu Hsi. He passed several civil service exams and achieved a position in the court. While still young he accepted wholeheartedly Chu Hsi's ideas and worked hard following Chu Hsi's program, trying to become a Confucian sage. He struggled mightily in the attempt to follow Chu Hsi's ideas to achieve that goal. He practiced "quiet sitting" and did his best to master the educational system advocated by Chu Hsi. Ultimately, the method of Chu Hsi simply did not work for him. Wang Yang-ming found Chu Hsi's method purely theoretical, too artificial, too far removed from the demands of real life. In 1508 Wang Yang-ming experienced something like a Buddhist insight experience (*wu* or *satori*) which provided the realization that things in the external world are no more than objects of which we are aware. Things are objects of consciousness, objects of the mind. Reason and knowledge exist only in the mind.

Although he admired Chu Hsi, Wang Yang-ming did point out problems with Chu Hsi's system of thought. Wang Yang-ming treated the ideas of Chu Hsi as those of a fellow philosopher, not an idolized sage whose ideas should never be challenged. This caused problems for him among the other scholars and officials at court.

Because Chu Hsi stresses reason and the careful investigation of things in the world, Wang Yang-ming felt that in subsequent Neo-Confucian thought, investigation of universal principles dominated the school, and so genuinely spontaneous and natural moral behavior had been unfairly minimized. Wang Yang-ming's focus is on moral values, which he thought were innate in the mind. Wang was sure that we all know the difference between good and evil while still very young. This knowledge is not the result of reason or rationality. It is intuitive. To gain knowledge is to act spontaneously, without hesitation between thought and act.

Like other Confucians, Wang Yang-ming agrees with Mencius/Meng-tzu that human beings are born originally pure and good, not neutral and most certainly not evil. He argues that we are born with innate knowledge of goodness;

we know the difference between good and evil from birth. Moral intuition is built into human nature. His approach to moral action is grounded in either a Confucian value of loving kindness (*jen*), or perhaps the Chinese Buddhist value of loving egoless compassion (*karuna*), or both.

The Unity of Knowledge and Action

Wang Yang-ming's insight experience led him to assert that knowledge and action are not two separate things, as previous thinkers had assumed. There is a smooth continuum from knowledge to action; they are two ends of an ongoing process. Knowledge is informed choices which lead to action. Knowledge is not purely theoretical. If one knows what action is proper, one will automatically act. Wang Yang-ming explains to his student:

According to my interpretation, to *know* is to resolve to *do*; to *do* is to put *knowledge* into practice. *Knowing* is the initiative of *doing*; *doing* is the realization of knowing.[43]

This is especially true when it comes to morality. One does not simply know what is right and know what is good; according to Wang Yang-ming, moral action follows because action is the completion of moral knowledge. To know the good is to do the good.

For Wang Yang-ming, true or genuine knowledge is action that proceeds from active benevolence or love (*jen*/*ren*) that constitutes the basis of our human nature according to Confucius and Mencius. A human being cannot be said to know of the virtue of filial piety if that person does not *behave* with loving respect for parents, for elder family members and others. The virtues must be acted upon and lived, not merely understood abstractly.

Knowledge is the beginning of action and action is the completion of knowledge. Learning to be a sage involves only one effort. Knowledge and action should not be separated.[44]

Wang Yang-ming Criticizes Chu Hsi's "Quiet Sitting"

The Chinese Buddhists have a tendency to stress *prajna*-wisdom or liberating knowledge as the key to sagehood. Wang Yang-ming disagrees. He places action as the key instead of insight or wisdom. Chu Hsi saw meditation as a means of moral training and a manifestation of moral seriousness. Originally Wang Yang-ming was trained in "quiet sitting" as well, but later he de-emphasized it. Wang asserts that all knowledge exists for the sake of action. It is not quiet meditation, pure reason or insight-filled knowledge that makes one a sage, but it is one's spontaneous behavior (many teachers in the Ch'an school seems to have felt the same). A sage eliminates self-centeredness (both Confucian and Buddhist thinkers agree on this), and manifests good character.

Perhaps because of the stress on action, Wang Yang-ming criticizes the stress on quiet sitting found in Chu Hsi and his followers. To sit quietly in cross-legged meditation seemed too passive and an abandonment of the necessity of a Confucian to actively engage in political affairs.

However, Wang Yang-ming did not reject all meditation. In order to eliminate selfish desires that cloud the innate mind's understanding of goodness, one can practice his type of meditation often called "tranquil repose" or "sitting still" (*ching-ts'o*/*jingzuo*). This is similar to the practice of Ch'an Buddhist meditation *ts'o-ch'an*/*zuochan* which was practiced in Buddhist monasteries throughout China during Wang Yang-ming's lifetime.

---

[43] Carsun Chang, *The Development of Neo-Confucian Thought: Volume 2* (New York: Bookman Associates, 1962), p. 36.

[44] Wing-tsit Chan, *A Source Book in Chinese Philosophy* (Princeton, NJ: Princeton University Press, 1963), p. 674.

Wang Yang-ming On the Fundamental Mind

Wang Yang-ming stresses the importance of mind or consciousness, and so he is often described using the Western philosophical label "Idealist" which means that all we can ever know are our own ideas ("idealist" is more accurately "idea-ist"). What are things like before our minds encounter them? Wang Yang-ming held that objects do not exist entirely apart from the mind because the mind shapes the understanding. It is not the world that shapes the mind, but the mind that gives reason to the world. Therefore, the mind alone is the source of all reason. He understood this deep inner mind to be the deepest part of human nature, an inner light, an innate moral goodness and an understanding of what is genuinely good.

This Fundamental Mind sounds similar to the Buddhist idea of intrinsic "Buddha-nature."[45] Wang Yang-ming asserts that if one can go deep within consciousness and find one's Fundamental Mind, one has found the original purity and goodness of our common humanity. "In the 'great man' the *jen* of the universe is identified with the *jen* of the individual, providing unity of all things."[46] We humans are not different from the rest of nature; one's clear character is manifest when one finds the Fundamental Mind, one realizes all things as having "one body with Heaven and Earth."[47]

It should be clear that much of Wang Yang-ming's thought is very compatible with the Ch'an Buddhist practice and system, and later followers of Wang Yang-ming stressed spontaneity and tended to exhibit a rather wildness of character, and acknowledged that they had much in common with Chuang-tzu's philosophical Taoism and Ch'an Buddhism.

Wang Yang-ming On the *Great Learning* Text

Wang's analysis of the Confucian classic entitled the *Ta Hsueh* (Great Learning), involves three completely interconnected claims, called the "Three Major Chords" which are (1) manifesting clear character, (2) loving people, (3) abiding in the highest good. Although the labels sound different, the explanations reveal that they are three perspectives on one's original nature, one's Fundamental Mind.

(1) The first chord is "manifesting clear character," which consists in returning to your original nature, a nature which is fundamentally good and naturally feels a oneness and love for all creation, recognizing the unity of all things. "To manifest the clear character is to bring about the substance of the state of forming one body with Heaven, Earth, and the myriad things."[48] It is your original nature to do so.

(2) The second chord, "loving people," is also derived from Wang Yang-ming's assertion that human beings are one with Heaven and Earth. We love our own parents, and then we strive to love all parents as though they were our own parents; we love our siblings and strive to love all those who are also siblings.

(3) The third chord is to "abide in the highest good," which is simply to live by manifesting your original nature/character, and to love all human beings and all things. Wang writes: "As the highest good emanates

---

[45] Recall that in chapter 20, we discussed the Ch'an master Bodhidharma who is supposed to have said that "Direct pointing at the essence of a human being. Seeing into the deepest part of your nature is attaining Buddhahood."

[46] Wing-tsit Chan, *op. cit.*, p. 659.

[47] This idea that all things are "one body with Heaven and Earth" was first expressed in the *Chuang-tzu* in chapter 2. Chuang-tzu says: "Heaven and Earth came into being with me together, and with me, all things are one." When we are completely absorbed in the moment, we are in harmony with the Tao and we lose anxieties, worries vanish, and make no distinction between "self" and "other."

[48] Wing-tsit Chan, *op. cit.*, p. 660.

and reveals itself, we will consider right as right and wrong as wrong. Things of greater or less importance and situations of grave or light character will be responded to as they act upon us." He also writes, "It is the original substance of the clear character which is called innate knowledge of the good."[49]

Wang Yang-ming argued that by studying our own nature, anyone (not just court scholars) could discover their own Fundamental Mind and achieve the wisdom of a superior person or even a sage. Every one of us is capable of becoming the equal of Confucius or Mencius. Wang asserted that the writings of Confucius and Mencius were useful guides to living a good life, but were not absolute truth. Wang asserted that careful analysis could reveal actual flaws in the great Confucian classics. An educated farmer who followed the Three Major Chords could be wiser than a court scholar who had memorized all the Confucian classics, but had little experience in the actual world of daily life.

Needless to say, the court's Confucian scholars were horrified by these "dangerous ideas" which claimed that scholars were not superior to farmers and soldiers. Wang Yang-ming's writings also spurred his followers to take up the study of philosophical Taoism and especially Ch'an Buddhism. In the highly political court, followers of Chu Hsi and followers of Wang Yang-ming would clash.

22.11 NEO-CONFUCIANISM AFTER WANG YANG-MING

The Sung/Song (960-1279) is the period of Chu Hsi and his School of *Li* of Neo-Confucianism. The period after the Sung/Song (960-1279) is the Mongol Yuan Dynasty (1271-1368), when the Mongols led by Kublai Khan from the north conquered and ruled China. The Ming dynasty (1368-1644) followed the collapse of the Yuan, and that was the time of Wang Yang-ming.

The Ming Dynasty ended in 1644, and was followed by the Ch'ing/Qing Dynasty (1644-1912), the very last dynasty in Chinese history.[50] This is when a non-Chinese group from the north called the Manchus ruled China and managed to bring about a period of stability, peace, and prosperity. The Manchu rulers had great respect for scholarship, and they patronized scholars and institutions of learning with many gifts. Thanks to government funding, it became entirely possible for a person with skills in scholarship to devote his life to abstract scholarly studies of ancient texts, ancient language and phonology which had little or no relevancy to life. Too many Neo-Confucian scholars gloried in incredible feats of memorization and arcane research, and this tendency provided an impetus for change with the next Neo-Confucian thinker, Tai Chen/Daijen.

TAI CHEN (1723-1777).

Tai Chen/Daijen lived during the Ch'ing/Qing dynasty (1644-1912), a dynasty under non-Chinese Manchu rule. Tai Chen/Daijen is the last great Neo-Confucian philosopher. He reacted against the rationalism and "quiet sitting" of Chu Hsi, and rejected the "Fundamental Mind" idealism of Wang Yang-ming. Tai Chen feels that the error of the previous Neo-Confucians was an obsessive concern with abstract principles. Tai Chen came to emphasize the empirical realm of things we can see, hear, touch, taste, and smell. Spiritual principles are not divorced from the world of human affairs. To make spiritual progress is to do a detailed and analytical investigation of things, of daily events. "A thing is an affair or event. When we talk about an event, we do not go beyond daily affairs such as drinking and

---

[49] Wing-tsit Chan, *ibid.*, p. 661.

[50] For more on these key eras, see Jonathan Porter, *Imperial China: 1350-1900* (Lanham, MD: Rowman & Littlefield, 2015).

eating. To neglect these and talk about principle is not what the ancient sages and worthies meant by principle."[51]

NEO-CONFUCIANISM AFTER T'AI-CHEN/DAIJEN.

In the decades after T'ai-chen, Ch'ing/Qing dynasty China began to experience difficulties, both internally and externally with ongoing problems with Western powers. In 1793 Great Britain tried to arrange trading agreements with China, but the Chinese emperor declared that Europe had nothing that China wanted or needed. By 1830 British businesses were exporting, selling, and smuggling opium to Chinese citizens,[52] and when the Chinese government tried to stop the selling of opium, Britain declared war on China. This was known as the First Opium War (1839–1842). The self-confident certainty of the innate superiority of the Chinese civilization was shaken to the core when it was discovered that the Chinese military was no match for Western weapons on the ground and no match for Western navy warships. The Qing navy, composed entirely of wooden sailing junks, had no chance against the modern tactics and firepower of the British Royal Navy. British ground soldiers, using muskets and artillery far more advanced that the Chinese army, easily outmaneuvered and outgunned Ch'ing/Qing forces in ground battles.

In 1842 the Ch'ing/Qing rulers surrendered. It was a decisive, humiliating blow to the self-confident pride of Chinese superiority.[53] In the surrender document China agreed to pay reparations, to allow unrestricted European access to Chinese ports, and ceded Hong Kong Island to Great Britain. The conflict revealed many inadequacies in the Qing government and provoked widespread rebellions by the population in the 1850s against the already hugely unpopular regime.

For the next six decades, in varying degrees, Great Britain, Russia, France, Italy, Austria, Germany, and the United States pretty much did as they pleased in China and had even managed to coerce the government into signing off on what are generally viewed as gross violations of Chinese sovereignty in these unequal treaties. Each nation harbored its own imperial ambitions regarding China and China of the Ch'ing/Qing dynsty was no longer in a position to resist foreign domination or defend itself against the vastly superior Western military forces. China was descending into a semi-colonial state under Western powers.

We should note that non-Chinese religions other than Indian Buddhism did make their way into China. Nestorian Christianity traveled the Silk Route in the T'ang dynasty and flourished for a while. Later, under Mongol rule, the Nestorian branch of Christianity gradually disappeared. Muslim traders made their way into China, especially during the Yuan dynasty (1271–1368) and maintained a strong presence. Even Juadaism had a presence in China during the Northern Sung/Song dynasty (960–1127), but gradually faded. Roman Catholic Jesuits under Matteo Ricci impressed imperial Chinese with their knowledge of science and especially astronomy, which was particularly important for the Chinese who considered their emperor as the lord of "all under heaven." These Chinese scholars studied the heavens for omens. Into the Ch'ing/Qing dynasty (1644–1912), especially in the late 1600s Jesuit influence persisted, but later in 1724 Christianity was proscribed by the court. Protestant missionaries also came to China, but had little success in converting the Chinese during this period.

---

[51] John Koller, *Oriental Philosophies*, 2nd. ed., p. 324.

[52] For more on the role of Britain selling opium in Ming and Ch'ing/Qing dynasty China, see Yangwen Zheng, *Social Life of Opium in China* (New York: Cambridge, 2005). Another book is Richard J. Grace, *Opium and Empire: The Lives and Careers of William Jardine and James Matheson* (Montreal: McGill-Queen's University Press, 2014).

[53] As noted previously, there was nothing unique about the Chinese view of its own civilization. The same held true for the Europeans when they first encountered Asia. Anthony Pagden writes, "Europeans have always looked on their own culture as privileged, and upon all other cultures as to some degree inferior. There is nothing remarkable about this." Anthony Pagden, *European Encounters with the New World: From Renaissance to Romanticism* (New Haven, CT: Yale University Press, 1993), p. 199.

22.12   THE CH'ING/QING DYNASTY (1644–1912) ENDS

The Ch'ing/Qing dynasty was the last imperial dynasty in Chinese history. By the 1880s and 1890s, the Qing dynasty was increasingly paralyzed, the state was in dire need of massive reform, and the people were growing increasingly restless. In the absence of a strong central government, warlords came to dominate much of the Chinese landscape.

The government officials were often corrupt, and the wealthy who were able to pay bribes lived well. The poor did not. When Western powers began to attempt to turn China into a colony of the West, the reaction of the populace was profoundly negative. The long-suffering peasants were not willing to watch their nation succumb to the West's ambitions to divide up China's wealth. The Chinese populace was beginning to blame Western missionaries, diplomats, soldiers, and engineers for the enduring state of crisis in Ch'ing China.

Then there was the Sino-Japanese war of 1894–1895. China had traded with Japan for nearly fifteen-hundred years, and always considered Japan a small unimportant feudal island country for which the Chinese had little or no respect. The long-standing arrogance of the Chinese towards the Japanese islands and the Japanese people (who the Chinese regarded as inferiors) was long a sore spot for the Japanese.

The Japanese had learned much from the West and for many decades Japan had modernized itself along Western lines. The Chinese military forces were unable to defend themselves against Japan. Losing the Sino-Japanese War was a major turning point for the Ch'ing/Qing government. The Japanese military convincingly destroyed the recently modernized Chinese navy, which the Ch'ing/Qing government believed to be the strongest naval force in Asia. In defeating the Chinese forces and the Chinese navy, Japan showed that it was no longer the tradition-bound feudal nation that the Chinese remembered. The Chinese sense of itself as a superior civilization was shattered by their defeat at the hands of the Japanese in 1894–1895. The new Japan was able to do just the same as the Western nations in their military, economic and technological achievements.[54]

The Boxer Rebellion

In late 1899, Americans heard about the local Chinese movement calling itself the "Fists United in Harmony" (which Westerners called the Boxer rebellion),[55] in which powerless peasants in northeastern China (who were the ethnic Han) took up arms against the Manchu overlords (who were not Han Chinese) of the Ch'ing/Qing government. Leaders expressly encouraged attacking and killing Westerners in China, especially the many Catholic and Protestant missionaries who had supported Western imperialistic attempts at dividing up China. The Franciscan missionaries saw all Chinese religions as the presence of Satan, and understood their duty to disrupt Satan's powerful presence. These missionaries interpreted the local and household Chinese gods as manifestations of Satan's machinations. These same missionaries built their Christian churches on the old sites of Chinese temples, symbolic of the victory of Christianity over Satan and victory over traditional Chinese religions which were called evil.

It was easy for these peasants to focus their resentment and blame arrogant westerners for the enduringly chaotic situation in China. These peasants in northeastern China thought the solution was to exterminate foreigners.[56] The rallying cry of the Boxers was "Expel the foreign devils." Peasants looted, pillaged, and murdered with the

---

[54] An excellent book on this is Heung Shing Liu, *China in Revolution: The Road to 1911* (Hong Kong: Hong Kong University Press, 2011). See also S. C. M. Paine, *The Sino-Japanese War of 1894-1895: Perceptions, Power, and Primacy* (2005).

[55] There are many good books on the Boxer Rebellion and the ambitions of the so-called Western Great Powers in China. A recent and valuable book is David J. Silbey, *The Boxer Rebellion and the Great Game in China* (New York: Hill and Wang, 2012) and also Joseph W. Esherick, *The Origins of the Boxer Uprising* (Berkeley: University of California Press, 1987).

[56] An interesting book dealing with both sides of the Boxer Rebellion is Anthony E. Clark, *Heaven In Conflict: Franciscans and the Boxer Uprising in Shanxi* (Seattle: University of Washington Press, 2014).

Ch'ing/Qing military unable to stop the them. The Boxers (Westerners called them "Boxers" because they practiced martial arts and believed religious Taoist magical claims that the Boxer-followers could not be hurt by Western rifle bullets) then joined with Qing imperial forces in pitched battle against European forces. The new rallying cry was "Support Ch'ing/Qing; destroy foreigners."

Western military forces with an interest in China coordinated their response to the rebellion. By late summer 1900, an eight-nation alliance consisting of Great Britain, Russia, Japan, France, Italy, Austria, Germany, and the United States had landed an army of more than fifty thousand troops on Chinese soil. The once-mighty Chinese state suffered the indignity of a multilateral, imperial occupation lasting for roughly the next year as the rebellion was crushed, order restored, and the teetering Qing dynasty preserved. Ultimately, the Western powers imposed the punitive Boxer Protocol on China while preserving, at least for a time, the imperial status quo.

The Western military powers had triumphed over one of the greatest civilizations in world history. For the next several decades, the West, now including Japan, continued to divide up China's territory, handing out spoils to shore up more important relationships, and ignoring the desires and needs of the Chinese populace. In short, the Western nations exploited China as the Qing state grew even weaker and the nation drifted toward civil war.

When China came face to face with the humiliation of a defeat by Japanese armed forces, followed a few years later by complete defeat and occupation by western military powers, the certainty of the Chinese that their way of life made them the best, the most civilized, the most moral, and the most powerful nation was shattered. It became apparent that the Confucian educational system, looking backwards to the teachings of the long-gone legendary Golden Age of three-thousand years before, stressing ancient ritual, rigid social morality, and proper obedience to power, could not deal with the challenges of this new technological world.

The Chinese intellectuals realized that the overwhelming military might of the Western powers came from critical thinking, applied science and objective empirical investigation, not blind trust in ancient religions. Traditional Confucian education tended to ignore modern ideas, always looking to the past. Although China had produced many brilliant scientists and many wonderful inventions, historically, Confucianism in the imperial court had not placed any value on the study of science and technology. The list of important Chinese discoveries in science and technology (including gunpowder) is quite astonishing, but the Chinese did not pursue the technology to convert those discoveries into the mighty weapons of the West.[57] Certain that China had nothing to learn from any other culture, the Chinese court put no effort into studying Western technology until the Western powers easily dispatched the Chinese military and the Ch'ing rulers were powerless before Western military technology.[58]

It seemed clear to many in power in China that a new, more Western form of education was needed if China was to survive and protect itself against the might of the European and American powers. China did not want to become a colony of a Western power, as had India and Sri Lanka (Ceylon), and much of South America.

---

[57] The Chinese had printing presses five-hundred years before the Gutenberg bible. The ancient Chinese were the first to discover the solar wind and the circulation of the blood and even to isolate sex hormones. Chinese engineers invented the suspension bridge and the ancient Chinese had a crude but effective seismograph. The Chinese discovered iron and created the iron plough. The Chinese drilled for natural gas, and invented the parachute. Ancient China's contributions in the fields of engineering, agriculture, astronomy, medicine, technology, mathematics, water transportation, and music continue to astonish westerners who began to study the important discoveries of the Chinese. The amazing scientific accomplishments of China have been studied in the monumental multi-volume series by Joseph Needham, *Science and Civilization in China* (Cambridge University Press). A valuable overview of the findings is Robert Temple and Joseph Needham, *The Genius of China: 3,000 Years of Science, Discovery, and Invention* (Inner Traditions Press, 2007). A book which covers the ancient history but with more stress on the scientific background for contemporary China's economic strength is Sterling Seagrave, *Lords of the Rim* (Putnam, 1995).

[58] A recent valuable book offers an extensive review of the literature including several different perspectives and differing analyses to account for the recent dominance of the West rather than the East. The author, Jonathan Daly, writes, "China was probably the most inventive and technologically advanced society in premodern times, the longest-lasting great empire in history, and by far the world's richest, most populous, and most powerful country until a couple of centuries ago" (p. 135). Factors such as technological strength, a politically fragmented Europe, Judeo-Christian values, individualism, competition, geography, capitalism, imperialism, land development, and inexpensive labor in China are discussed. See Jonathan W. Daly, *Historians Debate the Rise of the West* (London and New York: Routledge, 2014).

CHAPTER 22: NEO-CONFUCIANISM

Faced with the reality of Western foreign power threatening to dominate China, state support of Confucian temples and Confucian education faded. Many Chinese intellectuals wanted to maintain Confucian ethics while eliminating all the backward-looking aspects, but others in power wanted all traces of Confucianism destroyed to make room for Western style improvements. They perceived Confucianism as keeping alive a culture and literature that looked only to the past, punishing change or novelty, hobbling China's ability to deal with the challenges of the future and all of the changes that must occur for China to combat Western power and influence. When the Ch'ing/Qing government structure fell, so too did the public system of Confucian ceremony and Neo-Confucian education.[59]

In 1911, the imperial system came to an end and the Chinese tried to create the Republic of China, with many Chinese attempting to institute Western forms of democracy as the Republic of China. However, ultimately it was the influence of Western Marxism which was to dominate and control China.

Chinese scholars began to learn English, French, German, and other Western languages and traveled to study in the major universities of Europe and the United States. Western philosophy and science were studied, and the American philosophical movement of pragmatism was popular for a while. In other words, the intellectual genesis for reform in China came not from China; it was from Europe. The cries for gradual reform were overwhelmed by those who advocated revolution. Revolutionaries reacted to the crippling Boxer Protocol imposed by Western powers and responded by cries to overthrow the Ch'ing/Qing Manchu rulers and improve the lives of the people. Inspired by the revolution in Russia, Chinese Marxists began actively to achieve their goals. As the Marxists gained control over China, they considered anything resembling religion to be the opium of the masses, and did their best to destroy all traces of Neo-Confucianism, Confucianism, Taoism, and Buddhism. Their activities increased once they became the new rulers of China.

The twentieth and twenty-first century developments in Chinese religion tended to occur outside the mainland. Recent developments have appeared in non-mainland Chinese communities, such as Taiwan, Singapore, and Hong Kong. These include Fa Lun Gong and Fo Kuang Shan.

Mao Tse-tung and Marxism

As a young man, Chairman Mao (Mao Tse-tung/Mao Zedong 1893–1976) toyed with the idea of a Western style democracy for a while, but ultimately felt that European Marxist ideas were the best solution to modernize China. Inspired by the Russian revolution, in the 1920s Mao worked for a similar violent revolution in China.[60] A revolution began which was to finally terminate with the Marxist defeat of the Republic in 1949. Scholars have estimated that Mao's policies as they were carried out between 1949 and 1976 resulted in the death of between 40 and 70 million Chinese.[61]

With Mao, the Confucian belief system was under a new attack. Karl Marx's rejection of religion was reflected in Mao's policies. The Communists charged Confucianism with being a rigid and inflexible elitist religion which privileges the wealthy and powerful over the common people. After the revolution, Chinese schools no longer taught the ideas of Confucius, but instead branded him a slave-owner. It is true that in the past, a Confucian education was the key to monetary and social success, and that such an education was impossibly expensive for any other than the sons of a very wealthy family to pursue. Such an education had been completely out of reach for the great majority

---

[59] Some have found a resurgence of Confucianism and Neo-Confucianism in contemporary China. For example, Kenneth Hammond and Jeffrey Richie, eds., *The Sage Returns: Confucian Revival in Contemporary China* (New York, NY: SUNY Press, 2015).

[60] There is a great deal of literature on Mao and Maoism. For example, see Timothy Cheek, ed., *A Critical Introduction to Mao* (New York: Cambridge University Press, 2010). A sober analysis of Mao is Andrew G. Walder, *China Under Mao: A Revolution Derailed* (Cambridge, MA: Harvard University Press, 2015).

[61] Jonathan Fenby, *Modern China: The Fall and Rise of a Great Power, 1850 to the Present* (Ecco, 2008), p. 351 "Mao's responsibility for the extinction of anywhere from 40 to 70 million lives brands him as a mass killer greater than Hitler or Stalin put together, his indifference to the suffering and the loss of humans breathtaking."

of Chinese. Records indicated that over ten-thousand Protestant and Catholic missionaries were thrown out of China, leaving an estimated one million Protestant Chinese, and perhaps as many as three million Roman Catholic Chinese. The Communist party placed limits on remaining Christians in China.

From the earliest years, Mao rejected the traditional Chinese attitude which devalued women. Reflecting this, Chinese Marxism criticized Confucianism for teaching that males are more important and more valuable than females, and for forbidding education to women. Marxism criticized this practice as unfairly oppressive and resulting in a loss of the abilities of half of the population, the female half.

The Cultural Revolution of 1966–1976

Well-educated Chinese valued critical thinking, and valued the ability to question the claims made by those in authority. To criticize the Communist party seemed to be allowed during the early days of the revolution. Mao, fearing that he was losing control over the communist revolution, instigated the Cultural Revolution of 1966–1976. Chinese Marxists demonized the well-educated, the scholars and intellectuals. During the Cultural Revolution, Marxist students (the Red Guard) reviled and humiliated their professors and destroyed educational institutions which the Communist Party thought might criticize those in authority. Highly trained surgeons, physicists, and professors were sent to work in mines, or in the rice fields and their classrooms became empty. For ten years almost no medical doctors or highly-educated science students were produced in China. For many decades the repercussions of the Cultural Revolution reverberated negatively throughout China. The chaos caused by the cultural revolution also had the unanticipated consequence of spawning anti-bureaucratic movements, and there were those who took advantage of the breakdown of public order to criticize the Communist government. They were severely repressed.

> The Cultural Revolution began for the most part as a revolution from above... but as the movement continued, many long-standing social and political issues resurfaced in a new circumstance in which public order had virtually collapsed. More than a decade and a half after the victory of the Communist-led revolution, popular resentment of bureaucratic privileges and cadre abuses of power was widespread, and many citizens were only too eager to take advantage of the newly proclaimed right to rebel against established authorities.[62]

The modern Chinese reluctance to allow organized religions is at least partly a reaction to the recognition that any large social movement (such as the Cultural Revolution) will ultimately lead to a political confrontation with the Communist party state. If any form of religion is to be allowed in China, it should support the Communist party and the state. Western scholars have pointed out that despite Mao's violent and destructive attack on old China, on Buddhism and Confucianism, Mao cultivated an image of himself as a semi-divine Confucian sage in the mold of the legendary Sage-Kings of the Chou dynasty, a benevolent ruler who was a poet and a philosopher, an exceptional leader who practiced Confucian virtues of duty, sacrifice, and self-cultivation. In China under Mao, Maoism came to fulfill the function of a national religion.[63] After Mao's Great Leap Forward (1958–1960), the state apparatus deified Mao: Mao Zedong was an all-knowing leader to whom everyone should display fervent and unquestioning loyalty. It was illegal to even suggest that any ruler anywhere was as great as Mao. The cult encouraged various rituals, including daily

---

[62] This quote is from a recent analysis of the cultural revolution and its unintended consequences: Yiching Wu, *The Cultural Revolution at the Margins: Chinese Socialism in Crisis* (Cambridge: Harvard University Press, 2014), p. 51.

[63] A careful study of the religion of Mao is Daniel Leese, *Mao Cult: Rhetoric and Ritual in China's Cultural Revolution* (Cambridge: Cambridge University Press, 2011). Professor Leese notes that Mao died in 1976, but he quotes Deng Xiaoping at the 1958 Chinese Communist Party Congress: "Love for the Leader is essentially an expression of love for the party, the class and the people, and not the deification of the individual" (p. 48). As noted above, the love for Mao can be likened to the Japanese deification of the emperor in the Meiji era. Following Mao's Great Leap Forward (1958–60) the Mao cult blossomed into adulation for Mao Zedong as a charismatic, all-knowing leader to whom everyone should display fervent and unquestioning loyalty. It was illegal to even suggest that any ruler anywhere was as great as Mao. All of this demonstrates the problems which can arise when any human anywhere or at any time is deified or treated as deserving of unquestioning loyalty.

morning and evening pledges to Mao, and even "loyalty dances."

In mainland China, students at all levels of thought were educated to follow the official Maoist interpretation of Marxism. Marxist criticism of Confucianism, Taoism, and Buddhism was officially encouraged. Critical thinking applied towards Marxism was severely discouraged. In recent times, the Chinese educational system appears to be changing as China moves into the next decades of the twenty-first century.[64]

Current population estimates in China suggest that there are 1.3 billion Chinese. Recent surveys suggest that there are perhaps 200 million Buddhists and Taoists/Daoists in mainland China today, perhaps fifty million Protestants, and ten million Roman Catholics. The Muslim population is estimated to be perhaps as many as twenty-five million. Approximately 175 million are listed as followers of "little tradition" Chinese religion, followers of shamanism and other forms of folk religion.[65]

In the areas beyond the Chinese mainland, like Taiwan and Singapore, Confucian temples and ritual are still maintained, but Confucianism as a political system has pretty well disappeared. Some of the families maintain their own private Confucian temples. Now that Hong Kong has reverted back to Chinese governmental control, it remains to be seen what will happen to its Confucian roots. Confucian ideas remain important in parts of east Asia, especially modern South Korea.

In modern mainland China, important aspects of Confucianism still supplies the pattern for correct social and family behavior. It continues in the presuppositions of the Chinese value system about respect for the elderly and ancestors, continues in assumptions as to how a family should behave and how one should conduct social relationships, but the political and philosophical dominance of Confucianism is gone.[66]

22.13 CONTEMPORARY CHINESE RELIGIONS

Fo Kuang Shan/Fo Guangshan

In Chinese cultures away from the mainland Communist regime, new forms of Buddhism have arisen. Probably the most famous example is the Fo Kuang Shan (Fo Guangshan) or FKS, which is based in Taiwan. Founded in 1967, and gaining considerable popularity in the 1980s, Fo Kuang Shan considers itself a humanistic Buddhism, which is to say that instead of worrying about the Pure Land after we die, or placing its focus on the attainment of awakening in some future life, FKS asserts that its goal is to improve life in this world. Today, Fo Kuang Shan is headquartered in Taiwan, where it operates institutions which educate the youth from kindergarten to the university level. It has a large number of monastic leaders who proselytize and attempt to carry out the organization's goals. In 1989 FKS organized a world-wide organization called the Buddha Light International Association, which has established temples in Australia, South Africa, and thirty other countries.[67]

---

[64] A good treatment is Joseph W. Esherick, *China: How the Empire Fell* (2013), and his earlier volume, Esherick, *Reform and Revolution in China* (1998).

[65] These estimates come from a book on religion in contemporary China by Ian Johnson, *The Souls of China: The Return of Religion after Mao* (New York: Pantheon Books, 2016).

[66] For recent scholarship on this topic, see Donald S. Lopez, ed., *Religions of China in Practice* (Princeton, 1996).

[67] David Chappell, "New Buddhist Movements" in Kevin Trainor, ed., *Buddhism* (London: Oxford University Press, 2004), p. 214.

CHAPTER 22: NEO-CONFUCIANISM

Fa Lun Kung/Falun Gong

This contemporary Chinese religion draws upon many influences, especially Taoist physical exercises and Taoist medicine, Buddhist meditation, and Confucian ideas of self-cultivation. The movement was initiated in China in 1992, and is also known as Fa Lun Ta Fa/Falun Dafa. The founder, Li Hongzhi (b. 1951) studied *ch'i-kung/qigong*, an ancient system of physical and breathing exercises which are related to the Chinese martial arts, and which are believed to increase longevity, health, and strength through stretching and other exercises. Li Hongzhi also utilized meditation, and the Falun Gong (whose name in Chinese is the three characters for "truth" or "teaching" + "wheel" + "energy") movement arose out of these. The central idea is the *falun*, or truth-wheel, which is believed to be an invisible spiritual wheel located just below the navel, that can be activated by one proficient in Falun Gong techniques. When the *falun* wheel begins to turn, it draws energy from the universe which is stored in the human being. When the wheel turns in the opposite direction, that stored energy is sent throughout the body and even can extend to others.

There are numerous physical exercises, some performed from a standing position, and others done while seated. Similar to the religious Taoist ideas out of which Falun Gong arose, practitioners believe that advanced adepts can gain not only health and long life, but also gain paranormal powers such as reading another's mind, seeing things at a great distance, hearing conversations many miles away, and the sort of physical invulnerability portrayed in modern martial arts movies.[68] Similar Chinese religious movements in the past which claimed physical invulnerability for its followers (like the Boxer Rebellion) actually resulted in peasant military action which destabilized the Chinese government as a result of revolts. An attempt to change society brought it into conflict with the Communist authorities. In April 1999 followers came into open conflict with party leadership, and the government did its best to put a stop to the religion., and it is felt that for this reason the Chinese government banned Falun Gong.

In recent decades there has been a new reappraisal of the philosophy of Confucianism in Chinese intellectual circles, and a marked growth in the appreciation of the great Confucian thinkers of the past.[69]

22.14 SUMMARY OF THE CHAPTER

The early political dominance of Confucianism during the Han dynasty (206 B.C.E. - 220 C.E.) was weakened after the fall of the Han rulers, and Taoism and Buddhism slowly came to exert influence politically and philosophically. The Confucians retained a strong presence in the court, but were no longer the only important group politically. Later, in the Sung/Song dynasty (960-1279) the Confucians would regain a great degree of control because the Civil Service Examination system promoted Confucian scholars into the government.

The power of Buddhism was strong during the Sui (581-618) and T'ang (618-906) dynasties, but several Buddhist sects were seriously weakened by the An Lu Shan rebellion of 755, and then weakened again in the 845 persecution. In this period, Confucian scholars began to search for modifications of Confucian doctrine so that the Confucian thinkers could compete with, and exceed Buddhist and Taoist metaphysics.

The Confucian Han Yu (768-824) and his pupil, Li Ao, continued the attack. Li Ao criticized Buddhism as a foreign religion, and rejected Taoism claiming that it was unconcerned with human goodness. However, Li Ao was not able to create a purely Confucian theory of reality.

Chou Tun-I/Zhou Dunyi (1017-1073) advocated a theory of *li*, an absolute principle. The Ch'eng brothers, Ch'eng Hao/Cheng Hao (1032-1085) and Ch'eng I/Cheng Yi (1033-1107), developed the School of *Li*, the Chinese

---

[68] Michael Molloy, *Experiencing the World's Religions*, Second Edition (Mountain View, Ca.: Mayfield Publishing Company, 2002), p. 473.

[69] See Kenneth J. Hammond and Jeffrey L. Richey, *The Sage Returns: The Confucian Revival in Contemporary China* (State University of New York Press, 2015)

name for what we have called Neo-Confucianism.

Chu Hsi/Zhu Xi (1130–1200) is the dominant Neo-Confucian thinker, and his ideas became the official Neo-Confucian philosophy until the end of the nineteenth century. Chu Hsi was a rationalist who synthesized almost all the elements of previous thinkers into a single coherent philosophy.

Wang Yang-ming (1472–1529) rejected the stress on rationality, and advocated ethics and regaining one's Fundamental Mind. Many Chinese Buddhists felt quite comfortable with the meditation exercises advocated by Wang Yang-ming.

Tai Chen/Daijen (1723–1777) is the last great Neo-Confucian School of *Li* philosopher, and he rejected the theoretical aspects of his predecessors and put his stress on the everyday details of our lives.

For the past several hundred years, imperial China has faced numerous social, political, economic, and military problems. As pointed out, predatory foreigners have had a role in China's troubles, but it would be a mistake if one did not note that the more important difficulties were caused by China itself. As mentioned previously, massive political corruption and powerful territorial warlords took advantage of incompetent rule. This was followed by savage fighting between the newly formed republic and the Marxist-Leninist Communists led by Mao, combined with a fourteen-year invasion from Japan. Four years of civil war after 1945 led to the Maoist era, with its purges and repression which killed millions; the disastrous Great Leap Forward; a famine that killed perhaps tens of millions of Chinese; and the anti-intellectual excesses of the Cultural Revolution.

Confucian and Neo-Confucian thought did not prepare China adequately to defend itself against the military strength of Western powers, and as a result in the early decade of the twentieth century China attempted to modernize and discarded all forms of political Confucianism and Confucian education. When Maoism took over in 1949, Buddhism and Taoism were rejected officially, Buddhist and Taoist temples were vandalized and destroyed, and Confucius minimized and vilified. The attitudes towards the Confucian heritage have become more positive in recent decades, and many claim to see a resurgence of Confucian values in China's future.

22.15 TECHNICAL TERMS

ch'i/qi	material force, matter, as well as life-energy (pronounced "chee").
li	"principle" or "the pattern or rational principle which all things must follow."
T'ai-chi/Taiji	Great Ultimate (pronounced "tie-jee").
Chu Hsi	Zhu Xi (pronounced "ju-shi")
Wang Yang-ming	

22.16 QUESTIONS FOR FURTHER DISCUSSION

(1) For most of its history, Neo-Confucianism looked to the ancient past as having the answers to all important questions. Are there any similar attitudes found in Western thought or Western religions?

(2) The Neo-Confucians searched for the one single underlying principle (*li*) which could make sense out of all phenomena. Modern physicists sometimes talk about the great Theory of Everything, a theory can which explain the four basic forces of nature, and unify quantum mechanics and physics in the macro world (as with the recent celebration following the demonstration of the existence of the Higgs boson). What are the similarities between the Neo-Confucian approach towards ultimate principles and that of modern physics? What are their differences?

(3)   The Chinese decided that Confucian and Neo-Confucian ideas were impractical when dealing with the military might of Western powers. If you had been emperor of China, how would you have established the educational system? Would you have included any Confucian ideas or practices? Which ones? Why? Why not?

SELECTED BIBLIOGRAPHY

NEO-CONFUCIAN SOURCES

Chan Wing-tsit, *A Source Book in Chinese Philosophy* (Princeton, N.J.: Princeton University Press, 1963)

Chang, Carsun, *Development of Neo-Confucian Thought* (New Haven: College and University Press, 1963)

Chang, Carsun, *The Development of Neo-Confucian Thought: Volume 2* (New York: Bookman Associates, 1962)

de Bary, Wm. Theodore, W. T. Chan and Burton Watson, *Sources of Chinese Tradition*, 2 volumes (New York: Columbia University Press, 1960)

Fung Yu-lan, *A History of Chinese Philosophy* in two volumes, tr. by Derk Bodde, (Princeton, N.J.: Princeton University Press, 1952–1953).

Gardner, Daniel K., *Learning to Be a Sage: Selections from the "Conversations of Master Chu, Arranged Topically" by Chu Hsi* (Berkeley, CA: University of California Press, 1990)

Van Voorst, Robert E., *Anthology of World Scriptures*, 6th ed. (Belmont, Ca.: Wadsworth/Cengage Learning, 2008)

STUDIES IN NEO-CONFUCIAN THOUGHT AND HISTORY

Bell, Daniel A., *China's New Confucianism: Politics and Everyday Life in a Changing Society* (Princeton, NJ: Princeton University Press, 2010)

Bell, Daniel A. and Hahm, Chaibong, eds., *Confucianism for the Modern World* (London: Cambridge University Press, 2003).

Chan, Wing-tsit, *A Source Book in Chinese Philosophy* (Princeton, NJ: Princeton University Press, 1963)

Chang, Carsun, *Development of Neo-Confucian Thought* (New Haven, CT: College and University Press, 1963)

Chang, Carsun, *The Development of Neo-Confucian Thought: Volume 2* (New York: Bookman Associates, 1962)

Chappell, David, "New Buddhist Movements" in Kevin Trainor, ed., *Buddhism* (London: Oxford University Press, 2004)

Cheek, Timothy, ed., *A Critical Introduction to Mao* (New York: Cambridge, 2010)

de Bary, Wm. Theodore, W. T. Chan and Burton Watson, *Sources of Chinese Tradition*, 2 volumes (New York: Columbia University Press, 1960)

de Bary, Wm. Theodore, *The Unfolding of Neo-Confucianism*

Fenby, Jonathan. *Modern China: The Fall and Rise of a Great Power, 1850 to the Present* (Ecco, 2008)

Gardner, Daniel K., *Learning to Be a Sage: Selections from the "Conversations of Master Chu, Arranged Topically" by Chu Hsi* (Berkeley, CA: University of California Press, 1990)

Gregory, Peter N., *Tsung-mi and the Sinification of Buddhism* (Honolulu: University of Hawai'i Press, 2002) Gregory does some interesting comparisons between Neo-Confucian thinkers and the ninth century Buddhist scholar, Tsung-mi.

Hammond, Kenneth J. and Jeffrey L. Richey, *The Sage Returns: The Confucian Revival in Contemporary China* (State University of New York Press, 2015)

Koller, John, *Asian Philosophies* (NJ: Pearson/Prentice Hall, 2007) 5th ed.

Koller, John, *Oriental Philosophies*, 2nd ed.,

Leese, Daniel, *Mao Cult: Rhetoric and Ritual in China's Cultural Revolution* (Cambridge: Cambridge University Press, 2011)

Lopez, Donald S., ed., *Religions of China in Practice* (Princeton, 1996)

Needham, Joseph, *Science and Civilization in China*, Vol. II (London: Cambridge University Press, 1956)

Seagrave, Sterling, *Lords of the Rim: How Offshore Chinese Networks Became the World's Richest People Over Two Thousand Years* – Newly Revised Edition (Bowstring Books, 2014)

_____, *Lords of the Rim 2010: The Invisible Empire of the Overseas Chinese* (CreateSpace Independent Publishing, 2010)

Silbey, David J., *The Boxer Rebellion and the Great Game in China* (New York: Hill and Wang, 2012)

Shun, Kwong-Loi & David Wong, eds., *Confucian Ethics: A Comparative Study of Self, Autonomy and Community* (New York: Cambridge, 2004)

Temple, Robert, and Joseph Needham, *The Genius of China: 3,000 Years of Science, Discovery, and Invention* (Inner Traditions Press, 2007)

Wang, Robin R., *Yinyang: The Way of Heaven and Earth in Chinese Thought and Culture* (London: Cambridge, 2012)

Wu, Laurence C., *Fundamentals of Chinese Philosophy* (New York: University Press of America, 1986)

Yong Huang, *Why Be Moral? Learning from the Neo-Confucian Cheng Brothers* (New York: SUNY Press, 2014)

Zheng, Yangwen, *Social Life of Opium in China* (New York: Cambridge, 2005)

Ziporyn, Brook, *Ironies of Oneness and Difference: Coherence in Early Chinese Thought; Prolegomena to the Study of Li* (SUNY series in Chinese Philosophy and Culture, 2013)

_____, *Beyond Oneness and Difference: Li and Coherence in Chinese Buddhist Thought and Its Antecedents* (SUNY Series in Chinese Philosophy and Culture, 2014)

Religion in Modern China

Bush, R. C., *Religion in Communist China* (1970).

Chan, Wing-tsit, *Religious Trends in Modern China* (New York: Columbia Univ. Press, 1953).

Chandler, Stuart, *Establishing a Pure Land on Earth: The Foguang Perspective on Modernization and Globalization* (2002)

Chau, Adam Yuet, ed., *Religion in Contemporary China: Revitalization and Innovation* (New York: Routledge, 2011)

Fisher, Gareth, *From Comrades to Bodhisattvas: Moral Dimensions of Lay Buddhist Practice in Contemporary China* (Honolulu, HI: University of Hawai'i' Press, 2014)

Huang, Julia, *Charisma and Compassion: Cheng Yen and the Buddhist Tzu Chi Movement* (2009)

Laliberto, Andre, *The Politics of Buddhist Organizations in Taiwan* 1989–2003 (2004)

Madsen, Richard, *Democracy's Dharma: Religious Renaissance and Political Development in Taiwan* (2007)

Welch, Holmes, *The Buddhist Revival in China* (Cambridge: Harvard Univ. Press, 1968).

_____, *Buddhism Under Mao* (Cambridge: Harvard Univ. Press, 1972)

Wu, Yiching, *The Cultural Revolution at the Margins: Chinese Socialism in Crisis* (Cambridge: Harvard University Press, 2014)

Yü Chün-fang, *The Renewal of Buddhism: Chu-hung and the Late Ming Synthesis* (1981).

Zhi, Ji, "Buddhism in the Reform Era: A Secular Revival?" in *Religion in Contemporary China: Revitalization and Innovation*, ed. Adam Yuet Chau (New York: Routledge, 2011)

CHAPTER 22: NEO-CONFUCIANISM

PART IV: JAPAN

CHAPTER 23: JAPANESE THOUGHT AND SHINTO

23.1 OVERVIEW OF THE CHAPTER

Do not assume that people in Japan share the same religion and spiritual assumptions as people in India and China. You will discover that although there are influences and similarities, there are also significant differences. Japan is a group of four main islands and numerous smaller islands off the coast of Korea, China and Russia. These islands have been inhabited for as far back as 30–35,000 years when Japan was physically connected to the Asian mainland. About 12,000 years ago, the marshy land bridge was submerged. It was then that Japan became separate islands.

For most of their history, the Japanese did not think of Buddhism or the native Shinto practices as "religions" in the sense that westerners use the term. In fact, in the late 1800s after studying Christianity, the Japanese denied that Shinto was a religion, and instead considered it as scientific.[1] Despite these observations, we in the West tend to label Shinto as a world religion, and so we will use the term "religion" in this chapter, although noting that the term is potentially misleading.[2]

The earliest layers of Japanese concern with supernatural forces are clearly shamanistic, and those layers persist in the popular folk traditions found throughout Japan. It is also true that folk religions in Korea, in Mongolia and in China were profoundly shamanistic, so shamanism is an important feature of the Far Eastern cultures (although found in Western religions as well). Although Japan has imported much from the Chinese and Korean mainland, this process happened over long time spans and the Japanese assimilated and changed the newly arrived cultural artifacts to fit the Japanese ways. Borrowing and assimilating foreign cultures has always been a major force in the life of the Japanese.

The concept of religion as people in the West use the term is not found in the classical Japanese world-view. It was not until the seventeenth century when Christian missionaries came to Japan that the Japanese had to coin a new term to try to capture the common Western sense of "religion," and that Japanese term is *shukyo*.[3] In English it would be "authoritative lineage" + "teaching" or perhaps "ancient sect" + "respected teaching" or "institutional

---

[1] For more on this, see Jason Josephson, *The Invention of Religion in Japan* (Chicago: University of Chicago Press, 2012).

[2] We have discussed problems with the term "religion" previously. When we talk about "religion" we tend to make the Eurocentric assumption that there must be some universal essence to all religions, and despite numerous attempts to define that essence, no such essence has ever been found. Even the question "What is religion?" is based on assumptions that are very controversial. The religious categories we use to answer this question are historically specific and culturally relative, not universal. Daniel Dubuisson argues that the word "religion" is too Western in its associated meanings to be useful outside a European context. Scholars have argued that both "religion" and "religious experience" are a relatively late and distinctively Western inventions. For example, see Daniel Dubuisson, *The Western Construction of Religion: Myths, Knowledge, and Ideology* (Johns Hopkins University Press, 2007), or Tomoko Masuzawa, *The Invention of World Religions: Or, How European Universalism Was Preserved in the Language of Pluralism* (University of Chicago Press, 2005), or Brent Nongbri, *Before Religion: A History of a Modern Concept* (Yale University, 2013)

[3] In Japanese the term *shukyo* renders "religion," however the Japanese two-character compound *shukyo* (*zongjiao* in Chinese) is not ancient; it was created by Jesuit missionaries in Japan. Because the Japanese did not have words for anything quite like Christian beliefs, the missionaries made up the two-character compound in an attempt to capture the Western concept of religion. Interestingly, the literal meaning of *shukyo* is something like "tenets-teachings," "sectarian-tenets" or "lineage-teaching," a respected teaching handed down in a line of teachers. According to Professor Dan Lusthaus, the compound implies reverence for an institutionalized ancestral dogma. The Chinese borrowed the two-character compound from the Japanese.

doctrine" + "tenets." Of course none of these resemble the meaning that Western people ascribe to the term "religion," although it might be historically accurate.

Japanese cultural attitudes towards supernatural beings do not resemble the common Western religious attitudes. There are no commandments and the gods do not issue moral rules. The gods do not punish immoral behavior. There are official political and religious myths which permeate the culture, but there are no claims one must accept on faith. Japanese religions do not demand followers obey priests, and do not impose rules on moral behavior such as contraception, sexual behavior, stem cell research, or abortion. These things are guided by tradition. These are not controlled by priestly authorities who claim to speak for a god.

Traditional Japanese folk activities were not focused on faith, on dogma, or doctrine. When we use the Euro-centered term "religion" to describe Shinto, we must realize that religion in Japan is about benefits and about ritual activities, not beliefs. Japanese people participate in local community folk rituals and celebrations which generally belong to the perspective called Shinto, they visit shrines where they announce themselves to spirits, they freely participate in several forms of Buddhism, and may request a Christian wedding as well as a Buddhist funeral. In spite of participating in these activities, the great majority of Japanese consider themselves non-religious in the Western sense of the term.

The emperor of Japan was not only the head of the government and the head of the official Shinto sect of Japanese religion, he and his family were also promoted as divinities in human bodies. Japanese state Shinto utilized the power of holy texts and scriptures to support the divine status of the ruling family, to support the family's unquestioned right to rule and unify the country under their rule, to clarify the status of the huge variety of spirits and divinities called *kami*, and to explicate the relationship between *kami* and ordinary human beings. Throughout the history of Japan, any climactic event that could be interpreted favorably was seen as irrefutable evidence of the divinity of the imperial family.

Like the United States, modern Japan is a secular nation without an official state religion endorsed by the government. In 1945, a strict separation of church and state was imposed upon Japan by the United States at the end of World War II, and this strict separation is enshrined in the Japanese constitution. There have been a number of new religions following World War II, but the majority of contemporary Japanese do not consider themselves religious and are not affiliated with any religious group. The majority of younger Japanese have little interest in, or knowledge of the details of either Shinto or Buddhism. Fewer than 1% of the Japanese belong to Christian denominations. There is not any exclusive identification with any single religion.

In this chapter, we'll focus on the folk tradition and organized Shinto. In the next chapter, we'll discuss Japanese Buddhism and recent developments in Japanese religion.

JAPANESE HISTORICAL PERIODS

PRE-HISTORIC ERA (10,000 B.C.E.-350 C.E.)
      Jomon Era - about 10,000 B.C.E. to 350/250 B.C.E.
      Yayoi Era - approximately 250 B.C.E. to 250 C.E.
      Kofun Era - about 250 C.E. to 600 C.E.

PROTO-HISTORIC ERA (3rd century B.C.E. thru middle of 7th century C.E.)
      ASUKA (538-671 C.E.) Introduction of Buddhism from Korea.

CLASSICAL ERA (mid-7th through 12th century C.E.)
      NARA (672-780) Earliest sects established.
      HEIAN (781-1184) Tendai and Shingon established.

MEDIEVAL PERIOD (13th-18th centuries).
      KAMAKURA (1185-1338) Jodo, Shinshu, Nichiren, Zen.
      ASHIKAGA (1338-1568) Civil war, dark ages.
      MOMOYAMA (1568-1614) Hideyoshi, Tokugawa Iyeyasu (dictators).
      TOKUGAWA (1615-1867), also known as the Edo Period. Dominance of Buddhist church;
            Portuguese expelled; ports closed. 1867-1868
            Feudalism abolished & monarchy restored.

MODERN PERIOD (19th century to the present)
      MEIJI (1868-1911)
      TAISHO (1912-1926)
      SHOWA (1927-1988).
      HEISEI (1989-present).

23.2 A HISTORICAL OVERVIEW OF JAPANESE THOUGHT

      One way to organize the development of Japanese thought and spirituality is in terms of historical eras. The first era would include the earliest prehistoric times, followed by a decentralized unification of Japanese civilization prior to significant Chinese influences (prior to the 7th century C.E) and the beginning of the divine ruling family. Then there is a period of significant Chinese influence, roughly the ninth to the thirteenth centuries. This is followed by the era where Japan slowly begins to close off and assimilate these cultural influences, becoming a decentralized isolated feudal society. Certainly, Chinese influences predominate, including Buddhism, but by the thirteenth century, these strands would begin to be reshaped as Japan began to focus inwardly and accommodate the Chinese influences, and new and different Japanese forms of Buddhism arise. Finally, nineteenth century Western attitudes and influences began to reshape Japanese thought after the middle 1800s.

      During this period of Western influences, Japan evolved to a self-consciously modernizing nation that successfully assimilated Western technology, economic organization, military and political structures. With modernity came industry, warfare, imperial ideology, and a particularly exploitative attitude to the world's resources.

CHAPTER 23: JAPANESE SHINTO

23.3 THE HISTORICAL PERIODS OF JAPANESE SPIRITUALITY

THE FIRST PERIOD: The Prehistoric Era

Japan is composed of four main islands and a large number of smaller islands off the coast of Korea, China and Russia.[4] The Korean peninsula is only about 120 miles (200 km.) from the nearest Japanese island. However, Japan was not always islands in the sea; until about 12,000 years ago Japan was physically connected to continental Asia by a low marshy plain. Human beings and animals could and did walk from the Asian mainland to the peninsula that was Japan.

The very earliest inhabitants came to Japan 30,000–35,000 years ago. Archaeologists have found physical evidence of the earliest human inhabitants in shell-heaps along the seacoast. Very probably some the early inhabitants were also mountain dwellers who lived by hunting and gathering. Several different migrating groups came to Japan over the centuries.

Sea levels began to rise about 12,000 years ago and Japan became a group of islands separated from continental Asia. After the oceans rose, several distinct waves of new immigrants arrived at the Japanese islands on boats. The population expanded yet the amount of land that could be successfully cultivated to feed the population could not keep pace with this growth because almost two-thirds of Japan is mountains. Besides lumber, there are few natural raw materials on the islands of Japan, and consequently the Japanese had to depend upon external sources for raw mineral resources. The beautiful densely wooded Japanese forests and mountains made agriculture difficult. When rice-growing became essential, the population became most dense in those areas capable of growing rice, portions of the islands of Honshu, Kyushu and Shikoku.

Japan is part of a geological structure called the Pacific Ring of Fire which means that originally the islands were created by shifting geological plates and volcanic eruptions. It is the slipping of the active plates on the ocean floor which creates the devastating earthquakes, such as the terrible quake in March of 2011. Destructive tsunamis can and do result.

These geological features are also responsible for the vicious typhoons. Exceptionally stormy seas separate the islands of Japan from the edge of the mainland. For human beings who inhabit the islands, boat travel to and from the mainland was dangerous,[5] and living on the Japanese islands in an environment of earthquakes and typhoons offered little certainty in life. In that environment, one cannot help but be aware that all things are transient. One's home can be destroyed in an instant, and the climate can change from balmy to destructive overnight. In such a world, life is dangerous. These same conditions persist in the modern era. This awareness of transiency has clearly influenced the Japanese world views.

Among these very first inhabitants of Japan was the Ainu culture, a hunting, fishing, and gathering economy. The Ainu peoples may have been linked with prehistoric northern Asia and with Alaska, and perhaps Europe. It is believed that the early Ainu world-view was shamanistic with a special reverence for bears. As wave after wave of new immigrants came into Japan, the Ainu were pushed farther and farther north. Even today there is a small population of Ainu people still living in the far northern island of Japan.

---

[4] Hokkaido is the northmost island; then the largest island Honshu where Tokyo and Kyoto are found. Shikoku and Kyushu are the southern islands. There are many other smaller islands as well.

[5] As noted in the introductory paragraph, in the entire history of Japan, no invading army has ever conquered Japan via the sea from the mainland.

CHAPTER 23: JAPANESE SHINTO

The Jomon Era—approximately 10,000 B.C.E. to 350/250 B.C.E.

The Jomon culture[6] dominated the southern islands of Japan for nearly nine thousand years. That is a lot of time to develop and grow. The Jomon people were originally hunters, fishermen, and foragers, and the world's first known potters. Archaeologists have noted phallic emblems which were plentiful in these times, suggesting procreation, fruitfulness and fertility among humans and the crops. Throughout its history, Japan has always been comfortable with phallic and other procreative imagery.

Later Japanese mythology puts the mythical first emperor in the Jomon era. The legend is that Jimmu Tenno lived about 660 B.C.E., which (if this person actually existed) would be in this later Jomon time period.[7] Twelve-hundred years later the government-supported Shinto organization taught that the royal family was divine and descended from this mythical emperor Jimmu Tenno.

The Yayoi Era—approximately 250 B.C.E. to 250 C.E.

Approximately 250 B.C.E. another major wave of immigrants called the Yayoi came to Japan via Korea and dominated Japan for about five-hundred years. The Yayoi brought rice agriculture, iron and bronze; they brought potters and the wheel. The evidence indicates that most probably their society was matrilineal. During the Yayoi period, the dead were interred in jars (a custom typical of Korea during these times).

Recent findings based upon genetic studies of ancient DNA in fossilized bones of Jomon and Yayoi shows that both Yayoi and Jomon genes contributed to the contemporary Japanese gene pool.[8]

The Kofun Era—about 250 C.E. to 600 C.E.

The previous matrilineal Yayoi culture was completely overridden by the next group to immigrate into Japan, the Kofun people. The Kofun peoples established themselves as an elite ruling class, and they erected huge earthen tumulus burial mounds ("Kofun" means tomb). They were a very strong and highly defined warrior-based horse-riding Asian culture, which caused a complete transformation in Japanese civilization, going from about 250 C.E. to 600 C.E.

It is during this period that the fundamental social unit in Japan became the clan, and each clan claimed descent from a different supernatural spirit (*kami*) whose worship was led by the clan chief. In Japan, the group with the highest status was the warrior (unlike China where the scholar had the highest status and the warrior had low status). A seventh century book of Japanese peerage shows virtually one-third of the noble families in Japan claimed descent from a Chinese or Korean founding ancestor.[9] In addition, each clan had its ancestral divinity or spirit, and it was female shamans who divined the desires and wishes of the ancestral beings.

The end of the Kofun period came about 350 C.E. as the various clans jockeyed for power. One clan, the Yamato, justified its attempt to rule all of Japan by claiming that it was directly descended from the single most important of all the supernatural divine spirits which shared the island with the people, the *kami* spirit named **Amaterasu**, the Sun Goddess. Although powerful, the Yamato clan did not have sufficient military strength to enforce its rule until several centuries later.

---

[6] Junko Habu, *Ancient Jomon of Japan* (New York: Cambridge University, 2004).

[7] Of course, when the Japanese myth of the divine emperor was created, no one in that time period knew of Jomon civilization; that knowledge comes from recent archaeological explorations.

[8] John Travis, "Jomon Genes: Using DNA, researchers probe the genetic origins of modern Japanese," in *Science News*, Vol. 151, February 15, 1997, pp. 106-107.

[9] Bradley K. Hawkins, *An Introduction to Asian Religions*, p. 287.

CHAPTER 23: JAPANESE SHINTO

THE CLASSICAL PERIOD (mid-seventh through twelfth century C.E.) AND THE FOUNDATION OF INSTITUTIONAL SHINTO

In the Classical Period, the Yamato clan manipulated the folk religion of Japan to solidify its power by enshrining its leaders as divinities descended from *kami* spirits. The Yamato clan claimed the right to rule all of Japan because it was directly descended from Amaterasu, the Sun Goddess. The myth of the divinity of the emperor was used to unify the various clans under the divine authority of the Yamato clan. The same myth also brought a sense of pride and an awareness of the special virtues of the Japanese people, and it legitimized the power of the ruling clan, the Yamato, and its divine sovereign. This myth, that the Japanese are a unique, superior, and especially virtuous people, dominated Japanese culture into the twentieth century.[10]

It was during the Classical Period that the sophisticated civilization of T'ang (618–906 C.E.) China was introduced into Japan. In China, the Chinese court system kept detailed written records of all proceedings. There was no written Japanese language yet, so the Japanese court record-keepers and aristocrats learned to read and write Chinese in order to keep records. As a result, the politically powerful could read the great Chinese poetry, Chinese history, Chinese laws and manners, Chinese philosophy, and religion. They also collected and imitated Chinese black-ink art, and built temples in the Chinese style. The effect was overwhelming. The upper-class Japanese embraced everything flourishing in T'ang (618–906 C.E.) and Sung (960–1279) dynasty China, and that included aspects of Confucianism, religious Taoism, and Buddhism.[11]

After the introduction of Buddhism into Japan, the rulers drew upon Chinese Buddhist rituals and ideas, plus shamanistic folk religion to develop the state religion of Shinto, using it as a tool to solidify its position and cement central authority.

Although the Yamato emperor took on the role of high-priest of a newly institutionalized state religion called Shinto, the royal Yamato clan was not able to maintain its power. Beginning in the seventh century, the rival Fujiwara clan gained so much military strength that the Yamato emperor no longer ruled; he became a heavenly religious symbol to venerate and official head of government but with no actual political authority. Because the monarch was essential to state religion, Yamato royal family rulers were not killed, but merely tolerated and manipulated as puppets.

THIRD PERIOD: MEDIEVAL PERIOD (thirteenth–eighteenth centuries): THE MILITARY RULE JAPAN

During the Medieval period, military warlords ruled Japan. The state-supported Shinto organization was tied tightly to the Yamato royal family, which no longer was in control of the country and could no longer distribute lavish financial support. As a result the most important Shinto shrines lost their main source of financial patronage, and state Shinto declined in importance. Buddhist temples grew stronger. It was common for Buddhist temples to be built on Shinto shrine lands and gifts to these Buddhist temples was not only to the Buddhist group, but also provided additional financial support to the Shinto priests.

State-supported Shinto may have lost much of its influence, but the myth that the emperor was divine did protect his life and the lives of his family through the following centuries. The heavenly sovereign was not killed, but merely moved aside to a ceremonial position with no power.

---

[10] The perceptive reader will notice that many cultures in the modern world promulgate the same sorts of myth. Sociology scholars have pointed out that the United States has a "Frontier Myth" that inspires most cowboy movies, and an "Immigration Myth" that leads us to believe that the United States in its past was unusually welcoming and tolerant making it unique and special. That belief tends to be unquestioned, and when challenged, many are offended.

[11] As we saw in a previous chapter, there were several forms of Buddhism in China; the Pure Land, the T'ien-t'ai, the Hua-yen, and the Tantric Chen-yen (in Japanese, Shingon, that is, "true word" or *mantra*) school. Each of these was imported into Japan as separate schools, however the esoteric forms of Chinese Buddhism gained special prominence in Japan. At this time in China philosophical Taoism did not exist separately but its ideas had been absorbed into Ch'an Buddhism.

During this period several forms of Buddhism came to enjoy the support of the new military rulers, especially Zen (or Ch'an in China), Tendai (T'ien-t'ai in China), and Shingon (Chen-yen, esoteric Buddhism). The influence of Pure Land Buddhism spread throughout the general population. The Neo-Confucian philosophy of Wang Yang-ming (1472-1529) which stressed the unity of knowledge and action came to influence the ethic of the *samurai* warriors. In Japan Wang Yang-ming's name is pronounced Oh-yo-mei, and the school of Oyomei exerted influence on many Japanese reformers.

Originally, the emphasis of popular Shinto was to support the authority of the Yamato royal family. Shinto priests asserted that if proper rituals were conducted and paid for, native divinities called *kami* could grant wishes and protect the nation and its people. Shinto *kami* offered financial success, good health, favorable business conditions, and even good scores in final examinations at school. Shinto shrines also sold small figures, or talismans, which were supposed to provide spiritual protection or a relationship with a beneficial *kami*. The power of the amulets would slowly wear away, and the petitioner would need to buy another within the year.

It was during the later years of this medieval period that European powers and Americans saw Japan as a great source of potential wealth derived from trade, and wanted to bring the country under their spheres of influence. Europeans began trade in the early 1500s. By the late 1500s the Japanese powers pushed away the threat of Western influences with the slogan "revere the emperor and expel the barbarians."

On July 8, 1853, four American warships under Commodore Matthew Perry anchored off the Japanese coast and demanded that Japan open itself to foreign trade and commerce or suffer military consequences.[12] This initiated a crisis in the Japanese government.

The ruling clans of Japan were unable to deal with the military threats from the West. As a result of the American Admiral Perry and the threat of very powerful Western military attacks, it was believed that a strengthening of the imperial family's centrality and importance could unify the nation against the Western barbarians. The governing bodies arranged it so that the royal family regained its power and state-supported Shinto was used to strengthen the unifying influence of a divine ruler. State Shinto was a tool to stimulate nationalistic fervor.

THE MODERN PERIOD (19th–21st centuries): THE EMPEROR RETURNS TO POWER

Following 1868, traditional feudal structures were abolished officially and the royal family monarchy was restored to political power. State Shinto was encouraged and supported once again by the government and controlled by the government. After 1868 the emperor was openly worshiped as a god and state-supported Shinto religion was imposed upon every family and every school. School teachers at all grade levels led each class in prayers addressed to the divine emperor.[13]

With the imperial family once again the center of institutional Shinto, shrines became even more important, and the people believed that Shinto priests controlled access to powerful *kami* who offered the possibility of many benefits. The Japanese were taught that their *kami* gods would protect them from military harm, and that their duty was to embrace the will of their divine emperor. Among many intellectuals the Neo-Confucian philosophy of Oyomei (Wang Yang-ming 1472-1529) influenced reformers, scholars, politicians, and even exerted influence upon the Japanese *bushido* military code of conduct for a warrior. The School of Oyomei affected many Japanese thinkers.

During this period which the Japanese call the Meiji era (1868-1911), Japan evolved from a decentralized, isolated feudal society to a self-consciously modernizing nation that successfully assimilated Western technology, economic organization, and military and political power. The Japanese were encouraged to learn the Western spirit and master Western science, technology, and political ideas.

---

[12] George Feifer, *Breaking Open Japan: Commodore Perry, Lord Abe and the American Imperialism of 1853* (New York: Harper Collins, 2006).

[13] Many books detail this period. For example, see Helen Hardacre, *Shinto and the State: 1888-1988* (New York: Princeton University Press, 1991).

CHAPTER 23: JAPANESE SHINTO

The Japanese quickly discovered that Western military power was not due to Western religion but rather it was independence of thought and questioning religious authority which were primary features of Western critical analysis which led to Western advances in science which in turn led to military dominance. In the flush of modernization, some Japanese thinkers advocated freedom of speech, freedom of assembly, and freedom of belief, and welcomed the open clash of ideas as essential to Japan making progress.[14] In 1875, a Japanese thinker advocated the recognition that the emperor was not really a divinity,[15] but this idea did not take hold.

Politicians reshaped official institutional Shinto into a cult of patriotic support. To be a patriotic citizen was to fulfill the will of the divine emperor. To be a good Japanese meant that each citizen must wholeheartedly and unreservedly support the god-emperor in all of his undertakings, including a series of wars.[16] After the Shinto-inspired resurgence of nationalism in 1890, the Japanese army won military victories over China in 1894–1895 and victories over Russia 1904–1905. This was perceived as irrefutable evidence that the Japanese emperor was indeed divine and because of this it was only right that Japan should rule neighboring countries. The next focus was strengthening Japan against the perceived threat posed by Western powers and culture. Christianity was not seen as a positive source of Western power; instead it was seen as a tool serving the interests of Western colonialism, Western economic and military powers.

The process of nationalistic wars eventually led to the Japanese bombing of the American naval base in Hawaii, Pearl Harbor, on December 7, 1941. American and Japanese forces fought hotly-contested battles throughout the Pacific for the next several years. Following the dropping of two American atomic bombs on the cities of Hiroshima and Nagasaki in 1945, the Japanese surrendered and World War II came to an end.[17]

The United States imposed several conditions of surrender; the emperor had to go on radio and renounce his divinity and strict separation of church and state was imposed. The Japanese government wrote into its constitution that it was forbidden to support any religion financially or politically. This separation of church and state forced a disruption of many traditional Japanese religious patterns, and the Japanese belief in their divine emperor and their own unique national identity was seriously weakened. Officially modern Japan is a secular nation, but in the post-war period several new religions arose out of the chaos and became important. These are discussed in the next chapter.

23.4 SUPERNATURAL SPIRITS: THE *KAMI*

It seems typical of all early civilizations to have an awareness of places which appear to be special, to be unusual, to possess a special aura, to be sacred. Some places, some objects, and some beings are numinous. These special places and objects were referred to as *kami*, but the term *kami* also referred to sentient beings who possessed the power to control forces of nature. The forces of creation were referred to as *kami*. Some animals could be *kami*. Local communities had special reverence for elements in nature such as a nearby mountain or mountain pass, or a cave, or a rock, or a tree. These sacred objects or areas were where the realm of spirits interacted with the realm of nature. The realm of spirits was especially pure, and it was essential that contamination from the human world not be allowed to

---

[14] Bob Tadashi Wakabayashi, *Modern Japanese Thought* (London: Cambridge University Press, 1999), p. 4.

[15] *Ibid.*, p. 4, p. 8.

[16] See Marius Jansen, ed., *The Emergence of Meiji Japan* (New York, Cambridge University Press, 1995).

[17] The decision to use atomic bombs against Japanese populations has remained a topic of serious discussion ever since the events. For example, see Wilson D. Miscamble, *Most Controversial Decision: Truman, the Atomic Bombs, and the Defeat of Japan* (New York: Cambridge University Press, 2011). The nationalistic fervor of the Japanese people in support of the total war ideology of Japanese imperialism is discussed in Louise Young's *Japan's Total Empire: Manchuria and the Culture of Wartime Imperialism* (Berkeley: University of California Press, 1998).

sully these places and objects. Pollution angered local *kami*.

The Japanese term *kami* is commonly rendered as "god" or "gods" in English, but as was true for many of the other non-Western religions, the word "god" or "gods" is not very useful.[18] The Japanese use two different characters to render *kami*: one of them means "superior" or "upper" and the other is "sacred" or "divinity."

Kami are often anthropomorphic deities, but their character and their nature is not clearly described; rather their qualities are very vague and loose. Very few *kami* have a name, or a character or personality.[19] There are many kinds of *kami*, some of which are good, most of which are neither good nor bad, and some are plainly mischievous and even malevolent. Most of the time *kami* are not so much seen as they are sensed. Anything that gives us a feeling of awe, a feeling of being in the presence of unusual power is a sign that we are in a locale sacred to *kami*. Anything which is unusual, strange, inexplicable, out-of-the-ordinary, and especially awe-inspiring, can be the indicator of the presence of *kami*. When someone feels such a presence, they can tie a straw rope around a rock, or a tree to mark the spot as special. It is not just good things which are *kami*; evil and mysterious things can be *kami* as well.

Kami were the source of all that was inexplicable in human lives. If contamination were to come into contact with the spirit realm or things important to the spiritual realm, then the consequences could range from misfortune to disaster. Illness, destruction, typhoon, earthquakes and tsunami could result. The people believed that constant rituals of purification were essential if the community were to survive.

Kami-spirits can live anywhere, and not only in heavenly realms. Traditionally the Japanese believed that all natural objects harbored some sort of *kami*-spirit and that we humans share our world with great forces and beings. Divinity was ascribed to powerful and awe-inspiring elements such as sun, moon, storms, oceans . . . but a home for a divine spirit was also ascribed to mountains, caves, rocks, streams, trees, and flowers, and even to a patch of ground in a farmer's field, the water-well, and one's own home including the cooking pot (or a modern office building). The world we inhabit was composed of visible and invisible realms, and both are populated with numerous natural and powerful non-human sentient *kami*, in addition to humans and the other animals. A traditional text claims there are 80,000 *kami*, although perhaps this is just a way of saying that there are uncountably many. This could be described as a form of polytheism, but perhaps just as well it is a variety of pantheism.

Amaterasu, the Sun Goddess, is a *kami*, but so too mud, sand, and even vermin can be *kami*. A great many natural objects, like seas, grass, trees, rocks, mountains, and rivers, have been called *kami*; animals have been identified as *kami*; even some departed charismatic human beings who embodied cultural virtues or engendered admiration are called *kami*. The ancient ancestors of Japanese clans have been considered *kami*.

Departed ancestors are not automatically *kami* although certain extraordinary ancestors might be *kami*.

Some extraordinary ancestors might become *kami* after their death, but this was not common. Most of our own ancestors do not elicit awe and reverence during their lifetimes. It is believed that these ancestral departed spirits may remain to interact with the human realm, especially their descendants. Despite the dangers of life in Japan, Japanese religion was not based upon fear of nature or fear of the gods of nature. Instead the Japanese religious impulse tends to be an aesthetic appreciation of nature and an unwillingness to annoy or anger those myriad powerful beings with whom we share our universe. The *kami* are spirits, infused with vague super-human powers such as the ability to control the weather. Like the rest of the world the Japanese believed that changes in the weather, especially typhoons, were generated by *kami* (a typhoon is called a "*kami*-wind," a "divine-wind," or *kami-kaze*).

---

[18] To be consistent, Western Christians should then call their own assortment of angels and saints "gods" because these, like *kami*, are supernatural beings with magical powers.

[19] For some of the named *kami* see Jess Hoda, *Shinto Kami: Deities of Japanese Shinto* (CreateSpace Independent Publishing, 2016).

In fact, even in modern times, when Japanese people go to a Shinto shrine believed to be inhabited by a spirit being, a *kami*, they have little concern for the exact nature of the *kami* with whom they are interacting. Usually no one knows a name to associate with the *kami*, and there may not be a single story to tell about that *kami*. The key point is that Japanese go to a shrine seeking benefits. Perhaps an important examination is upcoming and the student requests help from a *kami*. Perhaps a family member is ill. Is one's business in need of help? Ask a *kami* for help. Has someone been married, or graduated, or been born? Celebrate the event with *kami* and ask that *kami* protect them. Notice that the person at the shrine is likely to experience a sense of awe, a sense of peace, a nuance of heightened reality, and they find the traditional gestures of reverence to be appropriate and meaningful.[20]

Based on what we know about the history of the Japanese, it is very likely that the ancient attitudes towards nature included an aesthetic appreciation of the beauty found everywhere in nature, and it was not only Japanese poets and artists who experienced a delicate sensitivity to the constantly changing beauties of nature. Japanese civilization has cultivated a heightened aesthetic appreciation of nature. It is most likely that early Japanese pantheism is a religion of love and gratitude rather than a religion of fear — the earliest rites and rituals were praising and thanking as well as placating and mollifying the divinities.

23.5 THE CLOSENESS OF HUMAN BEINGS, *KAMI*, AND NATURE

A distinctive attitude of Japanese religion is the relationship between *kami*, human beings, and nature, which is unlike the common Western view. Western people are used to a religious hierarchy of very strict separation between gods and humans and nature. In Japanese sensibilities, the triad of gods (*kami*), humans, and nature, are on a nearly equal level, forming a triangle of harmonious interrelationships. Since we share this world with powerful anthropomorphic beings and forces, human beings must avoid things offensive to the *kami*. Purification, rituals, and charms date back to the earliest periods in Japanese pre-history, and these practices have gone on to shape Japanese Buddhism as well. Ritual purity is central: if one is contaminated, dirty, or unclean, then one is offensive to the *kami* who share our immediate environment and one needs cleansing and purification. Purification rituals were designed to remove things offensive to *kami*.[21]

23.6 THE JAPANESE CREATION STORY

The traditional Japanese beliefs about the origins of the Japanese islands and the Japanese people are found in the folk religion mythology. Since approximately 600 C.E. the rulers of Japan encouraged the people to believe that their sovereign was descended from the gods, that he and his family were divine. They also taught the people that the entire Japanese nation was homogeneous in its makeup and unique among all the world's peoples.[22]

---

[20] H. B. Earhart, "A Brief Introduction," from *Japanese Religion*, 3rd Edition.

[21] This great stress on pollution and ritual purification is one aspect which separates Japanese Buddhism and Japanese culture from Chinese Buddhism and Chinese culture.

[22] Modern DNA analysis indicates that this belief is not quite justified. It reveals that Japanese society was made up of several distinct waves of immigrants. Present-day Japanese are predominantly Mongolian, but several separate groups made up the Japanese people. Genetic evidence suggests that the early Jomon people had much in common with the people who came from Siberia, Mongolia, and the people who settled Tibet only a few thousand years ago. Linguistically, the spoken Japanese language belongs to the same language family as the Korean language but is not related to spoken Chinese. Apart from the use of Chinese graphic characters, grammatically Japanese has no relationship to Chinese and belongs to an entirely different family of languages.

CHAPTER 23: JAPANESE SHINTO

In the creation myths of Japan, *kami* spirits participated in the formation of the world out of chaos (somewhat like the gods of Greek and Roman mythology). For Japanese mythology, the world was **not** created out of nothing by a divinity. Japanese creation myths bear no similarity to creation stories in Western religions. In fact, there is more than one distinct origin myth in Japanese religion. One such origin tale tells that the gods did not create the earth, but rather the *kami* arise out of the earth. Heaven and earth were not separated at the earliest time, but gradually the purer aspects of matter rise to form heaven, and the heavier parts settle to form earth.[23] Something sprouts from earth, and becomes a god. Six generations later, it gives rise to the primordial couple, and male-female reproduction begins.

The predominant story tells of the brother and sister pair of *kami* named Izanagi ("he who invites") and Izanami ("she who is invited"). Brother and sister deities mate, and give birth to the islands of Japan and all the numerous *kami* spirits who inhabit our world. The islands of Japan are a heavenly home for *kami* but that heavenly home is also shared with human beings. Izanami then gives birth to the god of fire, and loses her life in the flames. Izanagi tries to descend into the underworld to recover her, but fails. He returns from the underworld and purifies himself in the salty waters of the ocean. As he washes, he produces another generation of *kami* divinities. The goddess of the sun, Amaterasu, is born of his left eye, and the moon god is born from his right eye; the god of hot summer winds, the storm god, is born of his nostrils. The storm god then performs marvelous exploits to rescue and save the Japanese people.[24]

Amaterasu, the sun goddess, sends her divine *kami* grandson Ninigi to rule the Japanese islands but Ninigi has to battle against human beings and human forces which create chaos. According to legend Ninigi landed on the island of Kyushu (closest to Korea) and he brought the central symbols of the royal family, a mirror (symbolizing the sun and the sun goddess), a sword (symbolizing the virtue of the warrior), and a curved stone or jewel (symbolizing fertility), to Japan. Ninigi married a local princess, and she gave birth to two sons. Three generations later, Ninigi's great grandson, Jimmu Tenno,[25] was born about 660 B.C.E.[26] Thus the myths tell us that it required three generations of descendants before the Ninigi line subdued the violent and destructive humans and established themselves as royalty. The first emperor is descended from the sun goddess, so he is semi-divine. According to legend, Jimmu Tenno was the first emperor of Japan and the direct ancestor of the current emperor of Japan.

In historical fact, the evidence is that an actual imperial line did not begin to emerge in Japan until more than a thousand years later. However the Amaterasu /Ninigi legends provided a ready-made mythology of origin to justify the ruling position of the Yamato clan and family. The result (supported by the state throughout Japanese history) was a belief in a deep and abiding natural bond between the *kami*-religion and the Japanese people, the Japanese nation, and the Japanese emperor (even when the emperor no longer ruled but served merely as a figure-head).

Myths affect the way people understand themselves, their culture, and their world. These stories from the ancient past which claim to be historical truths gives the people a sense of unity and pride in the Japanese nation. All world civilizations have religious and political myths which inspire nationalistic sentiment and pride in one's nation as special. It worked this way in Japanese history, unifying the people in the belief in the god-given superiority of the

---

[23] We have seen something similar in Chinese thought, where *yang* energy went upwards to form the heavens, it is light, fire, life, movement. The *yin* aspect of reality is heavy and descended to form the earth we inhabit, it is water, death, stillness.

[24] These tales are recounted in the Shinto text, *Kojiki* (Record of Ancient Matters). The myth combines the goddess of the sun, the moon god, and the wind god, into a harmonious triad.

[25] Ten-no means "heavenly" + "sovereign." This term applied to the divine rulers of Japan is usually translated as "emperor" in English.

[26] On February 11, 1940 the militarized Japanese government celebrated the 2,600th anniversary celebration of mythical Emperor Jimmu as historical fact. A book which deals with this topic is Kenneth J. Ruoff, *Imperial Japan at It's Zenith: The Wartime Celebration of the Empire's 2,600th Anniversary* (Ithaca: Cornell University Press, 2010).

Japanese emperor, the special virtue of the Japanese nation and the Japanese people. These myths are what allow the citizens to die for the sake of the ruler, for the sake of one's god, for the sake of the nation. Of course, the myths of a country do serve to legitimize the power of the rulers.[27]

In spite of the mythology, before the line of emperors emerged, women may have been the rulers of early Japan. Historical evidence strongly suggests that the earliest rulers were most likely women shamans who served the gods and were the channel of communication between the *kami* and the people. A Chinese record from 298 C.E. describes a Queen Himiko, child of the sun, as a shaman and ruler of Japan.[28]

23.7 RELIGION IN JAPAN: FIVE MAJOR STRANDS

There has never been a single common core of religious tradition shared by all Japanese. Japanese religion is richly synergetic. The religious world-view of Japan can be thought of as a rope composed of at least five interwoven strands. These include (1) Little Tradition folk religious practices, (2) institutional Shinto which deified the emperor, (3) Chinese Confucianism, (4) Chinese Buddhism, and (5) religious Taoism/Daoism. These are explained below.

(1) "Little Tradition" Folk Religion

The oral strand of Japanese religion is composed of numerous traditional beliefs and practices existing outside highly organized and structured religion. There never was a single religious tradition; only many similar traditions separated by distance and time. These go back to the past before written languages, emerging out of the teachings of the shamans and priests. Male and female shamans believed they shared the world with *kami* spirits and that they could communicate with these *kami*; rituals, sacrifices, and rites could be used to appease these divinities. Certain symbols like the sun and moon were especially important to the interaction of sacred realms and human realms. There is a clear element of sun-worship in early Japanese religion (as explained above, the sun goddess Amaterasu has a special connection to the ruling family of Japan).

Some of these ancient beliefs and practices are associated with hunting and rice agriculture. The Japanese have many nature myths, and as noted above, the sun has a role of special importance for farming communities. The oral folk tradition includes community celebrations of thanks for successful crops and celebrations connected to the yearly planting and harvesting cycles, and new year's celebrations. The oral tradition has creation myths, clusters of local deities, purification rituals, and charms. Fertility of the soil and fertility of farm animals are also of central importance. The community asked for heavenly blessings, asked for crops, abundance of food, and good weather. If rituals and prayers did not bring good crops, it was regarded as a sign of the displeasure of the *kami* due to some polluting infraction by a member of the community.

(2) The "Grand Tradition" of Institutional Shinto

The second of the five strands influencing Japanese religious world views is the uniquely Japanese official state religion called "The Way of the *Kami* spirits," or **Shinto**. Shinto is one of the major world religions, but as we shall see, it is quite unlike most of the formal religions which westerners tend to associate with the term "religion." Shinto is especially associated with Japanese myths, with rituals which are so ancient that they are lost in time, with priests who concern themselves with purification and cleanliness, with shrines dedicated to many different spiritual forces,

---

[27] Political myths are found in today's world as well as ancient Japan. We can spot the Japanese myths, but the myths of our own political culture are the ones that are difficult to recognize. For example, see Meffrey S. Victor, "Political Myths that Influence Voters" in *Skeptical Inquirer*, Vol 36, No. 4 (July/August 2012), pp. 48-51.

[28] Julia Ching, "East Asian Religions" in Willard Oxtoby, ed., *World Religions: Eastern Traditions*, Second Edition, pp. 344-345.

and with spiritual beings called *kami*.

The second strand of Japanese religion, Grand Tradition Shinto, is based upon ancient pre-historic assumptions and wide variety of practices of the first strand, Little Tradition Shinto, but in its developed forms it has also been influenced by aspects of Chinese Buddhism (including esoteric Buddhist practices) and religious Taoism. Its continuing influence is still found in the numerous shrines found in contemporary Japan.

The Grand Tradition of Shinto is a formal religion which concerns itself with promoting and teaching government sponsored myths, with state-mandated rituals, with ceremonial cleanliness and purification, with shrines in honor of national and local *kami*, with priests who interact with spirits, and with placating *kami* or obtaining benefits from *kami*. This second strand of formal institutional Shinto did not create a completely new form of religion in Japan, but organized and re-structured its pre-existing pre-historic folk heritage, combined with Buddhist and Chinese influences, into a distinctive tradition designed to support the authority of the ruling family.

(3) Chinese Confucianism

In 607 the Japanese court opened an embassy in China, and the Chinese responded by establishing an embassy in Japan. The result was the beginning of a vast exporting of Chinese culture into Japan. The Japanese deeply respected the high culture of China and those Japanese who traveled to China and returned to Japan brought with them the Chinese teachings of filial piety towards elders and ancestors,[29] social and family ethics, formal ceremonial interaction, theories of ruling, stress on loyalty to the traditions of the past, and loyalty to one's superior. The Confucian stress on virtue, benevolence and obedience to authority provided the basis for Japanese education based upon Chinese education models, and Chinese government institutions and policies. The value of Confucianism was that it could provide for social, cultural, and governmental harmony. The result was that in Japan, social and political identity was grounded in Confucian notions. However, few Japanese recognized this as the teaching of one particular school of Chinese thought called "Confucianism." To the Japanese those practices seemed inseparable from civilized Chinese culture and simply seemed to be the "Chinese way." As a result, Confucianism became deeply embedded into everyday behavior and belief in Japan, even though the Japanese did not think of it as a separate school of thought in China.

There was a major difference between the society of Japan and China. In China, it was the literati, the well-educated scholar gentry who had high social status, and the soldier was on the bottom of the social ladder. Japan was just the reverse; a military society dominated by the warrior ethos, and Chinese Confucianism was modified to reflect the Japanese hierarchy with the warrior on top. Chinese stress on loyalty becomes loyalty to one's clan leader, loyalty to one's military superior. The Japanese stressed the superior-subordinate relationship between lord and vassal, between husband and wife, between male and female. In virtually every relationship, there is superior and inferior, and the superior has more power, more rights, and more privileges than the inferior. The duty of each inferior is to be submissive. The Japanese saw the most important relationship not between father and son, but rather ruler to ruled, reflecting the belief in Japan that the emperor was divine, and that the citizen owed unquestioning loyalty and obedience to the emperor and to all their superiors.

Later during the Tokugawa era (1615-1867), Neo-Confucianism was encouraged, and the Neo-Confucian scholar Chu Hsi's (1130-1200 C.E.) version of this thought system[30] was used as an official ideology for education, where the Japanese stressed rationality, patriotism, good government, and a rational ethic. Others stressed reverence, purity of mind, prayer, and loyalty to the emperor.

Thus the third strand of Japanese religion is the teachings of Confucius and later Neo-Confucian ideas, which stressed filial piety, respect for one's ancestors, loyalty to one's superior, appropriate ceremonial interaction, education,

---

[29] Reverence for ancestors seems not to have been in Japan until after the influence of Chinese Confucianism.

[30] Discussed in chapter 21 of this book.

politics and a deep abiding respect for past traditions and the ruling family. Confucianism provided a foundation for Japanese social, cultural, and governmental harmony. In fact, Chinese Confucianism ceased to exist as an independent tradition in Japan, except as an object of study among Japanese scholars.

(4) Chinese Buddhism

Chinese Buddhist schools, scriptures (*sutras*), beliefs, and rituals, combined with Buddhist philosophical texts, provided a remarkably sophisticated philosophical framework unlike anything found in Japanese folk religion or formal Shinto. Although Buddhism began in India around 500 B.C.E., it would not influence Japanese thought until a thousand years later. The main sources of Japanese Buddhism were first from sixth century Korean Buddhism and then eighth century Chinese Buddhism. After Chinese forms of Buddhism were adopted, later, several distinctively Japanese forms of Buddhism emerged.

As we discussed in previous chapters, Chinese Buddhists taught a wide variety of practices including devotion to Amitabha Buddha, contemplative cross-legged seated meditation, the claim that we all have the Buddha-nature, and ideas such as a causally interconnected world of interdependent processes where all things are impermanent and empty of any enduring essence. However, in Japan the Buddha was first interpreted as a sort of powerful godlike *kami* magician with even more magic than native *kami*, whose powers could be used to ensure political tranquillity, health and prosperity, protection in battle, and protection from natural calamities.

Buddhism in Japan did have a central authority, but that authority was not a Buddhist priest. The central authority was the government. Each Japanese Buddhist group had the equivalent of a clan leader, and each leader was separate from the other Buddhist groups. Japanese Buddhists seem to have shared the clan attitude typical of Japanese culture, where loyalty is a vertical relationship between superior and inferior. A Buddhist priest's loyalties were to his superior priest in his own group. There was no sense of unity or cooperation between Buddhist groups, no single buddha or deity which all Buddhists accepted, and various Buddhist groups disagreed with one another. In the name of loyalty to one's leader, occasionally there were violent battles between groups of monks for political power and influence. In this sense Buddhist groups often functioned more like regimented clans than monastic organizations.

In addition, Chinese Buddhist culture supplied the understanding of the afterlife as re-birth determined by karma, provided the goal of becoming an awakened sage, or a Buddhist bodhisattva, and belief in the efficacy of Tantric secret rituals and *mantras*, and all of this affected Japan. This will be discussed in detail in the next chapter, on Japanese Buddhism.

(5) Religious Taoism/Daoism

The fifth strand of the rope which constitutes the religious world-view of Japan, one which also reflects the Chinese influence upon the Japanese world view, is non-contemplative, or religious Taoism (*Tao-chiao*). In absorbing Chinese culture, the Japanese also adopted popular "Little Tradition" Chinese astrology and cosmological notions, adopted geomancy, alchemy, and shamanistic medicine, believed that there existed potions which could bring about longevity, tried to establish which days were lucky and which were unlucky, and practiced fortune-telling or divination, all loosely connected to religious Taoism from China. This is especially evident in the yin-yang duality as an ordering principle for understanding nature and human beings, including medicine. Religious Taoism supplied theories of yin/yang sexual energy as the basis of health and provided magical numbers of power and luck. Of course, these very same notions were popular Chinese religious practices associated with cosmological notions, alchemy, longevity, and divination, associated with *Tao-chiao* or religious Taoism. The Japanese government had an official "Bureau of Yin and Yang" reflecting this influence (divination).

Notice that the five strands of Japanese thought never existed in isolation from one another. Japanese thought is an ongoing process of continual influence, and no one of them can account for the process called "Japanese religion" and the Japanese world-view.

Christianity, which first entered Japan in the sixteenth century, did not contribute to the formation of traditional Japanese religion. Although Christianity had some very limited success in the early centuries, the Japanese authorities could not help but notice that Christian priests would arrive, would teach and covert, but their activities seemed to precede Western political colonization. This had happened repeatedly around the globe, so Japanese leaders regarded the Christian religion as a tool of Western colonialism and an obvious threat to the Japanese government. In addition Christian presuppositions have been difficult for Japanese to adjust to. These are discussed in more detail at the end of this chapter.

23.8 THE TWO FORMS OF SHINTO

As was pointed out earlier, the term "Shinto" names a mixture of both native folk religion (the first strand of Japanese religion) and the state religion of a divine emperor, combined with foreign elements from China, and the result was a national tradition common to all Japanese, which co-existed with other religious beliefs such as Buddhism. Thus we might argue that there are two forms of Shinto:

(1) Little Tradition Shinto is the traditional body of many different popular shamanistic practices which arose long before the Japanese royal family or the arrival of Buddhism into Japan (in the sixth century C.E.).

(2) The Grand Tradition of state Shinto is an institutional religion fostered by the ruling classes with priests, shrines, scriptures, and charms, which has the semi-divine emperor as its head. Formal Shinto is an organized and elaborate cult closely bound up with the ruling family and its political system. Chinese Buddhism exerted a great deal of influence upon the eventual structure and ritual practices of state Shinto.

Unlike Buddhism, both forms of Shinto are systems of ceremony, of ritual, of practice, not concerned with philosophy, or doctrines, or speculation. They focus upon anthropomorphic deities (*kami*), whose characters are confused and shadowy, whose powers are ill-defined, and whose place of habitation either unknown or indistinguishable from that of ordinary beings. The worship of the goddess of the sun plays an important role, and both forms of Shinto are especially concerned with agricultural interests.

The "Little Tradition" of Japanese Shinto Religion

Early in human history, it seems as though everyone believed that what we think of as natural forces were controlled by supernatural powers and spirits which interacted with human lives. These spirits could send down blessings and benefits, or cause disasters. Blessings and catastrophes were both explained by the actions of *kami* spirits. The Japanese did not have a name for this traditional folk religion of Japan.

As we have discussed previously in the context of other world religions, the term "Little Tradition" has been used to describe the oral and traditional religious beliefs and practices existing outside highly organized and structured religious institutions.[31] It is the way of life and practices of ordinary people, not the elite well-educated class. Folk religion rituals are associated with fertility, with seasonal changes, with agriculture and rice production, with hunting, with fishing, and with the weather. They are concerned with benefits, and have rituals for healing and for producing male heirs. In folk religion, there is neither interest in nor opportunity for the study of actual history or careful

---

[31] Many points in this discussion are based on Robert Ellwood, *Cycles of Faith: The Development of World Religions* (Altamira Press, 2003), p. 143.

CHAPTER 23: JAPANESE SHINTO

philosophical analysis.

The popular traditions include local shaman who cultivate trance states and engage in divination or fortune telling. Like other folk religions, there is no founder or group that established this ancient religion. There is no central authority or official head of folk religion. In fact, there was no formal church, no formal beliefs, and nothing resembling theology or philosophy. The folk tradition is about behavior, not beliefs.

This enduring tradition accepts a world filled with spirits who can and do interact with humans. The spirit realm is perfectly pure, and is offended by anything that is polluting. Thus folk religion also puts great stress on contamination and purification rituals and charms, and these have gone on to shape the formal state-supported Japanese religion called Shinto and have influenced Buddhism in Japan as well. The more recent religion of the "common people" inherited much of the beliefs of the prehistoric period combined with state-supported Shinto traditions, and borrowed from organized religions of Buddhism, Taoism, and Confucianism.

Little Tradition religion in Japan involved reverence and aesthetic appreciation for nature. It is ceremonial ritualism based on animistic beliefs, purification rituals, and magical spells and charms. It has no scriptures, no doctrines, no god-given moral mandates, and no concern with theory or other intellectual aspects. The focus in Japanese folk religion is on spiritual healing and expelling demons, on curses, spells and charms, on purification rituals, and beliefs and practices transmitted through family, community, and charismatic figures like shamans and wise women. Purification rituals, and magical charms, and such practices date back to the earliest periods in Japanese pre-history, and these practices have influenced Japanese Buddhism as well. Many of the oral tradition rituals deal with sickness, and rituals for avoiding illness and danger. One ongoing danger in Japanese homes was the threat of fire. The beautiful traditional homes were made of wood and paper, and very flammable. The same fire that heated tea could turn a home into a roaring inferno in a few minutes. People paid shamans and priests for charms to ward off fire, and in modern times one can buy charms to lessen the danger of traffic accidents.

Purification, Rituals, and Charms.

A major difference between Chinese religions and Japanese religion is the stress in Japan on ritual purification and magical charms, which anthropologists date back to the earliest periods in Japanese pre-history. These influences have gone on to shape certain aspects of the character of Japanese Buddhism as well.

Many of the Japanese community rituals are associated with seasonal changes, and especially with agriculture and rice production, but also with fishing, hunting, and those activities necessary to ensure that we survive another year.

There are priestly and family rituals to deal with sickness, avoiding danger, with ensuring a safe birth of a child, and other similar activities. Western scholars who came to Japan to study Shinto were surprised to find Japanese Shinto priests chanting familiar-sounding *mantra*-like phrases in their rituals. Listening carefully, they found that these chants are Japanese pronunciations of Indian Sanskrit phrases. In other words, the original chants from India were meaningful Sanskrit. But when the Chinese Buddhists adopted them, the Chinese did not understand Sanskrit so they interpreted the sounds as magical phrases with supernatural power (*mantras*). Then the Japanese, Buddhist and Shinto alike, chanted the same phrases, using Japanese pronunciations, still believing that the sounds themselves had magical power.

Another aspect of popular Japanese religion is reliance on objects which one could purchase and which were believed to have special powers. One can go to a Shinto priest and purchase a talisman or charm, sold to ward off fire, or prevent illness, or prevent traffic accidents.

The oral tradition of Japanese Shinto religion and the Grand Tradition both put stress on ritual purity. When people do things which dirty or contaminate themselves, they offend *kami*, and rituals are required to restore them to a state of acceptable purity.

In addition to native *kami*, popular Japanese beliefs accepted the possibility that humans who had died before their time could return as vengeful spirits (similar to Chinese beliefs). Warriors killed in battle, those required to commit ritual suicide, women who had died in childbirth, and children who had died and foetuses who had been aborted, all must have rituals performed to keep their angry spirits pacified. Spirits need to be controlled and even exorcized. Shinto priests specialized in such rituals.

Traditional folk religion was different local communities with no common requirements of belief or faith. It was simply what people in the local community do. Oral religion was a common community possession, but there was no formal moral code, no dogma, and no sacred texts. The *kami* play no role in morality.

Although there was no centralized church, the folk religion traditions often had hereditary priests who conducted rituals intended to interact with the parallel realm of spirits. Later, the oral tradition incorporated adaptations of the formal organized structured religious traditions created by the governmental hierarchy. These affect the Japanese with their annual community celebrations, and their work and home ethics. Family and community are one primary focus of folk religion.

Folk religion did emphasize relationships between *kami* spirits and humans but was not concerned with politics or ruling clans. Local community practices had no interest in political authority and folk religion did not teach the people to be obedient to a local lord or a sovereign. As disparate local traditions, there was no single most important *kami* which citizens could focus upon.

Institutional Shinto

Institutional Shinto arose and assumed its basic shape only after the appearance of Buddhism in Japan, after the seventh century when many important changes were occurring in Japanese society. One of those changes developed as a result of the influence of highly organized Chinese Buddhism upon the ruling clans. At that time in Japan, the Yamato clan had fought their way to dominance over the others, and needed some principles which would strengthen its position. It needed something that could teach the people that they had a divine obligation of obedience to the feudal lords and the ruler. This would help to support the clan authority.

A formal government-controlled hereditary priesthood was established, and a detailed mythology was created, elaborated and written down. A whole pantheon of gods was listed, and by the tenth century of the common era, Shinto rituals were established in accord with the official mythology of the past (many of these Shinto rituals drew upon esoteric Chinese Buddhist sources).[32] Additional major Shinto shrines were built and supported financially by the government. The influence of Grand Tradition Shinto continues in the numerous shrines found in contemporary Japan.

Japanese Religion and Government Institutions

The strand of folk religion was not concerned with ruling or rulers, but when the royal family created institutional Shinto, they explicitly placed the emperor as not only the head-priest but also as a human divinity. This Japanese concern with the religious authority of the ruling family and its political power did not affect Shinto alone. When Buddhism was adopted by the Japanese aristocracy, it too was made subservient to the government. In India, Indian Buddhists rejected government authority, and in China the Chinese Buddhists argued that they ought to be independent of governmental interference. In Japan it was considered obvious that the divine royal family and the government should control all aspects of every tradition in Japan. Of course, there were similar events in Europe, when the church and royalty made claims that kings ruled by "divine right" and the notion of a religious leader such as the Catholic Pope was superior to all kings.

The ruling Yamato clan needed a unifying influence, something to bring together the disparate local communities. Traditional folk religion could not do this because it was too decentralized, did not emphasize unity and

---

[32] Japanese historian Kuroda Toshio argues that the governmental separation of Shinto and Buddhism during the Meiji era obscured the fact that "Shinto was largely a sectarian departure from the world view of esoteric Buddhism (*kenmitsu bukkyo*)." See his "Shinto in the History of Japanese Religion," in the *Journal of Japanese Studies*, 1981, 7, 1: 1-21.

cooperation, did not teach obedience to a sovereign, and there was no single unifying ritual or most important *kami* to unify the people and teach them to support the rulers.

The ruling clans realized that the Sun Goddess, Amaterasu, would be ideal for unifying the people because she was a central *kami* for much of popular religion. The emperor and his clan claimed to be descended from the first legendary emperor, Jimmu Tenno (whose traditional dates are 660 B.C.E.), the great grandson of the Sun Goddess's grandson, Ninigi. Thus the Japanese royal family would be semi-divine, descended from the creator *kami*, for whom the folk traditions of the Japanese people already performed rituals. If the sovereign ruler is divine, then one owed unquestioning obedience to the divinity.[33] The Japanese took their primary *kami* involved in their creation myth, goddess Amaterasu (whose shrine at Ise is one of most important), and turned her into an ancestor.[34]

Institutional Shinto is a direct result of the need of the clan to strengthen its imperial authority and consolidate its control over the islands of Japan. It utilized an ancient mythology of *kami* and divine origins to justify its ruling position and inculcate the religious duty of obedience to authority. It also used clusters of nature deities who protected the ruler and the people. It also collected powerful esoteric rituals to deal with the spirit realm.

Out of earlier legends, a formal Shinto mythology was created and written down in the *Kojiki* ("Record of Ancient Events," 712), and in the *Nihongi* ("Chronicle of Japan," 720). Although everyone in Japan knew that there were uncountably many *kami*, a select group of *kami* found in the folk tradition were elevated to highest importance and their names listed, resulting in a pantheon of gods. Later, specific *kami* were assigned to occupy various shrines called *kami*-halls. Under the influence of Chinese Buddhism, a Shinto priesthood took shape. Influenced by Chinese models, Shinto liturgies arose by the tenth century of the common era, and state-supported Shinto shrines were built.

The emperor took on the role of divine high-priest of a newly institutionalized state religion called the "Way of the *kami* spirits," or Shinto. Because the government taught that the monarch is a semi-divine descendant of the first emperor who was descended from the *kami* who created the Japanese islands, he is the divine leader of all of Japan. At this time in Japanese history, the emperor was both the spiritual head of the country, and the political head of government, so Japan was a theocracy. The heavenly sovereign was responsible for ritual purity and for maintaining the cosmic order via administrative propriety. A variety of Shinto ritual observances played an important part. Every spring the emperor engages in ceremonial rice-planting on the palace grounds, which is intended to guarantee fertility of the soil and richness of the rice harvest for all farmers. Myths and rituals have been deliberately stressed by the imperial family and the ruling classes to ensure strong even unquestioning loyalty to the rulers of Japan.

The Sea of Japan

In spite of the powerful influences of rulers, generals, and lords, geography and climate often have the most enduring effects on social order. Japanese thought is profoundly affected by the Sea of Japan, and the Japanese religious views were shaped and constrained by their environment of islands in a stormy sea. We noted before that Japan has never been successfully invaded by ships from the mainland. The typhoon winds (*kamikaze*, divine-winds) swirling around the sea foiled each invasion attempt. Since *kami* control the weather and the winds, the Japanese people saw each failed invasion of Korean or Mongolian warriors as convincing evidence of divine protection offered by the emperor's *kami* ancestors, which in turn reinforced the belief in the divinity of the emperor. This implied that local Japanese *kami* defeated the gods of Korea and Mongolia, so they were superior to mainland deities, which means that

---

[33] The various details of this complex system of myths is explained in Richard Bowring, *The Religious Traditions of Japan 500-1600* (New York: Cambridge University Press, 2005).

[34] Note that in China, the Shang dynasty ruling family elevated its first ancestor to the status of a deity, Shang-ti. In Japan, they took an important deity and turned her into an ancestor.

the nation of Japan was superior to mainland Asia.[35] With such beliefs, the strength of institutional Shinto increased.

Japanese mythology stresses a *kami*-blessed land and a royal family of divine origins, and the Japanese people were encouraged to think of themselves as unique among world populations, and to be proud of their long heritage. So, until recently, institutional Grand Tradition Shinto served as a national political religion, which stressed loyalty and obedience to the imperial line and reverence for the divine origins of the imperial family and emperor. In addition the Japanese also have numerous local non-political religious practices and traditions. As we have noted, both folk and institutional forms have been called "Shinto." However, as is very clear to the reader, neither form of Shinto has anything like the great creeds, confessions, and doctrinal works of Western religions of Europe and the Americas.

23.9 THE INTRODUCTION OF BUDDHISM

It was shortly before the formation of institutional Shinto that the Korean country of Paikche sent gifts of Buddhist texts and statues to the new Japanese court. The Koreans stressed that the Buddha offered magical protection for the new ruler and his interests. The Japanese court understood the Buddha to be a sort of super-*kami*, a magician with even more magical power than native *kami*, and a protective deity who could be used to ensure political tranquillity, health and prosperity, protection in battle, and protection from natural calamities. After a rocky beginning,[36] eventually Buddhism became an official religion among the ruling Japanese aristocracy and the upper-classes and Buddhism became much more tightly intertwined with government than it had ever been in India or China.

Once the Japanese realized that the Koreans received Buddhism from China, Japanese Buddhist priests and scholars traveled directly to China to study. They returned to Japan and brought with them knowledge of the Chinese model of governmental administration and control, important because Japan was a country still experimenting with centralized authority. Esoteric forms of Chinese Buddhism were important in China during this period, and these were imported into Japan, as was Pure Land Buddhism. The newly forming Shinto adopted many elements of esoteric Buddhism, and Buddhist temples were frequently built within Shinto compounds. Shinto shrines were also built within Buddhist temples. Buddhist sutras were chanted within Shinto shrines. *Kami* were accepted as manifestations of buddhas.[37] Shinto was understood to be a local Japanese manifestation of eternal Buddhist truths. As long as Buddhism dominated Japan, Shinto was secondary to Buddhist truths.

However, beginning in the fifteenth century, Shinto thinkers were arguing that Japan was the source of all civilization, and that therefore Buddhism must have been derived from Shinto and therefore Buddhism must be subordinate to Shinto. Yoshida Kanetomo (1435–1511) wrote:

> Prince Shotoku [who ruled when Buddhism was adopted into Japan] stated in a memorial that Japan was the roots and trunk [of civilization], China its branches and leaves, and India its flowers and fruit. Similarly, Buddhism is the flowers and fruit of all laws. Confucianism their branches and leaves, and Shinto their roots

---

[35] When Christian proselytizers told the Japanese the story of an angry god who flooded the world and drowned the people, the Japanese knew that their island had never been flooded, and therefore the Japanese *kami* spirits had protected their ruler and the islands, and so their *kami* were more powerful than the Christian gods.

[36] The details are explained in the next chapter, on Japanese Buddhism.

[37] For example, Amaterasu, the Sun Goddess, was interpreted as the feminine aspect of the Shingon Buddha, Mahavairocana, the Great Sun Buddha.

and trunk. Thus all foreign doctrines are offshoots of Shinto.[38]

From the seventeenth century onwards, the Japanese began to minimize the contribution of China[39] to their own civilization, and instead took pride in the distinctively Japanese aspects of their culture. Ultimately this grew into a great revival of Shinto as it became an official part of the government. Institutional Shinto was not merely one religion among many, nor was it merely the most important religion. As a cult of veneration of a divine emperor as the ruler of the universe, it was above all religions.

23.10 MODERN SHINTO

Modern Shinto is a conglomeration of numerous different beliefs, rituals and celebrations. Institutional Shinto did not create completely new forms of religion in Japan, but organized Japan's pre-existing pre-historic heritage, along with Buddhist and other Chinese influences, into a distinctive tradition consciously intended to unify, manipulate and control the people. Prior to World War II, this aspect persisted in modern Shinto in the form of government-supported shrines and rituals venerating important *kami* enacted in such shrines, or rituals performed by the emperor. This is Shrine Shinto. Although no longer government supported, Shrine Shinto persists.

The separate local religious festivals and practices which are completely non-political, continued on independently of state-supported institutional Shinto. Modern Shinto also celebrates a wide variety of separate local festivals related to agriculture and local *kami*-centered community celebrations. There are household *kami* and village *kami* to be venerated and celebrated. Even in modern times, this aspect of folk Shinto is rituals and celebrations still associated with the periods and patterns in rice growing. Planting is a festival, harvesting is a festival. The rice harvest is the main festival, during which new rice is offered up to the *kami* as thanksgiving. Many other practices which form folk Shinto include several forms of ritual purification, fortune-telling, astrology derived from Chinese sources, spirit possession, and magical healing done by shamans who can manipulate *kami*.

In addition, there are some modern Japanese religions which draw upon Shinto roots for inspiration, but seem equally shamanistic. These examples of sect Shinto arose within the folk tradition and often have women as founders. The founder may have had a profound transforming religious experience, and then he or she exhibits unusual powers for healing or magic. These religions are not celebrated in Shinto shrines; they are local and just use local meeting halls for the congregation. Tenrikyo is an example of sect Shinto.[40]

THE SHINTO PRIESTHOOD IN CONTEMPORARY TIMES

For most Shinto priests, priesthood is a part-time occupation. Shinto priests were not full-time religious officials unless they were in charge of major political shrines. Even priests who lived at shrines usually combine ordinary jobs with their priestly duties. Any civil official might have to discharge some religious function—the only requirement being that he purify himself first so that he does not offend the *kami*. Traditionally Shinto priests wear white robes, symbolic of purity, although some robes are gray, pink, or a turquoise blue.

---

[38] Tsunoda, ed., *Sources of Japanese Tradition* (New York: Columbia University Press, 1958), p. 271.

[39] A valuable summary on the complex relationship between imperial China and imperial Japan is June Teufel Dreyer, *Middle Kingdom and the Empire of the Rising Sun: Sino-Japanese Relations, Past and Present* (Oxford: Oxford University Press, 2016). Dreyer argues that neither nation will accept the other as an equal, and neither will accept a position of inferiority to the other.

[40] Julia Ching, "East Asian Religions," *op. cit.*, p. 351.

CHAPTER 23: JAPANESE SHINTO

The position of a Shinto priest is most often hereditary, reflecting the Japanese emphasis on family lines. A Shinto priest officiating at a shrine had the power to summon the *kami*, and would do so at the beginning of a particular ceremony. At the close of the ceremony, the priest would send the *kami* away (often symbolized by opening and later, closing, the doors to the *kami*-hall which contained the sacred symbol of the *kami*.)[41] The priests have the power to bless worshipers, which they do by waving a wand with small pieces of white paper attached. The wand purifies the people in attendance, and purifies the area.

It was unacceptable for a Shinto priest to come into contact with sickness, with death, or with mourning, if the priest was going to be in contact with *kami*. It was thought that *kami* were offended by these, and so these were contaminating.

SHINTO SHRINES (*jinja*)

Technically, there are no Shinto temples, only shrines. **Temples** (*-tera* or *-ji*) are Buddhist, and **shrines** (*jinja*) are Shinto. The earliest sacred places of folk religion were locations which had something special or disconcerting about them. People felt that there was something unusual about a particular spot, or perhaps something frightening or awe inspiring. Perhaps powerful *kami* dwelt here; possibly ancestral spirits dwelled here. The *kami* who occupied these places might be visible, but most likely were invisible. They might take the form of an animal, or even a human form.

The early locus of Shinto activity was most probably not buildings at all; rather a sacred space was marked off with one or more *Do Not Enter* markers intended to symbolically block people from approaching too closely. A straw rope might be tied around a stone or a tree to mark the place. To trespass into these sacred places was to raise the ire of the *kami*, and disaster could follow.

Later on, two buildings were erected on many of those special sacred spaces. The first was the worship hall primarily for priests, but sometimes used by people; the second is the *kami*-hall which contained a sacred object (usually either a mirror, comma-shaped gem or stone, or sword) symbolic of the presence of the enshrined *kami*. Worshipers believe that the *kami* sometimes reside in these symbolic treasures. The treasures are not usually part of the public display, and smaller shrines may not have these at all. The Shinto shrine at Ise is one of most important of all the Shinto shrines, for it is there that the Sun Goddess *kami*, Amaterasu, is enshrined.

As is typical of non-Western religions, there are no weekly Sunday services which people are expected to attend. Japanese families do not make regular weekly visits to Shinto shrines, or Buddhist temples. Families go to local shrines during major events in the life of the family. In the very first outing from the house, the month-old child is presented to the local *kami*. When a family comes to a Shinto shrine, everyone purifies themselves with sacred water (rinsing their mouth and their hands), then a financial donation is made, and then one climbs the stairs, pauses reverently, and then pulls a thick rope attached to a large bell. Then they clap their hands twice, summoning the *kami* spirit who resides in the temple. The family will bow and pray, or perhaps chant. When they finish, they bow again, make a donation to the priest, and depart. If they have requests, they may write a request on a piece of white paper and tie it to the branches of a nearby tree.

As the children grow up, major events in their lives are celebrated by visits to shrines. On the occasion of a personal crisis, it was appropriate to visit the local shrine to ask for help from one's ancestors or local *kami*. It should be clear that the Japanese view *kami* as sacred powers which can sustain and influence an individual's life for the better. When a Japanese goes to a Shinto shrine to summon a *kami*, he or she has little concern for the exact nature of the *kami* with whom they are interacting.

---

[41] H. B. Earhart, *Japanese Religion: Unity and Diversity* , 3rd Edition, p. 34.

CHAPTER 23: JAPANESE SHINTO

SHINTO CEREMONIAL EVENTS (*matsuri*) DURING THE YEAR

As noted above, Buddhist temples and Shinto shrines are not the sites of weekly religious services, as in Western religions. There is no single day of the week which is sacred to a particular *kami* (or buddha). But there are numerous seasonal and yearly festivals, many of them agricultural. In Japanese, these ritual festivals and celebrations are *matsuri*, where offerings are made to *kami*. In return, the *kami* is expected to reciprocate and give blessings and protection. Many of these community festivals involve singing and dancing, parades, food and drink, music performances, and often have obvious fertility associations, such as phallic objects carried in processions. Periodic festivals are held which linked the individual home religious center with the community religious group.

Four of the most ancient festivals occur seasonally, at spring associated with rice planting, and fall, associated with harvest. The rice harvest is the main festival, during which new rice is offered up to the *kami* as thanksgiving. In addition there are the mid-year and new-year festivals. The mid-year and new years festival are especially important because people can wash away spiritual pollution or defilement of the previous six months.

The new-year holiday celebration has become one of the most important of all. *Kami* are invited into the home, which must be thoroughly cleaned. The family goes to the local Shinto shrine and members pray for success for the next year. They make formal visits to relatives and friends, renewing relationships. As the old year is renewed to become a new year, New Year's holiday celebrates the renewal of life. In addition the Obon festival in August invites the spirits of the departed back to enjoy the celebration, and receive ritual offerings of food and drink.

However, not all of the festivals are of ancient Japanese origin; many of the ceremonies are Chinese in origin. For example, the following Shinto festivals also correspond to Chinese traditional holidays determined by Chinese Taoist numerology:
the first day of the first month, New Years
the third day of the third month, girl's festival (or doll's festival)
the fifth day of the fifth month, boy's day
the seventh day of the seventh month, the Star festival
ninth day of the ninth month, the chrysanthemum festival

Japanese Shinto festivals are occasions of laughter and celebration and are more like carnivals than somber religious events. Japan has a very sophisticated culture of gift-giving, so occasions of gift-giving are very important. It is for this reason the Western holiday of Christmas was adopted into the New Year's festivities and is celebrated by the non-Christian Japanese with abandon, even though Christianity itself is of very minor importance in the frame of Japanese religions.

Both forms of Shinto participate in these festivals. Local community festivals are important, and there are even individual cults. The state supported aspects of Shinto are visible in the nation-wide celebrations of New Years and the celebration of every significant event in the life of the royal family.

PURIFICATION IN MODERN SHINTO

In Shinto, anyone who has come into contact with something offensive, or who does something that is forbidden by or annoying to the *kami* violates *kami*-inspired taboos and in the process becomes impure and contaminated. In Shinto, the prohibition against contamination was very strong; a corresponding ritual process of decontamination, or purification, was used to remove the contamination.

A person becomes polluted by doing something or touching something which is offensive to *kami* yet such acts might be necessary and unavoidable. It might be something as simple as eating foods like onions which annoyed the *kami*. Coming into contact with unclean things such as sickness, sores, tumors, or eruptions, or even dirt, wounds, childbirth, injury, and sexual intercourse, required cleansing. Sexual intercourse is not offensive to *kami*. Rather, sex involves substances separated or discharged from the human body, and these fluids are ritually impure and offensive to *kami*. Spilled blood is defilement, but it matters not whether you were stabbed, or you did the stabbing. It is the blood which is offensive, not the behavior.

Because there are many behaviors that are contaminating and prohibited, there is much need for purification. Originally, eating meat was not contaminating, but probably because of the influence of Buddhism, it became defiling. Wounding and killing (even accidentally) required cleansing. Diseases such as leprosy or tumors require purification. Incest (children by same father but different mother were not considered too close to marry so did not count as incest) and sexual relations with animals are contaminating. Encounters with things which creep can need purification. Also requiring purification are calamities originating from the acts of *kami*, but also calamities due to birds and animals, and calamities due to spells of witchcraft. All required cleansing.

What Is Defiling Is Not Necessarily Immoral.

In the Shinto world-view, one does not undergo purification because he or she has done something morally wrong. It is not moral guilt which is washed away; it is pollution or contamination. As is clear, in Shinto we find no distinction between "ceremonial impurity" and "moral impurity," no distinction between civil offenses and religious offenses. The Shinto code is not ethical and it is not legal; rather it is ceremonial and customary.[42] There is no concept of moral failure or moral guilt, because there is no moral divinity who judges us, or issues moral commands. If we offend a *kami* we merely purify ourselves. The Japanese religions never had a concept like "original sin," and never believed that we humans are fallen and corrupt creatures. The Japanese never thought that humans had been expelled from a paradise by an angry and jealous deity. The Japanese islands are the homes of *kami* and in a sense, we humans share a divine garden with gods.

Human beings are good, the world is good, the body is good, and sexual activity is good. Both Japanese Shinto and folk traditions are comfortable using sexual imagery, and phallus-shaped stones and wood carvings symbolic of fertility are found in many shrines and are carried by young girls and grandmothers in local seasonal public processions. There are no Shinto moral rules concerning birth control, divorce, abortion, or stem cell research. Shinto priests have no concern with which sexual activities occur between lovers.

As discussed previously, sexual intercourse is defiling, but it is equally defiling whether it occurred within marriage or extra-maritally (adultery), or even rape. It is not sex that is offensive; it is the bodily fluids involved which cause the need for purification.

Shinto is an agricultural religion of life and growth, so death was viewed as contamination. Life and growth are good; that which interferes, sickness and death, is polluting. Contacting corpses is polluting. After one touched a corpse, one had to be cleansed. The house where a person had died was also contaminated and needed the services of a Shinto priest to purify the home. In the ancient past, the contamination of death was considered so severe that the home had to be abandoned and the inhabitants had to build a new home. This applied even to the imperial palace. Until the beginning of the eighth century, the Japanese imperial palace was moved to different site upon the death of a sovereign.

Three Methods for Purification

Purification rituals depend upon whether one is a layman, or a Shinto priest. The less severe contaminations can be dealt with by the person himself, or herself, and do not require priestly intervention. More serious contamination requires the services of a Shinto priest. There are special ceremonial duties which the priests are to perform in the shrines, so it is essential that the priest not offend *kami* who have been summoned.

---

[42] The English term "ethics" comes from the Latin "ethos," customary attitudes specific to a particular culture. The term "morality" comes from the Latin "mores," again social and customary behavior determined by a group or culture.

It is important to note that the ritual is what purifies, and one's state of mind is not important. An internal attitude of repentance is not required; what is required is that the ritual be performed correctly, precisely, even beautifully, by a qualified priest, in order to impress the *kami*.

Cleansing the Body and Mind

Cleansing is a process by which an ordinary person can remove less severe contamination, or unintentional defilements acquired by contact with unclean things. When a supplicant approaches a Shinto shrine, water is provided for purification of body and mind. The ritual process is not complicated: you take a bamboo ladle and use it to pour water on your hands, and rinse your mouth with water, and finish by wiping your hands with a white handkerchief. A similar practice is used in Buddhist-influenced teahouses.

The majority of Japanese were farmers, and a farmer must get dirty, and one's home will get dirty, so appropriate cleansing is important. Ordinary people become ill or diseased, and family members tend to their needs; these conditions also need cleansing. Encountering bodily fluids requires washing. Coming into contact with death will also require cleansing. Our bodies, our clothing, and our homes must be clean, and purified.

Obviously, washing, sweeping, dusting and all forms of cleaning are religious activities, not merely house-cleaning. Even activities like repaying debts and officially apologizing to those we have offended are essential if one's character is to be pure and clean. In modern Japanese society, one cannot help but notice the Japanese stress on bathing, the hot baths, even the traditional warm wash cloth offered on Japanese airplanes at the end of a flight, and a similar warm cloth offered in traditional Japanese restaurants at the end of a meal.

In the ancient past, ritual cleansing was accomplished by the person bathing in the place where a running river emptied into the sea.[43] The combination of salt plus running water was most important. Later, these two features separated out. Salt by itself became an instrument for purification. So too, running water is used for purification.

Exorcism of Negative Energies

This pertains to contamination so severe that it requires rituals performed by a Shinto priest. For example, in a house where someone had died, the Shinto priest would not perform a funeral, but after the period of mourning the priest was necessary to purify the home. Also, in a location where misfortune has occurred, such as a place where a workman has been injured or killed, a Shinto priest is brought in to exorcize the negative influence and reestablish a healthy working environment. When one has become polluted because of a civil offence, or a religious offence, a priest was required to remove pollution. The Shinto priest will wave a stick to which pieces of white paper have been attached. The priest will sprinkle salt, or salt water on the person. The person will then make offerings to the priest. In more recent times, the person merely presented money to the priest, the priest would brandish a wand, and pronounce a formula of purification (similar to a legal fine). The distinction between civil and religious offences was unclear — the same fine and wand wave would expiate either error.

Abstention

Abstention is avoiding contamination, and is primarily a duty of priests, although it will apply to ordinary people as well under certain circumstances. Shinto priests interact with the *kami* much more frequently than ordinary people because the priests preside over shrines and perform many different rituals which summon *kami*. Because of this, Shinto religion requires a Shinto priest to avoid sources of pollution prior to presiding over shrine rituals. A Shinto priest must avoid activities which would offend *kami*, even when such behavior is part of everyday life. The duty of Shinto priests is to abstain from such behavior if they are going to be active in a shrine ceremony.

---

[43] This reflects the environment in the ancient past, when the Japanese people primarily lived along the ocean as fisherman; the place where pure running water mixed into salty sea water was the instrument of purification. This is also seen in the origin myth of Izanagi who purifies himself in the ocean waters after his trip to the underworld.

Priests must avoid contact with things like sickness, death, and even mourning — these were also unacceptable for they obstruct birth and life. It is for this reason that in Japan, funerals are most often performed by Buddhist priests.[44]

The Shinto priests who preside over rituals and festivals (*matsuri*) must be free of contamination. Before presiding over Shinto rituals, priests could only eat food cooked over a fire which had been purified. Certain foods were to be avoided such as garlic or onions. According to tradition, for three days prior to the ritual, the priest must strictly avoid sources of pollution. For three days before officiating, the priest cannot consume alcohol.

Priests could only eat food cooked over a purified fire. Their clothing must have been purified. For three days before the celebration, they must remain indoors and away from noise, dancing, and singing. For three days the Shinto priest must abstain from sexual relations with his wife. The priest can wear only ritually purified garments. The priest must remain indoors and closet himself away from ordinary society, and that included staying away from noise, dancing, and singing.

For about the last four hundred years, traditions decree that marriages are Shinto rituals (in the home or in a hotel), and it is very rare for Shinto priests to be involved in funerals. The main exception is funeral rites for the emperor, always performed by the most powerful Shinto priests.

23.11 THE IMPORTANCE OF THE FAMILY

Traditionally, the family has been one of the most important basic religious units in Japanese culture. However, we must not think of "family" as two parents and two children. As in India, China, and southeast Asia, traditionally the family has been what we call the extended family. Even if they did not live under the same roof, the family included three or even four generations with several sets of related parents and their children. The relationship did not need to be biological. The family unit could also include children who were adopted to carry on the family name. Sometimes even the people who worked for the family were included as family members. In contemporary Japan the family structure has been changing, and the importance of the extended family is not as strong as it was in the past.

As in China, family stresses continuity, so it includes both living members and departed ancestors. Influenced by popular Chinese religion, Japanese religion came to accept the idea that ancestors exist in a heavenly realm, so deceased family members can interact with and have an effect upon their descendants.

We can appreciate the importance of the family in Japanese religion, because unlike China, the Japanese Buddhist and Shinto priesthoods became organized along hereditary lines, and temples and shrines became family-dependent.

Homes have Buddhist altars and Shinto altars

Priests presided over community celebrations, but priests were not necessary for most family religious practices. Often, modern Japanese homes will have one or two shrines in them. The great majority of family residences would have a home Buddhist altar, called a *butsu-dan*, and also a Shinto shrine, called a "god-shelf," or *kami-dana*. There was no conflict between these. Homes could and did have both, and these home altars have long been the center of family religious practices.

23.12 THE BASIC JAPANESE WORLD-VIEW IS NOT DUALISTIC

In general, the Japanese world-view does not see the world in terms of "either/or" absolutes. Western society

---

[44] This is changing in modern Japan, where now there are professional undertakers.

tends to say "either you are with me or you are against me," "either you love God or you hate God," things are either Godly or on the side of Satan. This either/or duality is rarely found in Japanese thought. There is a clear tendency in Japanese thought not to think in terms of absolutes; not to think in terms of yes or no, true or false, either this or that, black and white with no shades of gray in between. Rather Japanese tend to see things happening in a situation and relative to that situation. Between extremes there are a wide range of in-between positions.

Do not confuse this with the Western philosophical position of moral relativism. The Japanese are not arguing that morality depends on how you feel, or that something is morally right for me and morally wrong for you. Rather, they are stressing flux, change, and the possibility of different perspectives. There is an interdependent connectedness, an aesthetic complexity to all the world which goes far beyond simple contradictories like good and evil. We all realize that it is not true that things are either beautiful or ugly with nothing in between. The Japanese perception has more in common with aesthetics and artistic values, not with binary logic and absolutes.[45]

Nevertheless, there are values which are perceived as independent of perspective. For example, the Japanese tended to interpret loyalty to one's superior as one of those things which did not permit shades of grey. This is seen in the tales of loyal samurai warriors who committed suicide when their leader was killed in battle or forced to commit *harakiri* (ritual suicide) by royal decree.

Japanese Religions are Not Exclusive

It is typical of Western religions to claim to possess absolute truth, to assert that their religion is the only one that is perfect and correct, and thus all other religions are heretical and evil. In general the Japanese world view tends to not be exclusive the way Islam and Christianity are. Traditionally, Japanese people did not think of themselves as belonging to one system of thought or practice to the exclusion of the others. Most Japanese participated in several of those traditions with no problem. Japanese often see themselves as belonging to two and sometimes three different religious denominations simultaneously. One can participate fully in Buddhism and Shinto with no conflict.

The reason is that different religions meet different needs and tend to operate in different areas of life. Shinto is basically festive and concerned with the things in this life that bring joys and deep social relationships involving family and community; this is the reason that traditionally marriages have been performed in a Shinto ceremony. Shinto is about community and festivals.

Buddhism is considered to be more concerned with the deeper, more profound and even ultimate mystery of existence and the ultimate destiny of a human being – thus it is more about the individual and the meaning of existence. Buddhism is associated with meditation, philosophy, and with funerals. Family memorial services are presided over by Buddhist priests. Of course, there are Confucian customs which also persist.

There has been a wide variety of approaches to each of these religious forms. There is a tendency for followers to pick and choose among the various strands of religion, forming a more personal religion which best works for the individual. Someone who is analytic and philosophical may gravitate towards the intellectual aspects of Buddhism, Taoism, and Shinto, which make sense to them. In the same way, someone with a more devotional personality is free to choose those aspects of Buddhism, Taoism, and Shinto, which most strongly appeal to him or her. The individual is the one who unifies these strands of Japanese religion. "Japanese women and men usually have found religious fulfillment not in one tradition by itself but in the total sacred power embodied in a number of traditions."[46]

Respect for Tradition is Essential to the Japanese World-View

The world may be one of unceasing flux and change, but a kind of stability is possible in the midst of change. The world cannot be locked down and made fixed, but human institutions can give continuity between the generations. Enduring traditions provide the stable foundation of Japanese spirituality.

---

[45] Robert Ellwood, *Introduction to Japanese Civilization* (Routledge), ch. 4.

[46] *Ibid.*

Some of the traditions are perhaps hundreds of years old, and some might even be thousands of years old. For example, most families have traditions associated with the local Shinto shrine and the Buddhist temple visited by the family, and also many traditions concerning one's community. Local family temples bear names of one's own ancestors who are visited on formal and informal occasions. Family members will return to family shrines and temples on solemn and important occasions throughout each member's lifetime. In later feudal times, additional traditions concerned feudal lords and the feudal hierarchy were promulgated. The religious traditions of Shinto ritual and Buddhism provide symbols of stable identity to the Japanese.

23.13 MODERN JAPANESE RELIGION

Modern Japan is a secular nation, and public opinion polls and surveys indicate that interest in religion is at a considerably lower level than in the United States. However, modern Japan is full of shrines and temples in all the ancient cities. Sometimes the shrines are large and impressive, and sometimes they are just about the size of a tall birdcage. These shrines are well-kept-up, clean, obviously in use. Clean fresh offerings of flowers or food can be found on the altars; the bigger temples will be filled with visitors, worshipers, and tourists.

Why do Japanese go to shrines and temples? Attending shrines and temples is a tradition, and it is good to follow tradition.[47] It can also give one a feeling of peace. Shinto has innumerable *kami*, but there is not a sharp distinction between the *kami* and human beings. Buddhism tends to be less god-oriented, but in the popular mind buddhas and bodhisattvas are very much like *kami*.

In Japan, it has been customary for a person (or family) to participate in both Shinto festivals and Buddhist memorial services and to practice Confucian ethics and follow beliefs of religious Taoism and folk religion.[48]

As we have noted before, no single strand of Japanese religion claims to satisfy all the needs of every personality. The numerous strands of Japanese religion never existed in isolation from one another. There has been a wide variety of approaches to each of these religions; followers generally pick and choose among the various strands of religion, forming a unified religion which best works for the individual. Even the religions themselves change over time. For example, Buddhism in Japan has been responding to the secular pressures of business and modernity, and this will be discussed in the next chapter.

There is an appeal of modern Shinto to twenty-first century Japanese, even in the secular nation of Japan. Shinto draws deeply on the sense of reverence for nature, and the Japanese people resonate to that appreciation of nature. The fact that Shinto does not have a moral code means that each individual can make his or her own decisions on moral issues without church officials imposing their own views. The lack of Shinto dogma means that a great deal of flexibility is available to followers who can draw from their local traditions. Shinto rituals have appeal for those who are moved by ritual, or who appreciate the beauty of ritual performances. One can participate wholeheartedly in Shinto festivals celebrating nature and seasonal change without the follower having to give up his or her other religious affiliations.

Several post World War II new religions have drawn upon Shinto roots, including Tenrikyo ("heavenly reason teaching") and Omotokyo ("great origin teaching").

---

[47] Why do many agnostics and atheists put up Christmas trees and exchange gifts? These are family traditions, times of joy and celebration. Peace on Earth, Good Will to Men. Tradition.

[48] Earhart, *op. cit.*, p. 4.

CHRISTIANITY IN JAPAN

Catholic priests came to Japan in the 1500s and made an attempt to convert the Japanese. In Japan the original interest in Christianity was primarily military and political, because the missionaries were accompanied by merchants who sold firearms! Japan did not have reliable guns. In a nation of archers and swordsmen, a gun or rifle can make a huge difference to the outcome of a battle. It permits assassination from a distance, and bodyguards are no longer able to protect a leader with certainty. Some clans compelled members to convert to Christianity so that the clan leaders could have special access to weaponry from merchants.

Catholicism was active from 1549–1597 and by 1650, it was politically proscribed and prosecuted. The reason was because of the fear of the Japanese who had seen Christian priests enter into a country, begin to convert followers to Christianity, and then the missionaries were followed by military and political forces which established political dominance for Western nations (India, Sri Lanka, China, South America, Hawaii, and so forth).

Fearing that missionaries were precursors to colonization, the military rulers of Japan ordered Christian missionaries and other foreigners, out of the country in 1587, and again 1597, and again 1614 and 1651. The prohibition against Christian proselyting was not withdrawn until 1873.

Philosophically, Christianity was difficult for Japanese to adjust to. The Christians said an essential part of their religion was the claim that all human beings are sinners, and are born stained with original sin. The Japanese thought that even if one believed that to be true, it was not serious because the impurity of original sin was obviously a kind of contamination, which could be eliminated by Shinto purification rituals. There was no need for a savior, a church, or a Christian priest.

Also, although Christianity has numerous supernatural spiritual beings with supernatural powers like angels and saints (which the Japanese thought of as additional *kami*), Christianity asserts that there is only one god, and this has serious social consequences which would undermine Japanese civilization. If there is only one god (the god of Christianity), then the emperor could not be a god and yet to accept the divinity of the emperor was part and parcel of home life, of school, and just being Japanese. Every aspect of Japanese society (and Japanese uniqueness) insisted that the emperor is divine (the belief in the divinity of the emperor endured until the Japanese surrender after World War II).

There was yet another thing about Christianity with which the Japanese had difficulty. In Asian cultures, the father is always higher in status than the son. In Christianity, the father god and the son god were equal. This made no sense in a society dominated by ideas of Confucian filial piety and hierarchy.

Another reason that the Japanese tended not to adopt Christianity was partly because of its rather aggressive attitude of non-toleration of other religions. This was especially true for its conversion policies which not merely required a Japanese individual changing from her or his prior religion, but also the convert was expected to engage in a vigorous condemnation of all those family members who remained Buddhists, or Shintoists, or Confucianists, or all three combined. To condemn one's parents and family went against everything that Japanese society believed. Christianity seemed morally inferior to Japanese religion because the Christian priests did not share the values of family harmony, did not practice filial piety, and was not willing to co-exist with other religions. So being a Christian required the convert to abandon all that made him or her Japanese. It required the convert to damage the family harmony and unity, which was a terrible thing to do.

In Japanese society, blind loyalty to superiors was a virtue cultivated and valued in society and in tales of heroes. Remaining loyal even in the face of death is a virtue much prized in Japanese civilization and the same behavior is seen over and over in Japanese society within families, within clans, politically, as well as in religion. There are many famous tales of loyal *samurai* who committed suicide (*harakiri*) when their leader was defeated or executed. This stress on loyalty also played a role in Christianity, because once converted to Christianity, many Japanese converts remained loyal to their new religion and refused to disavow Christianity even when it was made illegal. This is the Japanese Confucian tradition of complete loyalty to higher authority (even in the face of death) and so, just as *samurai* refused to disavow their feudal lords when the battle was lost, and died as a result, many Japanese Christians remained loyal to their tradition.

During the Meiji period (1868-1911), Protestant missionaries entered Japan as soon as Admiral Perry's 1853 American armada threatened military force to compel opening up Japan for Western trade interests. But state Shinto as religion was reestablished in 1868, and the Shinto priests, once again stressing the divinity of the emperor, criticized foreign religions as disrespectful of the imperial family, disrespectful of Japanese (mythological) history, and disrespectful of traditional family values.

It is during the Meiji period when Japan quite intentionally and consciously evolved from a decentralized, isolated feudal society to an industrialized modern nation that needed to understand and assimilate Western scientific technology based on empirical observations and testing, and critical thinking. Also Japan studied carefully European and American economic organization, and military and political power. Japan successfully assimilated Western technology, economic organization, military and political structures. With modernity came industry, modern techniques of warfare, imperial ideology, and a particularly exploitative attitude to the world's resources. All of these were the Japanese attempt to become "civilized" based on Western world-views.

Initially, an uncritical acceptance of everything Western meant adopting Western religions as well as Western science and culture. In this time period, many Japanese associated Christianity with attaining the benefits of westernization; later the Japanese students realized that one can be analytic, scientific and industrialized and still reject Christianity. This was especially true for those Japanese who came to the USA to study, and discovered that many Christians rejected the very things that the Japanese considered essential to modernization: the findings of science and the use of critical analysis. Instead it was the agnostics and atheists who valued these things. Following World War II, Japanese attitudes began to place more much emphasis on ecological modernity.

Modern day Japanese, although rejecting the divine origins of the ancient imperial family, still have the enduring feeling that the Japanese people are a unique and special historical entity. This reflects Shinto religious heritage of 1,000 years or more.

23.14 SUMMARY OF THE CHAPTER

We have traced the earliest beginnings of the Japanese world-view to many thousands of years before the oceans began to rise and isolated Japan from the mainland. The belief that we share this world with many unseen spirits who can help or harm us, is not unique to Japanese religion. However, in Japan the assumption that various spirits (*kami*) share our lives became the foundation for two of the five strands that make up Japanese religion, and affected the other strands.

The Folk Tradition of Japanese Shinto religion has many stories about various *kami* and how they created the Japanese islands, and how they are related to the royal family of the emperor of Japan. The priests of the local traditions are in charge of community health and are consulted on matters of importance to the various families. On occasions requiring serious ritual purification the Shinto priest is essential. Festivals connected with agriculture are especially important to the little tradition.

Institutional Shinto ("the Way of the *Kami* Spirits") draws much of its inspiration from the Little Tradition, but it was adapted by the government to provide a firm foundation for the absolute and unquestioned authority of the royal family to rule. This form of state Shinto is government-created and government-supported. Priests are appointed by politicians. Priestly families draw their authority and income from the state. Originally Shinto teachings were imposed by the dominant political clan leaders, teachings which gave the emperor absolute authority to rule. Later, when military warlords took control, Shinto rituals were celebrations where the emperor would appear, but functioned only as a figurehead. In the nineteenth century, the emperor was returned to power and once again the imperial line was in charge of the nation. Institutional Shinto was resurrected to provide complete political and religious control over the Japanese nation. This was halted in 1945 at the end of World War II.

Confucianism came to Japan from China, and the Japanese equated Confucianism with the ideal form of government, and the ideal structure of family and society. Although Buddhism came to Japan via sixth century Korea originally, two-hundred years later Japanese Buddhist priests traveled to China and brought back the major traditions of Chinese Buddhism, which changed the way the Japanese thought of spirituality and religion. Major Buddhist figures were re-interpreted to become exceptional *kami* spirits with the power to save the nation.

The magical aspects of religious Taoism were also imported into Japan and provided a mechanism to divine the future. Religious Taoism also supplied theories of sexual energy as the basis of health and provided magical numbers of power and luck. Religious Taoism also influenced popular shamanistic religion as well as exerting some political power by claiming to give the rulers insights into future events.

All the strands of Japanese religion accept the parallel realm filled with *kami* spirits who can influence our lives for better or worse. These *kami*-spirits are not infinitely powerful, they are not morally perfect, and they are not creators of the cosmos. Nevertheless, some are so powerful that they can control aspects of nature such as storms and earthquakes and we do not want to anger them. Whether powerful or not, *kami* live in and share our world and must be treated with respect. If behavior would be offensive to a *kami* spirit, then people who engage in such behavior need to purify themselves so as to no longer offend *kami*.

We have seen that Japanese religion is a constantly interacting and changing mixture of five different strands of influence, including ancient traditional shamanistic religious practices, formal institutional Shinto, Chinese Buddhism, Chinese Confucianism, and religious Taoism. State-supported institutional Shinto drew upon the oral folk traditions, combined with aspects of Chinese Buddhism and Confucianism to create a religion ruled by the emperor. The government supported formal Shinto stresses the divinity of the ruling family and offers celebrations in honor of numerous *kami*. The folk tradition of Shinto stresses ritual purification and festivals of celebration.

Folk religion and institutional Shinto exist side by side, and are not in conflict. Institutional Shinto was manipulated by the Japanese rulers after 1868 to support Japanese military aspirations, and the deification of the ruling family was only repudiated after the defeat of Japan in 1945, marking the end of World War II.

Traditionally, the Japanese way of thinking about human beings and their world has been profoundly shaped by the closeness of members of the Japanese family. Within the family, as a group the family can visit a Shinto shrine, and communicate with *kami* spirits. As a family, or individually, family members can pursue questions about the ultimate meaning of life or the universe through the various traditions of Buddhism. Confucian views dominate family interaction in Japan in much the same way as they did in China. These different traditions are not in conflict. One picks and chooses among them depending upon one's needs and one's personal inclinations. At least, this was the way of Japanese religion until World War II.

Japanese religion is not a religion of absolutes. It is not exclusive. The various religions cooperate because they satisfy different needs in different ways. And when it comes to how one should guide one's life, the answer is "tradition." The way that the ancestors have done things is where we should start to find the best way to find a good life.

23.15 TECHNICAL TERMS

Ainu (ai-nuu)   One of the earliest groups to inhabit Japan, whose racial characteristics are closer to Caucasian than Mongolian.

Amaterasu (ah'-mah-te-rah'-sue) Shining in Heaven, the Sun Goddess, the mythical ancestor of the royal family.

Bodhisattva   an Indian Buddhist term for someone who chooses to return lifetime after lifetime to help suffering people. The line between a bodhisattva and a *kami* is not drawn very clearly in the minds of most Japanese.

Ise (ee'-say)   The home of Amaterasu, the most important shrine, located in southeastern Honshu.

Izanagi (ee'-za'-nah'-gi)   "He Who Invites," the male god who with his sister gives rise to Japan.

Izanami (ee'-za'-nah'-mee)   "She Who Is Invited," the female goddess who with her brother gives rise to Japan.

jinja (jin'-ja)   A Shinto shrine.

Jomon   An early group of fishers who inhabited Japan approximately between 10,000 B.C.E. to 300 B.C.E. The Jomon people were the world's first known potters. The name Jomon refers to the coiled "cord-pattern" pottery decoration.

kami (kah'-mee) A spirit being, a being who shares our world. Anything that gives us a feeling of awe, a feeling of being in the presence of unusual power, anything which is unusual, strange, inexplicable, out-of-the-ordinary, and especially awe-inspiring, can be called *kami*. Shinto priests are the shamanistic intermediaries between the more important *kami* and the nation and community.

Kofun   A third century C.E. group of immigrants into Japan who erected huge earthen tombs ("Kofun" means "tomb").

Kojiki (koh'-ji'kee)   The earliest chronicle of formal Shinto.

matsuri (mah'-tsu-ri)   Shinto festivals.

miko   female shamans who transmitted spirit messages, performed healings, and did fortune-telling, later replaced by male priests. Currently the term means "witch" or "sorceress."

Nihongi (nee-hohn'-gee) A chronicle of Japanese history, again the formal scripture of state-supported Shinto.

Shinto   The way of the *kami* spirits which exists in two forms, the oral folk tradition and the official state-supported religion headed by the emperor. "Shin" means god or *kami*-spirit. "To" (pronounced "toe") is the Japanese pronunciation of the Chinese Tao/Dao, the "way."

Yayoi   A wave of immigrants who came to Japan via Korea about 250 B.C.E.

23.16 QUESTIONS FOR FURTHER DISCUSSION

(1)   We have seen that the Japanese world view is not quite like most traditional religions. How has the fact that the Japanese islands have never been invaded successfully by an army on the ocean affected the Japanese religious world-view?

(2)   Sociologists of religion distinguish a "Little Tradition" and a "Grand Tradition" in all world religions. Discuss the differences between these as they appear in the Japanese religious world-view.

3)   We have seen that in Japan, the ruler claimed to rule because he was descended from a divinity. Is there any similar approach found in the history of kings in Europe?

4)   When rulers claim to be divine (as the Roman emperors often did), or claim authority because of their connection with a divinity (a minister, priest, or pope), we expect their behavior to accord with their divinity. There seem to be no moral expectations about the semi-divine emperor of Japan. What do you think accounts for this?

5)   We have seen that the Japanese perceived Western Christian religion as a political danger to the country. What aspects of Christianity gave this impression?

SELECTED BIBLIOGRAPHY

JAPANESE SHINTO THOUGHT

Bowring, Richard, *The Religious Traditions of Japan 500–1600* (London: Cambridge University Press, 2005)

Breen, John, and Mark Teeuwen, *A New History of Shinto* (Wiley Blackwell, 2009)

_____, *Shinto In History: Ways of the Kami* (London: Routledge, 2013)

Dreyer, June Teufel, *Middle Kingdom and the Empire of the Rising Sun: Sino-Japanese Relations, Past and Present* (Oxford: Oxford University Press, 2016)

Hardacre, Helen, *Shinto and the State, 1868–1988* (New York: Princeton University, 1991)

Hoda, Jess, *Shinto Kami: Deities of Japanese Shinto* (CreateSpace Independent Publishing, 2016)

Kasulis, Thomas P., *Shinto: The Way Home* (Honolulu: University of Hawaii Press, 2004)

Littleton, C. Scott, *Understanding Shinto: Origins, Beliefs, Practices, Festivals, Spirits, Sacred Places* (Watkins, 2011)

Moore, Charles, *The Japanese Mind* (Honolulu: University of Hawaii Press, 1982).

Ono, Sokyo, and William P. Woodard, *Shinto: The Kami Way* (Rutland, VT: Tuttle, 2004)

Picken, Stuart, *Shinto: Japan's Spiritual Roots* (Tokyo: Kodansha, 1980).

Rankin, Aidan, *Shinto: A Celebration of Life* (Mantra Books, 2011)

Wakabayashi, Bob Tadashi, ed., *Modern Japanese Thought* (London: Cambridge University Press, 1999)

Young, Louise, *Japan's Total Empire: Manchuria and the Culture of Wartime Imperialism* (Berkeley: University of California Press, 1998).

Yamakage, Motohisa, *The Essence of Shinto: Japan's Spiritual Heart* (Kodansha USA: 2012)

CHAPTER 24: JAPANESE BUDDHISM AND MODERN JAPANESE RELIGIONS

24.1 OVERVIEW OF THE CHAPTER

In the previous chapter, we discussed the oral folk tradition and the state-sponsored Shinto sect, two important strands of Japanese religion. However, Japanese Institutional Shinto did not arise independently of Buddhism. The introduction of Chinese Buddhism into Japan during the Asuka era (538-671) profoundly affected Japanese Shinto religious rituals and practices, and in turn, Shinto would have an enduring effect upon Buddhism in Japan.

For example, the primary function of early Japanese Buddhism was to provide rituals to protect the ruling family and the nation. Buddhism was adopted by the wealthy and powerful ruling clans long before it became popular among the people, precisely because it was thought that Buddhist gods (*kami*) were powerful protectors. For many centuries Shinto faded while various forms of Chinese Buddhism and later Japanese Buddhist developments would come to dominate the daily life of the Japanese, alongside the folk tradition of celebration and community festive interaction with local *kami* spirits.

In fact, in the population the Buddhist buddhas and bodhisattvas were assumed to be new *kami* spirits, and these spirits would serve pretty much the same function as the other spirits with which they were so familiar. Notions of liberation from the cycle of birth-and-death, or elimination of suffering, were simply unknown to the average Japanese citizen. Awakening or enlightenment did not play a role in converting Japanese to the Buddhist system. It was benefits promised by these new Buddhist *kami* which had the greatest appeal.

As mentioned above, the ruling classes adopted Buddhism long before the population, and the ruling class believed that Buddhist spirits would offer protection for the state and the clan from bad luck and evil *kami* spirits. In traditional Shinto, the *kami* offered benefits. So too the new Buddhist *kami* would offer benefits to those who performed rituals and festivals.

In this chapter we will pay special attention to the history and doctrines of the major schools of Japanese Buddhism. Several of these clusters of Buddhist teachings originated in China, including the esoteric Shingon (*mantra*) Buddhism, and the Tendai (stressing the philosophy of emptiness and the *Lotus sutra*). Some are Japanese revised versions of Chinese Buddhist groups, including Pure Land forms of Buddhism (which originated in China but two forms of Pure Land Buddhism developed in Japan), two forms of Zen (imported from the Ch'an teachers of China), and the Nichiren sect (a uniquely Japanese form of rather militant Buddhism). The chapter will conclude with a discussion of modern religions in Japan following World War II.

CHAPTER 24: JAPANESE BUDDHISM

JAPANESE HISTORICAL PERIODS

Pre-Historic Era (10,000 B.C.E. - 350 C.E.)
Proto-historic (third century CE thru middle of seventh century CE)
Second Period: the Classical (mid-seventh thru twelfth century CE)
    538 The first introduction of Buddhism to Japan
Third Period: Medieval Period (thirteenth - eighteenth centuries)
    Triumph of Buddhism and the subordination of Shinto
    Pure Land (popular religion) and Zen (upper well-educated and samurai class).
    Confucianism becomes so tightly integrated into both Buddhism and Shinto that it ceases to exist as an independent tradition.
    Shinto enjoys a revival during the later medieval.
Modern Period: nineteenth - twenty-first centuries.
    Japan evolved from a decentralized, isolated feudal society to a self-consciously modernizing nation that successfully assimilated Western technology, economic organization, and political power.
    Shinto forced into a cult of patriotism before World War II.
    Formation of numerous new religions as the disruption of traditional patterns of worship and national identity.

JAPANESE ERAS

ASUKA (538-671) Introduction of Buddhism from Korea.
NARA (672-780) Earliest sects established.
HEIAN (781-1184) Tendai and Shingon established.
KAMAKURA (1185-1338) Jodo, Shinshu, Nichiren, Zen.
ASHIKAGA (1338-1568) Civil war, dark ages.
MOMOYAMA (1568-1614)
TOKUGAWA (1615-1867) Crystallization of Buddhist church;
    Portuguese expelled; ports closed. 1867-1868
    Feudalism abolished & monarchy restored.
MEIJI (1868-1911)
    Yokohama port is open to trade with the west.
    Japanese begin close study of western science, politics, and philosophy.
TAISHO (1912-1926)
SHOWA (1927 - 1988).
HEISEI (1989 - present)

24.2 INTRODUCTION TO JAPANESE BUDDHISM

Among the most important influences upon Japanese religion and Japanese culture were the several different clusters of teaching approaches based on particular sutras in China, clusters which flourished during the T'ang (618-906 C.E.) and Sung (960-1279) dynasties. According to traditional accounts, Buddhism first entered into Japan between 538–552 C.E. during the Asuka Era (538–671).[1] A different traditional account gives the year 577 when a Japanese envoy brought back Buddhist texts and Buddhist teachers from Korea to Japan.

In the middle of the sixth century C.E., Korea was in the midst of a civil war and in an attempt to gain allies, one of three Korean states sent gifts of Buddhist texts and a statue of Shakyamuni Buddha to the ruler of Japan (seeking military aid from Japan). An important Japanese clan rejected these foreign icons and texts, but following that rejection Japan was visited with natural disasters. The ruler reasoned that the disasters occurred because the mighty foreign god (*kami*) named Buddha was offended, and so the symbols and rituals of Buddhism were adopted by clan leaders.

The Japanese Court Adopts Buddhist Rituals

Rituals were performed to honor this foreign divinity, in the same manner that rituals were performed to local *kami* (gods, spirits). Hence, in Japan Buddhism started out as an elite state religion intertwined with and subservient to government in a way never seen before in India, and even more subservient than in China.[2] The early forms of Japanese Buddhism were understood as a set of powerful rituals which could protect the ruler and protect the nation from harm. In addition to state rituals, early Buddhism in Japan also focused on funeral rites, the worship of sacred relics, and put stress upon the law codes of China. There was no interest in lessening suffering or attaining enlightenment or nirvana.

The Japanese could not help but interpret Buddhism through the eyes of their own folk religious beliefs, and so the Buddha was not thought of as a wise sage teaching a pathway to liberation. Instead, the Japanese thought the Buddha to be a sort of super god with even more magical power than native gods (*kami*). Buddhist moral precepts were then interpreted as taboo-behavior which offended the Buddha.

During this early period, Buddhism was not a popular religion of the people. The primary responsibility of a Japanese Buddhist monk or nun was to perform rituals of worship focused on an image of a Buddha, hoping that the Buddha would respond with gifts and protection. In addition, the Japanese cultural stress on ritual purity to wash away contamination came to have an enduring influence on Japanese forms of Buddhism. As noted in the chapter on Chinese forms of Buddhism, in general Chinese Buddhists did not share this concern with ritual purity.

The earliest forms of Buddhism in Japan were adopted by the powerful clan leaders with ties to Korea, and the influence was top-down. The clan structure of Japanese civilization ensured that the Buddhist and Shinto priesthoods became organized along hereditary lines, with temples and shrines the property of particular families of priests. Loyalty to one's immediate Buddhist superior became expected, the same way a warrior was loyal to his clan leader or general. From its earliest days, Japanese Buddhism was always subservient to the state and involved with politics.

---

[1] Different Japanese sources give the date of both 538 and 552 for the introduction of Buddhism into Japan.

[2] "Japanese Buddhism, from its very inception, was subject to a degree of autocratic state control that surpassed anything seen in early Buddhist China. Government oversight of all aspects of Buddhist activity encouraged competition, if not open strife, among individual teachers, lineages, and temples as they contended for the patronage of the court and the aristocratic families in what was often a zero-sum game. State control was but one of the several factors that led to the overriding sense of lineal and sectarian identity that came to characterize Japanese Buddhism. The Japanese Buddhist monastic institution quickly evolved into multiple independent and somewhat exclusionary schools, formally recognized and superintended by the central government, each holding to distinctive modes of dress, liturgy, ritual and doctrine, and each governed by its own centralized ecclesiastic organization." Robert H. Sharf, *Coming to Terms with Chinese Buddhism* (Honolulu: University of Hawai'i Press, 2002), p. 8.

CHAPTER 24: JAPANESE BUDDHISM

Bodhisattvas Become Important in Japan

Throughout much of Japanese history, but especially during the early centuries, buddhas and bodhisattvas were thought to be powerful *kami*-gods with the ability to control natural forces. In addition to the historical Buddha, Shakyamuni, there was the Buddha of the Western Paradise, **Amida** (Amitabha), and the great Sun Buddha, Dainichi nyorai (**Mahavairocana** Buddha).

In addition to the major Buddhas, several Mahayana bodhisattvas gained special importance in Japan. One was the benign and motherly **Kannon**, the bodhisattva of loving compassion. In India, Kannon was originally the male bodhisattva Avalokitesvara, the helper of Amitabha Buddha. In China, Avalokitesvara became the female Kuan-yin/Kwan-yin/Guanyin. In Japan, the two Chinese characters pronounced "Kuan-yin" are pronounced "Kannon". Kannon responds to suffering, and responds with miracles in desperate situations. Kannon also gives the state of fearlessness, a quality highly valued by the samurai class.

Another important bodhisattva is the medicine god, **Jizo** (in Sanskrit, he is Ksitigarbha). Although the beginnings of the worship of Jizo is in the twelfth and thirteenth centuries, statues and images of Jizo proliferate in modern Japan. He has the power to rescue tormented souls from Buddhist hells, and carries a staff to force open the gates of hells. He protect travelers and children. He also takes care of the souls of those aborted.[3] In Chinese Taoist and Japanese mythology, people who die before their allotted time can become angry vengeance-filled demons. Rituals done to Jizo can help soothe or pacify the spirits, or perhaps free them from their demon state. Temples can be paid to perform rituals for such unhappy spirits. Jizo can guide anyone who asks on the great journey of life. He is a savior and a guide to paradise. Jizo's name can be translated as "Earth Womb," "Earth Matrix," "Earth Store," or perhaps "Earth Treasury."

The bodhisattva **Miroku** (Maitreya) was the Buddha of the future, sitting in heaven waiting to come to earth and teach. We have discussed his importance in early Buddhism and in later Mahayana Buddhism in India and China.

Eventually there would be eight separate schools of Japanese Buddhism, and perhaps fifteen smaller sub-groups of Buddhism. In this chapter we will discuss the most important of these.

24.3 BUDDHISM DURING THE NARA PERIOD (672–780)

Although Buddhism was first introduced into Japan via Korea, the Japanese soon learned that China was the source for Buddhist thought. China had recently become unified during the Sui (581-618) and T'ang (618-906) dynasties, and during that period of relative stability its cultural influence began to spread. The Japanese sent monks to China to learn more about Buddhism, where they also learned the Chinese language and Chinese mores. Chinese culture transformed the Nara era (672-780) court and the Japanese government in many different ways.

One important influence of China upon Japan was in the area of writing. There had been no written language in Japan prior to the introduction of Chinese Buddhism. The Japanese court adopted the Chinese tradition of recording important events, and Japanese scholars learned to read and write Chinese in order to keep court records. This provided literate elite Japanese access to Chinese poetry, history, philosophy, religion, science, technology and medicine. Japanese Buddhist monks learned to read and write classical Chinese, and used this skill to communicate with the Chinese, especially with Chinese merchants and Chinese Buddhist teachers. This also guaranteed that the canonical language of Japanese Buddhism would be Chinese, not Sanskrit from India. Thus, the Chinese understanding of and interpretations of Buddhism were the only forms practiced in Japan.

---

[3] An excellent book on this bodhisattva is Jan Chozen Bays, *Jizo Bodhisattva: Guardian of Children, Travelers & Other Voyagers* (Boston: Shambhala, 2003). See also Hank Glassman, *The Face of Jizo: Image and Cult in Medieval Japanese Buddhism* (Honolulu: University of Hawai'i Press, 2012).

CHAPTER 24: JAPANESE BUDDHISM

Early Indian Buddhism is Not Important

As Buddhism developed in Japan, the Mahayana ideas were accepted and the Mahayana bodhisattva pathway intertwined with Japanese beliefs about rituals of purification, folk-religion and the world filled with spirits. If you recall, in India the Mahayana branch used the insulting term "Hinayana" (inferior branch of Buddhism), to refer to the earlier conservative forms like Theravada Buddhism. The Japanese never questioned the Mahayana claim that the more conservative Theravada was an inferior form of Buddhism, so the ancient teachings of early Buddhism, the Four Noble Truths and the Noble Eightfold Path, were pretty much ignored in Japanese Buddhism.

Chinese Buddhism is the Foundation for Japanese Buddhism

Japanese monks traveled to China to study using their abilities to read and write classical Chinese, and Chinese Buddhist scriptures were imported into Japan. The wide variety of sacred texts[4] ascribed to the Buddha (sutras) and commentaries written in Chinese were studied avidly. The Japanese knew nothing about the wide variety of Buddhist approaches in early Indian Buddhism, and simply adopted Chinese views about sutras and teachings.

As we learned in previous chapters, different Mahayana Buddhist sects in India and in China had different buddhas as the center of their worship, and different Buddhist sutras to serve as their primary authority. Since Mahayana sutras often disagreed with one another, these Japanese Buddhist groups who clung to one sutra were often confronting Buddhist groups which adopted another sutra. The tendency was for a group to claim its buddha as the most important, so the basic Japanese teaching of loyalty to one's clan became loyalty to one's Buddhist temple or abbot (these became one's family or clan).

Loyalty is a key virtue in Japanese civilization

As mentioned before, Japanese culture taught citizens to be loyal unto death to the proper superior. This carried over into Japanese Buddhist monasteries. Monks were not loyal to the religion of Buddhism; they were not loyal to Buddhist doctrines and teachings. In feudalistic Japanese society, one is loyal to one's superior. The loyalty of a monk was to his monastic superior, not to fellow Buddhists. Each monk was expected to be loyal to his own abbot and his own group, loyal unto death. The confrontations between Japanese Buddhist sects of Tendai and Shingon turned violent from time to time with armies of military monks battling one another.

Following the Chinese model, Buddhist monasteries and monks did not pay taxes, so Buddhism became economically strong, and like China, many monks become unproductive and indolent, and temples become parasitic. This would cause problems for Japanese rulers similar to the problems caused by similar situations in China.

Early Buddhism in Japan in the first centuries was not about common people; it was about monks and their relationships with those in power. It would be later in the twelfth century when some Buddhists became missionaries whose focus was upon converting ordinary people into what they claimed was the only one true form of Buddhism.

24.4 THE RELATIONSHIP BETWEEN SHINTO AND BUDDHISM

After the introduction of Buddhism during the Nara period, not only were central buddha figures identified as Japanese spirits (*kami*), but Japanese Buddhist priests had no problem identifying Shinto gods as Buddhist bodhisattvas, and Shinto shrines became more Buddhist in many ways. Traditional *kami* could be reinterpreted as particular manifestations of buddhas and bodhisattvas, so popular Shinto rituals could be understood as Buddhist

---

[4] The sacred scriptures of Buddhism are called *sutras*, and typically they begin "Thus I heard . . ." and were treated as the actual memories of the students of the Buddha (in the same way the Gospels of Christianity are treated as actual memories of followers).

rituals. Popular Shinto deities could be absorbed into Buddhism with no problem. Similarly, buddhas and bodhisattvas could be understood as *kami* spirits, so buddhas can be worshiped in Shinto shrines. Rituals of worship for the buddha of the future, Miroku (Maitreya) could be performed by Shinto priests and understood as honoring a Shinto *kami*, but equally well the rituals in honor of Miroku could be performed by Buddhist priests in Buddhist temples.

In addition to the Shinto influences, Japanese Buddhist religion slowly became dominated by the Chinese understanding and schools of Mahayana Buddhism, especially the philosophical Hua-yen, the Madhyamaka school called T'ien-t'ai, and esoteric Buddhism. This came to have a significant influence on the strength and power of Shinto in the court. Because the primary purpose of institutional Shinto had been to support the authority of the emperor and the ruling clan, when the emperor lost power to military rulers, so too did the formal and institutional Shinto religion lose political power, although it continued to exert influence in the areas of agriculture, fertility and national celebrations. Shinto priests at shrines would recite Buddhist prayers, offer reverence to statues of *kami* as though they were buddhas, and even burn incense. Shinto shrines often adopted red-roofed Chinese Buddhist temple architecture.

For political and military reasons, by the ninth century the emperor and his clan became a mere figurehead of the Japanese nation, lacking any real power or authority. In the twelfth century other clans, or families, had official authority to rule in the name of the emperor. Because the emperor was supposed to be descended from the grandson of the *kami* Amaterasu and was the divine head of institutional Shinto, his presence was essential to perform important state rituals for the protection of Japan and fertility of the soil and the success of the crops.

The emperor was the heavenly sovereign, he was a divinity and could not be replaced or killed, but the royal family was marginalized for approximately forty generations. The status of the emperor would not change significantly until 1868 when a coup occurred, unseating the ruling Tokugawa family and restoring the emperor to power in what is called the Meiji Restoration.

24.5 CHINESE BUDDHIST SECTS DURING THE NARA (672–780)

The early history of Buddhism in Japan begins in the Nara era (672–780). It is a tale of the complex interactions between Chinese Buddhist influences and native Shinto attitudes. These two combined to shape early Japanese Buddhism into a strongly formalistic and liturgical religion under the control of the government.

The primary function of Japanese Buddhist priests was to perform spells, produce magical images, perform complex magical gestures, all to preserve and protect the ruler, the ruling clans, and the elite in society. In exchange, Japanese Buddhist monks expected state support and patronage, and received both. However the different Buddhist groups had to compete with one another for this patronage.

The wealthy and powerful families sponsored Buddhist art and the creation of buddha statues, in order to gain favors from buddhas and bodhisattvas, and to cultivate good karma, or merit. Buddhist temples did rituals on behalf of their patrons. The same patrons also performed rituals in honor of Shinto *kami* spirits.

Chinese schools of Buddhism arrive in Japan

Uniquely Chinese forms of Buddhism were still developing in China during the seventh century. The earliest forms of Chinese Buddhism imported into Japan included several Chinese sects which did not last long in China. Different Japanese emperors associated themselves with different Buddhist sects. During the Nara period, the Kegon (Flower Garland, known as Hua-yen in China) school came close to being the official state religion. The Yogachara Hosso school had so much power for a while that the ruling empress (766) of Japan almost abdicated in favor of her Hosso Buddhist advisor.

In Japan, the Buddhist church was under the control of the government, in the same way that formal Shinto was. Ecclesiastical titles were awarded by the court, so monks who aspired to power and high rank tended to be conformist and flatterers, and at the same time they entered into the court intrigues. There was a consolidation of political power and ritual, and decorative magnificence and increasing corruption. Power and politics had rewarded opportunistic Buddhist priests firmly subservient to whichever clans were the locus of power. Buddhism served the elite and claimed to provide salvation for the highest members of society. In those early centuries, Japanese Buddhist priests had no concern with awakening or the cessation of suffering. Japanese Buddhism had little appeal to ordinary farmers and fisherman, and had not yet begun to exert a spiritual influence upon the aesthetic sensibilities of society. The two dominant schools of Buddhism during the Nara and subsequent Heian periods were the Tendai and Shingon.

24.6 THE HEIAN PERIOD (781–1184)

During the early Heian era, the influence of China remained strong. The Chinese writing system was modified and adapted to create the ability to write the actual spoken Japanese language (the Japanese spoken language does not belong to the same grammatical family as Chinese). Chinese poetry, art and architecture were reshaping Japanese culture. City planning techniques were being adapted to Japanese cities.

A profound awareness of change, transiency[5] and the fleeting beauty of life came to dominate Japanese aesthetics, seen especially in the greatest classic Japanese novel, Lady Murasaki's *The Tale of Genji* (ca. 1010) with its stress on the power of things in the world to evoke a strong emotional reaction within the onlooker. Basing themselves on Chinese T'ang dynasty gardens, the Japanese began constructing extraordinary gardens whose beauty and naturalness continues to influence Japan and the West even into contemporary times.

In the same period, two important sects of Chinese Buddhism were established in the new capital of Kyoto, the center of imperial power. One was the Tendai (based on the Chinese T'ien-t'ai and the *Lotus sutra*) and the other was the esoteric Shingon school (based on the Tantric Chinese Chen-yen tradition). Shortly after the Tendai and Shingon forms of Chinese Buddhism were well established, Japan would turn its attention away from the influence of China for almost three-hundred years until the Kamakura period (1185–1338) when two new forms of Chinese Buddhism would enter Japan.

24.7 TENDAI BUDDHISM

A Japanese monk named Saicho (Dengyo Daishi, 766–822) traveled to China in 804 C.E. and studied Chinese T'ien-t'ai Buddhism and also practiced Ch'an forms of upright seated meditation. In 807 C.E. he returned to Japan and established his Tendai temple on Mt. Hiei to the north-east of Kyoto, the capital city of Japan.[6] Like the Chinese T'ien-t'ai school, Saicho's Japanese Tendai Buddhism stressed the Mahayana *Wonderful Dharma of the Lotus sutra* (whose title in Japanese is *Myoho renge kyo* - *myo* is wonderful; *ho* is truth, teaching or *dharma*; *renge* is lotus, and *kyo* is sutra). Saicho was not a rigid adherent to one sect alone. In addition to his study of Chinese T'ien-t'ai doctrines, Saicho openly sought after Buddhist truth in other Chinese Buddhist schools, so he incorporated new doctrines and beliefs, especially drawing upon the esoteric Tantric Shingon school.

---

[5] Recall the central Buddhist insight that "all things are impermanent."

[6] This location was at least partly determined by the Chinese pseudo-science of *feng-shui* (geomancy), because it was thought that the temple in the north-east would protect the capital from evil forces emanating from that direction. Chinese mythology asserted that both northeast and southwest are inauspicious directions, for they lack heavenly *yang* and earthly *yin* essences. Chinese homes should face south, where the *yang* is most vital. Chinese and Japanese Buddhist temples utilized the same orientations.

CHAPTER 24: JAPANESE BUDDHISM

Tendai Thought

The *Lotus sutra* was the most important scripture for Japanese Tendai Buddhism. The text was devotional and philosophical but also magical. For example, the Buddha preached the *Lotus* to 12,000 *arhats* (who had achieved nirvana but not buddhahood), to 6,000 nuns, to 8,000 bodhisattvas (who sought buddhahood), and 60,000 *devas* (divinities or gods). The god Brahma was there, attended by 12,000 dragons, and uncountably many other supernatural beings and creatures. As the Buddha talked, a ray of light was emitted from his forehead revealing 18,000 pure lands with a Buddha presiding over and preaching in each one.

Although Mahayana Buddhism had a tendency to feel that there were two branches of Buddhism, the superior or great vehicle, and the inferior or little vehicle, the *Lotus sutra* asserted that there was only one vehicle of Buddhism, not two. Tendai called itself the "One-Vehicle School" and aimed at including all forms of Buddhism within one comprehensive scheme.

One Tendai belief was one shared with most other Mahayana sects. Tendai asserted that the Buddha had three different bodies: a mortal human body (*nirmanakaya*) which we associate with Shakyamuni Buddha (another name for Siddhartha Gautama who lived in the fifth century B.C.E.), a bliss body (*sambhogakaya*) which experiences the bliss of Nirvana in a Buddha paradise, but most important was his "cosmic body" (*dharmakaya*) which is eternal and persists after the (apparent) physical death of Buddha.[7]

Tendai asserts that all living things possess the Buddha-nature which means that everything has the potential to attain enlightenment and nirvana. Tendai accepted Nagarjuna's Madhyamika view of *svabhava-sunyata* (all things are devoid of unchanging substance, "empty" of essence) that all things arise from numerous causes and nothing has an independent essence, substance, or soul. Things are real, but reality is "emptiness" (*sunyata*).

Tendai Buddhist monks accepted a list of moral precepts which included the practice of filial piety (clearly a Chinese concern) towards parents, teachers, and clergy. They also gave special value to the ruler and like the other Buddhist sects, they promised peace and prosperity to the nation.

The Triple Truth of Tendai

To say that all things are *svabhava-sunyata*, empty of unchanging essence, does not mean that things do not exist or that things are unreal. Based on a quote from a text by the Indian philosopher Nagarjuna, Tendai says that there is a Triple Truth: (1) all things are empty of unchanging essence, yet (2) at the same time things do exist, albeit provisionally. The (3) third truth is the truth that transcends both emptiness and temporariness.[8] As its basic tools, Tendai utilized the two practices of seated focused concentration, or cross-legged mediation, and liberating wisdom or insight. Finally, the influential idea of the age of the "decay of the teaching" appears in the *Lotus* sutra.

---

[7] These Three Bodies of the Buddha can be understood metaphorically as well. There are lines from a poem which goes "Your own nature is provided with the Three Bodies." The Japanese Zen teacher Hakuin (1685-1768) said "The pure Dharmakaya is your nature; the perfect Sambhogakaya is your wisdom; the myriad Nirmanakayas are your activities." Quoted from Isshu Miura and Ruth Fuller Sasaki, *The Zen Koan* (New York: Harcourt Brace, 1965), p. 67.

[8] The "Triple Truth" seems to arise from a mistranslation of a verse by Nagarjuna:
   We state that whatever is dependent arising, that is emptiness.
   That is dependent upon convention. That itself is the middle path.
Nagarjuna's Sanskrit verse states the causality (dependent co-origination) is the same thing as emptiness (*sunyata*), and this is also the Middle Way of Buddhism. This was translated into Chinese, which the Chinese T'ien-t'ai school understood to be teaching three truths, emptiness, dependent origination (the conventional), and a third and highest truth which transcends both, i.e., the Middle Way. The quote is from chapter 24, verse 18, discussed in chapter 10 of volume 1 of this book. This translation is from David Kalupahana, *Nagarjuna: The Philosophy of the Middle Way* (New York: State University Press of New York, 1986), pp. 339-341. Compare this with the translation of Jay Garfield, *The Fundamental Wisdom of the Middle Way* (New York: Oxford University Press, 1995), pp. 304-308.

CHAPTER 24: JAPANESE BUDDHISM

The Three Periods of the Dharma-Teaching

The *Lotus* says that the farther away we get from the lifetime of the Buddha, human abilities will decline and the world will enter into dark ages of ignorance.[9] This situation can be schematized into three different periods:

(1)   Period of the True Dharma (about 500 years; thought to end about 50 C.E.). The term dharma refers to the Buddhist teachings that lead to awakening and nirvana. During this period ordinary people have profound abilities and can become enlightened easily; serious Buddhist students are guaranteed of attaining liberation. This is true for five hundred years; after this period, enlightenment is no longer easily available because people's abilities begin to decline.

(2)   Period of the Semblance of the Dharma, Counterfeit or Quasi-Dharma (thought to end about 1050 A.D.). During this period, human abilities have declined and deep understanding is no longer possible but the teaching resembles genuine Buddhism closely, and enlightenment is still possible—just very difficult. This is the time period of the last bodhisattvas and philosophers like Nagarjuna and Vasubandhu.

(3)   Period of the Decay of the Dharma (beginning after 1050 C.E.). Fifteen hundred years after the death of the Buddha, human nature will have decayed so much that almost no one has the discipline or wisdom to attain enlightenment by his or her own efforts. In this period, we are just common mortals with no special gifts or skills — upon whom could people rely to achieve liberation, or was it hopeless?

Tendai Teaches *Mappo*, the Evil Times of Decline

In Japanese, this third era of the Decay of the Dharma is called *mappo* (in Chinese, *mo-fa* or *moshi*, "final age"), the period of the serious decline of the highest teaching or *dharma*. During this third period, human beings are degenerate, overcome by passions, and lack the ability to understand the highest teachings, and cannot generate enough spiritual energy to make real progress towards nirvana. The world will fall into a state of increasing disorder and it cannot be improved.

Tendai teachers claimed that it was possible to achieve liberation by a combination of special rituals, secret incantations or *mantras*, ritual hand gestures, visualization of Buddha-lands, and seated meditation. Monks could contact supernatural divinities in other realms who could assist those who ask for help. They did not teach the Four Noble Truths or the Noble Eightfold Path because the Japanese believed that these teachings belonged to the inferior schools of Buddhism.

Later Developments in Tendai

In the late ninth century, a bitter rivalry developed between two groups of Tendai followers, and both sides used warrior-monks who brawled and fought with one another. Violence increased until, during the eleventh century, the major temples and Shinto shrines had standing armies of *akuso*, or "vicious monks." Mt. Hiei, the home of Tendai Buddhism, became especially violent with a standing army of several thousand troops, both monks and mercenaries. They would march into the capital terrorizing citizens, demanding special rights, demanding special titles, and even demanding land.

A Tendai monk named Ryonin (1072-1132) placed special emphasis on chanting the name of the Buddha of the Pure Land, Amida Buddha, as a device to help poor degenerate human beings in this age of pain and disorder. This practice of calling on Amida Buddha became incorporated into Tendai rituals and spread to other temples as well.

---

[9] In the Hindu world that Buddhism grew out of, there was the idea of the three times which included the time of creation (presided over by Brahma), the sustaining period (Vishnu presides), and then the time of dissolution and destruction, the *kali yuga*, presided over by Shiva. Did this have an influence over Buddhist thought?

24.8 ESOTERIC SHINGON BUDDHISM

Several teachers of Tantric Buddhism had recently gained influence in the Chinese court just when Japanese monks were traveling to China to study Buddhism. The Chinese court required Confucian rituals to be practiced constantly, and so they valued those teachers who claimed to have expertise in secret ritual technology. These Tantric monks invoked deities and chanted magical formulae, so these were labeled monks with skill in Chen-yen/Zhenyan, two Chinese characters which literally mean "true word" (a Chinese attempt to capture the meaning of the Indian Sanskrit term *mantra*). These ritual-based techniques and *mantras* of esoteric Buddhism were believed to offer supernatural protection for the ruler and the nation. In eighth century China, these secret techniques were still relatively new. Although there does not seem to have been an actual "school" of Tantric Buddhism in China, state-controlled Buddhism in Japan created very separate and strict sects and temple lineages, and this did affect the Japanese version of esoteric Buddhism.

The Japanese monk Kukai (Kobo Daishi 773–835) was fascinated by one of the Chinese teachers, and brought back to Japan these secret Tantric invocations used in rituals, and magical texts.[10] In Japan Kukai claimed to have been entrusted with a secret teaching and described it as coming from an exalted lineage of esoteric masters.[11] The two Chinese characters "Chen-yen" are pronounced "Shin-gon" in Japanese, so in Japan, this became the separate sectarian lineage of Shingon Buddhism. Although Shingon Buddhism became very powerful in Japan, Chen-yen Buddhism does not seem to have been a separate lineage and virtually disappeared in China after the 845 persecution.

As we have seen before, a chanted *mantra* is a word or phrase believed to contain magical power, and perhaps capturing an insight that cannot be expressed in ordinary language. The Shingon school understood a *mantra* to be a profound ideal conceived in a Buddha's mind but not expressible in words.[12]

Like the other forms of Tantric Buddhism, Japanese Shingon saw itself as a higher doctrine which transcended all forms of Buddhism which had come before. These earlier forms had teachings which could be expressed in words. However, the Shingon tool of *mantra* went beyond the limits of language. Therefore Shingon believed that it transcended both early Buddhism (which they called the "Inferior Vehicle" or Hinayana) and surpassed all prior Mahayana doctrines.

Kobo Daishi / Kukai

The Japanese monk Kukai (Kobo Daishi 773–835) traveled to China and for two years studied the esoteric Tantric Chen-yen (*mantra*) techniques of ritual chanting, ritual imagery, bright colors, sensuality and magnificent ceremonies. Kukai brought all of this back to Japan and established the home of esoteric Chinese Buddhism on Mt. Koya, 40 miles (approximately 64 kilometers) outside the capital of Kyoto.

---

[10] An important student of esoteric Buddhism in China was the monk Hui-kuo (746–805), who was the teacher of the Japanese monk Kukai (774–835). Kukai studied in China and then when he returned from China, he asserted that he brought a special secret transmission to Japan. In Japan, Shingon Buddhism became exceptionally important and politically powerful lineage tradition, or "school," whereas in China there were many teachers who used Tantric methods but it is unclear if they thought of themselves as teachers in a distinctly separate lineage of esoteric Buddhism. If it ever was a separate school in China, Tantric Buddhism quickly faded. See Robert H. Sharf, *Coming to Terms with Chinese Buddhism* (Honolulu: University of Hawai'i Press, 2002), Appendix 1: "On Esoteric Buddhism in China," pp. 263–278)

[11] "Japanese scholars have been perplexed at the apparent absence of any explicit reference in Chinese sources, including the writings and translations of the great 'Tantric patriarchs' of the T'ang, to the self-conscious esoteric tradition that Kūkai claimed to have inherited." Robert Sharf, *op. cit.*, p. 271.

[12] Esoteric Buddhism was discussed in *Asian Thought*, Volume 1. In chapter 5 we discussed Tantric Hinduism, in chapter 11 esoteric Indian Buddhism, and in chapter 12 we discussed Tibetan forms of Tantric Buddhism.

However, Kukai did not simply transfer Chinese Tantric Buddhism intact to Japan. Kukai formulated a system which included elements of the "Flower Garland" Kegon (Hua-yen) school, the Three-Treatises Sanron (Madhyamaka), the "Consciousness-Only" Hosso (Yogacara), combined with Chinese Chen-yen Tantric beliefs and practices and very special rituals which the Chinese Chen-yen teachers revealed to Kukai, claiming that they had been obtained from secret Indian sources. Kukai was Japanese and was raised with the ideas about *kami*, and these too figured into the Shingon system. Each *kami* spirit could be understood as a manifestation or appearance of a buddha or bodhisattva.

The basic techniques of Kukai's Shingon Buddhism utilizes esoteric rituals, *mantra* and *dharani* ("incantation," phrases to avert evil, heal illness and bring about blessings), divination, magic, *mandala* images, sexual symbols, symbolic finger manipulations (*mudra*), and other useful and skillful devices (*upaya*) to symbolically illustrate the highest truth. In addition esoteric rituals were also for the purpose of protecting the powerful patrons from rebellion, and from natural disasters like typhoons, windstorms and earthquakes.

The Buddhist sutras which teach these sorts of devices are usually preached by a great cosmic Buddha whose name is Mahavairocana ("Great Sun" pronounced Maha-vai-RO-chana), or in Japanese, *Dai-nichi*. For Shingon, the historical Buddha, Siddhartha Gautama, was merely one of many manifestations of the eternal Great Sun Buddha.[13] Mahavairocana is the Buddha-nature inherent in all things. Mahavairochana is the third body of the Buddha, the *dharmakaya*, the ultimate nature of reality and the ultimate truth. But Mahavairocana does not exist apart from the mind.

Mantras are a means to unite one with Mahavairocana. By chanting these, and reciting and meditating upon these, one can achieve awakening. Even the title of a sutra can be a *mantra*. Shingon puts great stress on esoteric symbolic and iconographic representations of truth. Shingon believes that certain hand and finger positions (called *mudra*) have magical powers.

Shingon Buddhism came to have great appeal for the Japanese, at least partly because of its magical elements: *mantras*, or incantations, divination, exorcism, and its elegant mysterious rituals performed secretly in hidden rooms in the temple, hidden from all but those who had been initiated into the highest secrets. Public rituals were rich in pageantry, brilliant in color and movement, and appealing to the aristocrats in the capital of Kyoto. Not every Japanese who attended these very popular rituals was devout; a visit to a temple to observe these rituals was primarily a pleasure trip, more like attending a play or music event.[14]

Perhaps more than any other Buddhist sect, Shingon seemed to have an affinity for Shinto, with bodhisattvas identified with *kami* spirits. A major Shinto writer of the 1300s declared that Shingon Buddhism came to prominence in Japan, but faded in China, because of the fact that Shingon Tantric Buddhism was so compatible with traditional Shinto.[15]

Tantric Shingon Buddhism became very nationalistic, claiming the Japan was the original home of all the gods (*kami*) and the original home of the buddhas as well. This would make Japan the most important location for Buddhism, more important than India or China.

Kukai is credited with inventing the Japanese syllabary called *kana* allowing Chinese characters to be used for nouns and verb roots, and *kana* to be used for inflections like verb endings. Kukai is also credited with bringing tea to Japan.

---

[13] The student will recall that the Shinto Sun Goddess, Amaterasu, was the mythical founder of the Japanese royal family. It did not take long for Amaterasu to be understood as the *yin* or feminine aspect of the Great Sun Buddha, Mahavairocana, who contains both masculine and feminine. Shingon Buddhism became very close to Shinto.

[14] Conrad Schirokauer, *A Brief History of Japanese Civilization* (New York: Harcourt Brace, 1992), p. 60.

[15] *Ibid.*, p. 86.

24.9 THE END OF HEIAN ERA AND NEW BUDDHISM (late 1100's).

As the Heian (781-1184) period was coming to an end, life was increasingly difficult as clans warred against one another for power. In 1156 a destructive civil war between clans intensified. At the end of the Heian era, one clan defeated its rivals, destroyed many of the temples in Kyoto during the battles and established a new capital in the city of Kamakura around 1175. A much more bitter war in 1180 decimated much of the countryside, ultimately ushering in the new Kamakura era.

The new ruling clan took action to defend itself against the military power of the Buddhist groups situated in the old capital city of Nara, where the standing temple armies of several temples were destroyed and the temples themselves were burned.[16] The power of the emperor was officially handed over to the military in 1192, when the emperor appointed the clan leader, General Yoritomo, to be the delegated power behind the throne, the *shogun* (ruling general), who then was authorized to rule Japan. He used his power to appoint men loyal to himself to positions of power throughout the provinces. It was a warrior elite clan that took control of the government. From this time until the nineteenth century, Japan was ruled by a military aristocracy.

Mappo, The Decline of the Dharma

The idea of the *mappo* period of the decline of the highest teaching or *dharma* (sort of a dark ages) and an age of increasing disorder as taught in the *Lotus sutra* began to exert more appeal. Buddhism in Japan became quite pessimistic. The times during the Heian era were evil; people and politics had degenerated. The evidence of *mappo* was everywhere. Deadly conflict which decimated the major cities and countryside was evidence of *mappo*. Political and religious corruption was evidence of *mappo*. The subservience of Buddhist monks and priests to political power and to serving the wealthy, was seen as evidence of the decline of human abilities. Society was in chaos, and there were accompanying natural disasters such as typhoons, earthquakes, and famine.

It is important to realize that the Buddhist idea of *mappo* did **not** promise that eventually things would get better. Rather, the world will just continually spiral down farther and farther for ten-thousand years and we will have a hell on earth. Everything worthwhile and valuable in this world will decline. Such a decline means that people lack the ability to have any control over their lives, or liberate themselves to achieve the goals of Buddhism, as previous generations had done. In such a world, humans can no longer comprehend or master the liberating insights and doctrines of Buddhism because of the decline of human abilities.

If people accept the idea that in this last age individual effort and intellect are doomed to fail, then forms of Buddhism which rely on self-effort gradually will lose much of their appeal. The Nara schools of Buddhism, the Tendai and Shingon, were about self-effort, but were also the province of the aristocracy and the elite. As happens so often in human history, power had a corrupting influence and both Nara schools of Buddhism had become preoccupied with materialistic matters involving land, politics, power and financial advantage. These schools of Nara and the Buddhism of the Heian era were out of touch with the world of the ordinary Japanese.

With the older Buddhist schools no longer at the center of power, several new forms of Buddhism became popular, including Zen Buddhism, two devotional forms of Pure Land Buddhism, and Nichiren Buddhism. During the earlier periods a few monks had devoted themselves to working with the common people, but they did not have broad acceptance. However, this changed. At least some Buddhist priests successfully took on the role of missionaries, taking on the role of converting and tending to the needs of ordinary people. The primary focus of the devotional schools would be faith, not rituals, not scholarship, not meditation.

---

[16] These were the Todaiji and Kofukuji temples in the city of Nara.

These more devotional forms of Buddhism denied the claim that the Buddhist priests were superior, were special people able to offer salvation to those who paid for it. It was now the individual who could achieve the goals of Buddhism directly, without a priestly hierarchy.

24.10 THE KAMAKURA (1185–1338) AND ASHIKAGA (1338–1568) SHOGUNATES

The older forms of Heian Buddhism, originally in Nara and then centered in the capital of Kyoto, particularly the Tendai and Shingon, had been corrupted by political power and were quite uninterested in the spiritual needs of the people. Political upheavals and social turmoil mark the end of the Heian period, and the fact that Tendai and Shingon had loyally catered to the powerful elites, and were irrelevant to the needs of ordinary people set the stage for new forms of Buddhism to become popular.

Three new developments would occur during this period. New Buddhist leaders appeared during the Kamakura period who attracted many followers both among the intellectual elite and among the common people. These leaders turned away from fancy ceremonies aimed at the wealthy and powerful elite, and put less stress on the church-state institutions. One of these developments involved Zen Buddhist monks who would stress the power of insight and meditation to bring about awakening, and would not stress faith. The two dominant figures in Zen were Eisai (1141-1215) and Dogen (1200-1253). The second development would stress devotion and faith in the Buddha of the Western Paradise. The Pure Land leaders would be Honen (1133-1212) and Shinran (1173-1262). During this same era a quite militant form of Japanese Buddhism was founded by the monk Nichiren (1222-1282). Nichiren condemned all forms of Buddhism other than his own, and wanted the state to execute all Buddhists who did not follow his own form of Buddhism.

24.11 THE ZEN TRADITION IN JAPAN

The practices of the Chinese Ch'an or Zen school of Buddhism were first introduced into Japan in the seventh century, but did not take root at that time. Zen would not become truly established in Japan until the twelfth century.[17] The Japanese had little interchange with China for several hundred years, but now in the twelfth century Japanese monks once again traveled to Sung China (Sung dynasty 960-1279), and the influence of China once again became important in Japan.

Chinese Ch'an Buddhist Schools

In this era, there were two major streams of Chinese Ch'an Buddhism, the Lin-chi (Linji) and the Ts'ao-tung (Caodung). Both forms were brought to Japan, where in Japanese the same Chinese characters were pronounced as "Rinzai" and "Soto."[18] Zen appealed to the military leaders now ruling Japan, warriors who had less concern with elaborate esoteric Shingon and Tendai rituals and *kami* spirits. The warrior class was not interested in the abstract philosophic approach of the other sects, but rather concerned with direct action and immediate experience which rendered the samurai fearless in battle. Zen Buddhism offered the immediate and self-transforming insight experience of *satori* which seemed to be just what a warrior needed.

---

[17] A detailed historical and philosophical analysis of Zen in Japan can be found in Heinrich Dumoulin, *Zen Buddhism: A History: Vol. 2 Japan* (New York: Macmillan, 1990).

[18] A later Chinese school called the Huang-po or Obaku teaching was brought to Japan during the Ming dynasty, and although it has nowhere near the number of followers as Rinzai and Soto, there are still a few Obaku temples in Japan. See Heinrich Dumoulin, *Zen Buddhism: A History: Vol. 2 Japan.*

Ch'an was the dominant Buddhist school in China during the Sung dynasty (960–1279), profoundly influencing art, poetry, and philosophy. From the middle of the twelfth century on, a steady exchange of Japanese and Chinese monks developed which would bring the Japanese into contact with flourishing Ch'an schools. Ch'an Buddhist monks often accompanied trade missions from China to Japan. It was during this period, during the twelfth and thirteenth centuries, when the Japanese Zen would become influential in Japan. There were two Japanese monks who were especially important to this process: Eisai (1141–1215) and Dogen (1200–1253).

24.12 EISAI: RINZAI ZEN IN JAPAN

In China, the Lin-chi line was dominant, and for several hundred years different Ch'an monks and students came to Japan bringing Lin-chi Ch'an, but Ch'an did not take root in the Heian era. That began to change with the Japanese monk Eisai (1141–1215). Eisai had been a Tendai monk at Mt. Hiei, but was not satisfied with esoteric Tendai teachings and practices. During this era there was a great pessimism in Japan, the belief that the age of the decay of the *dharma* made all effort useless, but Eisai did not accept this. Even if it was a time of decay, he thought that the correct place to seek the Buddhist truth is in the awakening experience of the Buddha. He traveled to China 1168 as a member of a Tendai delegation seeking that experience and was deeply impressed by the spirit of Ch'an/Zen in Sung China but did not stay in China for an intensive study.

Twenty years later Eisai made a second trip to China in 1187, and devoted himself to the Lin-chi lineage's *koan* study and seated meditation Zen practice, and after four years of study, he finally received the seal of authority in the Lin-chi sect which gave him permission to teach. He returned to Japan as an authorized Zen teacher (*roshi*, respected teacher, or master) and built the first Lin-chi/Rinzai temple in 1191. Eisai also had an enthusiasm for tea; he brought tea seeds back to Japan, and encouraged tea drinking by monks, thus beginning a very close association between Zen and the tea ceremony.

Toward the end of the Heian era, many Japanese Buddhist monks accepted that this was a degenerate age of *mappo* and that Buddhist practices would not be sufficient to bring awakening. As a result many did not practice *zazen* meditation and were not observing the Buddhist precepts which apply to monks, and this was perceived as a decline of the quality of the Buddhist priesthood. Eisai believed that the foundation of Zen practice lies in the observation of all the moral precepts of Buddhism, so he encouraged reform.

The politically powerful Tendai sect on Kyoto's Mt. Hiei had no interest in reform, and so was opposed to the new Zen understanding brought by Eisai, fearing Zen popularity could threaten the Tendai influence on the aristocrats and the powerful clans. So, periodically the Tendai monks succeeded in having the Zen sect banned.

One military ruler (*shogun*) was so deeply impressed by Zen that he appointed Eisai head of the Kenninji Zen temple in Kyoto in 1202. Kyoto, the ancient capital, was dominated by the more ancient Buddhist sects of Tendai and Shingon, and because of this, Eisai had to make concessions to the other older more established sects. In the Kenninji temple, in addition to the Zen hall, there was a hall where the rituals and rites of both Tendai and Shingon were celebrated. For this reason, Eisai's Rinzai sect was not a purely Rinzai Zen sect as it had existed in China; rather it was a respectful combination of Chinese Lin-chi practices combined with esoteric Japanese Shingon and Tendai Buddhism, and used the practice of chanting the name of Amida Buddha, the Buddha of the Western Paradise.

Eisai had many students, most of whom combined Tendai and esoteric practices with Zen practices. In the following centuries, many other Japanese monks traveled to China, and brought back other lineages of Ch'an in China. The Zen sect created many world-famous rock gardens and black-ink paintings.

The goal of Rinzai Zen is Satori

As was discussed in Chapter 21, the prior chapter on Chinese Ch'an, the Ch'an tradition claims there exists an unbroken lineage of teachers going all the way back to the Buddha himself, and each Ch'an master had achieved the identical awakening *bodhi* experience of all the Indian predecessors.[19] The Japanese accepted this, and paid careful attention to their own teaching lineages, connecting each Japanese teacher to one of the Chinese lines.

Satori in Rinzai Zen

We also saw that the Chinese tradition tends not to refer to the Indian Sanskrit term for enlightenment, *bodhi*, but rather to the Chinese character *wu*, a term which the Japanese render into the noun *satori*. As Eisai learned in China, *satori* is not a once-and-for-all complete and total awakening.[20] *Satori* is often identified with the euphoria which comes from a breakthrough insight into the nature of the self or the nature of the world. Zen monks could have several experiences, each deeper than the previous. They are often described as *kensho*, "seeing one's own true nature," or obtaining a glimpse of one's Buddha-nature. Thus *satori* seems to be euphoric insight experiences of varying intensity and depth, not a one-time complete unexcelled awakening experience. Insight is not identical with euphoria; one can be awakened without the positive emotional release that sometimes follows understanding clearly. Euphoria is **not** the goal; insight is the goal. Ch'an teachers stress lifelong practice.[21]

Eisai learned that the Chinese Lin-chi Ch'an masters do not seem to have had any interest in escaping from the world, and did not think that the awakened sage transcended or rejected the world of cause and effect. The Chinese Ch'an Buddhist teachers asserted that awakening gave you a correct understanding of the true nature of reality, and allowed you to live fully in the this reality of flowing change, and impermanence.

So, Zen *satori* is not the same thing as complete unexcelled awakening in early Indian Buddhism. But it is grounded in *kensho*, a glimpse into one's own true nature, and one's true nature is that of a Buddha.

Koan Practice in Japanese Zen Buddhism

In chapter 21 we discussed the Chinese Ch'an technique of a *koan*[22] (pronounced ko-an), which literally means a "public case" in the same way a settled point of public law is a legal precedent which can be used to decide current legal cases. Much of that discussion on Chinese Ch'an *koan* use also applies to Japanese Zen and *koan* study. In Japan, it was the Rinzai school which put the greatest amount of stress on the study of *koans* as a means to awakening, although the Soto school also used these unusual questions.

---

[19] As discussed in chapter 21 on Ch'an, scholarship during the past 90 years has revealed that this claim is pure mythology. There never was such a lineage, either in India or China.

[20] Indian Buddhism refers to the Buddha's experience as complete unexcelled awakening (*samyaksambodhi*). This is not the meaning of *wu* or *satori*.

[21] The Chinese and Japanese traditions utilize a series of woodblock prints that lay this out in an artistic way, called the Ten Ox-Herding Pictures, reproduced in numerous books. The Japanese Zen master Dogen also placed great stress on continuing practice.

[22] In Chinese this is a *kung-an/gongan*, but the Japanese pronunciation *koan* (ko-an) has been used in the West since the 1930s, and appears in English dictionaries.

Zen rock garden at Ryoan-ji

The popular explanation of a *koan* is an enigmatic question the teacher asks of the student which requires the student to plumb the depths of the most important issues in life, but which is worded so that logic alone will not provide the connection between question and reply. The student cannot look up an answer in a reference book or a Buddhist scripture. The student is able to answer the question only when the student has a new perspective, an insight into the self, the world, or the interconnection of self and world and their mutual relativity.

One of the greatest of all the Japanese Rinzai Zen teachers was Hakuin[23] (1685–1768) who, along with his successors, organized Japanese *koan* study and emphasized the necessity of seeing into one's own true nature (*kensho*) as the essential prerequisite for Zen understanding. Hakuin understood Zen practice as having two parts. The first part was all of one's training prior to the abrupt emotional breakthrough called *kensho* (seeing into one's own true nature).[24] The second part was all the training thereafter. Hakuin says:

Seeing into our own real nature is the first principle for Zen monks. Therefore, always keeping foremost in our minds the koan that we have been given, we never cease seeking kensho day and night, night and day. . . . If you wish to seek Buddha, you must first have insight into your own real nature. . . . Under no circumstances search among the teachings of the sutras or in written words. Never ask your teachers to explain.[25]

---

[23] For more on Hakuin, see Norman Waddell, *Wild Ivy: The Spiritual Autobiography of Zen Master Hakuin* (Shambhala, 1999).

[24] This echoes the Chinese Ch'an stress on "sudden awakening" as a first step of Ch'an Buddhist practice.

[25] This quote draws on three separate quotations from Hakuin, all taken from Isshu Miura and Ruth Fuller Sasaki, *Zen Dust* (New York: Harcourt Brace, 1966), p. 41, 42, 43.

Koans[26] are a skillful teaching device the Zen master uses to get us to shift our perspective from the single view of ordinary people to the multi-perspectives of the insightful. In doing so, we come to get a glimpse of our true nature, to realize it by direct experience. In Zen there is no list of claims we are asked to believe on faith. "Koans are about manifesting that and actualizing that [nature] in everything we do"[27]

Japanese Zen teachers drew upon numerous collections of Chinese *koans*, and Hakuin (1685–1769) and later generations of his followers began to organize the *koans* into three main groups, structured on whether the koan leads to insight into the world, the relationship between self and the world, or transcending both. Unlike the Chinese lineages, the Japanese Zen teachers organized those three main approaches of *koan* study into five more specific groups of *koans*. To become a Zen teacher the student must go through the *koans* in each of the five of these groups, and then master additional steps. The first beginning steps of Rinzai Zen are when the student is given one of the basic *koans* which provoke a *kensho* experience. Traditionally, one of these *koans* would be given when the student first enters the monastery:

(1)   Thinking neither of good nor of evil, at this very moment what was your original aspect before your father and mother were born?
(2)   A monk asked Master Joshu: "Has the dog a Buddha-nature or not?"
        Joshu answered: "Mu."[28]
(3)   Hakuin Zenji used to say to his disciples: "Listen to the sound of the Single Hand!"[29]

The Traditional Five Groups of Koans

Having penetrated into and passed one or more of those first koans, one has experienced a "sudden-insight" into his or her nature (*satori*), and is now ready to deepen that initial insight and begin organized study. The student begins with the first of the five groups of *koans*, (1) *koans* intended to give the student insight into the oneness of all things. Until one can see past the discriminations into a state of non-separation, one has not made progress. With the first group, the student comes face to face with a world of undifferentiated processes. An example of these includes the following:

A monk once said to Dairyo Osho: "The physical body decomposes. What is the indestructible Dharmakaya?"
Dairyo answered with this verse:
        Blooming mountain flowers
        Are like golden brocade;
        Brimming mountain waters
        Are blue as indigo.[30]

---

[26]   In the paragraphs that follow the author's explanation of *koans* will utilize writings of several contemporary American Zen teachers who have successfully penetrated through the hundreds of *koans* in their practice, and whose answers have been accepted by their teachers. It is an object of belief in contemporary Japanese Zen that contemporary teachers have the identical understanding of the teachers of the past, but there is no way to show it is so. These authors are providing an emic explanation of the *koan*. There are numerous etic studies of the *koan*, including Steven Heine and Dale S. Wright, eds., *The Koan: Texts and Contexts in Zen Buddhism* (London: Oxford University Press, 2000).

[27]   John Daido Loori, *Two Arrows Meeting in Mid Air: The Zen Koan* (Rutland, Vt.: Charles E. Tuttle, 1994), p. xxiv

[28]   This very popular beginning *koan* has a book devoted to it: James Ishmael Ford, Melissa Myozen Blacker, eds., *the book of MU: essential writings on zen's most important koan* (Boston: Wisdom Publications, 2011).

[29]   Isshu Miura and Ruth Fuller Sasaki, *The Zen Koan* (New York: Harcourt Brace, 1965), p. 44.

[30]   *Ibid.*, p. 48.

Having achieved clarity about the flowing processes we call reality, the (2) second group of *koans* functions to bring about awareness of the other side of the coin, the "complex interlockings of differentiation." Although there is abstract principle, there are also individual things, each of which exemplify the universal. An example of this second group is this:

A monk asked Master Joshu: "What is the meaning of Bodhidharma's coming from the West?"

"The cypress tree in the garden," Joshu replied.[31]

The (3) third group of *koans* focus specifically on language, on the words and phrases of the earlier generation of Zen teachers, and how language is related to the world. The world of the interaction of abstraction and concrete is explored. A great Chinese master is quoted as saying "Men of immeasurable greatness are tossed about in the ebb and flow of words." Zen master Miura says that "if you are caught in the entanglement of words, you will lose your freedom." Here's an example of a *koan* belonging to this third section:

A monk asked Nansen: "Is there a truth that has not been preached to men?"

"There is," said Nansen.

"What is this truth?" asked the monk.

Nansen answered: "This is not mind, this is not Buddha, this is not a thing."[32]

(4) The fourth category are those *koans* which are considered especially difficult to penetrate into, even if the student has understood all the previous *koans*. These reveal that no matter how many *koans* we have already resolved, our understanding and insight can still go deeper. Even though the student has made enormous strides towards understanding her own true nature, there are still more layers more to penetrate into. These *koans* are not for beginners. "Not until we have penetrated these *nanto* ["difficult to pass through"] koans one by one can we be said to be true monks."[33]

The Japanese Zen master Hakuin says this about one who has been able to penetrate all of these *koans*:
Now you may pass your days in tranquillity, drinking tea when there is tea, eating rice when there is rice. If there is nothing further to do, that is all right; if there is something to do, that is all right. The patriarchs cannot lay their hands on you, and you can spend ten thousand ounces of gold."[34]

Enkan's Rhinoceros-horn fan (there is no such thing as a "rhinoceros-horn fan") is an example of these *koans*:
One day Enkan Osho called to his attendant and said: "Fetch me my rhinoceros-horn fan."

"The fan has been broken," said the attendant.

"If the fan has been broken, then bring me the rhinoceros itself."

The attendant had no reply.

John Tarrant, an authorized Zen teacher who writes about this *koan* explains,

Most of life is inconceivable; even your left hand cannot be fully conceived of though it can be very useful. And if you try hard to conceive of what your hand does, it won't play piano very well. The inconceivable is the source of all that comes into being. This koan is not about making what is

---

[31] *Ibid.*, p. 50.

[32] *Ibid.*, p. 55, p. 56.

[33] *Ibid.*, p. 57.

[34] *Ibid.*, p. 58.

unknown, known. Instead, it is an exercise in relying on and making friends with the inconceivable, using a casual event to start an exploration into the unlit realms.[35]

Tarrant also explains, "If you are stuck in some way or in a tight corner and can't imagine a way out, this koan might help. It doesn't require you to know where you are going, or need a solution that makes sense in terms of the problem."[36]

(5) The fifth group of *koans* seem to be more philosophical, because these *koans* are based on the *Five Ranks* of a Chinese Ch'an master named Tung-shan (Tozan in Japanese).[37] Tozan is one of the two founders of the Chinese Ts'ao-tung or Soto Zen school. The label for this group of koans is "going beyond."[38] Zen master Miura says:

> The study of the Five Ranks is more nearly like a severe and final examination, for he who undertakes this study will be called upon not only to review all that he has previously come to understand, but to clarify, correlate and deepen still further the insight he has attained. He will have to polish again each facet of his spiritual jewel, which he has cut so laboriously and painstakingly. But, in doing so, he will see for the first time the total inclusiveness, perfect symmetry, and matchless beauty to which it has been brought under the training devised by the old masters.[39]

In Japanese Zen, *koan* study does not end here. For many Zen organizations, after going through the five groups of traditional koans, there is more to be done before one is a certified Zen *roshi*, a respected Zen teacher.[40] The next stage involves essential Buddhist moral precepts which are treated as *koans* to be resolved. Assuming that the Zen monk has realized an unusual depth of insight, how is the Zen monk to behave in the world? Can you express your insight when you awaken in the morning, as you eat breakfast, as you drive to school or work, as you talk to your friends, and as you go to sleep? The senior Zen student will now treat "Do not destroy life" as a koan to penetrate into. "Do not steal" is then the next koan. The process continues until all are clarified.

Gerry Shishin Wick is an American with a Ph.D. in physics who has gone through the traditional *koan* process, and is now recognized as a *roshi* or respected Zen master. Dr. Wick's Zen training process under a Japanese teacher is very much like what we have described above. He writes:

---

[35] *Ibid.*, p. 61. The quote is from a Western Zen teacher who has written a book on Zen *koans*: John Tarrant, *Bring Me the Rhinoceros and Other Zen Koans to Bring You Joy* (New York: Harmony Books, 2004), p. 48.

[36] *Ibid.*, p. 53.

[37] A really excellent and technical book dealing with the Five Ranks is Alfonso Verdu, *Dialectical Aspects in Buddhist Thought: Studies in Sino-Japanese Mahayana Buddhism* (University of Kansas: Center for East Asian Studies, 1974). Verdu also explains the Chinese Hua-yen (Japanese: Kegon) inspiration for these Five Ranks. Another primary source is Ross Bolleter, *Dongshan's Five Ranks: Keys to Enlightenment* (Boston: Wisdom Publications, 2014).

[38] A basic source which summarizes these five, with lengthy examples and explanations, is Isshu Mirura and Ruth Fuller Sasaki, *The Zen Koan* with a summary on pages 46-76. See also Eido Shimano, "Zen Koans" in K. Kraft, ed., *Zen: Tradition and Transition* (New York: Grove Press, 1988).

[39] Isshu Miura and Ruther Fuller Sasaki, *op. cit.*, pp. 62-3.

[40] As has been pointed out earlier, ideally Zen requires the student to pass through all of these *koans* and more before being certified as a *roshi*, a respected Zen teacher. In actual fact, teachers have been given the title "*roshi*" by mail and have even purchased the title. Do not assume that a Zen *roshi* is a perfectly enlightened Buddha after passing all the *koans*. Even in official Japanese Zen temples, they are not. They are Zen teachers, and they are respected. Nothing more is expected of a *roshi*.

CHAPTER 24: JAPANESE BUDDHISM

I spent over twenty years studying with Taizan Maezumi Roshi. Much of that time was devoted to examination and appreciation of about seven hundred koans during our face-to-face encounters in the private interview room. In the system of koans presented by Maezumi Roshi, we start with two hundred "miscellaneous" koans designed to bring the student to experiential realization of oneness of all things. These koans are drawn from various sources including traditional collections and more obscure sources. . . . Next we study the *Gateless Gate* which contains forty-eight koans. Then there are the hundred koans of the *Blue Cliff Record* followed by the hundred koans of the *Book of Equanimity*. . . . Next we study the fifty-three koans of *The Transmission of Light*, which detail the enlightenment experiences of the Zen Ancestors from Shakyamuni Buddha to Master Dogen. Next we appreciate the Five Ranks of Master Tozan with about fifty koans and testing points. The final collection is a series of one hundred koans based on detailed examination of the sixteen bodhisattva precepts which are transmitted during ceremonies for both laypeople and monks when they commit to the Way of the Buddha."[41]

Resolving a Zen koan

Although we can talk about "solving" or "answering" a *koan*, those who have passed through *koan* study suggest that it might be more correct to say that the student penetrates into the *koan*. In a not-so-obvious fashion, a *koan* raises an issue or a point. The student is to offer a response which elucidates an issue raised in the *koan*. As such, often the answers do not make sense to someone who has not explored the issue deeply. For the person with insight into the *koan*, the connection between the question and the student's response is clear. The student answers the *koan* by adopting a new perspective which gives the student some insight into the nature of the self, the nature of the world, and the interaction between self and the world.

The Sound of the One Hand

One of the most famous of the Zen *koans* originated in Japan with Zen master Hakuin (1686-1769). Traditionally Hakuin's *koan* is one of three given as the very first to a student who has just begun study. It is based on a Chinese proverb on the necessity of teamwork: "A single hand does not make a clap." We all know that you need both hands to make the sound of clapping. The *koan* asks, "What is the sound of one hand clapping?" Logically, we know that to produce a sound, one hand has to be in a relationship with the other hand. Logically, the answer is that there is no sound, but if you answer "no sound," your Zen teacher will not accept your answer. If you use one hand so that your fingertips pat your palm, you have got the wrong answer. Clearly this *koan* is exploring distinctions, differentiation, and dualistic thinking patterns, but the satisfactory understanding of a student cannot be merely intellectual; the teacher can ask the student to demonstrate understanding.[42] The answer must be immediate with no hesitation for analysis and logic.

Koans are not restricted to the Zen teachers of the ancient past. New *koans* continue to appear, sometimes current, sometimes right out of today's news. For example, a Japanese Zen teacher living in Los Angeles might ask: "When you are driving on the freeway, where is your mind?"[43]

---

[41] Gerry Shishin Wick, *The Book of Equanimity: Illuminating Classic Zen Koans* (New York: Wisdom Publications, 2005), pp. 1–2.

[42] This is one of the most famous examples of a *koan* in books on Zen. It originated in Japan with the Rinzai teacher Hakuin (1686-1769). This *koan* on the sound of the one hand does not appear in any traditional *koan* collection. The teachers in the Hakuin line passed this on orally: "Listen to the sound of the Single Hand!" Miura and Sasaki, *Zen Dust, op. cit.*, p. 44.

[43] Joshu Sasaki (1907-2014), a Rinzai Zen teacher.

The answer to a *koan* can be in words, but it can also be a shout, a nod, a smile, the blinking of an eye, pushing one's foot down on the floor, waving the arms, slamming a door, bowing, or even holding up a flower.

The Two Functions of a Koan

Koans function in at least two different yet related ways:
(1) to initiate some insight, realization or attainment by the student;
(2) to allow the teacher to determine the depth of the student's realization.

(1) Resolving a *koan* initiates insight.

In order to gain enough clarity to answer the question posed by the teacher, the student needs a spiritual realization, a *satori*. In order to penetrate or resolve a *koan* the student needs to gain a different perspective, freeing herself from prior conditioning and assumptions, thereby providing a glimpse of the way things really are and a break-through into a deeper understanding. Many of the classic *koan* stories end with the monk obtaining *satori*, or insight as a result of the *koan*.

(2) The teacher can use a *koan* to test the depth of the student's understanding.

In theory, a student with a profound awakening to his or her own true nature can answer each and every *koan*. "If you break through one koan, hundreds and thousands of koan have all been penetrated at once."[44] The student presents the answer to the koan. At that moment, the Zen teacher can test the depth of the student's understanding by asking further follow-up *koans* which a student with deep understanding should be able to answer. When the teacher finally comes to a follow-up *koan* that the student cannot answer, the limits of the student's understanding have been reached, and the *koan* process begins again when the teacher assigns a new *koan*.

Each of these subsequent questions can probe the depth of the student's understanding, but also can help the student to clarify that original insight, to help the student to cling less and less to her attainment, and continue the study of *koans*. The ultimate and ideal goal is that the self-centered ego is no longer the center of one's personality. The Zen tradition uses meditation in the process of resolving a *koan*. The most common explanation for how to probe a *koan* from those who have done so successfully is the following:

> The only way through the koan, no matter what koan, is to be the koan. The only way through a barrier is to be the barrier. If the barrier is fear, the only way to the other side of that barrier of fear is to be that fear. If the barrier is pain, the only way to the other side is to be the pain. When you are the pain, when you are the barrier, the barrier fills the whole universe. The whole relativistic system disappears. When the barrier fills the universe, there's nothing outside it. It includes everything. The world of differentiation disappears. . . . The way to work with any koan, . . . is to be the koan, be the barrier. Don't separate yourself.[45]

In the Mahayana Buddhist traditions dating all the way back to India, the technique of *upaya*, "expedient means" or a special teaching trick, is stressed. It is clear that the apparent irrationality of the Ch'an *koan* is a sort of skillful teaching trick, *upaya*, a special device to help the student achieve insight.[46]

---

[44] Shibayama Zenkei, *Zen Comments on the Mumonkan* (New York: Harper & Row, 1974), p. 23.

[45] John Daido Loori, *Two Arrows Meeting in Mid-Air* (Rutland, VT: Charles Tuttle, 1993), p. 319.

[46] The ability to utilize a skillful teaching device, or *upaya*, is one of the skills of a buddha and bodhisattva. Using *upaya*, buddhas and bodhisattvas can lead people from this shore of *dukkha* to the other shore of Nirvana.

12.13 DOGEN: SOTO ZEN IN JAPAN

In addition to Eisai, the other great Zen pioneer was Dogen (1200–1253), who certainly is one of the most important figures in intellectual Japanese religious history. His surviving writings have generated great interest in contemporary times. Dogen was an intellectually gifted child, but both his parents had died before he was seven. On her deathbed, his mother urged him to become a Buddhist priest. In 1213, when he was age 13, Dogen was ordained by the Tendai school on Mt. Hiei. As a result of his study on Mt. Hiei, he wondered why, if Chinese Buddhism teaches that we are all born with the Buddha-nature, why do we need to practice to attain awakening? Why study to achieve enlightenment? His Tendai teachers could not give a satisfactory answer to the precocious youth.

According to the tales told in the Soto tradition, in the spring of 1223 Dogen traveled to China to seek an answer. He studied hard and in spite of extreme effort, he did not attain a transforming insight experience. Discouraged, he was about to return to Japan when he heard of a Ts'ao-tung/Caodung master named Ju-ching/Rujing (1163–1268). Dogen had finally found his own true teacher.

Although the lineage Ju-ching belonged to was the Ts'ao-tung (the two Chinese characters which the Japanese pronounce "Soto"), he had an independent mind and he despised sectarian rivalry and was critical of the abuses of the Buddhism of his time. Ju-ching had no interest in fancy rituals, secret teachings, mysterious *mantras*, hand waving manipulations, popular divinities or special doctrines. He taught Dogen that all any Zen student needs is directly in front of us; we merely need to see it clearly. We do that with the practice of seated meditation (*zazen*). There is no mysterious or supernatural "Buddha-mind" to be transmitted apart from the written words of the Buddhist sutras. Ju-ching did not like to label his teachings as "Ch'an" or "Zen" and rejected all sectarianism.

Although he was elderly, Ju-ching exhorted all his monks to work hard, telling his students stories about all the effort and hardships endured by Zen students in the past. The disciples of Ju-ching sat in silent focused meditation day and night. Dogen gave his utmost. Once one of the monks fell asleep while in the seated meditation *zazen* posture, and Ju-ching called out, "In Zen, body and mind are cast off.[47] Why do you sleep?" On hearing this, Dogen experienced a profound awakening experience, and soon after from Ju-ching he received the seal of transmission making him a successor to the patriarchs of the Soto sect, and authorizing him as a teacher. Dogen remained with Ju-ching for two more years, exemplifying his understanding that Buddhist practice is not a "once-and-for-all" experience, but rather is a lifelong learning process capable of endless deepening and broadening. One has a profound experience, and then the student continually deepens it, or authenticates it.

Dogen returned to Japan in 1227, but unlike previous Japanese monks who returned from China with new sutras and new rituals which would increase the monks personal importance, Dogen came back to Japan without new sutras, without new rites, without new sacred images. He had no intention of founding a new sect of Zen, but simply wanted to devote his life to the deepening realization of the truth of Buddhism in seated meditation. Dogen did not regard his practice as a special Buddhist school.[48] He called it "the great Way of the Buddhas and the patriarchs."

Dogen retired to a small rural temple to avoid the political problems of Kyoto sectarianism. However, this small rural temple where Dogen sat in quiet meditation and instructed others in the skill grew to become an important center for the practice of Soto Zen. Many gifted students were lured to study with him when they heard stories of Dogen's profound understanding of Buddhism and life.

---

[47] This line is an echo of a similar passage in chapter 6 of the philosophical Taoist classic, *The Chuang-tzu*, where we find "I have dropped the body and limbs and discarded intelligence and consciousness. Freed from the body and knowledge, I have become one with the Great Thoroughfare [Tao]."

[48] A good basic explanation of Dogen's thought can be found in Heinrich Dumoulin, *Zen Buddhism: A History – Japan* (New York: Macmillan, 1990). Another source on Dogen and his philosophy is Tanahashi, Kazuaki and Peter Levitt, eds., *Essential Dogen: Writings of the Great Zen Master* (Shambhala Publications, 2013). A discussion of a key text is Eihei Dogen, *Dogen's [Shobogenzo] Genjo Koan: Three Commentaries* (Berkeley, CA: Counterpoint, 2011).

CHAPTER 24: JAPANESE BUDDHISM

The politically powerful Tendai monks on Mt. Hiei viewed Dogen's success with alarm, and threatened the Soto Zen community of monks which had slowly gathered around him, so in 1245 Dogen moved again, this time to a far-away mountain retreat in the north named "Eternal Peace Temple," Eiheiji.[49] He continued teaching at Eiheiji until he died in 1253.

Although the original Chinese group was not the most important of the Ch'an sects in China, Dogen's Japanese Soto sect became the strongest of all Japanese Zen schools, despite the fact that Dogen tried to keep it as the non-sectarian teachings of the Buddha.

Dogen's Teachings

The problem that started Dogen's spiritual journey was the question "Why do we have to practice to attain awakening, if we are all born with a Buddha-nature?" In Buddhist philosophy, this is called the problem of the relationship between the awakened Buddha nature we have at birth, called innate awakening, and the profound life-changing insight experience resulting from practice, called acquired awakening.

Dogen resolved the problem while he studied in China. To provide a simple explanation, Dogen writes that one is innately awakened, but one has not yet realized the fact. Not aware of this fact, you seek outside yourself for happiness in ways that miss the point. When one does get a glimpse of one's own innate Buddha nature, one realizes that nothing was missing and no new facts had been acquired. You have a state of awareness which constitutes the enlightenment you were born with. It is your Buddha-nature. Most of the time you are unaware of it.

Becoming aware of this intrinsic nature is the awakening that a student realizes after extended meditation practice. Transformation occurs in the form of the practice. In one of his texts, Dogen writes: "As for the Buddha Way, when one first arouses the thought [of enlightenment], it is enlightenment, and when one first achieves perfect enlightenment, it is enlightenment. First, last, and in between, are all enlightenment."[50] The activity of that consciousness is intrinsic enlightenment.

Of course, Dogen was not the first to raise and resolve the problem. The Chinese Ch'an teachers had begun the process of de-mythologizing the phenomenon of awakening several hundreds of years before. The Chinese master Lin-chi (whose name the Japanese pronounce Rinzai) had taught that monks do not have to meditate for lifetimes; not even for decades. Strenuous and focused practice might someday culminate in a burst of profound comprehension, and all the categories we normally use are now seen as not ultimate, but merely conventional. The result is a transformation of the way one perceives the world.

Dogen on Buddha-Nature (*Tathagatagarbha*)

Tendai and Shingon Buddhist groups and teachers taught that we have or possess the nature of a Buddha, and there was a tendency to understand this as possessing some mystical inner entity, some supernatural power or transcendental reality. Dogen rejects this. Living beings do not possess a small 'inner buddha' within them. Dogen says that Buddha-nature is not something one possesses — one *is* Buddha-nature. There is no ultimate duality between the seer (self, student, practitioner), and the seen (a separate Buddha-nature). All is flowing processes, empty of unchanging inner essences. All things are Buddha-nature, just as they are. All things possess beauty, perfection, holiness, sacredness, just as they are. When you see things through the eyes of a Buddha, all things are perfect just as they are.

---

[49] Eiheiji is pronounced "eh-hey-ji." "Ji" means "temple."

[50] Francis H. Cook, *Sounds of Valley Streams: Enlightenment in Dogen's Zen- Translation of Nine Essays from Shobogenzo* (New York: SUNY Press, 1989), p. 12.

CHAPTER 24: JAPANESE BUDDHISM

There Is No Absolute Reality Beyond the Realm of Interdependent Processes

Like the previous generations of Ch'an masters in China, Dogen rejected the idea that awakening is a one-time experience of transcendence of the world of cause and effect. When seen clearly, this world of interdependent interconnected impermanence is Ultimate Reality. The awakened Zen master does not transcend impermanence. Achieving Buddhist awakening does not make one immune from change. One cannot evade ever-changing conditions; there is no alternative to the world of impermanence and conditioned phenomena.[51] The only solution is to affirm it unequivocally as one's own life. Things, impermanent phenomena, even death, are not transcended, not evaded, and not denied — rather they are radically affirmed and accepted.

This also means the acceptance of oneself as being that same reality, that same impermanence, without regret, fear, resentment, or antipathy.[52] All of these influences upon our lives are changing and none remains fixed. Influences wax and wane over time. The perceptive student may notice that what we describe is the essential claim of the emptiness doctrine of Nagarjuna (discussed in chapter 10 of Volume 1, *Asian Thought*).

Dogen is pointing out that nothing stands alone, separate. Nothing is independent. You do not have an unchanging essence, nor does anything else that has affected you. You are *svabhava-sunyata*, "empty of unchanging inner essence." You arise out of constantly changing conditions, and your constant changing is a constituent of what we call reality. You are what you are because of everything else, but in turn, you condition your environment, affecting others daily.[53] Everything is changing. The world is not static, not inert. The emptiness of all things appears to us as in the shape of a flying bird, a barking dog, a flower turning toward the sun, the nearby mountain or a cloud blowing overhead. Indeed, you and I are a crystalized expression of ever flowing reality, empty of inner unchanging substance.

Dogen believed that it is the practice of *zazen* or quiet seated meditation which allows us to recognize the profundity and mystery in all existence, and to thoroughly penetrate this dimension in our everyday life of eating, sleeping, and chopping firewood for our campfire.[54]

The Use of *koans* in Dogen's Soto Zen

For a long time it was common for authors to report that the Dogen school of Japanese Zen did not use the apparently irrational *koans* typically used in the Rinzai lineages. However Japanese scholars have known that Dogen collected and used a book with three-hundred *koans* taken from the Chinese collections, and that collection was published in Japan in 1934.[55] Dogen assigned these *koans* to his students, and the later Soto tradition also used another collection of koans called *The Book of Serenity*. The collection has been translated at least two times. One translation is by the late John Daido Loori who produced a lengthy translation of the *koans* that Dogen used with his students. The other is by another American *roshi*, Gerry Shishin Wick.[56] Dr. Wick had also penetrated all of these *koans*.

---

[51] *Ibid.*, page 28.

[52] *Ibid.*, page 19.

[53] *Ibid.*, p. 24.

[54] *Ibid.*, p. 25.

[55] The history of the *koan* text used by Dogen can be found in Steven Heine, *Dogen and the Koan Tradition* (New York: State University Press of New York, 1994).

[56] John Daido Loori and Kazuaki Tanahashi, *The True Dharma Eye: Zen Master Dogen's Three Hundred Koans* (Boston: Shambhala Press, 2005). See also Gerry Shishin Wick, *The Book of Equanimity: Illuminating Classic Zen Koans* (Boston: Wisdom Publications, 2005). Gerry Wick and John Loori studied together under Maezumi Roshi.

CHAPTER 24: JAPANESE BUDDHISM

The Soto school of Dogen seems to understand *koan* practice in the same way the Rinzai lineage did. A contemporary Zen master (*roshi*) writes: "So, what is the purpose of koans? Why do we study them? Our practice is to examine the very nature of the ignorance that causes us to grab onto the self—not only the self as we perceive it but also the self in relation to everything else."[57]

In order to penetrate a koan, the student must drop away attachments to images, beliefs, and projections. As Dogen Zenji said, "To study the Buddha Way is to study the self and to study the self is to forget the self." He is talking about the small ego-grasping self that hinders our free functioning in life. In order to drop that away, we have to see the fundamental nature of our mind and our self.[58]

Nevertheless, the primary practice of the modern Soto school of Japanese Zen is quiet sitting, or seated meditation.

Seated Meditation (*zazen*) According to Dogen

Dogen taught his students what he had learned from his teacher in China. The basic practice of Dogen's Soto Zen is *shikan taza* (often rendered "zazen only"). The Soto student sits in crosslegged meditation facing the wall, following the example of the legend of Bodhidharma's practice of "wall-gazing." Based on his own experience, Dogen saw this as essential to awakening. For Dogen, *shikan taza zazen* is not something one does in order to achieve awakening. *Zazen* is the realization and fulfillment of the Buddha's teaching.[59]

Although *zazen* may begin as one sits crosslegged in one's home, or possibly sitting with a group in a meditation hall, ideally *zazen* is something done in all activities. The state of focused concentration is extended to all of our encounters, all of our experiences. To the extent that one is able to focus *zazen* attention in all experiences, one also continually encounters the experience with an enlightened consciousness.[60]

Here is Dogen's own explanation of *zazen*, taken from Dogen's "General Teachings for the Promotion of Zazen":

"If you wish to attain enlightenment, begin at once to practice zazen. . . . Free yourself from all attachments, and bring to rest the ten thousand things. Think of neither good nor evil and judge not right or wrong. Maintain the flow of mind, of will, and of consciousness; bring to an end all desires, all concepts and judgments. Do not think about how to become a Buddha.
[Bodily position described]

. . .

Now that the bodily position is in order, regulate your breathing. If a wish arises, take note of it and then dismiss it. In practicing thus persistently you will forget all attachments and concentration will come of itself. That is the art of zazen. Zazen is the Dharma gate of great rest and joy."

The body finds itself in that state of relaxed attention in which sense and mind remain awake and yet are released in complete rest.

---

[57] Gerry Shishin Wick, *The Book of Equanimity*, p. 5.

[58] *Ibid.*

[59] For example, see Taigen Dan Leighton, *Zen Questions: Zazen, Dogen, and the Spirit of Creative Inquiry* (Wisdom Publications, 2002).

[60] Gerry Shishin Wick, *ibid.*, p. 14.

Do not practice zazen in order to achieve enlightenment; rather enlightenment is already contained within you as you "exercise," and so just sit in zazen in the full knowledge that you are already innately enlightened (even though there is an enlightenment experience which you do have).[61]

Enlightenment in Dogen's Zen

As Dogen explained above, *zazen* meditative practice is *not* a mechanism to attain a state of awakening or enlightenment. Awakening is not something outside of oneself which one should seek. Awakening is not an all-at-once experience which happens just once in one's life. Awakening is an ongoing experience of continual deepening, or continual authentication. Meditation, or *zazen*, is not a tool to achieve awakening. *Zazen* itself is an expression of intrinsic enlightenment. *Zazen* reveals that intrinsic enlightenment.

Buddhist Realization is a Life-long Practice

Dogen identifies awakening with life-long on-going focused *zazen* practice, and this means that awakening is not a once-and-for-all momentary experience. Being awakened, or clarity, expresses itself in everything we say and do. Francis Cook explains that enlightenment is simply the egoless uniting of the mind-body with its experience. An activity can be enlightened so long as one is identified with the experience; but the next activity becomes unenlightened when one becomes separated from one's experience. If awakening is a state of mental non-separation, mental oneness with some object or activity, there must be an ongoing effort to achieve this consciousness in moment after moment of activity and encounter.[62] The awakened life is one of continual authentication.

According to Dogen and Soto Zen, Buddhist practice is capable of endless deepening and broadening. Buddhahood is not to be sought outside oneself. To realize liberation, one need only find it within. The Japanese Zen school puts its stress on self-understanding and self-reliance. No one can save you but yourself. But, what is this "self" in a universe where everything is empty of unchanging inner essence? Dogen advises us to practice seated meditation if we want an answer to this question.

Funeral Rituals in Soto Zen

As was mentioned before, Japanese Shinto priests regarded an encounter with death to be contaminating, so Buddhist monks were the ones who performed funeral rituals, which were of great importance to ordinary people as well as the wealthy and powerful. Many were worried that their beloved parents might suffer in hellish realms because of bad karma. People believed that funeral rituals for deceased Soto priests and nuns were especially powerful. This was because a Buddhist priest or nun was an actual embodiment of the liberated mind of Shakyamuni Buddha himself. The Soto school devised a strategy of making any and every deceased person an ordained Soto monk or a nun, thereby giving them special status with very powerful funeral rituals. This certainly helped make Soto the most popular form of Zen in Japan.

The influence of Zen in Japan increased in the following Ashikaga (1338–1568) era and afterwards. It was a time of terrible civil war, filled with inequity and uncertainty for all levels of Japanese society. During this traumatic period many of the warriors and political leaders became very serious practitioners of Zen. It appears as though some of these powerful people achieved deep insight. There are many stories about these warriors who became Rinzai Zen students. The great sword master Miyamoto Musashi (1584–1645) is one famous person who studied Zen seriously.

---

[61] Heinrich Dumoulin, *Zen Buddhism: A History - Japan*, p. 161.

[62] *Ibid.*, p. 13.

24.14 JODO and JODO SHINSHU DURING THE KAMAKURA ERA (1185–1338)

The military had taken control of the government when they established their new capital in Kamakura, but things would not remain peaceful. Although the military *shogun* ruled in the name of the emperor, in 1221 the emperor raised an army in an attempt to reestablish his control and power over the other clans, but during the ensuing battles he was soundly defeated and as a result the military ruler's position was strengthened.

Times of civil war make life very precarious and difficult. It seemed clear that Japan and the world must be going deeper into the Period of the Decay of the Dharma (*mappo*). In the period of *mappo*, scholarly self-efforts could not succeed. What could a person do to escape the suffering? The answer is faith. Devotional forms of Buddhism became extended beyond the monastics into the lives of common people. Some Buddhists became missionaries, preachers, focusing on ordinary people and promising them the possibility of nirvana.

THE TWO PURE LAND SCHOOLS OF BUDDHISM

In previous chapters, we have discussed the Pure Land forms of Buddhism in India and in China. In Japan, the term "Pure Land" is **Jodo**, and the school of Pure Land Buddhism is Jodo Buddhism.

The Roots of Pure Land Are In India: A Review

In chapter 10 of Vol. I of *Asian Thought*, we discussed a group of monks in India who practiced visualization of the Pure Land of Amitabha Buddha. The source for this is the first century C.E. sutra *Sukhavati-vyuha* (Sutra of Infinite Life). The sutra told of the Western Paradise presided over by Amitabha Buddha who made 48 vows as he traversed the path leading to buddhahood. While still a bodhisattva and not yet a buddha, he vowed to establish a land of bliss wherein all beings could be free of *duhkha* (sufferings and troubles). In his 18th vow, he vows to come to the aid of all who think of him ten times. In his 11th vow he promises that humans will finally attain nirvana when born into the Pure Land. All that is needed is the recitation of the name of Amida Buddha. Even if one committed the worst offences, by reciting the name of Amida Buddha ten times, all offences would be erased and he or she could be reborn in the Pure Land. Despite these visualization exercises, no separate devotional sect of Buddhism devoted to Amitabha Buddha developed in India.

Pure Land Buddhism in China: A Review

The Chinese form of Pure Land (Ching-t'u/Jingtu) began around the fourth century in the common era when the Chinese Buddhist teacher Hui-yuan (334–417) had a vision of Amitabha's Pure Land as a result of using visualization meditative practices. The many teachers in the Pure Land lineage also used the *Lotus sutra*, and based on that sutra, the Chinese divided Buddhist history into "Three Periods of the Dharma (Teaching)."

(1) The Period of the True *Dharma* when people can become awakened easily and can understand Buddha teaching.
(2) The Period of the Semblance of the Dharma, the Counterfeit- or Quasi-Dharma—which ended about 50 C.E. Deep understanding is no longer possible; awakening is possible but very difficult.
(3) The Period of the Decay of the Dharma (*mappo*)—beginning somewhere between 500 C.E. and 1050 C.E.: ordinary people do not have the discipline or intelligence to attain enlightenment by their own efforts. What could one do?

The Chinese Pure Land Buddhist teacher T'an-luan felt that one could attain salvation or liberation only by relying on the power of Amida's Vow—it would be an egocentric error to believe that one could achieve the goal by himself or herself alone. Shan-tao/Shandao (613-681), the Third Chinese Patriarch of Pure Land, thought that liberation is available only to those who believed that they were "sinful, lowly persons, eternally involved in error, shut off from salvation."[63] One must get the sincere mind, the mind of deep faith, and the mind which sincerely desires rebirth in the Pure Land. Recite the name of and call upon Amida Buddha. Shan-tao recited it continuously throughout his life. Shan-tao advocated single-minded devotion to Amida Buddha, and rejected all other Buddhist practices.

In the early decades of the 1200s, the Japanese began to show new interest in trading with China, especially for Chinese luxury items, and this stimulated a renewed interest in Chinese religions and Chinese culture. It is during this period that Pure Land Buddhism became most important in Japan.

JODO: PURE LAND BUDDHISM IN JAPAN

Three hundred years before Pure Land Buddhism became an independent sect in Japan, the Tendai monk on Mt. Hiei, Saicho (Dengyo Daishi, 766–822), considered invoking the name of Amida (Japanese pronunciation of Amitabha) as one possible method of meditative practice. The Shingon Buddhism of Kukai understood Amida to be an aspect of Mahavairocana (Dai-Nichi Nyorai, The "Great Sun Buddha"). Even esoteric Shingon considered the Pure Land to be "The Palace of Vaicrocana."

In Japan, Pure Land Buddhism makes a distinction between (a) achieving liberation by **Self-Power** (relying on discipline, meditation and concentration, *koans* and the self-liberating power of one's own mind) and (b) achieving liberation by **Other-Power** (complete reliance on the power of a buddha to bring him or her to salvation). Pure Land Buddhism thinks that if students believe that they can achieve awakening by themselves, this is a manifestation of arrogance and pride, cultivating ego-centeredness. Pure Land says that in this era of *mappo*, students cannot depend on their own powers, but must rely on the power of another, the power of Amitabha to take them to the Pure Land. The Pure Land sutra teaches that one may be reborn in the Pure Land without extinguishing human passions, and once in the Pure Land, one can attain nirvana without hindrances.

The actual founders of the two Japanese Pure Land traditions were **Honen** (1133–1212) and his student **Shinran** (1173–1262). Both discovered the power of Pure Land teachings when they read books written four generations earlier by the Japanese monk Genshin (942–1017). Genshin had been a monk who worked with the common people, preaching to their concerns and needs. Genshin was enthralled by the vision of Amitabha's Western Paradise and wrote devotedly about the glories of the heavenly Pure Land, and the delights of those who were blessed to inhabit the realm. He also wrote about the varieties of hells and the suffering of the doomed. Genshin made many paintings of his vision of the Pure Land. He actually managed to organize the Pure Land imagery into a doctrine of liberation for all.

The Pure Land pathway for those of us with limited ability in this era of *mappo* (decay of the Buddha-dharma) simply required continuous and uninterrupted thought on Amida Buddha and his Pure Land. To continually have the Buddha in one's mind requires concentration and unification of the mind. Clearly, this is a visual meditative approach, stressing singlemindedness. Then one can practice purification. Purification leads to ultimate insight.

JODO: PURE LAND BUDDHISM OF HONEN

One of the most important founders of an independent school of Japanese Pure Land Buddhism was a Tendai priest named Honen (1133–1212), who was certain that he lived in the degenerate age of *mappo*, the last period of the decay of the true teachings of the Buddha. He was disgusted by Tendai Buddhism's obvious preoccupation with politics, power, and wealth. Honen read Genshin's description of the Pure Land and was certain that this Pure Land teaching was the true pathway for the age of *mappo*. He thought that the traditional Buddhist practices of following

---

[63] Al Bloom, *Shinran's Gospel of Pure Grace*, p. 14.

the Buddhist precepts, practicing seated meditation, studying and chanting sutras, and worshiping buddhas as *kami* were no longer effective.

During his lifetime, Honen was preoccupied with demonstrating the superiority of the simple practice of reciting the name of Amida Buddha. Honen read about Amida Buddha and his Forty-eight Vows and was struck by the insight that religious peace depends not upon one's own feeble strength but rather upon relying on the infinite compassion and supernatural strength of Amida Buddha. Honen believed that the vows of Amida Buddha gave us all a loving pattern or standard for religious faith and activity of the devotee. We all need to take Amida Buddha as a role model, and be more like Amida Buddha.[64]

Honen Stresses the Practice of Reciting

According to the eighteenth vow, anyone calling upon the name of Amida "even to ten thoughts" will be reborn in the Western Paradise. It is **not faith** in Amida that is effective; according to the vow, it is simply the **practice** of reciting the name, although faith will arise naturally later. Honen urged his followers to continue chanting the name of Amida for their entire lives.

This *mantra* must be recited continuously: *Namu Amida butsu* (Homage to Amida Buddha), also known as the *nembutsu* (*nem* is "to think of" or "keep in mind" and *butsu* is "buddha"). One does not have to be well-educated in order to chant the *nembutsu*, one did not need to have only good karma to chant the *nembutsu*. Even evil and depraved people could chant the *nembutsu*. Everyone could be saved.

Chanting the *nembutsu* with a sincere mind will guarantee rebirth in the Pure Land. Once the devotee has been reborn in the Western Paradise, it will be much easier to attain nirvana, and then one can re-enter the world of birth-and-death (*samsara*) and labor for the liberation of other sentient beings. It is possible for common people to be saved in the degenerate age of the buddha-dharma ("buddha-teachings"). If a human will simply recite the name of Amida Buddha, that chant is guaranteed to produce liberation.

According to Honen, no training in Buddhist philosophy was necessary for enlightenment, and there was no need for the strenuous meditation techniques as taught by Saicho and his Tendai sect. For Honen, Buddhist monks were no better than ordinary people, and were no closer to liberation than ordinary people.

The Tendai monks of Mt. Hiei were strongly opposed to Honen's radical and subversive ideas and burned his writings. The Shingon monks of Mr. Koya were also opposed. If Honen's ideas of the unimportance of ritual and philosophy were to spread, then esoteric Shingon ritual practices would be superfluous, as are all intellectual approaches. Because of the opposition of Tendai monks, Honen and his disciple Shinran were banished in 1207, but even in exile Honen continued teaching.

Honen did reject traditional meditation, ritual, and scholarship as worthless. Honen's method had only three requirements: recite the *nembutsu* mantra with (a) a sincere heart with genuine devotion, (b) with a deeply believing heart, and (c) with a desire to attain rebirth in Amida's Pure Land. One does not need to start with devotion. These three conditions will arise naturally if one believed in Amida's vow, and recited the name of Amida.

Recite *Namu Amida butsu* (the *nembutsu* mantra) continuously, even though one recitation might be enough. The sincere mind was essential but it was not permanent; the sincere mind could be lost. For example, if one doubted their eventual rebirth in the Pure Land, or doubted the vow of Amida, then one has lost the sincere mind. Thus, the efficacy of the recitation is neither permanent, nor necessarily cumulative and lasting.[65]

According to Honen, at moment of death, the follower will see Amida Buddha, and the last moment is of critical importance. Amida, or his helper Kannon (in Chinese, Kwan-yin/Guanyin), will arrive and escort the believer into a rebirth in the Pure Land.

---

[64] A good book on Honen is Soho Machida, *Renegade Monk: Honen and Japanese Pure Land Buddhism* (Berkeley: University of California Press, 1999).

[65] Bloom, *Shinran's Gospel of Pure Grace*, p. 21.

JODO SHINSHU: SHINRAN'S NEW SECT OF PURE LAND

The most important disciple of Honen was the passionate monk Shinran (1173–1262), who went on to found the New Sect (*Shinshu*) of the Pure Land (*Jodo*). Shinran was orphaned and when he was nine years old he went to study Tendai at Mt. Hiei. While he was a Tendai monk he devoted himself to rigorous meditation, but the only result was frustration and inner conflict. He achieved no spiritual benefits from his meditative efforts. Avoiding women and avoiding meat had produced no spiritual benefits either.

All of his life Shinran was deeply aware of the strong pull of sensuality and all the pleasures normally forbidden to a Buddhist monk. There was some indication that he believed that his passionate nature prevented him from attaining liberation. He felt that he was doomed to hells because of his passions, which made him a debased, depraved and unworthy person, and in the degenerate age of *mappo*, he knew that he could not liberate himself, by himself.

Shinran had a dream which told him to study with the monk Honen. As a result of the vision, he entered into Honen's group in Kyoto. Honen's teaching seemed to offer some chance of salvation for a person with a passionate nature otherwise doomed to hells. Warned by Tendai Buddhists that he would go to the Buddhist hells if he listened to Honen, Shinran replied that he was already doomed to go to hell no matter what.

Like Honen, Shinran rejected the vigorous meditative and deeply esoteric philosophical approaches to Buddhist enlightenment he had practiced on Mt. Hiei. Shinran rejected the aristocratic Self-Power approach of the older forms of Buddhism, and put his faith in the recitation of the *nembutsu* mantra, chanting *Namu Amida butsu*.

During the period when Shinran's teacher, Honen, was exiled in 1207, Shinran was also exiled to a different location and his life changed profoundly. Although it was not uncommon for Buddhist monks to have a concubine and even marry, these things were never to be made public. Quite publically Shinran married a nun and argued that the *nembutsu* worked for those who were married as well as anyone else.

He was no longer a priest, and for the first time the married Shinran came face to face with hard realities of common people's lives. He had been in a monastery since he was nine years old. He had never worried about food or clothing since he was nine years old. Now, because of his exile he was without the priestly advantages and privileges supplied by the state. Ultimately he devoted himself to preaching the Pure Land teachings of Honen to farmers, to fisherman, and to anyone who would listen. The last thirty years of his life were spent in Kyoto where he spent his final days writing. He died in 1262 and his ashes placed in the Honganji sect temple in Kyoto.

Doctrines of Shinran's form of Pure Land Buddhism.

The key insight of Shinran's New Sect of Jodo Buddhism was that in this degenerate age of the decay of the true teachings, the age of *mappo*, all human beings are ignorant and passion-ridden and their passions can never be eradicated. We are all self-centered; everything we do is selfish. We are motivated by pleasures, not spirituality. If this is the case, then no matter how hard we tried, no one could ever earn or achieve liberation by his or her own efforts. Shinran wrote, "[Beings] are defiled, evil and polluted, without a pure mind. They are false and vain and possess no mind of truth."[66]

Since no one can achieve liberation by herself or himself, it follows that one needs the help of a buddha to escape from *samsara* (the continuous cycle of birth and rebirth). Nothing a person can do will ever purify his/her spirit sufficiently to gain the insight of and assurance of awakening. Even when one tries to do good, one hopes for good karmic results so one's act is self-centered (and hence evil in Honen's eyes) because ultimately it was intended to be to one's own benefit. The monk wants to generate good karma or generate an insight into reality which will permit

---

[66] Al Bloom, *Shinran's Gospel of Pure Grace*, p. 33.

one to attain enlightenment and do away with suffering, or *duhkha*. Perfect goodness was not possible, and the search for it seemed self-centered to Honen.[67]

Those who believed that they lived in the age of *mappo* were certain that no one could liberate himself. No one can successfully achieve what the Buddha achieved. The Buddha was a proper role model during the first age of the true teaching. In that era, it was possible to take up the discipline, meditate, work strenuously, and, by your own efforts, realize our own Buddha-nature and attain complete awakening. None of that will work in the degenerate current age.

There is an infinite gulf between Amida Buddha's goodness and the depravity of a human being. Shinran's inspiration, the Chinese patriarch Shan-tao and his own teacher, Honen, had regarded Amida Buddha as the standard for religious faith. However, for Shinran, Amida was not a pattern or model for human beings to emulate, not a model for compassion and generosity. Rather, Amida was absolutely different from human beings; no human being could ever be compared to the perfect goodness of Amida's saving grace and no human could ever hope to emulate it successfully.[68]

Shinran's conclusion was that people cannot liberate themselves. It requires an absolute power completely different from all human beings. How can we tap into that power? Shinran's answer is that the attitude of the devotee is the essential feature. Beings, no matter how depraved, could perform the *mantra*, reciting of the name of Amida Buddha, *Namu Amida butsu*, and the name would cleanse the person from previous evil karma and obsessive concern with the passions. The infinite love and compassion of Amida/Amitabha will embrace all equally, the good and the evil.

Shinran Stressed Faith in Amida Buddha

Shinran's teacher, Honen stressed the **practice** of reciting the name which brings salvation, but Shinran stressed the **faith** as the essential ingredient. And, even the faith was a gift from Amida Buddha, acting upon us. "The act of faith itself [was made] the essential basis of salvation, and the act of faith was not made by the individual, but by the Buddha in that person" — because the traits of mind that are necessary for salvation were also given by the Buddha (along with the practice of recitation). Every aspect of religion derived ultimately from the Buddha himself. Bloom writes that "in order for the recitation practice to be effective, the devotee must reproduce in himself the sincerity, faith and aspiration which Amida Buddha (as Hozo) had cultivated when he practiced the austerities which established the Pure Land and the way of salvation for all beings."[69]

But, even if we can find that sincerity and faith, Shinran tells his followers, "Do not manifest the appearance of wisdom, goodness and purity externally [i.e., following the pattern or standard of Amida Buddha], because (we) are vain and false within."[70]

Shinran thought that the process of Pure Land liberation proceeded as follows: first, you had to convince the individual of his or her depravity and failure. The awareness of human obsession with sensual pleasures is the first step to salvation. Next the teacher must lead the followers through the important vows in the Pure Land sutra, ultimately arriving at the 18th Vow, where Amida vows that he will come to the aid of all who think of him ten times.

---

[67] It is possible that the influence of Japanese folk-religion and its attitude towards pollution and violating taboos of the *kami* spirits played a role in this. No one is ever perfectly pure. We are polluted continuously, and we just continue purifying ourselves as the occasion demanded.

[68] Bloom, *Shinran's Gospel of Pure Grace*, p. 30.

[69] *Iibid.*, p. 32.

[70] *Ibid.*, p. 33.

Traditional Buddhist Practices are Worthless

Shinran realized that this eighteenth vow of Amida makes traditional Buddhist practices irrelevant. Scholarship is of no value. Monasticism and meditation are of no value. Shinran himself lived as a common person. Celibacy is of no value. Shinran married a nun. Abstention from eating meat is of no value. Shinran ate meat. Abstaining from intoxicating beverages is of no value. No asceticism, no religious privation is required. There is no need to appease buddhas or gods in order to win their acceptance or assistance in gaining some goal. Yet Shinran continues to preach that one must decide to accept the way of salvation. Merely trust in Amida Buddha, who accepts the least worthy as well as the most righteous.

True Pure Land Teaching is where the individual relies entirely upon the vow of Amida, without a moment's doubt; salvation is entirely a gift which can never be deserved, and there was no act by which salvation could be guaranteed, assured, or attained.[71] Let go of self-centeredness. One must have no egotism, no pride, no striving for one's own salvation. Rely entirely on Amida Buddha. The entire process of salvation comes from the Buddha's side.

Faith is identified with *Namu Amida butsu*, the recitation of the name of Amida Buddha. Faith is confidence in Amida Buddha's vows. Faith is grounded in the religious awareness of the individual of his or her passion-filled nature and the need for Amida Buddha's compassion. Faith is completely and totally a gift of Amida Buddha. Faith is not generated by the human will; one does not will herself to have faith in Amida. In this age of *mappo*, human beings are fundamentally different from the Buddha. The wide gulf between mundane life and Buddha cannot be spanned by anything that a human being can do. Even to believe that you have a good nature (or the buddha-nature) was a fundamental obstacle or barrier to the attainment of enlightenment. Shinran thought that the unity of Buddha and humans came completely from the side of the Buddha, through the gift of faith as the transfer of his qualities of mind "It was by the Buddha's act of compassion that one attains Buddha nature."[72]

The power of the Name and Its Recitation

For Shinran, the name Amida Buddha embodies the total reality of the nature of Amida Buddha himself. Therefore, repeating the *nembutsu* mantra, *Namu Amida butsu*, has the power to cleanse and purify the evil, and bring good merit to the individual. According to Shinran, the name "mysteriously arouses faith in sentient beings when they hear it and become aware that it embodies Amida Buddha's compassionate intention to save all beings . . . . Amida is no longer the merely vocal element in the practice of recitation, but it is the mysterious activity of Amida Buddha within the minds of men."[73]

"One-calling" upon Amida.

One of the most important features which sets Shinran's New Sect of Pure Land apart from Honen's Pure Land is Shinran's belief that reciting one *nembutsu* with deep and abiding faith is all that is really necessary, not ten. The *nembutsu* recitation is not practiced by individuals for their own salvation — rather the Buddha's name reverberates through the universe, is heard by the individual, and the inner cause of faith is aroused. Once we have that faith, how do we manifest it? Faith is manifested in the recitation of the *nembutsu*, recitation of *Namu Amida butsu*, and faith is a gift.

If we have the gift of faith, why continue to chant the *nembutsu*? Shinran says that we continue to chant the name of Amida Buddha out of gratitude for the gift of faith and salvation and the Pure Land granted by Amida

---

[71] Some may notice similarities with the fifth century theology of St. Augustine concerning the gift of grace.

[72] *Ibid.*, p. 39.

[73] *Ibid.*, p. 55.

Buddha. Shinran stresses the deep sense of personal joy and gratitude which welled up within him as he reflected on the compassion and mercy he had received from Amida Buddha. Joy and gratitude were the outstanding traits of the life of faith. One responds by revealing to others Amida's compassion. One repays the debt by revealing this to others.

The Unique Elements in Shinran's Jodo Shinshu

Apart from chanting the *nembutsu* mantra just once, several other features set Shinran's sect of Pure Land/Jodo Buddhism apart. Shinran was married, so Jodo Shinshu allows married priests. Shinran ate meat, unlike the other Buddhist priests. Calling the name of Amida Buddha once was sufficient to guarantee that one can be reborn in the Pure Land because Shinran simplifies all Buddhas into one – Amida Butsu (Amitabha Buddha). Traditional Pure Land Buddhism felt that one was carried to the Pure Land after death, and there Amida Buddha would teach one how to achieve nirvana. Shinran disagreed with this. **Shinran thought that the Pure Land was nirvana**, and that the devotee acquired awakening at the entrance to the Pure Land.[74]

In 1252 a great 49 foot tall bronze statue of Amida Buddha was constructed in Kamakura, and paid for by donations from common people, not the government. Originally the statue was inside a large wooden temple, but in modern times it stands open. The statue is hollow and pilgrims and visitors can go inside and and are allowed to climb up a narrow stairway. The other great Pure Land deity, Kannon (Kwan-yin/Guanyin) was also very popular, and there are many great artistic sculptures of Kannon in Kamakura, Kyoto, and other cities throughout Japan.

Amida Buddha – Kamakura 1972

Over the centuries the New Pure Land sect of Shinran developed into the largest sect of Buddhism in Japan. Since the priests were allowed to marry, the leadership became hereditary and the two different branches of New Pure Land are each headed by descendants of Shinran.

Militant Pure Land Buddhism

In the sixteenth century, Pure Land followers (including masterless samurai) rose up against the existing powers whom they considered oppressors, and nearly overwhelmed government forces. Ultimately the followers were defeated and brought under control.

The Jodo Shinshu tradition later split into two separate lineage groups early in the seventeenth century, each grounded in a major temple. One is Higashi Honganji (Temple of the Original Vow: East), and the other is the Nishi Honganji (Temple of the Original Vow: West). In addition to these two major temples, there are some other less prominent branches.

24.15 THE NICHIREN SCHOOL OF BUDDHISM: THE LOTUS SUTRA

In addition to the Zen and Pure Land teachings, which originated in China, a new and very different form of Japanese Buddhism developed during the Kamakura (1185-1338) era. This was the Nichiren school of Buddhism, inspired by Saicho's (766-822) Tendai school, but it went in a very different direction from the earlier Tendai school.

---

[74] *Ibid.*, p. 79.

The founder of this school of Buddhism was Nichiren (Rissho daishi, 1222-1282), who was born into a family of poor fishermen. Like so many others, he was profoundly affected by the idea of the third period of the decay of the Buddhist teaching, called the age of *mappo* as taught in the *Lotus* sutra. This idea of the three periods of the teaching was important in Tendai Buddhism and the Pure Land sects. If we are living in a dark ages where individual intellect and individual effort are inadequate to make progress on the Buddhist pathway, how are we to achieve liberation in the age of *mappo*?

Many in Japan believed that this third period (*mappo*) had begun about 1050 C.E. Nichiren, born in 1222, was certainly living in the age of decay. The way Nichiren understood the age of *mappo*, during this period not only are people of limited ability, but actually they are depraved and evil. Evil humans have no chance of achieving salvation through their own efforts. As degenerate as we all are, during this age of the decay of the teaching, Nichiren believed that the only means of liberation is not the Self-Power of the Zen schools, and it is not chanting the name of Amida Buddha, but rather it requires complete and total belief in one book, the *Lotus sutra* itself. The follower does need to read or master the contents of the *Lotus sutra*; only have faith in the book and chant its title.

Chanting the Title of the *Lotus Sutra* is the Key to Salvation

Nichiren accepted the Tendai claim that the highest truth is found in only one book, the *Wonderful Dharma of the Lotus sutra* (in Sanskrit, the *Saddharma pundarika sutra*) or in Japanese pronunciation, the *Myoho renge kyo*. Saicho (766-822), founder of Japanese Tendai Buddhism, said that the *Lotus* sutra stresses the essential oneness of Buddhism, but Nichiren felt that all the other non-*Lotus* schools mistakenly emphasize only one incomplete aspect of the totality of Buddhism. Shingon Buddhism stressed the Sun Buddha, Mahavairocana, as the ultimate truth body of the Buddha (*dharmakaya*). The Pure Land followers stress the bliss-filled Western Paradise of Amida Buddha who is a different body of the Buddha, namely the "bliss body" (*sambhoga-kaya*) of Amida. The Zen school relied on individual efforts (Self-Power) to reproduce the actual awakening experience of the historical Buddha, Siddhartha Gautama, whose body is called the *nirmanakaya* (the human person Mahayana Buddhists know as Shakyamuni, the sage of the Shakya clan).

Nichiren's Buddhism is Intolerant of All Other Schools

Nichiren was profoundly intolerant of each of these earlier forms of Japanese Buddhism. He felt that each of these Buddhist traditions was incomplete, and each sect should be replaced by the only form of Buddhism that was of any value in the age of the decay of the teaching. Rather than calling upon the name of a single Buddha, like Mahavairochana, Amida, or Shakyamuni, one should call upon the name of the *Lotus sutra* which in Japanese is *Myoho renge kyo*. Nichiren invented a new *mantra*, a new chanted phrase of power (another *nembutsu*): *Namu Myo ho renge kyo*, "Reverence to the *Wonderful Dharma of the Lotus Sutra*." Have faith in the book, and chant the title of the book. It is the only practice of any value in the degenerate age of *mappo*.

Nichiren Buddhism Should Rule Japan

Nichiren's extended his vision of Buddhism into the political realm as well. Nichiren's self-confidence was legendary. He was certain that the only true form of Buddhism was Nichren's form of Buddhism. Not only that, but True (i.e., Nichiren) Buddhism was essential for the continuation of the existence of the nation of Japan itself. Reciting the title of the *Lotus sutra* was essential for the very survival of the Japanese nation. The nation of Japan must not tolerate other Buddhist faiths because this would lead to destruction. Of all the countries in the world, Japan was the only country where True Buddhism could be revived. The Essential Principle of Nichiren is the close relationship between properly practiced Nichiren Buddhism and the welfare of the Japanese people and the Japanese nation.

Nichiren asserted that if Nichiren Buddhism were not adopted as the one and only Buddhist religion of the nation, the Mongols would invade and destroy Japan. He continuously predicted a Mongol invasion. In 1266 the Mongol ruler Khubilai Khan dispatched messengers to the Japanese court, demanding their submission to his rule.

CHAPTER 24: JAPANESE BUDDHISM

Armies had attempted to invade Japan before, but the typhoons had always stopped and destroyed their fleet. The Japanese military rulers were determined to resist. Khubilai Khan then began to assemble a fleet of ships to be used to invade Japan.

Nichiren predicted that the next Mongol invasion would succeed in conquering Japan because of the false Buddhist beliefs of non-Nichiren sects. Political and spiritual salvation required the Japanese to give up evil non-Nichiren religions. Although this was the age of degenerate human beings, Japan was the only country in the world where the people are still pure enough to successfully revive the true faith of Nichiren Buddhism. Nichiren was absolutely certain that the salvation of the world depends upon Japan, and the salvation of Japan lay with Nichiren!

It is the Duty of the Government to Execute all non-Nichiren Buddhists

Nichiren did not accept Buddhist virtues of egoless loving compassion and non-violence, not in these evil times. In Kyoto he gave sermons in which he violently and virulently attacked all other forms of Buddhism. He even went so far as to assert that it is the duty of the government to see that non-Nichiren Buddhists be executed. He attacked the founder of Pure Land Buddhism, Honen, and calls him "the enemy of all the Buddhas." Nichiren's extreme position infuriated the common people who relied on the compassionate grace of Amida as taught by Honen and Shinran. Nichiren was mobbed. His life was in danger and he was obliged to flee to the city of Kamakura.

Nichiren was certain that he was correct in everything, and had no doubts. His followers understand him to be a person of great conviction and strength of character. He believed his teachings with his whole heart, and despite the fact that his life was in danger, he returned again to Kyoto, and continued his attacks. Now he attacked the Japanese government for not adopting Nichiren Buddhism, and finally he was banished by the government to the isle of Izu. While in Izu he studied the *Lotus* more intensively than ever, and in the text he found a description of a Buddha who would be persecuted during this terrible age of the decay of the *dharma*. He was certain that the *Lotus* was describing himself and predicting people's antagonism and their persecution of him during this pernicious age. More than ever before, he was certain that he was the salvation of Japan, and the trials of his life had been foretold in the *Lotus*.

When the period of exile ended, he was released from Izu by the government, and more certain than ever, he immediately resumed his virulent attack upon other sects, especially the Pure Land sects. As a result of this last attack, he was condemned to death in the year 1271. Then a miracle occurred. The legends say that lightning struck the executioner's sword, so he had a miraculous stay of execution. There are many tales about the miraculous escape of Nichiren which Nichiren Buddhists take as proof that his teachings must be true.

Nichiren then spent three years in exile (1271-1274) and became convinced that he was a manifestation of one bodhisattva, the Bodhisattva of Superb Action. In 1272 Nichiren wrote a text asserting that he was the pillar of Japan, the eye of Japan. He was the great container of religious truth that was the revivify the country and return it to the true faith.

Nichiren Himself Should Rule Japan

It seemed only logical to Nichiren that he should become the leader of the nation of Japan as well. He saw himself as the single divinely designated teacher for all the world in the age of *mappo*. He himself was the Bodhisattva of Superb Action who had been reborn in the time when the Japanese nation needed him. His intolerant teachings continued to anger the common people, so he identified himself with the Bodhisattva named Sadaparibhuta (Ever Abused), who was insulted and reviled.

Nichiren settled in Kamakura on west side of Mt. Fuji in 1274 – just before the great Mongol invasion which he had predicted so often. Thirty thousand Mongol warriors sailed for Japan on a fleet of ships, but only a few ships made it to the Japanese islands; the rest sank in storms. The invasion failed because of the heavenly divine typhoon winds (*kamikaze*) which protected the island nation. The great Khan once again sent envoys to the Japanese court demanding submission and surrender, and the Japanese executed his envoys. In 1281 Khan sent an estimated 140,000 warriors to crush the Japanese. For seven weeks the ships landed and the Japanese fought off the Mongols, but once again another great destructive storm of divine winds intervened and about half of the Mongol army was drowned.[75]

Nichiren had predicted a successful Mongol invasion, but in fact the invasion failed; it was not successful. However, for his followers, that the invasion had even been attempted was taken as proof of his status and enhanced his credibility. For the remaining years of his life, Nichiren taught that the *Lotus sutra* is the perfect holy scripture for the degenerate third age of *dharma*. Although people were incapable of achieving any spiritual goal by themselves, the *Lotus* offered a simple technique of chanting appropriate for the period of blindness of followers. The age of *mappo* was the right time to proclaim this Lotus-doctrine, for this is the age when it is most appropriate. Japan was the country where it should be taught, and thence spread to all over the world. Nichiren asserted that all other Buddhist systems, now being out-of-date, should bow out and honor the *Lotus* and the Nichiren sect. Nichiren died at his hermitage in 1282.

Nichiren Buddhism After the Death of Nichiren

Loyal followers of Nichiren continued to preach his messages, and they established a network of Nichiren temples throughout central Japan. Many of the followers of Nichiren Buddhism were as intolerant of one another as they were of the other Buddhist sects, and the result was a rather destructive factionalism. The Nichiren sect continues into modern times, and has several new forms in our world. The new religion of Soka Gakkai, Rissho Koseikai, and Nichiren Shoshu are all successful offshoots of these various factions.

24.16 THE ASHIKAGA AND MUROMACHI PERIODS
ASHIKAGA (1338–1568) Civil war, dark ages.
MUROMACHI PERIOD (after 1392)

An attempt was made to reestablish the rule of the emperor and the royal family, which continued for almost fifty years, but it came to an end in 1392. Families and clans engaged in warfare, some supporting the ruling clan, others supporting the effort of the emperor to regain control over Japan.

The various Pure Land and Nichiren schools continued to gain converts. The Zen sect continued to receive support and great Zen art and world-class gardens were designed during this period. Chinese Ch'an-influenced poetry and painting had a profound effect on Japanese art forms, especially the black ink style of painting and black-ink landscapes. Japanese Zen monks traveled to China during this period and brought back and preserved some of the greatest Chinese artworks of the Southern Sung/Song dynasty.

24.17 THE MOMOYAMA (1568–1614) and TOKUGAWA (1615–1867) ERAS

THE MEDIEVAL PERIOD

During the Tokugawa era, Buddhism was used purposefully by politicians to create a national religion to solidify the newly-won power of the Tokugawa clan. The Tokugawa regime created a hierarchy of Buddhist temples

---

[75] The Japanese military did not know whether there would be a third invasion attempt and continued to prepare militarily for an invasion for thirty more years until 1312. Khubilai Khan had died in 1294 and all invasion plans were dropped at that time. Buddhist temples and Shinto shrines all claimed credit for the Mongol failure, since their gods had created the storms.

and each family had to be registered with a local temple. Perhaps partially as a result of this politicization of the religion, and the need for Buddhist priests who wished to be successful to accommodate the political aims, Buddhism became less dynamic and less vital than before.

The patronage of the Tokugawa government provided lives of wealth and leisure for the majority of Buddhist monks and nuns who went along with their rules. The duties of monks was to perform rituals for departed ancestors, and funerals. The only requirement was that the monks and nuns had to acknowledge that they were subservient to the government, and the monks had to acknowledge that everyone in Japan must be subservient to the rulers as well.

The Tokugawa era was one of isolation from the West and from China as well. Buddhism became more Japanese than before. For the most part, Japanese Buddhism was not about suffering and the elimination of suffering. Over the centuries Buddhist temples had become family property. The father passed the temple on to his son. The temples and priesthood were a family business, like any other business. Priests were paid to perform funerals and rituals to keep the rulers healthy.

The great majority of temples were not expected help followers to learn Buddhist teachings on lessening pain and suffering, and the temples did not claim to offer a pathway to awakening. The Tokugawa regime had worked very hard to make all of Buddhism subservient to politics, and the majority of the monks and institutions were corrupted by politics and money.

Toward the end of the Tokugawa era, Chinese Neo-Confucian ideas were important, but it was Neo-Confucianism interpreted through the eyes of Japanese culture, especially concerning social regulation of the social classes (with samurai on the top, and farmers on the bottom). Showing proper loyalty to one's social superior and accepting one's place in the social order were values that were promulgated.

24.18 MEIJI RESTORATION AND REOPENING OF JAPAN TO THE WEST 1868

The Europeans and the north Americans wanted to reopen trade with Japan, and had visions of wonderful profits to anyone who could get the Japanese to open their ports and begin trading. Thus, the tensions between Western powers and the Japanese government controlled by the Tokugawa clan was growing stronger and stronger. All during the Tokugawa era (1615-1867), European traders and priests were kept out of Japan. The reason was that the obvious strength of Western weaponry was a clear threat to Japanese sovereignty. The Japanese made many attempts to understand and deal with Western power. The Japanese needed to study what made the West so strong, so powerful. Was it science? Was it their language? Was it their religion? Was Christianity one of the sources of the strength of the West? Or was Christianity a tool that westerners used in order to conquor another nation?

A movement called Kokugaku ("country" + "study of") argued that everything Japanese was superior to every other culture on the planet. The Kokugaku scholars had heard the Christian biblical story of Noah and the ark, and pointed out that Japan had never experienced a flood caused by an angry god to punish evil humans. That was proof that the Japanese was more pure and divine than Christians and that Japanese *kami* were more powerful than Western gods. It was clear that Japanese medicine had not produced the sort of breakthroughs that were found in the West; this was taken as additional evidence that the Japanese people were more pure and less contaminated and less polluted than the rest of the world, since such Western medical discoveries were claimed to be unnecessary in Japan.

Admiral Perry and his Warships Come to Japan

On July 8, 1853, four American warships under Commodore Matthew Perry anchored off the Japanese coast and demanded that Japan open itself to foreign trade and commerce trading, or suffer military consequences.[76] This initiated a crisis in the Tokugawa clan and the other military clans controlling the Japanese government. Although

---

[76] George Feifer, *Breaking Open Japan: Commodore Perry, Lord Abe and the American Imperialism of 1853* (New York: Harper Collins, 2006).

Japan was still under the control of military clans, these clans were deeply mired in outmoded traditions of the past and unable to deal with the military threats from the American military power. There was no creative central authority able to deal with the crisis. Fifteen years later, in 1867, the Tokugawa regime collapsed.

The new regime which replaced the Tokugawa was called the Meiji, and Meiji rulers wanted to break free from all the traditions of the samurai past which were perceived as making Japan unable to deal with demands of Europeans and Americans. As a result of the American Admiral Perry and the threat of Western military attacks, the new rulers believed that a strengthening of the ancient imperial family's centrality and importance could unify the nation against the Western barbarians. The divinity of the emperor needed to become a focal point for the nation. The new government designed a system whereby the ancient royal family regained its power and state-supported Shinto was patronized because it exalted the divinity of the ruler. Shinto came to enjoy a serious revival as a tool to stimulate nationalistic fervor.

Buddhism is Weakened

The Buddhism which had been subsidized by the previous Tokugawa rulers was now perceived as an anchor pulling Japan down. Buddhist priests had been required to be vocal supporters of the Tokugawa clan. The new regime declared that Buddhist institutions were corrupt and an obstruction to Japan's need to make scientific and technological advancement. State Shinto was to be strengthened and separated from Buddhism (associated with the previous regime). The new progressive motto was "Discard the Buddha, cast out Shakyamuni." There was some government persecution of Buddhism inasmuch as some officials even organized mobs which destroyed Buddhist temples and decapitated the statues found in the temple gardens. To counter this attack, Buddhism began to portray itself as philosophy and not superstitious religion. The Buddha was thought of more as a humanist than the founder of a devotional religion. The Zen school in Japan responded with university-educated Buddhist intellectuals (like D. T. Suzuki 1870–1966) explaining the tradition in terms that were modern and in ways that attracted Western scholars, artists, poets, and other practitioners. Although it has been argued that the great majority of Zen temples and institutions in Japan were not as modern as Suzuki portrayed them, Japanese Zen Buddhism became considered a modern system of thought as a result of these activities.[77]

Institutional Shinto is Made the Official Government Religion

The period of Japanese isolation during the Tokugawa era had meant that outside its own country Japan had no political power, and no influence. Of course, this weakened Japan's position in the world, and Japan had fallen behind in all the newest discoveries. The new ruling clans believed that institutional Shinto must be re-established as national religion, and the *kami* Amaterasu be once again worshiped throughout the land as the divine ancestor of the imperial family. Shinto replaced Buddhism in the political firmament. Institutional Shinto priests became government officials, and lavish government support was directed towards Shinto shrines instead of Buddhist temples. State-supported Shinto became the official national religion, and Buddhism was criticized and persecuted (for financial and moral corruption and for political and nationalistic reasons). Shinto priests tried to abolish Buddhism as decadent and foreign religion. The few Christians in Japan attacked Buddhism for not accepting Jesus as savior.

The Divinity of the Emperor

The divinity of the emperor became a centerpiece in strengthening Japan against Western power. Since earliest childhood the people were told that their duty was to support their divine emperor in any enterprise that he should undertake. In fact, their duty was to die for the nation to protect the imperial family. The religious nationalism of Shinto was taught in school, was placed in all school textbooks and flooded mass media. Now it was Shinto that was closely allied with politics and with government. During this period of transformation, Shinto priests became

---

[77] See David McMahan, *The Making of Buddhist Modernism* (Oxford: Oxford University Press, 2008).

bureaucrats and lived very well, no longer connected to the mass of people or their concerns. It was state Shinto that drifted away from the lives of common people and became corrupted with power.

The new government began to work to protect itself from Western colonization. It abolished the old feudal system. It embarked on a nation-wide program of industrialization, militarization, and tried hard to study the aspect of Western thought which accounted for the achievements of Western science. Japanese students began the study of Western politics, science, and philosophy. However, the Japanese rulers were encouraging State Shinto and right-wing propaganda that was pushing Japan toward militarism and, ultimately, war.

Buddhism is Transformed

Traditional Buddhism was not destroyed in Japan, but it was transformed. During the Meiji era, there were some spiritual Buddhist teachers whose lives commanded the respect of all who knew them. Meanwhile Shinto institutions became more and more political and less concerned with farmers. This contributed to a spiritual transformation which solidified Buddhism as the genuine religion of the mass of Japanese people, rather than Shinto.

From 1876 on, Buddhist priests began to travel to Europe and study a wide range of important subjects. These Japanese mastered French, German, and English as well. A tradition of extraordinary scholarship was inaugurated in Japan. Mastering Western methods of critical scholarship, Japanese professors were already skilled in classical Chinese, and now they became world-famous scholars in the fields of Asian thought and philosophy, Asian history, and philology.

24.19 THE TAISHO ERA

A New Era of Buddhist Scholarship

The Meiji period came to an end when the Meiji emperor died. His son was the new emperor, and the era name changed to the Taisho era (1912–1926). The study of European and American research and academic methods by Japanese scholars generated a genuine eruption of scholarly publications in Chinese and Japanese subjects. One major achievement between 1924 and 1934, during the Taisho era, was the publication of the encyclopedic collection of Chinese Buddhist texts in 65 volumes, commonly referred to as the *Taisho* collection. That was then supplemented with a continuation of the *Taisho*, a great collection of Japanese Buddhist texts in 45 more volumes.[78] Then separate indexes were published. Such scholarship required and generated fabulous encyclopedias and dictionaries in Japanese which are still essential to anyone doing research in Chinese or Japanese Buddhism, and the Japanese edition of the Chinese canon contains some ancient texts in the Chinese scriptures which had been lost in India.[79]

High quality Western-style Buddhist universities were founded, and Buddhist scholars were doing comparative philosophy, and making breakthroughs in Indian and Tibetan Buddhist philosophy and psychology. These scholars were working in original sources in Sanskrit, Tibetan, and Pali. However, this high level of scholarship had some negative repercussions. Ordinary farming people and businessmen had little concern with such academic topics.

Since the thirteenth century, Buddhist priests had been especially concerned with performing funerals, and popular Buddhism was grounded in faith and repetition of the *nembutsu* mantra, *Namu Amida butsu*. During this Taisho period (1912–1926), the work of Japanese Buddhist scholars was not particularly sympathetic to popular beliefs involving devotion to buddhas. The scholarship of these Taisho Buddhist priests was focused on historical accuracy,

---

[78] For more on the great collections of Buddhist works in Chinese and Japanese, see Jiang Wu and Lucille Chia, eds., *Spreading the Buddha's Word in East Asia* (Columbia University Press, 2015).

[79] We cannot help but note that all this work was done with pen and paper. In recent years these texts have been digitized.

critical analysis, and intellectual justification for claims. These Japanese scholars separated out mythology from history, and the result was tension between traditional piety of popular Buddhism and the newer more intellectual approaches. Scholars revealed that many popular beliefs had no historical justification, and no justification in the sacred texts. In fact, it was made clear that none of the Mahayana Buddhist texts were actually spoken by the historical Buddha, but were written many centuries later, and reflected different Buddhist groups arguing back and forth, each trying to supersede the others. Much of popular Buddhism was declared mere superstition. Uneducated and anti-intellectual priests were offended by this historical research, and called for a return to the fundamentals of the past, a return to traditional beliefs as taught by local Japanese Buddhist priests.[80]

24.20 CHRISTIANITY IN MODERN JAPAN

During the Momoyama (1568-1614) and early Tokugawa (1615-1867) eras, Catholic missionaries had traveled to Japan with traders and merchant ships, and made attempts to convert the Japanese. Catholicism spread very slowly from 1549-1650. Many of the converts understood the Catholic god to be another foreign powerful *kami* who could grant wishes and perform miracles to benefit followers.

In addition, many who converted to Christianity did so for very practical reasons, not religious reasons. The missionaries came to Japan on merchant ships which sold firearms, and firearms not only changed the balance of power but even changed the nature of war. Being a Christian gave one special access to firearms. But, firearms in the wrong hands was a very serious threat to political power. Political and clan leaders began to perceive Christianity as a threat to the stability of the state, as well as a threat to the national religion of Shinto, which deified the emperor.

The Japanese had observed other countries (for example, India, Sri Lanka, China, South America) where Christian priests had become successful in converting many people in a country, and then after the priests, Western businessmen and military forces spread throughout a country. Eventually the country became a colony of the West. Fearing that missionaries were precursors to colonization, Christianity, along with foreigners, were ordered out of the country in 1587, and again 1597, and again 1614 and 1651. Christianity was politically proscribed and prosecuted. The prohibition against Christian proselytizing was not withdrawn until 1873.

Protestant Christianity entered Japan as soon as Admiral Perry forced Japan to open up its ports for Western trade. But state Shinto as official religion had been re-established five years before in 1868, and the Shinto priests criticized Christian religions as foreign, disrespectful of the imperial family and being disrespectful of the Japanese history every student learned in school. Some of this was true. Western Christians disparaged the stories of the major *kami* spirits, Amaterasu and Izanami and Izanagi, calling them just mythology. The Japanese were insulted. Several Protestant sects of Christianity (i.e., Congregationalism) sent missionaries to Japan and sought converts, but also argued that by being a good Christian one was also being a good and loyal Japanese citizen. Apparently the majority of these Christians supported the goal of a Japanese empire extending into Korea, Japan, and even Russia.[81]

Faced with Western military might, the Japanese responded by studying the West to learn the secrets of Western military power. Studying the West included studying Christianity. Originally the Japanese associated Christianity with attaining the benefits of westernization; later they discovered that one can be analytic, scientific and industrialized without being Christian. Then the Japanese realized that some Christians were actually opposed to science and opposed to critical thinking. This also lessened the Japanese interest in Christianity.

---

[80] This would be similar to the sorts of tensions which appeared in Western religions when serious Christian biblical scholars pointed out that Jesus was not born on December 25th, and that the texts of the Bible could not have been written by the disciples whose names are attached to them, that early Christians had over a dozen gospels originally, and other similar problems.

[81] An interesting book exploring these support the Japanese Protestant Congregational converts gave to the Japanese empire of the late nineteenth and the first half of the twentieth century is Emily Anderson, *Christianity and Imperialism in Modern Japan: Empire for God* (London: Bloomsbury, 2014). Professor Anderson finds that this Congregational sect had an important role in shaping modern Japan.

CHAPTER 24: JAPANESE BUDDHISM

When the Japanese began to understand the implications of Christian doctrines, Christian dogma presented several difficulties. The Christians asserted that all people are born sinners, but as far as the Japanese were concerned, even if one believed that to be true, the original sin could be eliminated by Shinto purification rituals. One did not need Christian baptism or a Christian priest. One did not need a savior to die for one's original sin. The contamination of original sin was washed away easily.

The Christians insisted that there was only one god, so it followed that the emperor could not be a divinity. But one had to reject more than just the divine emperor. The *kami* who inhabited every area of Japanese life also would have to be rejected.

The Christians insisted that the stories found in their bible, their sacred book, were a genuine and true history of all human beings, but there was no record of such events in the Japanese historical texts, and there weren't any events even roughly equivalent in Japanese history. There was no story of a flood, no story of a Tower of Babel, no stories of Adam, Eve, serpents, or Lucifer. From the Japanese perspective, the bible was either a collection of Western myths, or, if these events had really happened to Christians but not to the Japanese, it was evidence of the superiority of Japan over the West and Christianity.

The newly arrived Protestant missionaries criticized the Catholic Jesuit missionaries and their doctrines, and the Christian groups fought among themselves, each attacking all the other Christian churches. Christians had theological disagreements and there was much in-fighting between sects. The better-educated Japanese generally considered Christianity to be philosophically and theologically inferior to Buddhism. They found what they felt to be many flaws and weak arguments which could not match up to sophisticated Buddhist analyses. When it came time to travel to the Western countries during the Meiji era, other Western thought forms were as attractive, or more attractive than Christianity, including agnostic philosophies and the atheism of Marxism.

We have seen that religions of Asia in general tend not to be exclusive. The Japanese were uncomfortable with Christianity partly because of its rather aggressive attitude of non-toleration of other religions including fellow Christians. Christian conversion policies required not merely changing from one's prior religion, but also condemnation of all those who remained Buddhists, or Shintoists, or Confucianists, or all three combined. Christianity was not willing to co-exist with other religions, and was unwilling to co-exist with other forms of Christianity.

Convinced of their own superiority, Christian missionaries of the early period were not willing to learn Japanese customs much less adapt to them. The Catholic Jesuit priests who came to Japan as missionaries had demanded that Buddhist temples be demolished, and Buddhist images destroyed.[82]

In the popular Japanese mind, Buddhist images were indistinguishable from Shinto imagery. Japanese mythology stresses a very ancient *kami*-blessed land and a royal family divinely descended from the Sun Goddess. The Japanese have been taught to be proud of their long heritage and converting to Christianity seemed to require the Japanese person to reject his or her own self-identity as a Japanese.[83]

However, once converted,[84] the Japanese tended to transfer their Japanese/Confucian tradition of loyalty (even in the face of death) to their new religion of Christianity, and they refused to disavow Christianity, just as samurai refused to disavow fealty to their feudal lords when the battle was lost, and the warriors committed ritual suicide as a result.

---

[82] Bowring, *The Religious Traditions of Japan, op. cit.*, pp. 430-435.

[83] Even modern day Japanese, although rejecting the divine origins of imperial family, still have feeling that Japanese people are a unique historical entity (H. B. Earhart, *Japanese Religion: Unity and Diversity* Third Edition, p. 197).

[84] A reading of Japanese history reveals that a significant number of early Christian conversions were forcible, imposed by warlords in order to gain trading advantages with the Portugese Catholic traders. The Jesuits arrived in 1543. After 15 years of proselytizing, the Catholic Jesuits reported having only ten converts.; forty years later (1582) they had 60 converts.

Institutional Shinto had taught every person that their duty was to support their divine emperor in whatever enterprise interested him. This state-supported Shinto campaign successfully generated a powerful resurgence of nationalism which culminated in military victories over China and then over Russia in 1904-1905. At this point the new focus shifted to strengthening Japan against Western powers and culture, and few Japanese were attracted to Christianity. As of the twenty-first century, less than 1% of the Japanese population are Christians.

24.21 NEW RELIGIONS: TENRIKYO

One of the most important of the modern Japanese religions is Tenrikyo. The folk and shamanistic roots of Tenrikyo are quite clear. The religion began a few decades before the Meiji restoration of the royal family, so it still belongs to the Tokugawa era. Tenrikyo is oriented around its founder, Ms. Nakayama Miki (1798-1887) who followers revere as a human *kami*. Originally Ms. Nakayama served as a trance medium for a rural countryside healer, inviting *kami*-spirits to enter her body and convey messages and healing influences. However, once in the trance state in 1838, she believed a *kami* named "Tenri O no Mikoto" (Heavenly-wisdom royal-divinity) had taken up permanent residence in her body, and she spoke in the voice of this *kami*. Followers began to accumulate, impressed by her healing powers evidenced in her songs and dance, and she created her own scriptures and sacred rites.[85] She believed she was conveying divine truths about how to live a happy life, an honorable life, a harmonious life filled with spirit blessings. Followers treated her and her life as the life of a goddess on earth. As a goddess, her writings were revelation. Her songs became sacred hymns, and her dances became liturgy and ritual gestures.[86]

After her death in 1887, the male members of Ms. Nakayama's family took over the leadership of the movement. In 1908, Tenrikyo was accepted as an official sect of Shinto, which gave it official standing and allowed it to avoid government persecution and proscription. After World War II, when the new Japanese constitution required separation of church and state, Tenrikyo became independent of Shinto again.

24.22 NEW RELIGIONS: SOKA GAKKAI

The Soka Gakkai religion began as a contemporary form of the Nichiren line of Japanese Buddhism. The name means "Value Creation Society." Like its Nichiren roots, unquestioning faith in the *Lotus sutra* is the foundation of the group. Soka Gakkai was founded by Makiguchi Tsunesaburo (1871-1944), who drew upon the writings of the Nichiren sect to develop a comprehensive theory of education and value.

Tsunesaburo noticed that some schools of philosophy put value upon an important triad: truth; beauty; goodness. He felt that philosophers had missed something very important. His triad was beauty, benefit (gain), and goodness. Money, success, status and achievement are important and can flow from sincere faith in the *Lotus sutra*.

After World War II, Soka Gakkai followers began serious efforts at proselytizing others into the group. The group started out targeting energetic young people who could be converted. In turn, the youthful enthusiastically converted great numbers of others. Since Nichiren followers were taught that the *Lotus sutra* is the source of absolute and eternal truth, it is imperative that people be converted to the new religion. Because Soka Gakkai possessed eternal truth, the second president of Soka Gakkai (Toda Josei 1900-1958) believed any means can be used to convert people. He encouraged followers to use aggressive and even violent tactics to force others to convert. Many American soldiers stationed in Japan were the target of conversion, and some did become followers of the *Lotus sutra*.

After Daisaku Ikeda became president in 1960, the emphasis shifted to peaceful persuasion. Each and every member of Soka Gakkai must: (1) remove all traces of any other religious tradition from their home; (2) recite the

---

[85] H. B. Earhart, *Japanese Religion: Unity and Diversity* (Third Edition), p. 172.

[86] *Ibid.*, p. 174.

Japanese pronunciation of the Chinese title of the Lotus sutra, *Nam-myo-ho ren-ge kyo*, before family altar twice a day, (3) actively convert others and bring them into the organization. Good luck in business, luck in gambling, sexual pleasures and other benefits accrue to those who follow these three guides.

The Soka Gakkai organization was very effective at conversion but also efficient in motivating its followers to become involved in politics as well. They sponsored the political party called Komeito or Clean Government Party. The extraordinary ability to organize and get things done was built around the older Japanese Nichiren and *Lotus sutra* ideal from the past.

The effectiveness of the Clean Government Party was such that politicians charged that the religion of Soka Gakkai was trying to take over the secular government. In the 1970s after Soka Gakkai used its political power to try and suppress a book critical of their religion, they were criticized heavily and their power weakened. The Soka Gakkai religious group officially disassociated itself from the Komeito party, and its political wing has declined in importance in recent years.[87]

In the USA, Soka Gakkai is called Nichiren Sho-shu (the New Sect of Nichiren Buddhism), and has many followers. There is a recent institution named Soka University in Orange Country in Southern California which welcomes students from all over the world. The school teaches human rights and the sanctity of life. The official goal is to teach young people to work for and achieve world peace.

24.23 RELIGION IN JAPAN AFTER WORLD WAR II

Shinto Religion Supported Japanese Militarism

Since the 1860s, every Japanese citizen had been taught that their ruler was a divinity, and it was their duty to obey their divinity. Patriotism became identified with religion and nationalism. They were taught that their country was blessed by the gods, that Japan was pure and special and because of this their emperor should rule the other Asian nations of Korea and China.[88] For all the years of formal education, every Japanese citizen was taught in school to worship and obey their divine Emperor, who was destined to rule all of Asia. Every day, every month, every year, teachers echoed the Shinto priests and the government, and it simply seemed unquestionably obvious that the divine ruler of Japan was destined to rule all.

War Between Japan and the United States

Japanese military forces attacked both Korea and China. In a frenzy of Japanese nationalism, the Japanese attacked the U.S. naval base at Pearl Harbor, Hawaii on Sunday, December 7th, 1941. Americans responded militarily, but also responded by requiring all those of Japanese ancestry to give up their homes and their businesses, and be interred for the duration of the war. Japan responded similarly, and those Americans in Japan were also treated as potential spies, and those Japanese who were opposed to the war were also interred.[89] After initial Japanese victories, American forces began to defeat Japanese forces in the Pacific.

---

[87] *Ibid.*, p. 180.

[88] There are many good books on this topic. For example, Yoshiaki Yoshimi, *Grassroots Fascism: The War Experience of the Japanese People*, translated by Ethan Mark (New York Columbia University Press, 2015), Sheldon Garon, *Molding Japanese Minds* (1997) and Louise Young, *Japan's Total Empire* (1998)

[89] W. Puck Brecher, *Honored and Dishonored Guests: Westerners in Wartime Japan* (Cambridge, MA: Harvard University, 2017).

CHAPTER 24: JAPANESE BUDDHISM

Throughout all of history, the Japanese islands had never once been conquered by an invading army. The divine *kami* spirits had always protected the islands and the divine ruling family. To the Japanese, this was proof of the divinity of their leader. As the war continued, the Japanese military was no longer successful in battle, and the tide of battle turned. The American military forces were able to bomb Tokyo.

As World War II was coming to an end, the Japanese believed that their heavenly sovereign was divine, and that *kami* related to the divine emperor would protect Japan against American military forces as they had done every time in the past. But the *kami* did not protect Japan. American military forces were able to fly over Japan and drop bombs on munitions plants and bridges. The situation was dire. Then two atomic bombs were dropped on Hiroshima and Nagasaki. Japan surrendered.

The surrender resulted in profound disorientation in Japan, both politically and religiously (because all organized religions in Japan supported nationalism). The *kami* had not protected the nation. Their priests and rulers had been wrong, or perhaps all of them had lied.

Separation of Church and State Following Japan's Surrender

One of the conditions of surrender imposed upon Japan by the USA was separation of church and state. Following the imposition of a secular state by American forces, Shinto was no longer the official state religion of Japan. Shinto was now a religious institution separate from the government. As such, Shinto was no longer the tool of militaristic nationalism. Shinto priests were no longer government officials, and government subsidies to shrines stopped. Painful and difficult decisions had to be made. Should emperor still be considered head of Shinto religion? Should the emperor be treated as a semi-divinity? The state continued to support the religious ceremonies of the royal family (quite expensive and elaborate), but should such support continue?

Shinto was not the only religion affected by World War II. Buddhist temples had lost their land holdings following World War II, and thus lost much of their financial support. Many temples were forced to sell temple treasures and art works to survive. Fewer Japanese entered the Buddhist temples as monks. Many Japanese families have hereditary ties to Buddhist temples, and it is difficult to sever these even when the modern Japanese does not feel close to Buddhism any longer. Following World War II, there was no great spiritual resurgence of Buddhism. In general, the younger Japanese have been indifferent to all religions.

The New Religions

The main religious thrust in Japan following World War II has been what scholars refer to as the "New Religions." Because they were neither Shinto nor Buddhist, and many were formed after World War II, these new religions escaped the negative stigma attached to Shinto and associated with Japan's defeat. Those new religions which had been persecuted by the government a hundred years ago for failure to support Shinto nationalism became more popular. New religious freedom following World War II gave the new religions the possibility to operate freely. New religions generally are not burdened with ancient problems, and thus could take shape to deal with contemporary problems without the baggage of outmoded past. New religions were truly Japanese, and thus appealed to the Japanese people more than foreign Western religions. New religions could be openly syncretic, taking the features that appealed to them from Christianity, Buddhism, Shinto or anywhere else.[90]

Buddhism in Modern Japan

There have been many forces which have affected Buddhism in the twenty-first century in Japan. The fact that the government no longer offered financial support for institutions and temples caused major problems following the

---

[90] An interesting book dealing with the continuity between the older religions and the New Religions is Helen Hardacre, *Kurozumikyo and the New Religions of Japan* (New York: Princeton University Press, 1981).

defeat of Japan in June, 1945, at the end of World War II. In the past one major source of income for temples was from a primary function of Buddhist priests, performing funerals, but in recent times the non-secular funeral home industry has greatly reduced the income for Buddhist temples. The domestic and global forces for modernity have intruded into all aspects of Japanese life, and organized Buddhism needed to respond to these forces. The need to revitalize the role of Buddhist priests in the secular society of Japan is clear. Some Buddhist groups have been attempting to deal with problems of a consumer-driven society by placing temples in shopping malls, or installing a café on temple grounds where people can gather informally in a relaxing serene atmosphere. Some Buddhist temples are taking up the problem of gender discrimination in Japan. Others have become socially active by helping families deal with the need for care for the elderly. Some Buddhist groups have offered counseling services, and others offer shelter for victims of domestic violence, and suicide prevention services.[91] Several have become involved in issues related to the atomic energy industry following the tsunami of March 2011.

24.24 JAPANESE BUDDHISM COMES TO THE WEST

Some forms of Japanese Buddhism were brought to the West by emigrants from Japan who serviced first-generation Japanese and second-generation Japanese in Hawaii and the west coast states of the continental U.S.A. Japanese Buddhist temples were established in the centers where there were large numbers of Japanese citizens. Pure Land Buddhism traveled to the West when Japanese workers came to California and Hawaii.

There have been several outreach attempts from Japanese followers to appeal to westerners. For example, the Japanese group Soka Gakkai (originally affiliated with the Nichiren school of Buddhism, but increasingly it is separating itself from Nichiren) has established an international organization called the International Value-Creation Society, and they have established a university in Southern California.

One of the most varied movements to come to the west were the various Zen schools, which came to the West in several different waves from several different sources. D. T. Suzuki (1870–1966) first came to the United States in 1893 bringing Rinzai Zen in the early decades of the twentieth century and wrote many important popular and scholarly books but did not open a monastery or train students. In 1906, the Japanese teacher Sasaki Shigetsu (1882–1945) came to the United States, and in 1930 he established the New York Rinzai group which came to be known as the First Zen Institute. The American Robert Aitkin (1917-2010) was interred in Japan during World War II, and discovered Zen at that time. After returning to his home in Hawaii, Aitkin and his wife continued to practice the Harada-Yasutani form called "Sanbo Zen," and ultimately his Japanese teacher acknowledged his insight and made him a *roshi*, a respected teacher. He and his wife Anne directed the Diamond Sangha Zen group (near the University of Hawaii) for many decades. The Diamond Sangha has continued on in Hawaii after the deaths of both of its founders.

In its Japanese form of Zen, this tradition has been very popular in Europe and North America, especially in the last decades of the twentieth century. Western poets, painters, and writers were intrigued by the Zen forms of Buddhism and one can find many Zen references in American literature, beginning in the 1950s and 1960s (such as Jack Kerouac's 1958 book *Dharma Bums*), in the writings of Peter Mathiessen (b. 1927) and in great American poets

---

[91] Several books deal with this topic. For example, see John K. Nelson, *Experimental Buddhism: Innovation and Activism in Contemporary Japan* (Honolulu: University of Hawai'i Press, 2013), Steve Covell, *Japanese Temple Buddhism: Worldliness in a Religion of Renunciation* (Honolulu: University of Hawaii Press, 2005); Richard Jaffe, *Neither Monk nor Layman: Clerical Marriage in Modern Japanese Buddhism* (Princeton, NJ: Princeton University Press, 2002).

such as Gary Snyder (b. 1931) and Allen Ginsberg (1926-1997). The avant-garde composer and artist John Cage (1912-1992) drew heavily upon Zen Buddhism classes he had taken with D. T. Suzuki for his inspirations.[92]

Interest in Zen was not merely in literature, poetry, and scholarship. Increasing Japanese nationalism impelled a Japanese Zen monk named Nyogen Senzaki (1876-1958) to come to the U.S. in 1905, and fifteen years later opened a meditation center in San Francisco.[93] Senzaki is the author of a popular volume entitled *Zen Flesh Zen Bones*. Later in 1930 a Japanese Rinzai teacher named Sasaki Shigetsu (1882-1945) established what became the First Zen Institute in New York. He was succeeded by the American-born Ruth Fuller Sasaki (1892-1967), who became a priest and translator in Japan, and facilitated study of Zen in Kyoto for several important future poets and scholars.[94]

Contemporary Zen teaching lineages in the USA tended to derive from the Japanese Soto tradition of Suzuki Shunryu, and several Rinzai Zen traditions (most stemming from the Japanese Rinzai teacher Soyen Shaku 1860-1919). The Zen of Maezumi Haku'yu (1931-1995), who established the Zen Center of Los Angeles in 1956, was a combination of Soto and Rinzai (the Sanbo Zen lineages). Maezumi-roshi had several American students who went on to become respected teachers, and *roshis*.[95] One major Rinzai group derived from Sasaki Joshu (1907-2014) who came to southern California in 1962 and opened his own Zen training center in 1968, and opened several practice communities in southern California.

The Soto tradition of Suzuki Shunryu (1904-1971) was established when he founded the Zen Center of San Francisco in the early 1960s. The community was quite successful and Suzuki's lectures were turned into a book and became one of the most important and popular books on Zen Buddhism, *Zen Mind, Beginner's Mind*. There are over a hundred American successors to these teachers, both male and female, such as the late Robert Aitkin (1917-2010), Charlotte Joko Beck (1917-2011), Jerry Shishin Wick, Jan Chozen Bays, Bernard Tetsugen Glassman, Joan Rieck, Henry Shukman, Melissa Blacker, and James Ford, and the influence of the Japanese style of Chinese Ch'an has been profound in north America. The Korean Ch'an (Seon) teacher Seung Sahn (1927-2004) established several successful groups and successors.

24.25 SUMMARY OF THE CHAPTER

This chapter discussed the history and teachings of several different schools of Japanese Buddhism, each of which was inspired by Chinese Buddhism during the T'ang (618-906 C.E.) and Sung (960-1279) eras. Although Buddhism originally entered Japan via Korea in the sixth century, it was China that shaped Japanese religion and Japanese culture.

We saw that the Japanese interpreted Chinese Buddhism as forms of their own native Shinto. Since Shinto was about rituals to propitiate *kami* spirits, so too Buddhist rituals must be to honor the *kami* deities of Buddhism. The early forms of Buddhism were understood as a set of powerful rituals which could protect the ruler and protect the nation from harm. In addition to state rituals, early Buddhism in Japan also focused on funeral rites and the

---

[92] For example, see Helen Westgeest, *Zen in the Fifties: Interaction in Art between East and West* (Reaktion Books, 1998), Ray Kass and Steven Addiss, *John Cage: Zen Ox-herding Pictures* (New York: George Brazilier, 2009), and Kay Larson, *Where the Heart Beats: John Cage, Zen Buddhism, and the Inner Life of Artists* (New York: Penguin, 2012).

[93] Nyogen Senzaki's teachers included Rinzai master Soyen Shaku and the influence of D. T. Suzuki.

[94] Isabel Stirling, *Zen Pioneer: The Life and Works of Ruth Fuller Sasaki* (Counterpoint Books, 2006).

[95] Several books have been written on American forms of Buddhism. One excellent book is Charles S. Prebish, *Luminous Passage: The Practice and Study of Buddhism in America* (Berkeley, Ca.: University of California Press, 1999), and Charles S. Prebish and Kenneth Tanaka, *The Faces of Buddhism in America* (Berkeley, Ca.: University of California Press, 1998). There is also Rick Fields, *How the Swans Came to the Lake* (Boulder, Co.: Shambala, 1981).

worship of relics. Japanese Buddhism was a strongly formalistic and liturgical religion under the control of the government. Japanese Buddhist priests performed spells, produced magical images, performed complex magical gestures, all to preserve and protect the ruling clans and the elite in society. Thus, Japanese Buddhism started out as an elite state religion intertwined with and subservient to government in a way never seen before in India or China.

During this early period, Buddhism was not a religion of the people, and Buddhist monastics were priests who performed rituals, not individuals seeking the end of suffering and the attainment of nirvana. The Japanese cultural stress on ritual purity came to have an enduring influence on Japanese forms of Buddhism (Chinese Buddhists did not share this concern with ritual purity).

The hierarchical clan structure of Japanese civilization ensured that the Buddhist and Shinto priesthoods became organized along hereditary lines, with temples and shrines the property of particular families of priests. Many Buddhist groups permitted priests to be married.

Several buddhas and bodhisattvas were understood to be *kami*-gods with the ability to control natural forces. The historical Buddha in India, Shakyamuni, was not stressed except in the Zen traditions. Instead, the stress was on the Buddha of the Western Paradise, **Amida** (Amitabha), and the great Sun Buddha, Dainichi nyorai (Mahavairocana Buddha). Several bodhisattvas were also of special importance. One was the goddess of loving compassion, the benign and motherly **Kannon** (Kwan-yin in Chinaj). Kannon responds to suffering, and responds with miracles in desperate situations. There was also the medicine god, **Jizo**, who has the power to rescue tormented souls from Buddhist hells, and protect travelers and children. He also takes care of the souls of those aborted. The bodhisattva **Miroku** (Maitreya) was the Buddha of the future, sitting in heaven waiting to come to earth and teach.

The major schools of Japanese Buddhism included the Tendai, the esoteric Shingon, the Jodo and Jodo Shinshu schools of Pure Land Buddhism, and the two Zen schools of Rinzai and the Soto. Then the monk Nichiren started his own unique form of Japanese Buddhism, a vigorous, intolerant, and even violent form of Buddhism which Nichiren based on Tendai and its source, the *Lotus Sutra*.

Tendai Buddhism came into Japan in the ninth century, and the major influence was the Chinese T'ien-t'ai school with its stress on Nagarjuna ("emptiness") and on seated meditation. The stress on the age of degeneracy, *mappo*, as taught in the *Lotus Sutra*, was to have an enduring effect on Tendai, Shingon, the Pure Land schools, and the Nichiren sect.

Shingon Buddhism, established by Kukai in the 800s, was the Japanese version of Chinese Tantric Buddhism, with particular stress on the chanting of magical *mantras* and public and secret performance of rituals. Tantric Shingon Buddhism claimed that Japan was the original home of all the gods (*kami*) and the original home of all the buddhas as well. This would make Japan the most important location for Buddhism, more important than India or China.

The military samurai clan leaders, *shoguns*, took over control of Japan in the 1100s, and minimized the power of the Tendai and Shingon schools of ritualistic Buddhism, which were so closely associated with the politics of the old court. Those events coincided with travels of several Japanese monks into China, in search of answers to their personal questions. As a result, in the 1200s two forms of Zen Buddhism were brought back to Japan from China. The Zen schools became popular with the samurai groups due to the Zen stress on self-control and meditation to bring about insight.

The more devotional aspects of Japanese Buddhism were found in the Pure Land schools of Honen and Shinran. Both accepted that the world was in the age of *mappo*, or the degenerate age where humans were so mean and fallen that no one had the ability to liberate themselves. Instead, we must rely on the grace of the Buddha of the Western Paradise, Amida. The Pure Land's primary practice was the recitation of a chanted mantra, *Namu Amida butsu*, or "Homage to Amitabha Buddha." Recited with faith, at the moment of death one would be greeted and carried to the Western Paradise of Amida Buddha.

In approximately the same period, a new and uniquely Japanese school of Buddhism began, headed by Nichiren (1222–1282), who also was profoundly affected by the idea of the age of *mappo* as taught in the *Lotus* sutra. Nichiren asserted that all humans are depraved and evil, and have no chance of achieving salvation through their own efforts. Nichiren believed that the only means of liberation is complete and total belief in the *Lotus* sutra itself. The follower does need to read or master the contents of the *Lotus* sutra; only have faith in the book and chant its title. Nichiren invented a new *mantra*, a new chanted phrase of power: *Namu Myo ho renge kyo*, "Reverence to the *Wonderful*

CHAPTER 24: JAPANESE BUDDHISM

Dharma of the Lotus Sutra." The early Nichiren school of Japanese Buddhism was extraordinarily intolerant of everyone who did not agree with Nichiren. He argued that all Buddhists who did not belong to his school should be put to death. He saw himself as the only true ruler of Japan. The newer religions of Soka Gakkai, Rissho Koseikai, and Nichiren Shoshu are all successful offshoots of these various factions which developed after Nichiren's death in 1282.

The chapter ended with a brief discussion of Japanese religions following World War II (1941–1945), when the USA forced separation of church and state into the Japanese constitution as a condition of surrender.

24.26 TECHNICAL TERMS

Amaterasu — The Shinto *kami* who is the ancestor of the royal family.

Amida — The Buddha of the Western Paradise, the main focus of Pure Land Buddhism.

Dainichi nyorai — The Great Sun Buddha, a central figure of Kegon Buddhism.

Hosso — The "Mind-Only" or Yogacara school of Japanese Buddhism, imported from China in the seventh century.

Jizo — The medicine Buddha.

Kami — Divine spirits essential to the Shinto religion.

Kannon — The bodhisattva Avalokitesvara, bodhisattva of compassion, and a helper of the Buddha of the Pure Land, Amida (Amitabha).

Kegon — The Japanese version of Chinese Hua-yen, or "Flower Garland" school of Buddhist philosophy.

koan — A puzzling question asked by a Zen teacher (roshi) of the student, whose purpose was to (1) initiate insight or (2) measure the depth of the insight. "What is the sound of one hand clapping?" is an example.

Mahavairocana — The great Sun Buddha, Dai-nichi. Pronounced Maha-vai-ro-cha-na.

Meiji Restoration — In 1868 the Tokugawa regime was replaced by the royal family and the emperor once again became the central power in the Japanese nation.

Miroku — The Japanese pronunciation of Maitreya, the name of the Buddha of the future

Mappo — The third period of the decline of the Buddha's teaching, when people's abilities to achieve spiritual goals has declined so severely that the world is filled with evil and will never get better.

Nembutsu — To bear in mind (nen) + Buddha (butsu). One does this by chanting *namu Amida butsu*, "homage to Amida Buddha." The basic practice of Pure Land Buddhism.

samurai — The powerful warrior class in Japan, with the highest status and importance.

Sanron — Three Treatise sect of early Japanese Buddhism, which stressed the Madhyamaka philosophy of Nagarjuna.

24.27 QUESTIONS FOR FURTHER DISCUSSION

1) We saw that when Japanese religion became associated with the ruling classes and politics, it seemed to have a negative effect on the priests and on the religion. What do you think is the cause of this?

2) When a religion is introduced from another culture, the people inevitably use the ideas of their native religion to interpret the new religion. Explain how we see this effect in the history of Japanese religions.

3) Japanese Rinzai monks took the approximately 1800 classic koans from the Chinese tradition, and organized and categorized them in terms of the goal of insight. How can we tell if the *koan* can help to produce insight into the world? Are any tests possible?

4) Japanese Rinzai monks took the approximately 1800 classic koans from the Chinese tradition, and organized and categorized them in terms of the goal of insight. The tradition believes that resolving the *koan* can produce insight into the true nature of the self, and help the student to be able to answer the question, "Who am I?" How could anyone tell if this is true? Can you think of any way to test this claim?

5) Which Japanese religions were a continuation of sects found in China, and which originated in Japan?

6) The Pure Land schools are the most popular in Japan. Explain two or three factors which might explain why these came to dominate Japanese Buddhism.

SELECTED BIBLIOGRAPHY

OVERVIEW

Dreyer, June Teufel, *Middle Kingdom and the Empire of the Rising Sun: Sino-Japanese Relations, Past and Present* (Oxford: Oxford University Press, 2016)

Earhart, H. B., *Japanese Religion: Unity and Diversity* (The Religious Life of Man), Third Edition (Belmont, CA: Dickinson Publishing Company, 1969)

Feifer, George, *Breaking Open Japan: Commodore Perry, Lord Abe and the American Imperialism of 1853* (New York: Harper Collins, 2006)

Hardacre, Helen, *Kurozumikyo and the New Religions of Japan* (New York: Princeton University Press, 1981)

Schirokauer, Conrad, *A Brief History of Japanese Civilization* (New York: Harcourt Brace, 1992)

JAPANESE BUDDHISM

Addiss, Stephen, Stanley Lombardo, Judity Roitman, eds., *Zen Sourcebook: Traditional Documents from China, Korea, and Japan* (Cambridge: Hackett Publishing Company, 2008)

Anesaki, Masaharu, *Nichiren: The Buddhist Prophet* (Gloucester, MA: Peter Smith, 1966; a reprinting of the original 1916 book)

Bays, Jan Chozen, *Jizo Bodhisattva: Guardian of Children, Travelers & Other Voyagers* (Boston: Shambhala, 2003)

Baroni, Helen Josephine, *The Illustrated Encyclopedia of Zen Buddhism* (New York: Rosen Publishing Group, 2002)

Bloom, Al, *Shinran's Gospel of Pure Grace*, (Tucon, AZ: University of Arizona Press, 1965)

Blum, Mark, "Shinran's Concept of *Shinjin* in the *Kyogyoshinsho*," in *Journal of Asian Culture, Graduate Students in Asian Studies at UCLA*, Vol. IV, Spring 1980, pp. 48-82.

Cook, Francis H., *Sounds of Valley Streams: Enlightenment in Dogen's Zen – Translation of Nine Essays from Shobogenzo* (New York: SUNY Press, 1989)

Dogen, Eihei, *Dōgen's [Shobogenzo] Genjo Koan: Three Commentaries* (Berkeley, CA: Counterpoint, 2011)

Dumoulin, Heinrich, *Zen Buddhism: A History: Vol. 2 Japan* (New York: Macmillan, 1990)

Ford, James Ishmael, and Melissa Myozen Blacker, eds., *the book of MU: essential writings on zen's most important koan* (Boston: Wisdom Publications, 2011)

Glassman, Hank, *The Face of Jizo: Image and Cult in Medieval Japanese Buddhism* (Honolulu: University of Hawai'i Press, 2012)

Heine, Steven, *Dogen and the Koan Tradition* (New York: State University Press of New York, 1994)

Heine, Steven, and Dale S. Wright, eds., *The Koan: Texts and Contexts in Zen Buddhism* (London: Oxford University Press, 2000)

Kurata, Hyakuzo, *Shinran* (Tokyo: Cultural Interchange Institute for Buddhists, 1964)

Leighton, Taigen Dan, *Zen Questions: Zazen, Dogen, and the Spirit of Creative Inquiry* (Wisdom Publications, 2002)

Loori, John Daido, *Two Arrows Meeting in Mid Air: The Zen Koan* (Rutland, Vt.: Charles E. Tuttle, 1994)

Loori, John Daido, and Kazuaki Tanahashi, *The True Dharma Eye: Zen Master Dogen's Three Hundred Koans* (Boston: Shambhala Press, 2005)

MacInnes, Elaine, *The Flowing Bridge: Guidance on Beginning Zen Koans* (Boston: Wisdom, 2007)

Miura, Isshu and Ruth Fuller Sasaki, *The Zen Koan* (New York: Harcourt Brace, 1965)

_____, *Zen Dust* (New York: Harcourt Brace, 1966)

Payne, Richard K., and Kenneth Tanaka, eds., *Approaching the Land of Bliss: Religious Praxis in the Cult of Amitabha* (Honolulu: University of Hawai'i Press, 2005)

Shibayama, Zenkei, *Zen Comments on the Mumonkan* (New York: Harper & Row, 1974)

Shimano, Eido, "Zen Koans" in K. Kraft, ed., *Zen: Tradition and Transition* (New York: Grove Press, 1988)

Soho Machida, *Renegade Monk: Honen and Japanese Pure Land Buddhism* (Berkeley: University of California Press, 1999)

Suzuki, D. T. [Daisetz Teitaro] *Essays in Zen Buddhism: First Series* (1927) (New York: Grove Press, 1994)

_____, *Essays in Zen Buddhism: Second Series* (1933) (New York: Samuel Weiser, Inc. 1953–1971)

_____, *Essays in Zen Buddhism: Third Series* (1934) (York Beach, Maine: Samuel Weiser, Inc. 1953)

_____, *An Introduction to Zen Buddhism* with a Foreword by C.G. Jung (London: Rider & Company, 1948).

_____, *The Training of the Zen Buddhist Monk* (New York: University Books, 1959).

_____, *Manual of Zen Buddhism* (London: Rider & Company, 1950, 1956. New York: Random House, 1960 and subsequent reprintings).

_____, *The Zen Doctrine of No-Mind* (London: Rider & Company, 1949. York Beach, Maine: Red Wheel/Weiser 1972).

_____, *Living by Zen* (London: Rider & Company, 1949.

_____, *Mysticism: Christian and Buddhist: The Eastern and Western Way*, (New York: Macmillan, 1957).

_____, *Zen and Japanese Culture*, (New York: Pantheon Books, 1959). A wonderfully interesting book.

Suzuki, D. T., Erich Fromm, Richard DeMartino, *Zen Buddhism and Psychoanalysis* (New York: Harper Collins, 1970)

Takuwa, Shinji, *Perfect Freedom in Buddhism: An Exposition of the Words of Shinran* (Tokyo: Hokuseido Press, 1968)

Tanahashi, Kazuaki and Peter Levitt, eds., *Essential Dogen: Writings of the Great Zen Master* (Shambhala Publications, 2013)

Tarrant, John, *Bring Me the Rhinoceros and Other Zen Koans to Bring You Joy* (New York: Harmony Books, 2004)

Ueda, Yoshifumi, ed., *Notes on Once-calling and Many-calling: A Translation of Shinran's Ichinen-tanen mon'i* (Kyoto: Shin Buddhism Translation Series, 1980)

_____, *The True Teaching: Practice and Realization of the Pure Land Way: A Translation of Shinran's Kyogyoshinsho*, Vol. IV (Kyoto: Shin Buddhism Translation Series, 1990)

Verdu, Alfonso, *Dialectical Aspects in Buddhist Thought: Studies in Sino-Japanese Mahayana Buddhism* (University of Kansas: Center for East Asian Studies, 1974)

Wick, Gerry Shishin, *The Book of Equanimity: Illuminating Classic Zen Koans* (Boston: Wisdom Publications, 2005)

Yoshioka, To-ichi, *Zen* (Kawamata, Japan: Hoikusha, 2002)

Buddhism in Modern Japan

Covell, Steve, *Japanese Temple Buddhism: Worldliness in a Religion of Renunciation* (Honolulu: University of Hawai'i Press, 2005)

Jaffe, Richard, *Neither Monk nor Layman: Clerical Marriage in Modern Japanese Buddhism* (Princeton, NJ: Princeton University Press, 2002).

Nelson, John K., *Experimental Buddhism: Innovation and Activism in Contemporary Japan* (Honolulu: University of Hawai'i Press, 2013)

Zen Buddhism and Christianity

Aitken, Robert and David Steindl-Rast, *The Ground We Share: Everyday Practice, Buddhist and Christian* (Triumph Books, 1994).

Blyth, R. H., *Buddhist Sermons on Christian Texts* (Tokyo: Hokuseido, 1958)

Borg, Marcus, ed., *Jesus and Buddha: The Parallel Sayings* (Berkeley: Seastone, 1997)

Boyd, James W., *Satan and Mara: Christian and Buddhist Symbols of Evil* (London: E. J. Brill, 1975)

Buddhist-Christian Studies, the official journal of the Society for Buddhist-Christian Studies, available online through Project Muse.

Cobb, John B., "Can a Christian be a Buddhist too?" in *Japanese Religions*, December 1978, pp. 1-20.

Dumoulin, Heinrich, *Christianity Meets Buddhism* (LaSalle: Open Court, 1974)

Enomiya-Lasalle, Hugo M., *Zen Meditation for Christians* (Open Court, 1974)

Graham, Dom Aelred, *Conversations: Christian and Buddhist* (Harcourt Brace & World, 1968).

_____, *Zen Catholicism* (Harcourt Brace & World, 1966).

Gross, Rita M. and Terry C. Muck, eds., *Christians Talk About Buddhist Meditation; Buddhists Talk About Christian Prayer* (Continuum, 2003)

Habito, Ruben, *Healing Breath: Zen for Christians and Buddhists in a Wounded World* (Wisdom Publications, 2006)

_____, *Living Zen, Loving God* (Wisdom Publications, 1995)

_____, "No Longer Buddhist or Christian," *Buddhist Christian Studies*, vol 10, pp. 231-237.

_____, *Total Liberation: Zen Spirituality and the Social Dimension* (Orbis Books, 2006)

Johnston, William, *Christian Zen* (Harper & Row, 1971)

_____, *The Still Point: Reflections on Zen and Christian Mysticism* (New York: Fordham University Press, 1970)

Kadowaki, Kakichi, "Ways of Knowing: A Buddhist-Thomist Dialogue," in *International Philosophical Quarterly*, December 1966, pp. 774-795.

_____, *Zen and the Bible* (Penguin, 1990).

Kennedy, Robert, S.J., *Zen Gifts to Christians* (Continuum International Publications, 2004).

_____, *Zen Spirit, Christian Spirit* (Continuum, 1996)

MacInnes, Elaine, *The Flowing Bridge: Guidance on Beginning Zen Koans* (Boston: Wisdom Publications, 2007)

Merton, Thomas, *Mystics and Zen Masters* (New York: Farrar, Straus and Giroux, 1967)

_____, *Zen and the Birds of Appetite* (Farrar, Straus and Giroux, 1968)

Nishitani, Keiji, *Religion and Nothingness* (Berkeley: Univ. of Calif. Press, 1982).

Roberts, Bernadette, *The Experience of No-Self* (New York: SUNY Press, 1993) A Christian experience of no-self.

_____, *The Path to No-Self* (New York: SUNY Press, 1991)

Spae, Joseph, *Buddhist-Christian Empathy* (Chicago: Chicago Institute of Theology and Culture, 1980) - Father Spae was the special advisor to the Pope John Paul on Eastern religions (the book has a lengthy bibliography).

Tillich, Paul and Hisamatu Shin'ichi, "Dialogues East and West" in *The Eastern Buddhist*, 1971, pp. 89-107, 1972, pp. 107-128, 1973, pp. 87-114.

Walker, Susan, ed., *Speaking of Silence: Christians and Buddhists on the Contemplative Way* (New York: Paulist Press, 1987)

Waldenfels, Hans, *Absolute Nothingness: Foundations for a Buddhist-Christian Dialogue* (New York: Paulist Press, 1980).

Zen and the Arts/Creativity

Awakawa, Yasuichi, *Zen Painting* (Tokyo: Kodansha, 1970)

Blyth, R.H., *Zen and Zen Classics* (5 volumes) (Tokyo: Hokuseido, 1960–1975)

Blyth, R.H., *Zen in English Literature and Oriental Classics* (Dutton, 1960)

Chang, Chung-yuan, *Creativity and Taoism* (Julian Press, 1963).

Fontein, Jan and M. Hickman, *Zen: Painting and Calligraphy* (Boston: Museum of Fine Arts, 1970).

Hisamatsu, Shin'ichi, *Zen and the Fine Arts* (Tokyo: Kodansha, 1971)

Iriya, Yoshitaka, "Chinese Poetry and Zen," in *Eastern Buddhist* vol. 6, no. 1, May 1973, pp. 54-67.

Shimano, Eido Tai and Kogetsu Tani, *Zen Word Zen Calligraphy* (Boston: Shambhala, 1995)

Suzuki, D. T., *Zen and Japanese Culture* (New York: Pantheon, 1959)

Oppenheimer, Mark, "Sex Scandal has American Buddhists Looking Within," *The New York Times*, 21 August 2010, p. A13.

PART IV

CHAPTER 25: CONCLUDING CHAPTER

In these volumes on Asian thought we have explored traditions whose world-view does not originate in either Jerusalem, the home of Judaism, Christianity, and Islam, but neither do these traditions have their origins in the Athens of Plato, Aristotle, and Socrates. In India, China, Japan, and Tibet, there never was anything like the sharp tension between these two approaches of Jerusalem and Athens, the tension between reason and faith, between science and religion, which dominates the history of Western thinking. In general, the world-view originating in Jerusalem rejected empirical observation, reason, science and logic in favor of faith and righteousness before God. Athens rejected faith in favor of reason, logic, empirical observation, and science. Thus the demarcation in the West between religion and philosophy applies perfectly well to the history of Western Christian civilization, but dividing non-western thought into these two rigid categories is simply not an appropriate structure to impose upon these non-western systems of thought. Trying to impose these categories gives us a distorted understanding of the ideas and their assumptions.

One important value which comes from studying Asian thought is that we see what the world looks like from many very different perspectives, from a very different set of assumptions about the world and the human beings who inhabit the world. In fact, many of the things that most people in the West assume to be both true and maybe universal, are not presupposed by India, China, Japan, or Tibet. For example, in the West, the common assumption is that we have one life, and when that is over, we are judged and will spend eternity in either heaven or hell. None of the non-western systems shares this cluster of beliefs. Most accept reincarnation (or rebirth), and when heavens and hells are a part of life after death, quite often they are thought to be temporary, not permanent.

Another example is our assumptions about the only acceptable ways to be religious. We have seen that in India, the belief was that one can be religious by acts of devotion, by expressions of faith, by the performance of ritual, but one can be religious by sitting in meditation (with or without a divinity involved), and one is being religious when one uses reason to investigate and challenge the claims and beliefs of one's own tradition. In the West, this last approach is understood to be non-religious, and perhaps even anti-religious. It is associated with philosophy. Here is a clear example where East and West conflict in their assumptions.

Because the dominant Western religions are grounded in a single infinitely powerful god, westerners tend to assume that all religions believe in a powerful personal god, a transcendent being who created the world. If you have read any of these chapters, you must have noticed that, as discussed in *Asian Thought* Volume I, in India the Samkhya and Advaita Vedanta traditions reject gods entirely and consider this a belief appropriate for those who are spiritually immature. The early Buddhists in India denied that the Buddha was a god, and in fact, understood gods as inferior to humans and in need of help. Philosophical Taoism associated with Lao-tzu and Chuang-tzu had no interest in gods or religious rituals, and no belief in life after death. The Ch'an Buddhists of China and the Zen Buddhists of Japan tend to ignore gods. The Confucians perform rituals, but their rituals are not in honor of gods in heavenly realms. Confucian rituals are about relationships with fellow human beings, not divinities. Apparently one can be religious and engage in rituals and yet have little or no concern with god or gods.

CHAPTER 25: CONCLUSION

People who share the Western world-view tend to assume that if the universe exists, there must have been a creator-god, a first cause. In India, some asked, "so where did that creator god come from?" "What is the source of all the gods?" For many in India, the source of all the gods is Brahman, which itself is an impersonal force, not a god. Another related response in India is that the universe has always existed, but expands for a few billion years, then contracts into a big crunch, after which it expands again. With this view, there never was a first cause.

If you cannot imagine a universe without a first cause, this is a failure of your imagination, not a fact about the universe. If you think of the cosmos as Nature, then asking about a first cause is a lot like asking "What is the first cause of the rain?" The answer is that these sorts of events occur naturally, and there is no first cause and no need for a first cause.

It has been common in the West for our religions to be exclusive. When a religion is exclusive, a follower must reject all other religions after one has committed oneself to a specific creed or faith. In fact, leaders within some Western religious traditions have been known to persecute and even kill those belonging to different sub-groups within the same religious traditions.

As you have seen, the majority of non-western systems are not exclusive in this same way. When it comes to popular religions, one can participate in more than one religion at the same time without hesitation. One can participate in rituals to gods other than one's own, with no problem. The Hindu sacred text entitled the *Bhagavadgita* explicitly says that it is perfectly fine to worship any god whatsoever from any religious tradition, for each and every one of the gods is an aspect of the one divinity.

Although some Asian systems rely on a savior of sorts (for example, Pure Land Buddhism and Nichiren Buddhism), the great majority do not. None of these systems ever heard of "original sin," so they do not need to be saved from it. The great majority do not accept the idea of "sin" as offending a god (Japanese Shinto is an exception, but there the problem is contamination, not sin). For the non-devotional systems in India, one's karma is caused by oneself, and good deeds will get one the karmic reward of the heavens. The Buddha in India declared that "no one can save you but yourself," and many of the subsequent Buddhist traditions are built on that. For the philosophical Taoists, all living things (including each and every one of us) arise out of the swirling patterns of nature and then we return back to those flowing patterns. There is no life after death. When one has harmony with nature, there is nothing left to do.

Even basic ideas about human nature diverge wildly from our usual Western assumptions. For many in the West, humans are created with a soul (a gift created by god in the image of god which gives one rationality, self-awareness, free-will and the ability to love freely), and we will be judged by god or by god's representative at our death, and sent to either heaven or hell. Similar ideas can be found in pre-Christian Persian religious beliefs (which historians and scholars say influenced both Judaism and Christianity). In India, some think we have an eternal unchanging soul (*atman*) which has been transmigrating forever, but this soul was never created by a god, and was not created in the image of any god. Early Buddhism argues critically and forcefully against the concept of an eternal soul. Taoists and Confucians have no concept of a unitary soul. In Western religions, that soul accounts for self-consciousness and free-will, two gifts from the Christian God. What Westerners find strange is that there was no concept of free-will in India, in China, Tibet, or Japan (or in Greek philosophy). Certainly, moral and social responsibility are a part of these cultures, but these concepts were not connected to religion or free-will, but only to social structures and community. The strongly moralistic Confucians find the foundations of morality to be built into nature, but not related to the gods. In Asian systems, morality in general tends not to be associated with divinities. There are no "Ten Commandments" issued by gods in any of these non-western traditions.

In the West we tend to value autonomy of the individual. We assume that the individual is more important than the group; in traditional China and Japan the group is always more important than the individual, especially the family group. Western stress on individual human rights and personal responsibility for decisions conflicts with those

394

CHAPTER 25: CONCLUSION

societies for whom group goals and values should control and direct our choices.[1] Although romantic love is known in all human societies, in non-western societies it was felt that the goals of the family must always take precedence over our personal emotions; thus the prevalence of arranged marriages (of course arranged marriages were common in much of European society). It is common for Western social institutions to be based on assuming autonomy of the individual self, but this idea seems unacceptably strange to many in the world.

We saw that the tension between faith and reason (so basic to Western religions) was not important in the majority of non-western religious traditions. In fact, the Madhyamaka Buddhists of India and Chuang-tzu in China challenged the Western assumption that rationality and logic could ever describe the spiritual nature of ultimate reality accurately. These non-western systems produce sophisticated philosophical arguments to demonstrate that there are limits to what language can accomplish, and those limits are especially clear in the case of religious language attempting to articulate precise religious claims and beliefs. Interestingly, neither Madhyamaka nor Chuang-tzu exempt their own words from this criticism. Perhaps better ways to express religious insights are poetry and art; certainly many in Asia have thought so.

The majority of the Asian systems we have discussed in these two books are older than the majority of Western religions and philosophical systems. Their longevity demonstrates that these have successfully satisfied the needs of followers at all levels of society. We have seen that these Asian systems of thought are not simplistic, they are not without intellectual depth and complexity. For thousands of years, these systems have exhibited the power to change the lives of followers for the better.

●

What can we conclude? After studying non-western systems of thought, we might conclude that the pathways of philosophy and religion are much more complex than we might have imagined, and that many ideas which Western societies assumed to be universal are not so universal after all.[2] In the past, cultures and religions were more isolated from one another, and beliefs and practices of non-western "others" were thought to be strange, even primitive. That ethnocentric view is no longer held by scholars. In the twenty-first century we now live in an interlocking world of religions, world-views, and cultural assumptions, and it is appropriate to realize that other systems have their own legitimacy, their own foundations, and often these are not compatible with Western views assumed to be universally true by Europeans and north Americans.

The disagreements and differences between Asian and Western are not so much about the facts, as about the underlying assumptions and presuppositions which provide the structure for how we interpret those facts. In Western society the majority of the people around us share our culture and share our religious traditions whose assumptions are to be accepted unquestioningly. Because of that, it is uncommon for us to recognize much less have to justify our assumptions. Reading about non-western religious traditions provides precisely that sort of valuable challenge.

After having read these chapters, it is hoped that the student has discovered that there are insights found in non-western thought systems which are valuable, and which can enrich one's life. These systems provide an alternative perspective other than the one that we in the West are so very used to. These differences are their value; we learn more from those who challenge and disagree with us than we learn from those who share our assumptions and conclusions.

---

[1] Some would argue that when westerners believe we have offended god or others, as individuals we feel guilt. In East Asia, the reaction is shame, for bringing disrepute on our family or our group.

[2] In the seventeenth and eighteenth centuries there was a discussion between rationalists and empiricists in epistemology (study of sources and limits of knowledge), and many of the rationalist Western philosophers argued that each and every one of us was born with the innate knowledge that the god of Christianity exists. Empiricists argued that such an idea taught from earliest childhood might seem to be innate knowledge that one was born with, but in fact it is just belief inculcated from an early age.

Credits

Introduction

Excerpt from Stephen Batchelor, *Confession of a Buddhist Atheist* (New York: Spiegel & Grau, 2010), p. 58.
Excerpt from Konrad Talmont-Kaminski, "The New Atheism and the New Anti-Atheism," *Skeptic*, Vol. 15, No. 1, 2009, p. 68.

Chapter 13

Quote from Roger Ames, "Images of Reason in Chinese Culture," in Eliot Deutch, ed., *Introduction to World Philosophies* (New Jersey: Prentice Hall, 1997), p. 256.
Quote from N. J. Girardot, *Myth and Meaning in Early Taoism* (Berkeley: University of California Press, 1983), p. 193.
Partial sentence quoted from Hans-Georg Moller, *Daoism Explained* (Chicago: Open Court, 2004), p. 150.
Ming dynasty rock inscription, translated in Philip Rawson and Laszlo Legeza, *Tao: The Eastern Philosophy of Time and Change* (London, Thames and Hudson Ltd., 1973), p. 8, p. 10.
Photo of the Great Wall of China and the terra cotta army by William Hillman (used by permission)

Chapter 14

Partial sentence quoted from Russell Kirkland, *Taoism: The Enduring Tradition* (London: Routledge, 2004), p. 75.
Partial sentence quoted from Chang Chung-yuan, *Creativity and Taoism: A Study of Chinese Philosophy, Art, and Poetry* (New York: Julian Press, 1963), p. 65.
Excerpt from Lawrence G. Thompson, *Chinese Religion: An Introduction*, 4th. ed. (Belmont, CA: Wadsworth, 1989), p. 12.

Chapter 15

Uncredited quotations from the Confucian *Analects* are translations by the author.
George Rowley, *Principles of Chinese Painting: Revised Edition* (Princeton NJ: Princeton University Press, 1974), p. 5.
Excerpts from the *Analects* in de Bary, Chan and Watson, *Sources of Chinese Tradition*, Volume 1 (New York: Columbia University Press, 1960), p. 28, 29, 31, 32, 89, 90, 105, 115, 176.
Excerpt from D. C. Lau, *Confucius: The Analects* (Penguin Books, 1979)
Excerpts from Simon Leys, *The Analects of Confucius* (New York: Norton, 1997), p. 6, 15, 105.
Excerpt from Arthur Waley, *The Analects of Confucius* (NY: Norton, 1938), VII:1, p. 123.
Excerpt from a translation by Laurence G. Thompson, *The Chinese Way in Religion* (Belmont CA: Dickinson, 1973), p. 17, p. 22.
Excerpt from Wm. Theodore DeBary, *The Unfolding of Neo-Confucianism* (New York: Columbia University Press, 1975), p. 3.
Excerpt from Hans-Georg Moeller, *The Moral Fool: A Case for Amorality* (New York: Columbia University Press, 2009), p. 9.
Excerpt from Wing-tsit Chan, *A Source Book in Chinese Philosophy* (New York: Princeton University Press, 1963), p. 13, p. 81.
Excerpts from Burton Watson, *Hsun-tzu: Basic Writings* (Columbia, 1963), p. 85, 86, 97.
Excerpt from A. C. Graham, *Disputers of the Tao* (LaSalle, Illinois: Open Court, 1989), p. 248, p. 305.
Excerpt from Burton Watson, *Hsun-tzu: Basic Writings* (Columbia, 1963), p. 85, p. 96, p. 97, p. 135, p. 157.
Excerpt from Arthur Waley, *The Way and Its Power* (London: George Allen & Unwin, 1968), p. 43.

Chapter 16

Poem quoted from Chang Chung-yuan, *Creativity and Taoism: A Study of Chinese Philosophy, Art, and Poetry* (New York: Julian Press, 1963, reprinted Harper Colophon Books, 1970; and again by Jessica Kingsley, Publishers, Philadelphia PA: 2011), p. 34, p. 90.

Excerpt from A. C. Graham, *Chuang Tzu: The Inner Chapters* (London: George Allen & Unwin, 1981), p. 6.
Excerpt from Paul J. Lin, *A Translation of Lao-tzu's Tao Te Ching and Wang Pi's Commentary* (Ann Arbor, MI: Michigan Papers in Chinese Studies 30, 1977), p. 152.

Chapter 17
Excerpt from Fung Yu-lan, *A History of Chinese Philosophy, Vol. I* (Princeton, N.J.: Princeton University Press, 1952), p. 221, p. 231, p. 244.
Excerpt from Burton Watson, *The Complete Works of Chuang Tzu* (N.Y.: Columbia University Press, 1970), p. 31, p. 40, p. 41, p. 43, p. 45, p. 46, p. 49, pp. 52–53, pp. 54–58, p. 78, p. 80, p. 81, p. 94–95, pp. 99–100, p. 140, p. 176, 177.
Excerpt from A. C. Graham, *Chuang Tzu: The Inner Chapters* (London: George Allen & Unwin, 1981), p. 4, p. 47, p. 56, p. 65.
Excerpt from Chang Chung-yuan, *Creativity and Taoism: A Study of Chinese Philosophy, Art, and Poetry* (New York: Julian Press, 1963), p. 36, p. 42, p. 47, p. 67.
Excerpt from Elaine Macinnes, *The Flowing Bridge: Guidance on Beginning Zen Koans* (Boston: Wisdom, 2007), p. 23.
Excerpt from Francois Jullien, *In Praise of Blandness: Proceeding from Chinese Thought and Aesthetics*, translated by Paula M. Varsano (New York: Zone Books, 2004), pp. 42–43.
Excerpt from John Wu, *The Golden Age of Zen* (New York: Doubleday Image, 1996), p. 39 and p. 41.
Excerpt from Martin Palmer, *The Book of Chuang Tzu* (New York: Penguin ARKANA, 1996), p. xvii.
Excerpt from Holmes Welch, *Taoism: The Parting of the Way, Revised edition* (Beacon Press, 1971), pp. 124–125.

Chapter 18
Excerpt from Michael Saso, *Taoism and the Rite of Cosmic Renewal* (Washington State University Press, 1972), pp. 13–14.
Excerpt from Philip Rawson and Laszlo Legeza, *Tao: The Eastern Philosophy of Time and Change* (London: Thames & Hudson, Ltd., 1973), p. 18.
Brief excerpt from Kwok Man Ho, Joanne O'Brien, *The Eight Immortals of Taoism* (New York: Meridian Books, 1991), p. 16.
Excerpt from Lu K'uan Yu, *Taoist Yoga: Alchemy and Immortality* (New York: Samuel Weiser, 1970), p. xii.
Excerpt from Akira Ishihara, *et. al*, *The Tao of Sex: A Translation of the Twenty-Eighth Section of the Essence of Medical Prescriptions* (Integral Publications, 1989), p. 156.

Chapter 19
Excerpt from Francis Cook, *Sounds of Valley Streams* (New York: State University of New York, 1989), page 6.

Chapter 20
Excerpt from Thomas Cleary, trans., *The Flower Ornament Scripture: A Translation of the Avatamsaka Sutra* (Boston, MA: Shambhala Publications, 1993), ch. 20, p. 452.
Excerpt from Thomas Cleary, *Entry into the Inconceivable: An Introduction to Hua-yen Buddhism* (Honolulu, HI: University of Hawaii Press, 1983), p. 145, p. 165.
Excerpt from Francis Cook, "Causation in the Chinese Hua-yen Tradition," *Journal of Chinese Philosophy* 1979, Vol. 6, No. 4, pp. 368–369.
Excerpt from Wing-tsit Chan, *A Source Book in Chinese Philosophy* (Princeton, N.J.: Princeton University Press, 1963), p. 411–412.

Chapter 21
Excerpt from Paul Reps, *Zen Flesh, Zen Bones* (Rutland, Vt.: Charles Tuttle, 1957), p. 95, p. 109.

Author's modification of the translation in John Wu, *The Golden Age of Zen* (New York: Doubleday Image, 1996), pp. 34–35, p. 63, p. 118.

Bodhidharma scroll from the nineteenth century from the Robert Zeuschner collection.

Hui-neng cutting bamboo art from the Robert Zeuschner collection.

Excerpt from Steven Heine, *Bargainin' For Salvation* (New York: Continuum, 2009), p. 15.

Excerpts from Ruth Fuller Sasaki and Thomas Yuho Kirchner, *The Record of Linji* (Honolulu: University of Hawaii Press, 2009), p. 160, p. 202, p. 222, p. 223.

Excerpts from Chang Chung-yuan, *The Original Teachings of Ch'an Buddhism*, p. 50, p. 92, p. 131, p. 134, p. 246, p. 292, p. 279.

Excerpts from Burton Watson, *The Zen Teachings of Master Lin-chi* (Boston: Shambhala, 1993), p. 26, p. 29, p. 33, p. 40, p. 52.

Excerpt from Urs App, *Master Yunmen* (New York: Kodansha International, 1994), page 169.

Excerpt from Suzuki Shunryu, *Zen Mind Beginner's Mind*, p. 34, p. 61, p. 97.

Excerpt from Ruth Fuller Sasaki, Yoshitaka Iriya, Dana Fraser, *The Recorded Sayings of Layman P'ang: A Ninth-Century Zen Classic* (New York: Weatherhill, 1971), p. 17,

Excerpt from Sheng Yen, "Chan, Meditation, and Mysticism," *Chan Magazine*, Autumn 2010, Vol. 30, No. 4, p. 8.

Excerpt from Sheng Yen, in *Chan Magazine*, Vol. 26, No. 4, Autumn 2006, p. 9.

Excerpt from Shen-Yen, *Chan Magazine*, vol. 2, no. 4 (Spring 1981), page 29.

Excerpt from Sheng-Yen, *The Infinite Mirror* (NY: Dharma Drum Publications, 1990), pp. 19-20.

Exerpt from Sheng Yen, "Transmission" in *Chan Magazine*, Spring 2009, Volume 29, Number 2, pp. 17–18.

Excerpt from Chang Chung-yuan, *Creativity and Taoism*, p. 57, p. 113, p. 114.

Excerpt from John Daido Loori, *Two Arrows Meeting in Mid Air: The Zen Koan* (Rutland, VT: Charles E. Tuttle, 1994), p. xxiv, p. xviii, p. 319.

Excerpt from Steven Heine, *Opening A Mountain: Koans of the Zen Masters* (NY: Oxford University Press, 2002), p. 6.

Photo of Ryoan-ji Zen rock garden by Robert Zeuschner, used by permission.

Excerpt from Robert Aitkin, *The Gateless Barrier* (Berkeley: North Point Press, 1991), p. 278.

Excerpt from Stephen Batchelor, *Confession of a Buddhist Atheist* (New York: Spiegel & Grau, 2010), p. 64.

Excerpt from Shibayama Zenkei, *Zen Comments on the Mumonkan* (New York: Harper & Row, 1974), p. 23.

Excerpt from Heinrich Dumoulin, *Zen Buddhism: A History, Vol. 1: India and China* (New York: Macmillan Publishing, 1988), p. 258.

Tom Wright, Jisho Warner, Shohaku Okamura, translators, *Opening the Hand of Thought: Foundations of Zen Buddhist Practice* (Boston; Wisdom Publications, 2004), p. xviii.

Excerpt from Zarko Andricevic, "Acceptance and Appreciation," *Chan Magazine*, Vol. 33, No. 4 (Autumn 2013), p. 18.

Excerpt from Irmgard Schloegl, *The Wisdom of the Zen Masters* (New York: New Directions, 1976), pp. 17–18.

Chapter 22

Excerpt from Carsun Chang, *Development of Neo-Confucian Thought* (New Haven: College and University Press, 1963), p. 96.

Excerpt from Carsun Chang, *The Development of Neo-Confucian Thought: Volume 2* (New York: Bookman Associates, 1962), p. 36.

Excerpt from John Koller, *Oriental Philosophies*, 2nd edition, p. 310, p. 319.

Excerpt from de Bary, *Unfolding of Neo-Confucianism*, p. 8, p. 10, p. 11, p. 14, p 17.

Excerpt from Laurence C. Wu, *Fundamentals of Chinese Philosophy* (New York: University Press of America, 1986), p. 240, p. 244.

Wing-tsit Chan, *A Source Book in Chinese Philosophy* (Princeton, NJ: Princeton University Press, 1963), p. 659, p. 660, p. 674.

Brief excerpt from Yiching Wu, *The Cultural Revolution at the Margins: Chinese Socialism in Crisis* (Cambridge: Harvard University Press, 2014), p. 51

Chapter 23

Excerpt from Bradley K. Hawkins, *An Introduction to Asian Religions* (Pearson Longman, 2004) p. 287.

Excerpt from Tsunoda, ed., *Sources of Japanese Tradition* (New York: Columbia University Press, 1958), p. 271.

Excerpt from H. B. Earhart, *Japanese Religion: Unity and Diversity*, 3rd Edition, p. 4.

Chapter 24

Excerpt from Isshu Miura and Ruth Fuller Sasaki, *Zen Dust* (New York: Harcourt Brace, 1966), p. 41, 42, 43.

Excerpt from John Daido Loori, *Two Arrows Meeting in Mid Air: The Zen Koan* (Rutland, VT: Charles E. Tuttle, 1994), p. xxiv, p. 319.

Excerpts from Isshu Miura and Ruth Fuller Sasaki, *The Zen Koan* (New York: Harcourt Brace, 1965), p. 44, p. 48, p. 50, p. 55, p. 56, p. 57, p. 58, p. 62, p. 63.

Excerpts from John Tarrant, *Bring Me the Rhinoceros and Other Zen Koans to Bring You Joy* (New York: Harmony Books, 2004), p. 48, p. 53

Excerpt from Gerry Shishin Wick, *The Book of Equanimity: Illuminating Classic Zen Koans* (New York: Wisdom Publications, 2005), pp. 1–2, p. 5, p. 14.

Excerpt from Shibayama Zenkei, *Zen Comments on the Mumonkan* (New York: Harper & Row, 1974), p. 23.

Photo of Amida Buddha by Robert Zeuschner

Photo of Zen Rock Garden at Ryoan-ji by Robert Zeuschner

Excerpts from Francis H. Cook, *Sounds of Valley Streams: Enlightenment in Dogen's Zen–Translation of Nine Essays from Shobogenzo* (New York: SUNY Press, 1989), p. 12, p. 19, p. 24, p. 28.

Excerpt from Heinrich Dumoulin *Zen Buddhism: A History: Vol. 2 Japan* (New York: Macmillan, 1990), p. 161.

Index

402

CPSIA information can be obtained
at www.ICGtesting.com
Printed in the USA
FSHW02n2114230618
49465FS

9 781635 617030